Governance, Directors and Boards

Corporate Governance in the New Global Economy

Series Editors: Kevin Keasey
Leeds Permanent Building Society Professor of Financial Services and Director of the International Institute of Banking and Financial Services, Leeds University Business School, UK
Steve Thompson
Professor of Strategic Management, Nottingham University Business School, UK
Mike Wright
Professor of Financial Studies and Director of the Centre for Management Buy-out Research, Nottingham University Business School, UK

1. Governance and Auditing
   Peter Moizer
2. Governance and Ownership
   Robert Watson
3. The Life Cycle of Corporate Governance
   Igor Filatotchev and Mike Wright
4. Governance, Directors and Boards
   Mahmoud Ezzamel

Future titles will include:

Governance: An International Perspective
Diane Denis and John McConnell

Corporate Governance: Political and Legal Perspectives
Mark J. Roe

Governance and Expropriation
Larry H.P. Lang

Governance and the Public Sector
Ron Hodges

Wherever possible, the articles in these volumes have been reproduced as originally published using facsimile reproduction, inclusive of footnotes and pagination to facilitate ease of reference.

For a list of all Edward Elgar published titles visit our site on the World Wide Web at www.e-elgar.com

Governance, Directors and Boards

Edited by

Mahmoud Ezzamel

Cardiff Professorial Fellow
Cardiff Business School, Cardiff University, UK

CORPORATE GOVERNANCE IN THE NEW GLOBAL ECONOMY

An Elgar Reference Collection
Cheltenham, UK • Northampton, MA, USA

Published by
Edward Elgar Publishing Limited
Glensanda House
Montpellier Parade
Cheltenham
Glos GL50 1UA
UK

Edward Elgar Publishing, Inc.
136 West Street
Suite 202
Northampton
Massachusetts 01060
USA

A catalogue record for this book is available from the British Library.

ISBN 1 84542 103 5

Printed and bound in Great Britain by MPG Books Ltd, Bodmin, Cornwall

Contents

Acknowledgements

The editor and publishers wish to thank the authors and the following publishers who have kindly given permission for the use of copyright material.

Academy of Management and Copyright Clearance Center for articles: Barry Baysinger and Robert E. Hoskisson (1990), 'The Composition of Boards of Directors and Strategic Control: Effects on Corporate Strategy', *Academy of Management Review*, **15** (1), 72–87; James D. Westphal (1999), 'Collaboration in the Boardroom: Behavioral and Performance Consequences of CEO-Board Social Ties', *Academy of Management Journal*, **42** (1), 7–24; Dan R. Dalton, Catherine M. Daily, Jonathan L. Johnson and Alan E. Ellstrand (1999), 'Number of Directors and Financial Performance: A Meta-analysis', *Academy of Management Journal*, **42** (6), 674–86; Mason A. Carpenter and James D. Westphal (2001), 'The Strategic Context of External Network Ties: Examining the Impact of Director Appointments on Board Involvement in Strategic Decision Making', *Academy of Management Journal*, **44** (4), 639–60; Wei Shen and Albert A. Cannella, Jr. (2002), 'Power Dynamics within Top Management and Their Impacts on CEO Dismissal Followed by Inside Succession', *Academy of Management Journal*, **45** (6), 1195–1206.

Administrative Science Quarterly for articles: Rita D. Kosnik (1987), 'Greenmail: A Study of Board Performance in Corporate Governance', *Administrative Science Quarterly*, **32** (2), 163–85; James Wade, Charles A. O'Reilly III and Ike Chandratat (1990), 'Golden Parachutes: CEOs and the Exercise of Social Influence', *Administrative Science Quarterly*, **35** (4), 587–603; Jeffrey A. Alexander, Mary L. Fennell and Michael T. Halpern (1993), 'Leadership Instability in Hospitals: The Influence of Board-CEO Relations and Organizational Growth and Decline', *Administrative Science Quarterly*, **38**, 74–99; James D. Westphal and Edward J. Zajac (1995), 'Who Shall Govern? CEO/Board Power, Demographic Similarity, and New Director Selection', *Administrative Science Quarterly*, **40**, 60–83; Edward J. Zajac and James D. Westphal (1996), 'Director Reputation, CEO-Board Power, and the Dynamics of Board Interlocks', *Administrative Science Quarterly*, **41**, 507–29; Donald C. Hambrick, Theresa S. Cho and Ming-Jer Chen (1996), 'The Influence of Top Management Team Heterogeneity on Firms' Competitive Moves', *Administrative Science Quarterly*, **41**, 659–84; William Ocasio and Hyosun Kim (1999), 'The Circulation of Corporate Control: Selection of Functional Backgrounds of New CEOs in Large U.S. Manufacturing Firms, 1981–1992', *Administrative Science Quarterly*, **44**, 532–62.

American Economic Association for article: Benjamin E. Hermalin and Michael S. Weisbach (1998), 'Endogenously Chosen Boards of Directors and Their Monitoring of the CEO', *American Economic Review*, **88** (1), March, 96–118.

Blackwell Publishing Ltd for articles: Jay Dahya, John J. McConnell and Nickolaos G. Travlos (2002), 'The Cadbury Committee, Corporate Performance, and Top Management Turnover', *Journal of Finance*, **LVII** (1), February, 461–83; Mahmoud Ezzamel and Robert Watson (2002), 'Pay Comparability Across and Within UK Boards: An Empirical Analysis of the Cash Pay Awards to CEOs and Other Board Members', *Journal of Management Studies*, **39** (2), March, 207–32.

Elsevier for articles: Michael S. Weisbach (1988), 'Outside Directors and CEO Turnover', *Journal of Financial Economics*, **20**, 431–60; David Yermack (1996), 'Higher Market Valuation of Companies with a Small Board of Directors', *Journal of Financial Economics*, **40**, 185–211.

Journal of Financial and Quantitative Analysis for article: Kevin F. Hallock (1997), 'Reciprocally Interlocking Boards of Directors and Executive Compensation', *Journal of Financial and Quantitative Analysis*, **32** (3), September, 331–44.

RAND Corporation for article: Benjamin E. Hermalin and Michael S. Weisbach (1988), 'The Determinants of Board Composition', *RAND Journal of Economics*, **19** (4), Winter, 589–606.

Sage Publications Ltd for article: Terry McNulty and Andrew Pettigrew (1999), 'Strategists on the Board', *Organization Studies*, **20** (1), 47–74.

University of Chicago Press for article: Charles J. Hadlock and Gerald B. Lumer (1997), 'Compensation, Turnover, and Top Management Incentives: Historical Evidence', *Journal of Business*, **70** (2), April, 153–87.

John Wiley and Sons Limited for articles: John A. Pearce II and Shaker A. Zahra (1991), 'The Relative Power of CEOs and Boards of Directors: Associations with Corporate Performance', *Strategic Management Journal*, **12** (2), February, 135–53; Brian K. Boyd (1994), 'Board Control and CEO Compensation', *Strategic Management Journal*, **15** (5), June, 335–44.

Every effort has been made to trace all the copyright holders but if any have been inadvertently overlooked the publishers will be pleased to make the necessary arrangement at the first opportunity.

In addition the publishers wish to thank the Marshall Library of Economics, Cambridge University and the Library of Indiana University at Bloomington, USA for their assistance in obtaining these articles.

Introduction
Boards of Directors: Composition, Dynamics and Effects

Mahmoud Ezzamel

Boards of directors are prevalent in both the for-profit and public sector organisations. Having a board is one of the legal requirements for incorporation and, as Hermalin and Weisbach (2003, p. 7) have suggested, nonincorporated entities tend to have a governing body of some type. According to this perspective, boards are the product of regulation, created to meet specific legal requirements, in particular to ensure their own independence and proper action. However, it is noteworthy that governing boards in general predate legal regulations, so their roles must extend beyond the purely legal and regulatory. As evidence of this, Hermalin and Weisbach (*ibid.*, p. 9) have noted that the size of boards of directors tends to be much larger than required by law. This leads them to suggest that 'boards are a market solution to an organizational design problem, an endogenously determined institution that helps to ameliorate the agency problems that plague any large organization' (*ibid.*, p. 9).

The agency problem is one of the most dominant and analytically developed theses in the literature on corporate governance. Prompted by the path-breaking work of Berle and Means (1932) on the separation of ownership from control in the modern, large organisation, a fundamental problem is immediately posited according to which the interests (capital) of diffused owners (shareholders) are depicted to be at the mercy of opportunistic managers. The question then is how to ensure that managers make decisions that are consistent with shareholders' interests. External and internal governance mechanisms have been suggested in the literature.

External solutions include capital markets and managerial labour markets. If capital markets perform the roles expected of them properly, then they should act as a powerful disciplining mechanism for recalcitrant and opportunistic managers. First, capital markets should flag the poorly performing firms of opportunistic or incompetent managers by down-valuing their securities. Further, such firms become obvious targets for more interventionist actions in the form of takeovers by other firms, a radical solution that immediately undermines the employment of managers of failing firms (Jensen, 1993). Similarly, efficient managerial labour markets are intended to be powerful disciplining mechanisms. If such markets are capable of placing valuations on managerial capital, then the expectation is that this would function as a powerful incentive for rational managers to act in the interests of shareholders, else the managerial labour markets will reflect their opportunistic behaviour in lower values (Fama, 1980). Both forms of external governance are not particularly welcome by managers; the discipline of capital markets results in them losing their jobs and reputations, and the discipline of managerial labour markets could result in public admonition reflected in lower managerial value.

By comparison, internal governance structures are a lesser evil. The classic solution of aligning shareholders' and managers' interests via the judicious application of carefully designed incentive schemes is particularly popular in most corporations. If there are some major shareholders in a firm, then these could be entrusted with the role of designing the requisite, optimally structured, incentive schemes. Note that even in this case boards of directors have a role to play, for the board becomes the stage upon which the significant shareholder plays the role of governance. In the majority of cases, however, there is a notable absence of such major shareholders, and we frequently encounter cases of diffuse share ownership. Hermalin and Weisbach (2003, p. 10) argue that in these situations boards of directors could play a major governance role: 'One idea explaining why boards have emerged is that the directors' mutual monitoring was critical for inducing shareholders to trust the directors with their money.'

This mutual monitoring by board members has much resemblance to some of the ideas underpinning the managerial labour market thesis (Fama, 1980) and the subsequent work of Fama and Jensen (1983a, 1983b) on governance. Whether the mitigation of agency problems is thought to be the outcome of optimally designed incentive schemes or the mutual disciplinary practices of board members upon each other, both explanations are driven by pure economic reasoning. These economic explanations offer powerful insights into many issues surrounding the existence of boards of directors, their functioning and the impacts they may have, and many of the contributions contained in this volume attest to precisely this importance. While I do not wish to diminish the power of such explanations, it is crucial to consider other roles of boards of directors, just as we have in moving from the purely legal explanations to embrace the economic. For example, a larger board size may indeed signify an economic response to specific agency problems, the argument being the larger the size of the board the more likely agency problems will be attenuated, for example via more adequate monitoring or separation of decision responsibilities. However, it is equally plausible that larger size boards of directors are also intended to enhance board legitimacy by creating the myth that the larger the board, the more diffused are the responsibilities of individual members and the less likely is collusive action among members of the board. Such actions, for example to increase board size, may therefore be purely ceremonial, to create an impression rather than to make a genuine change in the way the board makes decisions, allocates responsibilities or monitors actions.

The efficacy of external and internal governance mechanisms has been debated in the literature. Jensen (1993) in particular has launched a strong attack on internal governance schemes and provides some anecdotal evidence from the practices of a few large organisations, as well as more systematic evidence (the productivity of corporate R&D and capital expenditures) which point to what he calls the failure of internal control (governance) systems. He argues that few boards of directors have successfully performed their jobs properly: hiring, firing and compensating the chief executive officer (CEO) and providing high-level counsel. When the board succeeds in removing an opportunistic or an incompetent CEO, this seems to happen much too late. Jensen blames this failure on a board culture that is not conducive to corporate high performance (*ibid.*, p. 863): 'Board culture is an important component of board failure. The great emphasis on politeness and courtesy at the expense of truth and frankness in boardrooms is both a symptom and cause of failure in the control system.' Jensen goes on to list other reasons that explain why, in his view, board control fails. The additional reasons, other than board culture, include lack of availability of appropriate information and expertise to board members compared with the CEO; legal incentives that lead to minimisation of downside risk rather than maximising shareholder value; lack of management and board member equity holdings; oversize of the board that colludes against effective board monitoring; and the great percentage of internal directors that are likely to be more responsive to the CEO's desires than to protecting shareholders to avoid animosity and retribution from the CEO. To reform the board, he recommends that the CEO be the only inside director on the board, and for the board to be modelled along the characteristics of the boards of leveraged buyouts (LBO) associations and venture capital funds (ibid., p. 869).

Whether or not the ambitions and aspirations of Jensen for the reforming of boards of directors will ever see the light of day is something that can only be revealed in the future. What Jensen's work demonstrates without doubt, however, is the critical and central importance of boards of directors as internal governance mechanisms. This also explains why boards of directors have been the subject of academic enquiry for some time. Considered fundamental to any serious and systematic effort to govern the corporation, boards of directors have been at the centre of the corporate governance debate in terms of their composition and the dynamics of board member turnover and succession, their power vis-à-vis that of the CEO, their ability to ensure efficient decision making, their impact upon firm performance, and also their effect on top executive pay. This interest in boards of directors is not restricted to academia; regulators, the business press and investors, particularly institutional investors, all have a keen interest in issues related to boards of directors. Given the rising interest in boards of directors, it is not surprising that the *Journal of Management* felt it necessary, or at least desirable, to have a review paper of the literature on boards published in 1996 (Johnson, Daily and Ellstrand, 1996) only seven years after an earlier review paper (Zahra and Pearce, 1989). Even since the latter review paper appeared, many other valuable contributions have emerged.[1] This is therefore both an important and dynamic research area and it is hoped that this volume provides a sound basis for future researchers in this sphere.

As a reflection of the cross-disciplinary nature of research on boards of directors, the focus of this volume is on contributions drawn from the disciplines of economics, finance and management. Despite their importance, legal studies of boards of directors are beyond the scope of this volume. Most of the papers are positivistic pieces of research, that is they entail empirical tests of a number of hypotheses on the boards of directors. A few papers are of a theoretical nature and only one paper is a qualitative piece of work. This suggests that future work in this area could be further enhanced if, in addition to the positivistic research that forms the majority of this volume, more effort is directed towards theory as well as qualitative research on boards of directors.

In any edited volume of this nature, an element of selection of the contributions to be included is inevitable. Naturally, there are more papers dealing with boards of directors than those included here. The selection process was based on identifying papers that contribute as directly as possible to a distinctive area of research on boards of directors, and wherever possible to cover as wide an array of research methods and methodologies as possible. This is not to say, however, that other papers not included in the volume are of marginal interest. Rather, space limitations dictated that some contributions had to be left out, but many of these are discussed briefly in this chapter and are included in the reference list.

The contributions contained in this volume have been organised under four main headings:

I. Determinants of board composition and board dynamics.

II. Board characteristics and decision making.
III. Board characteristics and organisational performance.
IV. Board characteristics and CEO compensation.

The remainder of this chapter is organised around these key themes.

Part I Determinants of Board Composition and Board Dynamics

The question of board composition, in terms of who is represented on the board and how those represented are selected, has been central to many research agendas. One key reason for this is that the nature of board composition is likely to impact upon the manner in which the board functions and also on how power and influence are allocated and become manifest within the board. Selection of board members reveals further dimensions of power within the board in relation to who hires such important executive and non-executive directors. Issues of personal loyalty within the board and degree of independence loom large in this context. An understanding of board members' turnover and selection is therefore crucial in gaining a sound understanding of how boards function, the extent to which they are effectively governed and the shifts in power dynamics within the board.

The literature points to the critical role played by the CEO in selecting members of the board. Consider two possible scenarios (see Mace, 1971; Vancil, 1987). The first scenario involves a senior CEO who is near retirement. The literature suggests that it is likely in these cases for the CEO to recruit a number of internals to the board with a view to giving them exposure to corporate issues and making them visible to other board members. The second scenario is when a new CEO is appointed; here the concern for the new CEO is likely to be bringing in some external members to help give advice; also some internals who had ambition to become the new CEO may leave because they judge their chances of becoming CEO in the same firm to be minimal. Other arguments pertaining to changes in board membership are poor performance and change of markets. Poor performance provides an incentive to bring in new, fresh blood, thereby resulting in external members being added to the board. In contrast, entering new markets is assumed to favour internal members already on the board, and exiting a market is likely to lead to a loss in internal membership of the executive who served that market.

The paper by Hermalin and Weisbach (1988) was motivated by these arguments. They collected data on board composition for a sample of 142 firms for thirteen years, but conducted the analysis on the period 1972–1980. The results suggest that in the years just preceding and following a CEO change a number of insiders leave the board, and before a CEO change some insiders join the board. CEO selection tended to be drawn from those insiders who had joined recently, and following the appointment of a new CEO, losing insider candidates tended to leave, to be replaced by outsiders. Poor firm performance was also associated with the departure of some insiders, who were then replaced by outsiders. An explanation relating to agency theory and monitoring is that when the firm performs poorly, the dynamics of managerial labour markets ensure that new outsider members join to enhance monitoring over the board and the CEO, with some insiders leaving to make room for the new outsiders. It is also possible that insiders are fired because they are held responsible for the poor performance. When firms exit markets, a number of insiders also leave the board, and as leaving markets tends to be caused by poor performance, insiders may leave because they are held responsible for performance.

A number of studies have also shown that poor firm performance is associated with CEO dismissal (e.g. Coughlan and Schmidt, 1985; Warner, Watts and Wruck, 1988). Weisbach (1988) extended this work further by distinguishing between the roles of insider directors and outsider directors. His results show that the association between poor performance and CEO resignation was stronger for firms with outsider-dominated boards, compared with firms whose boards are dominated by insider directors. This result points to the strong possibility that outsider members of boards enhance board independence and monitoring power over CEOs. Such a finding is given even further credence and importance by the other observation that stock returns on the days of CEO resignation announcements were consistent with the view that firm value increased following the removal of bad management. Naturally, the empirical power of such an argument relies upon the extent to which results of event-type studies such as that conducted by Weisbach really capture the impact of the event of concern (removal of a badly performing CEO).

Dahya, McConnell and Travlos (2002) examine the impact of the Cadbury Code of Best Practice on the composition and size of boards of directors, and also on CEO turnover in the UK. Their analysis reveals a significant increase in board sizes and in the number and fractions of outside board members, and a significant decrease in the number and fraction of firms where the CEO is also the chair of the board of directors. They also found that CEO turnover increased following the issuance of Cadbury's report, with firms that adopted Cadbury's recommendations exhibiting the greatest sensitivity between increase in CEO turnover to firm performance. These results can be taken to indicate that the quality of board control has improved in the UK following the adoption of Cadbury's recommendations. However, the authors voice a note of caution in suggesting that prior research has shown that board composition affects the way in which boards of directors perform discrete tasks, such as hiring and firing top management and responding to hostile takeovers.

Research has suggested that situations of natural retirement for CEOs, in contrast to CEO dismissal, are characterised by significant influence exerted by the departing CEO in terms of grooming a new successor as an heir apparent (Vancil, 1987). Powerful retiring CEOs tend to groom successors, particularly insiders, who are similar to themselves (Zajac and Westphal, 1996). The paper by Shen and Cannella (2002) extends the work of Weisbach (1988) by specifically focusing upon power contests within the board that result in CEO dismissal. They proxied CEO power using duality (being both CEO and chair of the board) and CEO stock ownership. Yet, they do not explicitly model for power of other board members, particularly given their interest in power dynamics within the board. Rather, power dynamics are assumed to exist and underpin competition, in a tournament-like fashion, between the CEO and other board members. Their results show that for their sample, in 58 per cent of CEO dismissals successors were insiders. More importantly, the results show that non-CEO inside directors and non-CEO executive ownership were positively associated with CEO dismissal followed by inside succession, but neither influenced CEO dismissal followed by outside succession. This suggests that non-CEO senior executives play an important role in monitoring and disciplining the CEO.

Westphal and Zajac (1995) examined CEO/board power in the context of new director selection. They proxied CEO power as reflected in an insider ratio (number of employee directors divided by total board membership), duality and relative CEO/board tenure (the average board tenure divided by CEO tenure), and board power was reflected in non-CEO ownership relative to total ownership. Similarity between CEOs and their boards were measured along four dimensions: age, background, education and insider/outsider status. Their results suggest that when incumbent CEOs are more powerful than their boards, new directors appointed to the board are likely to be demographically similar to the incumbent CEO. In contrast, when the board is more powerful than the incumbent CEO, newly appointed directors resemble more closely non-CEO directors on the board.

In a subsequent paper, Zajac and Westphal (1996) examined the effects of interlocking directorates and director reputation on CEO/board relationships. They focused upon contexts for interorganisational power and their effects upon interorganisational ties, with the latter expected to spread knowledge and awareness about specific organisational changes, such as corporate strategy, organisation structure and the board's role in the organisation. Examining a large sample of US firms over a seven year period, their results suggest that variations in CEO/board power relationships across organisations have contributed to a segmentation of the corporate sector network. Internal organisational politics in the CEO/board relationship were found to significantly affect the selection and retention of directors as well as the formation and dissolution of the board. Companies with relatively high board control were attracted more to directors with prior experience in changes indicating increased board control over top management (governance changes), while companies with relatively passive boards were much less attracted to these directors. Consistent results were obtained for directors with less prior experience in governance-related changes. The results overall therefore indicate that the extent of directors' prior experience in governance changes provides an important basis for selecting or retaining directors.

Managerial succession, particularly at the level of the CEO, creates unavoidable instability in the board. Such instability could impact not only on the nature of the relationship between the CEO and the board, but also on the performance of the organisation in future years. Two papers in the volume explore this important issue of instability. Alexander, Fennell and Halpern (1993) examined the association between leadership instability (succession at the top of the board) with sociopolitical structures that define the relationship between the CEO and the board in hospitals as an example of not-for-profit organisations. Consistent with previous work, they found that unstable and declining hospitals experienced more instability in the position of the CEO compared with stable or growing hospitals. They also found that CEO power over the board was associated with leadership stability and that CEO contracts functioned as a structural mechanism of power exercised by the board over the CEO. This suggests that CEO power over the board and formal employment contracts operate as power-balancing mechanisms. This work also suggests that factors other than board governance mechanisms (the rational exercise of control by the board over top management) impact upon leadership instability; power relations between the CEO and the board also impact upon leadership stability.

Ocasio and Kim (1999) address the issue of board instability through the notion of circulation of corporate control. They viewed the selection of CEOs as both a political context for the top executive position and an ideological struggle among members of the organisation's political coalition over defining corporate agenda and strategy. They examined the selection of functional backgrounds (i.e. production, marketing, finance) of new CEOs in a large sample of US firms over the 1981–1992 period. Theoretically, the paper also contrasted the model of political dynamics (circulation of functional control) with the institutionalisation of power. The pattern of results was found to be inconsistent with the model of institutionalisation of power, whereby we should expect to observe entrenchment of the power of the functional units. Instead, Ocasio and Kim reported that the results were more consistent with the model of circulation of control (the instability in formal authority at the top of large organisations as the dynamic outcome of how contests for control play out among competing individuals, groups and identities).

The above discussion focused in the main upon CEO/board relationships, thereby acceding to the fact that CEOs play particularly crucial roles in running the modern organisation, and that the key dynamic is that between such CEOs and the rest of the board. This clearly could lead to the erroneous implication that the nature of representations on the board, other than that of the CEO, is of trivial consequence. This is obviously not the case; a standard measure of CEO/board control used in virtually all the above studies is the proportion of non-executives to total board membership. Moreover, some research has explicitly addressed the issue of stakeholder representations on the board. For example, Jones and Goldberg (1982) and Freeman and Evan (1990) have lamented the limited extent of stakeholder representation on boards of directors, and Luoma and Goodstein (1999) have reported a somewhat modest degree of stakeholder board representation for more recent periods.

Part II Board Characteristics and Decision Making

The previous section examined the factors that researchers identified as affecting the composition of the board of directors and the power dynamics between the CEO and the board, with their impact on CEO dismissal, appointment and other board recruitment. We examined factors affecting board composition, ranging from the purely economic and rational, through the institutional to the political. In this section, the focus is upon the impact of board composition, however determined, and decision-making style in organisations. If a connection between these two sets of parameters could be established, then it may be possible to manipulate board characteristics in particular directions in order to lead to more desirable types of decisions. Precisely what impact do board characteristics have on decisions made by the board? The range of decisions made by the board is clearly very broad, but it would be expected that strategic types of decisions loom particularly important, for after all boards of directors are expected to focus on crucial strategic decisions. This is reflected in the readings selected for this section, as most of them deal with strategic decision making. While the papers examined below in more detail focus directly and almost exclusively on the decision-making effects of board composition, other studies have provided some useful insights. For example, Westphal (1998) has shown that changes in the structure of the board that enhance board independence from management are associated with higher levels of CEO ingratiation and persuasion towards board members, which in turn serve to mitigate the effect of structural board independence on corporate strategy. But it is to the most direct effects of board composition on decision making, and in particular strategy, that we now turn.

Hermalin and Weisbach (1998) set the scene by developing an analytical model that explains situations when boards of directors can be effective monitors of CEO decisions and situations when they are weak at monitoring. They model board monitoring effectiveness as a function of its independence, the rationale being that the more independent the board is from the CEO the more likely that it will be effective in monitoring the CEO. Board independence, in turn, is modelled as a function of implicit or explicit negotiations between existing board directors and the CEO over decisions taken to fill vacancies on the board. To the extent that the CEO has greater relative power over the board selection process, this may be taken to imply that board independence is impaired and hence its ability to monitor the CEO is likely to be restricted significantly. This will also imply that the CEO's perceived ability is judged by other members of the board to be greater compared with that of potential successors.

The paper by Baysinger and Hoskisson (1990) examines the effects of the composition of the board on corporate strategy. They develop a model according to which ownership and control parameters impact on board composition, which in turn impacts on control emphasis, and through that on strategic choice outcomes. The study is theoretical in nature, and hence leads to the development of a number of important propositions that are not tested empirically. These propositions suggest that as outsider-dominated boards are likely to favour rewarding top management on the basis of objective financial measures, they will intensify managerial effort to maximise short-run profits and direct their efforts away from greater investment in R&D and towards greater diversification, and away from high-risk–return strategies favoured by shareholders. In other words, outsider-dominated boards will demotivate managers from making strategic decisions that involve higher expected risks and associated higher expected returns, in a sense resulting in a very cautious top management team. The corollary of this argument is that higher-risk decision strategies are to be found in boards of directors that are dominated by insiders.

The paper by McNulty and Pettigrew (1999) conducts a qualitative study of the contribution to strategy by the CEO and non-executive directors in a sample of UK organisations. The paper argues that non-executive (part-time) directors do not simply play the role of ratifying decisions made by powerful members of the board. Rather, non-executives are shown to be able to influence the process of strategic choice, change and control by shaping both the ideas that become incorporated in corporate strategy and also the methods and processes by which these ideas develop and evolve. McNulty and Pettigrew quickly note that the influence of non-executives on strategic choice is not without limits; rather, it is moderated by factors such as changing norms about corporate governance, the history of the organisation and its performance, the process and conduct of board meetings and the informal dialogues amongst directors between board meetings. While a qualitative paper of this type should not be expected to provide generalisations similar to those made by positivistic papers examined in this volume (even though its findings are based on interviews of 108 directors), it generates excellent insights about processes and informal dynamics that only qualitative research could provide.

The paper by Carpenter and Westphal (2001) specifically examines the impact of external network ties on the ability of boards of directors to impact strategic decision making. The working principle on which their argument is based is the sociological perspective that points to the importance of directors' networks of appointments to other boards in determining whether they have the strategic knowledge and perspective required to monitor and advise management in the strategic decision-making process. Their findings suggest that the monitoring and advising behaviour of directors depended on the strategic perspective and expertise provided by their appointments to other boards. Specifically, Carpenter and Westphal reported that strategically related board ties enhanced board involvement in firms facing relatively stable environments and strategically heterogeneous board ties enhanced involvement in firms facing relatively unstable environments. The value of the study lies in demonstrating how interlocking ties influence an organisation's corporate governance via the appropriate alignment of ties to the strategic needs of the organisation.

The paper by Kosnik (1987) provides an interesting study of the impact of board characteristics on the ability of the board to prevent managers from making a decision, namely to pay greenmail. Greenmail transactions refer to threats that a significant stockholder will challenge the incumbent management in a takeover or a proxy fight. Management could prevent this threat by paying a premium over the market price to buy back the stockholder's interest in a private transaction. Clearly, senior managers' ability to conduct significant greenmail transactions suggests weaker board govemance as these transactions are not likely to be in the best interest of shareholders. The results suggest that boards that were more effective in resisting greenmail had more outside directors, more directors with executive experience and more directors who represented interorganisational transactions, that is the firm having more contracts with its outside directors.

Part III Board Characteristics and Organisational Performance

While the preceding section reviewed papers related to the impact of board characteristics on organisational decision making, this section introduces papers specifically focused on the effects of board characteristics on organisational performance. The two areas are clearly strongly related: the decision-making process and the outcome of decisions are part of organisational performance. In this section, however, the aim is to emphasise traditional, bottom-line measures of performance. The value of making such connection between board characteristics and organisational performance lies in the basic argument that if governance reforms are aimed at improving organisational performance, then this should operate via reforms affecting the board of directors. In other words, if the effects of board characteristics are shown to be neutral to organisational performance, then our investigation should shift to other areas where the effects of board characteristics are manifest. By the same token, if board characteristics impact organisational performance, then it should become clearer how board characteristics could be manipulated in order to produce certain desired effects on organisational performance.

One of the most fundamental questions involving the board of directors and performance relates to whether the existence of boards is at all important to firm success. Earlier, the discussion briefly commented on possible motives or reasons for the existence of boards of directors, and various reasons, such as legal, economic (agency theory) and political/symbolic, have been advanced. At the very least, the economic rationalisation for the existence of boards should be supported by empirical evidence that shows that having boards adds value to organisational success. It could also be argued that even if the boards exist for purely legal reasons or political reasons, this should still contribute to better organisational performance. Breaking the law can involve the imposition of severe financial sanctions, or even threaten the viability of the organisation altogether, not to mention the high costs of legal suits. Similarly, symbolic and political roles for boards of directors could be associated with better performance as the legitimacy of the organisation is enhanced in the eyes of external constituencies, and maintaining political cohesion can foster better performance. There is therefore a *prima facie* case to suggest that boards of directors of certain enabling characteristics should produce favourable effects on organisational performance.

The question of whether boards of directors are a burden on corporate resources has given rise to a 'small is beautiful' view of board size; the smaller the board size the less costly it is to the organisation and the more successful the organisation is (Lipton and Lorsch, 1992; Jensen, 1993). Such a view is not only concerned with the direct costs of keeping large boards of directors, in terms of financial rewards to members, but also their associated indirect costs (perquisites). Very large boards of directors could at the limit be far too large to function smoothly, resulting in greater bureaucracy, less openness, slower decision making and less entrepreneurial risk taking.

The paper by Yermack (1996) was motivated by the desire to examine the impact of board size on corporate performance. His study of a large sample of US firms over a five year period suggests an inverse relationship between board size and firm value measured as Tobin's Q. This result appears to be robust to various controls of firm size, industrial classification, inside share ownership, growth opportunities and alternative governance mechanisms. The paper also reports other findings which are supportive of the above main result. Specifically, financial ratios related to profitability and operating efficiency were found to decline as the size of the board grew. Further, a small number of firms that announced significant reductions in board size exhibited significant excess stock returns around the announcement date, with the opposite reported for firms that announced an increase in the size of their boards. These results lend support to institutional investors, regulators and other constituencies campaigning for smaller size boards.

The paper by Dalton, Daily, Johnson and Ellstrand (1999) also examines the connection between the size of the board of directors and financial performance. Marshalling alternative theoretical perspectives to those advocated by Yermack, the authors make a case for the benefits to be gained from larger size boards. Thus, according to resource dependency theory, larger boards can be used to form environmental links to obtain greater amounts of critical resources for the organisation. Dalton *et al.* also note the theoretical advantages of smaller size boards before they empirically test these theoretical propositions using meta-analysis (correcting for statistical artefacts and aggregating results across studies to obtain an estimate of the true relationship between variables). Their results show a systematic relationship between board size and financial performance, thereby suggesting a non-zero, positive association between the two variables. This relationship held for large and small firms but the effects were reported to be greater for the latter. These results are therefore in contrast to those reported earlier by Yermack.

The paper by Pearce and Zahra (1991) developed a typology of a large sample of US firms to test the association between characteristics of boards of directors and corporate performance. They differentiated between caretaker, statutory, proactive and participative boards, and reported that the four board archetypes exhibited significant differences in the main characteristics studied: internal processes, decision-making styles, board effectiveness and contribution to corporate performance. Concerning corporate performance, Pearce and Zahra's results suggest that the highest corporate financial performance (earnings per share and the financial strength of the corporation's stocks) was associated with the participative type of boards. While not as strong, the same relation obtained for subjective ratings of performance (perceived company competitive position, overall company performance and overall company profitability). The implications of this work are therefore that it pays for companies to have boards that are participative in style, emphasising the norms of collegiality, shared leadership and participation.

Such boards tend to have a healthy representation of outside members and a separation between leadership and the rest of the board.

The paper by Westphal (1999) examines the extent to which lack of social independence enhances board involvement and firm performance by increasing the frequency of advice and counsel between CEOs and outside directors. Collaboration between members of the board and the scope for provision of advice are together therefore thought to be a key characteristic of boards of directors, impacting favourably upon their ability to manage organisations more effectively. The results suggest that social ties between the CEO and the board not only do not adversely affect the board's monitoring ability, but they also enhance the furnishing of advice and counsel from outside members of the board on important strategic issues. CEOs, it seems, are more likely to seek advice when they feel they can rely on the loyalty of members of the board as reflected in social ties. The results also show that CEO–board collaboration and control are independently and positively associated with subsequent organisational performance.

The paper by Hambrick, Cho and Chen (1996) examines the impact of a different set of board characteristics, namely top management heterogeneity, on management actions, competitive behaviour and firm performance. Their study used a fairly small number of airline firms, 32, but over an eight year period. Top management teams with greater measures of heterogeneity (in terms of functional backgrounds, education, company tenure) exhibited a greater tendency towards taking action and undertaking competitive initiatives. However, heterogeneous teams were slower in executing action compared with homogeneous teams. More importantly, heterogeneous teams were positively associated with changes in market share and changes in firm profits. These findings need to be placed with the broader literature exploring the impact of top management heterogeneity on organisational performance (see Murray, 1989, for negative effects and Eisenhardt and Schoonhoven. 1990, for positive effects).

Part IV Board Characteristics and CEO Compensation

The final collection of readings deals with the relationship between board characteristics and CEO pay. A number of interesting research issues emerge in this area. One of these issues relates to the power and effectiveness of the board in controlling the determination of compensation levels for the CEO. To the extent that the board is effective in monitoring the actions of the CEO and ensuring that these actions are consistent with shareholder wealth maximisation, then the board would link CEO compensation directly to firm performance. There is some evidence to suggest that boards of directors tend to ignore movements in the firm's share prices, possibly pointing to the board trying to encourage CEOs to focus on the long term (Kerr and Bettis, 1987). The effectiveness of the board in monitoring CEOs and influencing their pay may depend to a greater or a lesser extent on the degree to which interlocks exist. Another related issue is the extent to which pay dynamics are similar for the CEO and the rest of the executive directors on the board. That is to say, to what extent does the trajectory of CEO pay over time resemble that of the rest of directors? This important issue has implications for the notion of distributive justice and fairness. If CEOs' pay dynamics are much more favourable than those of the rest of the board of directors, then feelings of unfairness may permeate the board. To the degree that such feelings exist, this may also be taken as an indication of weak control by the board over the determination of CEO pay. Board control is a fundamental part of the internal governance mechanisms, and it is likely to be favoured by most companies to market-based discipline that operates via mergers and acquisitions. In this sense, strong boards could act to stave off possible takeover threats (Walsh and Seward, 1990).

The paper by Hadlock and Lumer (1997) provides an interesting historical analysis of the dynamics of top management turnover and the sensitivity of turnover to share returns, and finds this to be significantly smaller for the period 1933–1941 compared with modern periods (1974–1986). Interestingly, they also report that top management compensation has become more sensitive to variations in firm performance since the 1930s, suggesting that over time management incentives have become stronger under the control of the board, contrary to the findings of other researchers, for example Jensen and Murphy (1990). In seeking to explain the evidence on weak board control in the 1930s–1940s, Hadlock and Lumer suggest that regulatory and political constraints are not the only factors that determine the strength of internal control mechanisms (i.e. board control), and they surmise that their evidence may also bear witness to a 'survival of the fittest'-type outcome, with stronger incentive mechanisms dominating over time.

Boyd (1994) examines the relationship between board control and CEO compensation in order to identify the extent to which CEOs succeed in maximising their own salaries by circumventing board control. His results indicate that board control explains a significant part of CEO pay and therefore suggest that boards of directors are a key internal governance mechanism. Further, he reports that the ratio of inside directors was negatively related to CEO compensation, thereby providing support to the argument that insiders are not pawns of CEOs, in the sense that they do not side with CEOs or become intimidated by them to make decisions that favour CEOs. If internal governance mechanisms can be as effective as the study by Boyd suggests, and there are also supportive arguments elsewhere (see Mizruchi, 1983; Walsh and Seward, 1990), then, from the perspective of CEOs, independent, strong boards of directors could be a genuine, 'lesser evil' disciplinary mechanism than market-based governance.

The paper by Hallock (1997) examines the impact of reciprocally interlocking boards of directors upon CEO compensation. Reciprocal interlocks refer to situations when one director (either current or retired) from one firm sits on the board of another firm and vice versa. In addition to the interesting finding that 20 per cent of the large sample of firms he examined had reciprocal interlocking boards, Hallock reported that salaries of CEOs in firms with interlocked boards were higher than in other firms, although the difference is reduced substantially once CEO and firm characteristics are controlled for. The paper also suggests that the return benefits attributed to reciprocally interlocking boards were higher in the 1970s compared with the early 1990s, hence the benefits of interlocks may be phasing out.

Wade, O'Reilly and Chandratat (1990) test the power and independence of boards of directors by focusing on a specific type of pay to CEOs, that known as 'golden parachutes'. Golden parachutes refer to contracts between the CEO and the firm that offer additional compensation to the CEO if a change of control or ownership occurs; they are thus a form of insurance against takeovers. Hence, theoretically, the higher the risk of takeovers the more likely that we observe more of these golden parachutes. Such an economic explanation treats golden parachutes as a form of incentive. Alternative perspectives, however, suggest that the incidence of golden parachutes may be an indication of weaker boards of directors that fail to protect shareholders' interests by allowing CEOs to behave opportunistically. The authors provide empirical tests of this phenomenon and their results suggest that there is support for both theoretical positions, suggesting perhaps that the 'truth' lies somewhere in between. Larger firms were found to have a lower likelihood of the CEO having a golden parachute, a finding consistent with the argument that larger firms are less likely to be takeover targets. The results also show a negative relation between golden parachutes and takeover risks. Both these results are consistent with the economic explanation. However, the results also suggest that social influence of the CEO over the board was associated with the award of golden parachutes, indicating that weaker boards are more susceptible to CEO manipulation to secure golden parachutes. An earlier study of golden parachutes by Cochran, Wood and Jones (1985) reported that firms with comparatively higher percentages of inside directors were less likely to award senior managers with golden parachutes, pointing to a stronger, more proactive role for boards of directors that have greater representations of internal directors.

The paper by Ezzamel and Watson (2002) tests board/CEO relationships in a different way. Using a sample of UK firms, they examine the extent to which the pay to the CEO and other executive members of the board is influenced by external labour market comparisons and within-the-board pay comparisons. They argue that labour market pay provides an external benchmark and thus, firms that fail to keep in line with such external benchmarks are likely to have their executives bid away by other firms prepared to pay the 'going rate'. Within-the-board comparisons are based on the argument that some measure of comparability in the pay awards to all members of the board is essential if the firm is to observe justice and fairness in pay. The results lend support to both arguments. Ezzamel and Watson report that external labour markets and internal pay comparisons are important factors explaining both the CEO and other directors' pay awards. However, they also note that in the case of CEOs, there is evidence of asymmetric adjustment to prior period pay anomalies, where pay adjustments for the relatively underpaid CEOs show significantly greater sensitivity to external market pay comparison levels. This asymmetric pay adjustment results in a bidding-up of average CEO pay relative to other board members, a finding that may suggest that CEOs have greater leverage over boards when CEO pay is determined.

Conclusions

Boards of directors are in principle an important mechanism of governance and control in modern organisations. With the loss of direct owner control because of diffusion of ownership and the power of professional managers, boards of directors have the potential to function as an effective disciplining mechanism to ensure an alignment between the actions of managers and the interests of owners. If this potential is fulfilled, boards of directors are likely to be preferred to the harsher external market governance discipline that works mainly through takeovers and acquisitions. The question then is: do boards of directors effectively perform this governance role?

This volume brings together contributions from a diverse number of disciplines, in particular economics, finance and management, that deal with research issues related to boards of directors' composition, dynamics and effects; all being critical components of the governance role of boards of directors. Most of the papers are empirical, with only a few of a purely theoretical nature. Moreover, all but one of the empirical papers are quantitative. This suggests that there is a shortage of research of a purely theoretical nature and also of qualitative empirical research. Finally, most of the contributions employ US data bases, indicating the desirability of extending research efforts in this area much more significantly to other Western and non-Western economies.

Despite the above caveats, the contributions included in this volume provide an impressive and systematic body of knowledge on boards of directors that are extremely helpful in addressing the question posed above. The papers cover four major research areas: determinants of board composition and board dynamics; board characteristics and decision making; board characteristics and organisational performance; and board characteristics and CEO compensation. In this respect, these papers provide an indispensable source for researchers interested in understanding how boards of directors, are formed, their internal characteristics, how they operate, and how they impact organisational decision making and performance.

Note

1. Hermalin and Weisbach (2003) is a much more recent review paper, but the authors' main focus is on the economic literature and, as they themselves admit (p. 8), their review spends a 'disproportionate amount of time on our own work'.

References

Berle, A.A. and Means, G.C. (1932), *The Modern Corporation and Private Property*, New York: Macmillan.
Cochran, P.L., Wood, R.A. and Jones, T.B. (1985), 'The composition of boards of directors and incidence of golden parachutes', *Academy of Management Journal*, **28** (3), 664–671.
Coughlan, A.T. and Schmidt, R.M. (1985), 'Executive compensation, managerial turnover, and firm performance: an empirical investigation', *Journal of Accounting and Economics*, **7**, 43–66.
Eisenhardt, K.M. and Schoonhoven, C.B. (1990), 'Organizational growth: linking founding team, strategy, environment, and growth among U.S. semi-conductor ventures, 1978–1988', *Administrative Science Quarterly*, **35**, 504–529.
Fama, E.G. (1980), 'Agency problems and the theory of the firm', *Journal of Political Economy*, **88**, 280–307.
Fama, E.G. and Jensen, M.C. (1983a), 'Separation of ownership and control', *Journal of Law and Economics*, **26**, June, 301–325.
Fama, E.G. and Jensen, M.C. (1983b), 'Agency problems and residual claimants', *Journal of Law and Economics*, **26**, June, 327–349.
Freeman, R.E. and Evan, W.F. (1990), 'Corporate governance: a stakeholder interpretation', *Journal of Behavioral Economics*, **19**, pp. 337–359.
Hermalin, B.E. and Weisbach, Michael S. (2003), 'Boards of directors as an endogenously determined institution: survey of the economic literature', *Economic Policy Review*, **9** (1), 7–26.
Jensen, M.C. (1993), 'The modern industrial revolution, exit, and the failure of internal control systems', *Journal of Finance*, **48**, 831–880.
Jensen, M.C. and Murphy, K.J. (1990), 'Performance pay and top management incentives', *Journal of Political Economy*, **98**, April, 225–264.
Johnson, J.L., Daily, C.M. and Ellstrand, A.E. (1996), 'Boards of directors: a review and research agenda', *Journal of Management*, **22**, 409–438.
Jones, T.M. and Goldberg, L.D. (1982), 'Governing the large corporation: more arguments for public directors', *Academy of Management Review*, **7**, pp. 603–611.
Kerr, J. and Bettis, R.A. (1987), 'Boards of directors, top management compensation, and shareholder returns', *Academy of Management Journal*, **30** (4), 645–664.

Lipton, M. and Lorsch, J.W. (1992), 'A modest proposal for improved corporate governance', *Business Lawyer*, **48** (1), 59–77.

Luoma, P. and Goodstein, J. (1999), 'Stakeholders and corporate boards: institutional influences on board composition and structure', *Academy of Management Journal*, **42** (5), 553–563.

Mace, M. (1971), *Directors: Myth and Reality*, Boston: Harvard Business School Press.

Mizruchi, M.S. (1983), 'Who controls whom? An examination of the relation between management and boards of directors in large corporations', *Academy of Management Review*, **8**, 426-435.

Murray, A.I. (1989), 'Top management group heterogeneity and firm performance', *Strategic Management Journal*, **10**, 125–141.

Vancil, R. (1987), *Passing the Baton: Managing the Process of CEO Succession*, Boston: Harvard Business School Press.

Walsh, J.P. and Seward, J.K. (1990), 'On the efficiency of internal and external corporate control mechanisms', *Academy of Management Review*, **15**, 421–458.

Warner, J.B., Watts, R.L. and Wruck, K.H. (1988), 'Stock prices and top management changes', *Journal of Financial Economics*, **20**, 461–492.

Westphal, J.F. (1998), 'Board games: how CEOs adapt in structural board independence from management', *Administrative Science Quarterly*, **43**, 511–537.

Zahra, S.A. and Pearce, J.A. (1989), 'Boards of directors and corporate financial performance: a review and integrated model', *Journal of Management*, **15**, 291–334.

Zajac, E.J. and Westphal, J.D. (1996), 'Who shall succeed? How CEO/board preferences and power affect the choice of new CEOs', *Academy of Management Journal*, **39**, 64–90.

Part I
Determinants of Board Composition and Board Dynamics

[1]

RAND Journal of Economics
Vol. 19, No. 4, Winter 1988

The determinants of board composition

Benjamin E. Hermalin*

and

Michael S. Weisbach**

We identify factors that lead to changes among corporate directors. We hypothesize that the CEO succession process and firm performance will affect board composition. Our findings are consistent with both hypotheses. When their CEO nears retirement, firms tend to add inside directors (who may be possible candidates to be the next CEO). Just after a CEO change, inside directors with short tenures appear more likely to leave the board (they, perhaps, being the losing candidates). We also find that inside directors are more likely to leave the board and outside directors more likely to join after a firm performs poorly and when a firm leaves a product market.

1. Introduction

■ Recent attention has focused on what corporate boards of directors do, how their composition affects what they do, and what should be done to improve their effectiveness.[1] What has been ignored, though, is how boards get to be the way they are; the question of what determines who gets added or taken off a board has been left largely unanswered. Our goal here is to establish some empirical regularities about director selection in the hopes of partially answering that question.

Understanding how directors are chosen is crucial to understanding corporate organization and governance: who gets selected will, in turn, affect the roles the board can play and how effectively it can play them. Furthermore, knowing how board membership is currently determined makes it possible to evaluate proposed reforms in the board selection process, such as the ALI's (1982) or Dunn's (1987).

---

* University of California at Berkeley.

** University of Rochester.

We wish to thank participants in seminars at Chicago, M.I.T., NBER, and Rochester, as well as Sanjai Bhagat, Jim Brickley, Harry DeAngelo, Franklin M. Fisher, Jerry Hausman, Paul Healy, Cliff Holderness, Steve Kaplan, Mervyn King, Jeff Mackie-Mason, Kevin J. Murphy, Pat O'Brien, Jim Poterba, Ed Rice, David Scharfstein, Andrei Shleifer, Peter Temin, Jean Tirole, Rob Vishny, Jerry Zimmerman, and especially two referees and the Editorial Board for helpful comments. Hermalin acknowledges support provided by an NSF Graduate Fellowship and a Sloan Foundation Graduate Fellowship. Weisbach acknowledges support from MERC and the John M. Olin Foundation.

[1] ALI (1982), Brickley and James (1987), Brickley and Van Drunen (1987), *Business Week* (September 8, 1986), MacAvoy *et al.* (1983), Mace (1971), Morck, Shleifer, and Vishny (1988), Shleifer and Vishny (1986), and Weisbach (1988) are some examples.

In this article we ask whether firm performance, CEO tenure, and changes in market structure lead to changes in board composition. Our results suggest that outside directors are more likely to join and inside directors more likely to leave a board after poor firm performance, when firms leave product markets, and possibly when there is a new CEO.[2] We also find that as a CEO nears retirement, insiders will be added to the board, possibly to be "groomed" as candidates to be the next CEO (Vancil, 1987).

Section 2 develops the hypotheses to be tested. Section 3 describes our data. Section 4 presents the empirical results. Section 5 contains a discussion and conclusion.

2. Potential factors influencing director choice

■ Evidence from both academic and business sources (Mace, 1971; Vancil, 1987) suggests that the CEO plays a large role in choosing the board of directors. One concern of the CEO, particularly toward the end of his tenure, is the choice of his successor. Both the business press and some academic work (Mace 1971; Vancil, 1987) argue that "grooming" the next CEO is a major motive for adding insiders to the board. That is, insiders are added to give them exposure to a variety of corporate issues, as well as to make them more visible to the other board members. Broad exposure to the work and problems of other divisions is valuable experience for a potential CEO. In addition, greater visibility of potential CEOs will aid the board in evaluating and choosing the next CEO. Thus, the CEO facilitates the succession process through his choice of inside directors. Although some boards have only two insiders, the CEO and his "heir apparent," many boards include a number of "CEO candidates," who engage in a rivalry for the top job (or to be anointed heir apparent).[3]

The link between the board and the CEO succession process generates several testable hypotheses: toward the end of a CEO's tenure, insiders should be added to the board to facilitate the succession. Also, insiders who come to feel they have little chance to become the next CEO may leave the company.[4] At the beginning of a new CEO's tenure a number of insiders, losing candidates to become the new CEO, may leave, since they will not soon have another chance to become CEO. Since the new CEO is not ready or, perhaps, even able to begin his own succession process, he is not likely to wish to replace the departed insiders with other insiders. Also, the new CEO may wish to fill the board vacancies with outsiders who can offer good advice and counsel as he begins his job. Alternatively, a new CEO may have less freedom to choose his board than an established CEO, and hence may have to add outsiders to satisfy shareholders' desires for greater monitoring. Finally, the former CEO frequently stays on for a few years as chairman of the board, which further limits the new CEO's control of the board selection process.

A second set of explanations for board changes involves corporate performance: poor corporate performance can lead to an inside director's being fired, either at the urging of the shareholders and the rest of the board, or by the CEO in an effort to protect himself and the company. Thus, we would expect to see poor corporate performance leading to

---

[2] An outside director is a director whose full-time job is not with the firm (often the CEO of another firm), while an inside director is a director whose full-time job is with the firm. An explanation of how we operationalize this sometimes murky distinction appears in Section 3.

[3] The horse race among seven candidates, three of whom were added to the board, at General Electric to determine Reginald Jones' successor is an example of this (Vancil, 1987).

There are, of course, other motives behind the choice of board members. For example, the CEO may choose outside directors who will give good advice and counsel, who can bring valuable experience and expertise to the board, and who offer a contrast to the perspectives and opinions found within the firm. The CEO may use his choice of inside directors to enhance monitoring of subordinates or to reward valuable personnel.

[4] A possible example is the departure of two of three executive vice presidents of Allied Chemical after John Connor's rejection of the outgoing CEO's recommendation to make one of them COO and heir apparent. (Vancil, 1987).

resignations of insiders.[5] The insider's immediate successor on the board may or may not be an insider. To the extent that poor performance indicates a need for a fresh perspective or greater monitoring, a board vacancy following poor performance is more likely be filled by an outsider than by an insider.

Finally, if a firm exits a market, the insider who was in charge of that market is likely to lose his job or be demoted from the board. Therefore, there should be a positive correlation between a reduction in the number of markets in which a firm operates and the number of insiders who leave the board. When a firm enters a market, an insider who is already on the board, rather than the person in charge of the market, may be given the additional responsibility of managing that market. Consequently, we expect that entering a market will be less strongly correlated with the addition of insiders to the board.

3. Data

■ **An overview of the variables.** To study board composition we assembled a database on the boards of directors for a sample of NYSE-traded companies. We began with the 322 firms used by Weisbach (1988), all of which had data available on both earnings (from annual *COMPUSTAT*) and stock returns (from *CRSP*).[6] This data set contains detailed information about CEO tenure and turnover. For each firm in the sample we collected data from corporate proxy statements between 1971 and 1983. Because we were interested in the factors that determine board composition, we eliminated all firms whose board composition was likely to be affected by regulation. This restriction eliminated 23 public utilities, two airlines, and one railroad. Since banks and financial institutions have different board structures than do industrial firms, we eliminated 13 banks and financial institutions from our sample. We also required that each firm have a proxy available in Harvard's Baker Library for each year between 1971 and 1983. A total of 140 firms had missing proxies for at least one of the 13 years. The resulting sample contained 142 firms.[7]

For each of our 142 firms we gathered 13 years of data on their board composition. We classified each director according to his principal occupation. Full-time employees of the corporation were designated as insiders. Directors who did not work full-time for the corporation were classified as outsiders. Directors who were closely associated with the firm, but were not full-time employees, were designated as "greys." Greys either were related to an officer of the company or had extensive business dealings with the company (as reported on the proxy), which made their independence from management questionable. Directors who were classified as grey because of business dealings were often lawyers, bankers, consultants, or investment bankers. Because of the conflict-of-interest problems inherent in having investment bankers on the board (Mace, 1971), investment bankers were always designated as greys.

Our data collection procedure creates some relatively minor problems for determining composition. To economize on data-collection costs, we examined the 1971, 1974, 1977, 1980, and 1983 proxies to determine our set of directors for each firm. We then used the

[5] It is almost impossible for external observers to distinguish between firings and voluntary resignations. Corporations rarely announce publicly that they are firing top executives. Instead, they typically invent a face-saving explanation for the executive that is indistinguishable from a voluntary resignation. (See Weisbach (1988), Warner *et al.* (1988), or Vancil (1987) for evidence.)

[6] This data set in turn comes from a sample of 495 firms used by MacAvoy *et al.* (1983). The 495 firms represent all firms for which proxies were available in the Yale Library. 128 firms were excluded because they were not in the *Forbes* compensation surveys, which provide the data on CEO tenure and turnover we use below. Finally, 45 firms were excluded because they were missing earnings data from *COMPUSTAT*.

[7] In addition, we eliminated Chrysler Corporation because different directors represented different classes of stocks, rather than representing all shareholders. We felt this structure differed too much from the rest of the sample to be included.

other proxies to determine the year in which each of these directors joined and left the board. A problem with this procedure is that it undersamples directors with very short tenures (less than three years). For example, a director who joined the board in 1975 and left in 1976 would not be in our sample. Therefore, we are likely to miscalculate board composition occasionally because we fail to include some directors.[8] To the extent that this affects our results, it will bias us toward not finding strong relationships between our hypothesized determinants of board composition and actual composition, since it essentially creates errors in our dependent variables.

A second problem created by our collection procedure is that our data on when directors join the board are taken from proxy statements and are on a calendar-year, rather than a proxy-year basis (a proxy year is the year between mailing dates).[9] As the study of board composition is naturally done on the basis of proxy, rather than calendar years, some procedure was necessary for translating "joins" from a calendar-year to a proxy-year basis. If a company issues its proxies during the first half of the year, we assume that all directors who joined in that calendar year joined following the issuance of the proxy. If a company issues its proxies during the second half of the year, we assume that all directors who joined in that year joined before the issuance of the proxy. For example, if a firm issues its proxies in March, any join in the year 1975 is attributed to the 1975–1976 proxy year, but if it issued proxies in September, such joins would be attributed to the 1974–1975 proxy year.

We used and supplemented data from Weisbach (1988) to determine CEO tenures. This was done because our hypotheses predict that CEO tenure will be an important determinant of board composition. For the years within our sample period, we calculated CEO tenure by locating the exact date of any CEO change in the *Wall Street Journal Index.* We obtained the starting year for CEOs who started before 1971 from the *Forbes* compensation surveys or from *Who's Who in Finance and Industry.*[10]

As a measure of firm diversification, we use the number of different industries in which a firm operates, which we estimated by the number of four-digit SIC codes for which the firm was listed by *Standard and Poor's Register of Corporations.* Changes in diversification are measured by the proportional change in the number of four-digit codes.

The company information gathered from the proxies was supplemented by data on stock returns and earnings from *CRSP* and *COMPUSTAT.* The returns used below are the total return on a company's stock for the twelve months before the proxy year in question. If, for example, board changes between 1975 and 1976 are being analyzed for a firm with proxies mailed in April, we would use the returns over the year from April 1974 to March 1975 as an independent variable. These returns are adjusted for industry factors by subtracting from them a measure of the average return in the firm's industry. This measure is constructed by computing the average return of all firms in the given firm's two-digit SIC code on the *CRSP* tape for the relevant twelve-month period.[11]

The construction of the earnings measure is more complicated. Since our hypotheses suggest that changes in the composition of the board are likely to be related to deviations from average performance, we would like to use a measure of unexpected earnings. A large

---

[8] The fraction of directors who leave the board within three years of joining it (calculated by using only directors who joined in 1971, 1974, 1977, and 1980) is .1176 (with a standard error of .3226). The fraction who leave one year after joining is .0455 (.2086), and the fraction leaving after two years is .0468 (.2115). Given our method of calculation, these numbers tend to overstate greatly the probabilities of missing a director. Using these estimates, we calculate the number of directors we missed to be approximately 113, or 3% of the directors serving our 142 firms during the period 1971 to 1983.

[9] As a rule, proxies list only the (calendar) year in which a director joined.

[10] Occasionally precise starting and finishing dates were reported in the proxies as part of the CEO's biography. For those CEOs beginning before 1971, and for whom we only knew the starting year, we assumed that their tenure began July 1 of that year to minimize bias when carrying out certain calculations.

[11] We also have estimated our equations by using market-adjusted returns with similar results.

literature on the time-series behavior of accounting earnings (Ball and Watts, 1972; Foster, 1978) finds that annual earnings can be approximated by a random walk. This implies that changes in earnings are a good proxy for unexpected earnings.

The earnings variable used below is earnings before interest and taxes (*EBIT*).[12] We use this measure to prevent changes in capital structures or tax treatments from obscuring differences in earnings measures of performance. The change in *EBIT* is standardized by the book value of the firm's assets at the end of the previous year to control for size differences. Finally, to control for factors affecting earnings changes caused by industry effects, the average standardized earnings change is computed for all the firms on the *COMPUSTAT* industrial tape with the same two-digit SIC code as the given firm. This average is subtracted from the standardized earnings change for the test firm. The resulting variable provides a measure of unexpected earnings that should not be sensitive to the firm's size, industry, capital structure, or tax treatment.

□ **Descriptive statistics.** Table 1 provides a description of our data for the year 1977, the midpoint of our sample period. The median firm had 13 directors of whom 45% were outsiders. The percentage of outsiders ranged from 10% for General Instrument to 89% for Western Union. Board size varied between 4 (National Semiconductor) and 21 (Philip Morris).

Causal observation of this table reveals that some of the variables have skewed distributions. For example, the median CEO tenure is only 5.9 years, but one CEO (S. Rabb of Stop & Shop) was in office almost 47 years at the time of the 1977 proxy. Similarly, the inside members of the median board own slightly more than 1% of the stock, but for Campbell's Soup, insiders control almost 65% of the stock. It is important to recognize the importance of such outliers so that a few corporations do not drive the results.

Board composition has changed through time. A striking feature of our data is that between 1971 and 1983 there has been a substantial movement toward replacing insiders with outsiders. The average percentage of outsiders rose from 37.6% to 53.9%, while the average percentage of insiders fell from 49.1% to 34.3%.[13]

Table 2 gives a correlation matrix of some of the important variables in our data set.

TABLE 1 Variables on Firms and Their Boards of Directors Ranked by Percentile (Sample: 142 NYSE Companies in 1977)

	Percentile						
Data Item	1	10	33	50	67	90	99
Percentage Outsiders (%)	10.0	21.4	33.3	45.4	53.8	66.7	88.9
Board Size	4	10	12	13	14	17	21
CEO Tenure (Years)	0	1.5	4.8	5.9	7	19.8	46.8
Shareholdings of Insiders (%)	.00	.12	.39	1.13	2.89	28.59	64.89
Shareholdings of Top Management (%)	.00	.02	.11	.36	1.07	21.88	64.89
Shareholdings of Outsiders (%)	.00	.00	.01	.04	.21	1.83	27.68
Assets ($ Millions)	134	365	839	1214	1859	3839	93972

[12] This variable is constructed by adding data items 15, 16, 18, and 49 on the annual *COMPUSTAT* industrial tape.

[13] This trend confirms the results of other studies (Conference Board, 1973; Mruk and Gardinia, 1985). Since 1983, though, the pattern has reversed. Because of increased director-liability insurance costs, firms have begun to move back towards having more insiders on their boards (*Business Week*, September 8, 1986).

TABLE 2 Correlation Matrix of Variables about Firms and Their Boards of Directors (Sample: 142 NYSE Firms in 1977)*

Variable	CEO Tenure	Median Director Tenure	Stake of Top Management	Number of Industries	Market Value of Equity
Fraction Outsiders on Board	−.104 (1.17)	−.157 (1.72)	−.167 (1.82)	.136 (1.73)	.168 (2.18)
CEO Tenure	—	.242 (3.30)	.204 (2.70)	−.024 (.297)	−.072 (.825)
Median Tenure of Directors	—	—	.043 (.52)	−.090 (1.05)	−.088 (1.00)
Stake of Top Management[a]	—	—	—	−.205 (2.21)	−.094 (1.07)
Number of Industries[b]	—	—	—	—	−.033 (.38)

* *t*-statistics are in parentheses.

[a] Stake of top management includes the shareholdings of the present CEO as well as all former CEOs still on the board. It is measured as a fraction of the company's shares.

[b] The measure of the number of industries of a firm is the number of different four-digit SIC codes a firm is associated with in *Standard and Poor's Register of Corporations.*

The fraction of outsiders on the board is correlated with several variables: the median tenure of directors, the shareholdings of top management, and the number of industries in which the firm operates. All of these correlations are significant at least at the 10% level. The negative correlation between median board tenure and fraction of outside directors suggests that outside directors turn over more rapidly than do inside directors. This is not surprising: outside directors, because they are frequently CEOs of other firms, distinguished professors, retired politicians, etc., tend to be older than inside directors, who, except for the CEO, tend to be vice presidents. Consequently, the retirement rate for outside directors should be higher. Another explanation is that outside directorships are not the primary occupation of most outside directors. Therefore, they are more prone to resign as directors for reasons, either personal or professional, that would not be sufficient to cause inside directors to resign.

As noted in Weisbach (1988), the fraction of outside directors is negatively correlated with the shareholdings of top management. This fact is consistent with the view that monitoring by outside directors and the direct incentives created by management's stock ownership are substitute methods of control. This fact might be better explained, however, by the tendency of top management with a large stake in its firm to put family members on the board (the correlation coefficient between the fraction of the board related to top management and the shareholdings of top management is .5208, with a *t*-statistic of 8.9013). Since we never count family members as outsiders, this tendency necessarily reduces the fraction of the board who are outsiders. When we examined the correlation between the fraction of nonfamily board members who are outsiders and the shareholdings of top management, we found no significant relation (the correlation coefficient was −.0834, with a *t*-statistic of .9479).

4. Empirical specification and results

■ We expect the forces that determine board composition to affect insiders and outsiders differently. Consequently, we estimate separate equations for each type. Similarly, the forces that cause firms to add directors are different from those that cause firms to remove directors.

For this reason, we estimate separate equations for additions and departures from the board. Finally, we examine direct evidence on our conjecture that it is the succession process that motivates CEOs to add insiders to the board late in their tenure.

□ **Departures from the board.** To predict departures of director type i from the board, we estimate the following equation:

$$Depart_i = f(\text{CEO tenure}, \Delta\text{Earnings}, \text{Stock Returns}, \Delta\text{Industries}, \text{Median Director Tenure}_i, \text{Retirement Dummy}, \text{Number}_i, \text{Size of Firm}, \text{Period Dummies}).$$

The dependent variable is the number of departures of directors of a given type from the board from one proxy to the next.[14] The firm-years are pooled, with each firm-year representing a separate observation. Because we do not have data on the number of industries in 1971, we use 11 years of data for each firm. After omitting observations with missing data, we have 1,521 observations.

Because the dependent variable in our equations is the count of different events (departures from the board) rather than a continuous variable, ordinary least squares is biased and inconsistent. Therefore, we use a Poisson model (Hausman *et al.*, 1984) to estimate our equations. If λ is defined by $\log(\lambda) = X\beta$, where X is a vector of independent variables and β is a parameter vector, than a Poisson model assumes that the probability of n directors' leaving the board in a given year equals $(\exp(-\lambda)*\lambda^n)/(n!)$. This specification implies that the log-likelihood function is

$$L(\beta) = \sum_{i=1}^{N} \sum_{t=1}^{T} [C_1 - \exp(X_{it}\beta) + n_{it}X_{it}\beta],$$

where C_1 is a constant that does not affect the maximization process, n_{it} is the number of departures for firm i in year t, N is the number of firms, and T is the number of time periods per firm. The log-likelihood function is maximized over β to produce maximum-likelihood estimates.

Every company has its own history, traditions, and culture, which are likely to affect director choice. As these effects are not captured in the specification discussed above, we need to control for them in the estimation process. The logical way to do this is to include firm-specific fixed effects in the specification. A problem with this approach is that it ignores variation among firms and only uses within-firm variation. Since we have only 11 years of data for each firm, including fixed effects substantially lowers the amount of variation in our data. This will be particularly important when investigating the effects of factors that change slowly over time. As a result of this difficulty with fixed-effects estimation, we report each of our equations with and without fixed effects. With fixed effects the log-likelihood takes the form:[15]

$$L(\beta) = C_2 - \sum_{i=1}^{N} \sum_{t=1}^{T} n_{it} \log \{ \sum_{s=1}^{T} \exp[-(X_{it} - X_{is})\beta] \},$$

where C_2 is a constant that does not affect the maximization process.

A remaining specification issue concerns "adding-up constraints." One might think that we should estimate our additions and departures equations jointly, by imposing on the

[14] In a previous version of this article, we also used the percentage change of directors of a given type as the dependent variable. Since the results from these equations are economically identical to the ones reported here, we choose to report only the equations using the number of directors as the dependent variable.

[15] A derivation of this likelihood function can be found in Hausman *et al.* (1984, pp. 917–919).

estimation process the constraint that the total number of additions equal the total number of departures. Such a constraint does not seem to be borne out in our data, however. Of the 1,521 firm-years in our sample, 905 contain at least one departure from the board. In only 244 of these 905 firm-years does the number of additions to the board equal the number of departures. This suggests that board size is not fixed. Therefore, we chose not to impose constraints that are truly not constraints.[16]

The first independent variable is CEO tenure. Because our hypotheses focus on the beginning and end of a CEO's regime, we feel our hypotheses are best tested by using dummy variables for the different phases of a CEO's career. We have two dummy variables; the first indicates whether a CEO is in the lowest third of the sample in terms of his tenure (less than 4.5 years), and the second is the middle third (4.5 to 10 years). The omitted variable is for CEOs with at least ten years of experience.[17]

The measures of unexpected performance, changes in earnings and stock returns, are included for the two years before the proxy in question. We have experimented with longer lags on these variables, but as their coefficients were never significantly or meaningfully different from zero, we do not report these estimates.

The measure of the change in the numbers of industries in which the firm operates is broken down into its positive and negative components (i.e. $\Delta SIC = \Delta SIC_+ + \Delta SIC_-$, where ΔSIC is the proportional change in the number of industries, ΔSIC_+ (>0) is the positive component and ΔSIC_- (<0) is the negative component). We do this because adding industries and dropping industries are likely to be different types of events and there is no reason to suspect that the effects of the two on board composition are the same.

We include the median tenure of directors of a given type (e.g., median tenure of insiders or median tenure of outsiders) to control for the natural turnover process of the board.[18] As boards get older, there are likely to be more voluntary resignations, because age and professional norms limit the tenure of directors.

As we have suggested that board composition is intimately related to the CEO succession process, we attempt to control for retirements of CEOs. Since a large number CEOs retire at approximately age 65 (Weisbach, 1988), we include a dummy variable that is 1 if the CEO is between 62 and 66. This variable attempts to capture some of the "grooming" motivations for board change before a CEO change.

Because the number of directors of a given type who leave the board is likely to be related to the number of directors of that type on the board, we include the number of directors of the type in question in the equation. We also control for firm size in our equations. To measure size we use the market value of the firm's equity at the start of the proxy year.[19] Finally, to control for time trends, we include three period dummies.

The results are shown in Table 3 for departures of insiders and in Table 4 for departures of outsiders. The equations for insiders departing the board support the hypotheses discussed above. In the equations without fixed effects, the coefficient for a new CEO is positive and significantly different from zero at the 5% level: a new CEO leads to the departure of insiders.

[16] Since additions and departures may be correlated, however, we would have liked to estimate the additions and departures equations jointly and allow for correlations among the errors from the different equations. Unfortunately, that is impossible, given our fixed-effects Poisson specification—there is no consistent system estimator for this specification (unless the number of proxy years approaches infinity). By ignoring cross equation correlations, we admittedly lose efficiency but *not* consistency, so this problem is not serious.

[17] To test the robustness of our specification, we also estimate our equations by using a specification identical to the one reported except that it is linear in CEO tenure. The results (which are available from the authors on request) are consistent with those reported here.

[18] We have also estimated equations by using the median tenure of the entire board with similar results.

[19] We have also used the book value of the firm's assets with practically identical results.

TABLE 3 Poisson Estimates of Departures of Insiders from Boards of Directors (Sample: 142 NYSE Firms, 1972–1983)*

Independent Variable	Without Fixed Effects	With Fixed Effects
Intercept	−1.922	—
	(10.2)	
NEWCEO[a]	.257	−.099
	(2.77)	(.95)
MIDCEO[b]	.116	−.190
	(1.16)	(1.81)
$\Delta EBIT$[c]	.713	.570
	(.85)	(.77)
$\Delta EBIT_{-1}$	−.801	−.380
	(.97)	(.50)
Return[d]	−.493	−.359
	(3.30)	(2.78)
$Return_{-1}$	−.287	−.234
	(1.91)	(1.87)
ΔSIC_{+}[e]	.018	−.005
	(1.22)	(.38)
ΔSIC_{-}[f]	−.054	−.034
	(3.12)	(1.57)
MEDIN[g]	.009	.091
	(1.13)	(8.24)
RETIRE[h]	.212	.013
	(2.20)	(.15)
Number of Insiders on Board	.183	.369
	(13.2)	(15.0)
Market Value of Equity	.005	−.021
	(.54)	(.50)
Dummy If Year = 1972–1973	−.057	−.464
	(.51)	(4.85)
Dummy If Year = 1974–1976	−.114	−.387
	(1.14)	(4.40)
Dummy If Year = 1977–1980	−.113	−.219
	(1.14)	(2.65)
Number of Observations	1,521	1,521

* *t*-statistics are in parentheses

[a] *NEWCEO* is a dummy variable that takes the value 1 if the CEO has held his job for less than 4.5 years.

[b] *MIDCEO* is a dummy variable that takes the value 1 if the CEO has held his job for at least 4.5 years and less than 10 years.

[c] The variable $\Delta EBIT$ is the company's change in the earnings before interest and taxes weighted by the book value of assets in the most recent fiscal year before the potential resignation. This variable is adjusted for industry effects by subtracting from it the mean for all the firms on *COMPUSTAT* in the same two-digit SIC code.

[d] The variable *Return* is the return on the company's stock for the 12 months before the date the proxy was mailed minus the return on an equally weighted portfolio comprising all firms listed as having the same principal two-digit SIC code on *CRSP* for the same period.

[e] The variable ΔSIC_{+} isi the positive component of the change in the number of four-digit SIC codes over the period of the potential board changes weighted by the number of SIC codes at the start of the period.

[f] The variable ΔSIC_{-} is the negative component of the change in the number of four digit SIC codes over the period of the potential board changes weighted by the number of SIC codes at the start of the period.

[g] The variable *MEDIN* is the median tenure of the insiders currently on the board as directors.

[h] The variable *RETIRE* is dummy variable that takes the value 1 if the CEO is at least 62 and no older than 66 years old.

TABLE 4 **Poisson Estimates of Departures of Outsiders from Boards of Directors (Sample: 142 NYSE Firms, 1972–1983)***

Independent Variable	Without Fixed Effects	With Fixed Effects
Intercept	−2.702	—
	(14.8)	
NEWCEO	.171	.045
	(1.46)	(.35)
MIDCEO	.106	−.039
	(.95)	(.33)
$\Delta EBIT$	.472	−.528
	(.53)	(.65)
$\Delta EBIT_{-1}$	.944	.823
	(1.03)	(1.08)
Return	−.073	−.157
	(.57)	(1.42)
$Return_{-1}$	−.232	−.308
	(1.37)	(1.99)
ΔSIC_{+}	−.005	−.031
	(.23)	(1.34)
ΔSIC_{-}	.020	.033
	(.60)	(1.06)
MEDOUT[a]	.055	.161
	(4.59)	(11.6)
RETIRE	.201	.141
	(1.78)	(1.34)
Number of Outsiders on Board	.187	.383
	(12.3)	(14.2)
Market Value of Equity	−.012	.076
	(1.92)	(3.06)
Dummy If Year = 1972–1973	.268	.392
	(2.27)	(3.73)
Dummy If Year = 1974–1976	.151	.398
	(1.33)	(4.04)
Dummy If Year = 1977–1980	.043	.200
	(.39)	(2.17)
Number of Observations	1,521	1,521

* *t*-statistics are in parentheses.
[a] The variable *MEDOUT* is the median tenure of outsiders currently on the board as directors.

When the fixed effects are added, however, this effect disappears, possibly because much of the variation in CEO tenure is across firms, rather than within a given firm.[20]

Stock returns seem to affect the departure of insiders. The coefficient on stock returns for the year before the proxy year is negative (poor returns increase the number of insiders who depart) and significantly different from zero at the 1% level. The coefficient on returns for two years before the proxy is negative and significant at the 10% level. Poor performance, measured by stock returns, leads to the resignations of insiders. There does not appear to be an analogous effect for earnings changes, however. The coefficients on earnings changes are insignificantly different from zero. Nevertheless, a likelihood-ratio test of the hypothesis that the overall effect of the performance measures is zero is rejected at the 1% level ($\chi^2 = 15.79$).

[20] The within-firm variation in dummy variables is less than the between-firm variation because the values of the dummy variables stay the same for many years (e.g., a firm can have a "new" CEO or an "about to retire" CEO for 5 of its 12 firm-years).

Decreases in the number of industries in which firms operate appear to increase the departures of insiders from the board. The coefficients on the negative component of the change in SIC codes are negative and significantly different from zero in the specification without fixed effects. Presumably, this is caused by the departure of the insiders who were in charge of the exited industries. Increases in the number of industries had no effect on departures of insiders from the board. The coefficients on the positive component of the change in SIC codes are close to zero and not significant.

The number of insiders who leave the board is significantly and positively related to the CEO approaching retirement for the regression without fixed effects. This is consistent with the idea that as the CEO nears retirement and his replacement is announced, the losing candidates leave the firm for jobs elsewhere. The fact that this effect is not significant for the fixed-effects regressions is likely due to the lack of within-firm variation in the *RETIRE* variable (see footnote 20), although caution should be exercised when interpreting this variable's effect.

Thus, we see that poor stock returns, exiting industries, and possibly new CEOs and imminent CEO succession increase the chances of an insider's leaving the board. From Table 4, it appears that these factors do not play much of a role in the departure of outsiders. Indeed, the only significant variables in predicting the departure of outsiders are the median tenure of outsiders and the number of outsiders on the board. That these two variables are significant is not surprising, as they simply control for exposure to risk.

□ **Additions to the board.** When a new CEO takes office, the company performs poorly, and a company drops out of industries, insiders tend to depart. We argued previously that such departing insiders could potentially be replaced with outsiders. Now we examine additions to the board. We estimate the following equation for additions of directors of a given type:

$$Addition_i = g(\text{CEO tenure, } \Delta\text{Earnings, Stock Returns, } \Delta\text{Industries, Current Composition,}$$
$$\text{Retirement Dummy, Number of Vacancies, Size of Firm, Period Dummies}).$$

Again, we estimate the equations by using a Poisson model with and without fixed effects and use the same 1,521 observations as before.

The variables in the additions equations were, with two exceptions, also included in the departures equations: we include the current composition of the board and a measure of the possible number of vacancies. Current composition will affect who is added to the board, if management is wary of having boards that are extremely inside-dominated or extremely outside-dominated. We use the current proportion of outsiders as our measure of current composition.

Although not every departure is immediately filled, *ceteris paribus* someone is more likely to join the board following a departure than otherwise. Therefore, we would like to control for the number of departures preceding any addition to the board that we seek to explain. Unfortunately, given the information on the proxies, we cannot determine the sequence of departures and additions within a given proxy year (e.g., we cannot determine whether a given addition preceded or followed a given departure). We include in our specification the number of directors who left the board in the previous proxy year as an admittedly rough control for board vacancies.

One reason it is important to control for past departures is the following: imagine that, given a vacancy, top management always chooses, *independent of the circumstances,* to fill the vacancy with an insider with probability p and with an outsider with probability $1 - p$. Suppose further that no one is added to the board where there is not a departure. Then a regression of the number of type i directors added to the board that does not control for the number of vacancies would result in the spurious finding that the addition of type i

directors is related to the variables that determined the vacancies. Such a finding would give the misleading impression that who was being added to the board was *determined* by those variables, when, in fact, who was added was *independent* of those variables. To avoid that mistake, it is important to control for the number of vacancies. If, controlling for the number of vacancies, we find that the addition of type *i* directors is significantly related to a set of variables, then we can conclude that those variables do determine who gets added to the board, i.e., that the probabilities p and $1 - p$ are *not* independent of the circumstances.

The results from the addition of insiders equations are shown in Table 5. The CEO succession effect, measured by the dummy variable *RETIRE*, is positive and significant at the 5% level. This is consistent with the conjecture that CEOs use the period before their resignation as a grooming period, during which rival candidates to be CEO are added to the board. As hypothesized, the addition of directors is directly related to the previous departure of directors. The positive coefficient indicates that more insiders are added after previous departures of directors.

TABLE 5 **Poisson Estimates of Additions of Insiders to Boards of Directors (Sample: 142 NYSE Firms, 1972–1983)***

Independent Variable	Without Fixed Effects	With Fixed Effects
Intercept	−1.167	—
	(8.42)	
NEWCEO	−.027	−.350
	(.27)	(2.78)
MIDCEO	−.118	−.347
	(1.17)	(2.82)
$\Delta EBIT$	.698	−.358
	(.70)	(.37)
$\Delta EBIT_{-1}$	−.388	−.924
	(.42)	(1.01)
Return	−.314	−.307
	(1.91)	(1.98)
$Return_{-1}$	−.064	.020
	(.46)	(.14)
ΔSIC_{+}	.017	.008
	(1.00)	(.47)
ΔSIC_{-}	.005	.003
	(.15)	(.09)
PEROUT[a]	−.850	2.523
	(4.09)	(5.55)
RETIRE	.245	.267
	(2.48)	(2.40)
Number of Directors Who Left Last Year	.128	.026
	(4.35)	(.93)
Market Value of Equity	.021	.036
	(3.76)	(.98)
Dummy If Year = 1972–1973	.668	1.056
	(5.94)	(9.53)
Dummy If Year = 1974–1976	.240	.541
	(2.04)	(4.79)
Dummy If Year = 1977–1980	.285	.453
	(2.58)	(4.36)
Number of Observations	1,521	1,521

* *t*-statistics are in parentheses.

[a] The variable *PEROUT* is the fraction of outsiders on the board at the time of the initial proxy.

The effects of current board composition differ between the fixed-effects and the no-fixed effects regressions. But this apparent anomaly is not surprising because one would expect the between-firm variation and the within-firm variation to affect the results in opposite ways. When the fixed effects are included, the coefficient on the fraction of outsiders is positive. This means that when the fraction of outsiders is large *relative to the firm's historical norm,* firms look to reverse the trend and add insiders (i.e., return to their norm). When we exclude the fixed effects from the equation, the coefficient on *PEROUT* becomes negative. What appears to be happening is that the fraction of outsiders is a proxy for the omitted fixed effect. Firms that traditionally hire insiders (and thus have more of them on the board) are more likely to hire them in the future than are firms that traditionally hire outsiders.

Turning to the outsiders equations in Table 6, we see that the coefficients on *NEWCEO* are both positive and significantly different from zero at the 5% level in the equations without fixed effects and at the 10% level in the equations with fixed effects. This result suggests that newer CEOs are more likely to add outside directors than their more experienced counterparts.

TABLE 6 Poisson Estimates of Additions of Outsiders to Boards of Directors (Sample: 142 NYSE Firms, 1972–1983)*

Independent Variable	Without Fixed Effects	With Fixed Effects
Intercept	−1.01	—
	(8.32)	
NEWCEO	.225	.175
	(2.63)	(1.80)
MIDCEO	.172	.114
	(1.99)	(1.24)
$\Delta EBIT$	−1.522	−1.704
	(1.95)	(2.51)
$\Delta EBIT_{-1}$	1.052	1.108
	(1.41)	(1.80)
Return	−.117	−.048
	(.97)	(.47)
$Return_{-1}$	−.278	−.261
	(2.16)	(2.43)
ΔSIC_{+}	.004	−.006
	(.28)	(.43)
ΔSIC_{-}	−.047	−.053
	(3.09)	(4.42)
PEROUT	.217	−2.906
	(1.23)	(9.84)
RETIRE	.055	−.0002
	(.63)	(.004)
Number of Directors Who Left Last Year	.151	.125
	(7.27)	(6.00)
Market Value of Equity	.013	.009
	(2.54)	(.54)
Dummy If Year = 1972–1973	.141	−.324
	(1.55)	(3.63)
Dummy If Year = 1974–1976	−.010	−.343
	(.11)	(4.20)
Dummy If Year = 1977–1980	(.053)	−.108
	(.64)	(1.53)
Number of Observations	1,521	1,521

* *t*-statistics are in parentheses.

The estimates indicate that outsiders are added after poor performance. It seems to take longer for outsiders to be added than for insiders to leave, however. While the returns coefficients are all negative, the coefficient for returns immediately preceding the proxy are smaller than the coefficient on returns in the prior year. The coefficient for returns immediately preceding the proxy is not significantly different from zero in either equation. The coefficient on $Return_{-1}$, the returns between 24 and 12 months before the proxy, is significantly different from zero at the 5% level in both equations. The coefficient on earnings is negative and significantly different from zero in both equations. These results suggest that firms tend to add outsiders to their boards after poor performance, although perhaps with a lag.

There is an effect of exiting industries (decreases in the percentage of SIC codes) on the number of outsiders added to the board. The coefficient is negative and significantly different from zero at the 1% level, which implies that the more industries the firm exits, the more outside directors get added *ceteris paribus*. The coefficient on increases in the number of industries is once again close to and insignificantly different from zero. From this result and the earlier one, it appears that firms replace departing insiders with outsiders as they reduce the number of industries in which they operate, but do not change their board as they increase the number of industries in which they operate.[21]

□ **Director tenure and CEO succession.** In Section 2, we conjectured that the CEO succession process would play a significant role in director choice. The above evidence, that insiders are added toward the end of a CEO's tenure and that insiders leave just before and after a change in CEO, is consistent with our conjecture. In this subsection we consider some additional evidence.

If insiders are brought onto the board toward the end of a CEO's tenure to be groomed as potential successors, then the next CEO should tend to be chosen from these insiders with relatively short tenures. Table 7 gives the frequency with which inside directors become CEO, given their tenure at the time of a change in CEO. At the time of a change, a director with 4 to 6 years on the board was the most likely to become the new CEO. Directors with

TABLE 7 **The Relation between Inside Director Tenure and CEO Succession (Sample: 148 CEO Successions from 142 NYSE Companies, 1971–1983[a])**

Director[b] Tenure (Years)	Number of Directors	Number Becoming CEO	Proportion[c] Succeeding	Proportion[d] of All CEOs
0–3	261	43	.165	.291
4–6	156	42	.269	.284
7–9	109	26	.239	.176
10–12	75	18	.240	.121
13+	163	19	.117	.128
Total	764	148	.194	—

[a] All inside directors on the board at the time of a CEO change are included.
[b] Director tenure at time of CEO change.
[c] Proportion of directors with given tenure (at the time of the CEO change) who became CEO.
[d] Proportion of directors who became CEO with given tenure.

[21] This last result seems at odds with the positive simple correlation between percentage outsiders and number of SIC codes (Table 2). One explanation is that firms add outsiders only with a lag when they expand into new industries. We have attempted to uncover this process by using longer lags of changes in number of industries, but have been unsuccessful, most likely because there is a very low signal-to-noise ratio in these types of tests.

very short tenures (0–3 years) or very long tenures (greater than 12 years) were the least likely to become the new CEO.

To test the null hypothesis that there is no relation between director tenure and the probability of becoming CEO, we compute a χ^2-statistic from Table 7. The χ^2-statistic of 19.038 with 5 degrees of freedom implies that the null hypothesis can be rejected at the 1% level. Note that a director with 4 to 6 years on the board is only slightly more likely to become CEO than a director with a longer tenure (.269 versus .239 (7–9 years) and .240 (10–12 years)). The source of the significant χ^2-statistic is that directors with either very short or very long tenures are roughly half as likely to become CEOs as are directors with less extreme tenures. Although the probability that an *individual* inside director becomes CEO is approximately invariant with tenure (when we ignore very short or very long tenures), the probability that a new CEO will have a given tenure is *not* invariant with tenure. With probability .575, the new CEO was on the board for less than 7 years when chosen. The results in column 5 of Table 7 are consistent with the conjecture that candidates are brought onto the board before a CEO change, but, from column 4, we see that these newcomers are not the only candidates in the race.

Given that average CEO tenure is ten years, the data in Table 7 suggest that three out of four CEOs are succeeded by someone they put on the board. In addition, almost three out of five CEOs had been on the board less than seven years when they were promoted to CEO, so that the majority of future CEOs appear to be put on the board toward the end, rather than the beginning of the previous CEO's tenure. Finally, if we ignore directors with very short tenures ("too inexperienced") or very long tenures ("too old"), we see that every inside director stands roughly the same chance of becoming CEO. This last observation supports the widely held belief (cf. Mace, 1971) that only members of management who could potentially become CEO are added to the board.

We have argued that the tendency for insiders to leave after a CEO change might be explained by losing candidates for the CEO position leaving.[22] If this were true, then, given our findings about the tendencies for insider candidates to be added shortly before a CEO change, we should expect those insiders leaving shortly after a change to have shorter board tenures and to be younger than the average inside director at the time of his resignation.[23]

We test these hypotheses in Table 8. The top panel reports statistics on the distribution of tenure for three groups of insiders, none of whom ever became CEO. The mean tenure of those who leave within one year of a CEO change is 10.2 years, which is 2.5 years less than the mean tenure of the average director at retirement. This difference is significantly different from zero at the 5% level (t-statistic = 2.09). The difference between the means of those who leave within 3 years of a CEO change and a randomly chosen insider (1.9 years) is also significant (t-statistic = 2.22).

To be certain that the differences in means are not generated by a few outliers with extremely long tenures, we compute the median tenures upon leaving the board for our groups. The median tenure for the group of directors that left the board in the year after a CEO change is 7 years, 2 years shorter than the median tenure for the entire sample. We also compute the percentage of directors who leave after a short ($\leq$5 years) period. In the year after a CEO change, 36.6% of inside directors leaving the board have been there no longer than 5 years. This figure is 6.1% greater than the 30.5% of inside directors in the entire sample who leave within 5 years.

This evidence suggests that the directors who resign after CEO turnover tend to have shorter tenures than typical directors at resignation. This regularity is consistent with the

[22] The losers may leave because they see their future prospects diminished, because they find it difficult to work with the winner, or because the new CEO desires to hire his own people.

[23] It is considered desirable for a CEO to be in his midfifties when appointed (Vancil, 1987), and directors do not typically resign until age 65.

TABLE 8 **Tenures and Ages of Inside Directors Who Resign after CEO Succession (Sample: 142 NYSE Companies, 1971–1983)**

Variable	Measure	Group		
		Leave within 1 Year[a]	Leave within 3 Years[b]	Entire Sample[c]
Director Tenure at Resignation	Mean	10.2	10.6	12.7
	Median	7	8	9
	Percentage ≤ 5 Years	36.6	—[d]	30.5
	Number of Observations	142	232	747
Director Age at Resignation	Mean	56.7	57.4	60.3
	Number of Observations[e]	54	90	233

[a] This group contains all inside directors (excluding the CEO and all former CEOs) who were on the board at the time of a CEO change and resigned within 1 year of the CEO change.

[b] This group contains all inside directors (excluding the CEO and all former CEOs) who were on the board at the time of a CEO change and resigned within 3 years of the CEO change.

[c] This group contains all inside directors who were never CEO and resigned sometime during our sample period.

[d] A criterion for entry into the "Leave within 3 Years" group is that all directors in it must have been directors at the time of the CEO change. Because of this criterion, this group does not include directors who joined and quickly left the board shortly after the CEO change. If we were to include this statistic for this group, it would understate the number of directors who left with very short tenures. For this reason we omit it.

[e] The number of observations is smaller because firms were not required to include directors' ages in the proxy statements until the 1979 statement. All directors in the appropriate groups for which we have data are included.

notion that those directors were put on the board toward the end of the CEO's tenure as potential candidates to be the next CEO.

The lower part of Table 8 compares the ages of the directors who leave the board after CEO turnover with typical directors who leave the board. On average, those insiders who leave the board within one year of a CEO change were 3.6 years younger than average. This difference is significant at the 1% level (t-statistic = 2.63). The corresponding difference for those who leave within 3 years (2.9 years) is also significant (t-statistic = 2.73). These results indicate that the directors who leave the board following a CEO change are generally younger than typical directors when they leave the board. This supports the losing-candidates hypothesis.

5. Discussion and conclusion

■ We have hypothesized that board composition is determined by, among other things, the internal promotion and CEO succession processes, poor firm performance, and the participation of the firm in various product markets. We have provided some empirical support for each of these hypotheses.

The internal promotion and CEO succession processes have a number of effects on board composition. The years just preceding and following a CEO change see insiders leaving the board, although the sensitivity to model specification should be noted. Before a CEO change, insiders are also brought onto the board, possibly as part of the grooming process. We have found evidence that the new CEO tends to be drawn from these new insiders, though old insiders are also very much in the running. After the CEO is chosen, the evidence indicates that the losing candidates are prone to resign from the board. New CEOs, perhaps not yet ready to begin their own succession process or in need of advice, replace departing insiders with outsiders.

When firms perform poorly, they tend to remove insiders and add outsiders to the board. There are two explanations of these results. We have argued that firms may fire the insiders held responsible for poor performance. Having no sufficiently senior personnel—alternatively no one who might be a potential CEO—within the company to fill the vacancy, they fill it with an outsider. Thus, we see a correlation between poor performance and the removal of insiders and the hiring of outsiders. A similar argument holds when firms exit industries.

An alternative explanation for the performance and market participation results, as well as for the CEO tenure effects, can be derived from agency theory (Jensen and Meckling, 1976; Fama and Jensen, 1983): poor performance is an indication of poor management, and hence of the need for greater monitoring of management. Thus, in response to poor performance, the shareholders put (force the CEO to accept) more outside directors on the board to monitor management. To make room for these new outside directors, some inside directors must leave. Therefore, poor performance will cause insiders to leave the board and outsiders to join the board. Since exiting an industry is frequently the result of poor performance, the market-structure effects can be explained similarly.

An explanation for the CEO-tenure effects can also be derived from agency theory. A new CEO is an unknown quantity with relatively less power than an established CEO. Consequently, shareholders feel that a new CEO requires more scrutiny, so they will put more outsiders on the board to monitor him. In addition, shareholders are better able to put monitors on the board because the new CEO is not yet powerful enough to keep them off. A more established CEO is a known quantity, so less scrutiny is required. Furthermore, an established CEO is more powerful, and hence better able to control who gets a board seat.

We tend to believe the reasons discussed in Section 2, but we emphasize that there is little in the results to distinguish between the two sets of explanations. We have two principal reasons for not favoring the agency explanations. First, the institutional and business literature (Mace, 1971) argues convincingly that top management usually has the most say when it comes to choosing the board. Second, there is little or no direct evidence that outsiders exercise any control except in "crisis" situations (Mace, 1971; Vancil, 1987; Weisbach, 1988).[24]

To the limited degree that our results can help distinguish between the hypotheses of Section 2 and those of agency theory, we point to one piece of evidence. If shareholders respond to poor performance by adding new monitors, why do they not also replace the current monitors with new monitors, since poor performance could in part be due to a lack of vigilance on the part of the current monitors? Yet from Table 4 we see little evidence that poor performance leads to the resignation of outside directors (of the four measures of performance only one is significant and in only one specification). Nonetheless, the agency explanations are plausible, and future research should be devoted to distinguishing between the two sets of explanations.

References

American Law Institute. *Principles of Corporate Governance and Structure: Restatement and Recommendations. Tentative Draft No. 1.* Philadelphia: 1982.

Ball, R. and Watts, R. "Some Time-Series Properties of Accounting Numbers." *Journal of Finance*, Vol. 27 (1972), pp. 663–682.

Brickley, J. and James C. "The Takeover Market, Corporate Board Composition, and Ownership Structure: The Case of Banking." *Journal of Law and Economics*, Vol. 30 (1987), pp. 161–180.

[24] Some preliminary work by Hermalin and Weisbach (1987) fails to find any evidence of a relationship between board composition and firm performance (where performance is measured by Tobin's q).

——— AND VAN DRUNEN, L. "Residual Claims, Decision Rights, and Board Structure." MERC Working Paper 87-04, University of Rochester, 1987.

CONFERENCE BOARD. *Corporate Directorship Practices: Membership and Committees of the Board.* New York: 1973.

DUNN, D. "Directors Aren't Doing Their Jobs." *Fortune* (March 16, 1987), pp. 117–119.

FAMA, E. AND JENSEN, M. "Separation of Ownership and Control." *Journal of Law and Economics,* Vol. 26 (1983), pp. 301–325.

FOSTER, G. *Financial Statement Analysis.* Englewood Cliffs, N.J.: Prentice-Hall, 1978.

HAUSMAN, J., HALL, B., AND GRILICHES, Z. "Econometric Models for Count Data with an Application to the Patents-R&D Relationship." *Econometrica,* Vol. 52 (1984), pp. 909–938.

HERMALIN, B. AND WEISBACH, M. "The Effect of Board Composition on Corporate Performance." Mimeo, William E. Simon School of Business, University of Rochester, 1987.

JENSEN, M. AND MECKLING, W. "Theory of the Firm: Managerial Behavior, Agency Costs, and Ownership Structure." *Journal of Financial Economics,* Vol. 3 (1976), pp. 305–360.

MACAVOY, P., CANTOR, S., DANA, J., AND PECK, S. "ALI Proposals for Increased Control of the Corporation by the Board of Directors: An Economic Analysis" in *Statement of the Business Roundtable on the American Law Institute's Proposed "Principles of Corporate Governance and Structure: Restatement and Recommendations."* New York: Business Roundtable, 1983.

MACE, M. *Directors: Myth and Reality.* Boston: Harvard Business School Press, 1971.

MORCK, R., SHLEIFER, A., AND VISHNY, R. "Management Ownership and Market Valuation: An Empirical Evaluation." *Journal of Financial Economics,* Vol. 20 (1988), pp. 293–316.

MRUK, E. AND GARDINIA, J. *Organization and Compensation of Boards of Directors.* New York: Arthur Young, Inc., 1985.

SHLEIFER, A. AND VISHNY, R. "Large Shareholders and Corporate Control." *Journal of Political Economy,* Vol. 95 (1986), pp. 461–488.

VANCIL, R. *Passing the Baton: Managing the Process of CEO Succession.* Boston: Harvard Business School Press, 1987.

WARNER, J., WATTS, R., AND WRUCK, K. "Stock Prices and Top Management Changes." *Journal of Financial Economics,* Vol. 20 (1988), pp. 461–492.

WEISBACH, M. "Outside Directors and CEO Turnover." *Journal of Financial Economics,* Vol. 20 (1988), pp. 431–460.

[2]

Journal of Financial Economics 20 (1988) 431–460. North-Holland

OUTSIDE DIRECTORS AND CEO TURNOVER

Michael S. WEISBACH*

University of Rochester, Rochester, NY 14627, USA

Received January 1987, final version received July 1987

This paper examines the relation between the monitoring of CEOs by inside and outside directors and CEO resignations. CEO resignations are predicted using stock returns and earnings changes as measures of prior performance. There is a stronger association between prior performance and the probability of a resignation for companies with outsider-dominated boards than for companies with insider-dominated boards. This result does not appear to be a function of ownership effects, size effects, or industry effects. Unexpected stock returns on days when resignations are announced are consistent with the view that directors increase firm value by removing bad management.

1. Introduction

Boards of directors are widely believed to play an important role in corporate governance, particularly in monitoring top management. Directors are supposed to supervise the actions of management, provide advice, and veto poor decisions. The board is the shareholders' first line of defense against incompetent management; in extreme cases, it will replace an errant chief executive officer (CEO). Discussing boards' effectiveness in this role, Jensen (1986) claims that 'the internal control mechanism of corporations, which operate through the board of directors, generally work well' (p. 9).

Two recent studies, Coughlan and Schmidt (1985) and Warner, Watts, and Wruck (1988), provide some support for this view by showing that poor performance is associated with CEO turnover. These studies do not explore the differences in monitoring between the managers who serve as directors (inside directors) and directors who are not full-time employees of the company (outside directors). These outside directors are widely believed to play a larger role in monitoring management than inside board members. Fama

*I am grateful to Paul MacAvoy and Jim Dana for providing me with their data. I would like to thank participants in seminars at Harvard, MIT, Northwestern, Rochester, and UCLA, as well as Jim Dana, Franklin M. Fisher, Paul Healy, Cliff Holderness, Michael Jensen, Bob Kaplan, Steve Kaplan, Mervyn King, Kevin J. Murphy, Pat O'Brien, Rick Ruback, Ross Watts, Jerry Weisbach, and especially Ben Hermalin and Andrei Shleifer (the referee) for helpful comments. Special thanks go to my advisor, Jim Poterba, for reading countless drafts and providing invaluable support and advice throughout the project.

(1980, p. 293–294) argues:

> The probability of [top management colluding and expropriating shareholder wealth] might be lowered, and the viability of the board as a market-induced mechanism for low-cost internal transfer of control might be enhanced, by the inclusion of outside directors. The latter might be regarded as professional referees whose task is to stimulate and oversee the competition among the firm's top management.

This view has led to numerous calls for regulation of board composition to increase outside representation and hence the level of monitoring of management in American corporations [see, for example, the American Law Institute (1982)].

Economists have criticized such regulatory proposals.[1] Demsetz (1983a, p. B-6) argues that 'the board of directors can do very little to improve on the powerful incentives that presently guide management to serve the interests of shareholders'. He maintains that executive compensation contracts, which are designed to align shareholders' and managers' interests, and the pressures of the product and capital markets [Hart (1983)] already provide adequate monitoring of corporate managers. According to this argument, regulation of boards cannot improve and could possibly impose a harmful constraint on an optimizing management.

Understanding the role of the outside director remains an important and unresolved question. Unfortunately, most of the day-to-day actions of boards of directors are unobservable. Any attempt to isolate the different effects of outside and inside directors must either examine their effect on some aspect of firm performance or concentrate on the directors' observable actions. The most striking of such actions is the decision to remove a CEO.

This paper tests the hypothesis that inside and outside directors behave differently in their decisions to remove top management. It exploits the wide variation across firms in the composition of the board of directors to study how the relation between poor performance and management turnover varies with the makeup of the board. The findings suggest that firms with outsider-dominated boards are significantly more likely than firms with insider-dominated boards to remove the CEO on the basis of performance, as measured by such publicly available measures as earnings or stock returns.

The paper consists of seven sections. Section 2 reviews the role of boards of directors in the CEO succession process. Section 3 describes the data. The fourth section discusses the empirical specification. Section 5 presents an econometric model that explains CEO turnover using stock returns and earnings changes as measures of performance. It then tests to see whether this relation is the same for firms with different board types. Section 6 analyzes the

[1] See Andrews (1982), Demsetz (1983a), and MacAvoy, Cantor, Dana, and Peck (1983).

change in firm value associated with the announcement of CEO changes and tests whether the outside monitoring is causally related to the change in firm value. A brief conclusion discusses possible directions for future research.

2. Boards of directors as monitors of management

One important duty of the board of directors is to evaluate management. The board is responsible for evaluating the senior management of the corporation and replacing them if they fail to perform well. This task is likely to fall mainly on the outside directors. Inside directors' careers are tied to the CEO's and hence insiders generally are unable or unwilling to remove incumbent CEOs.[2] Harold Geneen (1984, p. 262), the longtime CEO of ITT, wrote: 'Certainly, none of the inside directors would substantially challenge his boss in the boardroom.'

Outside directors are responsible for removing bad management, but they may not have the incentives to do so. A recent *Business Week* editorial (Sept. 8, 1986) argues that outside directors without a significant stake in the firm have no incentive to cause trouble for management. However, outside directors are generally respected leaders from the business or academic community whose reputations suffer when they are directors of faltering companies. Like Fama (1980), Fama and Jensen (1983, p. 315) argue that

> outside directors will monitor the management that chooses them because outside directors have incentives to develop reputations as experts in decision control.... The value of their human capital depends primarily on their performance as internal decision managers in other organizations. They use their directorships to signal to internal and external markets for decision agents that (1) they are decision experts, (2) they understand the importance of diffuse and separate control, and (3) they can work with such decision control systems.

Outside directors thus will have an incentive to ensure the effective running of the company because being directors of well-run companies signals their competence to the market.

It may not be ideal, however, to have a board composed entirely of outsiders. Although outsiders may be best able to judge when to remove a CEO, inside participation on the board can improve the decision about who the successor should be. Inside board members are often potential future CEOs. Their inclusion on the board serves two purposes. First, it gives them experience that may prove valuable should they become CEO. Second, it gives

[2] Much of the discussion here and below is taken from Mace (1971). An alternative view is that insiders are much more likely to remove the CEO so they can take his place. This view is not consistent with the evidence in Mace (1971) or Vancil (1987).

the outside board members an opportunity to evaluate potential CEO candidates. Irrespective of the reasons for the CEO change, we might expect that boards combining inside and outside directors do a particularly good job of replacing management because this type board type allows for superior training of the inside directors and better evaluation of them by outside directors.

Most studies of the monitoring functions of boards of directors have used the case method. Perhaps the best attempt in the direction is Mace (1971).[3] He interviewed CEOs and directors to explore their functions and relationships. His results show that directors typically are not involved in important corporate decisions such as long-range planning or selecting other directors. Directors do serve as a valuable source of advice for many CEOs and were responsible for removing the CEO in what Mace called crisis situations. Mace emphasized that outside directors generally took the initiative to remove incumbent CEOs.

In addition to this case approach, there have been several attempts to identify quantitatively the effects of boards of directors on profitability. MacAvoy, Cantor, Dana, and Peck (1983), responding to the proposal by the American Law Institute (1982) for regulation of board composition, collected data on the composition of boards of directors for a cross-section of publicly traded companies. They compare two subsamples: those firms that met the proposed ALI regulations for a majority of outside directors and various other requirements, and all other firms. They tested whether the two subsamples differed in various performance measures: accounting profits, sales, and return on equity. Their results indicated no differences between the two types of firms. A problem with this approach is that the causality of the relation between board composition and firm performance is unclear. For example, if MacAvoy et al. had discovered that more profitable firms tend to have insider-dominated boards, we would not know whether inside directors cause good business decisions to be made or whether CEOs of unprofitable firms tend to invite outsiders onto the board to help solve their problems [Hermalin and Weisbach (1987a)]. This simultaneity problem makes the MacAvoy et al. results difficult to interpet.

A related study by Morck, Shleifer, and Vishny (1988) explores how stockholdings by boards of directors affect performance. They find that profitability, measured by Tobin's Q, is highest at moderate levels of share ownership by the board. In addition, they find that this result applies both to ownership by the firm's top officers and to ownership by the rest of the board.

[3] Vance (1983) performs a similar study. There also have been a number of studies that document the composition and compensation of boards. Two examples are Bacon (1975) and Mruk and Gardinia (1985).

This result may be due to the tradeoff between the agency costs resulting from misalignment of directors' and shareholders' interests and the costs of managerial entrenchment [Demsetz (1983b)]. Managerial entrenchment occurs when managers gain so much power that they are able to use the firm to further their own interests rather than the interests of shareholders. Demsetz argues that when CEOs are able to control the board, they are able to take on projects that are known to have negative net present values but provide utility for the CEO.

The extent of this entrenchment has been the subject of two recent studies. Coughlan and Schmidt (1985) and Warner, Watts, and Wruck (1988) estimate resignation equations for CEOs. Each study finds that poor performance by the company's stock increases the probability of a CEO's removal, although Coughlan and Schmidt find a much larger effect than Warner et al. However, neither paper provides any direct evidence that the board of directors is actively monitoring. A nonmonitoring explanation consistent with the evidence presented in these studies is that CEOs resign voluntarily from companies that are doing badly because of the difficulties of running a faltering company, including potential shareholder suits.

Warner, Watts, and Wruck (1988) also examine the residuals from a market model regression on the day the CEO change is announced. They find that the mean excess return is not distinguishable from zero, but that the variance of the excess return increases on the event day. This finding implies that the announcement contains information but that the information is good news for some firms and bad news for others. Warner et al. interpret this result as consistent with the announcement's providing information about both past and future performance.

Coughlan and Schmidt (1985) and Warner, Watts, and Wruck (1988) provide studies of the CEO succession process. Although both papers claim that the board of directors is responsible for the CEO changes, neither paper attempts to link the work with work on the composition of boards of directors done by MacAvoy, Cantor, Dana, and Peck (1983) and by Morck, Shleifer, and Vishny (1988).

3. Data

The data used in this study are an extension of the data collected by MacAvoy, Cantor, Dana, and Peck (1983). They assembled data on board composition for all corporations listed on the New York Stock Exchange with a proxy statement available on microfiche, a total of 495 publicly held corporations between 1977 and 1980. For each firm, directors were classified as either outside, inside, or grey. MacAvoy et al. classify directors who are full-time employees of the corporation as inside directors. They designate directors who neither work for the corporation nor have extensive dealings with the company as outside directors. Those directors who are not employees, but who may not be independent of current management because of extensive business dealings with the company or family relationships with management, are classified as grey. In the analysis below, the measure of outside domination of the board is the fraction of board members who are outsiders.[4]

These data on composition are matched with data on CEO succession. Once a year *Forbes Magazine* lists the names, compensations, ages, backgrounds, years with the company, and years as CEOs for the CEOs of all corporations it lists of the 500 largest corporations in several categories (sales, profits, etc.). I followed the identity of the CEO over a ten-year window from 1974 to 1983 for each firm in both the MacAvoy et al. sample and the *Forbes Magazine* surveys. All CEO changes were a cross-checked with the *Wall Street Journal* to get the exact date of the announcement of the change as well as the reason given by the company for the change.[5] Finally, the data were matched with financial data from the Center for Research in Security Prices (CRSP), giving a total of 367 companies.[6]

Table 1 shows the distribution of outsider representation for 1980. Firms are grouped according to the percentage of outsiders on the board. The distribution is centered around 50%, with few firms in the tails of the distribution. The largest concentration of firms – 61 (including 30 with exactly 50% outsiders) – is in the 45–50% range. To distinguish the differences between the firms on the basis of outside representation on the board, I divide the sample into approximate thirds. All firms in which outsiders make up no more than 40% of the directors are considered insider-dominated firms, all firms in which at least 60% of the board are outsiders are designated outsider-dominated firms, and firms with between 40% and 60% outsiders are considered mixed boards. According to this assignment procedure, 146 firms have mixed boards,

[4]An alternative measure is the fraction of insiders on the board. This alternative measure is highly correlated with the fraction of outsiders on the board, as the correlation coefficient between the two is −0.833 and the rank correlation is −0.823. The fraction of outsiders is used in the empirical work because of the claims in the institutional literature [see Mace (1971)] that grey directors do not monitor management.

[5]For the years 1974–1976 and 1981–1983, for which MacAvoy et al. did not collect any data, the board data were taken from the nearest available year (either 1977 or 1980). This approximation does not appear to be too inaccurate because board composition changes extremely slowly over time. For example, between 1977 and 1980, only 6% of the firms in the MacAvoy et al. sample changed the percentage of outsiders on their boards by at least 20%. When the equations are estimated on the 1977–80 subsample, the results are similar to those on the entire sample, although the coefficients are not estimated as precisely as with the entire sample.

[6]For some of the analysis, earnings data from the COMPUSTAT Industrial file were used, reducing the total number of firms to 322.

Table 1

The frequency of outsider representation on the boards of 367 NYSE firms in 1980.

Proportion of directors who are outsiders[a]	Number of firms
0–5%	1
5–10%	2
10–15%	6
15–20%	7
20–25%	11
25–30%	9
30–35%	23
35–40%	34
40–45%	37
45–50%	61
50–55%	18
55–60%	40
60–65%	26
65–70%	32
70–75%	28
75–80%	20
80–85%	7
85–90%	5
90–100%	0
Total	367

[a]The ranges are inclusive of the upper bound. For example, the 30 firms with exactly 50% outsiders are included in the 45–50% group rather than the 50–55% group.

compared with 93 insider-dominated boards and 128 outsider-dominated boards.[7]

Table 2 presents the reason given in the *Wall Street Journal* for the CEO resignations. Retirement (138 instances) is the most common. Perhaps the most striking feature of this table is that in only 9 of the 286 resignations was performance given as a reason why the CEO was replaced. In some of these nine cases, it was not the firm that mentioned performance but the *Wall Street Journal* which cited rumors that performance was the true reason.

Yet there is evidence that poor performance does precede CEO resignations. The findings of Coughlan and Schmidt (1985) and Warner, Watts, and Wruck (1988) both imply that poor stock performance tends to raise the probability

[7]There are many firms with exactly the same percentage of outsiders. Therefore, it was impossible to divide the sample into exact thirds without including two firms with exactly the same fraction of outsiders into different categories. This method of dividing the sample was chosen because of its simplicity. Alternate divisions, such as dividing the sample as equally as possible, yield similar results.

of a resignation. The same effect exists in my data. In the four quarters preceding retirements, market-adjusted returns were on average 4.8% lower than the average annual return from my sample. In the four quarters preceding all other resignations market-adjusted returns were 6.5% lower than average returns. Both differences are significantly different from zero but they are not significantly different from each other.

This suggests that companies do not announce the true reason behind their CEOs' resignations. Therefore, I ignore the stated reasons for resignation in constructing my sample. I do, however, eliminate the resignations for which I am able to corroborate the cause independently. Changes in CEOs caused by death and preceding a takeover are excluded because these 'resignations' are totally verifiable.[8]

One other variable that is highly correlated with the probability of a planned resignation is the age of the CEO. A nontrivial number of the resignations take effect on the CEO's sixty-fifth birthday. These resignations are likely to be actual retirements, unrelated to performance. Since the *Forbes* data on the age of the CEO are accurate only to within a year, all firms with CEOs aged 64, 65, or 66 were excluded.[9] Excluding these observations is likely to increase the signal-to-noise ratio and ultimately the precision of the estimates.[10]

4. Empirical specification

To test whether outside boards monitor management more effectively than inside boards and to compare the sizes of the effects across board types, I relate CEO resignations to performance measures. If a stronger relationship exists between poor performance and the probability of a CEO's being replaced for outsider-dominated than for insider-dominated boards, this would provide evidence that outsiders play a role in monitoring management. Find-

[8] The four public scandals and the five instances of CEOs taking prestigious positions elsewhere might also be considered verifiable. Excluding these observations from the sample does not change the results in any meaningful way.

[9] Excluding these observations does not meaningfully affect the results when stock returns are used as the explanatory variable. However, in the logits using earnings discussed below, excluding these observations drastically affects the results. This difference is possibly caused by CEOs who have compensation plans based on earnings. These CEOs have an incentive to manipulate the intertemporal structure of earnings to maximize their compensation. This strategy makes sense only if the resignation is anticipated, so it is not likely to be a problem in the case of an unanticipated removal. For a detailed study of how management can manipulate earnings to maximize their compensation, see Healy (1985).

[10] A number of resignations located in *Forbes* were not discussed by the *Wall Street Journal*. These resignations were also eliminated because it is impossible to isolate the date of the resignation accurately enough from the *Forbes* surveys.

Table 2

The principal reason given by the *Wall Street Journal* for CEO resignations; *sample*: 367 NYSE firms between 1974 and 1983.

Reason	Number of resignations
Retirement	138
Personal reasons	17
Death	12
Normal succession procedure	11
Illness	9
Performance mentioned	9
Policy or personality disagreement	8
Take prestigious appointment elsewhere	5
Followed by takeover	4
Scandal	4
Company policy to retire at 60	3
Merger	2
CEO purchased a subsidiary and will run it	1
No reason given	63
Total	286

ing the same relationship across different types of boards would imply that boards do not differ systematically in monitoring management.

I test this hypothesis using logit models to estimate the probability of a CEO change.[11] The logistic approach assumes that

$$\Pr(\text{CEO leaves his job}) = F(x\beta) = \exp(x\beta)/(1+\exp(x\beta)),$$

where x is a vector of variables (including a constant) that may affect the CEO's probability of losing his job, and β is a parameter vector. The distribution F is known as the logistic distribution. I use maximum likelihood to estimate the parameters. The log of the likelihood function for the logit model is given by

$$\log L = \sum C_i * \log[F(x_i\beta)] + \sum(1-C_i) * \log[1-F(x_i\beta)],$$

where C_i is a dummy variable equal to one if there is a resignation in a given firm-year.

[11] Ordinary least squares is not an appropriate statistical technique for this problem because the dependent variable is dichotomous. For a complete description of logit, see Amemiya (1985). Logit was used instead of probit to be consistent with the previous literature [Coughlan and Schmidt (1985), Warner, Watts, and Wruck (1988)]. The results are similar if probit is used instead of logit.

The first performance measure used is the return on the company's stock minus the return on a value-weighted market portfolio.[12] When stock returns are used as the performance measure, the logit equations are estimated using firm-quarters as the unit of observation and the return for the year prior to the quarter in question as the performance measure. This approach was adopted to minimize the time between the performance period and the potential resignation. The alternative approach of using annual data would have associated a resignation in, say, November 1982 with the performance of the stock in 1981, leaving eleven months between the measured predictive period and the event. If boards of directors do not remove CEOs for poor performance, it is plausible that the time lag would be relatively short. Therefore, annual data will, in general, paint a less accurate picture of the relationship between performance and removals than quarterly data.

5. Results of the prediction equations

5.1. Using stock returns as the performance measure

The removal equations with stock returns as predictors are shown in table 3. The first column indicates the relationship for the entire sample. The coefficient on the return variable is negative and significantly different from zero. This means that a poor stock return increases the probability of a CEO's losing his job. This result replicates the results of Coughlan and Schmidt (1985) and Warner, Watts, and Wruck (1988) with an effect smaller than the former and larger than the latter. The relationship between stock return and the probability of the CEO's being replaced implied in these equations is illustrated in the first column in table 4. For the median firm in the bottom decile of stock returns, with a return 33% lower than the market, the CEO has a 6% chance of losing his job, while the CEO of the median firm in the top decile that outperformed the market by 70% has a 3% chance of losing his job. Considering that CEOs leave their jobs for many reasons, the size of this difference seems fairly large.

The second column of table 3 examines the effect of stock returns on resignations across different board types. For the inside boards, the returns

[12]An alternative approach involves estimating market model parameters for each firm by estimating the equation

$$R_{it} = \alpha_i + \beta_i M_t + \varepsilon_{it},$$

where R_{t} is the return on firm i, M_t is the return on market portfolio, and α_i and β_i are the market model parameters. The residuals from this equation could be used as the performance measure. The reason this approach was not used is that if the parameters were estimated using data from several years prior to the resignation, the estimate of the α would likely be biased downward for firms with bad CEOs. For these firms, the residuals from the market model will not reflect true CEO performance.

coefficient is negative, but is small and not significantly different from zero. For mixed boards the coefficient ($-0.20 = -0.46 + 0.26$) is even smaller in absolute value and is also not significantly different from zero. However, there is a larger effect for outside boards. The coefficient ($-1.63 = -0.46 - 1.17$) is significantly different from zero at the 1% level and significantly different from the coefficients on either inside or mixed boards at the 10% level.[13]

The derivative of the probability of resignation with respect to stock returns illustrates the impact of board type. The derivative (evaluated at a return of 0.0) is -0.066 for companies with outside boards, -0.022 for companies with inside boards, and -0.010 for companies with mixed boards. This derivative, a measure of the responsiveness of the removal decision to stock performance, is three times as large for the companies with outside boards as for any other board type. Although the larger effect for inside boards than for mixed boards is unexpected, the difference between the two is not significant. The difference between the outside boards and mixed boards is significant at the 5% level. The difference between outside boards and inside boards is not significant at conventional significance levels.[14]

The probabilities of removal implied from these logit equations for each board type are shown in table 4. For outside boards the probabilities range from 7% for a firm in the bottom decile to 1.3% for a firm in the top decile. The difference between these probabilities is 5.7%, which is significant at the 1% confidence level. For inside boards the probabilities range from 5.7% to 3.6%, a difference of just 2.1%. This difference is not significant at any

[13] I use one-tailed tests here and below because there are many a priori reasons why outsiders would monitor better than insiders but few why insiders would monitor better than outsiders. The hypothesis is hence a 'one-tailed' hypothesis.

For the whole sample (including CEOs of all ages) the right-hand side of the estimated equation was

$$\underset{(36.4)}{-4.00} - \underset{(1.38)}{0.54}\,R + \underset{(0.36)}{0.19}\,R * D_{\text{mixed}} - \underset{(1.19)}{0.63}\,R * D_{\text{outside}} + \underset{(0.93)}{0.14}\,D_{\text{mixed}} + \underset{(0.25)}{0.04}\,D_{\text{outside}}.$$

(t-statistics are in parentheses.) The coefficient on outside boards is still significantly different from zero but is no longer significantly different from the coefficient on inside boards.

The equations shown in table 4 and below include dummy variables for each board type. These dummy variables make each of these equations equivalent to estimating separate equations for each board type. The equations are shown in this form to facilitate testing whether various effects differ across board types.

[14] The standard errors used here and below are calculated using the delta method [see Rao (1965)]. If a parameter vector w has a variance–covariance matrix V, and g is a differentiable function, then the variance–covariance matrix of $g(w)$ is approximated asymptotically by $G'VG$, where G is the Jacobian matrix of g. The numbers referred to in the text as t-statistics therefore do not actually have a small-sample t-distribution but are equal to the ratio of the parameter estimate and an asymptotic approximation of the standard error. Under the null hypothesis that the coefficient is equal to zero they have an asymptotic standard normal distribution.

Table 3

Logit equations predicting CEO turnover using stock returns;[a] *sample*: 12,997 firm-quarters between 1974 and 1983 (CEOs must be either younger than 64 or older than 66); asymptotic *t*-statistics in parentheses.

Variable	Coeff.	Coeff.	Coeff.	Coeff.
Constant	−4.39 (54.9)	−4.39 (31.4)	−4.60 (28.8)	−4.60 (28.8)
D_{mixed}[b]	—	0.13 (0.68)	0.22 (1.15)	0.23 (1.15)
$D_{outside}$[c]	—	−0.18 (0.86)	0.03 (0.13)	−0.03 (0.14)
Return[d]	−0.64 (2.28)	−0.46 (0.92)	−0.44 (0.88)	−0.45 (0.87)
Return * D_{mixed}	—	0.26 (0.39)	0.19 (0.28)	0.20 (0.29)
Return * $D_{outside}$	—	−1.17 (1.60)	−1.11 (1.52)	−1.07 (1.43)
$Return_{-1}$	—	—	—	−0.10 (0.20)
$Return_{-1}$ * D_{mixed}	—	—	—	−0.08 (0.11)
$Return_{-1}$ * $D_{outside}$	—	—	—	−0.44 (0.71)
Dummy if age > 66	—	—	1.28 (5.82)	1.29 (5.61)
Log likelihood	−846.76	−843.76	−830.88	−830.45

[a] The dependent variable is equal to 1 if there was a CEO change in a given quarter and 0 otherwise.

[b] D_{mixed} is a dummy variable that is 1 if the company's board contains between 40% and 60% outsiders.

[c] $D_{outside}$ is a dummy variables that is 1 if the company's board contains at least 60% outsiders.

[d] The variable *Return* is the return on a company's stock minus the return on a value-weighted market portfolio in the four quarters prior to the period.

conventional significance level. These implied probabilities again illustrate the monitoring effect of the outside directors.

The third column of table 3 includes a dummy variable for whether the CEO was past retirement age. (All CEOs at retirement age were excluded from the sample.) A possible objection to the results described above is that they are just proxies for effects due to age, a variable that seems likely to have an effect on the probability of retirement. Indeed, the coefficient on this age variable is significant and does increase the probability of retirement. It has little effect, however, on the estimates of the other coefficients.

The final column of table 3 includes the returns for two years prior to the resignation as explanatory variables. The variable $Return_{-1}$ is the market-

Table 4

Implied annual probability of resignation by marked-adjusted stock return decile and outsider representation on the board for 367 NYSE firms from 1974 to 1983.[a]

		Implied probability of resignation (standard error[b])			
			Percentage outsiders on board		
Decile	Return vs. market[c]	Entire sample	≤ 40%[e]	> 40%, < 60%[f]	≥ 60%[g]
1	−0.331	0.061 (0.00073)	0.057 (0.0128)	0.052 (0.0105)	0.070 (0.0141)
2	−0.204	0.056 (0.0054)	0.054 (0.0097)	0.051 (0.0082)	0.057 (0.0094)
3	−0.125	0.053 (0.0046)	0.052 (0.0082)	0.050 (0.0071)	0.050 (0.0076)
4	−0.065	0.051 (0.0042)	0.050 (0.0075)	0.050 (0.0065)	0.045 (0.0068)
5	−0.005	0.049 (0.0039)	0.049 (0.0070)	0.049 (0.0061)	0.041 (0.0063)
6	0.057	0.047 (0.0038)	0.048 (0.0068)	0.048 (0.0060)	0.037 (0.0061)
7	0.117	0.045 (0.0039)	0.046 (0.0070)	0.048 (0.0062)	0.034 (0.0060)
8	0.207	0.043 (0.0042)	0.045 (0.0076)	0.047 (0.0068)	0.029 (0.0060)
9	0.371	0.038 (0.0050)	0.041 (0.0094)	0.046 (0.0088)	0.022 (0.0061)
10	0.708	0.031 (0.0064)	0.036 (0.0132)	0.042 (0.0136)	0.013 (0.0056)

[a] Implied probabilities are obtained from logit equations that predict the probability of a CEO resignation in a given quarter using the market-adjusted returns for the four previous quarters as the independent variable. The probabilities are then multiplied by four to approximate annual probabilities.

[b] The standard errors are computed using the delta method [Rao (1965)].

[c] The *Return vs. market* variable is the return on the company's stock for the median stock in a given decile of the firms ranked in terms of stock returns minus a value-weighted market index.

[d] Estimated model: ln(odds of resignation) = −4.39 − 0.64 (market-adjusted return).

[e] Estimated model: ln(odds of resignation) = −4.39 − 0.46 (market-adjusted return).

[f] Estimated model: ln(odds of resignation) = −4.26 − 0.20 (market-adjusted return).

[g] Estimated model: ln(odds of resignation) = −4.57 − 1.63 (market-adjusted return).

adjusted return for the four quarters prior to the period covered in *Return*, i.e., the return between eight and five quarters prior to the quarter of the potential resignation. The estimates indicate that resignations are not sensitive to returns from previous years. This result, together with a similar one from Warner, Watts, and Wruck, suggests that boards react relatively quickly to poor performance in their decision to replace the CEO.

5.2. Using earnings as the performance measure

A second measure of corporate performance is accounting earnings. Despite the many problems with using earnings data as a measure of profitability [see Fisher and McGowan (1983), Solomon (1970), and Stauffer (1971)], earnings data have one large advantage over stock price data for the purposes of measuring the performance of the CEO: earnings data measure short-term profits. The stock price reflects the present discounted value of the expected future cash flows of the company. The stock price incorporates the market's estimate of the probability that a bad CEO will be fired. Therefore, the stock price of firms with bad CEOs is greater than it would be if the CEOs were given a lifetime job guarantee. If a company were known to be likely to replace bad management, e.g., if it had an outsider-dominated board of directors, this difference becomes even larger. This argument implies that using stock price data may underestimate the monitoring effect of outsiders. In addition, if boards of directors base executive turnover decisions on economic profitability, then a finding that accounting earnings data can predict CEO resignations is consistent with a relation between accounting profits and economic profits [Fisher and McGowan (1983)].

As the decisions to change CEOs are likely to be related to unanticipated changes in performance, I would like to use a measure of unexpected earnings. A large literature on the time series behavior of accounting earnings [see Ball and Watts (1972) and Foster (1978)] finds that annual earnings follow approximately a random walk. This implies that changes in earnings are an unbiased estimate of unexpected earnings.[15]

The choice of the appropriate earnings measure presents some difficulties. The measure used below is earnings before interest and taxes (*EBIT*).[16] This measure was used to prevent changes in capital structures or tax treatments from obscuring differences in earnings measures of performance. The change in *EBIT* is standardized by the book value of the firm's assets in the previous year (A_{-1}) to control for size differences.

Finally, to control for factors affecting earnings changes in the year of CEO turnover caused by industry effects, the average standardized earnings change is computed for all the firms on the COMPUSTAT industrial tape with the same two-digit SIC code as the test firm. This average is subtracted from the standardized earnings change for the test firm. The resulting variable provides

[15]An earlier version of this paper used earnings levels normalized by asset levels as the measure of performance. The results were all qualitatively identical. Earnings changes are used here because the appropriate benchmark for measuring CEO performance would seem to be the unexpected component of earnings.

[16]This variable is constructed by adding data items 15, 16, 18, and 49 on the annual COMPUSTAT industrial tape.

a measure of unexpected earnings that should not be sensitive to the firm's size, industry, capital structure, or tax treatment.[17]

The results from these logits are shown in table 5. The variable $\Delta EBIT$ reflects the most recent earnings change of which the board of directors has knowledge, and $\Delta EBIT_{-1}$ and $\Delta EBIT_{-2}$ the two prior changes. In the first column, earnings changes for the three years prior are used to predict resignations for the entire sample. The only variable with a significant coefficient is $\Delta EBIT_{-1}$. A possible explanation for this follows from the fact that CEOs can manipulate earnings streams [Healy (1985), DeAngelo (1987)] and have an incentive to report high earnings before their retirement. Since a large fraction of the resignations in my sample is likely to be planned in advance, high earnings changes for these firms might offset poor earnings change for the firms where the board of directors removes the CEO, obscuring the relationship between poor unexpected earnings for the year prior to the resignation and the probability of resignation.

The results broken down by fraction of outsiders are shown in the second column for the two earnings announcements prior to the resignation. The coefficients on the performance variables for inside and mixed are not significantly different from zero. The coefficient for outsiders is negative and significantly different from zero and from the insiders coefficient at the 5% level for $\Delta EBIT$ and at the 1% level for $\Delta EBIT_{-1}$.[18]

The implied probabilities of a CEO change calculated from this equation are similar to those from the returns equations. For the entire sample, the probability of resignation for a CEO with earnings changes in the bottom decile for two subsequent years is 0.071 in the following year. The probability of a CEO resignation in the year following two earnings changes in the top decile is 0.033. The difference between the two is satistically significant (t-statistic = 2.94). For the outside boards, the two probabilities are 0.135 and

[17]Because firms have fiscal years ending in months other than December, the timing of observations presents a problem. The unit of observation is taken to be a fiscal year. Since directors presumably know earnings before they are announced publicly, resignations occurring in the month of the announcement or the month before the announcement are said to have followed the announcement.

[18]For the whole sample (including CEOs of all ages) the right-hand side of the estimated equation is

$$\begin{aligned} &-\underset{(20.2)}{2.60} + \underset{(0.72)}{1.83}\ \Delta EBIT - \underset{(1.02)}{3.71}\ \Delta EBIT * D_{\text{mixed}} - \underset{(1.04)}{3.76}\ \Delta EBIT * D_{\text{outside}} \\ &\quad - \underset{(0.37)}{0.79}\ \Delta EBIT_{-1} + \underset{(0.67)}{1.94}\ \Delta EBIT_{-1} * D_{\text{mixed}} - \underset{(2.11)}{7.46}\ \Delta EBIT_{-1} * D_{\text{outside}} \\ &\quad + \underset{(1.06)}{0.18}\ D_{\text{mixed}} - \underset{(0.63)}{0.12}\ D_{\text{outside}} \end{aligned}$$

Using the entire sample, the coefficient on outsiders is still negative for both $\Delta EBIT$ and $\Delta EBIT_{-1}$. It is significant for $\Delta EBIT_{-1}$ but not for $\Delta EBIT$.

Table 5

Logit equations predicting CEO turnover using earnings changes and stock returns;[a] *sample*: 2,823 firm-years between 1974 and 1983 (CEOs must be either younger than 64 or older than 66); asymptotic *t*-statistics in parentheses.

Variable	Coeff.	Coeff.	Coeff.	Coeff.
Constant	−3.02 (31.6)	−2.92 (18.9)	−2.91 (18.9)	−2.89 (18.6)
D_{mixed}[b]	—	−0.05 (0.22)	−0.01 (0.05)	−0.10 (0.43)
$D_{outside}$[c]	—	−0.63 (2.31)	−0.16 (0.70)	−0.62 (2.24)
$\Delta EBIT$[d]	−0.33 (0.17)	3.04 (1.03)	—	4.18 (1.39)
$\Delta EBIT * D_{mixed}$	—	−3.95 (0.90)	—	−5.53 (1.22)
$\Delta EBIT * D_{outside}$	—	−10.08 (2.29)	—	−9.38 (2.04)
$\Delta EBIT_{-1}$	−5.23 (3.49)	0.58 (0.26)	—	0.63 (0.27)
$\Delta EBIT_{-1} * D_{mixed}$	—	−4.81 (1.41)	—	−4.82 (1.39)
$\Delta EBIT_{-1} * D_{outside}$	—	−14.52 (3.73)	—	−13.87 (3.29)
Return[e]	−0.35 (1.29)	—	−0.29 (0.73)	−0.44 (1.05)
Return * D_{mixed}	—	—	0.57 (0.97)	0.75 (1.21)
Return * $D_{outside}$	—	—	−1.38 (1.91)	−0.72 (0.86)
Log likelihood	−554.85	−547.17	−555.31	−544.39

[a] The dependent variable is equal to 1 if there was a CEO change in a given year and 0 otherwise.

[b] D_{mixed} is a dummy variables that is 1 if the company's board contains between 40% and 60% outsiders.

[c] $D_{outside}$ is a dummy variables that is 1 if the company's board contains at least 60% outsiders.

[d] The variable $\Delta EBIT$ is the company's change in the earnings before interest and taxes weighted by the book value of assets in the most recent fiscal year prior to the potential resignation. This variable is adjusted for industry effects by subtracting from it the mean for all the firms on COMPUSTAT in the same two-digit SIC code.

[e] The variable *Return* is the return on a company's stock minus the return on a value-weighted market portfolio in the four quarters prior to the period.

0.010. Again the difference between them is statistically significant (t-statistic = 3.80). For the inside boards, the poor earnings decrease the change of a resignation, as earnings changes in the bottom decile predict a 6.7% chance of a resignation and earnings changes in the top decile predict a 3.9% chance. However, the difference between these two numbers is not statistically significant (t-statistic = 1.45). That the difference is statistically significant for the outside boards but not for the inside boards is evidence that the outsiders engage in some monitoring.

These results show that there is a relation between both stock returns and changes in earnings and the probability that a CEO will be replaced for outsider-dominated firms but not for insider-dominated firms. Yet, the accounting literature has documented a well-known relation between stock returns and earnings [see Watts and Zimmerman (1985)]. A possible explanation for this result for earnings changes is that the significant coefficients on the changes in earnings just act as a proxy for the 'true' relation between stock returns and CEO changes.

To test this explanation I estimate equations including both earnings changes and stock returns as explanatory variables. A significant coefficient on changes in earnings in this equation would suggest that the boards of directors base their decision to retain a CEO in part on the component of changes in earnings not contained in stock returns.[19]

For purposes of comparison, I re-estimate the returns equation using annual data on the 322 firms with earnings data available in the third column. The results are qualitatively identical to the results presented in table 3. The coefficients for companies with outsider-dominated boards are all negative and significantly different from zero and from the coefficient on companies with insider-dominated boards.

In the fourth column, I include both earnings changes and returns. The coefficients on earnings changes for companies with outside boards are both negative and significantly different from both zero and the coefficient for companies with inside boards. Including returns in the equation does little to the coefficients on changes in earnings. However, the coefficient on returns for outsider-dominated companies is noticeably smaller when earnings changes are included. It is still significantly different from zero at almost the 5% level using a one-tailed test (t-statistic = -1.65), but is no longer significantly different from the coefficient for insider-dominated companies. Thus this equation provides support for the view that boards of directors look at

[19] The fact that the returns were computed quarterly and the earnings changes were computed on an annual basis presented a problem. The equations presented here use firm-years as the unit of observation. The returns are the market-adjusted returns for the year prior to the year of the observation and the earnings changes are exactly the same as discussed above. This method is employed instead of quarterly earnings changes because annual data are available for a larger fraction of my sample.

accounting numbers when evaluating a CEO's performance, possibly even more than at stock returns.

5.3. Controlling for shareholdings

A related concern is that shareholdings rather than the number of outside directors determine the board's level of monitoring. To test this hypothesis, I use data gathered by the Corporate Data Exchange (CDE) on the shareholdings of 456 *Fortune* 500 corporations for 1980.[20] Of these 456 firms, 220 are in the sample of firms used for the returns equations and 208 are in the sample used for the earnings equations. The CDE lists the shareholdings of each director with a stake larger than 0.2% of the total shares and identifies the top two officers of the corporation, usually the CEO and the chairman of the board. A deficiency of these data is that they do not distinguish between outsiders and insiders except for the top two officers. Nevertheless, the CDE data do provide some insights into the relations between board shareholdings, board composition, and CEO turnover.

A first pass at the CDE data merged with the composition data yields a strong relation between shareholdings and board composition. An ordinary least squares regression tells the basic story:

$$\underset{\textit{on board}}{\textit{Fraction of outsiders}} = \underset{(39.6)}{0.515} - \underset{(4.63)}{0.532}\ \underset{\textit{two officers}}{\textit{Stake of top}}$$

$$-\underset{(2.95)}{0.434}\ \underset{\textit{of board}}{\textit{Stake of rest}} + \underset{(0.032)}{0.00007}\ \textit{Assets},$$

$$R^2 = 0.111, \quad \text{Number of firms} = 236.$$

(t-statistics are in parentheses.) Even controlling for size, shareholdings by both the top two officers of the firm and the rest of the board decrease the number of outsiders on the board.[21]

The same correlation is illustrated in more detail in table 6. The top panel gives the average stakes of the top two officers and the rest of the board. In insider-dominated companies, the top two officers owned an average of nearly 8% of their company's stock in 1980, whereas in outsider-dominated companies, the top two officers owned an average of only 1.57%. The same effect is

[20] Many thanks go to Randall Morck, Andrei Shleifer, and Robert Vishny for providing me with their data, which are described in detail in Morck, Shleifer, and Vishny (1988).

[21] The stakes here are expressed as fractions, so that the equation would predict that a firm whose CEO holds 10% of the company's stock and whose board outside the CEO has negligible holdings would be predicted to have 47.8% outsiders on the board.

Table 6

The association between board composition and board shareholdings for 208 NYSE corporations in 1980.

(A) Average holdings by board type (%)

	Board type			Entire sample
	Inside[a]	Mixed[b]	Outside[c]	
Chairman & president	7.98	2.32	1.57	3.71
Rest of board	5.26	2.39	1.75	3.01

(B) The distribution of board stakes by board type

Board type	No. of firms	Number of firms with stake of board (excluding the stake of chair & president)			
		< 0.2%	≥ 0.2%, < 2%	≥ 2%, < 20%	≥ 20%
Inside	60	12	18	25	5
Mixed	80	31	30	16	3
Outside	68	21	32	14	1
Entire sample	208	64	80	55	9

[a] Inside boards have no more than 40% outsiders.
[b] Mixed boards have between 40% and 60% outsiders.
[c] Outside boards have at least 60% outsiders.

true for the rest of the board. In insider-dominated companies, the board other than the CEO and chairman owned 5.26% of the shares, whereas in outsider-dominated companies, they owned only 1.75%. Board holdings exclusive of the top two officers are broken down in the second panel of table 6. The pattern is the same as in the earlier columns. Insider-dominated firms have much greater ownership by directors than do outsider-dominated firms.

The relation between the CEOs' shareholdings and outsiders on the board is relatively easy to explain. The evidence presented above and in the institutional literature on boards suggests that CEOs have incentives to avoid including outsiders on the board. One explanation for this relation is that CEOs with more shares have more power in the firm and hence can keep outsiders off the board. A second argument follows from the Jensen and Meckling (1976) agency cost story. As a CEO's shareholdings grow as a fraction of his wealth, his interests become more aligned with the shareholders', so agency costs diminish. Thus there may be less need for monitoring by outside directors when the CEO has a large stake in the firm.

There are a number of explanations for the correlation between the holdings of the rest of the board and the composition of the board. One explanation is that when an outsider has a significant stake in the firm, further outside directors are not deemed necessary, because the first outsider already has significant incentives to monitor management. A second explanation is that ownership by inside directors and monitoring by outside directors are alternative mechanisms used by shareholders to control agency problems. Yet a third explanation is that family-dominated companies are generally both tightly held and insider-dominated. Hermalin and Weisbach (1987a) have shown for a subsample of 142 of the firms from this study that much of the relation between board ownership and composition can be explained by family directors.

Shareholdings might affect the CEO turnover process in several ways. When a CEO has more power in the firm, he is more difficult to remove. Since shareholdings are likely to be one source of a CEO's power, one might expect that a large stake in the firm would decrease the probability that a CEO is replaced. To test this hypothesis, I include the CEO's shareholding in the resignation equations.

The results from these equations are shown in the second column of table 7. In each case, increased shareholdings of the CEO reduce the probability that he resigns, although the reduction is not significantly different from zero. Nonetheless, including this variable in the equation does not affect the other coefficients.

Since board shareholdings are correlated with board composition, a possible objection to these results is that board composition may not be what determines monitoring levels, but that board composition is simply a proxy for shareholdings. Morck, Shleifer, and Vishny (1988) argue that directors will not monitor management without a significant stake in the firm. I test this hypothesis by examining whether the monitoring level depends on the shareholdings of the noncontrolling directors (other than the CEO and the chairman).

I divide the sample of firms into three subsamples based on the holdings of the noncontrolling directors. The first subsample has no noncontrolling directors with enough shares to be listed on the CDE director (i.e., no director has 0.2% of the shares). These 64 firms will be referred to as having negligible holdings. I split the remaining firms into two categories based on whether the noncontrolling directors hold more than 2% of stock. Although 2% is arbitrary, it seems plausible that in the 64 companies in which noncontrolling boards hold less than 2%, they may exercise some significant power over management. In the 80 companies where the noncontrolling directors hold less than 2% of the stock but enough to be listed on the CDE directory, these directors are likely to exercise much less control over management.[22]

[22] There are several problems with this approach. The most obvious is that I am using 1980 data to measure board control for 1974 to 1983. In doing so, I am implicitly assuming that board shareholdings do not change over this ten-year period. I also am not able to separate the shareholdings of outsiders and insiders. These equations are intended as a first pass at an important question, using the data that are available.

Table 7

Logit equations predicting CEO turnover using stock returns and management shareholdings;[a] *sample*: 8,862 firm-quarters between 1974 and 1983 (CEOs must be either younger than 64 or older than 66); asymptotic *t*-statistics in parentheses.

Variable	Coeff.	Coeff.	Coeff.	Coeff.
Constant	−4.34 (25.5)	−4.25 (23.6)	−4.19 (26.2)	−4.14 (20.7)
D_{mixed}[b]	0.03 (0.10)	−0.03 (0.13)	—	0.02 (0.09)
$D_{outside}$[c]	−0.18 (0.72)	−0.24 (0.92)	—	−0.19 (0.70)
Return[d]	−0.15 (0.26)	−0.15 (0.26)	−0.59 (1.00)	−0.10 (0.14)
Return * D_{mixed}	−0.48 (0.59)	−0.45 (0.55)	—	−0.53 (0.64)
Return * $D_{outside}$	−2.09 (2.32)	−2.08 (2.28)	—	−2.10 (2.19)
Stake of CEO	—	−1.28 (1.11)	—	−1.04 (0.84)
D_{Shnil}[e]	—	—	−0.22 (0.96)	−0.20 (0.83)
D_{Sh02}[f]	—	—	−0.32 (1.39)	−0.29 (1.16)
Return * D_{Shnil}	—	—	0.38 (0.45)	0.78 (0.88)
Return * D_{Sh02}	—	—	−1.08 (1.27)	−0.68 (0.75)
Log likelihood	−586.49	−585.84	−587.04	−583.88

[a]The dependent variable is equal to 1 if there was a CEO change in a given year and 0 otherwise.

[b]D_{mixed} is a dummy variable that is 1 if the company's board contains between 40% and 60% outsiders.

[c]$D_{outside}$ is a dummy variable that is 1 if the company's board contains at least 60% outsiders.

[d]The variable *Return* is the return on a company's stock minus the return on a value-weighted market portfolio in the four quarters prior to the period.

[e]D_{Shnil} is a dummy variable that is 1 if the directors collectively own less than 0.2% of the company's stock.

[f]D_{Sh02} is a dummy variable that is 1 if the directors collectively own between 0.2% and 2% of the company's stock.

In the third column of table 7, I estimate the resignation equations separating the samples by ownership level instead of by board composition. The results do not indicate that any one group engages in more monitoring than any other group. The boards with moderate levels of ownership appeared to do the most monitoring although the difference among the groups is not satistically significant. In the analogous earnings equations (not presented), the firms whose boards own negligible amounts of stock seem to do the most monitoring, although the effect appears only in the lagged earnings and not in the most recent earnings change. The two equations together do not lead to any clear conclusions about the role of shareholdings in motivating boards to monitor managers.

In the fourth column of table 7, I separate the sample both by composition group and by ownership group. The one result from these equations is that having outsiders on the board seems to have a large effect on its monitoring level. The coefficients are essentially unchanged from the original equations, shown in the first column of table 7.[23] The same result holds for the analogous earnings equation. Thus, the monitoring effect of the outsider-dominated boards does not appear to be a function of the ownership of the board. Rather, it seems that the composition of the board is what drives its level of monitoring.

5.4. *Additional tests*

One possible objection to the above results is that the CEO replacement relationship might vary systematically depending on a firm's size or industry. Since board composition is correlated with both firm size and industry, it is possible that the relationship discovered above is caused by board composition proxying for size or industry effects. To evaluate this interpretation, I control for size and industry effects in my equations. Since the results are not particularly revealing, they are not reported.

Including a measure of size in the equation has essentially no effect, either by itself or on the other variables. Since one might expect the strength of the monitoring relation to vary depending on the size of the firm, I also include terms interacting size and performance measures in the equation. These variables have no statistically or economically meaningful effect, either by themselves or on the other variables. Finally, I include dummies that are equal to one if the firm is in a certain SIC two-digit industry code. All industries with at least four firms in them are included. Including these dummies does not affect the basic result: the coefficient on outside boards is still significant at the 10% level in each equation.

An independent way of confirming that the results represent boards of directors firing CEOs and not simply that poor stock returns and earnings tend to precede resignations in general is to consider resignations that are caused by exogeneous forces. A finding that prior performance does not predict these resignations would provide support for the view that in the

[23] Because of the restriction that the firm must be included in the CDE directory, these equations are estimated on a smaller sample of firms and hence have slightly different parameter estimates. Therefore, I re-estimate the basic equations in the first columns of table 7. These estimates are the ones against which the ones in the later columns of table 7 should be compared.

previous cases, poor performance does cause the resignations. I therefore estimate the logit equations on the subsample of CEOs who are 64, 65, or 66 and are highly likely to resign because of mandatory retirement. The right side of the removal equation using returns is

$$\underset{(13.2)}{-\ 2.51} \ \underset{(1.21)}{-\ 0.82}\ \textit{Return} \underset{(0.76)}{+\ 0.69}\ \textit{Return} * D_{\text{mixed}}$$

$$\underset{(0.70)}{+\ 0.57}\ \textit{Return} * D_{\text{outside}} \underset{(1.04)}{+\ 0.26}\ D_{\text{mixed}} \underset{(1.16)}{+\ 0.29}\ D_{\text{outside}}.$$

(t-statistics are in parentheses.) The coefficient on returns for each of the groups is negative but the magnitudes are very small and none of the coefficients is significantly different from zero. The coefficient on outside boards is -0.25, which is less than one sixth of -1.63, the coefficient in the equation for the CEOs not of mandatory retirement age.

5.5. *Interpretations*

The results suggest that outside boards rely more frequently than inside boards on performance, at least as measured by publicly available measures, when making removal decisions. The obvious interpretation of these results is that the outside directors serve a monitoring role. A potential alternative explanation, however, is that some third factor simultaneously determines which companies have outside boards and which companies have CEO turnover after poor performance.

One factor may be the amount of 'power' the CEO has within the firm. Suppose some CEOs are weak, in the sense that they do not command much loyalty or control over their shareholders. Other CEOs are strong, because they do command such loyalty and control. Strong CEOs can impose their will on the director selection process, while weak CEOs cannot. Thus, we would expect that on average strong CEOs would have more insiders on their boards than weak CEOs. Similarly, strong CEOs would be less likely to be replaced following poor performance than would weak CEOs. According to this explanation, the relationship between the composition of the board and the correlation between poor performance and CEO turnover is spurious; both are actually caused by a third factor, the amount of power the CEO has within the firm.

This explanation, though, has an additional prediction that we can test. Suppose that strong CEOs leave office only when they retire voluntarily and weak CEOs leave office both when they are fired and when they resign voluntarily. If there are no systematic differences between the times when strong and weak CEOs choose to resign voluntarily, we would expect to see strong CEOs remain in office longer than weak CEOs. Thus, this differential power hypothesis predicts that the CEOs who resign with insider-dominated boards will have longer tenures than those who resign with outsider-dominated boards.

The data, however, do not confirm this prediction. The average tenure of CEOs who resign with insider-dominated boards is 11.7 years, while the average tenure of CEOs who resign with outsider-dominated boards is 9.7 years. This difference is not significantly different from zero (t-statistic = 1.50). Moreover, it is driven by a few outliers. The median tenure of CEOs who resign from outsider-dominated firms is actually longer than it is for insider-dominated firms; the median tenure is 9 years for outsider-dominated firms and 7.5 years for insider-dominated firms. The fact that there does not appear to be a systematic difference in the tenure of CEOs who resign between the two types of firms casts doubt on the hypothesis that the results are caused by some unobservable factor related to the power of the CEO within the firm.

Nevertheless, the question of how board composition is determined, and whether it is jointly endogenous with CEO removals, remains. The results can be plausibly explained by the following story: following poor performance, firms first respond by adding outsiders to the board. If poor performance continues, these outsiders remove the CEO. If the two stages are approximately contemporaneous and the unobserved forces that determine board composition are correlated with the ones that determine CEO removal, than the coefficient estimates in the CEO removal equations would be biased and inconsistent.

Indeed, results from Hermalin and Weisbach (1987) suggest that firms do add outsiders to their boards following poor performance. However, the effect is small – a firm with earnings changes in the bottom decile is predicted to increase the fraction of outsiders on its board by less than 1%. The effect of poor stock returns is similar. Since the change in board composition following poor performance is relatively small, and board composition changes very slowly over time, it is unlikely that the potential endogeneity of the board composition is a serious problem.

An interesting fact is that there is no significant difference in the overall number of resignations between board types. If anything, inside boards are more likely to remove CEOs than outside boards. The average probability of removal for an insider-dominated firm is about 5% annually; for an outsider-dominated firm it is approximately 4%. This fact, together with the results above, suggests that inside boards have reasons for replacing their CEOs unrelated to publicly available performance measures such as stock returns or earnings. Another explanation is that inside boards have better information about true performance than is reflected in publicly available measures. Yet a third explanation is that outside board members tend to be short-sighted and remove managers following one bad year, ignoring the fact that the manager may in fact be maximizing the long-term value of the firm. I will now test these various explanations.

6. Analysis of share price movements

6.1. Measuring price responses to announcement of resignations

If CEOs who are removed are in fact poor performers, then firm value should increase when the decision to remove them is made. Event studies are the traditional way to test hypotheses of this type.[24] This event study estimates the market model parameters α_i and β_i for each firm, using daily data occurring both more than 120 trading days before and 60 days following the resignation by running the following regression:

$$R_{ij} = \alpha_i + \beta_i M_j + \varepsilon_{ij},$$

where R_{ij} is the return of firm i's stock on day j and M_j is the return of a value-weighted market index on day j. The residuals from this predicted equation are computed on the days immediately surrounding the announcement of the resignation in the *Wall Street Journal*.[25] These residuals measure the percentage change in the expected future profits of the firm. A positive residual indicates that there has been good news about the firm's prospects unrelated to market factors. The cumulative abnormal residuals are computed for several 'event windows' and a test is performed to see whether their average across firms is significantly different from zero. This procedure tests whether the news about the sample firms conveyed to the market on the event day is on average good or bad. Through the estimation of the α_i and the β_i it controls for both systematic (market-related) risk and any possible anomalies such as the size effect [Banz (1981)].

The results of the event study are presented in table 8. The excess returns are shown for several event windows and broken down by board type and age

[24] The event study methodology was developed by Fama, Fisher, Jensen, and Roll (1969). The particular implementation adopted here follows Ruback (1982).

[25] For several of the firms, it was possible to isolate the month of the announcement but not the exact date. Usually, for these firms, there is an article describing the transition of power saying something like: 'Joseph Jones today replaced William Smith, who announced last August he would step down in December as chief executive officer of XYZ Corporation.' However, there was no article discussing the announcement in August. It was therefore possible to include the change in the prediction equations but not in the event study.

Table 8

Excess returns around the date of the announcement of CEO resignations; *sample*: 367 NYSE firms between 1974 and 1983; day 0 is the *Wall Street Journal* announcement date; *t*-statistics in parentheses.

Board types	Age restrictions	Event window 0 to 0	−1 to 0	to 1	−1 to 1	−3 to 3	Number of resignations
All	None	0.0016 (1.41)	0.0028 (1.77)	0.0022 (1.39)	0.0035 (1.77)	0.0027 (0.89)	259
All	Age < 64 or > 66	0.0017 (1.30)	0.0034 (1.79)	0.0037 (1.93)	0.0054 (2.29)	0.0039 (1.07)	153
Outside[a]	None	0.0049 (2.11)	0.0037 (1.09)	0.0062 (1.81)	0.0050 (1.19)	0.0060 (0.91)	83
Outside	Age < 64 or > 66	0.0045 (1.55)	0.0006 (0.15)	0.0105 (2.50)	0.0066 (1.28)	0.0080 (1.01)	44
Mixed[b]	None	0.0007 (0.40)	0.0043 (1.77)	−0.0002 (−0.10)	0.0033 (1.13)	0.0011 (0.25)	101
Mixed	Age < 64 or > 66	0.0015 (0.77)	0.0087 (2.82)	0.0002 (0.06)	0.0072 (1.90)	0.0021 (0.35)	62
Inside[c]	None	−0.0009 (−0.50)	−0.0001 (−0.57)	0.0012 (0.55)	0.0019 (0.79)	0.0011 (0.35)	75
Inside	Age < 64 or > 66	−0.0007 (−0.28)	−0.0010 (−0.28)	0.0019 (0.58)	0.0016 (0.41)	0.0022 (0.37)	47

[a]Outside boards have at least 60% outsiders. Of 367 firms in the sample, 128 have outside boards.

[b]Mixed boards have between 40% and 60% outsiders. Of 367 firms in the sample, 146 have outside boards.

[c]Inside boards have no more than 40% outsiders. Of 367 firms in the sample, 93 have inside boards.

of CEO. The excess returns are always positive and sometimes significantly different from zero. This result is different from Warner, Watts, and Wruck's (1988) finding that the mean of the excess returns was very close to zero. The entire sample and the entire sample excluding CEOs at mandatory retirement age are shown in the first two lines. The excess returns are positive and significantly different from zero for the three-day window from the day before the announcement to the day after the announcement. The excess returns are larger for cases where the CEO was not of retirement age. This suggests that more news is revealed by these resignations, which is reasonable, since retirements of 65-year-old CEOs tend to be anticipated.

The residuals are broken down by board composition in rows 3 through 8. Outside boards are shown in lines 3 and 4, mixed boards in lines 5 and 6, and inside boards in lines 7 and 8. The effects are positive for outside and mixed boards and close to zero for inside boards. The positive residuals for the outside boards are consistent with the hypothesis that outside boards improve firm value by replacing bad management. The positive residuals for the mixed boards are consistent with the argument discussed above that mixed boards allow both better training for future CEOs and better observation by outside directors of future CEO candidates. However, the difference between the residuals of different board types is not significantly different from zero. Thus it is impossible to conclude that outsiders add more to firm value than insiders do through their removal decisions.[26]

The excess returns from the market model provide weak evidence that outside and mixed boards increase their firms' values when they replace a CEO. This increase does not seem to be present for inside boards. These results are consistent with the hypothesis that outside boards engage in monitoring that improves firm value. The improvement for mixed boards is consistent with the argument that a combined board facilitates the evaluation of CEO candidates by the outsiders. The next section provides a test of these explanations.

6.2. *Explaining the share price responses*

The final test evaluates whether the event day residuals can be explained by the prior performance measures. If boards improve firm value by replacing bad CEOs, there should be a relation between the quality of the CEO and the change in firm value when he is replaced. If the performance measures are correlated with the quality of the CEO and all replacements for the CEO are expected to be of roughly the same quality, then the change in the value of the firm surrounding the event day will be correlated with the performance measure. The test measures whether the cases where the board replaces bad management are those cases where there is an improvement in firm value when the change is announced. A finding that there is a relation between prior performance and the event day residual for outsider-dominated firms but not for insider-dominated firms would provide additional confirmation for the results discussed above.

The test is performed by regressing the cumulative excess returns from the day before the *Wall Street Journal* announcement until the day following it on

[26] This argument presumes that the market is correctly valuing the firm prior to the resignation. Warner, Watts, and Wruck (1988) argue that if the market has only noisy information about firm value, the resignation of the CEO may signal that the CEO and hence the firm have been performing poorly. This signalling effect may cause a stock price to drop following a resignation even though the resignation increases firm value. Hence, the event study may not be the appropriate way to investigate whether CEO removals increase firm value.

the stock returns for the four quarters prior to the resignation.[27] The estimated equation is

$$\begin{aligned}\textit{Excess return} = &- \underset{(0.13)}{0.0010} + \underset{(1.66)}{0.0343} * \textit{Return} - \underset{(1.97)}{0.0555}\ \textit{Return} * D_{\text{mixed}} \\ &- \underset{(3.10)}{0.0924}\ \textit{Return} * D_{\text{outside}} + \underset{(1.24)}{0.0099}\ D_{\text{mixed}} \\ &+ \underset{(0.10)}{0.0009}\ D_{\text{outside}},\end{aligned}$$

$R^2 = 0.0776$, Number of observations = 153.

(t-statistics are in parentheses.) The relation between prior performance and the excess return surrounding the announcement of the CEO resignation is strongest for the companies with outside boards. The coefficient is significantly different from that for the inside boards at the 1% level and from zero at the 5% level. This implies that, for outside boards, it is exactly when the resignation is preceded by poor performance that firm value rises the most around the day the resignation is announced. There is no similar relation between prior performance and event day performance for companies with insider-dominated or mixed boards. The fact that the coefficient on the returns for mixed boards is not significantly different from zero is consistent with the story that the excess returns for the mixed boards are caused by good succession choices and not by throwing out bad CEOs.

7. Conclusions

The main result of this paper is that performance measures are more highly correlated with CEO turnover for firms in which outsiders dominate the boards of directors than for firms in which insiders dominate. Outsider-dominated boards tend to add to firm value through their CEO changes. This addition to firm value is largest when the change is preceded by poor

[27]An earlier version of this paper also included analogous tests using changes in earnings with similar results.

For this test, it is not appropriate to use the residuals from the estimated market model as the measure of performance. If the market model residuals are used, then those firms with negative returns prior to the resignation will be precisely those firms with low estimated values of the intercept term. Therefore, even though all the firms may perform about the same around the event day, it would seem as if there is a relation between prior performance and event day performance. This relation would be spurious, due to the estimation process and not to any decisions made by the boards of directors. For this reason the measure of excess return used for this test is the return on the stock minus the return on the market portfolio. In fact, the results are stronger if market model residuals are used because of this spurious effect.

performance. No similar results hold for insider-dominated boards. Furthermore, these results do not appear to be caused by differences in the ownership structure of the firm, the size of the firm, or the industry in which the firm participates.

Although the results discussed above are for CEO removals, there are many other ways in which outside directors can control the CEO's actions. One way is the choice of accounting policies. The board of directors has the final decision over the amount of discretion the CEO can take in manipulating accounting numbers, in particular the accruals, to maximize his compensation [Healy (1985)]. An interesting research project would test whether the ability of CEOs to manipulate accruals differs systematically depending on the board type. Similar projects could test agency cost explanations of dividends [Easterbrook (1984)] and capital structure [Myers (1984)].

References

Amemiya, T., 1985, Advanced econometrics (Harvard University Press, Cambridge, MA).

American Law Institute, 1982, Principles of corporate governance and structure: Restatement and recommendations, Tentative draft no. 1 (American Law Institute, Philadelphia, PA).

Andrews, K., 1982, Rigid rules will not make good boards, Harvard Business Review 00 34–46.

Bacon, J., 1975, Corporate directorship practices: Role, selection and legal status of the board (The Conference Board, Inc., New York).

Ball, R. and R. Watts, 1972, Some time series properties of accounting numbers, Journal of Finance 27, 663–82.

Banz, R., 1981, The relationship between return and market value of common stocks, Journal of Financial Economics 9, 3–18.

Coughlan, A.T. and R.M. Schmidt, 1985, Executive compensation, managerial turnover, and firm performance: An empirical investigation, Journal of Accounting and Economics 7, 43–66.

DeAngelo, L., 1987, Managerial competition, information costs, and corporate governance: The use of accounting information in proxy contests, Journal of Accounting and Economics, forthcoming.

Demsetz, H., 1983a, The monitoring of management, in: Statement of the Business Roundtable on the American Law Institute's proposed principles of corporate governance and structure: Restatement and recommendations (Business Roundtable, New York).

Demsetz, H., 1983b, The structure of ownership and the theory of the firm, Journal of Law and Economics 26, 375–393.

Easterbrook, F., 1984, Two agency costs explanations of dividends, American Economic Review 74, 650–659.

Fama, E., 1980, Agency problems and the theory of the firm, Journal of Political Economy 88, 288–307.

Fama, E. and M. Jensen, 1983, Separation of ownership and control, Journal of Law and Economics 26, 301–325.

Fama, E., L. Fisher, M. Jensen, and R. Roll, 1969, The adjustment of stock prices to the new information, International Economic Review 10, 1–21.

Fisher, F.M. and J.J. McGowan, 1983, On the misuse of accounting rates of return to infer monopoly profits, American Economic Review 73, 82–97.

Foster, G., 1978, Financial statement analysis (Prentice-Hall, Englewood Cliffs, NJ).

Geneen, H., 1984, Managing (Avon Books, New York).

Hart, O., 1983, The market mechanism as an incentive scheme, Bell Journal of Economics 14, 366–382.

Healy, P., 1985, The effect of bonus schemes on accounting decisions, Journal of Accounting and Economics 7, 85–108.

Hermalin, B. and M. Weisbach, 1987, The determinants of board composition, Unpublished manuscript (University of Rochester, Rochester, NY).

Jensen, M.C., 1986, The takeover controversy: Analysis and evidence, Midland Corporate Finance Journal 4, 6–32.

Jensen, M.C. and W.H. Meckling, 1976, Theory of the firm: Managerial behavior, agency costs and ownership structure, Journal of Financial Economics 3, 305–360.

Jensen, M.C. and R. Ruback, 1983, The market for corporate control: The scientific evidence, Journal of Financial Economics 11, 5–50.

MacAvoy, P.W., S. Cantor, J. Dana, and S. Peck, 1983, ALI proposals for increased control of the corporation by the board of directors: An economic analysis, in: Statement of the Business Roundtable on the American Law Institute's proposed principles of corporate governance and structure: Restatement and recommendations (Business Roundtable, New York).

Mace, M.L., 1971, Directors, myth and reality (Harvard Business School Press, Boston, MA).

Morck, R., A. Shleifer, and R. Vishny, 1988, Management ownership and market valuation: An empirical analysis, Journal of Financial Economics, this issue.

Mruk, E. and J. Gardenia, 1985, Organization and compensation of boards of directors (Arthur Young Inc., New York).

Myers, S., 1984, The capital structure puzzle, Journal of Finance 34, 575–592.

Rao, C.R., 1965, Linear statistical inference and its applications (Wiley, New York).

Ruback, R., 1982, The effect of discretionary price control decisions on equity values, Journal of Financial Economics 10, 83–105.

Solomon, E., 1970, Alternative rate of return concepts and their implications for utility regulation, Bell Journal of Economics 1, 65–81.

Stauffer, T., 1971, The measurement of corporate rates of return: A generalized foundation, Bell Journal of Economics 2, 434–469.

Vance, S.C., 1983, Corporate leadership – boards, directors, and strategy (McGraw-Hill, New York).

Vancil, R., 1987, Passing the baton: Managing the process of CEO succession (Harvard Business School Press, Boston, MA).

Warner, J.B., R.L. Watts, and K.H. Wruck, 1988, Stock prices, event prediction, and event studies: An examination of top management restructurings, Journal of Financial Economics, this issue.

Watts, R. and J. Zimmerman, 1985, Positive accounting theory (Prentice-Hall, Englewood Cliffs, NJ).

[3]

THE JOURNAL OF FINANCE • VOL. LVII, NO. 1 • FEB. 2002

The Cadbury Committee, Corporate Performance, and Top Management Turnover

JAY DAHYA, JOHN J. McCONNELL, and NICKOLAOS G. TRAVLOS*

ABSTRACT

In 1992, the Cadbury Committee issued the *Code of Best Practice* which recommends that boards of U.K. corporations include at least three outside directors and that the positions of chairman and CEO be held by different individuals. The underlying presumption was that these recommendations would lead to improved board oversight. We empirically analyze the relationship between CEO turnover and corporate performance. CEO turnover increased following issuance of the *Code*; the negative relationship between CEO turnover and performance became stronger following the *Code*'s issuance; and the increase in sensitivity of turnover to performance was concentrated among firms that adopted the *Code*.

THE CADBURY COMMITTEE WAS APPOINTED by the Conservative Government of the United Kingdom in May 1991 with a broad mandate to "... address the financial aspects of corporate governance" (*Report of the Committee on the Financial Aspects of Corporate Governance*, 1992, Section 1.8). The Committee was chaired by Sir Adrian Cadbury, CEO of the Cadbury confectionery empire, and included other senior industry executives, finance specialists, and academics. In December 1992, the Committee issued its report, the cornerstone of which was *The Code of Best Practice*, which presents the Committee's recommendations on the structure and responsibilities of corporate boards of directors. The two key recommendations of the *Code* are that boards of publicly traded companies include at least three nonexecutive (i.e., outside) directors and that the positions of chief executive officer (CEO) and chairman of the board (COB) of these companies be held by two different

* Dahya and McConnell are from Krannert Graduate School of Management, Purdue University, and Travlos is from Athens Laboratory of Business Administration and Cardiff Business School, Cardiff University. This paper has benefited from the helpful comments and suggestions of George Benston, David Denis, Diane Denis, Julian Franks, Paul Marsh, Robert Parrino, Ronan Powell, David Power, Raghu Rau, Andrew Stark, Jason Xiao, and seminar participants at Emory University, Purdue University, the University of Iowa, the University of Oklahoma, the EFMA (Paris) and the FMA (Orlando). McConnell acknowledges financial support from the Center for International Business Education and Research (CIBER) at Purdue University. Dahya acknowledges financial support received from the Nuffield Foundation. Travlos acknowledges financial support received from the Kitty Kyriacopoulos Chair in Finance.

individuals.[1] The apparent reasoning underlying the Committee's recommendations is that greater independence of a corporate board improves the quality of board oversight.

As of 2001, the *Code* has not been enshrined into U.K. law and compliance with its key provisions is entirely voluntary. Nevertheless, the *Code* is not without "teeth." First, the Cadbury Committee's report explicitly recognizes that legislation would very likely follow if companies did not comply with the guidelines of the *Code* (*Report of the Committee on the Financial Aspects of Corporate Governance*, 1992, Section 1.1). Second, the report has been given further bite by the London Stock Exchange (LSE), which, since June 1993, has required a statement from each listed company that spells out whether the company is in compliance with the *Code* and, if not, requires an explanation as to why the company is not in compliance.

To appreciate the significance of the Cadbury Committee and its recommendations, it is important to appreciate the environment surrounding the establishment of the Committee. First, the Committee was appointed in the aftermath of the "scandalous" collapse of several prominent U.K. companies during the later 1980s and early 1990s, including Ferranti, Colorol Group, Pollypeck, Bank of Credit and Commerce International, and Maxwell Communication. The broadsheet press popularly attributed these failures and others to weak governance systems, lax board oversight, and the vesting of control in the hands of a single top executive.

> The Cadbury Committee was set up in response to a number of corporate scandals that cast doubt on the systems for controlling the ways companies are run. The downfall of powerful figures such as Asil Nadir or the late Robert Maxwell, whose personal control over their companies was complete, raised fears about the concentration of power. (Self-regulation seen as the way forward, 1992)

Second, historically, executive (i.e., inside) directors have heavily dominated U.K. boards. For example, during 1988, for only 21 companies of the *Financial Times* (FT) 500 did outside directors comprise a majority of the board and, when boards are ranked according to the fraction of outside board members, outsiders comprised only 27 percent of the median board's membership (The Corporate Register, 1989). In comparison, outsiders comprised a majority of the board for 387 of the Fortune 500 companies. Furthermore, for the median board of the Fortune 500 companies, outside directors comprised 81 percent of the membership (Annual Corporate Proxy Statements). With

[1] The report also recommended: (a) full disclosure of the pay of the chairman and the highest paid director; (b) shareholders' approval on executive directors contracts exceeding three years; (c) executive directors pay be set by a board subcommittee composed primarily of outsiders; and (d) directors establish a subcommittee of the board, comprised mainly of outside directors, to report on the effectiveness of the company's system of internal control.

respect to the joint position of CEO and COB, the United Kingdom and United States historically are similar. For example, during 1988, a single individual jointly held the positions of CEO and COB for 349 of the Fortune 500 and for 328 of the FT 500.

At its issuance, the Cadbury Report was greeted with skepticism both by those who felt that it went too far and by those who felt that it did not go far enough. The general unease of those who felt it went too far can be summarized as a concern that the delicate balance between shareholders and managers is better left to the forces of competition. A less generous interpretation of this perspective, which was most frequently espoused by corporate managers, might be characterized as "leave us alone—we know best."

> There is danger in an over emphasis on monitoring; on non-executive directors independence . . . [and] on controls over decision making activities of companies (Green, 1994)

The general concern of those who thought that the report did not go far enough centered on the "voluntary" nature of the Report's recommendations.

> The Committee's recommendations are steps in the right direction. But . . . [s]hareholders, investors and creditors will have been disappointed that just when the corporate failures of recent years cried out for bold and imaginative legal reform, the body from which so much had been expected came up with a little tinkering and a voluntary code (Cadbury Committee Draft Orders Mixed News for Shareholders, 1992).

Against this background, this study empirically investigates the impact of the key Cadbury recommendations on the quality of board oversight in U.K. firms over the period 1989 through 1996.

We begin our investigation with the presumption that an important oversight role of boards of directors is the hiring and firing of top corporate management. We further presume that one indicator of effective board oversight is that the board replaces ineffective or poorly performing top management. Finally, we presume that corporate performance is a reliable proxy for the effectiveness of top management. With those presumptions in place, we empirically investigate the relationship between top management turnover and corporate performance before and after the Cadbury Committee issued its recommendations.

We assemble a sample of 460 U.K. industrial companies listed on the LSE as of December 1988. For each company, we collect data on management turnover, board composition, and corporate performance for up to seven years before and four years after the issuance of the Cadbury Report. With these data, we determine that the relationship between top management turnover and corporate performance is statistically significant both before and after adoption of the Cadbury Committee's recommendations, that is, poorer performance is associated with higher turnover. Importantly, for our purposes, this relationship is significantly stronger following adoption of the Committee's recommendations. Upon further exploration, the increased sensitivity of turnover to performance is due to an increase in outside board members among firms that complied with the key provisions of the *Code*.

The next section describes our sample selection procedure. Section II presents descriptive statistics for the sample. Section III presents the results of our empirical analysis. We reserve our literature review until Section IV, in which we present our conclusions in the context of prior related empirical studies.

I. Sample Selection

Our investigation focuses on top management turnover during the eight-year interval surrounding publication of the Cadbury Report in December 1992 (i.e., December 1988 through December 1996). To begin, we randomly selected 650 out of a total of 1,828 industrial firms on the *Official List* of the LSE as of year-end 1988 (Stock Exchange Yearbook, 1988–1996). For each of the 650 firms for which data are available in the *Corporate Register* for 1988, we determine the names of board members, the outside directors, the total shares held by the board, the total shares held by institutions, and the number of block shareholders, where a block shareholder is defined as any shareholder owning greater than three percent of the company's stock. Such data are available for 548 of the firms in the initial sample. Stock price and accounting data are taken from Datastream for the years 1985 through 1988. If such data are not available for the years 1985 through 1988, the firm is dropped from the sample. Forty-seven of the 548 firms were dropped because of insufficient stock price data; 41 were dropped due to insufficient accounting data. The resulting sample contains 460 firms. These firms are then identified according to their Financial Times Industry Classification (FTIC). The sample includes at least one firm from each of the 33 FTIC categories.

To keep the sample at 460 firms at all times, when a firm ceases to be listed, we search chronologically among newly listed industrial firms until we identify the first firm with book value of assets within plus or minus 20 percent of the book value of assets of the firm that ceased to be listed. For this firm to be eligible for our sample, we require that data be available on management identity, board composition, share ownership, and financial performance. Finally, we require that if the existing firm was (was not) in compliance with the *Code*, the replacement firm must (must not) be in compliance. In this way, a replacement firm was identified for each firm that ceased to be listed within at most four months of delisting. We continue this procedure each year from December 1988 onward, replacing firms that are no longer listed on the LSE, through the end of 1996.

For each firm in the sample, for each year, we collect the names of board members, the number of outsiders, the number of shares held by the board and by institutions, and the number of block holders from the *Corporate Register*. We take stock returns and accounting data from Datastream. For new firms, accounting data for three years prior to LSE listing are taken from filings with the LSE at the time of listing. The shares of some newly listed firms traded elsewhere prior to entering the LSE *Official List*. For these firms, stock price data are collected for up to three years preceding their listing dates. For other firms, we use price data beginning with their entry onto the *Official List*.

To determine top management turnover, we compare the names of top management from year to year over the time period December 1988 through December 1996. For each company, we identify the top executive as the individual with the title of CEO or Executive Chairman. In addition, we identify other board members as members of the top management team if the board member is an employee of the firm and holds the title of Chief of Operations or Managing Director. If the name of the top executive changes between successive years, we classify that as turnover in the top executive. For other members of the top management team, if a name disappears from the top management list, that event is deemed to be a turnover in the top management team excluding the top executive. If the top executive exits the list of top management and is replaced by another member of the top team, that event is considered turnover in the top executive position, but not turnover in the top management team. We do not count as turnover the event in which the position of Executive Chairman is split into the positions of CEO and COB. (Henceforth, we refer to the top executive position as the CEO.)

We further identify turnover as "forced" by examining articles in the *Extel Weekly News Summaries*, the *Financial Times*, and *McCarthy's News Information Service*. Turnover is labeled forced when (a) a news article states that the executive was "fired"; (b) an article states that the executive "resigned"; or (c) an article indicates that the company was experiencing poor performance. In addition, for criteria (b) and (c), the executive must be less than 60 years old and no other article can indicate that the executive took a position elsewhere or cite health or death as the reason for the executive's departure. All other turnover is labeled "normal."

In our tests, we employ both accounting earnings and stock returns to measure corporate performance. Specifically, as our measure of accounting earnings, we use three-year average industry-adjusted return on assets (IAROA). For each firm in the sample and for each year, we calculate return on assets (ROA) as earnings before depreciation, interest, and taxes (EBDIT) divided by beginning-of-the-year total assets. Then, for each firm with the same FTIC as the sample firm, we calculate ROA in the same way. Next, for each FTIC group for each year, we determine the median ROA. IAROA is calculated by subtracting the industry median ROA from the sample firm's ROA for each of the three years prior to a turnover event. The average of these three IAROAs is in our measure of accounting performance.

For measuring stock price performance, we use industry- and size-adjusted stock returns (ISARs), where ISARs are calculated by subtracting the daily stock returns of an industry- and size-matched portfolio from the return of the sample firm beginning 36 calendar months prior to, and ending 2 days prior to, the announcement of the management change. To construct the industry- and size-matched portfolio, for each sample firm, all other firms with the same FTIC code are ranked from largest to smallest according to their equity market values. The firms are then divided into four size portfolios. The differences between the return on the stock in our sample and the equal-weighted average return of the industry- and size-matched portfolio are calculated. The sum of these differences is the ISAR for that firm.

II. Characteristics of the Sample

To conduct our analysis, we split management turnover along two dimensions. First, we split turnover events into a pre-Cadbury time period (1989 through 1992) and a post-Cadbury time period (1993 through 1996). Descriptive data for these two samples are presented in the first set of columns in Table I.

Second, we classify the observations according to whether the firm that experienced the turnover was (or was not) in compliance with the two key provisions of the *Code*. This second classification scheme gives rise to three sets of firms. The first set includes 150 firms that were in compliance with the *Code* for each year that the firm is in our sample (hereafter, the "always-in-compliance" set). The second set includes 22 firms that were never in compliance with the *Code* during any year in which the firm is in our sample (hereafter, the "never-in-compliance" set). The third set includes those firms that came into compliance with the *Code* during a year in which the firm is in our sample (hereafter, the "adopted-Cadbury" set; 288 firms). Descriptive data for the first and second sets are split into pre- and post-Cadbury time periods. These data are presented in the second and third sets of columns in Table I. Descriptive data for the third set of firms (i.e., the adopted-Cadbury set) are split into pre- and post-Cadbury adoption time periods (i.e., $y - 4$ through $y - 1$ and $y + 1$ through $y + 4$, where y equals the year in which the firm came into compliance with the *Code*). These data are presented in the fourth set of columns in Table I.

The descriptive data include the mean and median of book value of assets, share ownership by the CEO, share ownership by the board, share ownership by institutions, number of block holders, board size, and number of outside directors. In terms of book value of assets, the three sets of firms are remarkably similar before and after Cadbury and to each other. (Other financial data [not shown] also exhibit little variation across the three sets of firms.)

In terms of share ownership, regardless of the category of investor, the fraction of shares held by that category is essentially unchanged from before to after Cadbury. Additionally, on this dimension, the always-in-compliance

Table I

Financial, Ownership, and Board Characteristics for 460 U.K. Industrial Firms over the Period 1989 through 1996

Descriptive statistics for a random sample of 460 publicly traded U.K. industrial firms over the period 1989 through 1996. The sample firms are classified into three sets based on whether they were (a) always in compliance with the Cadbury recommendations, (b) never in compliance with the Cadbury recommendations, or (c) adopted Cadbury recommendations. Sample firms in (a) and (b) are analyzed over two four-year periods, pre- and postpublication of the Cadbury Report (1989 through 1992 and 1993 through 1996). Sample firms in (c) are analyzed over two four-year periods, pre- and postadoption of the Cadbury recommendations ($y - 4$ through $y - 1$ and $y + 1$ through $y + 4$). The sample is taken from industrial companies included in the *Stock Exchange Yearbook*, the *Corporate Register*, and listed on the LSE. Firms that leave the sample between 1989 and 1996 are replaced by firms entering the LSE on the date closest to departure. Management and board characteristics are from the *Corporate Register*. Accounting information and share prices are from Datastream.

		Full Sample $N = 460$		Always in Compliance $N = 150$		Never in Compliance $N = 22$		Adopted Cadbury $N = 288$		
	Years	Mean	(Median)	Mean	(Median)	Mean	(Median)	Years	Mean	(Median)
Book value of assets	1989–1992	149.2*	(50.8)	148.8*	(48.8)	146.8	(45.3)	$y - 4$ to $y - 1$	150.1*	(50.7)
(£ million)	1993–1996	156.8	(56.7)	155.6	(53.2)	150.7	(49.2)	$y + 1$ to $y + 4$	158.6	(58.7)
Top executive ownership	1989–1992	2.23	(2.39)	2.22	(2.23)	9.93	(10.11)	$y - 4$ to $y - 1$	2.23	(2.44)
	1993–1996	2.24	(2.34)	2.09	(1.96)	8.34	(9.27)	$y + 1$ to $y + 4$	2.25	(2.43)
Board ownership	1989–1992	10.70	(10.96)	12.83	(12.60)	16.45	(15.93)	$y - 4$ to $y - 1$	9.79	(9.99)
	1993–1996	11.35	(10.83)	13.32	(13.01)	16.09	(15.99)	$y + 1$ to $y + 4$	11.09	(10.44)
Institutional ownership	1989–1992	21.39	(20.84)	22.55	(20.60)	16.37	(15.93)	$y - 4$ to $y - 1$	19.88	(19.82)
	1993–1996	20.04	(19.05)	22.09	(19.51)	16.29	(16.22)	$y + 1$ to $y + 4$	20.09	(20.44)
Number of block holders	1989–1992	2	(2)	3	(2.04)	1	(1)	$y - 4$ to $y - 1$	2*	(2)*
	1993–1996	3	(3)	3	(3.05)	1	(1)	$y + 1$ to $y + 4$	3	(3)
Board size	1989–1992	5.71	(5.00)*	6.69	(6.00)	4.53	(4.00)	$y - 4$ to $y - 1$	5.49*	(5.00)*
	1993–1996	7.29	(7.00)	7.41	(7.00)	5.02	(5.00)	$y + 1$ to $y + 4$	7.13	(7.00)
Percent outside directors	1989–1992	35.3**	(36.9)**	48.6	(43.4)	17.9	(15.4)	$y - 4$ to $y - 1$	26.1**	(25.7)**
	1993–1996	46.0	(43.1)	48.5	(45.8)	21.5	(20.9)	$y + 1$ to $y + 4$	46.6	(40.6)

** and * denote significance at the one and five percent levels, respectively, for both the t-statistic and Wilcoxon statistic. Tests are comparisons of before and after Cadbury values.

set and the adopted-Cadbury set are similar to the full sample and to each other. However, the never-in-compliance set has significantly more ownership by the CEO, significantly greater board ownership, significantly lower institutional ownership, and fewer outside block holders than the other two sets. Apparently, firms with greater "inside" ownership of shares are less likely to adopt the *Code*.

As regards board composition, for the full sample prior to Cadbury, 35.3 percent of directors are outsiders; after Cadbury, this figure is 46.0 percent. Almost all of this increase occurs in companies that came into compliance with the *Code*. For this set, the fraction of outsiders increases from 26.1 percent before adoption to 46.6 percent afterward. For the always-in-compliance set, the percentage of outside directors prior to Cadbury (48.6 percent) is nearly identical to the percentage afterward (48.5 percent). Finally, most of the increase in outside directors came about through an increase in board size as opposed to the replacement of inside directors with outside directors. The median board increases by two members, from five to seven for the full sample, and most of this increase occurs among the adopted-Cadbury set.

As regards the positions of CEO and COB (not shown), not surprisingly, there is considerable variation before and after Cadbury and across the various sets of firms. For the full sample prior to Cadbury, the CEO is also the COB in 36.5 percent of the companies; after Cadbury, that fraction drops to 15.4 percent. Of course, most of this change is due to the set of companies that became compliant with the *Code*. For this set, prior to Cadbury, a single individual held the position of CEO and COB in 39 percent of the firms; after adoption of Cadbury, in none of these companies did a single individual hold both positions.

A related question is when did firms become compliant with the key recommendations of the *Code*. At least some firms came into compliance every year throughout the interval 1989 through 1996, but the bulk of these firms, 202 out of 288, became compliant after 1992. Of these 202, 82 were in compliance with one or the other of the two key Cadbury provisions prior to becoming fully compliant. However, 160 were not in compliance with either recommendation prior to simultaneously adopting both provisions, and, again, most of these occurred after 1992.

III. Management Turnover

What our analysis shows thus far is that the informal arm-twisting associated with the Cadbury recommendations appears to have had considerable impact on the size and composition of boards of directors, and on the number of firms in which one individual holds the titles of CEO and COB. Indeed, as of 1998, 96 of the FT 100 and 90 percent of all LSE firms were Cadbury-compliant (The Corporate Register, 1998). The key questions to which we now turn are: What impact have these changes had on top management turnover and on the sensitivity of turnover to corporate performance?

A. Incidence and Rate of Top Management Turnover

Table II shows the incidence and rates of CEO turnover for the full sample and the three subsets. As in Table I, the data are arrayed into pre- and post-Cadbury time periods (1989 through 1992 and 1993 through 1996) and pre- and post-Cadbury adoption time periods ($y - 4$ through $y - 1$ and $y + 1$ through $y + 4$). The incidence of turnover is the number of instances in which we identify a change in the CEO. The rate of turnover is the annualized rate calculated as the incidence of turnover divided by 460 firms divided by four years. The first two rows present data on all CEO turnover and the second two rows present data on forced CEO turnover.

For the full sample, the incidence and rate of CEO turnover increase significantly from before to after issuance of the Cadbury Report. The increase in turnover is due to an increase in what we have classified as forced turnover. For example, for the full sample, the rate of all CEO turnover increased from 6.48 percent to 7.71 percent (p-value = 0.02), and the rate of forced CEO turnover increased from 3.10 percent to 4.30 percent (p-value = 0.04). Furthermore, the increase in CEO turnover is concentrated in the adopted-Cadbury set of firms. For this set of firms, the rate of all CEO turnover increased from 7.24 percent to 8.87 percent (p-value = 0.01), and the rate of forced CEO turnover nearly doubled, from 2.71 percent to 4.98 percent (p-value = 0.01). For the always-in-compliance set, the rate of CEO turnover is essentially unchanged from before to after Cadbury. For the never-in-compliance set, the rate of turnover declined modestly from before to after Cadbury, but, given the small sample size, we are inclined not to place much weight on this result. Thus, the increase in CEO turnover following Cadbury is primarily attributable to those firms that adopted the key provisions of the *Code of Best Practice*.

CEO turnover data are consistent with an argument that the Cadbury Committees' recommendations increased the quality of board oversight. That is, turnover, especially forced turnover, in the CEO position has increased and this increase is concentrated in the set of firms that adopted the key provisions of the *Code of Best Practice*. Of course, it could be that the increased management turnover that we document following Cadbury is random across firms. The pertinent issue for our purposes is whether turnover is correlated with corporate performance. That is, are the "right" managers being replaced? That is the key question to which we now turn.

B. Relationship between Top Management Turnover and Corporate Performance

Table III presents a preliminary look at the connection between forced CEO turnover and corporate performance, where performance is measured as three-year average IAROA as described in Section I. For each calendar year, firms are ranked from lowest to highest on the basis of their prior three-year average IAROA. For each year, observations are then sorted into

Table II

Incidence and Rates of CEO Turnover in 460 U.K. Industrial Firms, 1989 through 1996

CEO turnover for a random sample of 460 publicly traded U.K. industrial firms over the period 1989 through 1996. The sample firms are classified into three sets based on whether they were (a) always in compliance with the Cadbury recommendations, (b) never in compliance with the Cadbury recommendations, or (c) adopted Cadbury recommendations. Sample firms in (a) and (b) are analyzed over two four-year periods, pre- and postpublication of the Cadbury Report (1989 through 1992 and 1993 through 1996). Sample firms in (c) are analyzed over two four-year periods, pre- and postadoption of the Cadbury recommendations ($y-4$ through $y-1$ and $y+1$ through $y+4$). For each firm, the name of the CEO in the *Corporate Register* is compared from 1988 through 1996 to determine turnover. Turnover is classified as forced by examining news articles in the *Extel Weekly News Summaries*, the *Financial Times*, and *McCarthy's News Information Service*.

		Full Sample $N = 460$		Always in Compliance $N = 150$		Never in Compliance $N = 22$		Adopted Cadbury $N = 288$		
	Years	Incidence	Rate	Incidence	Rate	Incidence	Rate	Years	Incidence	Rate
All CEO Turnover	1989–1992	119*	6.48*	35	5.44	4	4.55	$y-4$ to $y-1$	80**	7.24**
	1993–1996	138	7.71	37	5.75	3	3.41	$y+1$ to $y+4$	98	8.87
Forced CEO Turnover	1989–1992	57*	3.10*	24	3.76	3	3.26	$y-4$ to $y-1$	30**	2.71**
	1993–1996	79	4.30	20	3.14	1	1.09	$y+1$ to $y+4$	58	4.98

** and * denote significance at the one and five percent levels, respectively, for both the t-statistic and Wilcoxon statistic. Tests are comparisons of before and after Cadbury values.

Table III

Forced CEO Turnover in 460 U.K. Industrial Firms Grouped by Quartiles of Performance, 1989 through 1996

Forced CEO turnover for a random sample of 460 publicly traded nonfinancial U.K. firms grouped into quartiles based on IAROA in the two four-year periods during the interval 1989 through 1996. IAROA is calculated as earnings before interest, taxes and depreciation divided by the total book value of assets less the median performance of firms in the same FTIC grouping. Three years of IAROA are averaged. Turnover is classified as forced by examining news articles in the *Extel Weekly News Summaries*, the *Financial Times*, and *McCarthy's News Information Service*. The sample firms are classified into three sets based on whether they were (a) always in compliance with the Cadbury recommendations, (b) never in compliance with the Cadbury recommendations, or (c) adopted Cadbury recommendations. Sample firms in (a) and (b) are analyzed over two four-year periods, pre- and postpublication of the Cadbury Report (1989 through 1992 and 1993 through 1996). Sample firms in (c) are analyzed over two four-year periods, pre- and postadoption of the Cadbury recommendations ($y-4$ through $y-1$ and $y+1$ through $y+4$).

		Interval							
		Quartile 1 (Lowest IAROA)		Quartile 2		Quartile 3		Quartile 4 (Highest IAROA)	
	Years	Incidence	Rate (%)	Incidence	Rate (%)	Incidence	Rate (%)	Incidence	Rate (%)
Full sample	1989–1992	33*	7.2*	15	3.3	9	2.0	0	0.0
	1993–1996	47	10.2	25	5.4	7	1.5	0	0.0
(a) Always in compliance	1989–1992	15	10.0	6	4.0	3	2.0	0	0.0
	1993–1996	15	10.0	5	3.3	0	0.0	0	0.0
(b) Never in compliance	1989–1992	2	9.1	1	4.5	0	0.0	0	0.0
	1993–1996	1	4.5	0	0.0	0	0.0	0	0.0
(c) Adopted Cadbury	$y-4$ to $y-1$	16**	5.5**	8	2.3*	6	2.1	0	0.0
	$y+1$ to $y+4$	31	10.8	20	6.9	7	2.8	0	0.0

** and * denote significance at the one and five percent levels, respectively, for both the t-statistic and Wilcoxon statistic. Tests are comparisons of before and after Cadbury values.

quartiles with quartile one containing the 115 firms with the lowest IAROA and quartile four containing the 115 firms with the highest IAROA.

For the full sample, both before and after Cadbury, the incidence and rate of forced CEO turnover increases as we move from the best to the poorest performing firms. Additionally, the data indicate that the increase in CEO turnover from before to after Cadbury that we document in Table III is due to an increase in turnover in the lowest two performance quartiles in the adopted-Cadbury set of firms. For example, for this set of firms, the rate of turnover in quartiles one and two increased by nearly 100 percent, from 5.5 percent to 10.8 percent (p-value = 0.01) and by almost 300 percent, from 2.3 percent to 6.9 percent (p-value = 0.04), respectively, from before to after adoption of Cadbury. In comparison, for the always-in-compliance set, in the same bottom two quartiles, the rate of turnover is essentially unchanged from before to after Cadbury.

The data in Table III are representative of the pattern of turnover (not shown) that emerges when we consider *all* CEO turnover and when we evaluate performance based on ISARs. That is, turnover is concentrated in the poorest performing quartiles of firms, and the increase in turnover is concentrated in the adopted-Cadbury set of firms.

C. Multivariate Analysis of the Relationship between Top Management Turnover and Corporate Performance

The final questions, to which we now turn, are whether the relationship between turnover and performance is statistically significant and whether the sensitivity of turnover to performance is greater following Cadbury. To answer those questions and to control for other factors that may influence managerial turnover, we estimate logit regressions with pooled time series, cross section data. Initially, we estimate regressions in which the dependent variable is 1 if a firm experiences CEO turnover during a calendar year and 0 otherwise. We estimate separate regressions for all turnover and for forced turnover. We estimate separate regressions using three-year prior IAROAs and three-year ISARs as our performance measures. We include yearly observations of four control variables: fraction of shares owned by directors, fraction of shares owned by institutions, number of block shareholders, and log of total assets.

The results of our regressions are presented in Tables IV and V. In Table IV, the performance variable is *logIAROA*. In Table V, performance is *logISAR*.[2] Panel A of each table presents regressions with all CEO turnover as the dependent variable and Panel B presents regressions with forced turnover as the dependent variable. In total, we have 20 regressions that have either *logIAROA* or *logISAR* as an independent performance variable. In each regression, the coefficient of the performance variable is negative and, with

[2] We also estimated the regressions with market model excess returns and CAPM excess returns as our measure of performance. The p-values of the coefficients are essentially unchanged.

two exceptions, each has a *p*-value of less than 0.05. Thus, CEO turnover is significantly negatively correlated with corporate performance: the poorer the firm's performance, the greater the likelihood that the CEO will depart his position. (We also estimate regressions separately for the pre- and post-Cadbury time periods [not shown]. In every regression, the coefficient of the performance variable is negative with a *p*-value less than 0.05. Thus, turnover is significantly negatively correlated with performance both before and after Cadbury.)

Of the four control variables, only the fraction of shares owned by directors regularly has a *p*-value less than 0.10. The coefficient of this variable is always negative, which indicates that, after controlling for performance, increased share ownership by the board reduces the likelihood that the CEO will depart his position.

We now turn to the effect of Cadbury on CEO turnover and the effect of Cadbury on the relationship between CEO turnover and corporate performance. The five regressions in each panel explore that question from different perspectives. The first regression in each panel is estimated for the full sample of firms and includes an indicator variable (*Dum for 1993–1996*) which takes a value of 0 for all observations before January 1993 (the pre-Cadbury period) and a value of 1 for all observations after that date (the post-Cadbury period) along with a performance variable, either *logIARCA* or *logISAR*, and the four control variables. In each panel, in the first regression, the coefficient of the indicator variable *Dum for 1993–1996* is positive with *p*-values ranging from 0.04 to 0.11. Thus, even after controlling for corporate performance, turnover is higher in the post-Cadbury period. However, as we observed in Table IV, increased turnover appears to be attributable to the set of firms that came into compliance with the Cadbury Committees' recommendations (the adopted-Cadbury set) as opposed to those firms that were always in compliance.

To determine whether the Cadbury/turnover relationship is due to a general phenomenon affecting all firms or whether it is due specifically to a change in board structures traceable to the Cadbury recommendations, we next estimate the regressions separately for the always-in-compliance set of firms and for the adopted-Cadbury set. The only difference in the regressions is that for the adopted-Cadbury set, the indicator variable (*Dum-for-Adopt*) takes on a value of 0 in all years prior to the year in which the firm came into compliance with the *Code* and a value of 1 for all subsequent years. These are the second and third regressions in each panel.

For the always-in-compliance set, the coefficient of the Cadbury dummy variable (*Dum for 1993–1996*) is always positive, but the *p*-values range from 0.79 to 0.92. Thus, publication of the Cadbury Report had a trivial impact, if any, on the rate of turnover among CEOs in firms that were already in compliance with the key provisions of the *Code*. For the adopted-Cadbury set, the coefficient of the indicator variable *Dum-for-Adopt* is always positive with *p*-values ranging from 0.06 to 0.08. Additionally, the magnitude of the coefficient is at least four times the magnitude of the coefficient of the

Table IV

Logit Regressions of CEO Turnover on IAROA and Status of Cadbury Compliance, 1989 through 1996

CEO turnover for a random sample of 460 publicly traded U.K. industrial firms in two four-year periods during the interval 1989 through 1996. IAROA is calculated as earnings before interest, taxes, and depreciation divided by the total book value of assets less the median performance of firms in the same FTIC grouping. Three years of IAROA are averaged. CEO turnover is classified as normal or forced by examining news articles in the *Extel Weekly News Summaries*, the *Financial Times*, and *McCarthy's News Information Service*. The sample firms are classified into three sets based on whether they were (a) always in compliance with the Cadbury recommendations, (b) never in compliance with the Cadbury recommendations, or (c) adopted Cadbury recommendations. Sample firms in (a) and (b) are analyzed over two four-year periods, pre- and postpublication of the Cadbury Report (1989 through 1992 and 1993 through 1996). Sample firms in (c) are analyzed over two four-year periods, pre- and postadoption of the Cadbury recommendations ($y - 4$ through $y - 1$ and $y + 1$ through $y + 4$). Accounting information and share prices are from Datastream. The dependent variable equals one when turnover occurs. *Dum for 1993–1996* equals one for the period 1993 through 1996. *Dum-for-adopt* equals one for the period following the adoption of the key recommendations of the Cadbury Report. The interactive dummy is *Dum-for-adopt* multiplied by logIAROA. *P*-values are in parentheses.

Variable	Total Sample $N = 460$	Always in Compliance $N = 150$	Adopted Cadbury $N = 288$	Adopted Cadbury $N = 288$	Adopted Cadbury $N = 288$
Panel A: Logit Regressions of All CEO Turnover on Log IAROA and Cadbury Status					
Intercept	−1.866 (0.08)	−1.849 (0.09)	−2.570 (0.00)	−2.799 (0.00)	−2.583 (0.00)
Performance variable					
Log IAROA	−2.034 (0.02)	−1.859 (0.10)	−3.180 (0.00)	−3.228 (0.00)	−3.019 (0.00)
Cadbury variable					
Dum for 1993–1996	0.457 (0.11)	0.055 (0.92)			
Dum-for-adopt			0.593 (0.06)	0.148 (0.66)	0.112 (0.72)
Dum-for-adopt × *logIAROA*				−0.739 (0.02)	0.038 (0.96)
Board variables					
Prop outsiders					0.331 (0.30)
Prop outsiders × *logIAROA*					−0.566 (0.08)
Dum for single CEO/COB					−0.062 (0.86)
Dum for single CEO/COB × *logIAROA*					−0.052 (0.89)
Board size					−0.039 (0.20)
Board size × *logIAROA*					−0.064 (0.08)

Control variables					
Board share ownership	−0.984 (0.04)	−1.092 (0.05)	−0.812 (0.08)	−0.844 (0.09)	−0.762 (0.12)
Institutional share ownership	1.294 (0.08)	1.027 (0.21)	0.985 (0.28)	1.032 (0.21)	0.597 (0.65)
Block holders	0.039 (0.60)	0.045 (0.48)	0.028 (0.72)	0.031 (0.68)	0.044 (0.46)
Log assets	−0.159 (0.02)	−0.122 (0.06)	−0.142 (0.05)	−0.139 (0.05)	−0.105 (0.12)
Observations	3,680	1,200	2,304	2,304	2,304
Log-likelihood	−572.89	−387.66	−454.11	−499.20	−501.58
Chi-square	86.45 (0.00)	37.10 (0.00)	60.84 (0.00)	70.36 (0.00)	70.93 (0.00)
Panel B: Logit Regressions of Forced CEO Turnover on Log IAROA and Cadbury Status					
Intercept	−1.745 (0.16)	−1.887 (0.10)	−2.995 (0.00)	−2.819 (0.00)	−2.493 (0.00)
Performance variable					
Log IAROA	−2.932 (0.00)	−2.293 (0.00)	−4.882 (0.00)	−4.659 (0.00)	−3.921 (0.00)
Cadbury variables					
Dum for 1993–1996	0.531 (0.08)	0.151 (0.79)			
Dum-for-adopt			0.631 (0.07)	0.164 (0.61)	0.132 (0.68)
Dum-for-adopt × logIAROA				−0.659 (0.06)	0.129 (0.68)
Board variables					
Prop outsiders					0.364 (0.30)
Prop outsiders × logIAROA					−0.618 (0.07)
Dum for single CEO/COB					−0.053 (0.87)
Dum for single CEO/COB × logIAROA					−0.103 (0.69)
Board size					−0.031 (0.25)
Board size × logIAROA					−0.058 (0.08)
Control variables:					
Board share ownership	−1.190 (0.01)	−1.114 (0.05)	−0.820 (0.10)	−0.854 (0.08)	−0.852 (0.08)
Institutional ownership	1.260 (0.10)	1.039 (0.22)	1.140 (0.15)	1.176 (0.15)	1.144 (0.15)
Block holders	0.051 (0.48)	0.076 (0.38)	0.044 (0.46)	0.049 (0.45)	0.043 (0.46)
Log assets	−0.131 (0.05)	−0.129 (0.06)	−0.166 (0.04)	−0.170 (0.04)	−0.189 (0.03)
Observations	3,680	1,200	2,304	2,304	2,304
Log-likelihood	−621.87	−485.07	−569.29	−588.65	−603.03
Chi-square	89.35 (0.00)	53.58 (0.00)	88.66 (0.00)	87.69 (0.00)	88.21 (0.00)

Table V

Logit Regressions of CEO Turnover on ISAR and Status of Cadbury Compliance, 1989 through 1996

CEO turnover for a random sample of 460 publicly traded U.K. industrial firms in the two four-year periods during the interval 1989 through 1996. ISARs are industry- and size-adjusted cumulative excess stock returns computed using daily stock returns beginning 36 calendar months prior to, and ending 2 days prior to the announcement of the top executive change. CEO turnover is classified as normal or forced by examining news articles in the *Extel Weekly News Summaries*, the *Financial Times*, and *McCarthy's News Information Service*. The sample firms are classified into three sets based on whether they were (a) always in compliance with the Cadbury recommendations, (b) never in compliance with the Cadbury recommendations, and (c) adopted Cadbury recommendations. Sample firms in (a) and (b) are analyzed over two four-year periods, pre- and postpublication of the Cadbury Report (1989 through 1992 and 1993 through 1996). Sample firms in (c) are analyzed over two four-year periods, pre- and postadoption of the Cadbury recommendations ($y-4$ through $y-1$ and $y+1$ through $y+4$). Accounting information and share prices come from Datastream. The dependent variable equals one when turnover occurs. *Dum for 1993–1996* equals one for the period 1993 through 1996. *Dum-for-adopt* equals one for the period following the adoption of the key recommendations of the Cadbury Report. The interactive dummy is *Dum-for-adopt* multiplied by logISAR. *P*-values are in parentheses.

Variable	Total Sample $N = 460$	Always in Compliance $N = 150$	Adopted Cadbury $N = 288$	Adopted Cadbury $N = 288$	Adopted Cadbury $N = 288$
Panel A: Logit Regressions of All CEO Turnover on Log ISAR and Cadbury Status					
Intercept	−3.194 (0.00)	−2.925 (0.00)	−2.639 (0.00)	−2.612 (0.00)	−2.495 (0.00)
Performance variable					
LogISAR	−0.019 (0.00)	−0.012 (0.03)	−0.022 (0.00)	−0.023 (0.00)	−0.019 (0.00)
Cadbury variables					
Dum for 1993–1996	0.519 (0.09)	0.066 (0.87)			
Dum-for-adopt			0.572 (0.08)	0.119 (0.77)	0.090 (0.85)
Dum-for-adopt × *logISAR*				−0.680 (0.05)	−0.144 (0.60)
Board variables					
Prop outsiders					0.262 (0.43)
Prop outsiders × *logISAR*					−0.573 (0.08)
Dum for single CEO/COB					−0.064 (0.82)
Dum for single CEO/COB × *logISAR*					−0.055 (0.85)
Board size					−0.037 (0.37)
Board size × *logISAR*					−0.050 (0.10)

Control variables					
Board share ownership	−0.930 (0.04)	−1.190 (0.02)	−0.804 (0.08)	−0.810 (0.08)	−0.850 (0.07)
Institutional share ownership	1.187 (0.13)	1.062 (0.16)	0.817 (0.40)	0.837 (0.34)	0.936 (0.22)
Block holders	0.059 (0.39)	0.072 (0.29)	0.039 (0.51)	0.031 (0.68)	0.039 (0.51)
Log assets	−0.087 (0.15)	−0.126 (0.04)	−0.077 (0.17)	−0.085 (0.16)	−0.087 (0.15)
Observations	3,680	1,200	2,304	2,304	2,304
Log-likelihood	−598.19	−491.39	−509.66	−584.02	−590.73
Chi-square	86.69 (0.00)	49.76 (0.00)	75.93 (0.00)	80.80 (0.00)	81.40 (0.00)
Panel B: Logit Regression of Forced CEO Turnover on Log ISAR and Cadbury Status					
Intercept	−4.892 (0.00)	−3.023 (0.00)	−1.538 (0.00)	4.624 (0.00)	4.291 (0.00)
Performance variable					
LogISAR	−0.030 (0.00)	−0.009 (0.07)	−0.049 (0.00)	−0.040 (0.00)	0.039 (0.00)
Cadbury variables					
Dum for 1993–1996	0.598 (0.04)	0.050 (0.86)			
Dum-for-adopt			0.538 (0.08)	0.227 (0.60)	0.030 (0.92)
Dum-for-adopt × *logISAR*				−0.590 (0.07)	−0.134 (0.65)
Board variables					
Prop outsiders					0.272 (0.39)
Prop outsiders × *logISAR*					−0.564 (0.08)
Dum for single CEO/COB					−0.060 (0.83)
Dum for single CEO/COB × *logISAR*					−0.039 (0.93)
Board size					−0.042 (0.34)
Board size × *logISAR*					−0.045 (0.10)
Control variables					
Board share ownership	−0.921 (0.05)	−0.925 (0.05)	−0.807 (0.09)	−0.840 (0.07)	−0.763 (0.13)
Institutional share ownership	1.040 (0.21)	1.100 (0.19)	0.638 (0.58)	0.635 (0.58)	0.567 (0.67)
Block holders	0.078 (0.25)	0.101 (0.07)	0.044 (0.48)	0.048 (0.47)	0.043 (0.47)
Log assets	−0.119 (0.07)	−0.142 (0.03)	−0.066 (0.26)	−0.061 (0.27)	−0.019 (0.31)
Observations	3,680	1,200	2,304	2,304	2,304
Log-likelihood	−629.65	−555.36	−581.41	−584.07	−588.82
Chi-square	117.41 (0.00)	48.37 (0.00)	50.21 (0.00)	50.46 (0.00)	50.61 (0.00)

Cadbury dummy (*Dum for 1993–1996*) for the always-in-compliance set. Thus, publication of the *Code of Best Practice* did not have an impact, per se, on the rate of turnover among top U.K. executives; rather, the effect was concentrated among those firms that altered their board structures to comply with the *Code*. This is not to say that the rate of turnover among top executives in firms that were always-in-compliance was "too low" either before or after Cadbury. The data only show that the rate of turnover for these firms did not change between the pre- and post-Cadbury periods. In comparison, the rate of turnover increased significantly among firms that came into compliance with the Cadbury recommendations during the period of this study.

To determine whether the increase in turnover is correlated with performance, we estimate a regression with only the adopted-Cadbury set of firms that includes the adopted Cadbury dummy (*Dum-for-Adopt*) and the adopted Cadbury dummy interacted with our measures of performance (either *Dum-for-Adopt* × *logIAROA* or *Dum-for-Adopt* × *logISAR*) along with our measures of performance (either *logIAROA* or *logISAR*) and our four control variables. These are the key regressions of our analysis and are given as the fourth regression in each panel.

The coefficient of the interaction variable indicates whether the increase in turnover among firms that adopted Cadbury is randomly distributed across those firms or is concentrated among the poorest performing firms. In each regression, the coefficient of the interaction variable is negative with p-values ranging from 0.02 to 0.07. Additionally, the coefficient of the adopted Cadbury dummy (*Dum-for-Adopt*) is reduced by 60 percent and now has p-values ranging from 0.60 to 0.77. These results indicate that the increase in CEO turnover is not random; rather it is (inversely) correlated with performance: After controlling for performance, the likelihood that the CEO will depart his position is greater once a poorly performing firm comes into compliance with the key provisions of the *Code*. The answer to the question of whether the "right" managers are leaving the firms appears to be yes, assuming, of course, that our measures of performance properly identify the right managers.

Thus far, we have employed an indicator variable to capture the key provisions of the *Code of Best Practice*. A further question is: Which of the key provisions is responsible for the increased sensitivity of turnover to corporate performance? To address that question, we estimate a final regression with the adopted-Cadbury set of firms in which we include annual observations on the fraction of outside directors (*Prop Outsiders*), an interaction between the fraction of outsiders and our measures of corporate performance (either *Prop Outsiders* × *logIAROA* or *Prop Outsiders* × *logISAR*), an indicator variable to identify observations in which the positions of CEO and COB are held by a single individual (equal to 1) or by two individuals (equal to 0) and an interaction between this indicator variable and our measures of corporate performance (either *Dum for Single CEO/COB* × *logIAROA* or *Dum for Single CEO/COB* × *logISAR*). These variables are designed to capture the changes brought about by the *Code of Best Practice*. Because adoption of the *Code* led to a general increase in board size, we also include the number of directors and an interaction between the number of directors and our measure of performance. These regressions, which also include a performance measure, *Dum-for-Adopt*, and the four control variables, are shown as the fifth regression in each panel.

According to the regressions, when the board composition and CEO/COB variables are included, the coefficients of the interaction of the *Dum-for-Adopt* and our measures of performance are not significant (p-values range from 0.60 to 0.96). Additionally, the coefficient of the fraction of outsiders on the board is positive, albeit not significant, in each regression (p-values range from 0.30 to 0.43). More interestingly, the coefficients of the interaction between the fraction of outsiders and our measures of performance are always negative, with p-values that range from 0.07 to 0.08. In contrast, in none of the regressions does the coefficient of the dummy for the CEO/COB or the coefficient of the interaction of this variable with our measures of performance begin to approach statistical significance (p-values range from 0.69 to 0.93).

Apparently, the increased sensitivity of turnover to corporate performance for the adopted-Cadbury set of firms (and the contemporaneous loss in significance of the interaction of *Dum-for-Adopt* with performance) is attributable to the increase in the fraction of outside directors. Splitting the responsibilities of the CEO and COB between two individuals appears to have had no effect on the rate of CEO turnover.

D. Spurious Correlation?

A question that may arise is whether the correlation between management turnover and corporate performance interacted with Cadbury compliance is spurious. More specifically, is it possible that both turnover and Cadbury compliance are caused by poor performance, perhaps because poorly performing firms adopt Cadbury to placate shareholders and, concurrently, dismiss top managers—a change in management that would have occurred even in the absence of Cadbury? Several analyses seem to indicate that this is not the case.

First, by construction, for the adopted-Cadbury set of firms, all postadoption CEO turnover follows compliance with the *Code*. This occurs because we use year-end data to determine whether a firm is in compliance. Only after the year-end in which the firm becomes compliant with the *Code* do we consider turnover to be postadoption. Thus, all post-Cadbury CEO turnover is postadoption. Related to this point, most postadoption turnover does not follow closely after Cadbury compliance. For example, for the 58 instances of postadoption *forced* CEO turnover, 18 occur within 12 months after the year-end of adoption, 23 occur in months 13 through 24, and 17 occur in months 25 through 36. Thus, forced CEO turnover is not clustered in the months immediately following adoption. The same is true for *all* CEO turnover. Second, corporate performance prior to adoption for those 288 firms that became Cadbury-compliant is not poor. For example, over the three years prior to adoption, both the mean IAROA and the mean ISAR are positive: They are +0.057 and +0.039, respectively, but neither is statistically significantly different from zero (p-values = 0.24 and 0.40). Thus, it is not just poorly performing firms that adopt Cadbury. Third, even for the set of 57 firms that came into compliance and then experienced forced CEO turnover, the three-year preadoption mean IAROA and ISAR are positive (+0.027 and +0.014), but not significantly different from zero (p-values = 0.55 and 0.69).

In sum, adoption of Cadbury and CEO turnover are not simultaneous, adoption of Cadbury is not concentrated among poorly performing firms, and firms that adopt Cadbury and have CEO turnover are not performing poorly prior to adoption. These analyses argue against spurious correlation.

E. How Much Additional Turnover?

To give some indication of the economic significance of the statistical relationship we document, we use the last regression in Panel A and Panel B of Table V to calculate the implied increase in the instances of total CEO turnover and forced CEO turnover for the adopted-Cadbury set of firms during years $y - 4$ through $y - 1$. The predicted instances of total CEO turnover are 95 and the predicted instances of forced CEO turnover are 54. These compare with actual total turnover of 80 and actual forced turnover of 30. Thus, the regressions imply all CEO turnover would be 20 percent higher and forced turnover would be 80 percent higher had these firms been in compliance with the *Code* over the four years prior to adoption.[3]

F. Corporate Performance and Turnover in the Top Team

As noted at the outset, we focus our discussion on turnover in the CEO position. However, we also gathered turnover data for the entire top team of managers. For the top team of managers, excluding the CEO, we conduct each of the same analyses as undertaken for the CEO. In general, the results for the top team (excluding the CEO) are similar to, albeit weaker than, those for the CEO. For example, the regressions reported in Tables IV and V for CEO turnover are also estimated for turnover in the top management team (excluding the CEO). The signs of the coefficients for these regressions (not shown) are identical to those of Tables IV and V; however, the p-values of the variables are not significant at traditional levels. For example, the sign of the Cadbury 1993 through 1996 dummy variable is positive with p-values that range from 0.16 to 0.20. Similarly, the sign on the *Dum-for-Adopt* variable is also positive in each regression, but has p-values that range from 0.17 to 0.24. The coefficient for the interaction of *Dum-for-Adopt* and our measures of performance in the same regression is always negative

[3] As a benchmark, we calculated the implied instances of total CEO turnover during years $y + 1$ through $y + 4$ to be 96 versus actual turnover of 98 and forced turnover to be 56 versus actual forced turnover of 58.

with p-values that range from 0.15 to 0.26.[4] In short, the regressions for turnover in the top management team (excluding the CEO) are consistent with those of turnover in the CEO, but the levels of statistical significance are weaker.

IV. Commentary and Conclusions

We initiated this study with a degree of skepticism. Given the potential bite associated with the recommendations of the Cadbury Committee, we are not surprised to observe a significant increase in board sizes, a significant increase in the number and fraction of outside board members, and a significant reduction in the number and fraction of firms with a single individual as CEO and COB. Further, because of prior studies on the relationship between corporate performance and CEO turnover, we also are not surprised to find a significant (negative) correlation between corporate performance and top management turnover both before and after Cadbury (Coughlan and Schmidt (1985), Warner, Watts, and Wruck (1988), Weisbach (1988), Gilson (1989), Martin and McConnell (1991), Murphy and Zimmerman (1993), Kaplan (1994), Kang and Shivdasani (1995), Franks and Mayer (1996), Huson, Parrino, and Starks (1998), Mikkelson and Partch (1997), and Denis and Sarin (1999)). We were, however, skeptical as to whether the observed changes in board composition would lead to changes in corporate decision making or to a change in the relationship between corporate performance and top management turnover.

Part of our skepticism may stem from the mixed results of prior studies on board composition and management turnover. For example, for 367 publicly traded U.S. companies, Weisbach (1988) determines that CEO turnover is more highly negatively correlated with performance in firms with outsider-dominated boards. Contrarily, for 270 publicly traded Japanese companies, Kang and Shivdasani (1995) find that the sensitivity of CEO turnover to performance is unrelated to the fraction of outside directors. Finally, Franks, Mayer and Renneboog (2000) examine CEO turnover for a sample of poorly performing U.K. firms for the period 1988 through 1993. They are unable to draw definitive conclusions as to whether or not CEO turnover is more sensitive to performance when the board comprises more outside directors.

The other part of our skepticism largely stems from our general expectation that, prior to Cadbury, market forces were likely to have propelled boards toward efficient structures. Thus, we are surprised to observe a significant increase in management turnover following Cadbury adoption, to find an increase in the sensitivity of management turnover to corporate performance following Cadbury adoption, and, especially, to find that the increase in sensitivity of turnover to performance is due to an increase in outside board members. These results are consistent with, and support, the argu-

[4] The results of our analyses of the top team excluding the CEO are available from the authors.

ment that the Cadbury recommendations have improved the quality of board oversight in the United Kingdom. However, a caveat is in order: Increased management turnover and increased sensitivity of turnover to our measures of performance do not necessarily mean an improvement in corporate performance. As observed by Bhagat and Black (1999), prior research on board composition and corporate performance generally appears to show that board composition does affect the way in which boards accomplish discrete tasks, such as hiring and firing top management, responding to hostile takeovers, setting CEO compensation and so forth (Klein and Rosenfeld (1988), Kaplan and Reishus (1990), Rosenstein and Wyatt (1990), Byrd and Hickman (1992), Shivdasani (1993), Denis and Denis (1995), Kini, Kracaw, and Mian (1995), Agrawal and Knoeber (1996), Cotter, Shivdasani, and Zenner (1997), Hermalin and Weisbach (1998), and Bhagat and Black (2000)). However, such studies generally show less (or no) connection between board composition and corporate profitability. Our study analyzes the effect of the Cadbury recommendations on a discrete board task. In a subsequent study, we intend to investigate whether the Cadbury recommendations have influenced corporate performance more generally.

REFERENCES

Agrawal, Anup, and Charles R. Knoeber, 1996, Firm performance and mechanisms to control agency problems between managers and shareholders, *Journal of Financial and Quantitative Analysis* 31, 377–397.

Bhagat, Sanjai, and Bernard S. Black, 1999, The uncertain relationship between board composition and firm performance, *Business Lawyer* 54, 921–964.

Bhagat, Sanjai, and Bernard S. Black, 2000, Board independence and long-term performance, Working paper, University of Colorado and Columbia Law School.

Byrd, John W., and Kent A. Hickman, 1992, Do outside directors monitor managers? Evidence from tender offer bids, *Journal of Financial Economics* 32, 195–221.

Cadbury committee draft orders mixed news for shareholders, 1992, *Financial Times*, June 2, p. 16.

The Corporate Register, 1989 to 1996, 1998 (Hemmington Scott Publications, London).

Cotter, James F., Anil Shivdasani, and Marc Zenner, 1997, Do independent directors enhance target shareholder wealth during tender offers? *Journal of Financial Economics* 43, 195–218.

Coughlan, Anne T., and Ronald M. Schmidt, 1985, Executive compensation, management turnover, and firm performance, *Journal of Accounting and Economics* 7, 43–66.

Denis, David J., and Diane K. Denis, 1995, Performance changes following top management dismissals, *Journal of Finance* 50, 1029–1057.

Denis, David J., and Atulya Sarin, 1999, Ownership and board structures in publicly traded corporations, *Journal of Financial Economics* 52, 187–224.

Franks, Julian, and Colin Mayer, 1996, Hostile takeovers and the correction of managerial failure, *Journal of Financial Economics* 40, 163–181.

Franks, Julian, Colin Mayer, and Luc Renneboog, 2000, Who disciplines managers in poorly performing companies? Working paper, London Business School.

Gilson, Stuart, 1989, Management turnover and financial distress, *Journal of Financial Economics* 25, 241–262.

Green, Sir Owen, 1994, Pall Mall Lecture on U.K. Corporate Governance, February 24.

Hermalin, Benjamin E., and Michael S. Weisbach, 1998, Endogenously chosen boards of directors and their monitoring of the CEO, *American Economic Review* 88, 96–118.

Huson, Mark R., Robert Parrino, and Laura T. Starks, 1998, Internal monitoring mechanisms and CEO turnover: A long term perspective, Unpublished manuscript, University of Alberta.

Kang, Jun-Koo, and Anil Shivdasani, 1995, Firm performance, corporate governance, and top executive turnover in Japan, *Journal of Financial Economics* 38, 29–58.

Kaplan, Steven N., 1994, Top executives, turnover and firm performance in Germany, *Journal of Law, Economics and Organization* 10, 142–159.

Kaplan, Steven N., and David Reishus, 1990, Outside directorships and corporate performance, *Journal of Financial Economics* 27, 389–410.

Kini, Omesh, William A. Kracaw, and Shehzad Mian, 1995, Corporate takeovers, firm performance, and board composition, *Journal of Corporate Finance* 1, 383–412.

Klein, April, and James Rosenfeld, 1988, Targeted share repurchases and top management changes, *Journal of Financial Economics* 20, 493–506.

Martin, Kenneth J., and John J. McConnell, 1991, Corporate performance, corporate takeovers, and top management turnover, *Journal of Finance* 46, 671–687.

Mikkelson, Wayne, and Megan Partch, 1997, The decline of takeovers and disciplinary management turnover, *Journal of Financial Economics* 44, 205–228.

Murphy, Kevin J., and Jerold L. Zimmerman, 1993, Financial performance surrounding CEO turnover, *Journal of Accounting and Economics* 16, 273–315.

Report on the Financial Aspects of Corporate Governance (With the Code of Best Practice), 1992 (Gee and Co. Ltd., London).

Rosenstein, Stuart, and Jeffrey G. Wyatt, 1990, Outside directors, board independence, and shareholder wealth, *Journal of Financial Economics* 26, 175–191.

Self-regulation seen as the way forward, 1992, *The Financial Times*, May 28, p. 17.

Shivdasani, Anil, 1993, Board composition, ownership structure, and hostile takeovers, *Journal of Accounting and Economics* 16, 167–198.

Stock Exchange Yearbook, 1989–1996 (London Stock Exchange, London).

Warner, Jerold B., Ross L. Watts, and Karen H. Wruck, 1988, Stock prices and top management changes, *Journal of Financial Economics* 20, 461–492.

Weisbach, Michael S., 1988, Outside directors and CEO turnover, *Journal of Financial Economics* 20, 431–460.

[4]

© *Academy of Management Journal*
2002, Vol. 45, No. 6, 1195–1206.

POWER DYNAMICS WITHIN TOP MANAGEMENT AND THEIR IMPACTS ON CEO DISMISSAL FOLLOWED BY INSIDE SUCCESSION

WEI SHEN
University of Florida

ALBERT A. CANNELLA, JR.
Texas A&M University

Following a power perspective, this study is a longitudinal examination of the antecedents of CEO dismissal followed by inside succession. Our theory highlights interest conflicts and competition within top management. We propose that CEO origin, CEO tenure, non-CEO inside directors, and senior executive ownership are important antecedents of CEO dismissal followed by inside succession. Evidence from a sample of 387 large U.S. corporations suggests that non-CEO senior executives frequently play an important role in CEO dismissal.

The influence of power in CEO dismissal and succession decisions is a major focus in current succession and governance research (Boeker, 1992; Boeker & Goodstein, 1993; Cannella & Lubatkin, 1993; Cannella & Shen, 2001; Ocasio, 1994; Zajac & Westphal, 1996). Theories of organizational politics highlight interest conflicts and power struggles within organizations, especially among senior executives (Lazear & Rosen, 1981; Pfeffer, 1981). For example, Fama (1980: 293–294) proposed that competition among top managers plays an important role in the internal monitoring of firms. Ocasio (1994), drawing on Pareto's (1968) circulation of power theory, reported that the likelihood of CEO turnover among companies with low performance increased with the proportion of inside directors. These scholars have noted that the presence of non-CEO inside directors on a board can facilitate the functioning of a corporation's internal monitoring system and reduce agency costs that stem from the separation of ownership and managerial control. However, much governance and succession research has questioned the effectiveness of internal monitoring by non-CEO top managers and concluded that a firm's senior executives are often allies of its CEO (Finkelstein & Hambrick, 1996; Walsh & Seward, 1990; Weisbach, 1988). Further, little research has directly focused on power contests within top management as an important cause of CEO dismissal. To advance understanding of the role that senior executives play in CEO succession decisions, in this study we explored the power dynamics within top management and examined their impacts on CEO dismissal followed by inside succession.

It is important to demarcate the boundaries of our study. Most CEO successions involve an incumbent's stepping down at an agreed-upon time, usually when he or she is around 60 to 65 years old (Cannella & Shen, 2001; Friedman & Singh, 1989). Often, a retiring CEO is replaced by an heir apparent who has been identified well in advance and groomed as president or chief operating officer by the CEO before the final promotion (Vancil, 1987). More importantly, powerful retiring CEOs exert a strong influence over successor selection and prefer successors, especially insiders, who are similar to themselves (Zajac & Westphal, 1996). Our study is not about these "ordinary" successions. Instead, it is about a subset of inside CEO successions resulting from power contests within top management groups in which the CEOs are dismissed and have no influence over successor selection. The relationships and the underlying processes we explored in this study thus differ importantly from those that figure in the extant literature on CEO succession in general.

THEORY AND HYPOTHESES

Much of the governance literature emphasizes interest conflicts between a company's management (as a group) and its shareholders and places the task of effective internal control of management primarily upon outside directors (Walsh & Seward, 1990). In this line of argument, when firm performance declines, often not only the capabilities of the CEO alone, but also those of the entire top management group, are called into question (Boeker & Good-

The authors thank Bob Hoskisson, Jing Zhou, Chao Chen, Fariborz Damanpour, and three anonymous reviewers for their helpful comments and suggestions.

stein, 1993). Further, this view implies that, because of the fear of losing their jobs, the senior executives of a firm have strong incentives to ally with its CEO and defend their positions (Dalton & Kesner, 1985). Although this managerial entrenchment argument has received empirical support (Boeker & Goodstein, 1993; Weisbach, 1988), it neglects important interest conflicts and competition within top management groups (Ocasio, 1994; Pfeffer, 1981).

A primary cause of interest conflicts and competition among top executives lies in their desire for power and career advancement. Senior executives are ambitious individuals who have high needs for power and achievement (McClelland & Burnham, 1976). As they move up the corporate hierarchy, their desire to become CEO and "run their own show" becomes even stronger (Pfeffer, 1981; Vancil, 1987). The extraordinary prestige and material benefits associated with the CEO title provide further incentives for senior executives to challenge the CEO of their company and to participate in a power tournament in the firm's internal labor market (Lazear, 1989; Lazear & Rosen, 1981). In addition, the external labor market generally evaluates executives' talent on the basis of the performance of their employing firms. When firm performance suffers, so does each senior executive's reputation and value in the external labor market (Fama, 1980). Senior executives thus, even if not direct power contenders themselves, have incentives to monitor the CEO's leadership and join others in taking action against the CEO when they perceive him or her to be less than capable.

The interest conflicts and competition between a CEO and other senior executives put the CEO at risk of power contests with senior executives (Lazear, 1989; Ocasio, 1994). Although such contests are not easily observable to outsiders, we argue that the power dynamics within top management will affect the occurrence of CEO dismissal as well as choices of successors. When senior executives successfully challenge a CEO and gain the support of outside directors, the CEO will be dismissed, and one of the contending executives will likely be promoted as the successor (Pfeffer, 1981; Sonnenfeld, 1988). This scenario is very different from the one widely discussed in much of the governance literature, in which outside directors initiate a power contest with a CEO or an entire top management group in the context of poor performance and subsequently appoint an outsider as the successor (Boeker & Goodstein, 1993; Cannella & Lubatkin, 1993; Weisbach, 1988). We believe that four factors particularly reflect the power dynamics that arise between CEOs and senior executives. Below, we develop hypotheses regarding the impacts of these factors on the occurrence of CEO dismissal followed by inside succession.

CEO Origin

CEO origin refers to whether an incumbent CEO was an employee of the firm he or she leads at the time of appointment as CEO (Kesner & Sebora, 1994). Origin has important implications for power dynamics within top management groups. Building strong social networks and coalitions within a firm is an essential task for those who aspire to be the CEO (Jennings, 1971; Vancil, 1987). When they are promoted to a firm's CEO position, inside successors not only have the approval of outside directors, but also have support within the top management group (though perhaps not complete support, owing to internal competition). In contrast, when outside CEOs take office, they lack the internal social networks and coalitions of inside CEOs. Accentuating this problem is the fact that senior executives from a firm's prior regime often have a hostile attitude toward outside CEOs because of the changes these outsiders may initiate (Boeker & Goodstein, 1993; Dalton & Kesner, 1985; Gouldner, 1954). In addition, because outside successors are often appointed in periods of poor performance and are expected to turn their firms around (Gabarro, 1987; Zajac, 1990), they are under pressure to take quick action in restructuring top management groups (Gouldner, 1954; Helmich & Brown, 1972). This intensifies interest conflicts between outside CEOs and senior executives. Thus, compared to inside succession, outside succession increases tension within a top management group and places the outside CEO at a higher risk of power contests with senior executives. The high expectations the board and other stakeholders have toward outside CEOs make them more vulnerable when challenges from senior executives emerge (Puffer & Weintrop, 1991). All else being equal, we expected a higher rate of CEO dismissal followed by inside succession among outside CEOs.

Hypothesis 1. CEO origin as an outsider increases the likelihood of CEO dismissal followed by inside succession.

CEO Tenure

New CEOs confront significant challenges upon taking office. Promotion to the CEO position typically leads to significant changes in both an executive's responsibility and task environment (Kotter, 1982). New CEOs must adjust to their new roles and quickly develop good working relationships with the other members of their top management groups, boards of directors, and powerful outside stakeholders (Vancil, 1987). The learning process is stressful and time consuming (Kotter, 1982). At the same time, new CEOs are charged with specific strategic mandates (Hambrick & Fukutomi, 1991), a charge that further increases the difficulty of their tasks. Finally, and perhaps most crucial for new CEOs, is their need to establish their authority in a top position (Gabarro, 1987).

Authority is legitimate power and is of two types—authorized power and endorsed power (Scott, 1995: 305–308). Authorized power is granted by those superior to the power holder (Weber, 1946), and endorsed power is granted by those subordinate to the power holder (Barnard, 1938). To establish their authority, new CEOs must be accepted by both their boards of directors and by subordinate executives. Although the official appointment represents authorization by the board of directors, it does not necessarily confer endorsement from subordinates (Barnard, 1938; Selznick, 1957). Further, the authorization of a board is likely to be somewhat tentative and can be revoked quickly if directors develop significant concerns about a new CEO's leadership capacity (Vancil, 1987). Indeed, because there is little proof of accountability in office, the leadership capacity of new CEOs is under close scrutiny by outside directors (Alderfer, 1986). Thus, until they can prove their competence and meet the expectations of both their boards and subordinate executives, the authority of new CEOs will be much weaker than that of established CEOs (Hambrick & Fukutomi, 1991; Ocasio, 1994).

The challenges facing new CEOs leave them vulnerable to power contests with rival executives. The fact that new CEOs need time to establish their authority in the top position (Selznick, 1957) provides an opportunity for ambitious senior executives to challenge them early in their tenures. Once incumbent CEOs have proven their leadership capacity and established their authority in office, the chance for senior executives to successfully mount a challenge is greatly reduced (Ocasio, 1994). Thus, CEOs are likely to face a higher risk of power contests with senior executives in the early years of their tenures, and we expected to see a higher rate of CEO dismissal followed by inside succession during that period.

Hypothesis 2. CEOs are at a higher risk of dismissal followed by inside succession in the early years of their tenures.

Non-CEO Inside Directors

Inside directors are directors who are also executives of the firm on whose board they serve. Although the effectiveness of inside directors in governance has been widely questioned (Walsh & Seward, 1990), theories emphasizing managerial interest conflicts and competition suggest that the presence of non-CEO inside directors has important implications for the power dynamics within top management. First, inside directors are the most likely and viable challengers of a CEO (Ocasio, 1994). A seat on the board gives an executive exposure to outside directors and enables them to build social networks and coalitions on the board (Jennings, 1971; Vancil, 1987). This development narrows the power gap between them and the CEO and lends them more confidence with which to challenge the CEO (Sonnenfeld, 1988). Second, for senior executives to successfully challenge a CEO and to advance their careers, they must be able to voice their concerns about the CEO to the corporation's board (Lorsch & MacIver, 1989). Non-CEO inside directors, if not challengers themselves, can function as conduits between senior executives and outside directors, making outside directors better informed about the concerns of these executives (Fama, 1980; Vancil, 1987). Finally, the presence of non-CEO inside directors limits a CEO's influence over a board and increases the chance for senior executives to successfully challenge the CEO. Inside directors have valuable firm-specific information about a firm's activities and market position (Fama, 1980). Through non-CEO inside directors, outside directors can reduce their reliance on the CEO and are more able to gain accurate information about the CEO and the firm's operations (Baysinger & Hoskisson, 1990). Thus, a CEO is likely under close monitoring when there are other senior executives on a board.

To protect their own interests, incumbent CEOs may try to use their positions to influence inside directors (Weisbach, 1988). However, interest conflicts between CEOs and ambitious inside directors can be inevitable. Although inside directors may have supported a CEO in the past, they may not continue to do so when their own career advancement is at stake. Prior research has indicated that under conditions of clear information about preferences and payoffs, coalition formation is often issue-oriented and temporary (Stevenson, Pearce, & Porter, 1985). Boeker (1992) found that even inside directors appointed by a CEO did not reduce the CEO's risk of dismissal. All else being equal, we expected to see a higher rate of CEO dismissal followed by inside succession among firms with higher proportions of non-CEO inside directors.

Hypothesis 3. The proportion of non-CEO inside directors increases the likelihood of CEO dismissal followed by inside succession.

Non-CEO Executive Ownership

As an important source of power (Finkelstein, 1992), stock ownership will affect both the incentives senior executives have to challenge their CEO and their credibility in doing so. Stock ownership by senior executives does not typically provide enough voting power to remove a CEO, but it increases the credibility of these executives' concerns about the CEO's leadership and helps them gain support from outside directors. Further, senior executives' stock ownership increases their influence in the selection of an inside successor following the dismissal (Boeker & Goodstein, 1993). In addition, stock ownership gives senior executives extra financial incentives to monitor the CEO and thus weakens the CEO's influence over them. Corporate governance scholars have emphasized using stock ownership to bond managerial actions to shareholder interests (Walsh & Seward, 1990). Stock ownership by executives has been reported to reduce agency problems in corporate restructuring (Johnson, Hoskisson, & Hitt, 1993). All else being equal, we expected a higher rate of CEO dismissal followed by inside succession among firms with higher levels of non-CEO executive ownership.

Hypothesis 4. Non-CEO executive ownership increases the likelihood of CEO dismissal followed by inside succession.

METHODS

The population for this study is large, publicly traded U.S. corporations. We initially selected a random sample of 512 publicly traded firms reporting at least $200 million in sales for 1988. After we deleted firms with missing data, a total of 387 firms remained, comprising the final sample used in the analysis. A *t*-test indicated no significant difference in annual sales between the final sample and the initial sample. Data were collected annually from multiple sources for the years 1988 through 1997. A primary data source for CEO turnover, successor selection, and board structure is the officer and director list provided in each firm's annual report to shareholders. Additional descriptive data on CEOs and their successors were collected from Dun & Bradstreet's *Reference Book of Corporate Management* and Dow Jones Interactive's Wall Street Journal and News Wires databases. Data on executive and director ownership were collected from proxy statements. Data on firm size and performance were gathered from COMPUSTAT and CRSP.

Measures

CEO dismissal followed by inside succession. Identifying CEO dismissals is a major challenge in succession and governance research because firms seldom fully disclose the true reasons behind CEO resignations (Denis & Denis, 1995; Fredrickson, Hambrick, & Baumrin, 1988; Weisbach, 1988). Given their importance in our study, we took two approaches to identify CEO dismissals. Our first approach relied on news reports (Parrino, 1997). We searched Dow Jones databases to collect all reports about each selected firm's CEO during a three-year period, from one year before to one year after the year of in which the CEO was succeeded. There are 340 successions in our sample, and we found news reports for 334 of these events. Of these 334, we first excluded successions that were consequences of a CEO's death or of clear health issues (14 cases), of a CEO's acceptance of a similar position at another firm (16 cases), or of a merger or acquisition (3 cases). We also excluded from our analysis four CEOs who were reported as serving on an interim basis.

Next, we analyzed the news reports and used the following three criteria to identify CEO dismissals. First, a CEO was directly reported as having been fired or forced out (11 cases). Second, a CEO was reported as having resigned unexpectedly or immediately, owing to poor performance, undisclosed personal reasons, or a desire "to pursue other interests" (35 cases). Lastly, we included each case in which a CEO was reported as taking early retirement and there was discussion of performance problems (18 cases) as a dismissal. Although a CEO may step down voluntarily when performance declines, our analysis of news reports suggests that this is rare. Further, a CEO may not have any option other than stepping down when performance pressure is very high. Thus, we classified a CEO turnover as a dismissal if it met any one of the above three criteria. We identified 64 dismissals in our sample on the basis of the news report analysis.

In our second approach, we used both CEO age and continuity as a board member at the time of turnover to identify CEO dismissals. Because many firms have retirement policies, some previous research has relied on CEO age to separate dismissals from retirements (Ocasio, 1994; Puffer & Weintrop, 1991). The age of 64 is often used as a cutoff point in making the decision: CEOs who leave office before the age of 64 are treated as dismissed, and those who depart later are treated as retired. An examination of our sample suggested that relying on CEO age alone to classify a departure as a dismissal or a retirement was too crude for our study. Many CEOs in our sample relinquished the CEO title at the age of 62 or 63 but kept directorship or the title of chairman of the board until the age of 64 or 65. These CEOs can hardly be treated as dismissed because it is unreasonable to keep a dismissed CEO on a board (Lorsch & MacIver, 1989). Given this, we used continuity as a board member as a second criterion, in addition to CEO age, to identify dismissal. A CEO's departure from a corporation was classified as a dismissal when the incumbent terminated his or her service as both CEO and board member before the age of 64 for reasons other than death or health, taking a similar position at another firm, or a merger or acquisition. We identified 75 dismissals using this approach.

We compared the CEO dismissals identified under the above two approaches and found that the 75 dismissals identified with the second approach (age and continuity observations) included all 64 dismissals identified with the first approach (news reports analysis). In other words, all 64 CEOs classified as dismissed on the basis of news reports left office before the age of 64 and simultaneously terminated their directorships. This finding gave us great confidence in the 64 dismissals identified via news reports. We then reexamined the news reports on the 11 nonoverlapping cases. Eight of these were reported as normal retirements in accordance with company policy; 2 were reported as early retirements occurring after corporate restructuring; and 1 was reported as an early retirement resulting from a need for restructuring. We elected to add only the last case to the dismissals. Thus, we identified a total of 65 CEO dismissals. We then created a dummy variable—*dismissal, insider*—to measure CEO dismissal followed by inside succession. It was coded 1 when a current executive of a firm became CEO after the predecessor's dismissal and 0 otherwise. There are 38 such events in our sample. Of these, 36 involved successors who joined their firms before their dismissed predecessors had been appointed as CEO, and only 2 involved successors who had joined their firms during their dismissed predecessors' tenures as CEO.

Predictor variables. CEO origin as an outsider was also measured as a dummy variable. In line with the discussion presented above, *outsider CEO* was coded 1 if a successor CEO was not an employee of the firm in which he or she took office at the time of succession, and 0 otherwise. The early years of CEO tenure were also measured as a dummy variable. In a qualitative study, Gabarro (1987) suggested that the process of CEOs' establishing authority in office generally takes from 30 to 48 months. Drawing on his study and our preliminary analysis, we selected five years of tenure as the cutoff in our coding. *Early years of tenure* was coded 1 for the first five years of a CEO's tenure and 0 otherwise. *Proportion of non-CEO inside directors* was calculated as the number of directors who were current executives of a firm, excluding the CEO, divided by the total number of directors (Daily, Johnson, & Dalton, 1999). *Non-CEO executive ownership* was calculated as the proportion of a firm's outstanding shares held by all executives other than the CEO who were listed in the company's proxy statement.

Control variables. Firm performance importantly influences the power dynamics at the top of a firm in that poor performance weakens a CEO's credibility and increases the likelihood of a power contest waged against the CEO (Boeker & Goodstein, 1993; Ocasio, 1994). However, because outside directors rely more heavily on financial performance to assess a CEO than do senior executives (Baysinger & Hoskisson, 1990), challenges to the CEO under conditions of poor performance may be initiated by outside directors rather than by senior executives. Given this concern, we did not develop hypotheses directly linking firm performance to power dynamics within top management and their impact on CEO dismissal followed by inside succession. Instead, because firm performance is widely believed to reflect a CEO's leadership ability (Puffer & Weintrop, 1991; Weisbach, 1988), we included it as a control variable representing CEO competence. We first chose an accounting measure of performance, *return on assets* (ROA), and calculated it as income before extraordinary items and discontinued operations divided by net assets. To control for industry effects (Dess, Ireland, & Hitt, 1990), following Edwards's (1995) recommendations, we included *industry ROA* in our analysis and measured it as the average ROA in the firms in a focal company's primary two-digit SIC category. We also selected a market-based measure of performance, *shareholder returns,* and measured it by compounding the daily returns to shareholders reported in the relevant CRSP tapes over each fiscal year. To further distinguish the impact of power from that of a CEO's human capital, we controlled for CEO's industry experience. *Industry experience* was coded 1 when a CEO had more than five years industry experience at the time of his or her appointment and 0 otherwise.

The corporate governance literature highlights

the view that boards of directors, and particularly their outside members, play an important role in CEO succession decisions (Walsh & Seward, 1990). Two variables, the proportion of outside directors and outside director stock ownership, have been extensively studied in previous research (Boeker & Goodstein, 1993; Johnson et al., 1993; Lorsch & MacIver, 1989; Ocasio, 1994; Weisbach, 1988). Because we included the proportion of non-CEO inside directors as a predictor, we chose to include only *outside director stock ownership* as a control. This measure was calculated as the proportion of a firm's outstanding shares owned by directors who were not current or past employees of the firm.

To control for the impact of CEO power, we collected information about CEO duality (Finkelstein & D'Aveni, 1994) and CEO stock ownership (Boeker, 1992). *Duality* was measured as a dummy variable with a value of 1 when a CEO also held the title of chairman of the board and a value of 0 otherwise. *CEO stock ownership* was calculated as the proportion of the firm's outstanding shares owned by the CEO. Finally, firm size may influence the power dynamics within top management because the CEO succession process at a large corporation may have become formalized or institutionalized (Ocasio, 1999; Vancil, 1987). We measured *firm size* as the natural logarithm of total sales and included it as our last control variable.

Analytical Methodology

In response to frequent calls for longitudinal studies in succession research (e.g., Datta & Rajagopalan, 1998; Finkelstein & Hambrick, 1996), we selected a continuous-time event history analysis to test our hypotheses. Event history analysis is an established methodology for analyzing dynamic process when the outcome of that process is a discrete event (Tuma & Hannan, 1984). It was appropriate for our study of the effects of the power dynamics within top management on CEO dismissal followed by inside succession because it takes into account the effect of time (that is, CEO tenure) in estimation. We conducted our analysis using the software package Stata, which provides maximum likelihood estimation of both monotonic and nonmonotonic parametric models of duration dependence (Stata, 1999). Further, Stata allows estimation of survival-time models with time-varying covariates and takes "right censoring" of data (loss of data on events occurring after the end of a study period) into account by using the information provided by the cumulative survival time of censored subjects. Although succession is a repeatable event from the perspective of a firm, it is nonrepeatable from the perspective of the CEO who is being succeeded (Boeker, 1992; Ocasio, 1994). CEO tenure thus was the duration measure in our event history analysis. To permit annual updating of the time-varying covariates, we divided CEO tenure into fiscal years (Ocasio, 1994, 1999). In our sample, CEOs appointed before 1988 were subjected to left truncation. To reduce the risk of an upward bias in the estimates, we collected tenure information for all the left-truncated CEOs and included all CEO-years, beginning in 1988, in our analysis (Tuma & Hannan, 1984). This procedure also reduced loss of information and increased the statistical power of the analysis.

A critical decision in event history analysis is to choosing an appropriate parametric model for the data (Yamaguchi, 1991). We started with the generalized gamma model. The survival and density functions for the three-parameter generalized gamma model are

$$S(t) = 1 - I\{k, k \exp[z/(k^{1/2})]\},$$

$$f(t) = [|k|/\Gamma(k^{-2})]\,[k^{-2}]^{1/k*k} \exp[k^{-2}(kz - e^{kz})], \quad \text{if } k \neq 0; \quad \text{or}$$

$$f(t) = 1/[(2\pi)^{1/2}] \exp[-z^2/2z] \text{ if } k = 0.$$

where $I(k, a)$ is the incomplete gamma function and $z = [\ln(t) - \lambda]/\sigma$. This model is implemented by parameterizing $\lambda_j = X_j\beta$ and treating the k and σ as ancillary parameters to be estimated from the data (Stata, 1999: 440). The hazard function of the generalized gamma distribution is extremely flexible, allowing for a large number of possible shapes including as special cases the Weibull distribution when $k = 1$, the exponential distribution when $k = 1$ and $\sigma = 1$, and the "log-normal" distribution when $k = 0$. We then estimated other functional forms, including Gompertz, Weibull, log-normal, exponential, and "log-logistic" models. Our analysis suggested that the generalized gamma model provided the best fit and had the largest log-likelihood with the smallest value on the Akaike information criterion (AIC; Akaike, 1974).

Previous research has consistently demonstrated that CEO dismissal is frequently the outcome of a power struggle between a CEO and outside directors (Boeker, 1992; Boeker & Goodstein, 1993; Cannella & Lubatkin, 1993). To test our theory and convincingly demonstrate that power dynamics within top management groups simultaneously influence CEO dismissal and subsequent inside succession, we conducted analyses not only on CEO dismissal followed by inside succession, but also on CEO dismissal followed by outside succession and CEO dismissal in general. The purpose was to examine the similarities as well as the differences between the factors influencing CEO dismissal followed by inside succession and those influencing CEO dismissal followed by outside succession. By comparing the results, we hoped to be able to better understand how the power dynamics within top management groups contribute to CEO dismissal, and the limits to that influence.

RESULTS

Table 1 reports variable means, standard deviations, and Pearson correlation coefficients for all observations (all CEO-years). Table 2 reports results from the event history analysis. Models 1 and 2 show results for CEO dismissal followed by inside succession; models 3 and 4, for CEO dismissal followed by outside succession; and models 5 and 6, for all CEO dismissals combined. Chi-squares for models 1 through 6 indicate strong model significance ($p < .001$).

We proposed that CEO origin as an outsider, early CEO tenure, the proportion of non-CEO inside directors, and non-CEO executive ownership would all increase the likelihood of CEO dismissal followed by inside succession. In model 1, in which ROA is the measure of performance, each of these four predictors displays a significant, positive impact. In model 2, where shareholder return is the measure of performance, three of the four predictors (except outsider CEO) display significant, positive impacts. These results support our hypotheses and suggest that CEO origin as an outsider, early CEO tenure, non-CEO inside directors, and non-CEO executive ownership all play important roles in heightening the likelihood of CEO dismissal followed by inside succession. In contrast, in models 3 and 4, where CEO dismissal followed by outside successor is examined, only early CEO tenure displays a positive impact. Outsider CEO, the proportion of non-CEO inside directors, and non-CEO executive ownership all are insignificant.

Among the control variables, while firm ROA and shareholder returns are negatively associated with both types of dismissal, outside director ownership, CEO ownership, and firm size are only negatively associated with dismissal followed by inside succession. CEO duality shows a positive association with dismissal followed by inside succession in model 2, but it is negatively associated with dismissal followed by outside succession in models 3 and 4. Finally, in models 5 and 6, in which both types of CEO dismissal are examined together, only four variables are significant. Outsider CEO and early CEO tenure both display positive impacts, and firm performance and CEO ownership both display negative impacts. Neither the proportion of non-CEO inside directors nor non-CEO executive ownership is significant.

DISCUSSION

This study helps advance understanding of the role of senior executives in CEO dismissal. Previous governance and succession research has examined either CEO turnover (Boeker, 1992; Ocasio, 1994; Weisbach, 1988) or successor selection (Boeker & Goodstein, 1993; Dalton & Kesner, 1985; Ocasio, 1999; Zajac & Westphal, 1996). Although there has been little direct examination of how CEO dismissal influences successor selection, firm performance has been consistently found to be negatively associated with CEO dismissal and positively associated with inside succession (Finkelstein & Hambrick, 1996; Kesner & Sebora, 1994). Given this finding, we expected to see a negative relationship between CEO dismissal and inside succession. Contrary to this logical inference, we found that 38 out of the 65 dismissed CEOs (58%) in our study were succeeded by insiders. Further, a comparison of the results reported above shows that the antecedents of CEO dismissal followed by inside succession and those of CEO dismissal followed by outside succession differ in important ways. Thus, to understand the role of senior executives in CEO dismissal, we believe that it is important to examine dismissal and successor origin simultaneously because they often reflect the outcome of the same power dynamic process (Pfeffer, 1981; Sonnenfeld, 1988).

The view that interest conflicts and power contests within top management groups are an important cause of CEO dismissal has not been a focus in empirical studies of CEO succession. Instead, most extant research concludes that executives are allies of their CEOs and that having several executives on a board leads to managerial entrenchment (Walsh & Seward, 1990; Weisbach, 1988). By examining CEO dismissal followed by inside succession and outside succession separately, this study garnered informative and revealing results. The two predictors capturing information about senior executives—the proportion of non-CEO inside directors and non-CEO executive ownership—both showed positive impacts on CEO dismissal followed by inside succession, but neither influenced the occurrence of CEO dismissal followed by outside succession. Given that we controlled for the impact of firm performance in our analysis, this finding suggests that having executives of a firm other than the CEO on its board and giving executives stock ownership

TABLE 1
Variable Means, Standard Deviations, and Correlation Coefficients

Variable	Mean	s.d.	1	2	3	4	5	6	7	8	9	10	11	12	13	14	15
1. Dismissal	0.02	0.15															
2. Dismissal, insider	0.01	0.11	.76														
3. Dismissal, outsider	0.01	0.10	.64	−.01													
4. CEO tenure	6.89	5.43	−.04	−.04	−.01												
5. Outsider CEO	0.08	0.27	.03	.03	.01	−.22											
6. Early years of tenure	0.52	0.50	.03	.03	.02	−.78	.23										
7. Proportion of non-CEO inside directors	0.14	0.12	−.02	.00	−.03	.00	−.07	.01									
8. Non-CEO executive ownership	0.04	0.08	−.01	.01	−.02	−.05	−.04	.04	.22								
9. Firm ROA	0.05	0.06	−.05	−.02	−.05	.08	−.09	−.06	.05	.03							
10. Industry ROA	0.03	0.02	.02	.02	.01	−.03	.02	.03	−.03	.02	.14						
11. Shareholder returns	0.13	0.24	−.12	−.07	−.10	.04	−.01	−.03	.00	−.02	.19	−.02					
12. Industry experience	0.99	0.11	−.003	.01	−.02	.07	−.39	−.08	.06	.02	−.02	−.02	.02				
13. Outside director ownership	0.03	0.07	.03	.02	.03	−.01	.03	−.01	.04	.02	.10	.02	.01	.02			
14. CEO ownership	0.03	0.07	−.03	−.04	−.01	.23	−.08	−.15	.15	.22	.02	.01	−.03	.03	.03		
15. Duality	0.84	0.37	−.05	−.02	−.05	.15	.02	−.11	−.10	−.12	.05	−.04	.06	−.04	−.12	.01	
16. Firm size	7.25	1.45	−.02	−.01	−.02	−.08	−.07	.08	.02	−.15	.02	−.01	.08	.05	−.21	−.26	.19

[a] Pooled data, with $n = 2{,}965$, are shown. Correlation coefficients greater than .04 or less than −.04 are significant at $p < .05$.

TABLE 2
Maximum Likelihood Estimates of Hazard Rate of CEO Dismissal[a]

	Dismissal Followed by Inside Succession		Dismissal Followed by Outside Succession		All Dismissals Combined	
Variables	Model 1	Model 2	Model 3	Model 4	Model 5	Model 6
Outsider CEO	0.42* (0.21)	0.04 (0.20)	0.15 (0.29)	0.21 (0.28)	0.68** (0.26)	0.63** (0.23)
Early years of tenure	1.07*** (0.23)	0.82*** (0.21)	1.03*** (0.17)	1.03*** (0.16)	0.97*** (0.18)	0.99*** (0.15)
Proportion of non-CEO inside directors	5.75*** (1.66)	4.46*** (1.35)	−0.64 (0.78)	−1.03 (0.77)	1.54 (0.99)	0.64 (0.66)
Non-CEO executive ownership	0.98† (0.63)	1.98** (0.74)	−2.70 (2.34)	−2.60 (2.26)	0.17 (0.94)	0.55 (0.88)
Firm ROA	−1.78† (0.96)		−4.22** (1.57)		−2.21* (1.03)	
Shareholder returns		−1.56*** (0.45)		−1.62*** (0.43)		−1.78*** (0.36)
Industry ROA	−0.15 (2.82)		0.83 (5.18)		5.68 (4.89)	
Industry experience	1.98 (8.32)	1.80 (4.87)	−0.47 (0.66)	0.21 (0.75)	0.74 (0.70)	0.82 (0.76)
Outside director ownership	−4.33*** (1.11)	−4.93*** (0.95)	0.45 (1.06)	0.38 (0.90)	−1.02 (1.03)	0.16 (0.77)
CEO duality	0.11 (0.21)	0.41** (0.14)	−0.44* (0.20)	−0.35* (0.18)	−0.16 (0.22)	−0.20 (0.18)
CEO ownership	−25.28** (9.22)	−34.68** (13.40)	−1.55 (1.63)	−1.32 (1.51)	−6.34** (2.26)	−5.79** (2.10)
Firm size	−0.20*** (0.03)	−0.21*** (0.04)	0.01 (0.06)	−0.01 (0.06)	−0.08 (0.05)	−0.02 (0.05)
Constant	−0.86* (0.42)	−3.68*** (0.74)	−3.06*** (0.59)	−3.18*** (0.49)	−2.71*** (0.69)	−3.32*** (0.45)
Log-likelihood	−131.45	−128.29	−98.39	−91.82	−211.96	−200.99
Model chi-square	60.85***	65.97***	36.00***	48.39***	54.16***	78.72***

[a] Standard errors are in parentheses; *t*-tests were one-tailed for hypothesized effects and two-tailed for control variables.
† $p < .10$
* $p < .05$
** $p < .01$
*** $p < .001$

can limit the CEO's influence and increase executives' incentives and ability to challenge the CEO.

A competing explanation for our results is that the positive impact of non-CEO inside directors on dismissal followed by inside succession does not reflect the power dynamics occurring between a CEO and senior executives. Instead, outside directors may have taken the lead in dismissing the CEO and subsequently picked an inside successor because there were sufficient inside candidates available. This alternative explanation has some appeal. However, if this scenario prevailed, we would observe a significant, negative association between the proportion of non-CEO inside directors and dismissal followed by outside succession, rather than the insignificant relationship found in this study. Similarly, without reference to power challenges to a CEO by senior executives, it is difficult to explain the positive impact of non-CEO executive ownership on dismissal followed by inside succession and its insignificant impact on dismissal followed by outside succession. We thus believe that the above results support our proposition that senior executives are potential power contenders and play an important role in CEO dismissal followed by inside succession. As to the insignificant impact of senior executives on dismissal followed by outside succession, our explanation is twofold. First, because their careers and personal wealth are at stake, senior executives may not resist outside succession if it is the best choice for their firm. Second, and more likely, senior executives may simply not have much influence when outside directors take the lead in CEO dismissal and successor selection.

Our results about the impact of outsider CEO and early CEO tenure are also informative. The positive impact of outsider CEO on dismissal followed by inside succession disappears when shareholder returns replace ROA as the performance measure. This result and the significant, negative impact of shareholder returns in model 4 together suggest that the higher risk of CEO dismissal followed by inside succession faced by outsider CEOs is primarily a consequence of their firms' low performance in the financial market. However, when all CEO dismissals are examined together, we still find a higher risk of dismissal among outsider CEOs even after controlling for firm accounting and market performance and CEO industry experience. We speculate that this higher risk of dismissal for outsider CEOs is a result of their lacking social networks and power bases within their new firms. Early CEO tenure shows a consistently strong and positive impact on both dismissal followed by inside succession and dismissal followed by outside succession. This finding corroborates the proposition that CEOs are in weak positions and are at high risk of power contests in the early years of their tenures (Ocasio, 1994).

The two control variables for aspects of CEO power provide additional clues about the power dynamics at the tops of firms. CEO ownership shows a negative impact on dismissal followed by inside succession, but it shows no impact on dismissal followed by outside succession. This result suggests that stock ownership increases a CEO's influence within top management. CEO duality shows a negative impact on dismissal followed by outside succession and some positive impact on dismissal followed by inside succession. This pattern suggests that although being chairman of the board increases a CEO's influence over outside directors, it may also increase the CEO's vulnerability to challenges from within the top management group, because duality makes it difficult for the CEO to blame others for low performance (Harrison, Torres, & Kukalis, 1988). Thus, we surmise that stock ownership and duality play different roles in a CEO's dealing with senior executives and outside directors. Finally, the negative impact of firm size suggests that power contests within top management are more frequent in smaller firms.

Limitations and Directions for Future Research

This study advances understanding of the role of senior executives in CEO dismissal, but it has limitations. First, like most researchers taking a power perspective, we did not directly observe the power dynamics leading to CEO dismissal discussed in our theory. Instead, we examined the antecedents and outcomes of that process. Although the results support our power-based arguments, it would be desirable to have field research to corroborate the findings of this study. Second, our identification of CEO dismissals was not based on firsthand information and may include some errors despite our efforts to avoid them. Third, given the focus of our study and constraints on the availability of financial information, we divided CEO tenure into fiscal years. Fiscal year may be a relatively coarse measure, despite its frequent use as a metric in organizational research. A finer measure of CEO tenure may be needed to facilitate closer examination of the power dynamics within top management during the early years of a CEO's tenure. Such a finer measure would be especially useful to test for the existence of the "honeymoon" between a new CEO and a board that is often discussed in the business press.

The internal monitoring argument of corporate

governance suggests that inside directors challenge a CEO when firm performance declines and the CEO's capability is questioned (Fama, 1980; Ocasio, 1994). In contrast, our results show that CEO dismissal followed by inside succession does not always derive from a CEO's lack of capability in that our power-related predictors displayed significant main effects after we controlled for firm performance and CEO industry experience in analyses. This finding suggests that outside directors need to closely monitor the power dynamics within top management and make sure that the competition is under control and contributes to firm operations. For management researchers, it will be important to examine the interaction between CEO capability and senior executive power in future research to fully identify the causal mechanisms underlying CEO dismissals. In addition, by demonstrating the effects of power dynamics within top management on CEO dismissal, our study suggests that there are important differences among inside CEOs. To better understand the performance consequences of inside succession, it is necessary to separate inside CEOs appointed following their predecessors' dismissal from those appointed following their predecessors' ordinary retirement (Shen & Cannella, 2002). This implication may be equally applicable to the study of the performance impact of outside CEO succession.

REFERENCES

Akaike, H. 1974. A new look at the statistical model identification. ***IEEE Transaction and Automatic Control,*** AC-19: 716–723.

Alderfer, C. P. 1986. The invisible director on corporate boards. ***Harvard Business Review,*** 64(6): 38–52.

Barnard, C. I. 1938. ***The functions of the executive.*** Cambridge, MA: Harvard University Press.

Baysinger, B. D., & Hoskisson, R. E. 1990. The composition of board of directors and strategic control: Effects on corporate strategy. ***Academy of Management Review,*** 15: 72–87.

Boeker, W. 1992. Power and managerial turnover: Scapegoating at the top. ***Administrative Science Quarterly,*** 37: 400–421.

Boeker, W., & Goodstein, J. 1993. Performance and successor choice: The moderating effects of governance and ownership. ***Academy of Management Journal,*** 36: 172–186.

Cannella, A. A., Jr., & Lubatkin, M. H. 1993. Succession as a sociopolitical process. ***Academy of Management Journal,*** 36: 763–793.

Cannella, A. A., Jr., & Shen, W. 2001. So close and yet so far: Promotion versus exit for CEO heirs apparent. ***Academy of Management Journal,*** 44: 252–270.

Daily, C. M., Johnson, J. L., & Dalton, D. R. 1999. On the measurements of board composition: Poor consistency and a serious mismatch of theory and operationalization. ***Decision Science,*** 30: 83–106.

Dalton, D. R., & Kesner, I. F. 1985. Organizational performance as an antecedent of inside/outside chief executive succession: An empirical assessment. ***Academy of Management Journal,*** 28: 749–762.

Datta, D. K., & Rajagopalan, N. 1998. Industry structure and CEO characteristics: An empirical study of succession events. ***Strategic Management Journal,*** 19: 833–852.

Denis, D. J., & Denis, D. K. 1995. Performance changes following top management dismissals. ***Journal of Finance,*** 50: 1029–1057.

Dess, G. G., Ireland, R. D., & Hitt, M. A. 1990. Industry effects and strategic management research. ***Journal of Management,*** 16: 7–27.

Edwards, J. R. 1995. Alternatives to difference scores as dependent variables in the study of congruence in organizational research. ***Organizational Behavior and Human Decision Processes,*** 64: 307–324.

Fama, E. F. 1980. Agency problems and the theory of the firm. ***Journal of Political Economy,*** 88: 288–307.

Finkelstein, S. 1992. Power in top management teams: Dimensions, measurement, and validation. ***Academy of Management Journal,*** 35: 505–538.

Finkelstein, S., & D'Aveni, R. A. 1994. CEO duality as a double-edged sword: How boards of directors balance entrenchment avoidance and unity of command. ***Academy of Management Journal,*** 37: 1079–1108.

Finkelstein, S., & Hambrick, D. C. 1996. ***Strategic leadership.*** New York: West.

Fredrickson, J. W., Hambrick, D. C., & Baumrin, S. 1988. A model of CEO turnover. ***Academy of Management Review,*** 13: 255–270.

Friedman, S., & Singh, H. 1989. CEO succession and stockholder reaction: The influence of organizational context and event content. ***Academy of Management Journal,*** 32: 718–744.

Gabarro, J. J. 1987. ***The dynamics of taking charge.*** Boston: Harvard Business School Press.

Gouldner, A. W. 1954. ***Patterns of industrial bureaucracy.*** Glencoe, IL: Free Press.

Hambrick, D. C., & Fukutomi, G. D. S. 1991. The seasons of a CEO's tenure. ***Academy of Management Review,*** 16: 719–742.

Harrison, J. R., Torres, D. L., & Kukalis, S. 1988. The changing of the guard: Turnover and structural change in the top management positions. ***Administrative Science Quarterly,*** 33: 211–232.

Helmich, D. L., & Brown, W. B. 1972. Successor type and

organizational change in corporate enterprise. ***Administrative Science Quarterly,*** 17: 371–381.

Jennings, E. E. 1971. ***Routes to the executive suite.*** New York: McGraw-Hill.

Johnson, R. A., Hoskisson, R. E., & Hitt, M. A. 1993. Board of director involvement in restructuring: The effects of board versus managerial controls and characteristics. ***Strategic Management Journal,*** 14: 33–50.

Kesner, I. F., & Sebora, T. C. 1994. Executive succession: Past, present & future. ***Journal of Management,*** 20: 327–372.

Kotter, J. P. 1982. ***The general managers.*** New York: Free Press.

Lazear, E. P. 1989. Pay equality and industrial politics. ***Journal of Political Economy,*** 97: 561–580.

Lazear, E. P., & Rosen, S. 1981. Rank-order tournaments as optimum labor contracts. ***Journal of Political Economy,*** 89: 841–864.

Lorsch, J. W., & MacIver, E. 1989. ***Pawns or potentates: The reality of America's corporate boards.*** Boston: Harvard Business School Press.

McClelland, D. C., & Burnham, D. H. 1976. Power is the great motivator. ***Harvard Business Review,*** 54(2): 100–110.

Ocasio, W. 1994. Political dynamics and the circulation of power: CEO succession in U.S. industrial corporations, 1960–1990. ***Administrative Science Quarterly,*** 39: 285–312.

Ocasio, W. 1999. Institutionalized action and corporate governance: The reliance on rules of CEO succession. ***Administrative Science Quarterly,*** 44: 384–416.

Pareto, V. 1968. ***The rise and fall of the elites.*** Totowa, NJ: Bedminster Press.

Parrino, R. 1997. CEO turnover and outside succession: A cross sectional analysis. ***Journal of Financial Economics,*** 46(2): 165–197.

Pfeffer, J. 1981. ***Power in organizations.*** Marshfield, MA: Pitman.

Puffer, S. M., & Weintrop, J. B. 1991. Corporate performance and CEO turnover: The role of performance expectations. ***Administrative Science Quarterly,*** 36: 1–19.

Scott, W. R. 1995. ***Organizations.*** Englewood Cliffs, NJ: Prentice-Hall.

Selznick, P. 1957. ***Leadership in administration.*** New York: Harper & Row.

Shen, W., & Cannella, A. A., Jr. Revisiting the performance consequences of CEO succession: The impacts of successor type, postsuccession senior executive turnover, and departing CEO tenure. ***Academy of Management Journal,*** 45: 717–734.

Sonnenfeld, J. A. 1988 ***The hero's farewell.*** New York: Oxford University Press.

Stata. 1999. ***Stata reference manual,*** release 6, vol. 3. College Station, TX: Stata.

Stevenson, W. B., Pearce, J. L. & Porter, L. W. 1985. The concept of "coalition" in organization theory and research. ***Academy of Management Review,*** 10: 256–268.

Tuma, N. B., & Hannan, M. T. 1984. ***Social dynamics.*** Orlando, FL: Academic Press.

Vancil, R. M. 1987. ***Passing the baton.*** Boston: Harvard University Press.

Walsh, J. P., & Seward, J. K. 1990. On the efficiency of internal and external corporate control mechanisms. ***Academy of Management Review,*** 15: 421–458.

Weber, M. 1946. ***From Max Weber: Essays in sociology.*** New York: Oxford University Press.

Weisbach, M. S. 1988. Outside directors and CEO turnover. ***Journal of Financial Economics,*** 19: 431–460.

Yamaguchi, K. 1991. ***Event history analysis.*** Newbury Park, CA: Sage.

Zajac, E. J. 1990. CEO selection, succession, compensation and firm performance: A theoretical integration and empirical analysis. ***Strategic Management Journal,*** 11: 217–230.

Zajac, E. J., & Westphal, J. D. 1996. Who shall succeed? How CEO/board preferences and power affect the choice of new CEOs. ***Academy of Management Journal,*** 39: 64–90.

Wei Shen *(wei.shen@cba.ufl.edu)* is an assistant professor of strategic management at the University of Florida. He received his Ph.D. in strategic management from Texas A&M University. His research focuses on corporate executive leadership development, succession, and the organizational implications of these phenomena.

Albert A. Cannella, Jr., is a professor and Mays Faculty Fellow at Texas A&M University. He received his Ph.D. in strategic management from Columbia University. His research focuses on executives, executive careers, leadership, succession, and the links between executive actions and organizational outcomes.

[5]

Who Shall Govern? CEO/Board Power, Demographic Similarity, and New Director Selection

James D. Westphal
Edward J. Zajac
Northwestern University

This study examines CEO influence in the board of director selection process and the theoretical mechanism by which CEO influence is presumed to affect subsequent board decision making on CEO compensation. We address both of these issues by linking political and social psychological perspectives on organizational governance. We propose that powerful CEOs seek to appoint new board members who are demographically similar, and therefore more sympathetic, to them. Using a longitudinal research design and data on 413 Fortune/Forbes 500 companies from 1986 to 1991, we examine whether increased demographic similarity affects board decision making with respect to CEO compensation contracts. The results show that (1) when incumbent CEOs are more powerful than their boards of directors, new directors are likely to be demographically similar to the firm's CEO; (2) when boards are more powerful than their CEOs, new directors resemble the existing board; and (3) greater demographic similarity between the CEO and the board is likely to result in more generous CEO compensation contracts. We discuss the implications of the strong effect of demographic similarity for corporate control issues.•

INTRODUCTION

The relative control of corporate boards of directors over management has long been a subject of theoretical analysis and debate in the organization theory, economics, and management literatures (e.g., Herman, 1981; Fama and Jensen, 1983; Mizruchi, 1983; Vance, 1983). A central question is whether boards are an effective management control mechanism (Fama and Jensen, 1983), or whether they are a "management tool" (Pfeffer, 1972: 219), a rubber stamp for management initiatives (Herman, 1981), and often surrender to management their major domain of decision-making authority, which includes the right to hire, fire, and compensate top management (Vance, 1983; Zajac, 1990).

While a variety of factors may facilitate management control over the board, the chief executive officer's (CEO's) dominance over the director selection process has often been considered a primary source of management control (Mace, 1971; Pfeffer, 1972; Kosnik, 1987). Bacon and Brown (1975: 28) concluded that "by and large, the chief executive controls who will come on the board while he is in power." More recently, in one of the few large-sample surveys of Fortune 500 directors, Lorsch and MacIver (1989: 21) reported that boards often have only limited influence over the new director nomination process. Finally, Wade, O'Reilly, and Chandratat (1990: 593) have suggested that CEOs enhance their influence over the board by appointing outside directors "sympathetic to [their] desires." While this view seems plausible, it raises several issues that require additional research attention. First, there is very little large-sample, empirical evidence regarding CEOs' role in the selection of new directors. Second, the theoretical basis for assuming that recently appointed outside directors are more

0001-8392/95/4001-0060/$1.00.

•
Both authors contributed equally to the paper. The helpful comments of Joe Baumann, Jerry Davis, Joe Moag, Mark Shanley, Brian Uzzi, Christine Oliver, and three anonymous *ASQ* reviewers are appreciated. We also thank Linda Pike for her excellent editorial work. An earlier version of the paper received the 1994 Best Paper Award in the Organization and Management Theory Division of the Academy of Management.

likely to be sympathetic to the desires of CEOs is not yet fully understood. The present study seeks to address both of these issues by showing how CEO control over the selection of new directors can increase subsequent compliance among board members. Specifically, we propose that a combination of social psychological and sociopolitical factors lead CEOs and existing board members to favor new directors who are demographically similar to them and that the relative influence of CEOs and existing boards will predict who is more likely to realize their respective preferences.

The study then addresses an important and tangible potential consequence of increased demographic similarity between the CEO and the board for board decision making: whether increased similarity results in a more generous level and mix of compensation in CEOs' contracts. The study links sociopolitical and social psychological perspectives on organizational governance and tests hypotheses on the antecedents and consequences of increased demographic similarity using longitudinal data on new director characteristics and change in CEO compensation among 413 Fortune/Forbes 500 companies from 1986 to 1991.

Demographic Similarity between the CEO and New Directors

Social psychological studies on performance evaluation and hiring practices consistently find bias in evaluation decisions in which the parties are demographically similar. In experimental and field research on hiring decisions, studies have demonstrated a positive relationship between applicant-rater similarity and the perceived quality of the applicant (Baskett, 1973; Wexley and Nemeroff, 1974). Additional evidence suggests that similarity frequently enhances interpersonal attraction (Byrne, Clore, and Worchel, 1966; Byrne, 1971). Early interpretations of these findings invoked a reinforcement model, arguing that similarity provides mutual reinforcement or "consensual validation" of each individual's beliefs (Byrne, Clore, and Worchel, 1966: 223), thus enhancing interpersonal attraction and producing bias in evaluation decisions.

More recently, theorists have used self-categorization theory (Tajfel and Turner, 1986; Turner, 1987) to explain the social psychological effects of demographic similarity (Jackson, Stone, and Alvarez, 1992; Tsui, Egan, and O'Reilly, 1992). From this perspective, people derive self-esteem and self-identity from perceived group membership. Given that demographic similarity provides a salient basis for group membership (Tsui, Egan, and O'Reilly, 1992), people may favor (e.g., prefer to hire) demographically similar individuals. Alternatively, people may seek to construct or maintain homogeneous groups in order to increase the salience of group membership, thus maintaining or enhancing their self-esteem and identity. This argument is consistent with the reinforcement perspective discussed above. Thus, according to both the similarity-attraction principle and self-categorization theory, incumbent CEOs should prefer demographically similar individuals for positions on the board.

These social psychological mechanisms can be quite powerful. Research has consistently shown that minimal categorizations (i.e., group categorizations based on irrelevant criteria) are sufficient to produce in-group bias, or discrimination toward in-group members (Tajfel and Turner, 1986; Messick and Mackie, 1989). Thus bias can occur even when CEOs strive to evaluate candidates on the basis of objective qualifications. CEOs may also favor similar board candidates for sociopolitical reasons. For instance, by deliberately identifying or promoting people with similar philosophies on strategy and administration, CEOs can subtly enhance board support for their initiatives and decisions or minimize the risk of dissension. Advocates of board reform have expressed concern over this potentiality, because a CEO could "use [his or her control over the nomination process] to choose board members who, at the very least, are not antagonistic to what he/she chooses to do" (Bacon and Brown, 1975: 29).

Similarly, CEOs may favor people with compatible leadership and communication styles, thus facilitating interaction and communication with the board (Wagner, Pfeffer, and O'Reilly, 1984; O'Reilly, Caldwell, and Barnett, 1989; Zenger and Lawrence, 1989). Kanter (1977: 58) made a similar argument about management promotion criteria: "One way to ensure acceptance and ease of communication was to limit managerial jobs to those who were socially homogenous. Social certainty, at least, could compensate for some of the other sources of uncertainty in the tasks of management." Further, difficulties in communication and interaction may heighten conflict and power struggles between the CEO and the board (Pfeffer, 1983; Alexander, Fennell, and Halpern, 1993). Although CEOs could prevail in these contests and enhance their power, board members clearly have an advantage in overt conflict, namely, their formal authority over management. Thus, in addition to endorsing candidates with similar attitudes and philosophies, CEOs may favor people with whom they can communicate easily should disagreements arise.

This study examines attitudinal and behavioral similarity in terms of similarity of particular demographic attributes. As noted by Pfeffer (1983), demographic variables furnish parsimonious representations of constructs that are otherwise difficult to collect and validate, especially for corporate directors and top management. Recent research employing demographic variables in the study of top management includes Bantel and Jackson (1989), Chaganti and Sambharya (1987), Finkelstein (1992), Fligstein (1987), Michel and Hambrick (1992), and Wiersema and Bantel (1992). These studies, and the organizational demography literature more broadly, view demographically similar individuals as developing comparable attitudes and a shared language by virtue of common experiences and similar choices (Rhodes, 1983; Useem and Karabel, 1986). A number of specific demographic characteristics are particularly salient in assessing demographic similarity between CEOs and their boards.

Functional background similarity. A number of empirical studies have established a link between functional

Who Shall Govern?

background and specific attitudes or behavioral tendencies. In a seminal study, Dearborn and Simon (1958) found evidence that executives selectively perceive and identify company problems depending on their functional area, suggesting that executives with primary experience in a particular functional area tend to have similar viewpoints on the sources of poor performance. Recently, Waller, Huber, and Glick (1995) found that top executives were more aware of changes in organizational effectiveness related to their own functional backgrounds; for instance, executives with a functional background in operations were more sensitive to changes in operational efficiency for the organization. Thus, functional background may influence executives' perceptions and beliefs about the most important strategic issues facing the firm. Moreover, Hitt and Tyler (1991) showed that experience in particular functional areas predicted differences in executives' strategic evaluations of possible acquisitions, indicating that functional background can influence executives' opinions or attitudes about important strategic decisions facing the firm.

In general, CEOs and directors sharing a particular functional background are thought to develop common schemata or belief structures relevant to strategic decision making (Dearborn and Simon, 1958; Walsh, 1988), prompting them to diagnose strategic issues comparably and prefer similar solutions (Hambrick and Mason, 1984; Bantel and Jackson, 1989). Moreover, although little direct evidence is available, several authors have suggested that functional background itself provides a salient basis for executive selection (Pfeffer, 1981; Useem and Karabel, 1986) or for psychologically differentiating oneself from others more generally (e.g., Tsui, Egan, and O'Reilly, 1992). As a result, differences in functional experience can lead decision makers to perceive dissimilarity, independent of actual attitudinal or behavioral dissimilarity.

Age similarity. Empirical research has demonstrated a relationship between age and a variety of work-related attitudes, including attitudes toward risk (Rhodes, 1983). Vroom and Pahl (1971) found a negative relationship between age and the value placed on risk in a sample of corporate managers, and Hitt and Tyler (1991) found similar results for top executives. Thus, as noted by Hambrick and Mason (1984), since risk posture is an important element of corporate strategy (Beatty and Zajac, 1994), age differences should predict differences in top managers' beliefs about the proper strategic direction for the firm. In fact, Hitt and Tyler (1991) found that age significantly predicted variation in executives' strategic evaluations of possible acquisitions. There is also evidence for a relationship between age and specific behavioral tendencies, such as managerial decision-making style. Taylor (1975) found that older executives sought more information before making decisions and took more time in making them. Wagner, Pfeffer, and O'Reilly (1984) noted that CEOs and directors of the same age cohort may hold a variety of work-related and non-work-related experiences in common, leading to shared attitudes and belief structures. There is also evidence that age itself provides a salient basis for group categorization

(Stangor et al., 1992), so that differences in age can create the perception of dissimilarity, independent of underlying attitudinal or behavioral differences.

Educational level similarity. Empirical research has linked educational level with a high capacity for information processing (Schroder, Driver, and Streufert, 1967), tolerance of ambiguity (Dollinger, 1984), and leadership style (Pinder and Pinto, 1974). Other research has provided more indirect evidence for a relationship between educational background and underlying attitudes or behaviors relevant to strategic decision making. Several studies have shown a relationship between education level and the rate of corporate innovation, or the likelihood of strategic change (e.g., Bantel and Jackson, 1989; Wiersema and Bantel, 1992). Advanced management education, in particular, may inculcate common beliefs and taken-for-granted assumptions about normative or proper strategic decision making (Hambrick and Mason, 1984). Hambrick and Mason (1984) also suggested that advanced education both encourages and indicates a preference for administrative complexity. Finally, Tsui, Egan, and O'Reilly (1992) have suggested that educational background itself provides a salient basis for psychological group identification (Tajfel and Turner, 1986), so that differences in education can create the perception of dissimilarity independent of actual attitudinal or behavioral differences.

Similarity in insider/outsider status. Executives with long tenures in a firm undergo common socialization experiences and experience similar work demands, thus developing common attitudes, management styles, and individual competencies (Pfeffer, 1983; Alderfer, 1986; Michel and Hambrick, 1992). Whereas insiders have acquired greater firm-specific knowledge than outsiders (Lorsch and MacIver, 1989: 81), the outsiders are more aware of alternative strategic approaches and technologies employed by other firms (cf., Fama and Jensen, 1983). Thus, as a result of different socialization experiences and knowledge bases indicated by insider/outsider status, outside directors and CEOs hired from outside the organization may be more likely to recognize opportunities for change in existing strategies or operational norms (cf., Dalton and Kesner, 1985), whereas directors and CEOs with longer organizational tenures tend to favor the status quo (Hambrick, Geletkanycz, and Fredrickson, 1993). Finally, given that the presumed differences between insiders and outsiders are well known to board members and top managers (cf., Vancil, 1987; Lorsch and MacIver, 1989), this characteristic should provide a very salient basis for group differentiation.

In general, based on the arguments developed above, CEOs should favor new director candidates who are similar in one or more of these characteristics, but whether they can act on their preferences in the director selection process depends on two factors: (1) While CEOs may prefer new directors who are demographically similar to them, CEOs also must have the requisite power vis-à-vis the existing board to act on these preferences and influence the new director selection process; and (2) existing boards may have their own preferences about new directors, also seeking to select candidates who are demographically similar to them, and their ability to influence the selection process will depend on their power relative to the CEOs'.

Demographic Similarity and CEO vs. Board Power

Although it is typically assumed that CEOs control the nominating process, so that the characteristics of new directors often resemble those of the CEO, it is also possible that relatively powerful boards appoint directors who reflect their own demographic makeup, thus attenuating the similarity between CEOs and new directors. One would expect that the subconscious, social psychological mechanisms leading CEOs to favor demographically similar director candidates would also influence the preferences of existing board members. Furthermore, to the extent that cohesive and united boards are better able to resist CEO influence (Alderfer, 1986), current directors may have an incentive to increase the homogeneity of board members by appointing demographically similar new directors. Thus, as with CEOs, both social psychological and political motivations may impel board members to favor demographically similar board candidates.

While it is often argued that CEOs typically control the nominating process, board involvement may be high in some companies. In Lorsch and MacIver's (1989) survey, the nominating committee played an important role in identifying director candidates in about one-third of the companies (see also Mace, 1971). CEOs and boards may effectively compete for their own kind of demographically similar new directors, and the success of either will depend on how much power or influence each has with respect to the other. A number of factors affect the distribution of power between the CEO and the board and are therefore likely to affect demographic similarity between incumbent CEOs and new directors, on the one hand, and between existing boards and new directors, on the other.

Insider ratio. Most researchers and advocates of board reform typically assume that outside directors will be less conciliatory toward CEOs (Lorsch and MacIver, 1989; Beatty and Zajac, 1994). Insider-dominated boards imply problematic board control over the CEO, since the CEO may be in a position to influence an inside director's career advancement within the firm. Thus insiders may be more willing to accommodate CEOs' preferences about new directors. Even if one disputes Fama and Jensen's (1983) view of outside directors as professional referees and experts in internal organizational control and views them, instead, as socially dependent on the CEO (Wade, O'Reilly, and Chandratat 1990), a heavy use of inside directors (i.e., top managers) still indicates comparatively weak board control over the CEO. Thus when boards are predominantly made up of outside directors, they are better able to constrain CEOs' preferences and act on their own preferences. This logic suggests the following related hypotheses:

Hypothesis 1a (H1a): The higher the ratio of inside directors to total directors, the greater the similarity between the CEO and new directors.

Hypothesis 1b (H1b): The lower the ratio of inside directors to total directors, the greater the similarity between existing board members and new directors.

Separate CEO and board chair positions. Managerial hegemony theorists and advocates of board reform have also long argued that when the CEO is also the board chair, it restricts the board's independence and increases CEO power (Vance, 1983; Crystal, 1991; Rechner and Dalton, 1991). In terms of selecting new directors, CEOs holding both positions have greater informal stature and heightened formal authority over board members (Harrison, Torres, and Kukalis, 1988), potentially minimizing the board's role in conducting or monitoring the director selection process (Rechner and Dalton, 1991). When the CEO and board chair positions are split, the board should have more power and, thus, influence in new director selection. This suggests the following hypotheses:

Hypothesis 2a (H2a): A dual position of CEO and board chairman is positively associated with demographic similarity between the CEO and new directors.

Hypothesis 2b (H2b): Separation of the CEO and board chair positions is positively associated with demographic similarity between existing board members and new directors.

Relative tenure. Several studies have hypothesized an effect for relative tenure (i.e., the tenure of board members relative to the CEO's tenure) on board power (e.g., Singh and Harianto, 1989; Wade, O'Reilly, and Chandratat, 1990). Long tenure as CEO or corporate director confers expert power through an increased familiarity with the firm's resources and methods of operation (Zald, 1969; Alderfer, 1986; Singh and Harianto, 1989; Finkelstein, 1992). Moreover, CEOs with high tenure may acquire a "personal mystique or patriarchy" (Finkelstein and Hambrick, 1989: 124), resulting in sanctions against questioning the CEO's authority. Finally, as discussed above, low-tenured directors who were appointed after the current CEO took office may feel beholden to or sympathetic toward the incumbent CEO (Finkelstein and Hambrick, 1989; Wade, O'Reilly, and Chandratat, 1990). Therefore, we hypothesize:

Hypothesis 3a (H3a): The higher the CEO's tenure relative to the board's (average) tenure, the greater the similarity between the CEO and new directors.

Hypothesis 3b (H3b): The lower the CEO's tenure relative to the board's (average) tenure, the greater the similarity between existing board members and new directors.

Directors' stock ownership. From an agency perspective (Fama and Jensen, 1983), board members should actively monitor the director nomination process to protect shareholder interests. When directors own stock, the interests of board members are more closely aligned with the interests of shareholders, providing directors with an additional incentive to challenge CEOs' new director recommendations, suggest alternative candidates, and work toward establishing greater board control over the nomination process. Moreover, voting rights afford additional power to owner-directors, and this power increases with the portion of total shares held (Zald, 1969; Finkelstein, 1992). In general, as Mace (1971: 195) suggested, "if one or more existing directors own or represent the ownership of substantial stock, the president's de facto power to select new directors may be challenged. In these cases the stock-owning directors are interested in adding new directors of *their* choice." Therefore:

Hypothesis 4a (H4a): The lower the stock ownership held by board members, the greater the similarity between the CEO and new directors.

Hypothesis 4b (H4b): The higher the stock ownership held by board members, the greater the similarity between existing board members and new directors.

Demographic Similarity and CEO Compensation

Demographic similarity between a CEO and the board may have important consequences for board decision making. This study examines its effect on CEO compensation policy. In effect, changes in CEO compensation contracts can be viewed as tangible manifestations of change in the demographic similarity of CEOs and their boards. While an agency perspective suggests that changes in top executive compensation will reflect changes in firm performance, there is considerable debate about the strength of the CEO pay-performance relationship (cf., Jensen and Murphy, 1990). As a result, theorists have increasingly explored behavioral explanations for the board's apparent failure to align pay with performance, such as that CEOs may rely on social influence tactics and norms of reciprocity to control the compensation-setting process (e.g., Finkelstein and Hambrick, 1988; Wade, O'Reilly, and Chandratat, 1990). We propose that relatively powerful CEOs may also affect the compensation-setting process more indirectly, by using their influence over the director nomination process to increase demographic similarity between them and board members, thus encouraging less critical board evaluations of CEO performance.

In evaluating CEOs, boards can attribute firm performance either to management or to uncontrollable factors in the firm's environment (Walsh and Seward, 1990; Kerr and Kren, 1992). The attribution of firm performance is an "ill-structured, complex problem" (Walsh, 1988: 873), and as a result, directors may rely on belief structures (Walsh, 1988) or cognitive schemata (Norman, 1976) in evaluating CEO behavior. To the extent that CEOs and board members share similar schemas or beliefs about the proper strategic direction for the firm (as indicated by demographic similarity), directors may attribute relatively good performance to the CEO's strategic wisdom, while attributing poor performance to environmental factors beyond management's control. In addition, the performance appraisal literature has consistently demonstrated that greater similarity in demographic characteristics between superiors and subordinates is associated with more favorable performance evaluations (Mobley, 1982; Pulakos and Wexley, 1983; Tsui and O'Reilly, 1989). Thus the increased possibility of biased performance appraisals and exaggerated perceptions of the value of a CEO that accompany relatively high demographic similarity between CEOs and boards may lead to more generous increases in total CEO compensation.

Increased demographic similarity between the CEO and the board may also affect the form or mix of CEO compensation by reducing the perceived need for performance-contingent CEO compensation. From an agency theory perspective, incentives that make CEO pay contingent on future firm performance are a primary mechanism by which firms reduce the so-called agency problem that arises in large corporations (Jensen and Meckling, 1976; Larcker, 1983). Such compensation includes stock options and performance plans that award shares of common stock or cash to the extent that specific performance goals are met (Jarrell, 1993). Given that demographic similarity enhances interpersonal trust (Kanter, 1977; Useem and Karabel, 1986), the perceived need to minimize shirking behavior and otherwise control CEO decision making with contingent compensation may be diminished when demographic similarity between the CEO and board is high. Thus increased similarity may lead to a decrease in the portion of total compensation that is contingent on firm performance, as well as an increase in total compensation.

More generally, while traditional indicators of CEO influence over the board, such as those discussed earlier, may still have a direct effect on CEO compensation arrangements, greater demographic similarity with board members may represent an additional, more subtle mechanism by which powerful CEOs affect their compensation. This discussion suggests the following related hypotheses:

Hypothesis 5a (H5a): Increases in demographic similarity between the CEO and the board will be positively associated with increases in CEO compensation.

Hypothesis 5b (H5b): Increases in demographic similarity between the CEO and the board will be negatively associated with increases in contingent compensation.

METHOD

Sample and Data Collection

This study uses a longitudinal research design to examine new director selection and change in CEO compensation from 1987 to 1990. The population includes the largest U.S. industrial and service firms, as listed in the 1987 Forbes and Fortune 500 indexes. The Forbes 500 uses multiple lists whose overlap depends on the specific size measure used. This study used those firms that appeared on lists of at least two size measures. Firms were excluded from the final sample if complete demographic data were unavailable for more than one-quarter of the outside directors in each year. This procedure yielded 413 companies. *T*-tests revealed no significant differences in size (measured as sales and number of employees) or performance (measured as return on assets and total stock returns) between the initial and final samples. Firms in this sample range in size from $487 million to $63 billion in sales and include both single-product firms and highly diversified conglomerates.

Demographic data were obtained from the *Dun and Bradstreet Reference Book of Corporate Management, Standard and Poor's Register of Corporations, Directors, and Executives,* and *Who's Who in Finance and Industry.* Data on board structure, ownership, and compensation were obtained from corporate proxy statements, and data from COMPUSTAT and CRSP were used to calculate performance and size measures. Data on director characteristics, CEO and board influence, and CEO compensation were collected for the years 1986 to 1991, inclusive. Directors were classified as "new" if they were listed in the *Standard and Poor's Register* in the current year but not in the prior year; new director status was corroborated with information from the *Dun and Bradstreet Reference Book.* This approach yielded a sample of 1,113 new directors for the period 1987 to 1990.

Dependent Variables

Demographic similarity. To develop measures of similarity between the new director and the CEO and board, we first created categorical measures for functional background, educational background, and insider/outsider status. Following Hambrick and Mason (1984) and others (e.g., Miles and Snow, 1978; Chaganti and Sambharya, 1987), we consolidated the various functional backgrounds into three core areas: output functions, which include marketing and sales; throughput functions, which include operations, R&D, and engineering; and peripheral functions, primarily law, finance, and accounting. We created a trichotomous measure of functional background, coded as one if the new director had primary experience in operations, engineering, or research and development, two if the new director had experience in marketing or sales, and zero if the new director's primary experience lay in peripheral functions. Each director's primary functional area was determined as the area in which he or she had the most experience (Chaganti and Sambharya, 1987).

We followed prior research (e.g., Chaganti and Sambharya, 1987; Murray, 1989; Michel and Hambrick, 1992) in assessing functional background primarily according to an individual's current and prior job titles, while also considering other aspects of his or her employment history, such as organizations worked for. When possible, we examined information from more than one data source in coding this variable. Although coding functional background entails a degree of subjectivity, Michel and Hambrick (1992) found a high correlation (.86) between the ratings of two different sets of coders. To ensure that reliability was similarly high in this case, we correlated the ratings of two different coders for a random sample of 75 directors. The correlation was .88, suggesting very high reliability.

To measure insider/outsider status of directors, we created a binary variable, coded as one if the director was not an employee of the organization, and zero otherwise. We coded CEOs as outsiders if they were not employed by the company or any of its subsidiaries prior to becoming CEO, consistent with prior research and common usage of the term among CEOs and directors themselves (Dalton and Kesner, 1985). Educational background was divided into four categories: (1) less than a bachelor's degree; (2) less than a master's degree; (3) less than a doctoral degree; and (4) a doctoral degree. The age of new directors was operationalized as a continuous variable.

To test hypotheses relating CEO and board influence to demographic similarity between CEOs and new directors, we created several dichotomous measures of similarity. Each variable was coded as one if the CEO and new director shared the same demographic category. For instance, *functional background similarity* (*CEO*) was coded as one if both the CEO and new director had primary experience in the same functional area, as defined above. *Educational level similarity* (*CEO*) was created similarly. *Age similarity* (*CEO*) was coded as one if the CEO and new director differed by less than one standard deviation (7.8 years, calculated from the pooled sample of directors).[1] Finally, *insider/outsider status similarity* (*CEO*) was coded as one if CEOs and new directors were both insiders or outsiders, and zero otherwise.

To assess the effect of CEO and board influence on the demographic similarity between existing board members and new directors, we created four continuous measures of similarity, using information on board members in the year the new director is appointed. In general, similarity between the board and the new director was assessed by aggregating similarity measures of all board-member-new-director dyads. *Age similarity* (*board*) was measured with an analog of the euclidean distance measure (i.e., the coefficient of variation) commonly used in research on organizational demography (Wagner, Pfeffer, and O'Reilly, 1984; O'Reilly, Caldwell, and Barnett, 1989):

$$\left[\sum_{j=1}^{n} \frac{(S_i - S_j)^2}{n}\right]^{1/2},$$

where S_i is the new director's age, S_j indicates the age of existing board member *i* (excluding the CEO), and *n* represents the number of existing board members. This measure was converted to an indicator of similarity by subtracting each firm's coefficient from the highest value in the sample.

For the categorical variables, we applied a variant of Blau's (1977) index of heterogeneity, defined as $(P_i)^2$, where P_i is the proportion of CEO-board-member dyads sharing the *i*th category (Murray, 1989). Thus, *functional background similarity* (*board*) between a new director and existing board members indicates the squared proportion of CEO-board-member dyads in which both individuals have primary experience in the same core, functional area; *education level similarity* (*board*) and *insider/outsider status similarity* (*board*) were calculated in the same way.

While the concept of board-new-director similarity may be less meaningful if the board itself is highly diverse, it seems reasonable to assume that if some pattern exists—even if only a slight tendency—in the distribution of values of a demographic characteristic among board members for some cases in the sample, the concept of board-new-director similarity is meaningful and our hypotheses can be tested. Similarly, we need only assume that CEOs and existing board members are not themselves highly similar, and thus do not hold identical preferences, in all cases. Given this,

1
In a separate model we used a more restrictive definition of age similarity (five years or less) and found that the results were substantively unchanged. Thus it appears that the findings are not sensitive to the chosen cutoff or criterion level for age similarity.

including cases in which the CEO is similar to a majority of existing board members on a given characteristic provides a conservative test.

Compensation. Total compensation comprises base salary, annual bonus, and the total value of long-term incentives granted in a given year (Crystal, 1984). Stock options were valued using the Black-Scholes (1973) method, which estimates option value based on the historical price volatility of the underlying security. Other grants, such as restricted stock and performance shares, were valued according to the market price at date of grant (Ellig, 1984). All compensation values were adjusted for inflation to represent 1990 constant dollars using the CPI. *Change in total compensation* was measured as the logarithm of compensation in the subsequent year minus the same measure in the prior year (Kerr and Kren, 1992). While change in compensation could also be measured from $t - 1$ to t, rather than $t - 1$ to $t + 1$, the calculation used here eliminates the possibility that increases in similarity occurred after compensation decisions were made in a given year. This measure indicates the growth rate in total compensation.

Compensation contingency was calculated for each year as the total value of long-term incentive grants divided by total compensation. *Change in compensation contingency* was calculated for each year as contingency in the subsequent year minus contingency in the prior year. Short-term bonuses were not included in this measure because they are notoriously vulnerable to tampering (Larcker, 1983). Although long-term incentives can be manipulated by lowering the strike price of a stock option or lowering the performance threshold for payouts under a performance plan, with the exception of a few celebrated cases (e.g., Apple Computer following the stock market crash in 1987), such manipulations are extremely rare in practice. Moreover, stock options are widely recognized in the empirical agency literature as an important source of contingent CEO compensation (e.g., Jensen and Murphy, 1990; Kerr and Kren, 1992). Nevertheless, since the potential for such abuse does exist for all firms in the sample, long-term incentives may be more precisely considered potentially contingent CEO compensation.

Independent Variables

CEO and board influence. The *insider ratio* was calculated as the number of employee directors divided by the total number of board members. CEO-board-chairman duality is a binary variable, coded as one if a CEO was also chairman of the board, and zero otherwise. *Relative CEO-board tenure* was calculated as the average board tenure of directors divided by the CEO's tenure. Finally, *directors' stock ownership* was measured as the percentage of total common equity owned by non-CEO directors. Because stock ownership can also be an important source of power for the CEO, we adjusted for CEO ownership in measuring this variable (Finkelstein, 1992).

Demographic characteristics and similarity. To test hypotheses relating similarity between the CEO and board to change in total compensation, four measures of *change in*

Table 1

Descriptive Statistics and Pearson Correlation Coefficients (N = 1652)

Variable	Mean	S.D.	1	2	3	4
1. Relative CEO-board tenure	.41	.43				
2. CEO-board chairman duality	.78	.41	.17			
3. Directors' stock ownership*	.01	.07	.45	.18		
4. Insider ratio	.28	.15	.11	.04	.16	
5. Return on assets	−2.76	5.58	−.15	−.05	−.10	−.03
6. Total returns	−4.55	15.29	−.03	−.07	−.02	.13
7. Background similarity (CEO)	.62	.49	.18	.23	.11	.12
8. Age similarity (CEO)	.64	.48	.22	.18	.26	.13
9. Eductional level similarity (CEO)	.68	.47	.06	.11	.18	.07
10. Insider status similarity (CEO)	.61	.49	.19	.24	.31	.17
11. Background similarity (board)	.10	.19	−.16	−.20	−.11	−.15
12. Age similarity (board)	19.38	3.35	−.07	−.17	−.19	−.07
13. Educational level similarity (board)	.20	.22	−.04	−.06	−.17	−.16
14. Insider status similarity (board)	.27	.21	−.19	−.20	−.18	−.20
15. Change in CEO-board similarity	.00	2.26	.13	.24	.21	.14
16. Change in total compensation	.15	.85	.07	.23	.22	.05
17. Change in compensation contingency	.02	.26	−.10	−.09	−.35	.17
18. Log of sales (in thous.)	6.73	1.21	−.02	−.01	−.04	−.17

* Mean and s.d. reflect actual values; correlations reflect inverse values.

CEO-board similarity were constructed for each year as similarity in the current year minus similarity in the prior year. The measures of (absolute) CEO-board similarity are analogous to the measures of CEO-new-director similarity discussed above. Since increases in the four measures of similarity were highly correlated (Pearson correlation coefficients > .6 in all cases), we created a single measure of increased similarity by summing the z-scores of all four change variables. We could also have limited this measure to include demographic information only on board members who serve on the compensation committee, but Lorsch and MacIver (1989: 65) suggested that the informal or formal evaluation of executives that informs compensation decisions is often accomplished in general board meetings. Moreover, other board members can clearly affect evaluations indirectly through informal conversations with committee members. An ideal approach might use data from all board members, with greater weight given to the characteristics of committee members, but the true influence weighting for committee membership would be difficult to determine and probably varies greatly across organizations.

Control Variables

Given that demographic similarity may play an especially large role in new director selection for the largest firms in the sample (Useem, 1984), *log of sales* was included as a control variable in analyses of CEO-new-director similarity and board-new-director similarity. Given possible relationships between various measures of firm performance and CEO compensation (e.g., Coughlan and Schmidt, 1985), we also controlled for performance in analyses of CEO compensation. *Total returns* was used as a market-based measure of firm performance, calculated as capital gains plus dividends accrued/paid during the year, divided by share price at the beginning of the year (Davis, 1991). *Return on assets* was also used as an operating measure of

Who Shall Govern?

Table 1 (*continued*)

5	6	7	8	9	10	11	12	13	14	15	16	17
.23												
−.15	−.19											
−.08	−.15	.60										
−.23	−.12	.68	.62									
−.24	−.13	.64	.61	.60								
.06	.05	−.10	−.07	−.02	.01							
−.02	.10	−.09	.01	−.10	−.13	.52						
.08	.16	−.14	−.17	−.10	−.15	.48	.45					
.03	−.01	−.12	−.08	−.11	−.06	.43	.59	.51				
−.19	−.17	.14	.06	.09	.10	−.18	−.10	−.11	−.08			
.04	−.03	.11	.10	.18	.07	−.07	−.05	−.08	.02	.18		
.17	.22	−.19	−.18	−.23	−.12	.11	.08	.05	.16	−.25	−.09	
−.06	−.06	.09	.15	.07	.03	.04	.01	−.02	.02	.14	.09	−.07

performance. Both measures were adjusted for primary industry performance at the two-digit Standard Industry Classification (SIC) code level.

To control for potential relationships between firm size and the level or form of CEO compensation, *log of sales* was also included in analyses of CEO compensation. Given prior findings showing a relationship between the relative power of the CEO and the level or form of CEO compensation (e.g., Finkelstein and Hambrick, 1989; Westphal and Zajac, 1994), we also included our measures of board power (insider ratio, separate CEO-board chair, relative CEO-board tenure, and directors' stock ownership) as control variables in the compensation equations. Finally, although the coefficients are not reported, we controlled for industry in all models by including dummy variables for each two-digit SIC code represented in the sample. Table 1 provides the means, standard deviations, and bivariate correlations for all data pooled.

Analysis

In testing hypotheses on the likelihood of CEO-new-director similarity, we used maximum-likelihood logit regression. Ordinary least squares (OLS) analysis is inappropriate when the dependent variable is categorical, because OLS assumes a linear additive model with normally distributed error terms, while the true probability model is nonlinear with binomially distributed errors (Aldrich and Nelson, 1984; Hosmer and Lemeshow, 1989). The logit function takes the following form:

$$\log [P_i/(1 - P_i)] = b_k X_{ik},$$

where P_i is the probability of CEO-new-director similarity on some attribute, X_{ik}s are independent variables, and b_ks are the estimated coefficients. Moreover, P_i is defined as:

$$\exp (b_k X_{ik})/[1 + \exp (b_k X_{ik})],$$

such that P_i increases monotonically with b_kX_{ik} and can assume any value between zero and one. OLS multiple regression analysis was used to analyze similarity between existing board members and new directors.

As discussed above, because the sample of new directors was not drawn randomly from the population of directors appointed from 1987 to 1990 and because data are not available on the representativeness of the sample, coefficient estimates could be biased. Although the sample of 413 firms appears to be representative of the population of Fortune/Forbes 500 firms, the sample of 1,113 new directors is not necessarily representative. To correct for any upward bias in parameter estimates resulting from nonrepresentative sampling and heteroskedasticity, we used Huber's variance correction procedure (White, 1980). This formula produces robust standard errors when clusters of observations (i.e., companies) are representative of a population but individual observations (i.e., new directors) are not necessarily representative.

To assess change in total compensation, we applied pooled cross-sectional time series regression (Sayrs, 1989). This technique is appropriate for analyzing a dataset composed of multiple organizations observed at multiple time points. To correct for heteroskedasticity and autocorrelated error terms, we used the two-staged generalized least squares (GLS) procedure offered in the LIMDEP program (Greene, 1993). This procedure partitions error variance into three components—random error in time, random error in space (e.g., across organizations), and random error not unique to time or space—and uses this information to derive efficient and unbiased parameter estimates (Sayrs, 1989). The GLS estimator takes the following form:

$$B = (X'S^{-1}X)^{-1}X'S^{-1}Y,$$

given

$$Y = X_{nt}B_k + u_{nt}, \text{ with } u_{nt} = y_t + u_n + e_{nt},$$

where y_t are random over time, u_n are random over cross sections, e_{nt} are random over space and time, and S is the sum of the variances of the three error components.

This model analyzes the effect of change in CEO-board similarity from year $t - 1$ to year t on change in compensation level/contingency from year t to year $t + 1$. All control variables were lagged by one year. Relationships are observed over a four-year time period, yielding 1,652 firm-years of data.

RESULTS

Hypotheses 1a through 4b predicted a positive association between CEO power and CEO-new-director similarity and, conversely, a positive association between board power and board-new-director similarity. In general, the results of logit and multiple regression analyses of demographic similarity provided in Table 2 provide strong support for these hypotheses. Higher insider-director ratios were significantly and positively related to CEO-new-director similarity for all demographic dimensions. Also, lower insider-director ratios were significantly and positively related to board-new-director similarity for all demographic dimensions. Supporting H2a and H2b, CEO-board-chairman duality was significantly and positively related to CEO-new-director similarity for all demographic dimensions except educational level. Also as predicted, separation of the CEO and board chair positions was positively associated with similarity between existing directors and new directors across the same three dimensions.

Table 2

Logit and Multiple Regression Analyses of Demographic Similarity of New Director with CEO and Board (N = 1113)*

Independent variable	New Director Demographic Similarity							
	Functional background		Age		Educational level		Insider/outsider status	
	CEO	Board	CEO	Board	CEO	Board	CEO	Board
1. Relative CEO-board tenure	.827***	–.045*	.957***	–.288	.338	–.008	1.341***	–.023*
	(.265)	(.022)	(.263)	(.200)	(.267)	(.010)	(.256)	(.011)
2. CEO-board chairman duality	.790**	–.079***	.724**	–.607**	.263	–.014*	.840**	–.027*
	(.275)	(.019)	(.274)	(.221)	(.280)	(.007)	(.276)	(.010)
3. Directors' stock ownership (inverse)	2.890	–.323*	3.913**	–3.518*	4.404**	–.221*	4.252**	–2.457**
	(1.533)	(.153)	(1.548)	(1.516)	(1.643)	(.112)	(1.615)	(1.012)
4. Insider ratio	.558	–.139*	.648*	–1.164	.668*	–.131*	.954**	–.124**
	(.367)	(.069)	(.319)	(.840)	(.394)	(.046)	(.392)	(.049)
5. Log of sales	.013	.004	.027	.046	.061*	.001	.027	–.002
	(.022)	(.002)	(.018)	(.027)	(.027)	(.001)	(.027)	(.001)
Constant	.400	.592***	1.363***	8.956***	.143	.129***	4.254***	.173***
	(.386)	(.122)	(.352)	(.213)	(.467)	(.031)	(.479)	(.031)
Chi-square†	36.18***	30.36***	25.49***	20.05***	21.86***	21.33***	31.63***	23.90***
Adjusted R-squared	–	.21	–	.16	–	.15	–	.18

*$p \le .05$; **$p \le .01$; ***$p \le .001$; t-tests are one-tailed for hypothesized effects, two-tailed for control variables.

* Standard errors are in parentheses. Chi-square values are reported for analyses of CEO-new-director similarity; F-values are reported for analyses of board-new-director similarity.

† The variance-covariance matrix was computed using Huber's correction procedure (White, 1980).

A very similar pattern of results emerged in support of H3a and H3b. Consistent with H3a, the longer the CEO's tenure relative to the average tenure of board members, the greater the demographic similarity between CEOs and new directors across three of the four measures of similarity. H3b was also supported for two measures of similarity: Relative CEO-board tenure is significantly and negatively related to demographic similarity between existing board members and new directors with respect to functional background and insider/outsider status. The results also support H4a: The lower the stock ownership among board members, the greater the demographic similarity between CEOs and new directors across all four dimensions of similarity. Moreover, consistent with H4b, directors' stock ownership was consistently and positively related to similarity between the new director and the board.

Taken together, the results suggest that relatively powerful boards are more likely to appoint demographically similar new directors, while also frustrating the attempts of CEOs to do the same. Conversely, the greater the CEOs' influence over the nominating process, the greater their ability to appoint demographically similar and therefore sympathetic individuals to the board. One might argue that these findings apply primarily to the selection of new outside directors and less to the selection of new insiders. Accordingly, in separate models, we examined whether relationships between relative power and similarity were significant for the subsample of new outside directors, but not for the subsample of new inside directors. The pattern of results was quite consistent across these subsamples and generally matched the pattern of results for the larger sample, although models of insider/outsider status similarity were necessarily excluded from these analyses.

With respect to the consequences of demographic similarity, Table 3 shows results of GLS regression analysis of change in CEO compensation. The first two columns provide results for compensation level; the last two columns provide results for compensation contingency. Models 1 and 3 include control variables only, while models 2 and 4 add the effect of change in CEO-board similarity.

Table 3

GLS Regression Analysis of Change in CEO Compensation (N = 1652)*

	Total compensation		Compensation contingency	
Independent variable	Model 1	Model 2	Model 1	Model 2
1. Change in CEO-board similarity		.037••• (.009)		−.011••• (.003)
2. Insider ratio	.231 (.156)	.226 (.156)	−.294 (.157)	−.169 (.158)
3. CEO-board chairman duality	.107• (.052)	.064 (.052)	−.043•• (.015)	−.026 (.014)
4. Relative CEO-board tenure	.161•• (.058)	.081 (.058)	−.039• (.017)	−.022 (.017)
5. Directors' stock ownership (inverse)	.710 (.381)	.713 (.382)	−.255• (.115)	−.254• (.115)
6. Total stock returns	.001 (.001)	.001 (.001)	.001 (.001)	.001 (.001)
7. Return on assets	.196 (.388)	.199 (.385)	.053 (.108)	.055 (.108)
8. Log of sales	.023•• (.008)	.022•• (.008)	−.002 (.002)	−.002 (.002)
F-value	3.75••	6.01•••	5.90•••	6.97•••
Adjusted R-squared	.18	.22	.21	.25

•$p \le .05$; ••$p \le .01$; •••$p \le .001$; t-tests are one-tailed for hypothesized effects, two-tailed for control variables.
* Standard errors are in parentheses.

H5a predicted that increased demographic similarity between the CEO and other board members leads to greater subsequent increases in the CEO's total compensation. Results strongly support this hypothesis (model 2). The results also support H5b, which posited a negative relationship between increased CEO-board similarity and subsequent change in compensation contingency (model 4). In general, then, the results show that greater similarity between the CEO and board is associated with more generous CEO compensation contracts, as indicated by subsequent increases in total CEO compensation and subsequent decreases in the portion of total CEO compensation that is contingent on firm performance.

Who Shall Govern?

Models 1 and 3 in Table 3 also show that the indicators of board control were generally negatively related to change in total compensation and positively associated with change in compensation contingency. These results, while not central to the present study, provide additional evidence, consistent with prior research, that powerful boards limit the CEOs' ability to dictate their own compensation arrangements (Finkelstein and Hambrick, 1988; Westphal and Zajac, 1994).

When change in CEO-board similarity is added to the equations (i.e., in models 2 and 4), however, coefficients for two of the three board-influence measures become statistically insignificant. In combination with the observed relationship between CEO influence and CEO-new-director similarity discussed above, these results provide suggestive evidence that change in CEO-board similarity may mediate the relationship between CEO influence over the board and subsequent changes in CEO compensation contracts. To ensure that results were not driven by scaling differences across the independent variables, we also estimated the effects of standardized influence and similarity measures on change in CEO compensation. The results were substantially unchanged.

DISCUSSION

This study provides strong and consistent evidence on the relationship between CEO and board power, demographic similarity and the selection of new directors. The study shows that social psychological and sociopolitical factors lead CEOs and existing board members to favor new directors who are demographically similar to them and that the relative influence of CEOs and boards predicts which party is more likely to realize his or her preferences in the new-director selection process. In addition, the study sheds light on the social psychological mechanism by which CEO influence can affect (intentionally or unintentionally) subsequent board decision making. Specifically, the findings indicate that (1) in firms in which CEOs are relatively powerful, new directors are likely to be demographically similar to the firm's incumbent CEO; (2) when the boards of directors are more powerful than the CEOs, new directors resemble the existing board, rather than the CEO; and (3) increased demographic similarity between CEOs and the board is likely to result in more generous CEO compensation contracts.

The first set of results provides direct evidence for the effect of CEO power (measured in multiple ways) on the demographic similarity of CEOs and new directors. These findings are consistent with social psychological studies on the hiring process, which suggest that CEOs (and boards) should favor new director candidates who share common group memberships with them (Byrne, 1971; Baskett, 1973; Tajfel and Turner, 1986). The findings are also consistent with a relatively deliberate, political process whereby CEOs increase board support for their decisions and minimize the risk of dissension by favoring individuals with similar philosophies on strategy and administration, as indicated by demographic characteristics (Kanter, 1977; Pfeffer, 1981).

The results also suggest that the preferences of existing board members about new directors parallel the preferences of CEOs. It appears that relatively powerful boards not only constrain the ability of CEOs to recruit similar new directors, but such boards are also more likely to appoint new directors who reflect their own demographic profile. From a social psychological perspective, these findings are unsurprising, given that board members are obviously no less vulnerable to subconscious, in-group biases than CEOs are. From a political perspective, however, the results may seem more surprising, since most governance researchers impute political motives only to CEOs' behavior, and not to board members' behavior. In any case, the findings suggest that CEOs and existing board members effectively compete for the characteristics of new directors.

The present findings are also consistent with qualitative research on the politics of strategic decision making (e.g., Eisenhardt and Bourgeois, 1988), which shows that demographic similarity provides an important basis for coalition formation. In the context of new director selection, powerful corporate actors seek to enlarge their coalition of support by recruiting people with similar demographic group memberships. More generally, this interpretation suggests that "power begets power" (Pfeffer, 1981: 304), whereby a priori sources of power over the director selection process provide an opportunity for political behavior (i.e., the opportunity to appoint demographically similar and therefore sympathetic people to the board). As a result, demographic similarity both reflects and reinforces the existing power distribution.

Having established the role of the relative power of the CEO and board in new director selection, we conducted additional post hoc tests to assess the extent to which CEOs or boards generally dominated the new director selection process, thus dictating the characteristics of new directors. For this analysis, we sought to predict the specific demographic characteristics of new directors as a function of the CEO's characteristics and the existing board's characteristics. These results, shown in the Appendix, suggest that there is a strong general correspondence between the characteristics of incumbent CEOs and those of new directors. The magnitude of these effects is also considerable. For instance, the likelihood that new directors will have an advanced management degree increases by 34 percent if the CEO also has one. The results are consistent across all demographic characteristics. Thus the findings support the notion that CEOs generally are able to influence the appointment of demographically similar new directors. In contrast, associations between existing board-member characteristics and the attributes of new directors are weak and inconsistent. These results, when considered with the earlier findings, suggest that demographic similarity between the CEO and new director is the general rule, rather than the exception, and that only firms with a high degree of board power are likely to counter this tendency. Thus, to the extent that demographic similarity between the CEO and board biases boards' evaluations of the CEOs' performance, the appointment of new directors may typically promote

Who Shall Govern?

CEO entrenchment rather than board control (Alderfer, 1986; Wade, O'Reilly, and Chandratat, 1990).

Consistent with these arguments, a third set of results indicated that increased demographic similarity between CEOs and board members was positively related to subsequent increases in CEO compensation and negatively related to increases in contingent compensation. Demographic similarity appears to enhance the boards' perception of the value of the CEO's leadership, while diminishing the perceived need for financial incentive alignment (Zajac and Westphal, 1995a). Moreover, there is suggestive evidence that changes in demographic similarity between the CEO and the board mediate the relationship between relative board influence (as indicated by our measures of board power) and subsequent change in CEO compensation contracts. Thus, while CEOs may still practice direct social influence or "internal entrenchment" practices (Wade, O'Reilly, and Chandratat, 1990; Walsh and Seward, 1990: 430), the appointment of demographically similar directors may represent another, relatively subtle and indirect mechanism by which CEOs influence board decision making. Accordingly, the findings suggest the need for corporate governance researchers to consider explicitly both the sociopolitical and social psychological dynamics in the relationship between the CEO and the board.

The strength of these results may be unexpected given how little demographic diversity typically exists among corporate elites. The standard deviation in age for directors in our sample is only six years, and nearly 60 percent hold an advanced degree, but as Wiersema and Bird (1993) noted, a high level of demographic homogeneity within a group may augment the salience of relatively slight demographic differences between people. Thus, for instance, given the constrained variation in age among directors in our sample, a new director candidate who is only ten years younger than the CEO and most directors on a board could nevertheless appear demographically distant, since, in relative terms, they are quite dissimilar. A high level of demographic homogeneity may actually promote out-group bias, confirming research on intergroup relations showing that out-group bias is more likely when the out-group status of others is relatively salient (Messick and Mackie, 1989).

This study has a number of implications for research on boards of directors. One implication is that the commonly made assumption that outside directors are more likely to exercise independent judgment in board decision making (Lorsch and MacIver, 1989) may be suspect, insofar as it ignores the possibility that—from a social psychological perspective—outside directors who are demographically similar to CEOs may be more akin to insiders. Thus normative debates on board composition should consider the more subtle role of demographic similarity in new director selection and subsequent board decision making

The present study also suggests that a relational demography approach (Tsui and O'Reilly, 1989) could provide a useful complement to traditional theoretical perspectives on corporate board member selection. For example, the likelihood that an individual will gain appointment to a particular corporate board may be contingent on his or her attitudinal and social compatibility with powerful actors in the organization (as indicated by demographic similarity), in addition to his or her social capital derived from other board appointments (Useem, 1984) or his or her organizational affiliation (Zajac, 1988). Similarly, this study also suggests alternative bases for compatibility. For instance, similar philosophies about strategy and administration, as indicated by shared functional background and other demographic characteristics assessed in this study, may largely compensate for membership in different socioeconomic classes. Future research could directly examine the relative importance of social and attitudinal similarity (e.g., socioeconomic status and functional background) as determinants of new director selection.

The theoretical mechanisms discussed in this study may also influence the selection of CEO successors. In more recent research, we found evidence that board power over departing CEOs decreased the likelihood of demographic similarity between new CEOs and their predecessors, while increasing similarity between new CEOs and the board (Zajac and Westphal, 1995b). Future research might investigate the circumstances in which this cycle of increased similarity between CEOs and boards is broken.

This study's findings highlight the potential importance of considering demographic variables in the analysis of corporate governance issues. Governance research has tended to emphasize legal, economic, sociological, or political perspectives. While such perspectives are clearly relevant, this study suggests that greater attention to the interplay of social psychological and sociopolitical processes can advance our understanding of the control of modern corporations.

REFERENCES

Alderfer, Clayton P.
1986 "The invisible director on corporate boards." Harvard Business Review, 64 (Nov./Dec.): 38–52.

Aldrich, John H., and Forrest D. Nelson
1984 Linear Probability, Logit, and Probit Models. Newbury Park, CA: Sage.

Alexander, Jeffrey A., Mary L. Fennell, and Michael T. Halpern
1993 "Leadership instability in hospitals: The influence of board-CEO relations and organizational growth and decline." Administrative Science Quarterly, 38: 74–99.

Bacon, Jeremy, and James K. Brown
1975 Corporate Directorship Practices: Role, Selection and Legal Status of the Board. New York: Conference Board.

Bantel, Karen A., and Susan E. Jackson
1989 "Top management and innovations in banking: Does the composition of the top team make a difference?" Strategic Management Journal, 10: 107–124.

Baskett, Glen D.
1973 "Interview decisions as determined by competency and attitude similarity." Journal of Applied Psychology, 57: 343–345.

Beatty, Randolph P., and Edward J. Zajac
1994 "Top management incentives, monitoring, and risk sharing: A study of executive compensation, ownership and board structure in initial public offerings." Administrative Science Quarterly, 39: 313–336.

Black, Fischer, and Myron Scholes
1973 "The pricing of options and corporate liabilities." Journal of Political Economy, 81: 637–659.

Blau, Peter M.
1977 Inequality and Heterogeneity. Glencoe, IL: Free Press.

Byrne, Donn
1971 The Attraction Paradigm. New York: Academic Press.

Byrne, Donn, Gerald L. Clore, and Philip Worchel
1966 "The effect of economic similarity-dissimilarity as determinants of attraction." Journal of Personality and Social Psychology, 4: 220–224.

Who Shall Govern?

Chaganti, Rajeswararao, and Rakesh Sambharya
1987 "Strategic orientation and characteristics of upper management." Strategic Management Journal, 8: 393–401.

Coughlan, Anne T., and Ronald M Schmidt
1985 "Executive compensation, management turnover, and firm performance." Journal of Accounting and Economics, 7: 43–66.

Crystal, Graef S.
1984 Questions and Answers on Executive Compensation. Englewood Cliffs, NJ: Prentice-Hall.
1991 In Search of Excess: The Overcompensation of American Executives. New York: W. W. Norton.

Dalton, Daniel R., and Idalene F. Kesner
1985 "Organizational performance as an antecedent of inside/outside chief executive succession: An empirical assessment." Academy of Management Journal, 28: 749–762.

Davis, Gerald F.
1991 "Agents without principles? The spread of the poison pill through the intercorporate network." Administrative Science Quarterly, 36: 583–613.

Dearborn, DeWitt C., and Herbert A. Simon
1958 "Selective perceptions: A note on the departmental identification of executives." Sociometry, 21: 140–144.

Dollinger, Marc J.
1984 "Environmental boundary spanning and information processing effects on organizational performance." Academy of Management Journal, 27: 351–368.

Eisenhardt, Kathleen M., and L. J. Bourgeois
1988 "Politics of strategic decision making in high-velocity environments: Toward a midrange theory." Academy of Management Journal, 31: 737–770.

Ellig, Bruce R.
1984 "Incentive plans: Over the long-term." Compensation Review, 16: 26–37.

Fama, Eugene F., and Michael C. Jensen
1983 "The separation of ownership and control." Journal of Law and Economics, 26: 301–325.

Finkelstein, Sydney
1992 "Power in top management teams: Dimensions, measurement, and validation." Academy of Management Journal, 35: 505–538.

Finkelstein, Sydney, and Donald C. Hambrick
1988 "Chief executive compensation: A synthesis and reconciliation." Strategic Management Journal, 9: 543–558.
1989 "Chief executive compensation: A study of the intersection of markets and political processes." Strategic Management Journal, 10: 121–134.

Fligstein, Neil
1987 "The intraorganizational power struggle: Rise of finance personnel to top leadership in large corporations, 1919–1979." American Sociological Review, 52: 44–58.

Greene, William H.
1993 Econometric Analysis. New York: Macmillan.

Hambrick, Donald C., Marta A. Geletkanycz, and James W. Fredrickson
1993 "Top executive commitment to the status quo: Some tests of its determinants." Strategic Management Journal, 14: 401–418.

Hambrick, Donald C., and Phyllis P. Mason
1984 "Upper echelons: The organization as a reflection of its top managers." Academy of Management Review, 2: 193–206.

Harrison, J. Richard, David L. Torres, and Sal Kukalis
1988 "The changing of the guard: Turnover and structural change in the top-management positions." Administrative Science Quarterly, 33: 211–232.

Herman, Edward S.
1981 Corporate Control, Corporate Power. New York: Cambridge University Press.

Hitt, Michael A., and Beverly B. Tyler
1991 "Strategic decision models: Integrating different perspectives." Strategic Management Journal, 12: 327–351.

Hosmer, David W., and Stanley Lemeshow
1989 Applied Logistic Regression. New York: Wiley.

Jackson, Susan E., Veronica K. Stone, and Eden B. Alvarez
1992 "Socialization amidst diversity: The impact of demographics on work team oldtimers and newcomers." In Barry M. Staw and L. L. Cummings (eds.), Research in Organizational Behavior, 15: 45–109. Greenwich, CT: JAI Press.

Jarrell, Gregg A.
1993 "An overview of the executive compensation debate." Journal of Applied Corporate Finance, 5: 76–82.

Jensen, Michael C., and William H. Meckling
1976 "Theory of the firm: Managerial behavior, agency costs, and ownership structure." Journal of Financial Economics, 3: 305–360.

Jensen, Michael C., and Kevin J. Murphy
1990 "Performance pay and top-management incentives." Journal of Political Economy, 98: 225–263.

Kanter, Rosabeth M.
1977 Men and Women of the Corporation. New York: Basic Books.

Kerr, Jeffrey L., and Leslie Kren
1992 "Effect of relative decision monitoring on chief executive officer compensation." Academy of Management Journal, 35: 370–397

Kosnik, Rita D.
1987 "Greenmail: A study of board performance in corporate governance." Administrative Science Quarterly, 32: 163–185.

Larcker, David F.
1983 "The association between performance plan adoption and corporate capital investment." Journal of Accounting and Economics, 5: 3–30.

Lorsch, Jay W., and Elaine MacIver
1989 Pawns or Potentates: The Reality of America's Corporate Boards. Boston: Harvard Business School Press.

Mace, Myles L.
1971 Directors: Myth and Reality. Boston: Harvard Business School Press.

Messick, David M., and Dianne M. Mackie
1989 "Intergroup relations." In Mark R. Rosenzweig and Lyman W. Porter (eds.), Annual Review of Psychology, 40: 45–81. Palo Alto, CA: Annual Reviews.

Michel, John G., and Donald C. Hambrick
1992 "Diversification posture and top management team characteristics." Academy of Management Journal, 35: 9–37.

Miles, Raymond E., and Charles C. Snow
1978 Organizational Strategy, Structure and Process. New York: McGraw-Hill.

Mizruchi, Mark S.
1983 "Who controls whom? An examination of the relation between management and boards of directors in large corporations." Academy of Management Review, 8: 426–435.

Mobley, William H.
1982 "Supervisor and employee race and sex effects on performance appraisals: A field study of adverse impact and generalizability." Academy of Management Journal, 25: 598–606.

Murray, Alan I.
1989 "Top management heterogeneity and firm performance." Strategic Management Journal, 10: 125–141.

Norman, Donald A.
1976 Memory and Attention. New York: Wiley.

O'Reilly, Charles A., III, David F. Caldwell, and William P. Barnett
1989 "Work group demography, social integration, and turnover." Administrative Science Quarterly, 34: 21–37.

Pfeffer, Jeffrey
1972 "Size and composition of corporate boards of directors." Administrative Science Quarterly, 17: 218–228.
1981 Power in Organizations. New York: Harper and Row.
1983 "Organizational demography." In L. L. Cummings and Barry M. Staw (eds.), Research in Organizational Behavior, 5: 299–357. Greenwich, CT: JAI Press.

Pinder, Craig C., and Patrick R. Pinto
1974 "Demographic correlates of managerial style." Personnel Psychology, 27: 257–270.

Pulakos, Elaine D., and Kenneth N. Wexley
1983 "The relationship among perceptual similarity, sex and performance ratings in manager subordinate dyads." Academy of Management Journal, 26: 129–139.

Rechner, Paula L., and Daniel R. Dalton
1991 "CEO duality and organizational performance: A longitudinal analysis." Strategic Management Journal, 12: 155–160.

Rhodes, Susan R.
1983 "Age-related differences in work attitudes and behavior: A review and conceptual analysis." Psychological Bulletin, 93: 328–367.

Sayrs, Lois W.
1989 Pooled Time Series Analysis. London: Sage.

Schroder, H. M., Michael J. Driver, and S. Streufert
1967 Human Information Processing: Individuals and Groups Functioning in Complex Social Situations. New York: Holt Rinehart and Winston.

Singh, Harbir, and Farid Harianto
1989 "Management board relationships, takeover risk, and the adoption of golden parachutes." Academy of Management Journal, 32: 7–24.

Stangor, Charles, Laure Lynch, Changming Duan, and Beth Glass
1992 "Categorization of individuals on the basis of multiple social features." Journal of Personality and Social Psychology, 62: 207–218.

Tajfel, Henri, and John C. Turner
1986 "The social identity theory in intergroup behavior." In S. Worchel and W. G. Austin (eds.), Psychology of Intergroup Relations: 7–24. Chicago: Nelson-Hall.

Taylor, Ronald N.
1975 "Age and experience as determinants of managerial information processing and decision-making performance." Academy of Management Journal, 18: 74–81.

Tsui, Anne S., Terri D. Egan, and Charles A. O'Reilly
1992 "Being different: Relational demography and organizational attachment." Administrative Science Quarterly, 37: 549–579.

Tsui, Anne S., and Charles A. O'Reilly
1989 "Beyond simple demographic effects: The importance of relational demography in superior-subordinate dyads." Academy of Management Journal, 32: 402–423.

Turner, John C.
1987 Rediscovering the Social Group: a Self-categorization Theory. New York: Basil Blackwell.

Useem, Michael
1984 The Inner Circle. Oxford: Oxford University Press.

Useem, Michael, and Jerome Karabel
1986 "Pathways to top corporate management." American Sociological Review, 51: 184–200.

Vance, Stanley C.
1983 Corporate Leadership: Boards of Directors and Strategy. New York: McGraw-Hill.

Vancil, Richard F.
1987 Passing the Baton: Managing the Process of CEO Succession. Boston: Harvard Business School Press.

Vroom, Victor H., and Bernd Pahl
1971 "Relationship between age and risk taking among managers." Journal of Applied Psychology, 55: 399–405.

Wade, James B., Charles A. O'Reilly, and Ike Chandratat
1990 "Golden parachutes: CEOs and the exercise of social influence." Administrative Science Quarterly, 35: 587–603.

Wagner, W. Gary, Jeffrey Pfeffer, and Charles A. O'Reilly, III
1984 "Organizational demography and turnover in top management groups." Administrative Science Quarterly, 29: 74–92.

Who Shall Govern?

Waller, Mary J., George P. Huber, and William H. Glick
1995 "Functional background as a determinant of executives' selective perception." Academy of Management Journal, vol. 38 (in press).

Walsh, James P.
1988 "Selectivity and selective perception: An investigation of managers' belief structures and information processing." Academy of Management Journal, 31: 873–895.

Walsh, James P., and James K. Seward
1990 "On the efficiency of internal and external corporate control mechanisms." Academy of Management Review, 15: 421–458.

Westphal, James, and Edward J. Zajac
1994 "Substance and symbolism in CEOs' long-term incentive plans." Administrative Science Quarterly, 39: 367–391.

Wexley, Kenneth N., and Wayne F. Nemeroff
1974 "The effects of racial prejudice, race of applicant, and biographical similarity on interviewer evaluations of job applicants." Journal of Social and Behavioral Science, 20: 66–78.

White, Halbert
1980 "A heteroskedasticity-consistent covariance matrix estimator and a direct test for heteroskedasticity." Econometrica, 48: 817–838.

Wiersema, Margarethe F., and Karen A. Bantel
1992 "Top management team demography and corporate strategic change." Academy of Management Journal, 35: 91–121.

Wiersema, Margarethe F., and Allan Bird
1993 "Organizational demography in Japanese firms: Group heterogeneity, individual dissimilarity, and top management team turnover." Academy of Management Journal, 36: 996–1026.

Zajac, Edward J.
1988 "Interlocking directorates as an interorganizational strategy: A test of critical assumptions." Academy of Management Journal, 31: 428–438.

1990 "CEO selection, succession, compensation and firm performance: A theoretical integration and empirical analysis." Strategic Management Journal, 11: 313–330.

Zajac, Edward J., and James D. Westphal
1995a "Explaining the explanations for CEO compensation: Substance and symbolism." Administrative Science Quarterly, vol. 40 (in press).
1995b "Who shall rule after a CEO succession? The likelihood and direction of changes in CEO characteristics." Working Paper, Northwestern University.

Zald, Mayer N.
1969 "The power and functions of boards of directors: A theoretical synthesis." American Journal of Sociology, 75: 97–111.

Zenger, Todd R., and Barbara S. Lawrence
1989 "Organizational demography: The differential effects of age and tenure distributions on technical communication." Academy of Management Journal, 32: 353–376.

APPENDIX

Logit Regression Analyses of New Director Characteristics (N = 113)*

	New Director Characteristics				
Independent variable	Operations background	Marketing/sales background	Age	Educational level	Insider/outsider status
1. CEO characteristic	.995***	1.493***	1.227***	1.981***	1.888***
	(.235)	(.263)	(.112)	(.139)	(.193)
2. Existing board member's characteristic	.675	1.313	.650*	.357	−.977
	(.361)	(1.178)	(.270)	(.365)	(.666)
Constant	1.948***	5.431***	.487	2.916***	2.244***
	(.151)	(.688)	(.299)	(.389)	(.307)
Chi-square†	56.12***	56.12***	96.68***	84.41***	82.98***

*$p \le .05$; **$p \le .01$; ***$p \le .001$.
* Standard errors are in parentheses.
† The variance-covariance matrix was computed using Huber's correction procedure (White, 1980). Chi-square values for functional background measures stem from one multinomial logit analysis (see analysis section).

[6]

Director Reputation, CEO-Board Power, and the Dynamics of Board Interlocks

Edward J. Zajac
Northwestern University
James D. Westphal
The University of Texas at Austin

This study advances research on CEO-board relationships, interlocking directorates, and director reputation by examining how contests for intraorganizational power can affect interorganizational ties. We propose that powerful top managers seek to maintain their control by selecting and retaining board members with experience on other, passive boards and excluding individuals with experience on more active boards. We also propose that powerful boards similarly seek to maintain their control by favoring directors with a reputation for more actively monitoring management and avoiding directors with experience on passive boards. Hypotheses are tested longitudinally using CEO-board data taken from 491 of the largest U.S. corporations over a recent seven-year period. The findings suggest that variation in CEO-board power relationships across organizations has contributed to a segmentation of the corporate director network. We discuss how our perspective can reconcile contrary views and debates on whether increased board control has diffused across large U.S. corporations.•

Have boards of directors of large U.S. corporations recently moved toward greater control of top managers? Recent discussions of corporate governance practices in the U.S. seem to vary widely in their answer to this question. For every research study or business press editorial pointing toward increasingly active boards, there appears to be a corresponding study or editorial arguing the opposite (Lorsch and MacIver, 1989; Davis, 1991; *Fortune,* 1993; *Wall Street Journal,* 1995a). The theoretical explanations used to support one or the other perspective range from a belief that public discourse and investor pressures have led to the diffusion of greater board independence across U.S. corporations (Useem, 1992; *Wall Street Journal,* 1995b) to the managerialist belief that managerial entrenchment and the cooptation of boards by powerful chief executive officers (CEOs) remain as strong as ever (Pfeffer, 1992; *Wall Street Journal,* 1995c).

Rather than debate the relative merits of such sweeping and rather one-sided perspectives on corporate governance, we suggest instead that a theory is needed that can simultaneously explain the coexistence and persistence of both board-controlled and CEO-controlled firms. We develop and test a theory that can explain such variation, based on an analysis of director appointments, whereby powerful actors in the CEO-board relationship affect the diffusion of board independence through the selection and retention of directors whose prior directorship experiences suggest differential sympathy for their interests. For instance, we propose that more powerful CEOs will avoid director candidates who have participated as directors in increasing the level of board monitoring and control over CEOs on other boards, while favoring new director candidates with prior directorship experience in protecting or bolstering CEO control.

With few exceptions (e.g., Mizruchi and Stearns, 1988; Davis, 1993), much of the corporate governance literature

0001-8392/96/4103-0507/$1.00.

•

Both authors contributed equally to the paper. We are grateful to Jerry Davis, Ranjay Gulati, Paul Hirsch, Willie Ocasio, Toby Stuart, Brian Uzzi, and seminar participants at Carnegie Mellon University, the Harvard Business School, and UCLA for comments and suggestions on earlier versions of this paper. The paper has also benefited from the helpful comments of Mark Mizruchi and the anonymous reviewers for *ASQ,* as well as the editorial assistance of Linda Johanson.

has taken board composition as a given, seeking to examine its implications rather than its determinants, but three distinct streams of research on boards could be invoked to examine the selection or retention of individual directors. One stream of research in organization behavior has typically examined the extent to which boards are a passive tool of management interests (Vance, 1968; Mace, 1971; Herman, 1981). Typical for this line of inquiry is examining how specific dimensions of board structure (e.g., the proportion of outside directors or the separation of CEO and board chair roles) can affect relative power and decision-making tendencies in the CEO-board relationship and thus affect the allegiance of board members to management's or shareholders' interests (Kosnik, 1987; Finkelstein and Hambrick, 1989; Wade, O'Reilly, and Chandratat, 1990; Mallette and Fowler, 1992). This line of research would suggest that the composition of boards will be determined largely by the attempts of powerful individual CEOs to coopt existing directors and influence the selection and retention of directors who are more likely to be sympathetic to that particular CEO's interests (Westphal and Zajac, 1995).

A second stream of research draws largely from organizational sociology and is concerned with determining the macro-structure of boards, i.e., the network of interlocking directorates (Ornstein, 1980), and its implications, such as the diffusion of particular organizational practices. From this perspective, internal power and influence dynamics between CEOs and boards are less relevant than how interlocking directorates may reflect interorganizational dependencies (Pfeffer and Salancik, 1978; Pennings, 1980; Zajac, 1988) or unity among members of the elite class (Koenig and Gogel, 1981; Mizruchi, 1982; Useem, 1982). Thus the best predictor of the specific composition of boards of directors is likely to reflect either interorganizational dependencies or social ties among members of the elite class. Empirical studies examining whether "broken" interlocks between resource-interdependent firms are reconstituted reflect an attempt to address such issues (Ornstein, 1980; Palmer, 1983; Palmer, Friedland, and Singh, 1986; Stearns and Mizruchi, 1986).

A third perspective on corporate governance that can address the question of director appointments is grounded in the agency conception of corporate boards as a generally effective, if imperfect control mechanism serving to protect shareholder interests (Fama, 1980). From this financial economics perspective, an efficient labor market for corporate directors acts as a motivating and disciplining device (Fama and Jensen, 1983). Directors seek to develop and maintain a favorable reputation as active representatives of shareholder welfare, thus enhancing their human capital on the boards on which they sit and increasing their attractiveness as candidates for board appointments at other firms.

While each of these largely nonoverlapping streams of research contributes to some understanding of changing board appointments, considering both the intraorganizational and interorganizational dimensions of board membership together would provide additional insights. We develop such a theoretical framework in this study, linking both intra- and interorganizational dynamics involving CEOs and boards of directors. This study contributes to the literature on CEO-board relationships by showing how director experience on other boards can affect decision making (i.e., director selection and retention) on a given focal board. It contributes to the literature on interlocking directorates by proposing and testing a new perspective on the formation and dissolution of board interlock ties that differs from the interorganizational resource dependence and intraclass unity approaches described above. While we share the view of intraclass theorists that interlocks can serve to "guide managerial behavior, socialize new directors into [the capitalist class] culture, and socially control deviant behavior" (Palmer, 1983: 42), we suggest that interlocks serve these functions for distinct and competing subcultures within the larger class of business elites. Finally, it contributes to the literature on director reputation by suggesting that while a director's prior experience can affect subsequent board appointments, such appointments may reflect a political rather than an economic rationality, in which both active *and* passive board members can thrive in a labor market for directors that is segmented by orientation toward management.

We test our perspective using longitudinal data taken from hundreds of large U.S. corporations over a recent seven-year period. Some research has suggested that this period coincides with the spread of increased board activism and shareholder orientation (Useem, 1992; Davis and Thompson, 1994; Zajac and Westphal, 1995) and an attendant increase in conflict between management and shareholder interests. In this context, a director's reputation for activism or passivity, along with the relative power of CEOs and boards, should be particularly relevant in influencing director selection and retention and thus the dynamics of board interlock formation and dissolution during this period.

INTERORGANIZATIONAL TIES AND INTRAORGANIZATIONAL POWER

Although researchers have drawn on a variety of theoretical perspectives to explain the diffusion of organizational phenomena through interlock network ties, recent discussions have tended to emphasize the role of such ties in spreading knowledge and awareness about specific organizational changes. As articulated by Galaskiewicz and Wasserman (1989: 456), network ties between boundary-spanning personnel, including board members, "act as a conduit to disseminate ideas and innovations." Empirical support for this argument has been found in studies investigating the likelihood of adopting poison pills (Davis, 1991), making specific kinds of corporate acquisitions (Haunschild, 1993), adopting the multidivisional form (Palmer, Jennings, and Zhou, 1993), or making campaign contributions to particular political candidates (Mizruchi, 1992).

On a deeper level, interlock ties may help spread more fundamental belief systems about corporate strategy, organizational structure, or the board's role in the organization, providing the foundation for a variety of organizational changes. Empirical research investigating the development of group norms has shown how the prior experiences of individual group members in similar contexts can provide the foundation for norms of the focal group (Bettenhausen and Murnighan, 1985). Thus board members who have participated in various strategic or structural changes on other boards bring those beliefs and the various, more specific scripts associated with them to the focal board, ultimately "negotiating" or advocating changes in board norms consistent with their beliefs (Bettenhausen and Murnighan, 1985). While governance scholars have noted the potential role of socialization experiences in affecting board decision making (Alderfer, 1986), such processes are frequently assumed to operate only within the focal board. Given that a large portion of corporate directors hold multiple board seats, however, and have held other directorships in the past (Useem, 1984; Mizruchi, 1992), the collective influence of directors' experiences on other boards may frequently outweigh the effect of socialization experiences on the focal board. Thus directors who have participated in structural changes that increase board control over management may help spread increased board control to the other boards on which they sit, either by raising awareness about specific changes or by moving board norms toward a behavioral model that favors active monitoring and oversight on behalf of shareholders. In effect, by virtue of their prior experiences, such directors "come to a normative understanding" that the role of corporate director requires monitoring and controlling management decision making, prompting them to initiate and encourage changes consistent with such behavior where they serve as outside director (Burt, 1987: 1289; Ocasio, 1996). Conversely, directors who have participated in structural changes that protect or enhance the CEO's control over the board may come to believe that outside directors should defer to the CEO's judgment on strategic issues, leading them to help maintain board norms that favor director passivity and loyalty to the CEO.

Director Experience and Change in Board Interlocks

Given that directors' relative experience with increased board control at other companies can affect their willingness to abide CEO control at the focal firm, powerful CEOs may seek to sustain CEO control by (1) avoiding director candidates who have participated in greater board control over management and (2) selecting, instead, directors whose experience on other boards reflects board passivity toward management. Conversely, powerful boards can perpetuate or increase their control over management by (1) avoiding directors who have been socialized into a passive board role, as indicated by their participation in allowing greater CEO control on other boards and (2) appointing individuals with prior experience in asserting board control. Moreover, individual board members should prefer activist new directors because, as Alderfer (1986) suggested, boards require unanimity and a sense of common purpose to control management decision making effectively, just as all groups require unanimity and cohesion to manage actors in their environment (Gladstein, 1984). Through selection and retention, then, powerful actors in the CEO-board relationship can "manage" board interlocks so as to reinforce or increase their control.

This argument is consistent more generally with the theoretical and empirical literature on power in organizations, which cites control over employee selection as an efficient means of building political coalitions (Pfeffer, 1981: 163; 1992). Managers can often build or protect their power bases more easily and cheaply by hiring or promoting individuals likely to support their personal, political interests than by trading favors with existing colleagues (Pfeffer, 1981). Drawing on this literature, several governance scholars have suggested that CEO control over the director selection process represents an important source of managerial entrenchment (Mace, 1971; Kosnik, 1987; Fredrickson, Hambrick, and Baumrin, 1988; Wade, O'Reilly, and Chandratat, 1990). For instance, Lorsch and MacIver (1989) and Finkelstein and Hambrick (1989: 124) noted that CEOs can "coopt" the board by favoring the appointment of "sympathetic" new directors. Although this process has typically been associated with CEO behavior, Westphal and Zajac (1995: 78) suggested that this process also applies to boards seeking to increase their monitoring and control by appointing new directors who are sympathetic to the orientation of existing directors. In effect, we propose that directors' experiences on other boards may furnish a relatively direct indicator of their relative "sympathy" toward either management or shareholder interests, thus providing a basis for director selection and retention.

An implication of this line of reasoning is that changes in relative control by the CEO or board may spread through the network of interlocking directorates in ways that have not been specified in prior research. We propose here that the diffusion of specific governance changes will depend on whether powerful actors in CEO-board relationships seek to deflect or encourage such diffusion. For example, the diffusion of a governance change that diminishes CEO control may be deflected by powerful CEOs by avoiding or eliminating interlock ties with prior "adopters." Similarly, powerful CEOs may also steer the diffusion of changes that protect or increase their control over the board by adding ties to prior adopters of such changes. As one director cited in Lorsch and MacIver (1989: 77) suggested, "The CEO shapes the board very much the way he wants, not only bringing people in, but also getting people he doesn't like off the board." Similarly, directors who sit on powerful boards are likely to prefer new director candidates who share their belief in active boards. As another director cited in Lorsch and MacIver (1989: 5) noted, "Directors today don't want colleagues like the old ones who rubber-stamped management's decisions."

In this way, contests for intraorganizational power can affect interorganizational ties: The actions of powerful corporate leaders seeking to influence the selection and retention of board members generate a "segmented" interlock network (Kaufman, 1986), with relatively few ties between active and passive boards and relatively dense ties between boards with similar power structures. Here, we examine the dynamic process by which this segmentation is maintained. We propose that a director's prior experiences on boards that have made changes that increase or decrease board control over management provide a strong indication of that director's likely subsequent behavior on other boards, affecting the relative attractiveness of that director in the following ways:

Proposition 1a: Directors who sit on boards that have recently moved to *increase* board control over management will have (1) fewer subsequent appointments to boards having low control and (2) more subsequent appointments to boards having high control.

Proposition 1b: Directors who sit on boards that have recently moved to *decrease* board control over management will have (1) more subsequent appointments to boards having low control and (2) fewer subsequent appointments to boards having high control.

In the remainder of this section, we develop specific testable hypotheses corresponding to the propositions offered above. While it is difficult to observe and measure directly the level of board control over management in large corporations, a number of indicators have been used in prior governance research to capture such differences across organizations. We consider five different indicators in this study: changes in the ratio of outside to inside directors, in board leadership structure, in diversification, in total compensation, and in compensation contingency. The first two are measures of board structure that assess board control over management, and the latter three are measures of strategy or policy that reflect attention to shareholder interests or managerial interests. Given that all five variables are visible to top managers and directors at other companies, they can provide a more salient basis for new director selection than less visible measures of actual board decision-making processes.

Change in the outsider ratio. Perhaps the most commonly used indicator of board independence from management is the ratio of outside to total directors. Governance researchers and champions of board reform have long contended that nonemployee or "outside" directors are better positioned to control management decision making than insiders (Fama and Jensen, 1983). As subordinates to the CEO, inside directors may be reluctant to challenge or question the CEO's position on an issue in board meetings, even when shareholder interests appear to be threatened (Fredrickson, Hambrick, and Baumrin, 1988; Hoskisson, Johnson, and Moesel, 1994). Outsiders should also be better able than insiders to judge managerial performance impartially, raising the likelihood that a poorly performing CEO will be dismissed (Boeker, 1992). Thus, increases in the ratio of outside to inside directors can be considered indicative of increased board control over management, while decreases in this measure should indicate greater board passivity in monitoring management decision making:[1]

Hypothesis 1a: Directors who sit on boards that have recently increased the ratio of outside to inside directors will have fewer subsequent appointments to boards having low control and more subsequent appointments to boards having high control.

1 For each of the hypotheses developed below, the two components of the hypothesis are related but distinct, such that a director can experience a change in appointments at low-control boards but not experience any change in appointments at high-control boards.

Hypothesis 1b: Directors who sit on boards that have recently decreased the ratio of outside to inside directors will have more subsequent appointments to boards having low control and fewer subsequent appointments to boards having high control.

Change in board leadership structure. It is also commonly suggested by organizational scholars and members of the business press that separating the CEO and board chair positions (i.e., allocating each position to separate individuals) should greatly increase the board's capacity to control management decision making (Vance, 1983; Harrison, Torres, and Kukalis, 1988; Crystal, 1991; Beatty and Zajac, 1994; Finkelstein and D'Aveni, 1994). Given that the board chair is nominally responsible for evaluating CEO decisions, allocating both roles to the same individual presents a conflict of interest (Kesner and Johnson, 1990; Zajac and Westphal, 1996). Moreover, board meetings represent the primary forum for directors to challenge CEOs' proposals (Lorsch and MacIver, 1989). By dictating an agenda that offers a limited opportunity for open debate, a CEO serving as board chair can easily minimize the level of board monitoring behavior (Demb and Neubauer, 1992). Conversely, an independent chairperson is better able to control management on behalf of shareholders. Thus, we hypothesize:

Hypothesis 2a: Directors who sit on boards that have recently separated the CEO and board chair positions will have fewer subsequent appointments to boards having low control and more subsequent appointments to boards having high control.

Hypothesis 2b: Directors who sit on boards that have recently combined the CEO and board chair positions will have more subsequent appointments to boards having low control and fewer subsequent appointments to boards having high control.

Change in corporate diversification. According to managerialist and agency researchers, top managers have personal incentives to pursue diversification beyond the level at which shareholder wealth is maximized (Hill and Snell, 1988; Jensen, 1988; Baysinger and Hoskisson, 1990). From the managerialist perspective, top managers may diversify into largely unrelated businesses to increase their personal power, compensation, and status (Marris, 1964). Agency theorists emphasize the link between diversification and reducing managerial risk (Amihud and Lev, 1981). By diversifying into unrelated businesses, managers can stabilize their investment portfolios while also reducing their employment risk. Shareholders should favor lower levels of diversification, because they can diversify their investment portfolios more easily than CEOs can diversify their employment. Thus, as nominal representatives of shareholder interests, relatively powerful boards of directors should resist managerial preferences for excessive corporate diversification (Hoskisson, Johnson, and Moesel, 1994). Conversely, as Jensen (1988) has suggested, board passivity may be partly responsible for inefficient diversification levels. Therefore, reduced corporate diversification provides an indication of greater shareholder representation and lower managerial control over board monitoring activity. Participation on boards that have overseen reduced corporate diversification would send a negative signal in the market for directors at CEO-dominated boards and a positive signal at companies with more active boards:

Hypothesis 3a: Directors who sit on boards that have recently decreased corporate diversification will have fewer subsequent appointments to boards having low control and more subsequent appointments to boards having high control.

Hypothesis 3b: Directors who sit on boards that have recently increased corporate diversification will have more subsequent appointments to boards having low control and fewer subsequent appointments to boards having high control.

Change in total compensation. The managerial and academic literatures on corporate governance have long attributed high levels of CEO compensation to board passivity and CEO entrenchment. Several studies have reported evidence that board independence from the top management is associated with smaller increases in CEO compensation (Finkelstein and Hambrick, 1989; Main, O'Reilly, and Wade, 1995; Westphal and Zajac, 1995). Changes in CEO compensation at large companies are well publicized and highly visible to managers and directors at other boards and thus may provide a salient indicator of the relative independence of the board from management. Participation on boards that have reduced the level of CEO compensation would therefore send a negative signal in the market for directors at CEO-dominated boards and a positive signal among companies with more active boards:

Hypothesis 4a: Directors who sit on boards that have recently decreased total compensation will have fewer subsequent appointments to boards having low control and more subsequent appointments to boards having high control.

Hypothesis 4b: Directors who sit on boards that have recently increased total compensation will have more subsequent appointments to boards having low control and fewer subsequent appointments to boards having high control.

Change in compensation contingency. Contingent compensation contracts include a variety of different incentive plans that link management pay to firm performance, thus aligning the interests of CEOs with the preferences of shareholders (Jensen and Meckling, 1976). According to agency theorists, long-term incentives such as stock options, performance shares, or restricted stock are a primary mechanism by which corporate boards protect shareholder interests against management excesses (Kerr and Kren, 1992; Gibbs, 1993; Beatty and Zajac 1994), and both economic and behavioral literatures on executive compensation suggest that, in general, CEOs should prefer less long-term incentive compensation in their pay packages. From a normative agency theory perspective, CEOs (as risk-averse agents) prefer less risk in their compensation contracts (Harris and Raviv, 1979). By making compensation contingent on future firm performance, long-term incentives add uncertainty to a CEO's compensation. Some empirical evidence suggests that passive boards make only limited use of long-term incentive compensation in designing CEO compensation contracts (Tosi and Gomez-Mejia, 1989), while increased board independence from management is typically followed by higher levels of contingent compensation (Westphal and Zajac, 1995). Membership on boards that have increased CEO compensation contingency should therefore decrease an individual's marketability among CEO-dominated boards, while increasing his or her attractiveness to relatively active boards:

Hypothesis 5a: Directors who sit on boards that have recently increased CEO compensation contingency will have fewer subsequent appointments to boards having low control and more subsequent appointments to boards having high control.

Hypothesis 5b: Directors who sit on boards that have recently decreased CEO compensation contingency will have more subsequent appointments to boards having low control and fewer subsequent appointments to boards having high control.

METHOD

Sample and Data Collection

The population for this study included top managers of the largest U.S. industrial and service firms, as listed in the 1986 *Forbes* and *Fortune* 500 indexes. We restricted our attention in this study to directors who were also CEOs, because recent evidence shows that CEO-directors play a pivotal role (relative to other directors) in determining the extent to which a board develops a passive or active orientation (Lorsch and MacIver, 1989: 18; Westphal and Zajac, 1997). The *Forbes* 500 uses multiple lists whose overlap depends on the specific size measure used; we included top managers of those firms that qualified according to two or more size measures. Directors were excluded from the final sample if complete diversification and compensation data were unavailable. This procedure yielded a final sample of 491 directors. *T*-tests revealed no significant differences between this sample and the larger population across any of the director, board, or firm attributes for which data were available on the larger population (i.e., director age, compensation level, board composition or leadership structure at the director's home company, or profitability or size—measured as log of sales—of the director's home company).

Data were collected for the years 1985 to 1992, inclusive. We obtained data on interlock ties, board structure, and CEO and outside director characteristics from the *Dun and Bradstreet Reference Book of Corporate Management, Standard & Poor's Register of Corporations, Directors, and Executives,* and *Who's Who in Finance and Industry;* compensation data came from proxy statements. Finally, we obtained diversification data from Standard & Poor's COMPUSTAT *Business Segment Tapes* and *Compact Disclosure;* size and performance data were provided by COMPUSTAT and the Center for Research in Security Prices (CRSP).

Independent Variables

We measured participation in increased board control across five different indicators. For each indicator, we first calculated the measure for each board in the sample in each year and then created measures of participation in increased board control for each year by comparing—for all boards on which the focal individual sits—the value of the given measure in year t with the value in year $t - 1$. Thus, for example, we first measured the outsider ratio in each year as the number of nonemployee directors divided by the total number of board members. We then calculated *participation in increased outsider ratio* as the number of boards on which the focal individual sits that increased the ratio of outside to inside directors from year $t - 1$ to year t. Board leadership structure was measured dichotomously, coded as 1 if the CEO and board chair positions are separate in a given year, and 0 otherwise. To measure *participation in CEO/board chair separation,* we calculated the number of boards on which the focal individual sits with combined CEO-board chair position in year $t - 1$ and separated CEO-board chair positions in year t.

In some cases, as in the outsider ratio, it was also possible to measure participation in increased board control as the *average* change across all boards on which the individual serves as director. We chose to treat each change as a dichotomous event for theoretical and empirical reasons. Theoretically, for most of the five measures, any change should represent a distinctive and visible event to managers and directors on other boards (exceptions are discussed further below). Empirically, the size of change is very restricted for several of our independent variables, e.g., boards rarely increase the outsider ratio by adding more than two individuals to the board, so that the magnitude of such increases is very similar across cases (Mizruchi and Stearns, 1988). Thus the count variables based on dichotomous change measures would be highly correlated with variables indicating the average, continuous change. Nevertheless, to ensure that our results did not hinge on one particular specification, we also conducted a separate analysis measuring participation as the average change in the relevant measure across all boards on which the individual serves as director (i.e., for those changes that can be measured continuously). The results were very similar to those reported below, suggesting that our findings do not depend on one particular specification of the independent variables.

To measure participation in reduced diversification, we used Palepu's (1985) entropy measure. This measure takes into account the number of segments in which a firm operates and weights each segment according to its contribution to total sales. It is defined as follows:

$$\sum_{i=1}^{n} P_i * \ln(1/P_i),$$

where P is the sales (dollar value) attributed to segment i and $\ln(1/P_i)$ is the weight for each segment i, or the logarithm of the inverse of its sales. We calculated reduced diversification as a decrease in the entropy measure exceeding one standard deviation, to capture relatively significant change and exclude change that reflects random alterations in segment sales levels (Amit and Livnat, 1988). The results were substantively similar using alternative thresholds, such as a decrease of one-half of one standard deviation. The standard deviation is based on change in diversification from year $t - 1$ to year t. *Participation in reduced diversification* was then measured as the number of firms where the focal individual serves as director that decreased diversification from the prior year to the current year.

To assess participation in increased compensation contingency, we first calculated contingency for each year as the total value of long-term incentive grants divided by total direct compensation. Short-term bonuses were not included in this measure because they are notoriously susceptible to manipulation (Healy, 1985), but stock options were included. Although it is possible for companies to "swap" higher-priced options for lower-priced options, thus diluting their incentive effect, this practice is extremely rare. We valued stock options using the Black-Scholes (1973) method, which estimates option value based on the historical price volatility of the underlying security. Other grants (e.g., restricted stock, performance shares, etc.) were valued according to the market price at date of grant (Crystal, 1984). All compensation values were adjusted for inflation to represent 1990 constant dollars using the Consumer Price Index. This approach to measuring compensation contingency is commonly used by compensation consultants (e.g., Crystal, 1984; Ellig, 1984).

By contrast, the simple correlation between CEO pay and firm performance is a very problematic measure of compensation contingency. The most serious problem is how to treat long-term incentives in such a measure. The value of long-term incentive grants (e.g., stock options, which confer the right to buy shares of common stock in the future) depends on *future* performance, while salary, bonus, and other forms of compensation depend on *prior* performance. Thus total compensation could not be correlated with performance over a single period. Researchers have sometimes attempted to avoid this problem by excluding long-term incentives from their measures of compensation. This approach is problematic in assessing the correlation between pay and performance, however, because long-term incentive compensation is the primary mechanism that companies use to make pay contingent on performance (cf., Ellig, 1984; Tosi and Gomez-Mejia, 1989; Kerr and Kren, 1992; Westphal and Zajac, 1995; Seward and Walsh, 1996).

We calculated *participation in greater CEO compensation contingency* as the number of firms where the focal individual serves as director that increased compensation contingency from the prior year to the current year. *Participation in reduced total CEO compensation* was calculated as the number of firms where the focal individual serves as director that reduced CEO total direct compensation from the prior year to the current year.

Finally, we created five parallel independent measures gauging participation in *reduced* board independence: *participation in decreased outsider ratio; participation in CEO/board chair combination; participation in increased diversification; participation in reduced compensation contingency;* and *participation in increased total compensation.* Increased total compensation does not exactly parallel decreased total compensation. Rather, we measured it as a positive change in the CEO's total direct compensation exceeding one standard deviation. This enables us to capture relatively distinctive and noticeable changes, since a large portion of companies in the sample increased total compensation in any given year. As with the diversification variables, the results were robust to alternative change thresholds, such as a positive change of one-half of one standard deviation.

Several control variables were included in the analyses. First, an individual's reputation or attractiveness in the director labor market may depend on the performance of companies where he or she has served as director (Fama, 1980). Accordingly, we included a control variable indicating the average profitability of firms at which the focal individual served as outside director in the prior year. We measured profitability as *return on assets,* industry-adjusted at the two-digit Standard Industry Classification (SIC) code level. From a human capital perspective (Becker, 1975), top managers' compensation at their home company may also indicate their worth as a corporate leader and, by extension, their value as an outside director. Alternatively, the level of a top manager's compensation could be viewed as reflecting the degree of board control at that individual's home company, thus providing another indicator of the individual's personal experience with greater or lesser board control. Thus we included the director's total direct compensation (*total compensation*) as CEO in his or her home company as a control variable in all models. This measure includes salary, short-term bonus, and the total value of long-term incentive grants.

Furthermore, because an individual's *age* might be taken as an indication of his or her likely openness to new ideas about board independence and control, we also controlled for age in all models. In addition, the total number of board appointments held by an individual could affect subsequent appointments in several ways. The total number of appointments a person holds might independently affect his or her prestige in the director labor market (Davis, 1993), but workload limitations may prompt CEOs with many appointments to decline further invitations. Accordingly, we controlled for the total number of directorships held in the prior year (*number of prior appointments*). Finally, we also controlled for director participation in CEO succession events (*participation in succession*) on other boards. Although Boeker (1992) suggested that succession is less indicative of board control than outright dismissal, which is more difficult for individuals outside the organization to detect, participation in succession may be related to some of the other indicators of board control used in this study (Harrison, Torres, and Kukulis, 1988) and thus is included as a control variable in all models. This variable is defined as the number of firms at which the focal individual serves as director that experienced CEO succession within the prior year.

Dependent Variables

Analyzing change in appointments to boards with high or low control over management required defining and identifying high- and low-control boards. We addressed this by developing an overall measure capturing the extent to which a firm's board displays a relatively enduring orientation toward board control (high control) or board passivity (low control). We began by standardizing the five indicators of board control discussed above and summing these five measures together for each board in the sample. This measure was calculated as the average value over a moving three-year period (i.e., year $t - 2$ to year t) to avoid measurement error that would otherwise arise from temporary fluctuations in relative control. We then distinguished between high- and low-control boards by taking the median split for this measure, separately for each year. Using this information, we constructed two dependent measures: *Additions/subtractions in appointments to boards with low control over management* and *Additions/ subtractions in appointments to boards with high control over management.*

We developed separate measures for additions and subtractions in appointments to examine the robustness of our results in predicting losses, as well as gains, in subsequent appointments and thus were able to assess director selection and retention, respectively. In creating these variables, we first calculated an overall change measure in each year as the number of appointments to boards with low or high control in year $t + 2$ minus the number of appointments to boards with low or high control in year t. We measured change in board appointments over a multiyear interval because employment contracts for directors limit the number of openings that are available in any given year. From the two overall change measures we then created four count variables indicating the net increase or decrease in appointments to low- or high-control boards over the two-year period. Table 1 provides the means, standard deviations, and bivariate correlations for all data pooled.

Analysis

We used poisson regression analysis to assess change in board appointments (Maddala, 1983). This technique is suitable for estimating models predicting the number of discrete occurrences (i.e., counts) of some event, in this case, additions or subtractions in board appointments. Separate models were created to analyze change in appointments to boards with high control or low control over management. The individual models analyze the effect that a board member's prior participation (from year $t - 1$ to year t) in each of the five governance-related changes in board structure and strategy or policy decisions has on subsequent additions or subtractions (from year t to year $t + 2$) in appointments to boards with high- or low-control orientations. All control variables were lagged by one year. We observed relationships over five time periods, yielding 2,455 CEO-years of data.

Table 1

Descriptive Statistics and Pearson Correlation Coefficients

Variables	Mean	S.D.	1a	1b	1c	1d
1. Participation in:						
a. Increased outsider ratio	.308	.550				
b. CEO/board chair separation	.206	.449	.15			
c. Reduced diversification	.176	.435	.06	.09		
d. Greater compensation contingency	.439	.611	.19	.16	.05	
e. Reduced total compensation	.173	.422	.21	.27	.19	.28
2. Participation in:						
a. Decreased outsider ratio	.173	.454	−.22	−.18	−.19	−.13
b. CEO/board chair combination	.100	.352	−.23	−.16	−.06	−.08
c. Increased diversification	.137	.413	−.09	−.12	−.18	−.06
d. Reduced compensation contingency	.092	.332	−.20	−.17	−.19	−.20
e. Greater total compensation	.091	.321	−.14	−.15	−.05	−.26
3. Average return on assets	.001	.059	−.09	.15	.06	.07
4. Total compensation (in millions)	1.875	2.218	−.11	−.17	−.08	−.13
5. Age	58.519	5.680	−.18	−.05	−.12	−.10
6. Number of prior appointments	4.388	3.212	.08	.11	.12	.07
7. Change in appointments to boards with high control						
a. Subtractions	.746	.767	−.15	−.27	−.23	−.16
b. Additions	1.094	.940	.14	.21	.25	.26
8. Change in appointments to boards with low control						
a. Subtractions	.873	.777	.27	.32	.18	.21
b. Additions	.944	.947	−.25	−.26	−.15	−.23

We also conducted a series of separate analyses using two other models: a generalized least squares (GLS) model and a negative binomial model. The results were substantively consistent with the results of poisson regression analysis reported below (i.e., the tests of statistical significance supported the same set of hypotheses).

RESULTS

Tables 2 and 3 report the results of poisson regression analysis of change in board appointments. The models in Table 2 predict change in appointments to boards with low control over management, while the models in Table 3 predict change in appointments to boards with high board control. As noted earlier, we provide two models in each table to reflect the fact that while our hypotheses apply to change in appointments, we can analyze such changes separately in terms of additions or subtractions to further assess the robustness of the findings. Hypothesis 1a, for example, predicted that participation in increasing the proportion of outside directors would lead to a decrease in appointments to boards with low control over management and an increase in appointments to boards with high control over management. The findings, as shown in Table 2, support this hypothesis: Participating in increasing the outsider ratio is negatively related to subsequent appointments to boards with low control over management. This holds true both in terms of fewer additions to new boards and more subtractions from current boards. The expected converse pattern of results emerged in models predicting appointments to boards with high control over management. The results in Table 3 show that participation in increasing the outsider ratio is positively associated with subsequent appointments to boards with high control over management (both in terms of more additions and fewer subtractions).

Board Interlocks

Table 1 (*continued*)

1e	2a	2b	2c	2d	2e	3	4	5	6	7a	7b	8a
−.30												
−.11	.17											
.01	.11	.13										
−.25	.27	.36	.20									
−.33	.09	.21	.19	.34								
−.12	−.08	−.08	.06	.09	−.12							
−.19	.02	.09	.11	.09	.21	.08						
−.14	.10	.15	.09	.10	.08	.07	−.03					
.05	.14	.06	.14	.10	.09	−.01	.07	.19				
−.07	.24	.29	.05	.22	.11	−.15	.16	.20	−.13			
.08	−.26	−.32	−.04	−.23	−.15	.13	−.09	−.19	.10	−.34		
.22	−.16	−.31	−.07	−.17	−.08	.06	−.20	−.17	−.10	−.38	.21	
−.18	.18	.32	.08	.15	.11	−.05	.18	.12	.14	.33	−.25	−.37

Table 2

Poisson Regression Models of Change in Appointments to Boards with Low Control over Management (*N* = 2455)[a]

Independent Variables	Change in Appointments: Subtractions	Additions
1. Participation in:		
a. Increased outsider ratio	.408 (.100)***	−.344 (.118)**
b. CEO/board chair separation	.531 (.157)***	−.417 (.174)**
c. Reduced diversification	.312 (.138)*	−.374 (.163)*
d. Greater compensation contingency	.270 (.102)**	−.408 (.151)**
e. Reduced total compensation	.389 (.162)**	−.450 (.226)*
2. Participation in:		
a. Decreased outsider ratio	−.170 (.086)*	.206 (.072)**
b. CEO/board chair combination	−.594 (.135)***	.393 (.142)***
c. Increased diversification	−.077 (.097)	.040 (.089)
d. Reduced compensation contingency	−.227 (.095)**	.208 (.081)**
e. Greater total compensation	−.256 (.140)	.280 (.154)
3. Average return on assets	.572 (.594)	−.524 (.612)
4. Total compensation	−.00002 (.00001)*	.00003 (.00001)**
5. Age	−.015 (.007)*	.010 (.005)*
6. Number of prior appointments	−.021 (.017)	.016 (.014)
7. Participation in succession	.195 (.389)	−.169 (.163)**
Constant	.273 (.175)	.755 (.312)**
Chi square	465.69***	488.18***

* $p \le .05$; ** $p \le .01$; *** $p \le .001$; *t*-tests are one-tailed for hypothesized effects, two-tailed for control variables.
[a] Unstandardized coefficients are reported. Standard errors are in parentheses.

Hypothesis 1b predicted opposite consequences from participating in decreasing outsider ratios as an outside director. Consistent with this hypothesis, the results indicate that experience with decreasing the outsider ratio is positively associated with subsequent appointments to low-control boards (more additions and fewer subtractions) and negatively associated with subsequent appointments to high-control boards (fewer additions and more subtractions). Taken together, the tests of hypotheses 1a and 1b are quite robust in suggesting that a director's prior experiences with a governance change involving altering the outsider ratio can result in predictable changes in subsequent appointments.

Table 3

Poisson Regression Models of Change in Appointments to Boards with High Control over Management (N = 2455)*

Independent Variables	Change in Appointments: Subtractions	Additions
1. Participation in:		
a. Increased outsider ratio	−.237 (.111)•	.214 (.106)•
b. CEO/board chair separation	−.527 (.157)•••	.363 (.174)•
c. Reduced diversification	−.370 (.139)••	.284 (.110)••
d. Greater compensation contingency	−.291 (.149)•	.425 (.112)•••
e. Reduced total compensation	−.179 (.171)	.329 (.211)
2. Participation in:		
a. Decreased outsider ratio	.478 (.073)•••	−.330 (.106)•••
b. CEO/board chair combination	.329 (.082)•••	−.641 (.137)•••
c. Increased diversification	.043 (.094)	−.035 (.113)
d. Reduced compensation contingency	.226 (.093)••	−.362 (.135)••
e. Greater total compensation	.203 (.182)	−.430 (.187)•
3. Average return on assets	−1.148 (.581)	1.169 (.621)
4. Total compensation	.00002 (.00001)•	−.00002 (.00001)•
5. Age	.012 (.006)•	−.016 (.007)•
6. Number of prior appointments	−.023 (.019)	.019 (.017)
7. Participation in succession	−.213 (.123)	.144 (.110)
Constant	.280 (.341)	.643 (.421)
Chi square	297.04•••	334.57•••

• $p \leq .05$; •• $p \leq .01$; ••• $p \leq .001$; *t*-tests are one-tailed for hypothesized effects, two-tailed for control variables.
* Unstandardized coefficients are reported. Standard errors are in parentheses.

A similar pattern of results emerged in support of hypotheses 2a and 2b. As shown in Tables 2 and 3, participation in separating the CEO and board chair positions is negatively associated with additional appointments to boards with low control over management and positively associated with subsequent subtractions, while for high-control boards, such experience is positively associated with subsequent additions and negatively associated with subsequent subtractions. Moreover, experience in combining the CEO and board chair positions is associated with fewer subsequent appointments to high-control boards (fewer additions and more subtractions) and more subsequent appointments to low-control boards (more additions and fewer subtractions).

Hypotheses 3–5 addressed the consequences of participating in additional strategy and policy changes that reflect greater (or lesser) board control over management. The findings generally support these hypotheses. For example, consistent with hypothesis 3a, participation in decreasing corporate diversification leads to fewer subsequent appointments to boards with low control over management (i.e., fewer additions and more subtractions) and also leads to more subsequent appointments to boards with high control (i.e., more additions and fewer subtractions). The results of testing hypothesis 3b, however, show that participation in increasing corporate diversification is not significantly related to subsequent change in board appointments to either high-control boards or low-control boards.

Hypotheses 4a and 4b, which addressed the effects on subsequent board appointments of a director's prior participation in increasing or decreasing total CEO compensation are generally supported. As hypothesis 4a argued, a director's prior participation in decreasing total CEO compensation is negatively associated with subsequent appointments to boards with low control over management (both in terms of fewer additions and more subtractions) and also is positively associated ($p \leq .10$) with subsequent appointments at high-control boards (but only in terms of additions). Hypothesis 4a is partially supported: Participation in increasing total CEO compensation is positively associated with subsequent appointments to low-control boards (more additions and fewer subtractions) and negatively associated with subsequent appointments to high-control boards (but only for additions).

The results strongly support hypotheses 5a and 5b. Experience with increasing CEO compensation contingency is negatively associated with subsequent appointments to boards with low control (fewer additions and more subtractions) and positively associated with appointments to high-control boards (more additions and fewer subtractions). Conversely, experience with decreased compensation contingency has the opposite effect. In general, therefore, the findings appear to provide robust evidence that participation in specific changes in board structure, corporate strategy, and CEO compensation that reflect change in relative control of CEOs and boards can differentially influence subsequent appointments to boards with high or low control over management.

The control variables yielded several interesting results. The average profitability (return on assets) of firms at which the focal individual served as outside director in the prior year is not related to subsequent change in appointments to boards with low control over management. Average profitability does increase appointments to high-control boards, however (significant at alpha = .10). The director's total compensation as CEO in his or her home company is positively related to appointments at low-control boards and negatively related to appointments at high-control boards. Moreover, older directors gain more subsequent appointments at low-control boards and fewer subsequent appointments to high-control boards.

We also examined the possibility that industry differences might affect our results. In separate analyses, we regressed the changes in board structure and CEO compensation on industry, designated as the company's two-digit SIC code. The industry factors did not significantly predict increased board control over management for any of the measures of board control; *t*-statistics ranged from .810 to 1.289. Thus it appears that our results are not driven by any tendency for boards to choose directors from related industries (e.g., to alleviate resource dependencies).

DISCUSSION

Overall, the findings of this study strongly support our notion that internal organizational politics in the CEO-board relationship can significantly affect the selection and retention of directors and, more generally, the formation and dissolution of board interlocks. The first set of results showed how a director's prior participation on boards engaging in specific changes in board structure and strategy or policy that reflect greater board control can affect subsequent change in board appointments. In general, prior experience with changes indicating increased board control over top management enhanced an individual director's attractiveness at companies with relatively high board control while decreasing his or her attractiveness at companies with relatively passive boards. This result was robust over five different indicators of increased board control: increases in the ratio of outside to inside directors, separation of the CEO and board chair positions, reduced corporate diversification, increased CEO compensation contingency, and decreased total CEO compensation. The results were also quite robust in terms of the type of change (i.e., additions and subtractions) in board appointments.

A second set of results showed the effect on subsequent board appointments of a director's prior participation in specific governance-related changes in the opposite direction, i.e., indicating greater CEO control over management. Overall, prior experience with such changes reduced a director's attractiveness to firms with relatively high board control while increasing his or her attractiveness to firms with more powerful CEOs and weak boards. Again, these results held for multiple indicators and for additions and subtractions in subsequent appointments. Taken together, these two sets of results provide strong evidence that prior experience with increased or decreased board control over management provides an important basis for selecting or retaining directors.

The control variables used in this study provide additional support for a sociopolitical perspective on director selection and board composition. For example, director age is also positively associated with subsequent appointments to low-control boards and negatively associated with appointments to high-control boards. Older directors may be perceived in the market for corporate directors as being more accepting of board passivity in controlling management and less likely to embrace newer perspectives reflecting more active board involvement and control in management decision making. Moreover, directors' own total executive compensation at their home company is positively related to subsequent appointments at companies with low board control and negatively related to appointments at companies with high board control. This suggests that highly paid CEOs may be perceived as individuals who are accustomed to weak board control, which would increase their attractiveness at low board-control companies and decrease their attractiveness at high board-control companies.

Board Interlocks

Finally, the results show that the profitability at companies on whose boards the focal director sits is unrelated to subsequent change in appointments at companies with low board control but is positively related to change in appointments to high-control boards. Thus it appears that an individual's attractiveness in the market for directors may be increased by sitting on boards of highly performing companies, as some financial economists have suggested (Fama, 1980), but this attractiveness applies only within the subsegment of boards with relatively high control over management. Our political perspective shares the economists' interest in the reputation of corporate directors, i.e., how prior director experience can provide a signal to other interested parties, but our theoretical framework is more nuanced. It suggests that reputational effects may be more complex than previously assumed. The market for corporate directors is not driven by a simple "ex post settling up" process in which "high-quality" (active and shareholder-oriented) directors are rewarded and "low-quality" (passive and management-oriented) directors are punished (e.g., Fama, 1980). Our results suggest, instead, that the market for directors in U.S. corporations can reward either type of director, and our theoretical perspective identifies the mechanisms than can generate and sustain such a segmented market for corporate directors.

This study contributes to research on corporate boards of directors by synthesizing three largely nonoverlapping theoretical literatures pertaining to board behavior: the economic literature on director reputation, the sociological literature on board interlocks, and the behavioral literature on CEO-board relationships. The findings show how powerful actors in CEO-board relationships can manage the content of board interlocks to maintain or increase their intraorganizational power. In this way, powerful CEOs can effectively exclude individuals who might import norms of active board monitoring and shareholder representation (i.e., at the expense of managerial preferences), while including individuals who have been socialized into a passive board role (Burt, 1987). In effect, our findings suggest that directors' experience on other boards may serve as a relatively direct reputational indicator of their "sympathy" (Finkelstein and Hambrick, 1989: 124) toward management or shareholder interests, thus providing a primary basis for director selection and retention. Moreover, this interpretation is consistent with the broader literature on power in organizations, which emphasizes control over employee selection and retention as an efficient means of building and maintaining political coalitions (Pfeffer, 1981).

The findings also have implications for theory and research on the formation of board interlocks. While theorists have typically emphasized the role of interorganizational dependencies or classwide interests in determining interlock ties (Useem, 1982; Palmer, 1983; Mizruchi and Stearns, 1988), the results of this study suggest that parochial political interests within the firm may also be an important determinant of interlock structure. In seeking to maintain or increase their influence in CEO-board relationships, powerful corporate leaders help maintain a "segmented" interlock network with relatively few ties between active and passive boards and relatively dense ties between boards with similar power structures. For example, 82 percent of the total number of ties observed are within-group ties, while only 18 percent are between-group ties. Thus, while our results could be viewed as consistent with the notion that interlock ties help elites to "close ranks" in the face of "deviant" behavior (Palmer, 1983: 42), interlocks appear to serve this function for competing subcultures within the broader class of corporate elites. The "rise of shareholder power" documented by Useem (1992: 19), Davis and Thompson (1994), and others (e.g., Zajac and Westphal, 1995) appears to have engendered a managerialist response that has affected the dynamic structure of board interlocks.

Our findings indicate that while organizational practices may spread through the network of interlocking directorates, powerful actors in CEO-board relationships can block or redirect the diffusion of those changes that diminish their control by cutting off interlock ties to other adopters of those practices and steering the diffusion of changes that protect or increase their control over the focal board by adding ties to prior adopters. The theoretical perspective and empirical findings of this study may generalize to the diffusion of other organizational phenomena by suggesting how *intra*organizational political interests can influence the course of *inter*organizational diffusion. Thus, while the role of existing social network ties in facilitating the diffusion of various structural and strategic changes within an organizational field is well understood (cf., Davis, 1991; Haunschild, 1993; Palmer, Jennings, and Zhou, 1993), future research could consider further the endogeneity of such ties, i.e., how they are created or severed and how they may reflect and reinforce the parochial political interests of already-powerful organizational decision makers.

Another question that merits additional research attention is the origin of CEO-board power relationships and how reversals in that relationship might occur. Beatty and Zajac (1994) noted, for example, that the small and young firms they studied (i.e., initial public offering firms) have compensation contracts and corporate governance mechanisms different from those found in large *Fortune* 500 firms. Qualitative and quantitative historical approaches might provide additional insight into how and why such changes occur over time and the implications of such changes on shifting the relative power balance in the CEO-board relationship.

We began our study by asking why increased board independence and control over top management may have spread to some organizations and not to others. We sought to answer this question by developing a cross-level theory of interlock tie creation and dissolution that explains the simultaneous coexistence and persistence of both board-controlled and CEO-controlled firms. Specifically, we showed how powerful CEOs and powerful board members seek directors whose prior director experiences (i.e., reputation) suggest a shared belief about board passivity or activity, respectively, and how this politically rational "matching" and segmentation process of like-minded individuals can influence the dynamic formation and dissolution of corporate interlock ties. These dynamics help to explain the fractured diffusion of increased board independence across large U.S. corporations. More generally, the findings illustrate the promise of developing "meso-level" theoretical frameworks integrating micropolitical factors and macro-social factors to explain organizational behavior. While such "meso-level" frameworks may be more complex than frameworks that address only micro or macro factors, they may offer the greatest potential to account for the simultaneous existence of what appear to be contradictory or opposing organizational phenomena.

REFERENCES

Alderfer, Clayton P.
1986 "The invisible director on corporate boards." Harvard Business Review, 64(6): 38–52.

Amihud, Yakov, and Baruch Lev
1981 "Risk reduction as a managerial motive for conglomerate mergers." Bell Journal of Economics, 12: 605–617.

Amit, Raphael, and Joshua Livnat
1988 "Diversification and the risk-return trade-off." Academy of Management Journal, 31: 154–166.

Baysinger, Barry, and Robert E. Hoskisson
1990 "The composition of boards of directors and strategic control: Effects on corporate strategy." Academy of Management Review, 15: 72–87.

Beatty, Randolph P., and Edward J. Zajac
1994 "Top management incentives, monitoring, and risk sharing: A study of executive compensation, ownership and board structure in initial public offerings." Administrative Science Quarterly, 39: 313–335.

Becker, Gary S.
1975 Human Capital, 2nd ed. New York: National Bureau of Economic Research.

Bettenhausen, Kenneth, and J. Keith Murnighan
1985 "The emergence of norms in competitive decision-making groups." Administrative Science Quarterly, 30: 350–372.

Black, Fischer, and Myron Scholes
1973 "The pricing of options and corporate liabilities." Journal of Political Economy, 81: 637–659.

Boeker, Warren
1992 "Power and managerial dismissal: Scapegoating at the top." Administrative Science Quarterly, 37: 400–421.

Burt, Ronald S.
1987 "Social contagion and innovation: Cohesion versus structural equivalence." American Journal of Sociology, 92: 1287–1335.

Crystal, Graef S.
1984 Questions and Answers on Executive Compensation. Englewood Cliffs, NJ: Prentice-Hall.
1991 In Search of Excess: The Overcompensation of American Executives. New York: W. W. Norton.

Davis, Gerald F.
1991 "Agents without principles? The spread of the poison pill through the intercorporate network." Administrative Science Quarterly, 36: 583–613.
1993 "Who gets ahead in the market for corporate directors: The political economy of multiple board memberships." Academy of Management Best Papers Proceedings: 202–211.

Davis, Gerald F., and Tracy A. Thompson
1994 "A social movement perspective on corporate control." Administrative Science Quarterly, 39: 141–173.

Demb, Ada, and F.-Friedrich Neubauer
1992 The Corporate Board: Confronting the Paradoxes. Oxford: Oxford University Press.

Ellig, Bruce R.
1984 "Incentive plans: Over the long-term." Compensation Review, 16: 26–37.

Fama, Eugene F.
1980 "Agency problems and the theory of the firm." Journal of Political Economy, 88: 288–307.

Fama, Eugene F., and Michael C. Jensen
1983 "The separation of ownership and control." Journal of Law and Economics, 26: 301–325.

Finkelstein, Sydney, and Richard A. D'Aveni
1994 "CEO duality as a double-edged sword: How boards of directors balance entrenchment avoidance and unity of command." Academy of Management Journal, 37: 1079–1108.

Finkelstein, Sydney, and Donald C. Hambrick
1989 "Chief executive compensation: A study of the intersection of markets and political processes." Strategic Management Journal, 10: 121–134.

Fortune
1993 "The king is dead: Why more boards are waking up and pushing out the CEO." January 11: 34–50.

Fredrickson, James W., Donald C. Hambrick, and S. Baumrin
1988 "A model of CEO dismissal." Academy of Management Review, 13: 255–270.

Galaskiewicz, Joseph, and Stanley Wasserman
1989 "Mimetic processes within an interorganizational field: An empirical test." Administrative Science Quarterly, 34: 454–479.

Gibbs, Philip A.
1993 "Determinants of corporate restructuring: The relative importance of corporate governance, takeover threat, and free cash flow." Strategic Management Journal, 14: 51–68.

Gladstein, Deborah
1984 "Groups in context: A model of task group effectiveness." Administrative Science Quarterly, 33: 334–365.

Harris, Milton, and Artur Raviv
1979 "Some results on incentive contracts with imperfect information." Journal of Economic Theory, 20: 231–259.

Harrison, J. Richard, David L. Torres, and Sal Kukalis
1988 "The changing of the guard: Turnover and structural change in the top-management positions." Administrative Science Quarterly, 33: 211–232.

Haunschild, Pamela R.
1993 "Interorganizational imitation: The impact of interlocks on corporate acquisition activity." Administrative Science Quarterly, 38: 564–592.

Healy, Paul M.
1985 "The effect of bonus schemes on accounting decisions." Journal of Accounting and Economics, 7: 85–107.

Herman, Edward S.
1981 Corporate Control, Corporate Power. New York: Cambridge University Press.

Hill, Charles W. L., and Scott A. Snell
1988 "External control, corporate strategy, and firm performance in research-intensive industries." Strategic Management Journal, 9: 577–590.

Hoskisson, Robert E., Richard A. Johnson, and Douglas D. Moesel
1994 "Corporate divestiture intensity in restructuring firms: Effects of governance, strategy, and performance." Academy of Management Journal, 37: 1207–1251.

Jensen, Michael C.
1988 "The takeover controversy: Analysis and evidence." In J. C. Coffee, L. Lowenstein, and S. Rose-Ackerman (eds.), Knights, Raiders, and Targets: 314–354. Oxford: Oxford University Press.

Jensen, Michael C., and William H. Meckling
1976 "Theory of the firm: Managerial behavior, agency costs, and ownership structure." Journal of Financial Economics, 3: 305–350.

Kaufman, Bruce E.
1986 The Economics of Labor Markets. Orlando, FL: Dryden Press.

Kerr, Jeffrey L., and Leslie Kren
1992 "Effect of relative decision monitoring on chief executive officer compensation." Academy of Management Journal, 35: 370–397.

Kesner, Idalene F., and Roy B. Johnson
1990 "An investigation of the relationship between board composition and stockholder suits." Strategic Management Journal, 11: 327–336.

Koenig, Thomas, and Robert Gogel
1981 "Models of the significance of interlocking corporate directorates." American Journal of Economics and Sociology, 38: 173–186.

Kosnik, Rita D.
1987 "Greenmail: A study of board performance in corporate governance." Administrative Science Quarterly, 32: 163–185.

Lorsch, Jay W., and Elaine MacIver
1989 Pawns or Potentates: The Reality of America's Corporate Boards. Boston: Harvard Business School Press.

Mace, Myles L.
1971 Directors: Myth and Reality. Boston: Harvard Business School Press.

Maddala, G. S.
1983 Limited-dependent and Qualitative Variables in Econometrics. Cambridge: Cambridge University Press.

Main, Brian G., Charles A. O'Reilly III, and James Wade
1995 "The CEO, the board of directors and executive compensation: Economic and psychological perspectives." Industrial and Corporate Change, 4: 293–332.

Mallette, Paul, and Karen L Fowler
1992 "Effects of board composition and stock ownership on the adoption of 'poison pills.' " Academy of Management Journal, 35: 1010–1035.

Marris, Robert L.
1964 The Economic Theory of Managerial Capitalism. London: MacMillan.

Mizruchi, Mark S.
1982 The American Corporate Network. Beverly Hills, CA: Sage.
1992 The Structure of Corporate Political Action: Interfirm Relationships and Their Consequences. Cambridge, MA: Harvard University Press.

Mizruchi, Mark S., and Linda Brewster Stearns
1988 "A longitudinal study of the formation of interlocking directorates." Administrative Science Quarterly, 33: 194–210.

Ocasio, William
1996 "Boards as normative arenas." Working paper, Northwestern University, J. L. Kellogg Graduate School of Management.

Ornstein, Michael D.
1980 "Assessing the meaning of corporate interlocks: Canadian evidence." Social Science Research, 9: 287–306.

Palepu, Krishna G.
1985 "Diversification strategy, profit performance, and the entropy measure." Strategic Management Journal, 6: 239–255.

Palmer, Donald
1983 "Broken ties: Interlocking directorates and intercorporate coordination." Administrative Science Quarterly, 28: 40–55.

Palmer, Donald, Roger Friedland, and Jitendra V. Singh
1986 "The ties that bind: Organizational and class bases of stability in a corporate interlock network." American Sociological Review, 51: 781–796.

Palmer, Donald A., P. Devereaux Jennings, and Xueguang Zhou
1993 "Late adoption of the multidivisional form by large U.S. corporations: Institutional, political, and economic accounts." Administrative Science Quarterly, 38: 100–131.

Board Interlocks

Pennings, Johannes H.
1980 Interlocking Directorates. San Francisco: Jossey-Bass.

Pfeffer, Jeffrey
1981 Power in Organizations. New York: Harper and Row.
1992 Managing with Power. Boston: Harvard Business School Press.

Pfeffer, Jeffrey, and Gerald R. Salancik
1978 The External Control of Organizations: A Resource Dependence Perspective. New York: Harper & Row.

Seward, James K., and James P. Walsh
1996 "The governance and control of voluntary corporate spin-offs." Strategic Management Journal, 17: 25–39.

Stearns, Linda Brewster, and Mark S. Mizruchi
1986 "Broken tie reconstitution and the functions of interorganizational interlocks: A reexamination." Administrative Science Quarterly, 31: 522–538.

Tosi, Henry L., and Luis R. Gomez-Mejia
1989 "The decoupling of CEO pay and performance: An agency theory perspective." Administrative Science Quarterly, 34: 169–189.

Useem, Michael
1982 "Classwide rationality in the politics of managers and directors of large corporations in the United States and Great Britain." Administrative Science Quarterly, 27: 199–226.
1984 The Inner Circle. Oxford: Oxford University Press.
1992 Executive Defense: Shareholder Power and Corporate Reorganization. Cambridge, MA: Harvard University Press.

Vance, Stanley C.
1968 The Corporate Director: A Critical Evaluation. Homewood, IL: Dow Jones-Irwin.
1983 Corporate Leadership: Boards of Directors and Strategy. New York: McGraw-Hill.

Wade, James B., Charles A. O'Reilly, and Ike Chandratat
1990 "Golden parachutes: CEOs and the exercise of social influence." Administrative Science Quarterly, 35: 587–603.

Wall Street Journal
1995a "Despite poor returns, Champion's chairman hangs on for 21 years." October 31: A1.
1995b "Irate shareholders target ineffective board members." November 6: B1.
1995c "How do you fire a CEO? Very, very slowly." January 20: B1.

Westphal, James D., and Edward J. Zajac
1995 "Who shall govern? CEO/board power, demographic similarity, and new director selection." Administrative Science Quarterly, 40: 60–83.
1997 "Defections from the inner circle: Social exchange, reciprocity, and the diffusion of board independence in U.S. corporations." Administrative Science Quarterly, vol. 42 (in press).

Zajac, Edward J.
1988 "Interlocking directorates as an interorganizational strategy: A test of critical assumptions." Academy of Management Journal, 31: 428–438.

Zajac, Edward J., and James D. Westphal
1995 "Accounting for the explanations of CEO compensation: Substance and symbolism." Administrative Science Quarterly, 40: 283–308.
1996 "Who shall succeed? How CEO/board preferences and power affect the choice of new CEOs." Academy of Management Journal, 39: 64–90.

[7]

Leadership Instability in Hospitals: The Influence of Board-CEO Relations and Organizational Growth and Decline

Jeffrey A. Alexander
University of Michigan, Ann Arbor
Mary L. Fennell
Pennsylvania State University
Michael T. Halpern
University of Michigan, Ann Arbor

This study tested whether leadership instability—a systemic pattern of frequent succession in the top management position of an organization—was associated with sociopolitical structures that define the relationship between the board and chief executive officer (CEO), controlling for temporal patterns of the organizational life-cycle stage. In organizations that are not profit maximizing and subject to considerable uncertainty, such governance properties were hypothesized to affect leadership instability independent of organizational growth or decline. Results of regression analyses demonstrate strong main effects of board-CEO relations, net of the impact of organizational life cycle, on leadership instability.•

Organizational analysts have demonstrated a long-standing interest in the issue of managerial succession because of its potential effect on organizational strategy, performance, and change (Grusky, 1963; Gamson and Scotch, 1964; Eitzen and Yetman, 1972; McEachern, 1975; Pfeffer and Salancik, 1977; Allen and Panian, 1982). Most of these studies have in common a focus on individual chief executive officer (CEO) succession rather than on patterns involving multiple turnovers of top managers in a given organization. Such patterns of succession are important, because they reflect an organizational property—leadership instability—the consequences of which may be deeply felt by an organization. Prior research had demonstrated that succession in top-level management is often accompanied by discontinuous change in the structure and strategy of the organization (Pfeffer, 1972; Meyer, 1978; Carroll, 1984; Singh, House, and Tucker, 1986; Finkelstein and Hambrick, 1990), but leadership instability may produce "so much change in the distribution of power and in structures and procedures that concerted action will be difficult, and change so disruptive, that organizational ability to cope with environmental requirements will be harmed" (Pfeffer, 1981: 327). Organizations may also suffer from frequent top-level managerial changes in the form of low morale, employment uncertainty, and internal political turmoil (Staw, 1980; Fredrickson, Hambrick, and Baumrin, 1988; Dwore and Murray, 1989). Finally, frequent CEO succession may suggest something about the distribution of power in an organization, its ability to attract and retain management talent, and the tendency to scapegoat in response to organizational problems (Gamson and Scotch, 1964; Pfeffer and O'Reilly, 1987).

A second attribute of much of the extant literature on managerial succession is the focus on functional associations between CEO turnover and organizational performance. Recent research on succession, for example, has attempted to demonstrate that the CEO turnover event is predicted by poor financial or market performance (Brown, 1982; Warner, Watts, and Wruck, 1982; Coughlan and Schmidt, 1985; Boeker, 1992). While such theoretical formulations have considerable intuitive appeal, they do not necessarily lend themselves to an examination of long-term leadership instability. While poor organizational performance, particularly when performance measures are based on yearly

0001-8392/93/3801-0074/$1.00.

•

This research was supported in part by grants from the National Science Foundation (#SES882-1592) and The Governance Institute. We would like to thank Clifford C. Clogg for his advice on analytic techniques and three anonymous *ASQ* reviewers for helpful comments.

observations of profits or sales, may have a modest impact on individual CEO turnovers (Fredrickson, Hambrick, and Baumrin, 1988), short-term performance is unlikely to be an important factor in understanding leadership instability over an extended period of time. We may need to consider a more systemic and long-term conceptualization of performance, such as the organizational life-cycle stage, defined by Whetten (1987) as temporal clusters of issues or problems that organizations must resolve and that tend to be sequentially linked. Life-cycle stages, such as growth or decline (Kimberly and Miles, 1981) may relate differentially to succession rates among top managers, such that different stages may represent different contexts affecting the level and type of uncertainty and stress faced by top managers and, consequently, their propensity to leave the organization (Cameron, Kim, and Whetten, 1987; Cameron, Whetten, and Kim, 1987). This raises the possibility that leadership instability may be explained by aspects of organizational life other than "the bottom line."

In this investigation, we explore the thesis that the stability of the CEO position depends on both the organization's life-cycle stage and the relative distribution of expertise, resources, and influence between the CEO and the board of directors. We are particularly interested in the influence of sociopolitical structures that define the relationship between the board and the top executive on leadership instability, controlling for life-cycle stage.

Theoretical Framework

Leadership instability in an organization can be defined in terms of the rate of succession in the CEO position over a specified time period. Whereas an orientation to individual succession would define serial turnovers as a series of independent, discrete events, leadership instability emphasizes succession frequency as a systemic organizational attribute. Examining leadership instability thus shifts the focus of any explanation to underlying organizational properties and to long-term patterns of organizational growth or decline. Particularly important in this regard are the sociopolitical structures that define the relationship between the organizational board of directors and top management.

Boards of directors are assumed to play an important role in corporate governance and are mandated to supervise the actions of management, provide advice, and veto poor decisions (Fama, 1980; Jensen, 1986; Weisback, 1988). In their control capacity, boards of directors are also responsible for removing ineffective management. The propensity to engage in such actions, however, is often more a function of influence relationships, cognitions about performance, and/or political action than the board's actual effectiveness as a rational management control system (Mace, 1971; Fredrickson, Hambrick, and Baumrin, 1988; Baysinger and Hoskisson, 1990). Some researchers have noted, for example, that the CEO may influence the board through the selective use of information, control over the board's agenda, and personal persuasion through access to key board members (Zald, 1969; Mace, 1971; Mizruchi,

1983). Whereas individual CEO succession may be influenced by the personal actions of the CEO vis à vis the board, the rate of CEO succession is more likely to be affected by structures that shape the enduring relationship between the CEO position and the board, irrespective of the attributes of the incumbents of either. These sociopolitical structures define power relationships, influence, information access, and decision-making orientations of the board and top management. Further, such sociopolitical structures tend to become established, self-perpetuating properties in organizations. Dominant coalitions have the ability to formulate constitutions, rules, procedures, and information systems that limit the potential power of others and thereby ensure their own continuing control (Thompson, 1967; Pfeffer and Salancik, 1977). Organizational influence structures thus become institutionalized and may be very stable over time.

We posit that governance structures that favor influence and control by the CEO may promote convergence on an established strategic direction and resistance to executive change, even in the face of environmental change or organizational decline or instability. Conversely, when sociopolitical structures assign primary power and authority to the board, the board may perpetuate this power through frequent replacement of the CEO, even under conditions of organizational growth or stability. As a test of these general propositions, we examined leadership instability in nonprofit hospitals between 1980 and 1988 in relation to sociopolitical features of hospital board-CEO relationships and organizational life-cycle stages.

Hospitals and Uncertainty in the Health Care Sector

Several considerations underlie our focus on leadership instability in hospitals in the 1980s. First, nonprofit hospitals operate under a set of operational and institutional constraints that preclude standard measures of profitability and financial viability as primary indicators of CEO effectiveness and organizational performance. As community service organizations, hospitals have multiple roles, including providing care to nonpaying indigent populations, teaching, and sponsoring research, as well as ensuring access to care to the community in general. The multiple goals of most nonprofit hospitals make it difficult to evaluate clearly whether a CEO is doing an effective job. For a study of leadership instability, this ambiguous situation may reduce the relevance of "objective" CEO evaluations and increase the potential importance of sociopolitical structures defining board-CEO relations.

Second, the 1980s were witness to a number of significant changes in the health care sector, including a radical shift in the payment structure for hospital services from cost-based to prospective payment, fragmentation of physician power and autonomy, shrinking capital markets, and rapid technological advancement (Kimberly and Zajak, 1985). Further, a reorientation in public policy from ensuring access to hospital care to containing hospital costs through competitive mechanisms resulted in increasing competition among health care providers for patients, physicians, and health care dollars. Focusing on hospitals during this period thus allows us to examine leadership instability in an industry experiencing considerable turbulence as a result of regulatory shifts, increased competition, and pressures for more efficient performance (Goldsmith, 1981; Goodstein and Boeker, 1991). For these reasons, hospitals provide a particularly good test of the study hypotheses, but we expect them to apply to all organizations in which demands are made both for efficiency and social responsibility and in which governing boards and CEOs are held at least minimally accountable by either shareholders or communities.

Hypotheses

Hypotheses for the study derive from the literature on managerial succession, governing board structure and behavior, and organizational power. These hypotheses consider the effects of board-CEO relations on leadership instability and are built around three key dimensions of the sociopolitical structure of board-CEO relations: locus of power and influence between the CEO and the board, internal versus external focus of the board, and consistency between the cognitive orientations of the board and top management.

CEO power and influence vis-à-vis the board. Previous research has emphasized the importance of CEO power and its relationship to the succession and tenure of top management (Pfeffer and Salancik, 1977; Allen and Panian, 1982; Finkelstein and Hambrick, 1990). Although CEO power has typically been expressed as the extent of equity ownership in the firm, in not-for-profit organizations power is more appropriately manifested in the ability of the CEO to influence key decisions within the organization and by the control of the CEO over the selection of board members who are sympathetic to the CEO's strategic orientation or style of management (Perrow, 1963; Middleton, 1987). The relationship of CEO power vis-à-vis the board and leadership stability is a straightforward one. The greater the influence the CEO has over the board and its decision making, the less likely those decisions will reflect adversely on top management and, consequently, the lower the level of leadership instability. CEOs who are in a powerful position with respect to the board can more convincingly argue their positions, put themselves in a favorable light, dictate the agenda for the board, and generally control the outcomes of board decisions. CEOs can enhance their influence over the board through a number of mechanisms, including active (voting) membership on the board, membership on key board committees, and participation in the selection of new board members. Thus, our first hypothesis:

Hypothesis 1: Hospitals whose CEOs are positioned to exercise influence over the board and its decision making will experience less leadership instability than those hospitals whose CEOs are not.

It has also been argued that environmental uncertainty and turbulence compel the top management of organizations to engage in more risk-taking behavior (Hall and Mansfield, 1971; Starbuck, Greve, and Hedberg, 1978; Cameron, 1983). Such risk taking may manifest itself in the form of unpopular decisions, such as downsizing certain functions of the organization or engaging in untried, new ventures. A formal employment contract between the board and the CEO may afford top management more risk-taking license to respond to turbulent and complex environments. The presence of a contract makes top management less subject to capricious action by the board, which may wish to sanction the CEO for short-term negative performance in the pursuit of long-term strategic goals. The contract, in effect, provides the CEO with some employment stability by giving him or her time to develop and implement programs that may result in short-term disruption of organizational performance but may lead to longer-term benefits for the organization. To the extent that such managerial action is inconsistent with the orientation of many community boards toward maintaining the status quo, contracts may provide a mechanism to engage in such action and, at the same time, ensure the stability of leadership in the organization.

Alternatively, employment contracts may provide the board with a formal mechanism for circumscribing the behavior of the CEO so that it is consistent with board expectations and continued board power. Contracts may contain quite specific provisions about terms of employment and management performance criteria. If board expectations are not being met, the contract simply is not renewed. Thus, employment contracts may be an institutional mechanism for controlling the CEO and perpetuating the board's power by circumscribing the prerogatives of the CEO or shaping the premises of decision making in the organization (Mizruchi, 1983). These arguments suggest two alternative hypotheses:

Hypothesis 2a: Hospitals whose CEOs have formal employment contracts with the board will experience less leadership instability than those hospitals whose CEOs have no formal contracts with the board.

Hypothesis 2b: Hospitals whose CEOs have formal contracts with the board will experience more leadership instability than those hospitals whose CEOs do not have formal contracts with the board.

Internal vs. external focus of the board. The literature on organizational governance maintains that two basic functions may be performed by organizational boards (Zald, 1969; Pfeffer, 1972). The first, buffering and boundary spanning, derives from the board's ability to link the organization to critical resources on which it is dependent or to provide a buffer between professional staff of the organization and the public (Price, 1963). Zald (1969) maintained that the second function is the opposite of such boundary-spanning and buffering roles and consists of the board's role in administration and management. In this role, the board primarily serves to set policy for the organization and to act as an internal control to ensure that those policies are carried out. Although the literature differs as to the conditions under which the board will assume one role over the other, there are consistent findings that suggest that the size and composition of the board are related to the function that the board is expected to serve. In general, board size will be larger when the board is used to link the organization to its environment and smaller when the organization is less closely tied to its environment and when the board is used for management control. Pfeffer (1973) found that larger boards were associated with community influence and fundraising as criteria for board-member selection, whereas knowledge of hospital administration was emphasized as a selection criterion most often among smaller boards. Given that larger, more heterogeneous boards tend to serve a cooptive function by linking the organization to its environment and/or buffering the organization from environmental disturbances, it follows that such boards will be more outwardly focused and less concerned with internal policy making and control functions. Smaller, more homogeneous boards, by contrast, are more likely to take an active role in organizational policy making as well as exercising internal control over hospital management.

From a functional perspective, CEOs may be better able to manage a large, diverse group of individuals when there is disagreement and fragmentation among board members. The CEO can gain relative advantage in power and influence through a number of political strategies, including coalition building, selective channeling of information, and "dividing and conquering." Board members' assessments of top management may therefore be manipulated by management when the board is large and diverse (Mintzberg, 1983). Finally, there is evidence to suggest that larger groups are less action oriented than smaller groups (Clendenin, 1972). Thus, the larger the board, the less likely it will be to exercise control over the CEO.

We argue, then, that large, representational boards, characterized by a greater number of members and wider variation in occupational backgrounds, will be less engaged in rendering decisions related to major internal changes in the organization, including the succession of the CEO. Conversely, smaller, more homogeneous boards will be more likely to exercise their internal control prerogatives, which include replacing top management. We hypothesize, then:

Hypothesis 3: Hospitals whose boards are characterized by large size and greater occupational heterogeneity will experience less leadership instability than those characterized by small size and greater occupational homogeneity.

Compatibility between orientations of board and CEO. The literature on organizational governance suggests that board members whose backgrounds and orientations are similar to those of the CEO will provide greater support for managerial action and decisions than will boards whose membership is not reflective of management orientations. Such compositional features have been found to relate strongly to outcomes such as managerial succession, resistance to takeover attempts (Kosnick, 1987, 1990), and profitability of the firm. We expect the correspondence between board members' orientations and the CEO's orientations to be an important factor in determining the stability of leadership in the organization. Specifically, corresponding orientations between board members and the CEO will reduce uncertainty regarding managerial action and strategies, increase communications and coordination, and generally improve the flow of information between the board and top management. Similarly, when board members' views and orientations are generally inconsistent with top management's, situations are likely to result that are characterized by greater conflict and more instability in the organization. Thus, the lack of correspondence between the orientations of top management and board members may severely undercut the power base of top management and lead to greater leadership instability in the organization.

Loyalties and agency relations on governing boards has been discussed largely in terms of insider versus outsider representation on the board. Insiders (organizational managers) are assumed to ally themselves with the CEO, whereas outsiders are presumed to exercise more objective control and monitoring over management. This dichotomy has oversimplified this issue insofar as constituencies within organizations may have different agendas or orientations, some of which may be in conflict with those of the CEO (Cochran, Wood, and Jones, 1985; Wade, O'Reilly, and Chandratat, 1990). Similarly, outside board members may hold views that are in consonance with those of the CEO, owing to social or political alliances or comparable experience with the uncertainties and complexities of managing large organizations. Thus, the insider-outsider distinction becomes less important for explaining executive stability than the backgrounds and agendas of specific groups represented on the board.

In hospitals, we expect that the correspondence between CEO and board orientations will increase as a function of the number of corporate representatives on the board. These individuals are more likely to be sympathetic to the strategic orientations of top management in complex organizations and would be more likely to support the CEO during periods of turbulence or decline. In contrast, board representatives from the hospital's medical staff are likely to hold views in opposition to those of the management of the hospital. It has been well documented, for example, that hospital management and medical staff often hold conflicting views on cost containment. Managers are concerned with increasing productivity and reducing costs in hospital operations, while physicians are typically concerned with acquiring expensive new medical technology and support staff to assist in their medical practice. We suggest that this situation is likely to result in increased conflict and a weakening of the political power of the CEO. Such conditions, in turn, will undermine the stability of executive leadership in the hospital:

Hypothesis 4a: Hospitals whose boards contain a greater number of members with corporate backgrounds will experience less leadership instability than hospitals whose boards contain fewer corporate representatives.

Hypothesis 4b: Hospitals whose boards contain a greater number of members from the active medical staff will experience more leadership instability than hospitals whose boards contain fewer members from the active medical staff.

Life-cycle stage and leadership instability. Controlling for the life-cycle stage, as we do in this study, reflects and refines the view that organizational performance is a primary determinant of leadership instability. Rather than focusing on single observations of profitability or return on investment, we emphasize the organization's long-term pattern of growth, decline, stability, or instability. These patterns or stages represent potentially important contexts reflecting the degree and type of uncertainty faced by the organization, its management, and its board. In addition, emphasizing the dynamics of the organization's resource base rather than its output is more appropriate for organizations like hospitals that are subject to multiple goals, vague performance criteria, and the interests of multiple stakeholders (Kanter and Summers, 1987). The health care literature suggests, in fact, that growth is a common performance criterion for management, boards, and medical staff of hospitals, in view of the ambiguity and complexity surrounding output-based measures of performance (Pfeffer and Salancik, 1978; Young and Saltman, 1985).

Long-term patterns of growth and decline have been conceptualized and measured in the literature on organizational life cycles (Cameron, Kim, and Whetten, 1987). Four stages have been identified in this literature: growth, decline, stability, and instability. Growth and decline are often conceptualized as those sets of conditions in which a substantial increase or decrease in an organization's resource base occurs over a specified period of time. Instability has been empirically defined as nontrivial, rapid, discontinuous, or fluctuating change in an organization's resource base; stability is the absence of change or a trivial amount of change. These stages are not necessarily sequential or tied to a developmental notion of biological life stages; organizations can and do pass into and out of different stages and re-enter earlier stages.

We follow the lead of prior research on decline and top management turnover (Whetten, 1981; Greenhalgh and Rosenblatt, 1984) in predicting that the instability of hospital leadership will be greatest when the organization itself is experiencing a period of instability, or turbulence. This occurs because turbulence introduces the vagaries of a fickle resource base, which in turn puts considerable stress on buffering, planning, and other rational actions of top management. Leadership instability will be increased during such periods as a function of this increased stress on CEOs and the inherently more difficult task of managing under highly variable resource conditions.

By contrast, organizations operating in periods of decline may experience less uncertainty than those operating under more turbulent conditions (Cameron, Kim, and Whetten, 1987). The primary response mandated by conditions of decline is for the CEO to acquire and manage resources. The responsibility for actually absorbing the costs of decline, however, falls disproportionately on organizational members and is expressed in employee cutbacks, reorganization, and the consolidation of functions. The top manager's job is essentially to control and oversee this process. Decline, therefore, may be experienced as less ambiguous and less threatening for top managers than high turbulence.

Growth periods have similarities to periods of decline. Organizational action in periods of growth has been shown to be similar to that in periods of decline in that managers' primary function is to acquire resources (Cameron, 1983). We therefore would not anticipate that leadership stability would be affected by growth, positively or negatively, because the locus of organizational response to growth, as to decline, is the organization's members rather than top management. These arguments suggest that leadership stability will be greatest in hospitals experiencing turbulence but will be relatively unaffected by the uncertainties caused by operating in growth or decline stages.

Control Variables

Hospital CEO turnover results from both voluntary and involuntary exiting (Weil, 1990; Weil and Timmerberg, 1990; American College of Healthcare Executives, 1991). Among hospital CEOs who voluntarily left their organizations, the most common reasons cited were job-related moves (e.g., promotions or transfers), desire for new challenges, and advances in career opportunities or compensation. A second reason cited for voluntary turnover was dissatisfaction with the job, a category incorporating personality differences and uncertainty about the future of the hospital. By contrast, the dominant reasons for involuntary turnover included organization-related factors such as restructuring or the dissatisfaction of senior management or the board, as expressed in differences in vision, management style, or personalities. In light of this research, selection of the control variables for our study was based on developing appropriate analogs to the traditional determinants of individual succession, which capture potentially important structural, historical, and operating contexts thought to affect the degree of long-term leadership instability in organizations.

Responsibility to higher authority. Many of the preceding arguments about the relationship of board attributes and leadership instability are predicated on the assumption that the board is empowered to hire and fire the CEO and assume major responsibility for management oversight. If, however, the board is accountable to higher authority, such as a religious body, unit of local government, or holding company, these responsibilities may be shifted upward in the organizational hierarchy. Managerial control systems regulated by higher administrative or governance authorities are more likely to rely on standardized performance indicators that do not reflect fully the complexity of organizational operations, the decision-making processes of the chief administrator, or exogenous factors affecting organizational performance. Reliance on such narrowly defined performance criteria and the physical distance between management and those monitoring management may promote more frequent CEO turnovers, all things being equal.

Size. Inconsistent effects of organizational size on CEO turnover have been reported in the literature (see Gordon and Becker, 1964). In the context of the current study, however, we argue that because of greater slack, large organizations are more stable and better able to absorb the impact of internal and environmental disruption. Smaller organizations, by contrast, operate with less financial buffering and are thus more sensitive to such disturbances (Cameron, Whetten, and Kim, 1987). In addition, career patterns among hospital executives suggest that positions in larger hospitals represent the endpoint for many management careers, while smaller hospitals are frequently used as stepping stones to more prestigious jobs in other institutions (Weil and Timmerberg, 1990). For both reasons, larger hospitals may have greater stability in their executive leadership.

Multihospital-system membership. Multihospital systems, defined as two or more hospitals owned, leased, or sponsored by a separate administrative entity, practice management rotation among their units or between units and corporate headquarters. Thus, high rates of CEO turnover in these organizations may be a function of the internal labor market of the system rather than board-CEO relations or patterns of organizational growth or decline. We anticipate that hospitals operating for a longer time under multihospital-system control will experience higher rates of leadership instability. Our focus is not on hospital entry or exit from a multihospital system per se but on the length of time a hospital is part of such a system.

Contract management. Contract management arrangements are situations in which an outside firm provides top-level management and support staff for a hospital for a limited time (typically two to three years). These differ from the board-CEO employment contract, which is a contractual agreement between the board of the hospital and the CEO it hires to manage the institution. A contract management arrangement consists of a formal agreement between a hospital and an external management firm for general management services, which include but are not limited to providing a qualified top executive. Although both types of contracts are for a prespecified period (e.g., three years), they can be and frequently are renewed if the board chooses. Hospital CEOs provided by a management firm will typically rotate after the contract period ends, assuming the hospital does not renew the contract. Even within a contract period, it is easier for the board to replace the incumbent CEO if problems or disagreements arise. The board has less commitment to the management of the hospital under a contract arrangement than when the board itself searches for and hires a hospital manager. We therefore expect hospitals operating for longer periods under contract management arrangements to experience higher rates of leadership instability. As with multihospital-system membership, we are primarily concerned with the length of time a hospital was exposed to such administrative arrangements rather than its entry into or exit from such arrangements. These entries or exits may be associated with individual CEO successions but are too delimited temporally to account for multiple CEO successions.

Competition. Organizations, including hospitals, will vary in the extent to which they operate in competitive or noncompetitive markets. Hospitals, in particular, are assumed to compete for patient admissions and physician affiliations with other hospitals in geographically proximate (local) markets (Garnick et al., 1987). We expect that organizational leadership will be less stable in difficult, competitive environments because boards may use frequent managerial succession to cope with critical contingencies and uncertainties facing the organization (Pfeffer and Salancik, 1977; Kesner and Dalton, 1985).

Previous CEO succession. Because the study examines patterns of leadership stability over a defined period of time, it is possible that "left censoring" of the dependent variable (i.e., some hospitals experienced CEO turnover before the study period) may influence the degree of stability or instability in hospital leadership. A hospital may be more likely to experience few successions in the 1980–1988 period simply as a function of a recent succession at the end of the 1970s. In a more substantive vein, an organization's historical experience with CEO tenure and succession may shape patterns of turnover among top administrative officers. Hospitals with long-tenured CEOs in a prior era, for example, may be more likely to retain their CEOs in subsequent periods. For these reasons, we included in the model a variable that captures the number of years prior to 1980 in which the most recent CEO succession occurred.

METHOD

Sample and Data

We used data from two primary sources: the American Hospital Association (AHA) Annual Surveys of Hospitals (1970 through 1988) and the AHA Governing Board Surveys (1985 and 1989). The AHA Annual Survey of Hospitals is administered in the fourth quarter of each year to all AHA registered and nonregistered facilities (N = 6,800). Except for minor modifications, the survey remained unchanged throughout the study period (1980–1988). This survey covers areas related to facilities and services and their use, staffing, finances, and administration. The Governing Board Surveys were sent jointly to the CEOs and board chairs of all 5,800 community hospitals in 1985 and 1989. The contents of the surveys were essentially identical from year to year. Survey items covered a variety of topics, ranging from board composition and structure to board-CEO and medical staff relations.

The sample used for the current study was a panel subset of 1,534 community hospitals that met three criteria: first, hospitals must have been in operation continuously between 1980 and 1988, inclusive. This allowed for a common base period over which leadership instability could be assessed; second, hospitals must have responded to both the 1985 and 1989 Governing Board Surveys. This gave us two separate points for assessing the stability of governing board-CEO relationships and potential changes in these relationships. Finally, only not-for-profit hospitals were included in the study sample. Governing boards of investor-owned hospitals are typically advisory boards to multihospital systems and not empowered to hire or fire their CEOs (Alexander and Schroer, 1985). The ability to make decisions about CEO succession is a basic control function related to the board's role in maintaining leadership stability (Zald, 1965; Zald and Hair, 1972).

The sample of hospitals was compared with the population of nonprofit community hospitals on three variables: regional location, bed-size category, and ownership. Only minor differences obtained between the sample and the population in the distribution of hospitals by census regions. Similarly, few differences were observed in comparing the two groups on the basis of bed-size categories. The sample has a slightly smaller proportion of hospitals in the two smallest categories (62.2 percent in the panel sample versus 68.5 percent in the population) and a greater proportion in the two largest categories (37.8 percent versus 31.5 percent, respectively). The sample therefore may be somewhat biased toward larger hospitals. No significant differences were observed between the study sample and the population of hospitals on hospital ownership and control. A majority of hospitals in both groups were secular not-for-profit hospitals (51.5 percent in the panel sample and 50.4 percent in the population), followed by governmental hospitals (33.1 percent and 36.1 percent) and religious not-for-profit hospitals (15.4 percent and 13.4 percent).

Variables

Leadership instability. The dependent variable for this study was the total number of CEO turnovers occurring at a given hospital during the 1980–1988 period. We do not distinguish between voluntary and involuntary exits by CEOs because both types of succession may reflect the influence of sociopolitical structures defining the relationship between the board and the CEO; for example, CEOs may leave because they were fired by the board, were pressured by the board to resign, or because they sought employment elsewhere due to excessive constraints imposed by the board. We do not expect a high number of CEO turnovers in the study period to be due to retirements. Hospitals look to hire younger managers who presumably have many years of their career ahead of them, and the literature indicates that after age 45 it becomes increasingly difficult for a hospital manager to obtain a position as CEO. Whereas retirement may be the cause of any one succession during the study period, it is unlikely that multiple successions can be attributed to the retirements of more than one CEO in a given hospital. Other causes of termination such as death and illness introduce a potential disturbance in measuring aggregate rates of turnover over the study period, but we have found nothing to suggest that such environmentally controlled forms of succession are not randomly distributed over the hospitals surveyed in our study.

Changes in the hospital CEO were determined by comparing hospital CEO names in consecutive years of the AHA Annual Survey of Hospitals. A potential limitation of this methodology is that no more than one CEO turnover per year can be detected. Although we consider multiple successions in a given year unlikely, our methods may nevertheless result in a somewhat conservative estimate of the actual number of CEO turnovers in the sample and population of hospitals. The distribution of leadership instability in the study sample indicates that 28 percent (427) of the hospitals experienced no CEO successions during the study period. Thirty-four percent of the hospitals had one succession, 22 percent two successions, 10 percent three successions, and 5 percent four or more successions. The distribution of CEO turnovers is quite similar for the entire population of nonprofit community hospitals (N = 5,311). Among all such hospitals during the 1980–1988 period 22 percent experienced no turnover; 32 percent had one succession; 23 percent had two turnovers; 13 percent experienced three turnovers, and 9 percent experienced four or more CEO turnovers.

Governing board—CEO relations. Many of our independent variables are related to relatively abstract concepts such as power, influence, and cognition. Whereas it may be possible to measure these constructs directly using obtrusive methods, because these data are sensitive, such measures would yield substantial measurement error, response bias, and difficulties of access (Frederickson, Hambrick, and Baumrin, 1988). Our general measurement strategy, therefore, was to use objective, structural measures of these constructs, on the assumption that these structures give rise to and determine the condition of the sociopolitical constructs discussed in the theory.

Nine indicators were constructed from the 1985 Governing Board Survey to characterize the relationship between hospital CEOs and governing boards. These nine measures are summarized in the Appendix. The concepts expressed in hypotheses 2a and 2b and 4a and 4b were measured by three discrete indicators: whether or not hospital boards maintained a formal, written employment contract with the CEO (hypotheses 2a and 2b); the number of board members whose occupation was corporate executive; and the number of board members who were also members of the active medical staff of the focal hospital (hypotheses 4a and 4b). We assessed the proportional representation by corporate executives and medical staff members by controlling for board size in the multivariate model.

To reduce the data and prevent problems of multicollinearity in the regression analyses, we created two factor-score indices from six of the governing-board measures, using principal components factor analysis with varimax rotation. The six variables loaded on two factors. *CEO power/influence over the board* was defined by the three variables pertaining to CEO influence and participation on the governing board [CEO role on governing board (.72), CEO membership on the board executive committee (.71), and CEO influence in board member selection (.73)]. The second factor, *board size and heterogeneity,* was defined by governing board size (.69), diffusion of board member selection responsibility (.62), and occupational heterogeneity of board members (.62). The two indices had alpha coefficients of .79 and .66, respectively.

All governing-board measures were constructed from data from the 1985 Governing Board Survey, to model leadership instability over the 1980–1989 period. Based on the premise that power and influence structures are institutionalized in organizations (Pfeffer, 1981), it was assumed that board characteristics remained relatively stable for the period of study. This assumption was tested empirically by examining the inertia coefficients of the board variables (Nielsen and Hannan, 1977; Fennell, 1982).[1] These inertia coefficients indicated that board characteristics are primarily a function of their prior (lagged) values, showing a substantial amount of stability. These results do not suggest that there is no change in board composition or membership. Other research clearly demonstrates that individuals leave and are replaced on hospital boards. Central to our analysis, however, is that very little structural change occurs in the governing boards of hospitals, particularly in those attributes that potentially affect the relationship between the board and the CEO. Corroborating support for the relative stability of board structural characteristics is provided by Boeker and Goodstein (1991), who found that in a study of 290 California hospitals between 1980 and 1986, the percentage of physicians, business executives, and hospital executives on boards changed by an average of only 1 percent per year, with very little variation among sample hospitals.

Life-cycle stage. Stage measures are based on the number of annual inpatient admissions to the hospital. Admissions are considered vital internal resources to the hospital that reflect its ability to compete and grow in its local market. Further, admissions take into consideration the role of physicians in channeling resources (patients) to the hospital, a situation markedly different from, say, universities, where students directly enroll to receive services.

Following Cameron and his colleagues (Cameron, Kim, and Whetten, 1987; Cameron, Whetten, and Kim, 1987; Whetten, 1987), we elected to measure life-cycle stages categorically to obtain clearer distinctions between the major stages. Although we recognize that by grouping hospitals by categories of growth and decline, some variance is lost, we felt that this was less important than retaining conceptual clarity and consistency with the predictions of past literature. This approach is also consistent with our underlying theory that leadership instability is predicted not so much by a linear continuum between good and poor performance as by the type of uncertainty created for the organization during particular stages of the organization's life cycle. We chose to use a five-year period as the appropriate length of a stage, so as to measure patterns of growth and decline over a sufficiently long period to capture trends and avoid short-term aberrations, yet a short enough period to relate temporally to the dependent variable (Cameron, Kim, and Whetten, 1987).

Hospitals were placed in one of four mutually exclusive stage categories for the period 1980–1984: decline, growth, stability, or instability. Effects of life-cycle stage on leadership instability were lagged to reflect the fact that stages of organizational growth or decline become known to organizational decision makers only after a sustained period. We developed and tested measures based on two lagged performance periods in our analysis. The first, 1975–1979, proved to be inconsequential in terms of predicting leadership instability during the study period. Measures

1

Values for each board attribute in the 1989 survey were regressed separately on their 1985 values, while suppressing the intercept in the regression. In interpreting these stability analyses, the closer the beta coefficient value is to 1, the more stable the governance attribute over time. Coefficient estimates for the five board attributes in 1985 ranged from .70 for CEO power/influence to .97 for insider representation on the board. R-square for these over-time regressions were all over .50, and differences in variances were never greater than .01. Although there is no generally accepted standard for stability analyses, taken together, these comparisons on autocorrelation coefficients, R-squares, and variances suggest the governing board measures were quite stable from 1985 to 1989.

based on the second period, 1980–1984, proved more robust and were adopted for this analysis. Life-cycle stage was determined by patterns of adjusted admissions of hospitals in the sample, where adjusted admissions are the sums of admissions and equivalent admissions attributed to outpatient services (product of admissions and ratio of outpatient revenue to inpatient revenue). This adjustment was necessary to standardize the assessment of critical internal resources among hospitals that differ in their strategic emphasis on inpatient or outpatient care.

To partial out the effects of industrywide change from true growth or decline during the 1980–1984 period, we compared patterns of change in adjusted admissions for an individual hospital to mean changes for that hospital's industry comparison group. Nine mutually exclusive comparison groups were formed on the basis of ownership category (secular not-for-profit, religious not-for-profit, or government), and within each ownership category, three groups were formed based on hospital bed size (less than 100 beds, 100–299 beds, 300 or more beds). Hospitals showing increases in adjusted admissions of more than 5 percent above the average change for their comparison groups for at least three of the four consecutive-year pairs (1980–81, 1981–82, 1982–83, and 1983–84) were categorized as growers, while those showing decreases of more than 5 percent below national averages for at least three of four year pairs were designated as decliners (Cameron, Kim, and Whetten, 1987). Hospitals showing at least one pair of consecutive years with adjusted admissions growth greater than 5 percent and at least one year pair of adjusted admissions decline greater than 5 percent with respect to their comparison groups were classified as unstable. All remaining hospitals were classified as stable (i.e., less than 5 percent over or under national change averages for most of the five-year period). The resulting stage categories, then, reflect hospital growth or decline net of industry trends, standardized by hospital size and ownership groupings. Numbers of adjusted admissions for this time period were taken from the 1980–1984 AHA Annual Survey of Hospitals.

Measures of all other control variables derive from several data sources and are summarized in the Appendix. Means and zero-order correlations are presented in Table 1.

Models

Given the infrequency of turnover events (most hospitals experienced 0 or 1 turnover), we tested our hypotheses using Poisson regression. The count of turnovers is denoted by Y_i, and we assume that each Y_i follows a Poisson distribution with $E(Y_i) = \lambda_i$. The regression model predicts the log of the intensity rate, λ_i, as a function of the observed covariates, x_i. λ_i can only take nonnegative values, and the natural way to model it is parameterized as a log-linear function of the covariates:

$$\lambda_i = \exp \beta' x_i ,$$

implying that log λ_i is equal to $\beta' x_i$. The probability

Leadership Instability

Table 1

Intercorrelations and Descriptive Statistics of Study Variables*

Variable	Mean	S.D.	1	2	3	4	5	6	7	8	9	10	11	12	13	14	15
1. CEO power/influence	−.02	.83															
2. Board size-heterogeneity	.01	.63	.39														
3. CEO contract	.39	.49	−.01	.01													
4. Corporate representation	2.13	3.31	.24	.51	.01												
5. Medical staff (M.D.) representation	1.67	1.89	.19	.41	.03	.27											
6. Higher authority	.49	.50	.18	.02	−.01	−.02	.00										
7. Competition (market)	9.40	19.37	.17	.21	.00	.29	.30	.06									
8. Yrs. in contract management	1.08	2.34	−.21	−.11	−.07	−.14	−.08	−.04	−.15								
9. Yrs. in multihospital system	1.38	2.36	.38	.19	−.07	.08	.08	.35	.08	−.17							
10. Organization size	195.15	176.30	.33	.38	.02	.45	.33	.12	.44	−.23	.28						
11, Succession lag	5.61	3.67	.05	.09	−.05	.10	.07	−.04	.02	−.18	−.01	.13					
12. Decline	.03	.18	−.01	−.02	−.02	−.01	−.01	.01	−.04	−.02	.02	−.04	−.01				
13. Growth	.10	.29	−.08	−.08	−.01	−.07	−.07	−.03	−.09	.07	−.04	−.15	−.06	−.06			
14. Stability	.43	.50	.15	.17	−.00	.16	.14	.04	.12	−.13	.08	.28	.10	−.17	−.29		
15. Instability	.46	.50	−.11	−.14	.01	−.13	−.12	−.02	−.07	.12	−.07	−.21	−.09	−.17	−.13	−.41	
16. Leadership instability	1.33	1.21	−.15	−.14	.06	−.14	−.06	.04	−.07	.33	−.00	−.15	−.16	.04	−.00	−.15	.15

* Correlations greater than + or −.05 significant at $p < .05$.

associated with any observed event count (number of turnovers) is:

$$\Pr(Y_i = y_i, \lambda_i) = \lambda_i^{y_i} e^{-\lambda_i}/y_i!, \quad i = 1, 2, 3, \ldots n,$$

where λ_i is the mean and the variance of the dependent variable. The product of these terms over *i* gives the likelihood function that is maximized. The Poisson regression model is a standard one for event-count data of this type (Tuma and Hannan, 1984; McCullagh and Nelder, 1989; Agresti, 1990), and its use is suggested here because the order and spacing of the dependent variable are automatically taken into account and because the skewness in the distribution of *Y* presents no special difficulties.

Three models were specified. The first specified leadership instability as a function of six of the control variables: board accountability to higher authority, years in contract management, years in multihospital system, market competition, organization size, and succession lag. The second Poisson function tested for the influence of life-cycle stage while controlling for the effects of covariates contained in model 1. Model 3 contained the five variables representing the sociopolitical structure of board-CEO relations, as well as life-cycle stage and other control variables.

RESULTS

Table 2 presents results of the Poisson regression analyses for the three models we specified. Model 1 results indicate that four of the control variables exercise statistically significant effects on the dependent variable. As anticipated, both years in contract management and years in multihospital systems were positively and significantly associated with leadership instability. Also, as expected, larger hospitals were significantly less likely to experience leadership instability than smaller hospitals. Finally, the greater the number of years since the most recent CEO turnover in the 1970s, the lower the leadership instability during the study period. No significant effects obtained for board accountability to higher authority or for market competition.

In model 2, three life-cycle stage variables were added to the model containing the six covariates. Consistent with our

Table 2

Poisson Regression Results (Unstandardized Coefficients): Effects of Board Attributes on Leadership Instability (*N* = 1534)

	Model 1		Model 2		Model 3	
Variables	Coefficient	S.E.	Coefficient	S.E.	Coefficient	S.E.
Constant	−5.60***	(.06)	−5.74***	(.07)	−5.88***	(.08)
Control variable						
Higher authority	−0.07	(.05)	−0.07	(.05)	−0.07	(.05)
Succession lag	−0.02***	(.01)	−0.02***	(.01)	−0.02**	(.01)
Yrs. in contract management	0.09***	(.01)	0.09***	(.01)	0.09***	(.01)
Yrs. in multihospital system	0.03**	(.01)	0.03**	(.01)	0.04***	(.01)
Competition (market)	0.08E-2*	(.01E-1)	0.09E-2	(.01E-1)	0.05E-2	(.01E-1)
Organization size	−0.06E-2***	(.02E-2)	0.05E-2**	(.02E-2)	−0.03E-2	(.02E-2)
Life-cycle stage						
Decline			0.29**	(.12)	0.28**	(.12)
Growth			−0.03	(.08)	−0.04	(.08)
Instability†			0.19***	(.05)	0.18**	(.05)
Board-CEO relations						
CEO power/influence					−0.09**	(.03)
Board-CEO contract					0.16***	(.05)
Board size-heterogeneity					−0.10*	(.05)
Medical staff (MD) representation					0.02	(.01)
Corporate representation					−0.01	(.01)
Model chi-square	194.19		215.03		250.53	
D.f.	6		9		14	

* $p \leq .05$; ** $p \leq .01$; *** $p \leq .001$.
* $E - a = 10^{-a}$.
† Suppressed category = stability.

expectations, hospitals experiencing unstable periods displayed significantly higher levels of leadership instability relative to hospitals in stable periods. Our results indicate, however, that declining organizations also exhibit levels of leadership instability significantly higher than hospitals in stable stages. Finally, organizations characterized as growers are not significantly different from stable organizations in their lower level of leadership instability.

While individual life-cycle-stage variables obtained acceptable levels of statistical significance in the model, we also tested whether or not the growth and decline stages were meaningful predictors of leadership instability. This was done by performing a chi-square test based on the difference in the chi-square values for the model containing the six covariates (model 1) and the model containing the covariates plus the three stage variables (model 2). This test is analogous to the standard *F*-test used to determine whether a set of variables contributes marginally to the proportion of variance explained when using ordinary least squares. Results of the test were significant ($X^2 = 20.84$, 3 d.f. $p < .01$), indicating that the life-cycle-stage categories were significant contributors to the explanatory power of the model.

In model 3, we tested the hypothesized relationships between board attributes and leadership instability, controlling for the stage variable and the six other covariates. Consistent with the prediction in hypothesis 1, which posited that greater CEO power and influence over the board would lower leadership instability, the CEO power and influence coefficient was negative and significant ($p < .05$). Hypotheses 2a and 2b proposed contrasting effects of CEO-board employment contracts on leadership instability. In support of hypothesis 2b, the CEO contract variable was positive and highly significant, indicating that the presence of such contracts increased the instability of leadership in hospitals. Hypothesis 3 predicted that greater stability of hospital leadership would be associated with larger board size and greater occupational heterogeneity. Controlling for the effects of the covariates, life-cycle stage, and the other board attributes, the coefficient for the board size and heterogeneity index was negative and statistically significant ($p < .01$), thus providing strong support for the hypothesis. Hypotheses 4a and 4b predicted, respectively, that corporate representation and medical staff representation on the board would exert opposite effects on leadership stability. Consistent with our predictions, a greater number of corporate representatives was associated with lower leadership instability in hospitals, while greater medical staff representation was associated with higher leadership instability. Neither of these results, however, was statistically significant.

We tested the explanatory power of the board variables as a group, using the model chi-square difference between models 2 and 3. Results indicated that the board variables were significant contributors to the explanatory power of the model ($X^2 = 45.50$, 5 d.f., $p < .001$). We also considered whether or not the effects of CEO-board relationships on leadership instability are conditioned by the organization's life-cycle stage. Two sets of analyses were performed to explore this possibility: (1) an analysis of multiplicative interaction terms incorporating stage and various board variables, and (2) partitioning the hospitals into subsamples based on life-cycle stage (growers, decliners, etc.). The analysis of cross-product interaction terms produced no clear pattern of results. The pattern of results from the subsample analyses was mixed. Leadership instability in growing hospitals and in unstable hospitals was unaffected by most of the governance variables, whereas declining hospitals were somewhat more sensitive to the sociopolitical aspects of board-CEO relations. Hospitals in stable cycles, however, showed significant associations with several board-CEO variables, including CEO power and influence (negative), CEO employment contract (positive), and board size/heterogeneity (negative).

DISCUSSION

In this study we have examined leadership instability as a long-term characteristic of hospitals and have proposed an explanation of leadership instability that incorporates both the organization's life-cycle stage and the sociopolitical structure linking top management and governing boards. Our results indicate that both types of variables exercise significant effects on leadership instability. First, the effects of long-term growth or decline on leadership instability generally parallel previous work that demonstrates a functional relationship between decline in organizational performance and CEO succession. Our findings indicate that unstable and declining organizations experience more instability in the CEO position over time than either stable or growing organizations. Second, the relational structure linking CEOs and governing boards also significantly explains variation in leadership instability, and these effects obtain net of the effects of life-cycle stage.

We examined CEO power and influence in terms of a number of potential influence channels through which the CEO could affect board decision making: membership on the board, membership on the executive committee, and involvement in the selection of new board members. Our results confirm that CEO power over the board is associated with leadership stability. Although we couched these arguments in terms of power and influence, at the heart of any board-CEO relationship is the need to acquire, control, or coordinate the flow of information. Under conditions of uncertainty, problems of bounded rationality become more acute (Galbraith, 1977). At base, informational needs are vastly increased under conditions of uncertainty and change, and thus more coordinated decision making between the two components of organizational governance, top management and the board, are required. Increased coordination attenuates the ambiguity associated with management roles, emergent strategies, and assignment of priorities to organizational goals and objectives. The likelihood of the board misinterpreting or misrepresenting managerial action is reduced if the board and top management work closely together as a unit, as opposed to operating in separate spheres of action. Integration of board-CEO decision making reduces the probability that the actions and expectations of management and the governing board will be at odds and thus lead to conflicts between the board and the CEO. As Williamson (1985: 1220) observed, "to the extent that management participation on the board permits reviews on the merits [or failures of management decision making] to be done more responsibly, it serves to safeguard an employment relation that would otherwise be exposed to excessive risk."

Another crucial aspect of the relative influence of the CEO and the board is the existence of a formal contract. We had proposed that the CEO contract could function as either a mechanism of CEO power over the board (hypothesis 2a) or of board control over CEOs, providing a structural mechanism for performance monitoring (hypothesis 2b). Our results support the latter interpretation, as the existence of a formal contract seems to increase levels of CEO turnover, thus suggesting that perhaps such contracts are used by boards to specify terms of employment, management performance, and board expectations. Contracts may lead to increased CEO instability if they provide boards with easily accessed termination procedures. Taken together, it would appear that CEO power over the board (through decision-making influence) and formal employment contracts between the board and the CEO operate as power-balancing mechanisms. Both have an impact on CEO turnover, but their effects are opposite. In fact, the more a CEO participates in decision making with the board, the more opportunities exist for the board to observe and evaluate the process of decision making by the CEO, as well as the outcomes of such decisions (Williamson, 1985).

The functional role of the board was examined indirectly through an analysis of board size and heterogeneity. We argued that internally focused boards tend to be smaller and more homogeneous and that such boards are less likely to function as a link to the hospital's environment. Our results confirm expectations that larger, more heterogeneous boards are associated with top-management stability, perhaps because such boards are actually less likely to become involved in decisions concerning the succession of CEOs and are more likely to be controlled by the CEO. Larger boards tend to be found in not-for-profit organizations and have traditionally been more concerned with external representation than with internal monitoring and decision making (Middleton, 1987; Delbecq and Gill, 1988). The larger the board, the less likely it is to exercise control over the CEO and the more likely the organization is to experience long-term leadership stability.

Our findings give additional credence to the notion that leadership instability is influenced by factors other than the rational exercise of control by the board over top management. Rationally based control in complex organizations is difficult because information about the relationship between managerial behavior and organizational performance is often hidden in the "complex causality" that determines any organizational outcome (Oviatt, 1988: 218). At issue is the board's ability to discriminate between outcomes or profiles that are attributable to managerial action (or inaction) and those that are exogenously determined. Under ideal circumstances, the control mechanisms employed by the board protect management from circumstances or outcomes over which it has no control or from short-term problems that are the results of investments in long-term goals (Eisenhardt, 1985). In organizations in which uncertainty is high or strategic goals are not easily defined and measured, formalized control systems are perhaps less useful in making such distinctions, and other factors become more salient.

This paper has made the case that the board-CEO relationship is a critical factor in the stability of the executive management position in organizations. This thesis, in part, is based on the premise that such relationships are structured through the bylaws, operating procedures, and historical norms that define power, influence, and access to information in organizational settings. This does not mean, however, that other constituencies exercise no influence over the stability of the CEO's position. In hospitals, for example, the medical staff is invested with a great deal of power, owing to their professional training, centrality to the production core of the organization, and relative immunity from administrative control. The ability of the CEO to manage the medical staff of the hospital effectively undoubtedly contributes to CEO tenure and succession, even though individual physicians and the medical staff of the hospital are not authorized to hire and fire the CEO. Even if such actions are proposed by the medical staff, they must be channelled through the board and are thus subject to the sociopolitical structures that define board-CEO relations. In the future, this picture may change.

Although, historically, the medical staff has operated somewhat like a wild card in the bureaucratic structure and governance of hospitals, recent trends in the medical care sector point to more formally structured relationships between physicians, hospital boards, and hospital management. Growth in the number of more complex governance structures in health care, such as preferred provider organizations, hospital-physician joint ventures, and diversified health systems, suggests that physicians will be more likely to act as partners with CEOs and will be financially as well as professionally tied to the fate of these organizations. The traditional role of physicians as powerful entrepreneurs, situated both inside and outside of the hospital, will be modified, and their inside role will become both more important and more formalized in relation to top management and the governing board. Research is needed on how this nexus of relationships is changing and how such change will affect leadership instability over time.

We have assumed that most of the turnovers included in our measure of leadership instability reflect either voluntary departure or involuntary dismissal and that retirements, deaths, or illness-related turnovers are randomly distributed over hospitals. Involuntary dismissals, however, have been viewed as a unique form of turnover (Boeker, 1992) and may be influenced more strongly by the power relationships and long-term cycles of growth, decline, or instability examined here. Dismissals can become an institutionalized form of scapegoating, contributing both to higher leadership instability over time and to the dysfunctional consequences of high turnover discussed by Fredrickson, Hambrick, and Baumrin (1988). Voluntary exits may reflect similar processes when such exits are preemptive departures, made in response to the expectation of dismissal or poor relationships with the board. Our data do not distinguish between voluntary exits and dismissals, and to the extent that these two types of exits may represent different turnover processes, our analysis of leadership instability may be masking different effects. If the processes underlying dismissals and preemptive exits are similar, however, the conclusions we have drawn here may be generally valid.

CONCLUSION

This analysis has considered leadership stability as a systemic organizational characteristic with long-term implications for the sociopolitical structures linking governing boards and top management and organizational growth or decline. Unlike examinations of individual succession as discrete turnover events, a focus on long-term leadership instability allowed us to examine the relationship between long-term rates of turnover and organizational cycles of growth, decline, stability, and instability, as well as relational properties of governing boards and top management. Such board-CEO relationships are particularly important in organizations such as hospitals, where indicators of CEO performance are ambiguous and where environmental conditions are characterized by high levels of uncertainty.

Although we have chosen to focus on long-term patterns of growth or decline in the organization's resource base and on the structural relationships between the board and the CEO, there are obviously a number of different stakeholder groups inside and outside of hospitals to whom the CEO is at least nominally accountable, including the medical staff, the nursing staff, local community groups, and local industry or business leaders. It is quite probable that each of these groups may emphasize different indicators of CEO performance, which may or may not correlate with long-term growth or decline in admissions. Within any given hospital board, the representatives of such groups may, in fact, come to dissimilar assessments of any given CEO. A careful examination of multiple constituencies and the performance measures they prefer, however, would likely require a more case-intensive study of micro-level CEO performance evaluations. Further, such a study would need to focus on the evaluations of individual CEOs by specific groups, rather than on long-term patterns of leadership instability. Such a case-study analysis of CEO performance assessment would complement, but not replace, the analyses reported here.

Current developments in the health care sector are moving hospitals more in the direction of the corporate model and a bottom-line emphasis on organizational performance. Board structures and the relative influence of CEOs and boards may have to change to balance the need for risk taking and long-term viability with short-term gains. Clearly we do not know what influence these governance relationships may have on the long-term survival of organizations in this rapidly changing sector. Following other writers (Fredrickson, Hambrick, and Baumrin, 1988), we have assumed that high rates of leadership instability over a prolonged period of time lead to internal disruption and declines in organizational performance, perhaps even to organizational failure. It is not clear, however, what the consequences are of protracted leadership instability on long-term survival, particularly for organizations experiencing extreme upheaval in their technical and institutional environments (Alexander and D'Aunno, 1990). It is possible that under such environmental conditions very low rates of CEO succession may also have serious dysfunctional consequences, such as impaired flexibility and a stagnant or ossified strategic capacity. Future research will need to examine in more detail the causal structure linking leadership instability, the board-CEO relationship, and long-term organizational survival.

REFERENCES

Agresti, Alan
1990 Categorical Data Analysis. New York: Wiley.

Alexander, Jeffrey, and Thomas A. D'Aunno
1990 "Transformations of institutional environments: Perspectives on the corporatization of U.S. health care." In Stephen Mick (ed.), Innovations in Health Care Delivery: New Insights into Organizational Theory: 53–85. San Francisco: Jossey-Bass.

Alexander, Jeffrey, and Kathryn Schroer
1985 "Governance in multihospital systems: An assessment of decision-making responsibility." Hospital and Health Services Administration, 30(2): 9–20.

Allen, Michael P., and Sharon K. Panian
1982 "Power, performance, and succession in the large corporation." Administrative Science Quarterly, 27: 538–547.

American College of Healthcare Executives
1991 Hospital Chief Executive Officer Turnover 1981–1990. Chicago: Foundation of the American College of Healthcare Executives.

Baysinger, Barry and Robert E. Hoskisson
1990 "The composition of boards of directors and strategic control: Effects on corporate strategy." Academy of Management Review, 15: 72–87.

Boeker, Warren
1992 "Power and managerial dismissal: Scapegoating at the top." Administrative Science Quarterly, 37: 400–421.

Boeker, Warren, and Jerry Goodstein
1991 Organizational performance and adaptation: Effects of environment and performance on changes in board composition." Academy of Management Journal, 34: 805–826.

Brown, M. Craig
1982 "Administrative succession and organizational performance: The succession effect." Administrative Science Quarterly, 27: 1–16.

Cameron, Kim S.
1983 "Strategic responses to conditions of decline." Journal of Higher Education, 55: 122–144.

Cameron, Kim S., Myung U. Kim, and David A. Whetten
1987 "Organizational effects of decline and turbulence." Administrative Science Quarterly, 32: 222–240.

Cameron, Kim S., David A. Whetten, and Myung U. Kim
1987 "Organizational dysfunctions of decline." Academy of Management Journal, 30: 126–138.

Carroll, Glenn R.
1984 "Organizational ecology." In Ralf E. Turner and James F. Short (eds.), Annual Review of Sociology, 10: 71–93. Palo Alto, CA: Annual Reviews.

Clendenin, W. D.
1972 "Company presidents look at the board of directors." California Management Review, Spring: 60–66.

Cochran, Philip L., Robert A. Wood, and Thomas B. Jones
1985 "The composition of boards of directors and the incidence of golden parachutes." Academy of Management Journal, 28: 664–671.

Coughlan, A. T., and R. M. Schmidt
1985 "Executive compensation, managerial turnover, and firm performance: An empirical investigation." Journal of Accounting and Economics, 7: 43–66.

Delbecq, Andre L., and Sandra L. Gill
1988 "Developing strategic directions for governing boards." Hospital and Health Services Administration, 33: 25–35.

Dwore, Richard B., and Bruce P. Murray
1989 "Turnover at the top: Utah hospital CEOs in a turbulent era." Hospital and Health Services Administration, 34(3): 333–351.

Eisenhardt, Kathleen
1985 "Control: Organizational and economic approaches." Management Science, 31: 134–149.

Eitzen, D. Stanley, and Norman R. Yetman
1972 "Managerial change, longevity, and organizational effectiveness." Administrative Science Quarterly, 17: 110–116.

Fama, Eugene
1980 "Agency problems and the theory of the firm." Journal of Political Economy, 88: 288–307.

Fennell, Mary L.
1982 "Context in organizational groups: The case of hospital clusters." Journal of Health and Social Behavior, 23: 65–84

Finkelstein, Sydney, and Donald C. Hambrick
1990 "Top-management-team tenure and organizational outcomes: The moderating role of managerial discretion." Administrative Science Quarterly, 35: 484–503.

Fredrickson, James W., Donald C. Hambrick, and Sara Baumrin
1988 "A model of CEO dismissal." Academy of Management Review, 13: 255–270.

Galbraith, Jay R.
1977 Organization Design. Reading, MA: Addison-Wesley.

Gamson, William, and N. Scotch
1964 "Scapegoating in baseball." American Journal of Sociology, 70: 69–76.

Garnick, Deborah W., Harold Luft, James C. Robinson, and Janice Tetreault
1987 "Appropriate measures of hospital market areas." Health Services Research, 22: 69–89.

Goldsmith, Jeff C.
1981 Can Hospitals Survive? The New Competitive Health Care Market. Homewood, IL: Dow-Jones-Irwin.

Goodstein, Jerry, and Warren Boeker
1991 "Turbulence at the top: A new perspective on governance structure changes and strategic change." Academy of Management Journal, 34: 306–330.

Gordon, G., and S. Becker
1964 "Organizational size and managerial succession: A reorganization.' American Journal of Sociology, 70: 215–223.

Greenhalgh, Leonard, and Zehava Rosenblatt
1984 "Job insecurity: Toward conceptual clarity." Academy of Management Review, 9: 438–448.

Grusky, Oscar
1963 "Managerial succession and organizational effectiveness." American Journal of Sociology, 69: 21–31.

Hall, Douglas T., and Roger Mansfield
1971 "Organizational and individual response to external stress." Administrative Science Quarterly, 16: 533–547.

Jensen, Michael C.
1986 "The takeover controversy: Analysis and evidence." Midland Corporate Finance Journal, 4: 6–32.

Leadership Instability

Kanter, Rosabeth M., and D. V. Summers
1987 "Doing well by doing good: Dilemmas of performance measurement in nonprofit organizations and the need for a multiple constituency approach." In W. W. Powell (ed.), The Nonprofit Sector: A Research Handbook: 154–166. New Haven, CT: Yale University Press.

Kesner, I. F., and D. R. Dalton
1985 "The effect of board composition on CEO succession and organizational performance." Quarterly Journal of Business Economics, 24(2): 3–20.

Kimberly, John R., and Robert H. Miles
1981 The Organizational Life Cycle. San Francisco: Jossey-Bass.

Kimberly, John R., and Edward J. Zajac
1985 "Strategic adaptation in health care organizations: Implications for theory and research." Medical Care Review, 42(2): 267–302.

Kosnik, Rita D.
1987 "Greenmail: A study of board performance in corporate governance." Administrative Science Quarterly, 32: 163–185.
1990 "Effects of board demography and directors' incentives on corporate greenmail decisions." Academy of Management Journal, 33: 129–150.

Mace, M. L.
1971 Directors, Myth and Reality. Boston: Harvard Business School Press.

McCullagh, Peter M., and John A. Nelder
1989 Generalized Linear Models, 2d ed. New York: Chapman and Hall.

McEachern, W. A.
1975 Managerial Control and Performance. Lexington, MA: D. C. Heath.

Meyer, Marshall
1978 "Leadership and organizational structure." In M. Meyer and Associates (eds.), Environments and Organizations: 220–232. San Francisco: Jossey-Bass.

Middleton, Melissa
1987 "Nonprofit boards of directors: Beyond the governance function." In W. W. Powell (ed.), The Nonprofit Sector: 141–153. New Haven, CT: Yale University Press.

Mintzberg, Henry
1983 Power in and around Organizations. Englewood Cliffs, NJ: Prentice-Hall.

Mizruchi, Mark S.
1983 "Who controls whom? An examination of the relation between management and boards of directors in large American corporations." Academy of Management Review, 8(3): 426–435.

Nielsen, François, and Michael T. Hannan
1977 "The expansion of national education systems: Tests of a population model." American Sociological Review, 42: 479–490.

Oviatt, Benjamin M.
1988 "Agency and transaction cost perspectives on the manager-shareholder relationship: Incentives for congruent interests." Academy of Management Review, 13: 214–225.

Perrow, Charles
1963 "Goals and power structures. An historical case study." In Eliot Freidson (ed.), The Hospital in Modern Society: 112–146. New York: Macmillan.

Pfeffer, Jeffrey
1972 "Size and composition of corporate boards of directors: The organization and its environment." Administrative Science Quarterly, 17: 218–228.
1973 "Size, composition, and function of hospital boards of directors: A study of organization-environment linkage." Administrative Science Quarterly, 18: 349–364.
1981 Power in Organizations. Marshfield, MA: Pitman.

Pfeffer, Jeffrey, and Charles A. O'Reilly, III
1987 "Hospital demography and turnover among nurses." Industrial Relations, 26: 158–173.

Pfeffer, Jeffrey, and Gerald R. Salancik
1977 "Organizational context and the characteristics and tenure of hospital administrators." Academy of Management Journal, 20: 74–88.
1978 The External Control of Organizations: A Resource Dependence Perspective. New York: Harper and Row.

Price, James G.
1963 "The impact of governing boards on organizational effectiveness and morale." Administrative Science Quarterly, 8: 361–377.

Robinson, James C., and Harold Luft
1987 "Competition and the cost of hospital care, 1972–1982." Journal of the American Medical Association, 257(23): 3241–3245.

Singh, Jitendra V., Robert J. House, and David J. Tucker
1986 "Organizational change and organizational mortality." Administrative Science Quarterly, 31: 587–611.

Starbuck, William H., A. Greve and B. L. T. Hedberg
1978 "Responding to crisis." Journal of Business Administration, 9: 111–137.

Staw, Barry M.
1980 "The consequences of turnover." Journal of Occupational Behavior, 1: 253–273.

Thompson, James D.
1967 Organizations in Action. New York: McGraw-Hill.

Tuma, Nancy B., and Michael T. Hannan
1984 Social Dynamics. New York: Academic Press.

Wade, James, Charles A. O'Reilly, III, and Ike Chandratat
1990 "Golden parachutes: CEOs and the exercise of social influence." Administrative Science Quarterly, 35: 587–603.

Warner, J. B., R. L. Watts, and K. H. Wruck
1982 "Stock prices, event prediction, and event studies: An examination of top management restructurings." Journal of Financial Economics, 20: 461–492.

Weil, Peter A.
1990 "Job turnover of CEOs in teaching and nonteaching hospitals." Academic Medicine, 65: 1–7.

Weil, Peter A., and John Timmerberg
1990 "Hospital CEO turnover: Modelling more or less desirable places to work." Health Services Management Research, 3: 208–217.

Weisback, M. S.
1988 "Outside directors and CEO turnover." Journal of Financial Economics, 20: 431–460.

Whetten, David A.
1981 "Organizational responses to scarcity." Educational Administration Quarterly, 17: 80–97.
1987 "Organizational growth and decline processes." In W. Richard Scott (ed.), Annual Review of Sociology, 13: 335–358. Palo Alto, CA: Annual Reviews.

Williamson, Oliver E.
1985 The Economic Institutions of Capitalism: Firms, Markets, and Relational Contracting. New York: Macmillan.

Young, David W., and Richard B. Saltman
1985 The Hospital Power Equilibrium: Physician Behavior and Cost Control. Baltimore: Johns Hopkins University Press.

Zald, Mayer N.
1965 "Who shall rule? A political analysis of succession in a large welfare organization." Pacific Sociological Review, 8: 52–60.
1969 "The power and functions of boards of directors: A theoretical synthesis." American Journal of Sociology, 75: 97–111.

Zald, Mayer N., and Feather D. Hair
1972 "The social control of general hospitals." In Basil S. Georgopoulos (ed.), Organizational Research on Health Institutions: 51–81. Ann Arbor, MI: Institute for Social Research, University of Michigan.

APPENDIX: Variable Measures

CEO role on governing board (ordinal scale): not a board member (0), a nonvoting (ex-officio) board member (1), a voting board member (2), chair of board (3).

CEO membership on the board executive committee (dummy variable): not a member or no board executive committee (0), member of the executive committee (1).

CEO influence on board member selection (ratio variable): the number of organizational bodies involved in member selection to which the CEO belongs (range from 0 to 3), divided by the total number of bodies involved in board member selection (range from 1 to 8).

Governing board size: number of individuals serving as members of the board of trustees of the hospital.

Diffusion of board member selection responsibility: number of organizational bodies involved in the selection of new board members. Selection involvement consists of appointing, nominating, or electing board members. Organizational bodies include board nominating committee, board executive committee, governmental body, hospital board, hospital's corporation or association, hospital medical staff, local community, and parent corporation board.

Occupational heterogeneity of board members: breadth or concentration of occupations represented on the governing board calculated as percentage of board membership of each of 14 mutually exclusive groups squared, and then summed (similar to Herfindahl index). The maximum value of the index is one if the entire board consists of one occupational group. Smaller values indicate a more heterogeneous board. Occupational categories assessed were physicians, other health professionals, hospital's CEO, religious, lawyer, educator, banker/financier, independent business person, corporate executive, farmer/rancher, government official/agency representative, labor official/representative, homemaker.

Written CEO-board employment contract (dummy variable): no written contract (0), contract (1).

Board members with corporate affiliation: number of board members occupationally classified as corporate executives.

Medical staff representation on board: number of board members who are physicians with active staff privileges at the hospital.

Leadership Instability

Board accountability to a higher authority (dummy variable): no accountability to higher authority (0), accountability to higher authority (1). Higher authorities include local, county, or state government, governing boards of holding or parent company, religious orders, universities, or for-profit corporations.

Hospital (market) competition: number of other community hospitals within 15-mile radius of the local hospital. This measure of competition is based on the assumption that hospitals operating in close geographical proximity are likely to experience greater market pressure as a result of competition for patient admissions and physician affiliations. Fifteen miles is the maximum distance physicians are expected to travel in order to admit patients to a hospital (Garnick et al., 1987; Robinson and Luft, 1987).

Contract management: number of years in the study period (1980–1988) that hospital was involved in a contract management affiliation.

Multihospital-system affiliation: number of years in study period (1980–1988) that hospital was a member of a multihospital system (excludes contract management affiliation).

Hospital size: number of hospital beds, set up and staffed for use (1985 AHA Annual Survey).

Lagged CEO succession: number of years prior to 1980 since the most recent CEO turnover; range from 1 (CEO turnover in 1979) to 11 (no CEO turnover from 1970 to 1979).

[8]

The Circulation of Corporate Control: Selection of Functional Backgrounds of New CEOs in Large U.S. Manufacturing Firms, 1981–1992

William Ocasio
Northwestern University
Hyosun Kim
Massachusetts Institute of Technology

We develop a conceptual model of the circulation of corporate control—the instability in formal authority at the top of large corporations. According to our model, chief executive officer (CEO) selection is both a political contest for the top executive position and an ideological struggle among members of the firm's political coalition over defining the corporate agenda and strategy. We apply the model to analyze the selection of functional backgrounds of 275 new CEOs in large U.S. manufacturing firms from 1981 to 1992. Results show that the circulation of control adds to previous explanations based on strategic contingencies and institutional isomorphism. Furthermore, we find evidence of an ideological and political obsolescence of financial CEOs and a change in the strategic contingencies that previously favored finance and the financial conception of control. Results suggest that conceptions of control are best understood as styles, rather than institutions, as these conceptions are neither taken for granted nor isomorphic across industries or the manufacturing sector, but are subject to sectoral variation, contestation, and change.•

During the 1960s and 1970s, executives with financial backgrounds gained prominence in U.S. industrial enterprises, attaining the highest levels of the organizational hierarchy and achieving control over how the corporate purpose was conceived, defined, and executed (Hayes and Abernathy, 1980; Fligstein, 1987). The rise of finance personnel to positions of formal authority led to a transformation in critical outcomes and strategies in large corporations (Fligstein, 1985, 1990; Davis and Stout, 1992; Fligstein and Brantley, 1992; Mizruchi and Stearns, 1994). The rise to power of financial CEOs altered the agenda and direction of large U.S. industrial corporations and led to an articulation of corporate assumptions, values, and goals that Fligstein (1990) has termed the finance conception of control. According to this conception, the corporation is a portfolio of diversified businesses earning differential returns. It focuses on attaining short-term profitability, using financial tools to evaluate existing product lines and divisions and engaging in mergers and acquisitions as central elements of corporate strategy (Fligstein, 1987, 1990).[1]

The decade of the 1980s, however, was characterized by widespread changes in corporate governance, including hostile takeovers (Davis and Stout, 1992), corporate restructurings (Useem 1993), and the decline of conglomerate forms of organization (Davis, Diekmann, and Tinsley, 1994). These changes were accompanied by ideological challenges to the finance conception of control and the view of the corporation as a portfolio of business assets that could be managed through the use of economic and financial indicators. The question is whether the rise in the prominence of financial CEOs and the finance conception of control continued during the 1980s and early 1990s. To explore how these economic and ideological changes affected prevailing conceptions of control, we studied the selection of functional backgrounds of new CEOs in U.S. manufacturing firms during 1981–1992. In doing this, we extend and develop earlier theory on intraorganizational political dynamics and apply it

0001-8392/99/4403-0532/$1.00.

•
We thank Ron Burt, Linda Johanson, Mark Mizruchi, Don Palmer, Dick Scott, Ed Zajac, four anonymous reviewers, and seminar participants at Chicago GSB, MIT-Sloan, Wharton, and Kellogg for their very helpful comments and suggestions.

1
The finance conception of control, although associated with CEOs from financial backgrounds, is inconsistent with modern finance theory. Contemporary finance theory stresses that financial diversification is best undertaken by individual investors rather than by corporations (Brealy and Myers, 1991). The term used by management scholars to refer to the finance conception of control is portfolio planning or portfolio management (Haspelagh, 1982).

to the study of stability and change in CEOs' functional backgrounds.

We analyze the contests for control among elite members of functional groups within organizations (Perrow, 1970; Zald and Berger, 1978; Fligstein, 1987; Chaves, 1993). Our study complements recent research that highlights political struggles between the CEO and the board of directors (Wade, O'Reilly, and Chandratat, 1990; Westphal and Zajac, 1995) but focuses instead on the conflicts within top management (Hambrick, 1994). We develop a conceptual model of changes in corporate control—the circulation of corporate control—that highlights the obsolescence and contestation of executive power, as corporate elites vie for status, position, and control of the organizational hierarchy (Ocasio, 1994). We contrast our model with the model of the institutionalization of power (Salancik and Pfeffer, 1977; Pfeffer, 1981). While both models rely on political, cultural, and social psychological mechanisms, they vary in how they explain stability and change in power in organizations and the rise and fall of alternative conceptions of control (Fligstein, 1990).

POLITICAL DYNAMICS IN ORGANIZATIONS

Institutionalization of power. The institutionalization of power (Salancik and Pfeffer, 1977; Pfeffer, 1981; Boeker, 1989) is the dominant model of political dynamics in organization theory.[2] It highlights the ability of powerful individuals and groups to entrench themselves in the formal positions of authority and to increase their control of the corporation over time. The institutionalization of power is shaped by symbolic as well as material forces that operate both within the organization and at the level of the organizational field. According to this theory, conceptions of control (Fligstein, 1990) serve to institutionalize the power of dominant groups, as the goals and orientation of the governing subunit become infused with value (Selznick, 1957) and corporate elites protect and enforce these values by implementing programs and selecting executives consistent with dominant ideologies. Institutional forces create both normative and mimetic pressures for isomorphism (DiMaggio and Powell, 1983), as the power of the dominant group becomes culturally embedded within the field's dominant conception of control (Fligstein, 1987, 1990).

Circulation of corporate control. In large industrial corporations control of formal authority and the means of administration resides in corporate elites, the corporation's senior executives or top management. These corporate elites are subject to intraelite conflict, circulation, and change as diverse individuals and factions contend for control over the organization's dominant ideology and ruling coalition (Michels, 1962; Zald and Berger, 1978; Hambrick, 1994; Ocasio, 1994).[3] The circulation of corporate control—the instability in formal authority at the top of large corporations—is the dynamic outcome of how contests for control play out in a changing environment among contending individuals, groups, and identities (White, 1992). While at any one point, one individual and function will gain control over the firm's political coalition, the leadership in the dominant coalition will change across generations of executives, as different issues and

2
The model of institutionalization of power, while influenced in part by institutional sociology, also draws on several other theories, including resource dependence, escalation of commitment, and strategic contingencies theory (Salancik and Pfeffer, 1977; Pfeffer, 1981). Both cultural and political theories are part of the model. Perhaps a more descriptive and less confusing term for it would be the model of entrenchment of power. In this paper we will continue to use the original term used by Pfeffer (1981) but want to explicitly state that any discussion or test of the model of the institutionalization of power in this paper is *not* intended as pertaining to or to be a test of institutional theory or the new institutionalism.

3
Corporate elites are also subject to contests for control with external factions, as in the case of hostile takeovers, which became common during the 1980s. External contests for control, while important mechanisms for elite circulation, are beyond the scope of this paper.

problems come to the forefront and require attention in the firm's environment (March, 1962; Cyert and March, 1963; Ocasio, 1997). Which individuals and groups are in positions of authority over the dominant coalition over the long run is inherently unstable, as the outcome of recurring political struggles will lead to sequential attention to the firm's issues and problems, with resulting fluctuations in executive power.

The circulation of control is guided by two interrelated mechanisms: obsolescence and contestation (Ocasio, 1994). Obsolescence refers to the relative stability in schemas, ideologies, and conceptions of control held by executives and the functional subunits they represent, at the same time that the firm's economic, political, and cultural environments are changing. Ocasio (1994) identified two sources of obsolescence that lead to a circulation of power of individual executives: technical and political obsolescence. Technical obsolescence occurs as the ability of executives to provide satisfactory solutions to the strategic contingencies faced by organizations declines over time. Political obsolescence refers to executives' continued reliance on their original sources of power, without deriving new bases of social and cultural capital to sustain their power as the firm's political environment changes. An additional source of obsolescence is ideological obsolescence. Conceptions of control represent organizational ideologies that both guide corporate action and serve to legitimize the power and control of elite actors (Fligstein, 1990, 1996). Ideological obsolescence occurs as challenges to existing ideologies increase over time, and new ideological models serve to justify political contests by alternative elite groups.

Closely linked to obsolescence is contestation among competing factions and organizational elites. Contestation refers to the emergent and recurrent struggles for position and control among contending individuals, groups, and identities within organizations (White, 1992). Unlike the model of the institutionalization of power (Pfeffer, 1981), which assumes that at any point in time executive power is taken for granted, the model of the circulation of control assumes that the power of executives is subject to challenge, political struggle, and contestation (Jackall, 1988). While political struggles among executives are often hidden behind the bureaucratic ethos of organizations, executive succession brings them to the forefront, with internal contests for power and control over the corporation increasing over time (Ocasio, 1994) and triggered by changes in the organization and its environment (Tushman and Romanelli, 1985).

According to the theory, obsolescence and contestation occur within organizations, organizational fields, and societal sectors. The circulation of corporate control is thereby a cross-level process that applies to the recurrent struggles among individuals, intraorganizational groups, and interorganizational groups for command and control of formal authority and the means of administration in society. Individual contests for power are shaped by local contests among organizational subunits that in turn are shaped by interorganizational contests for control at the level of the industry and the organizational sector. The outcomes of these political struggles serve to define who gains formal authority over the corporation and what the critical problems are that the organization must face. According to this view, resource dependencies and structural contingencies are not objective criteria but are historically situated social constructions that are themselves the subject of conflict between contending factions.[4]

Circulation of functional backgrounds. According to the model of the circulation of control, CEO succession and selection trigger a contest for control among contending factions of the firm's dominant political coalition (White, 1992; Ocasio, 1994). The selection of CEOs with particular functional backgrounds reflects two interrelated contests for control: the competition for formal authority at the top of the corporate hierarchy and the intellectual and ideological struggle over the definition and formulation of corporate purpose, strategies, and goals. The outcome of these contests is shaped by the degree of obsolescence associated with the functional backgrounds of previous CEOs versus the functions of contending subunits. The technical, ideological, and political obsolescence of functional subunits decreases the ability of groups to maintain their power and control over the corporation over time and across multiple generations of executives. Furthermore, the degree of obsolescence is shaped by the relative power and position of the functional units at the level of the industry and sector.

Our theory of the circulation of control presents an extension and modification of the pure model of circulation of power previously developed by Ocasio (1994). At any one time, the prevalence of entrenchment versus political change, and thus the degree of circulation among functional units, is contingent on environmental circumstances (Virany, Tushman, and Romanelli, 1992). Ideological struggles also play an important role in elite circulation, as ideological obsolescence at the sectoral level is likely to affect the perceived obsolescence of executives at both the industry and organizational level. These ideological struggles are particularly likely to affect financial executives during the period studied, as challenges to the financial conception in manufacturing led to increased obsolescence of finance CEOs and decreased ability of finance executives to entrench themselves.

Conceptions of control as contending styles. We follow White (1992) in distinguishing two forms of cultural conceptions in organizations: styles and institutions. We define a style as a cultural frame used by actors with a common role or structural position both to guide their behavior and attain status and power for themselves and for other actors occupying equivalent roles. White (1992: 17, 166–167) portrayed styles as profiles or formulas that integrate behavior across disparate network populations and that emerge in fluid social contexts characterized by a wide variety of formations and stochastic processes. Styles constitute a particular identity for actors and serve as cultural resources in their social and political contests. For example, according to this view, conceptions of control are styles that reflect the cultural frames used by production, marketing, operations, and finance personnel in U.S. industry to make sense of reality, solve the problems of the corporation, and attain status, power, and wealth.

4
According to both the model of the institutionalization of power and the circulation of control, resource dependencies and strategic contingencies affect the ability of executives to exert power at any one time. They differ, however, in whether resource dependencies are likely to lead to political entrenchment (Salancik and Pfeffer, 1977) or whether they result in political circulation as structural contingencies change (Cyert and March, 1963).

Table 1 summarizes key differences between institutions and styles. White distinguished styles from institutions as the former emerge under conditions of ambiguity and are maintained by the structural positions of actors with a particular style. Styles, unlike institutions, are not taken for granted but are subject to emergent contests for control among actors with different styles. While both institutions and styles provide cultural frames to guide organizational action, they vary in the strength of their cultural assumptions, the degree to which they are isomorphic across organization fields, and in how they shape organizational inertia. Institutions are relatively inert, and change is exogenous, infrequent, and episodic. Styles, in contrast, are subject to frequent endogenous change and short-term fluctuations The greater cultural control that characterizes institutions relative to styles is reflected in differences in the sources of power, the stability of dominant elites, and the degree of elite hegemony over the organization and organizational field.

The circulation of corporate control implies that conceptions of control are not institutionalized but are best characterized as contending styles subject to intra- and interorganizational struggles for control. Fligstein's conceptions of control could be interpreted, however, as either styles or institutions While Fligstein's (1987, 1990) earlier formulations imply that conceptions of control become institutionalized across the U.S. industrial sector (see also Davis, Diekmann, and Tinsley, 1994), his more recent work (Fligstein, 1996) suggests both greater fluidity and impermanence and that conceptions of control are more of a cultural tool (Swidler, 1986) that elites employ to gain power and control, rather than a taken-for-granted rule (Meyer and Rowan, 1977; Zucker, 1977). In examining the applicability of alternative models of political dynamics we consider whether alternative conceptions of control in the U.S. manufacturing sector are best understood as styles, as in the model of the circulation of control, or as institutions, as in the model of the institutionalization of power.

The circulation of corporate control can be characterized as the process of contestation among different styles over the prevailing theory to guide the governance of organizations, handle the ambiguity associated with executive positions, and control the formal command posts in organizations. Economic and political contingencies trigger contests for control

Table 1

Comparison of Institutions versus Styles

Characteristics	Institutions	Styles
Cultural assumptions	Taken for granted	Contested
Degree of isomorphism	Strong	Weak
Degree of inertia	Strong	Weak
Nature of change	Episodic	Frequent fluctuations
Sources of power	Formal and informal rules	Structurally equivalent actors
Degree of dominance	Hegemonic, large majorities	Relative; plurality or small majority
Elite dynamics	Entrenchment of power	Impermanence of power

among different factions tied to different styles (White, 1992). Under conditions of adversity or ambiguity, latent political and ideological differences among members of the corporation's dominant coalition become manifest (Ocasio, 1994). Predominant styles become increasingly challenged, leading to temporal instability and impermanence in power and control over the organization. Individual contests for power are shaped by local contests among contending styles and subunits, which in turn shape and are shaped by interorganizational contests for control at the level of the industry and the organizational sector.

The model of the circulation of corporate control and its emphasis on styles has close similarities to Oliver's (1992) model of deinstitutionalization. Both emphasize changing external dependencies and conflicting internal interests as drivers of organizational change. But there are important differences. First, the model of the circulation of control, unlike Oliver's model of deinstitutionalization, emphasizes contestation among multiple distinct styles or cultural frames. Deinstitutionalization, in contrast, refers to the erosion of legitimacy of one particular activity or procedure (Oliver, 1992). In the model of the circulation of control, multiple styles may be legitimate, and their rise and fall may occur independently of their legitimacy. While a decline in legitimacy is a sufficient condition to result in a decline in a particular style, it is not a necessary condition. Second, Oliver's (1992) conception of institution is broader than that used in this paper. Unlike Oliver, we rely on Meyer and Rowan's (1977), Zucker's (1977), and DiMaggio and Powell's (1991) emphasis on both cultural persistence and hegemonic control as necessary characteristics of institutions. We follow White (1992) in a more restrictive use of the term institution that distinguishes institutions from cultural tools or frames used by strategic actors to gain power and control (Swidler, 1986).

Circulation of Control in U.S. Industry, 1981–1992

Fligstein (1987, 1990) documented the changing patterns and conceptions of control in top executive positions from 1919 to 1979: the early dominance of manufacturing (or production) from 1919 to 1939, followed first by the rise of sales and marketing presidents from 1939 to 1959, and subsequently by finance executives and the finance conception of control. While Fligstein emphasized exogenous structural contingencies and external institutional forces (DiMaggio and Powell, 1983), the model of the circulation of corporate control suggests that internal political dynamics have an independent role in explaining the rise and fall of elite subunits. This model suggests that the rise and fall of the power and control of diverse subunits found by Fligstein (1987, 1990) reflects periods of relative dominance and entrenchment of diverse styles or conceptions of control followed by elite circulation and endogenous contests for control over the corporation.

An examination of the writings of management intellectuals (Guillén, 1994) in the 1980s and early 1990s suggests the emergence of ideological challenges to the finance conception of control. In a widely influential article, Hayes and Abernathy (1980) attributed the loss of international competitiveness of American industry to the excessive reliance on portfolio management practices and short-term financial controls at the expense of long-term investments in technology and production. They associated this financial orientation with the rise of finance (and legal) executives to CEO positions in large manufacturing companies. The conglomerate movement of the 1960s and the portfolio management techniques that became popular in the 1970s were presented as reasons for "managing our way to economic decline" (Hayes and Abernathy, 1980: 67).

Faced with increasing competition from Japanese and foreign firms, declining profits, and the recurring loss of market share and competitive advantage in key industrial sectors, including motor vehicles, consumer electronics, machinery, and office equipment, the popular business and management literatures sought alternative models of managerial practice during the 1980s and early '90s. It is beyond the scope of this paper to document the multiple approaches offered, but some of the best-selling concepts included theory Z (Ouchi, 1981), strong corporate cultures (Deal and Kennedy, 1982), "sticking to the knitting," (Peters and Waterman, 1982), the value chain (Porter, 1985), lean production systems, (Womack, Jones, and Roos, 1990), organizational learning (Senge, 1990), core competence (Prahalad and Hamel, 1990), and business reengineering (Hammer and Champy, 1993). While the solutions offered differed widely, they all shared a strong critique of the detached management practices associated with portfolio management, short-term financial controls, and unrelated diversification and an increased emphasis on the implementation of large-scale changes to established production processes and operating practices. By the late 1980s, strategy researchers and practitioners had settled on the resource-based view of the firm (Wernerfelt, 1984) and the related concepts of core competence and dynamic capabilities as dominant approaches to strategic management and control. These alternative conceptions favored CEOs with either production or operations backgrounds at the expense of financial executives and the finance conception of control. For example, those executives with production (including manufacturing) and technical backgrounds were seen as best able to manage the portfolio of competences (Prahalad and Hamel, 1990) and develop and implement the necessary resources for competitive advantage. Alternatively, executives with operational backgrounds, typically those with experience in administration and divisional general management, were seen as better able to implement organizational restructuring (Useem, 1993), which involved changes in the operations of the various organizational divisions.

Our hypotheses focus on how technical, political, and ideological obsolescence led to the decline in power of financial CEOs, relative to those from other backgrounds, in the U.S. manufacturing sector during the 1980s and early 1990s. Our approach reflects the view that explaining stability and change in the power of functional units does not involve identifying historically invariant causal sequences but, rather, involves specifying how the generative social mechanisms identified—obsolescence and contestation over contending functional styles—interact with the prevailing economic, cultural, and political context to generate specific outcomes. We subscribe to Tilly's (1997: 73) view that "[social] regularities lie in the generating mechanisms rather than in the recurrence of whole structures, the repetition of whole sequences, the reappearance of the same unilinear processes." This approach is consistent with the call for models in organization theory that reflect the historical particulars of the structures and processes studied (Davis and Stout, 1992). This approach also reflects the ontological assumptions behind White's (1992) theory of identity and control, which provides an underlying metatheory for our analysis. According to White, contests for control among contending identities (in our case, functional units) constitute the regularities that generate social action. The particular structures, sequences, and outcomes that result from these contests for control are contingent on the prevailing cultural meanings and value systems, the contingencies that provoke the contests for control, and the social position and location of the various identities. Consequently, the hypotheses presented reflect the prevailing historical conditions of the sector during the period studied.

Hypotheses

The intellectual and ideological challenges to the financial conception of control provided a repertoire of alternative styles (White, 1992) that fostered the circulation of corporate control and the decline in finance CEOs and the rise of production and operations. But the 1980s and early '90s were also characterized by the rise of institutional investors and the mobilization of shareholder power (Useem, 1996), structural changes that ostensibly favor a financial orientation. The corporate reorganizations associated with the rise of stockholder interests typically involve large-scale changes in either production or operations, strategies typically associated with CEOs from production or operations backgrounds. This study examines whether finance CEOs were able to maintain their ascendancy or whether the challenges to their conception of control were associated with their decline in power relative to those from either production or operations.

Strategic contingencies. According to the structural contingencies model (Hickson et al., 1971), positions of power will flow to groups best able to meet the critical problems and contingencies faced by the organization in its environment. According to this view, the financial conception emerged as a solution to problems of control in firms with strategies of related and unrelated diversification, large numbers of mergers (and divestitures), and the multidivisional forms of formal structure (Fligstein, 1985, 1987, 1990). The rise of the financial conception of control was linked during the 1960s and '70s to the use and formulation of portfolio management techniques and financial controls by CEOs with financial backgrounds.

According to the model of the circulation of control, organizations are political coalitions that sequentially attend to problems in their environments (Cyert and March, 1963). This implies first that previous strategic contingencies will no longer be effective in sustaining the power of dominant functional subunits. This suggests, during the period studied, that finance CEOs became technically obsolete with a decline in their ability to utilize prevailing conceptions of control to meet changing organizational contingencies. Consequently, the technical obsolescence of finance CEOs led to a decline in their ability to gain power in firms with related or unrelated diversification, multidivisional structures, or high levels of merger and divestiture activity. Our predictions here are consistent with Fligstein's (1987), who found that the size and statistical significance of these variables varied during different time periods in which the various conceptions of control became dominant, consistent with the model of the circulation of corporate control. We use these hypotheses to examine whether Fligstein's findings of the dominance of the financial conception of control from 1959 to 1979 can be replicated for the subsequent time period or whether, consistent with technical obsolescence and the circulation of corporate control, the challenges to the finance conception limited the ability of these strategic contingencies to favor the selection of new CEOs from financial backgrounds:

Hypothesis 1: During the 1980s and early 1990s, the strategic contingencies associated with the finance conception of control—multidivisional structures, related and unrelated diversification, and high numbers of mergers and acquisitions—did not lead to increased selection of new CEOs from finance, relative to other backgrounds.

The sequential attention to goals (Cyert and March, 1963) implicit in the model of the circulation of control suggests that new contingencies will arise over historical time. During the 1980s and early 1990s, U.S. manufacturing firms were faced with increasing challenges from foreign imports, decreasing their profitability and international competitiveness. The financial conception of control did not provide direct solutions to competitive problems, and the alternative models that favored either production CEOs, based on resources and competencies, or operations executives, based on organizational restructuring, were more likely to be favored in those industries facing a larger proportion of imports:

Hypothesis 2: During the 1980s and early 1990s, the greater the proportion of foreign imports at the industry level, the greater the selection of production and operations CEOs relative to those from finance.

The effects of foreign competition on the selection of functional backgrounds of new CEOs are likely to be moderated by the financial performance of the firm (Cyert and March, 1963). Given the premise that organizational restructurings are associated with failures of performance (Useem, 1993; Donaldson, 1994) and that organizational restructurings are more likely to be associated with CEOs from operations backgrounds, we expect the effects of foreign competition on the selection of functional backgrounds of new CEOs to be moderated by the firm's performance. Alternatively, for firms with good financial performance, the strategic contingencies associated with imports are more likely to lead to a focus on a firm's distinctive resources (Wernerfelt, 1984; Prahalad and Hamel, 1990), particularly from manufacturing and research and development, and, consequently, an increase in CEOs from production and technical backgrounds.

We expect both a main effect for decreases in performance leading to increases in operations backgrounds and an interaction effect between performance and foreign imports, with firms with poor performance in import-intensive industries favoring operations CEOs and those with good performance in import-intensive industries favoring production CEOs:

Hypothesis 3a: During the 1980s and early 1990s, a decrease in firm-level financial performance will lead to an increase in the selection of new operations CEOs relative to CEOs with other backgrounds.

Hypothesis 3b: During the 1980s and early 1990s, an increase in financial performance in industries with greater import intensity will lead to an increase in the selection of production CEOs relative to those from operations.

Decline in isomorphism: Obsolescence at the industry level. Technical, cultural, and political forces may interact to lead to similarity in the selection of functional backgrounds of CEOs among firms in the same industry. Institutional theory (DiMaggio and Powell, 1983) posits the role of coercive, normative, and mimetic pressures in leading to isomorphic tendencies in organizational characteristics within an industry. Technical and economic differences among industries may also account for isomorphism. Finally, the intraorganizational power struggle may be shaped at the industry level. Once a set of actors gains dominance and institutionalizes their power, their subunit counterparts within the same industry may use this fact as a basis for gaining power in their respective firms.

According to the model of the circulation of control, isomorphism in functional backgrounds of CEOs is a temporary phenomenon that is unlikely to persist over time and is subject to challenge and contestation. A decline in the power of financial CEOs within an industry may affect the ability of that group to retain control over formal positions of authority in an individual organization relative to other functions within the firm. Given the ideological and technological obsolescence posited for finance, a decline of institutional isomorphism for financial CEOs may be expected relative to those from other backgrounds:

Hypothesis 4: During 1981–1992, isomorphism in the selection of functional backgrounds of CEOs at the industry level will be lower for CEOs from financial backgrounds than for CEOs from other backgrounds.

Annual fluctuations in styles and functional backgrounds. The model of the circulation of corporate control highlights the instability in political dynamics in organizations and the impermanence of alternative styles or conceptions of control. An important distinction in viewing conceptions of control as styles rather than institutions resides in their being subject to short-term trends as fads and fashion create temporary changes in which different managerial styles rise and fall in rates of adoption (Abrahamson, 1996). While changes in styles reflect short-run fluctuations, changes in institutions reflect long-term trends and transformations. Conceptions of control are subject to short-term fluctuations in styles annually, as the influence of business periodicals and publications and the direct social influence of other manufacturing firms affect the selection of new CEOs with a particular background:

Hypothesis 5: The likelihood of selection of a CEO from a particular background will be directly related to the proportion of CEOs from the same background selected by other firms in the sector during the same year.

Organizational-level political dynamics. As suggested earlier, our model of the circulation of corporate control allows for both stability and change in functional backgrounds to be observed, with periods of entrenchment followed by elite circulation as new subunits rise to power. We focus on intraorganizational dynamics to evaluate Fligstein's (1987: 56) content on that conceptions of control account "not just for organizational change, but organizational stability. This means that what is in place will tend to stay in place. . . . Any changes in that story could potentially undermine the rationale for any given organization and such revisions will be undertaken only under dire circumstances." Thus, we follow his suggestion to examine whether subunit power is stable over time (Fligstein, 1987: 57).

A pure model of the institutionalization of power implies persistence in the power of the subunit, with increased entrenchment over several generations of predecessor CEOs. A pure model of the circulation of power implies no persistence in the power of functional units. The circulation of corporate control implies periods of temporary entrenchment interspersed with periods of circulation and change in managerial elites. Elite circulation will increase as the ideological challenges to the subunit increase. This implies that during the 1980s we will find increased circulation of power and decreased entrenchment for financial CEOs relative to the marketing and production categories:

Hypothesis 6a: During the 1980s and early 1990s, CEOs from financial backgrounds will be less likely to be succeeded by CEOs from the same background than by those from other backgrounds.

According to the model of the circulation of corporate control, intraorganizational power is unlikely to persist across multiple generations of CEOs. The impermanence and instability in power are particularly likely for those backgrounds or styles that are most subject to contestation, i.e , for financial CEOs during the 1980s and early 1990s. To test for this effect of long-term entrenchment, we examine how the backgrounds of the two past incumbents influence the background of new CEOs and compare the effects of the entrenchment of financial CEOs with those of other backgrounds:

Hypothesis 6b: During the 1980s and early 1990s, CEOs from financial backgrounds will experience decreased long-term stability in power relative to those from other backgrounds, as measured by the stability in backgrounds across two generations of predecessor CEOs.

DATA AND METHOD

Sample

Our population included all 280 manufacturing firms listed in the *Forbes Sales 500* for 1980, the first year in which data on the functional backgrounds of CEOs were collected by *Forbes*. The sample was limited to manufacturing to account for sectoral difference in the determinants of CEO background. Among the original companies in the population, 29 companies were dropped due to missing data, for a total of

251 companies in the sample studied. We examined CEO succession events in large manufacturing firms from 1981 to 1992. To avoid sample selection bias, the CEOs of these companies were tracked through 1992, even if they were dropped from the *Forbes 500.* By 1992 a total of 79 firms, or 30 percent of the sample firms, were acquired, merged with other companies, went bankrupt, or became privately held. One hundred and ninety companies experienced at least one CEO succession during the period, and a total of 275 succession events occurred between 1981 and 1992.

Measures

Functional background of CEOs. A primary source for information on CEOs' functional backgrounds was *Forbes'* annual survey of CEOs' compensation, published since 1980.[5] The CEO succession events were identified based on the changes in the name of CEOs. *Forbes* asked the CEOs to identify their functional background as well as their salary level. *Forbes* used nine categories to classify backgrounds of CEOs: technical, production, sales, marketing, finance, operations, medical, journalism, and legal. In our analysis, the classification has been collapsed into five categories: (1) production and technical, (2) marketing and sales, (3) finance, (4) legal, and (5) operations and other. Categories were grouped based on both sensitivity analysis and on the interrelatedness between functions. The production and technical category includes CEOs from manufacturing, engineering, and research and development. These three functions presuppose a technical background in science and engineering for members of the respective subunits. Marketing and sales are related functions that are commonly joined together in many, if not most firms. Operations is grouped with the remaining categories to constitute the baseline group for comparison purposes. While legal is treated as a separate category in the descriptive analysis, for consistency with Fligstein's analysis and because there were too few new CEOs from legal backgrounds to treat them as a separate category, we collapsed legal into operations for the multinomial logistic regressions. In results not shown here, however, we reestimated the models following Hayes and Abernathy's (1980) and Hambrick and Mason's (1984) influential treatments, which grouped finance and legal in the same functional category. Note that both groups work closely together in the acquisitions and divestitures of companies, which is a central hallmark of the financial conception of control. The results were substantially the same whether legal was grouped with finance or with operations.

Since some of the companies in our sample dropped out of the *Forbes 500* list after 1980, we also used *Who's Who in Finance and Industry* and proxy statements to identify CEO backgrounds that we could not obtain from *Forbes* magazine. These sources were also used to identify the functional backgrounds of predecessor CEOs whose tenure ended before 1980. The titles of previous executive positions were used to code the CEO's functional background, following the classification system developed by *Forbes*.

Strategic contingencies. Following Fligstein (1987), we included corporate strategy and structure as measures of the

5
The results were compared with the coding of functional backgrounds offered by *Business Week*, which began annual coding of functional backgrounds in 1987. *Business Week's* coding is in general agreement with *Forbes'*, showing 21 percent of the firms in 1992 with finance and legal CEOs, lower than production and technical and marketing and sales. A difference resides in their classifications for operations and others, which changed from 51 percent in 1987 to 13 percent in 1988. This recoding of operations CEOs into other categories is unexplained. While there are differences in the two sources, both *Business Week* and *Forbes* show that finance CEOs were no longer dominant by the late 1980s.

strategic contingencies affecting a CEO's functional background. Strategy and structure were identified using information from annual reports and 10Ks. Following Rumelt (1974) and Fligstein (1987), we coded corporate strategy as product-dominant, related diversification, and unrelated diversification (conglomerate) strategy. A firm was classified as product-dominant when it had one line of business accounting for more than 70 percent of revenues. Firms with related diversification strategies had multiple lines of related businesses, with no single business accounting for 70 percent of revenue. Firms with unrelated diversification strategies were engaged in unrelated business, and no one business accounted for 70 percent of revenue. These strategies were coded as dummy variables, with product-dominant as the omitted category.

Another measure of corporate strategy was the three-year average of the number of *mergers and divestitures* undertaken by the firm. Because top management attention is required to execute each of the mergers and divestitures, their combined sum provides a measure of the strategic contingency facing the corporation. Data on mergers and divestitures were coded from *Moody's Manual*. We conducted sensitivity analysis, running the models with separate measures for mergers and divestitures. Although the models are not nested, so a formal comparison is not possible, the separate measures did not improve the fit of the model, even with three additional degrees of freedom.

For the structure variable, we compared the effects of a *multidivisional structure* with all other categories, including functional form and holding company. The titles of top officers and the description of companies' business reported in annual reports, 10Ks, and proxy statements were used to identify whether or not a company had a multidivisional form.

Isomorphism. We began with two-digit Standard Industrial Classification (SIC) codes to calculate industry-level mimetic effects, and there were 19 industries by two-digit SIC code level. Because some industries had too few companies, which made the isomorphism variable unreliable, we collapsed some two-digit SIC code level industries. The collapsed industries included (1) Food and Tobacco, (2) Textile and Apparel, (3) Wood and Furniture, (4) Miscellaneous Manufacturing, and (5) Oil and Petrochemical Refining industries. As a result, the original 19 industries were reduced to 14. Following Fligstein (1987), we captured isomorphism in the functional background of new CEOs by calculating the proportion of CEOs with technical and production, sales and marketing, and finance and legal backgrounds within each industry. The proportion of CEOs with operations and all other backgrounds was the omitted category. Since firms are more likely to mimic successful companies than poorly performing companies, we used manufacturing companies that were listed in *Forbes Sales 500* for each year to calculate this variable. In computing the proportion measure, the company was left out of the calculation when it was included in the *Forbes Sales 500* for that year. Thus, the proportion of CEOs with each functional background captures the pure effect of the subunit control that existed in the industry for each year. The measure is more appropriate than industry dummy variables in capturing isomorphic effects because it captures not only the similarity of cultural environments for companies within industries, but also the relative strength of mimetic pressure within each industry. The model was also estimated with industry dummies, with no change in the findings for the political dynamics measures. The inclusion of industry dummies, however, changes the effects of the isomorphism variable.

Firm and sector performance. Two measures of economic performance were included in the analysis. *Return on assets* (ROA) measured as the return on firm assets, adjusted for industry average, was used as a measure of firm performance. Other performance measures, including Tobin's Q were also evaluated, but no significant effects were found. ROA measures were obtained from COMPUSTAT. Given the increasing attention to foreign competition in the U.S. manufacturing sector, we included an import measure in the analysis. The import variable is simply the amount of imports divided by total output in each industry, by 4-digit SIC code. The import and output variables for each industry were obtained from the U.S. Department of Commerce, Bureau of Economic Analysis. The natural logarithm of the import variable was used in the analysis.

Annual trends. The effects of annual trends and fluctuations in the functional backgrounds of new CEOs were captured by calculating the proportion of CEOs with technical and production, sales and marketing, and finance backgrounds for each year. The proportion of CEOs with operations and all other backgrounds was the omitted category. As for the isomorphism variable, in calculating the total number of CEOs for each functional background, we excluded the background of the CEO for the particular firm year being coded. Thus, the variable captures annual variations in the rate of selection of functional backgrounds for each year and offers a measure of which subunit may be more in fashion during any particular period.

The annual trend variable differs from the isomorphism variable in two ways. The former applies to the level of the manufacturing sector, while the latter applies to the industry. The annual trend variable also accounts for the effects of short-term fluctuations in conceptions of control, consistent with the model of circulation. This differs from a historical trend variable, which assumes monotonic changes in the prevalence of conceptions of control, more consistent with the view of conceptions of control as institutions. The annual changes in selection of functional backgrounds were most variable for marketing and sales, which had the largest number of new CEOs during 1981–1983 but declined significantly thereafter.

Political dynamics. The political dynamics of the CEO succession process were captured by the functional backgrounds of the last two CEOs in office. These two variables measure the stability in power of functional subunits in the firm across generations of CEOs. By including the background of the two previous CEOs, we could test whether the determination of functional backgrounds can be modeled as a simple Markov process or whether previous history affects the determination of who controls the top executive position. The functional backgrounds of previous CEOs were collected the same way as functional backgrounds of new CEOs. Operations and all other backgrounds of previous CEOs was the omitted category.

We used the previous history of functional backgrounds to determine, at the organizational level, the political obsolescence of prevailing conceptions of control. According to the political coalition view of the firm that underlies the circulation of control, the selection of any one background will entail a quasi-resolution of conflict, but every new succession triggers a new conflict or contest among contending functional units. While political obsolescence is not directly observed, the instability in power of functional subunits across generations of CEOs is consistent with the view that power is impermanent, and historical sources of power become obsolete over time.

Control variables. *Organizational size*, measured as the logarithm of assets as reported in COMPUSTAT was used as a control variable. We tested other control variables and potential sources of strategic contingencies, including firm age, employment growth, R&D spending, and advertising spending, but these variables were either not statistically significant or only marginally significant and did not materially change the remaining results. Given the relatively large number of variables included in the models estimated, we do not

Table 2

Means, Standard Deviations, and Correlation Coefficients*

Variable	Mean	S.D.	1	2	3	4	5	6	7	8	9	10
1. Production & tech. CEO	.28	.45										
2. Marketing & sales CEO	.19	.40	−.31									
3. Finance CEO	.15	.35	−.26	−.21								
4. Operations CEO	.38	.49	−.49	−.39	−.32							
5. Log of assets	8.15	1.10	.19	−.02	−.08	−.10						
6. Related diversification	.41	.49	.03	.02	.01	−.05	−.11					
7. Unrelated diversification	23	.42	−.04	.02	−.12	.01	−.04	−.46				
8. Multidivisional structure	74	.44	.09	−.05	−.05	.00	.10	.19	.14			
9. Mergers & divestitures	1 15	1.31	−.08	−.06	.01	.12	.13	.09	.14	.13		
10. Percent prd. & tech. in ind.	24	.13	.20	−.22	.09	−.07	.26	−.27	−.01	−.07	−.17	
11. Percent mkt. & sales in ind.	18	.13	−.09	.14	.00	−.03	−.28	.18	.07	.05	.20	−.61
12. Percent finance in ind.	15	.09	−.07	.08	−.02	.01	−.05	−.05	.06	−.05	−.06	−.03
13. Percent operations in ind.	31	.13	−.06	−.03	−.08	.14	.10	.08	−.02	.08	.07	−.29
14. ROA	04	.07	.01	.11	.06	−.14	.02	−.06	.07	.07	.03	−.04
15. Log of imports	−2 51	1.34	.08	−.21	.10	.03	.02	−.27	.03	.00	−.18	.33
16. ROA * log of imports	−.11	.23	.08	−.19	.01	.08	−.01	−.07	−.03	−.05	−.07	.14
17. Percent prd. & tech. in year	23	.09	.12	−.07	−.10	.02	.15	−.03	.11	.14	.02	.14
18. Percent mkt. & sales in year	.16	.11	−.09	.24	−.03	−.09	−.17	.01	.02	.03	−.25	−.16
19. Percent finance in year	.14	.06	−.09	.03	.18	−.06	−.14	−.01	−.11	−.07	.02	−.03
20. Percent operations in year	.48	.11	.04	−.18	.01	.10	.12	.02	−.05	−.10	.21	.05
21. Past CEO prod. & tech.	.26	.44	.34	−.16	−.14	−.08	.12	−.03	.02	.04	−.09	.19
22. Past CEO mkt. & sales	.21	.41	−.21	.27	−.03	−.01	−.01	.14	−.09	−.05	.12	−.23
23. Past CEO finance	.16	.36	−.08	.00	.07	.02	.01	.01	.05	.03	−.02	.08
24. Past CEO operations	.27	.44	−.14	−.01	.16	.03	−.04	−.01	.01	.00	.04	−.04
25. 2nd past CEO prod. & tech.	.21	.41	.06	−.08	−.14	.11	.14	−.05	.00	−.02	−.02	.01
26. 2nd past CEO mkt. & sales	.21	.41	−.13	.31	−.06	−.09	.08	.13	−.03	.02	.14	−.17
27. 2nd past CEO finance	.13	.33	.03	−.06	.06	−.03	.02	−.03	.06	.08	.07	.05
28. 2nd past CEO operations	.25	.43	−.02	−.08	.02	.06	−.11	−.02	−.05	−.07	−.07	−.04
29. Multiple CEO successions	.35	.48	.02	−.04	.10	−.06	.13	.03	−.10	−.09	.17	.13

* The approximate cutoff for significance at the .05 level applies to correlations equal to or greater than .12 or equal to or less than −.12.

include these other control variables in the results presented. An indicator variable was also included as a control to record firms that have experienced multiple CEO successions during the sample period.

Modeling Procedure

We used multinomial logistic regression available in STATA to test the hypotheses. Multinomial logistic regression estimates simultaneous logistic regression models, with pairwise comparisons of each functional category with the base category. The base category was new CEOs of operations and other backgrounds. Therefore, the model estimates parameters of given predictor variables for the likelihood of new CEOs of technical and production, marketing and sales, and finance backgrounds, respectively, versus the base category, operations and others. In determining statistical significance, we must consider not only the individual parameter estimates but also a comparison of parameter values across the equations estimated.

RESULTS

Table 2 presents descriptive statistics: means, standard deviations, and correlation coefficients for the 275 succession events included in the sample. Table 3 presents the distribution of functional backgrounds of CEOs for the 251 firms in our sample. Data are presented for 1961, 1971, and 1981–1992. In 1981 finance and legal were the dominant functions, followed by operations and others, then marketing and

Table 2 *(continued)*

11	12	13	14	15	16	17	18	19	20	21	22	23	24	25	26	27	28
–.19																	
–.30	–.35																
.12	.07	–.15															
–.28	.12	–.09	–.25														
–.17	–.01	.08	–.87	.52													
–.11	–.11	.12	–.08	.14	.07												
.15	.15	–.32	.09	–.10	–.10	–.24											
–.01	.11	–.05	.07	–.05	–.03	–.66	.03										
–.05	–.12	.24	–.06	.01	.06	–.24	–.78	–.04									
–.10	–.05	–.05	–.05	.03	.05	.07	–.11	–.02	.06								
.18	–.01	.04	.08	–.20	–.12	–.11	.09	.11	–.06	–.30							
–.08	.01	.01	–.01	.08	.02	.09	.00	.00	–.08	–.24	–.22						
–.07	.06	.09	–.07	.08	.08	–.04	–.07	–.04	.12	–.36	–.32	–.26					
.03	–.05	–.08	–.02	–.05	–.02	–.07	.04	.03	.01	.25	–.10	–.04	–.08				
.11	–.07	.10	.11	–.09	–.14	–.06	–.07	.02	.10	–.22	.21	–.02	.10	–.28			
–.04	.05	–.01	.05	.07	.02	.07	–.03	–.03	–.01	–.10	–.01	.09	.06	–.20	–.21		
.05	.00	.00	–.08	.02	.09	.14	.00	–.09	–.07	.05	–.06	–.01	.01	–.27	–.30	–.22	
.10	–.09	.16	–.14	.15	.15	.07	–.43	.02	.42	.06	–.03	–.07	.16	.07	.16	.01	–.12

Table 3

Distribution of Functional Backgrounds of CEOs from 1961 to 1992

Functional backgrounds	1961	1971	1981	1982	1983	1984	1985	1986	1987	1988	1989	1990	1991	1992
Production and technical	24%	19%	20%	21%	22%	21%	22%	23%	23%	24%	25%	25%	25%	24%
Marketing and sales	23%	22%	21%	23%	22%	22%	22%	20%	19%	18%	18%	18%	18%	18%
Finance and legal	33%	31%	34%	30%	27%	26%	26%	23%	21%	21%	21%	22%	22%	21%
Finance	19%	19%	22%	20%	18%	18%	17%	17%	16%	16%	16%	17%	17%	16%
Legal	14%	12%	12%	10%	9%	8%	9%	6%	5%	5%	5%	5%	5%	5%
Operations and others	20%	28%	24%	27%	29%	30%	31%	34%	37%	37%	36%	36%	36%	37%

sales, and production and technical. Table 3 shows a decline in finance and legal by 1983, accompanied by an increase in the proportion of both operations and others and production and technical. Finance and legal were no longer the dominant categories, being surpassed by operations and others. By 1987, finance and legal were also surpassed by production and technical. Finance and legal dropped to 21 percent by 1992, compared with 24 percent for production and technical and 37 percent for operations and others. The drop was greater for legal than for finance backgrounds. Finance backgrounds dropped from 22 percent in 1981 to 16 percent in 1992. The corresponding decrease in legal was from 12 percent to 5 percent. The results are robust across alternative samples. Similar results were found for manufacturing firms in the *Forbes 500* (including newcomers to the *Forbes 500* after 1980 and excluding firms who dropped out of the *Forbes 500*) and for the top 100 industrial firms (including services and retailing), the populations used by Fligstein (1987). In all cases, the period of the 1980s and early 1990s showed a decline in both finance and legal CEOs relative to other backgrounds.

These results provide evidence that during the 1980s and early 1990s, financial CEOs failed to maintain their relative position in large U.S. manufacturing companies. At the sectoral level, the decline in financial CEOs as both production and operations CEOs increased provides evidence of the circulation of corporate control. Production and technical backgrounds, which had declined since the 1940s, experienced a relative increase during the 1980s. Operations CEOs experienced the greatest gain, from 24 percent in 1981 to 37 percent in 1992, but this followed a decline from 1971 to 1981. This pattern of findings suggests that functional backgrounds are subject to recurrent patterns of rise and decline, with limited stability in the power and dominance of any one background.

Stability and Change in Functional Backgrounds

Table 4 presents a classification of the functional backgrounds of new CEOs by the backgrounds of their predecessors. This tabulation describes the intraorganizational mobility in the backgrounds of the CEOs appointed from 1981 to 1992. The diagonal in the table represents the cases of stability in functional backgrounds of CEOs, with 100 out of 275

Circulation of Control

Table 4

Distribution of Functional Backgrounds of New CEOs by Background of Prior CEO, 1981–1992*

Functional background	Prior prod. & tech.	Prior mkt. & sales	Prior finance	Prior legal	Prior operations & others	Total
Production and technical	38	6	8	10	16	78
	54%	11%	19%	40%	20%	28%
Marketing and sales	6	23	8	2	14	53
	9%	40%	19%	8%	18%	19%
Finance	4	7	9	2	18	40
	6%	12%	21%	8%	23%	15%
Legal	2	1	2	1	3	9
	3%	2%	5%	4%	4%	3%
Operations and others	20	20	16	10	29	95
	29%	35%	37%	40%	36%	35%
Total	70	57	43	25	80	275

* Percentages below frequency counts refer to percent of column totals.

succession events, or 36 percent of the sample. The proportions of backgrounds of previous CEOs and successors from the same background are 21 percent for finance, 4 percent for legal, 36 percent for operations and others, 40 percent for marketing and sales, and 54 percent for production and technical. These compare with a proportion of 15 percent for finance among the 275 succession events, 3 percent legal, 35 percent operations and others, 19 percent for marketing and sales, and 28 percent for production and technical backgrounds. These results support hypothesis 6a, on the limited stability of CEOs from financial backgrounds. Only the production and marketing categories show statistically significant effects for stability in the functional backgrounds of new CEOs, as confirmed by a log linear analysis of the classification counts, shown in table 5. Neither financial nor operations CEOs evidence significant entrenchment during this period. Overall, instability, rather than stability in power, is the norm for functional backgrounds of new CEOs. At the organizational level, 64 percent of all CEO selections resulted in changes in functional backgrounds.

The results in tables 4 and 5 provide initial support for the importance of intraorganizational political dynamics and for the circulation of corporate control. Both production and technical and marketing and sales backgrounds increased with prior experience with CEOs of the same background,

Table 5

Log Linear Analysis of Intraorganizational Stability of Functional Backgrounds of CEOs in U.S. Manufacturing Firms*

Functional stability	Coefficient	Standard error
Production and technical	1.550***	.307
Marketing and sales	1.336***	.342
Finance	.358	.428
Legal	.070	1.084
Operations and others	−.380	.294

*** $p < .001$.
* Parameters for functional origins, destinations, and constant term not shown.

providing evidence of entrenchment at the organizational level. No entrenchment was found, however, for CEOs from finance and legal or operations and other backgrounds. The finance and legal backgrounds, which had been dominant in the 1960s and 1970s were not able to maintain control over the top command position in the firm during the 1980s and early 1990s, consistent with the model of the circulation of corporate control. The log linear analysis also shows that the stability of functional backgrounds was significantly greater for production and marketing than for other backgrounds. Notably, operations backgrounds, which are now relatively prevalent, were also not able to entrench themselves during the period studied.

Determinants of Functional Backgrounds of New CEOs

Table 6 presents the results of multinomial logistic regression models of selection of functional backgrounds of new CEOs. Two alternative models are presented: model 1 includes the results of the structural contingency and isomorphism hypotheses only and replicates Fligstein's analysis for the 1981–1992 period; model 2 adds the additional variables identified in this paper: annual fluctuations in the selection of new CEOs, the political dynamics variables, the effects of ROA, imports, and their interactions.

Table 6 also shows the statistical significance of the variables included in the two models, as measured by the chi-square contrast. Significance must be assessed not only for individual parameters but also for the differences among parameters of the same variable across the different outcomes of the dependent variables (i.e., across the three functional categories). We estimated significance by calculating the chi-square contrasts between models 1 and 2, respectively, and an alternative specification that omits the specified independent variable as a determinant of the three categories of production and technical, marketing and sales, and finance.

The overall comparison of models 1 and 2 shows that the model of the circulation of control significantly adds to the baseline model. The chi-square contrast between models 1 and 2 is 104.99 with 36 degrees of freedom, statistically significant at the .001 level. These results show that the model of the circulation of control adds to the understanding of the determinants of functional backgrounds in Fligstein's (1987) study. We found similar results, not reported here, by reestimating model 2 without the variables that were not significant in model 1, conserving degrees of freedom.

Strategic contingencies. Model 1 uses four measures of strategic contingencies—multidivisional structure, related diversification, unrelated diversification, and mergers and divestitures—to analyze the determinants of functional backgrounds of new CEOs. As shown in table 6, mergers and divestitures was the only variable found to be statistically significant in model 1 (overall significance at the .05 level), with negative coefficients on production and marketing backgrounds relative to operations and other categories, significant at the .05 level. The coefficient of mergers and divestitures on finance CEOs (relative to operations and others) is negative but not statistically significant. These effects show that firms with large numbers of merger and divestiture ac-

Circulation of Control

Table 6

Multinomial Logistic Regression of Functional Backgrounds of New CEOs, 1981–1992*

	Baseline model				Circulation of control model			
Independent variable	Prod. & tech.	Mkt. & sales	Finance	Chi-square contrast	Prod. & tech.	Mkt. & sales	Finance	Chi-square contrast
Strategic contingencies								
Multidivisional	0.334	−0.344	−0.054	2.23	0.326	−0.899	−0.241	1.20
	(0.405)	(0.408)	(0.453)		(0.447)	(0.487)	(0.494)	
Related diversif.	0.611	0.246	−0.036	2.69	0.639	−0.574	0.351	4.61
	(0.409)	(0.435)	(0.471)		(0.451)	(0.542)	(0.526)	
Unrelated diversif.	−0.030	0.087	−0.984	2.93	−0.325	−0.240	0.874	1.86
	(0.462)	(0.491)	(0.620)		(0.503)	(0.566)	(0.653)	
Mergers & divestitures	−0.379••	−0.362••	−0.012	9.46••	−0.362••	−0.419••	0.009	8.37••
	(0.157)	(0.158)	(0.155)		(0.172)	(0.194)	(0.176)	
Log of imports	–	–	–	–	−0.226	−0.38•	0.020	3.89
					(0.192)	(0.227)	(0.246)	
ROA	–	–	–	–	19.591•••	0.507	14.4•	10.14••
					(6.643)	(6.280)	(8.232)	
ROA * log of imports	–	–	–	–	6.61•••	0.134	4.123	8.92••
					(2.390)	(2.207)	(3.096)	
Isomorphism								
% Production & technical	4.932•••	−2.796	4.201••	17.44••••	4.441••	−0.652	3.734•	8.23••
	(1.666)	(1.843)	(2.061)		(1.813)	(2.079)	(2.206)	
% Marketing & sales	2.974•	2.327	2.863	4.42	3.246•	1.844	2.805	3.82
	(1.679)	(1.705)	(2.053)		(1.839)	(1.929)	(2.129)	
% Finance	−0.049	2.455	0.688	1.97	−0.697	2.413	−1.847	2.41
	(2.000)	(1.874)	(2.355)		(2.167)	(2.226)	(2.606)	
Annual fluctuations								
Annual percentage prod. & tech.	–	–	–	–	2.827	4.858	3.502	2.97
					(2.553)	(3.349)	(3.220)	
Annual percentage mkt. & sales	–	–	–	–	1.054	8.096•••	3.995	12.40•••
					(1.986)	(2.413)	(2.439)	
Annual percentage finance	–	–	–	–	2.009	6.251	11.017••	6.28•
					(3.808)	(4.768)	(4.708)	
Political dynamics								
Prior CEO prod. & tech.	–	–	–	–	0.953••	0.130	−0.880	9.92••
					(0.427)	(0.634)	(0.665)	
Prior CEO mkt. & sales	–	–	–	–	−1.222•	0.918•	−0.600	10.64••
					(0.595)	(0.513)	(0.576)	
Prior CEO finance	–	–	–	–	−0.532	0.486	−0.382	2.38
					(0.532)	(0.595)	(0.546)	
Second prior CEO prod. & tech.	–	–	–	–	−0.615	−0.406	−1.867••	7.10•
					(0.463)	(0.599)	(0.729)	
Second prior CEO mkt. & sales	–	–	–	–	0.107	1.790•••	−0.674	15.28•••
					(0.552)	(0.551)	(0.637)	
Second prior CEO finance	–	–	–	–	0.350	0.531	−0.723	1.05
					(0.534)	(0.690)	(0.615)	
Size								
Log of assets	0.449•••	0.356••	−0.058	11.71•••	0.486•••	0.217	0.180	7.41•
	(0.157)	(0.180)	(0.197)		(0.180)	(0.217)	(0.214)	
Multiple CEO successions	0.110	0.215	0.417	1.14	−0.362	−0.419	0.009•	4.63
	(0.347)	(0.394)	(0.406)		(0.172)	(0.194)	(0.176)	
Constant	−5.832••••	−3.346••	−2.019		−7.590••••	−7.803•••	−6.074••	
	(1.575)	(1.655)	(1.893)		(2.155)	(2.679)	(2.684)	
Chi-square		60.16				165.15		104.99••••
D.f.		27				63		36

•$p < .10$; ••$p < .05$; •••$p < .01$; ••••$p < .001$.
* Standard errors are in parentheses.

tivities are less likely to select production and marketing CEOs than either those from finance or operations and others. Both merger and divestiture activities were widely prevalent during the 1980s and remain an important determinant of the functional backgrounds of new CEOs. But this strategic contingency is now as likely to favor CEOs with operations backgrounds as CEOs from finance. The effects of mergers and divestitures remain in model 2, with the variable remaining significant at the .05 level.

The general findings provide support for hypothesis 1, on strategic contingencies no longer favoring finance CEOs and contributing to the circulation of corporate control. Contrary to Fligstein's (1987) findings for the previous two decades, no support is found for the effects of multidivisional form or related or unrelated diversification (conglomerates) in explaining the CEO's functional background. These effects were central to the dominance of the financial conception of control during the 1960s and 1970s, as finance CEOs were more likely in conglomerate firms and those with multidivisional structures. The effects of multidivisional form and unrelated diversification variables on finance CEOs are now negative, although not statistically significant. Interpreting findings that fail to reject the null hypothesis is often treacherous, because the lack of statistical significance could be due to the low power of the test. But for these two variables, the maximum likelihood estimates of the effects are in the opposite direction from those obtained by Fligstein (1987) for 1959–1979. While there are differences in the samples between the two studies, the changes in explanatory power between different time periods suggest that the effects of structural contingencies on subunit power are not independent from the dominant ideologies and conceptions of control for each time period. This interpretation is consistent with Fligstein's finding that the effects of structural contingency variables varied with the dominant conceptions of control. For example, he found that multidivisional firms favored both marketing and finance presidents during 1939–1959 when the marketing conception prevailed, but only finance presidents during the 1959–1979 period, when the financial conception became dominant. The failure of multidivisional structures and unrelated diversification strategies to result in an increased likelihood of finance CEOs during the 1980s and early '90s suggests a decline in the financial conception of control, which articulated a link between these contingencies and financial executives.

Model 2 adds new strategic contingencies for economic performance, imports, and their interaction. The main effect of imports is not significant, and hypothesis 2 is not supported. The main effects of ROA are positive for production at the .01 level and for finance at the .10 level. This suggests that increased performance will lead to increases in production and, to a lesser extent, financial CEOs relative to operations CEOs. With a decline in performance, however, the proportion of operations CEOs increases, consistent with hypothesis 3a. The interaction effects of ROA and imports is significant at the .01 level for production, consistent with hypothesis 3b, with an overall level of significance for the interaction effect at the .05 level. The combined results show that poor economic performance increases the likelihood of operations CEOs, associated with organizational and operational restructuring. Strategic contingencies associated with increased imports at the industry level will increase the likelihood of production CEOs for firms with high levels of economic performance and of operations CEOs for firms with poor economic performance.

Isomorphism. An examination of the industry isomorphism variables in model 1 shows that the effects of the proportion of firms in an industry with a CEO of a given background had an effect on the selection of new CEOs only for the proportion of CEOs from production and technical backgrounds. In model 1, the effect is statistically significant at the .01 level for the production and technical isomorphism variable and not significant for the others. The industry isomorphism effect for production and technical is significant at the .01 level for the coefficient of production and technical relative to the baseline category, as well as relative to marketing and sales. The evidence for the institutionalization of production CEOs at the industry level is complicated by the fact that the differences with finance are not statistically significant—the greater the proportion of production and technical CEOs in an industry, the greater the proportion of new CEOs from finance, significant at the .05 level. Industries with large proportions of production CEOs are almost as likely to have finance CEOs as production CEOs. Also, the effects of the proportion of marketing CEOs and proportion of finance CEOs are not statistically significant in model 1. The effects of the isomorphism variables remain in model 2, with a significance level of .05 for production, and no effect for the other categories. The results of the isomorphism variables in model 1 are consistent with hypothesis 4, on the circulation of corporate control for financial CEOs at the industry level, with lower levels of organizational field entrenchment than CEOs from production and technical.

Annual fluctuations in functional backgrounds. Hypothesis 5, on the effects of annual fluctuations in management styles shaping the circulation of corporate control, receives support for marketing and sales CEOs, as well as finance CEOs. Annual fluctuations serve to differentiate marketing and finance CEOs from operations; the annual percentage of production and technical CEOs has no statistically significant effect on production and technical CEOs. The effects of the annual percentage of marketing and sales CEOs has a statistically significant effect at the .01 level for the selection of marketing and sales CEOS and is also significant at the .01 level across all backgrounds. The annual percentage of finance CEOs has a significant effect at the .01 level on the selection of finance CEOs; the overall significance level is at the .10 level. These findings suggest that annual fluctuations in managerial styles contribute to the instability in power of the various conceptions of control.

Political dynamics. The political dynamic variables in model 2 show how the history of the functional background of the two previous CEOs affects the functional background of new CEOs selected. The model allows an examination of how intraorganizational power may persist or change across several generations of CEOs. The effects of the immediate predecessor in model 2 support the entrenchment of power at the corporate level for production and technical CEOs and marketing and sales CEOs, significant at the .05 level, but not for finance CEOs. While the individual coefficients of prior marketing and sales on marketing and sales (relative to the baseline category) are statistically significant at only the .10 level, the effects on marketing and sales relative to both production and technical and finance CEOs are statistically significant at the .05 level. This suggests that the persistence of marketing CEOs is more likely to result in fewer production and finance CEOs, rather than fewer CEOs from operations and other backgrounds. At the corporate level, the subunit power of production and technical and marketing and sales become entrenched, as the subunit once in power is more likely to maintain the position of CEO. For CEOs with prior backgrounds in finance, the differences between the categories are not statistically significant.

The results of the prior CEO variable provide support for hypothesis 6a, which states that during the period studied, CEOs from financial backgrounds will be less likely to be succeeded by CEOs from the same background relative to those from other backgrounds. To test this hypothesis formally, we examine the differences between the coefficients of entrenchment for production and technical and finance CEOs (.953 and −.382, respectively). The chi-square contrast between model 2 and a constrained model that equates the value of the two coefficients is significant at the .01 level. The chi-square contrast between model 3 and a constrained model that equates the values of the prior marketing and sales CEOs with the prior finance CEOs (with values of .918 and −.382, respectively, in model 2) is statistically significant at the .05 level. Comparing the coefficients across equations shows that stability in finance CEOs is significantly lower and their impermanence in power is significantly higher than for production and technical and marketing and sales CEOs.

Long-term persistence across two generations of previous CEOs was found only for the marketing and sales categories. While the second previous generation of CEOs from production and technical backgrounds decreased the subsequent proportion of finance relative to operations, they did not increase the proportion of CEOs in the same production and technical category itself. The statistical significance of the second prior CEO from a production and technical background, significant overall at the .10 level, with all three coefficients negative, suggests that these firms will have a significantly higher proportion of CEOs from operations backgrounds. While production and technical CEOs increased in total from 1981 to 1992, this increase did not reflect any long-term entrenchment at the corporate level of CEOs from this functional background but, rather, a long-term shift to operations CEOs, consistent with the circulation of corporate control. Marketing and sales was the only background with long-term entrenchment of CEOs in power, as measured by the background of the second previous CEO. The effect on the selection of marketing and sales CEOs is significant at the .01 level, as is the variable across all categories. The long-term entrenchment of marketing and sales CEOs occurs even though marketing and sales CEOs were not dominant across the manufacturing sector. These results are not consistent with the model of the institutionalization of power, which would imply that long-term entrenchment is associated with increased dominance and sectoral-level institutionalization. The long-term entrenchment of marketing and sales, while not predicted a priori, is consistent with the model of the circulation of control. While both operations and, to a lesser extent, production and technical CEOs rose in power during the 1980s, their power was not taken for granted and remained contested. Contestation of power was less likely, however, in those firms with histories of selecting marketing and sales CEOs, leading to increased entrenchment of marketing and sales CEOs in those firms.

There is no support, however, for the historical entrenchment in power of CEOs across all backgrounds, as these results do not hold for either production and technical or finance CEOs. Hypothesis 6b is supported by a comparison of the persistence of the second previous CEO from marketing and sales with finance (with coefficients of 1.790 and −.723, respectively). The chi-square contrast between model 2 and a constrained model that equates the values of the second prior marketing and sales CEOs with the second prior finance CEOs on their own respective backgrounds is statistically significant at the .01 level. Consistent with the model of the circulation of control, the results show that for the period studied, intraorganizational power is significantly less stable and more impermanent for finance CEOs than those from marketing and sales.

Control variables. Firm asset size, included as a control variable, increased the selection of new CEOs from production and technical backgrounds, relative to both finance and the base category, significant at the .01 level in models 1 and 2. The effects of asset size also increased the selection of marketing and sales CEOs in model 1, significant at the .05 level, but the effects were no longer significant in model 2. One possible explanation is that during the time period studied the power of production and technical subunits increased for manufacturing firms and that larger firms were more likely to lead these sectoral changes. Another possibility is that asset size reflects a strategic contingency associated with investments in fixed capital and that for the time period studied, CEOs from production and technical background were seen as best able to meet the challenges of large capital investments. In contrast, size had no effect in Fligstein's (1987) study, although his sample differed, because it included retailing and service firms and was limited to the top 100 firms for each decade. Our control variable for multiple CEO successions was not statistically significant in either model 1 or model 2.

DISCUSSION AND CONCLUSIONS

This paper contributes to the analysis of changes in functional backgrounds and conceptions of control in U.S. manufacturing and to the examination of the underlying intraorganizational political dynamics. The theoretical contribution of this paper is a new model of political dynamics, the circulation of corporate control, contrasted with the model of the institutionalization of power. While prior functional backgrounds were found to affect the backgrounds of new CEOs, we found no simple universal pattern of entrenchment or circulation of power across all backgrounds. We found, instead, that both processes occurred for different backgrounds and at different levels of analysis. The pattern of results is inconsistent with the strong version of the model of the institutionalization of power, in which political dynamics lead to entrenchment of the power of functional units at the level of the sector, the industry, or the firm. Instead, the overall pattern of results is more consistent with the model of the circulation of control. We found, at the sectoral level, an overall decline in financial CEOs during the period, a declining effect of strategic contingencies associated with the finance conception of control, and annual fluctuations in managerial fashions affecting the selection of functional backgrounds of new CEOs. At the industry level, institutional isomorphism effects were only found for CEOs with production and technical backgrounds. At the organizational level, the ability of functional units to entrench themselves varied among function, but these effects were significantly lower for finance and operations than for production or marketing.

Whither finance? We found that finance CEOs have declined from 22 percent in 1981 to 16 percent in 1992. Furthermore, the determinants of financial CEOs found by Fligstein (1987), the multidivisional firm, related and unrelated diversification, and proportion of firms with financial CEOs, no longer hold for the 1981–1992 period. Only the number of mergers and acquisitions is higher for finance CEOs than for production and technical or marketing and sales CEOs, but this variable no longer distinguishes financial executives from those with operations and other backgrounds. Finally, there is no evidence of entrenchment of power for CEOs with financial backgrounds. The combined findings all suggest a decline in finance CEOs and the financial conception of control since 1981.

The failure of finance CEOs to persist during the 1980s shows quite a distinct pattern. No entrenchment was found at either the industry or corporate level, consistent with the model of the circulation of control. The strategic and structural contingencies that explained the rise of finance CEOs to top executive positions from 1959 to 1979 in Fligstein's (1987) study were no longer valid during the 1981–1992 period. The related diversification and multidivisional firm measures, while not statistically significant, were in the opposite direction from prior findings. This historical change is consistent, however, with Fligstein's (1987) finding that the effects of strategic contingencies on subunit power depend on the conceptions of control that dominate during each time period. More specifically, these results suggest that the intellectual and ideological challenges to the finance conception have severed the link between the contingencies associated with diversification strategies and multidivisional structures and the ability of finance CEOs to effectively meet the challenges confronted. This interpretation is supported by the effect of the annual fluctuations variable on the selection of finance CEOs relative to operations CEOs. Field-level changes in the dominance of finance led to a decline of finance CEOs relative to operations CEOs. There was also partial support for decline in firm-level profitability leading to selection of operations CEOs relative to finance CEOs.

The pattern of the circulation of financial CEOs since 1981 is tied to the ideological challenges to financial elites and to their association with portfolio management and the financial conception of control. We found that the decline in power of finance CEOs at the level of the sector, industry, and firm and the ideological challenges to the financial conception of control and to portfolio management during the same period were accompanied by a blurring of the distinct identity of finance from operations. While the selection of financial CEOs can be distinguished from production and technical and marketing and sales by the lower merger and divestiture activity in firms that select CEOs from these two functional categories, finance cannot be distinguished from operations and others along this dimension. Instead, as discussed earlier, the decline in finance relative to operations is accounted for by annual fluctuations in sectoral level support for finance relative to operations and by lower rates of return on assets, supporting operations CEOs relative to finance CEOs.

To explain the decline in finance as a separate identity in the CEO selection process we propose two interrelated explanations for further study. First, the ideological challenge to the financial conception of control and to portfolio management weakened the theory behind the financial style. Portfolio management declined in legitimacy in U.S. industry, decreasing the ability of finance CEOs to rely on portfolio management as a means of attaining power. This ideological challenge altered both the organizational practice of managing the firm as a portfolio of financial assets and the political dominance of financial CEOs, identified with the financial conception. Second, financial CEOs are now more likely to have a Master's in Business Administration (MBA) as a general management degree, rather than obtaining their financial identity through on-the-job training and identification with the finance function. The MBA identity for finance CEOs may be increasingly indistinguishable from a general managerial and MBA identity for operations CEOs, as financial executives have abandoned their identification with portfolio management practices. CEOs from production and technical and marketing and sales may have closer links to these distinctive functions. Further research is required to examine the direct linkage among these changes in ideology and educational background, the decline in the practice of portfolio management, and the decrease in financial CEOs during the 1980s and early 1990s.

The circulation of corporate control? This study builds on and modifies Fligstein's (1987, 1990) analysis of changes in conceptions of control and CEOs' functional backgrounds, but our findings suggest a more fluid process of CEO selection than does his account. The complex pattern of entrenchment and circulation of CEOs from different backgrounds is consistent with the model of the circulation of control developed here. While a more comprehensive test of the model would require an examination of longer historical time periods, the overall pattern of results support the model. Consistent with the model, the political entrenchment of functional subunits was found to be a temporary phenomenon unlikely to persist across multiple generations of executives. As expected, neither the institutionalization nor the circulation of power were found to be invariant sequences that occur for all backgrounds and across all time periods. The results show instead that, during the period studied the ability of finance and operations CEOs to maintain their control and command over formal authority was limited.

In particular, the circulation of corporate control explains the decline in financial CEOs during the 1980s and early 1990s. Ideological challenges to financial CEOs, coupled with increasing foreign competition led to increased circulation of financial CEOs and instability in their power. The study showed that under conditions of poor economic performance, CEOs with operations backgrounds were more likely to be selected, but operational CEOs were also unlikely to entrench themselves in their positions. In addition, the results show that for firms with favorable economic returns, CEOs with production backgrounds were more likely, particularly if firms were facing the threat of increased imports in their industry. Alternatively, firms with poor economic performance favored operations CEOs, and this effect was heightened in industries with a large number of exports.

We interpret the findings on changing conceptions of control in U.S. industry to imply neither institutionalization nor taken-for-grantedness in either the power or the theory behind any particular conception. While the 1970s saw the rise of finance and the finance conception and the 1980s the rise of both operations and production, neither our results nor Fligstein's (1987, 1990) seem to support the view that any one background or conception of control became institutionalized. While some aspects of the finance conception of control may have become institutionalized, such as the multidivisional firm and mergers and acquisitions, there is little evidence that the conception as a whole, with its emphasis on portfolio management and the prominence of financial CEOs, ever became taken for granted or hegemonic. Although operations CEOs rose in prominence during the 1980s, they were neither hegemonic nor institutionalized, and their level of entrenchment was lower than for CEOs from production or marketing backgrounds. Given the lack of institutionalization of the finance or other conceptions of control, we cannot characterize the rise and decline of functional backgrounds as institutionalization and deinsitutionalization (Jepperson, 1991; Oliver, 1992). Instead, functional backgrounds of CEOs are best characterized not as institutional features of the U.S. industrial landscapes but as styles (White, 1992) that are subject to contestation.

Consistent with the view of conceptions of control as styles, the cultural assumptions behind prevailing conceptions were contested, the degree of isomorphism was weak for all backgrounds except production, there was limited inertia in background selection, frequent fluctuations reflecting current fashions, and no one function established hegemony over the U.S. manufacturing sector. The findings are also consistent with Jacoby's (1990: 839) view that "control conceptions [do] not neatly follow in serial stages." Rather than being consistent with the view that changing conceptions of control are episodic changes in prevailing institutions, with successive periods of institutionalization and deinstitutionalization, the findings are more consistent with the model of frequently fluctuating styles with limited entrenchment.

Circulation of Control

Although the findings are consistent with the model of the circulation of control and prevailing conceptions as styles rather than institutions, more research is needed to validate these findings. In particular, future research should examine the process of the circulation of control under various changes in prevailing economic, cultural, and political environments. In addition, more fine-grained analysis of the underlying processes of contestation and obsolescence is required. While we have assumed in this paper that every CEO succession and selection reflects a contest for control, these contests were not directly observed but were inferred from the data. Similarly, obsolescence was inferred from the instability in the power of functional backgrounds across generations of CEOs and across historical changes in prevailing ideologies and structural changes in the importance of strategic contingencies. The measures of intraorganizational political dynamics, in particular, while an important proxy, do not fully capture the complex processes that are affecting the obsolescence of functional backgrounds.

The circulation of styles contending for ideological and political control can be contrasted with the institutionalization of insider CEO selection in U.S. industrial corporations. Vancil (1987), Cannella and Lubatkin (1993), and Ocasio (1999) have studied the selection of insiders versus outsiders as CEOs and found both formalization of insider selection and persistence and entrenchment of insiders in a majority of large U.S. industrial corporations. While recent anecdotal evidence suggests that outsider selection may be increasing, the selection of insider candidates as CEOs was taken for granted in most corporations during 1960–1990. While insider selection is highly institutionalized in U.S. corporations, the same cannot be said about the selection of functional backgrounds of new CEOs, which is better characterized as a contest among contending styles.

Further research is needed to establish the conditions under which conceptions of control become taken for granted and institutionalized and those under which they fluctuate and remain contested. We have several theoretical speculations on what these conditions might be. First the degree of hegemony across organizations is likely to increase the entrenchment of a prevailing conception. The greater the diversity in prevailing conceptions across organizations, the lower the likelihood that any one conception will become entrenched and stable over time. While neither financial CEOs nor the portfolio management style were ever predominant or hegemonic across U.S. industry, other characteristics, such as the focus on short-term profitability and the multidivisional structure, were more widely diffused and are, according to this hypothesis, more likely to remain entrenched and to persist over time. Second, formalization is likely to increase the taken-for-grantedness of organizational forms and conceptions and their cultural persistence (Zucker, 1977). While insider selection becomes formalized in the internal labor market for CEOs (Vancil, 1987; Ocasio, 1999), the choice of a particular functional background is not part of the formal rules of CEO selection in any organization.

Third, the impermanence in power of particular functions and the contestation among styles does not imply that all styles are equally legitimate or that any individual style can gain power in U.S. industrial corporations. To the degree that opposing functional groups within an organization are structurally equivalent with members of incumbent groups, increased circulation among contending styles is likely. In many corporations, finance, production, marketing, and operations executives below the rank of CEO or chief operating officer are the structurally equivalent groups that are all part of the firm's dominant coalition and potential candidates for CEO. Managers and executives from other functions, human resources, for example, are not structurally equivalent to the dominant coalition members, their styles and conceptions of control are less legitimate, and their exclusion from the CEO position is highly institutionalized.

Finally, intraelite contestation, while limiting the political entrenchment of any individual or function within the dominant coalition, helps deflect external challenges to the dominant elite and restricts the ability of nonelite groups to gain power and ascendancy or provide alternative styles or conceptions. The contestation and circulation among dominant coalition members thereby strengthens their oligarchic control (Michels, 1962) and the institutionalization of the status, power, and material wealth of the coalition as a whole. The circulation of control does not, by itself, transform the corporation or restructure its institutions. During the 1980s and early 1990s, finance CEOs and the finance conception declined, but the corporation's focus on profitability and financial gain continued. There is little doubt, however, that the circulation of control influenced the changing strategies of the corporation.

REFERENCES

Abrahamson, Eric
1996 "Management fashion." Academy of Management Review, 21: 254–285.

Boeker, Warren
1989 "The development and institutionalization of subunit power in organizations." Administrative Science Quarterly, 34: 388–410.

Brealey, Richard A., and Stewart C. Myers
1991 Principles of Corporate Finance, 4th ed. New York: McGraw-Hill.

Cannella, Albert A., and Michael Lubatkin
1993 "Succession as a sociopolitical process: Internal impediments to outsider selection." Academy of Management Journal, 37: 763–793.

Chaves, Mark
1993 "Intraorganizational power and internal secularization in Protestant denominations." American Journal of Sociology, 99: 1–48.

Cyert, Richard M., and James G. March
1963 A Behavioral Theory of the Firm. Englewood Cliffs, NJ: Prentice-Hall.

Davis, Gerald F., Kristina A. Diekmann, and Catherine H. Tinsley
1994 "The decline and fall of the conglomerate firm in the 1980s: The deinstitutionalization of an organizational form." American Sociological Review, 59: 547–570.

Davis, Gerald F., and Suzanne K. Stout
1992 "Organization theory and the market for corporate control." Administrative Science Quarterly, 37: 605–633.

Deal, Terrence E., and Allan A. Kennedy
1982 Corporate Cultures: The Rites and Rituals of Corporate Life. Reading, MA: Addison-Wesley.

DiMaggio, Paul D., and Walter W. Powell
1983 "The iron cage revisited: Institutional isomorphism and collective rationality in organizational fields." American Sociological Review, 48 147–160.
1991 "Introduction." In Walter W. Powell and Paul J. DiMaggio (eds.), The New Institutionalism in Organizational Analysis: 1–38. Chicago: University of Chicago Press.

Donaldson, Gordon
1994 Corporate Restructuring: Managing the Change Process from Within. Boston: Harvard Business School Press.

Fligstein, Neil
1985 "The spread of the multidivisional form." American Sociological Review 50: 377–391.
1987 "The intraorganizational power struggle: Rise of finance personnel to top leadership in large corporations, 1919–1979." American Sociological Review, 52: 44–58.
1990 The Transformation of Corporate Control. Cambridge, MA: Harvard University Press.

Circulation of Control

1996 "Markets as politics: A political-cultural approach to market institutions." American Sociological Review, 61: 656–673.

Fligstein, Neil, and Peter Brantley
1992 "Bank control, owner control, or organizational dynamics: Who controls the large modern corporation?" American Journal of Sociology, 98: 280–307.

Guillén, Mauro F.
1994 Models of Management: Work, Authority, and Organization in Comparative Perspective. Chicago: University of Chicago Press.

Hambrick, Donald C.
1994 "Top management groups: A conceptual integration and reconsideration of the 'team' label." In Barry M. Staw and L. L. Cummings (eds.), Research in Organizational Behavior, 16: 171–174. Greenwich, CT: JAI Press.

Hambrick, Donald C., and Phyllis P. Mason
1984 "Upper echelons: The organization as a reflection of its top managers." Academy of Management Review, 2: 193–206.

Hammer, Michael, and John Champy
1993 Reengineering the Corporation: A Manifesto for Business Revolution. New York: Harper Collins.

Haspelagh, Phillippe
1982 "Portfolio planning: Uses and limits." Harvard Business Review, 60: 58–73.

Hayes, Robert H., and William Abernathy
1980 "Managing our way to economic decline." Harvard Business Review, 58: 67–77.

Hickson, D., C. R. Hinings, C. A. Lee, R. E. Schneck, and J. M. Pennings
1971 "A strategic contingencies theory of intraorganizational power. "Administrative Science Quarterly, 19: 22–44.

Jackall, Robert
1988 Moral Mazes: The World of Corporate Managers. New York: Oxford University Press.

Jacoby, Sanford M.
1990 "Competition management." Science, 250: 839–840.

Jepperson, Ronald L.
1991 "Institutions, institutional effects, and institutionalism." In Walter W. Powell and Paul J. DiMaggio (eds.), The New Institutionalism in Organizational Analysis: 143–163. Chicago: University of Chicago Press.

March, James G.
1962 "The business firm as a political coalition." Journal of Politics, 24: 662–678.

Meyer, John W., and Brian Rowan
1977 "Institutionalized organizations: Formal structure as myth and ceremony." American Journal of Sociology, 83: 340–363.

Michels, Robert
1962 Political Parties. New York: Free Press.

Mizruchi, Mark S., and Linda Brewster Stearns
1994 "A longitudinal study of borrowing by large American corporations." Administrative Science Quarterly, 39: 118–140.

Ocasio, William
1994 "Political dynamics and the circulation of power: CEO succession in U.S. industrial corporations, 1960–1990." Administrative Science Quarterly, 39: 285–314.
1997 "Toward an attention-based view of the firm." Strategic Management Journal, 18: 187–206.
1999 "Institutionalized action and corporate governance: The reliance on rules of CEO succession." Administrative Science Quarterly, 44: 384–416.

Oliver, Christine
1992 "The antecedents of deinstitutionalization." Organization Studies, 13: 563–588.

Ouchi, William G.
1981 Theory Z: How American Business Can Meet the Japanese Challenge. Reading, MA: Addison-Wesley.

Perrow, Charles
1970 "Departmental power and perspectives in industrial firms." In Mayer N. Zald (ed.), Power in Organizations: 59–89. Nashville, TN: Vanderbilt University Press.
1991 "A society of organizations." Theory and Society, 20: 725–762.

Peters, Tom J., and Robert H. Waterman
1982 In Search of Excellence. New York: Harper and Row.

Pfeffer, Jeffrey
1981 Power in Organizations. Marshfield, MA: Pitman.
1992 Managing with Power: Politics and Influence in Organizations. Boston: Harvard Business School Press.

Porter, Michael E.
1985 Competitive Advantage: Creating and Sustaining Superior Performance. New York: Free Press.

Prahalad, C. K., and Gary Hamel
1990 "The core competence of the corporation." Harvard Business Review, 68 (May-June): 79–91.

Rumelt, Richard P.
1974 Strategy, Structure, and Economic Performance. Boston: Harvard Business School Press.

Salancik, Gerald R., and Jeffrey Pfeffer
1977 "Who gets power—and how they hold on to it: A strategic-contingency model of power." Organizational Dynamics, 5: 3–21.

Senge, Peter M.
1990 The Fifth Discipline: The Art and Practice of the Learning Organization. New York: Doubleday.

Selznick, Philip
1957 Leadership in Administration. Evanston, IL: Row, Peterson.

Swidler, Anne
1986 "Culture in action: Symbols and strategies." American Sociological Review, 51: 273–286.

Tilly, Charles
1997 "History and sociological imagining." In Kai Erickson (ed.), Sociological Visions: 67–82. Lanham, MD: Rowman & Littlefield.

Tushman, Michael L., and Elaine Romanelli
1985 "Organizational evolution: A metamorphosis model of convergence and reorientation." In L. L. Cummings and B. M. Staw (eds.), Research in Organizational Behavior, 7: 171–222. Greenwich, CT: JAI Press.

Useem, Michael
1993 Executive Defense: Shareholder Power and Corporate Reorganization. Cambridge, MA: Harvard University Press.
1996 Investor Capitalism: How Money Managers Are Changing the Face of Corporate America. New York: Basic Books.

Vancil Richard F.
1987 Passing the Baton: Managing the Process of CEO Succession. Cambridge, MA: Harvard Business School Press.

Virany, Beverly, Michael L. Tushman, and Elaine Romanelli
1992 "Executive succession and organizational outcomes in turbulent environments: An organizational learning approach." Organization Science, 3: 72–91.

Wade, James, Charles A. O'Reilly, and Ike Chandratat
1990 "Golden parachutes: CEOs and the exercise of social influence." Administrative Science Quarterly, 35: 587–603.

Wernerfelt, Birger
1984 "A resource-based view of the firm." Strategic Management Journal, 5: 171–180.

Westphal, James D., and Edward J. Zajac
1995 "Who shall govern?: CEO/board power, demographic similarity, and new director selection." Administrative Science Quarterly, 40: 60–83.

White, Harrison C.
1992 Identity and Control: A Structural Theory of Action. Princeton, NJ: Princeton University Press.

Womack, J. P., D. T. Jones, and D. Roos
1990 The Machine That Changed the World: The Story of Lean Production. New York: Rawson.

Zald, Mayer N., and Michael A. Berger
1978 "Social movements in organizations: Coup d'etat, insurgency, and mass movements." American Journal of Sociology, 83: 823–861.

Zucker, Lynne G.
1977 "The role of institutionalization in cultural persistence." American Sociological Review, 42: 726–743.

Part II
Board Characteristics and Decision Making

[9]

Endogenously Chosen Boards of Directors and Their Monitoring of the CEO

By BENJAMIN E. HERMALIN AND MICHAEL S. WEISBACH *

How can boards be chosen through a process partially controlled by the CEO, yet, in many instances, still be effective monitors of him? We offer an answer based on a model in which board effectiveness is a function of its independence. This, in turn, is a function of negotiations (implicit or explicit) between existing directors and the CEO over who will fill vacancies on the board. The CEO's bargaining power over the board-selection process comes from his perceived ability relative to potential successors. Many empirical findings about board structure and performance arise as equilibrium phenomena of this model. (*JEL* D23, D73, G39, K22, L29)

Corporations are not governed by the process that corporate law would seem to imply. Corporate law states that shareholders choose the board of directors, but, in practice, shareholders almost always vote for the slate proposed by management.[1] Moreover, this slate is approved by, if not chosen by, the very CEO these directors are supposed to monitor (see, e.g., Myles L. Mace, 1971; Jay W. Lorsch and Elizabeth MacIver, 1989; Ada Demb and F.-Friedrich Neubauer, 1992). The resulting governance system has been criticized as ineffective in controlling management (see, e.g., Martin Lipton and Jay W. Lorsch, 1992; Michael C. Jensen, 1993).

Given these apparent shortcomings, it is easy to forget that the current system is, nonetheless, the market solution to an organizational design problem (albeit one that must be solved under legal constraints—e.g., all firms must have boards with certain powers).[2] Thus, as George J. Stigler and Claire Friedland (1983) argued, before any criticism of current practice is taken too seriously, a thorough understanding of the market forces that have led to its existence seems necessary. This, in part, is what we propose to do here.

The previous literature has focussed on what boards do, without asking how they get to be the way they are. However, the answers to these questions are invariably linked. For instance, a board packed with the CEO's relatives will be less effective than one made up of large shareholders. To understand corporate governance, the questions of director choice and director function must be answered simultaneously.

To capture this simultaneity, we assume that the board and the CEO negotiate over both the

* Hermalin: Haas School of Business and Department of Economics, S545 Student Services Building No. 1900, University of California, Berkeley, CA 94720; Weisbach: Department of Finance, College of Business and Public Administration, McClelland Hall, Room 315R, University of Arizona, Tucson, AZ 85721. The authors thank James Brickley, Aaron Edlin, Robert Gibbons, Charles Hadlock, David Hirshleifer, Steven Kaplan, Vojislav Maksimovic, Canice Prendergast, Anil Shivdasani, Sunil Wahal, Jerry Weisbach, two anonymous referees, and seminar participants at the University of Alberta, University of Arizona, Boston College, University of California-Berkeley, UCLA, University of California-San Diego, University of Chicago, Cornell University, Dartmouth College, Hong Kong University of Science and Technology, University of Illinois, Indiana University, University of Maryland, University of Rochester, and the Winter Econometric Society for their helpful comments and suggestions on earlier drafts.

[1] Even when shareholders do challenge management's slate of directors in a proxy fight, Harry and Linda DeAngelo (1989) find that they win a board seat only about one-third of the time.

[2] Mark Roe (1994) expands on the role of legal and political constraints. These, however, are better suited to explaining cross-country differences in corporate governance than the intracountry differences that are our focus.

CEO's wage and the identity of new directors. These negotiations could be explicit. Alternatively, in keeping with the institutional literature (see, e.g., Mace; Lorsch and MacIver; Demb and Neubauer), these negotiations could be implicit—the CEO could nominate new board members subject to a tacit understanding about the set from which they may be chosen. Were the CEO to violate this understanding, the board would refuse to approve his nominees. The CEO's bargaining power in these negotiations comes from his *perceived* ability relative to a replacement.

These negotiations determine the board's level of independence. Independence is important because a director's willingness to monitor the CEO increases with his or her independence. Monitoring provides information about the CEO used by the board in deciding whether to retain or to replace him. In this model, therefore, both the structure of the board and its actions are endogenously derived.

To evaluate the model's realism, we compare its predictions to existing empirical findings. Some of the model's predictions are:

1. A CEO who performs poorly is more likely to be replaced than one who performs well.
2. CEO turnover is more sensitive to performance when the board is more independent.
3. The probability of independent directors being added to the board rises following poor firm performance.
4. Board independence declines over the course of a CEO's tenure.
5. Accounting measures of performance are better predictors of management turnover than stock-price performance.

These predictions are consistent with existing studies of large corporations.

Predictions 1 and 2 match the empirical evidence on CEO turnover. A number of papers (e.g., Anne T. Coughlan and Ronald M. Schmidt, 1985; Jerold B. Warner et al., 1988; Jensen and Kevin J. Murphy, 1990), find that CEO turnover is negatively related to prior performance. In addition, Weisbach (1988) finds that the sensitivity of CEO turnover to performance is greater for firms with a higher proportion of outside directors, presumably because these firms' boards are more independent of management than are boards dominated by inside directors.[3]

While prediction 1 follows from other models (e.g., David Hirshleifer and Anjan V. Thakor, 1994), prediction 2 is more novel. The intuition behind it is that new CEOs require more monitoring than old ones, since less is known about their ability. More independent boards have a greater tolerance for this added monitoring, so they can afford to be tougher with an incumbent CEO whose performance is marginal.

Prediction 3 is consistent with the pattern of director turnover found by Hermalin and Weisbach (1988). They also find that the proportion of outside directors on the board decreases over the CEO's career. This finding suggests that board independence declines over a CEO's tenure, consistent with prediction 4.

Prediction 3 follows because poor performance lowers the board's assessment of the CEO's ability, reducing his bargaining position and thus increasing the probability that the CEO will be forced to accept more independent directors. Similar logic explains prediction 4: If a CEO keeps his job, then retaining him must be worth more to the directors than replacing him. This means that this CEO is, to some extent, a rare commodity, which gives him bargaining power vis-à-vis the directors. He is, therefore, able to bargain for a board that is more favorable to him.

Prediction 5 is consistent with both Weisbach (1988) and Murphy and Jerold L. Zimmerman (1993), who estimate equations predicting management changes using both stock returns and earnings and find that earnings do a better job. Intuitively, earnings are a function of current management only, but stock returns reflect both current management and the expectation of future management changes.

[3] Outside directors are nonmanagement directors not otherwise affiliated with the firm and inside directors are management or directors with close ties to the firm (e.g., ex-CEOs of the firm). Some researchers also include a third category, "grey" or "affiliated," intermediate in presumed independence between outsiders and insiders.

In addition, the analysis suggests the following predictions, which have not yet been empirically tested.

1. There should be long-term persistence in corporate governance. In particular, changes that either strengthen or weaken board independence should be "permanent" in that they change the long-term bargaining strength of the board against management.
2. The stock-price reaction to management changes should be negative if the manager is fired on the basis of private information and positive if the manager is fired on the basis of public information.
3. A CEO's salary should be insensitive to past performance at relatively low levels of past performance, but sensitive at relatively high levels of past performance.

The first prediction is consistent with anecdotal evidence of long-term patterns in corporate governance. When a firm has an extremely able CEO, he will be able to use his bargaining position to ensure a relatively weak board throughout his career. Consequently, his successor will inherit a relatively weak board. Thus, the model suggests that there will be long-term persistence in firms' governance practices and long-term interfirm heterogeneity in these practices as well.

The second prediction potentially explains why empirical studies have found no consistent stock-price reaction to management changes (see Warner et al.): there have been no controls for whether the dismissals were due to private or public information. Our prediction follows because a change in management conveys information about both the board and the CEO. If the board bases its firing decision on private information, then a firing reveals that a CEO who was previously seen as better than the expected value of a replacement is not. Expectations of new management are lower than the previous expectations of old management, so the stock price falls. In contrast, if the firing is based on public information, then nothing new is revealed about the CEO, but the firing conveys good news about the board's independence, so the stock price rises.

The third prediction comes from the structure of the bargaining game in our model. When the CEO is either new or a mediocre performer, the lower bound on his wage binds (a bound stemming from a limited-liability assumption). As performance increases, the CEO's bargaining position increases as well, allowing him to capture a fraction of the rents in the form of a higher wage.

Although we focus on explaining phenomena related to boards of directors, the model we develop is fairly general. It extends the job-matching model of Boyan Jovanovic (1979) by allowing for *endogenous* monitoring decisions. Among its features is a formalization of the argument that new workers are more valuable than older, better-known workers, ceteris paribus, because the former have a greater option value (see Proposition 2 below).

The paper has the following organization. The next section reviews some previous work on boards of directors. Section II introduces our model. We extend it in Section III, subsection A, by allowing the board to prefer the incumbent CEO to replacements. In Section III, subsection B, we consider how various governance activities affect the firm's stock price and how measures of firm performance will correlate with governance activities. Section IV considers a reinterpretation of our model that eschews bargaining and ensures that turnover is always optimal from the shareholders' perspective. Many of our results continue to hold under this alternative interpretation, although we lose the ability to analyze management capture of the board. Section V considers some policy prescriptions that have been offered to correct the perceived failings of boards (e.g., requirements that directors be paid in stock rather than cash). Our model predicts that many of these policies will be ineffective. We conclude in Section VI.

I. Boards of Directors in Corporate Governance: Existing Theory and Evidence

Adolph A. Berle, Jr. and Gardiner C. Means (1932 p. 87) observed that the separation of ownership and control inherent in a diversely held corporation leads to a board of directors controlled by management. They argued that:

> ... control will tend to be in the hands of those who select the proxy committee

> and by whom, the election of directors for the ensuing period will be made. Since the proxy committee is appointed by the existing management, the latter can virtually dictate their own successors.

Management's apparent control of the board selection process led Berle and Means, as well as more contemporary authors such as Jensen, to question whether directors can be effective monitors.

A counterargument is that directors' concern for their reputations in the managerial or directorial labor market causes them to be effective monitors (Eugene F. Fama, 1980; Fama and Jensen, 1983). Steven N. Kaplan and David Reishus (1990) find evidence consistent with this argument: directors of poorly performing firms, who therefore may be perceived to have done a poor job overseeing management, are less likely to become directors at other firms. On the other hand, as Bengt Holmstrom (1983) shows, reputational concerns need not correct all agency problems and can, in fact, create new ones.

To resolve these conflicting arguments about board effectiveness, an empirical literature assessing the board's role has developed. Unfortunately, measuring the day-to-day effect of board independence on corporate profits is made difficult by simultaneity problems, since board independence itself changes because of corporate performance (see Hermalin and Weisbach, 1991, for further discussion).[4] This literature has been more successful analyzing the relation between corporate decision-making in specific circumstances and some measure of the board's independence, such as its composition in terms of insiders and outsiders or other characteristics correlated with independence (e.g., directors' shareholdings). For instance, Brickley et al. (1994a) find that board composition affects their decision to adopt poison pills; John W. Byrd and Kent A. Hickman (1992) find that the greater the fraction of outside directors, the better the stock market's reaction to their firm's tender offers for other firms; and Weisbach finds that the sensitivity of CEO turnover to firm performance increases with the fraction of outside directors on the board. Anil Shivdasani (1993) suggests that outside directors who own a substantial number of shares and who hold more corporate directorships (presumably measuring the value they place on their reputations) are better at negotiating a favorable deal for shareholders who face a takeover bid. Lastly, Kevin Hallock (1997) finds that firms whose boards are interlocked (contain a CEO on whose board the firm's CEO serves) tend to pay their CEOs more. He argues that interlocked directors are less independent and, consequently, give the CEO a larger fraction of the rents than would other directors.

While the empirical literature on boards is fairly well developed at this point, there has been little formal modeling of the board. Existing papers have considered important issues about the board's conduct, but have ignored the process by which boards get to be the way they are (see Hirshleifer and Thakor, 1994; Vincent A. Warther, 1994; Brickley et al., 1994b; Thomas H. Noe and Michael Rebello, 1996). Our view is that such modeling is useful, but it ignores the fundamental question of how boards can, in many instances, be effective monitors of the CEO despite being chosen through a process partially controlled by him.

II. The Model

We model the board selection process as a bargaining game between the CEO and the board. We assume no active role for the shareholders (although some of them could be directors). Consistent with practice, shareholders simply ratify the slate put forward by the company. We discuss shareholder activity, particularly in crisis situations, later.

[4] Some papers that nonetheless attempt to estimate the day-to-day effect are Paul MacAvoy et al. (1983) and Barry D. Baysinger and Henry N. Butler (1985). Also see James A. Brickley and Christopher M. James (1987), Stuart Rosenstein and Jeffrey G. Wyatt (1990), William Brown and Michael T. Maloney (1992), Omesh Kini et al. (1994), Anup Agrawal and Charles R. Knoeber (1996), Sanjai Bhagat and Bernard Black (1996), James R. Booth and Daniel N. Deli (1996), Kenneth A. Borokhovich et al. (1996), David Yermack (1996), James F. Cotter et al. (1997), Robert Gertner and Kaplan (1997), David Mayers et al. (1997), and April Klein (1998) for related empirical work.

A. *Timing*

The game has multiple stages with the following timing.

1. At the start of the game, the firm has a new CEO. The *commonly* held prior distribution about his ability, α, is normal with mean zero and variance $1/\tau_0$ (τ_0 is the *precision* of the distribution). We set the mean to zero for convenience, but without loss of generality.
2. The first realization of earnings, x_1, occurs. Earnings are distributed normally with a mean equal to the CEO's true ability, α, and a variance equal to $1/r$.
3. Based on x_1, the board updates its estimate of the CEO's ability. The board may at this stage decide to fire the CEO and hire a replacement. The prior distribution of *any* replacement CEO's ability is normal with mean zero and variance $1/\tau_0$.
4. The CEO (either the incumbent or the replacement) negotiates with the board over filling vacancies on the board and his wage, w.[5] If the bargaining is unsuccessful, the CEO is fired and a replacement is hired. If a replacement is hired at this stage, the board bargains with him about the filling of vacancies on the board.
5. The board may then acquire a private signal, y, about the CEO. The probability that the board acquires this signal depends on the intensity with which it monitors the CEO. The signal is distributed normally with a mean equal to the CEO's ability, α, and a variance equal to $1/s$.[6]
6. If the board acquires the signal, it updates its estimate of the CEO's ability. Based on this posterior estimate, the board may decide to fire the CEO and hire a replacement.
7. The second realization of earnings (profits gross of the CEO's compensation), x_2, occurs. Again, earnings are distributed normally with a mean equal to the CEO's true ability and a variance equal to $1/r$. The random variables $y - \alpha$, $x_1 - \alpha$, and $x_2 - \alpha$ are independently distributed.

B. *Preferences and Ability*

The CEO in charge at stage 7 receives a control benefit of $b > 0$. A CEO who is dismissed prior to this stage (or not hired) receives a benefit of 0.

The CEO is also compensated with a wage, w, determined by the bargaining process between him and the board. This wage is paid *regardless* of whether the CEO survives to stage 7. A critical assumption is that the CEO is protected by limited liability; specifically, the wage must be nonnegative (i.e., $w \geq 0$).

A CEO's ability is fixed throughout his career. We follow Holmstrom (1983) by assuming that the CEO, like the board, knows only the *distribution* of his ability (i.e., that it is a normal distribution with mean zero and precision τ_0). We justify this assumption by noting that the uncertainty about a CEO's ability in a *particular* job is largely uncertainty about the match between him and the firm, which is similarly unknown to both the board and the CEO.

We assume that each director, i's, utility is

$$(1) \qquad \theta_i x_2 - \kappa_i d(p).$$

The constant $\theta_i > 0$ equals the director's marginal utility from firm profits, x_2.[7] We imagine that directors put different weights on profits for two reasons. First, directors' incomes depend on their own shareholdings. Second, di-

[5] We treat the creation of vacancies on the board as exogenous. This is fairly realistic, since many vacancies arise for presumably exogenous reasons such as death, illness, or reaching the customary retirement age. We also do not explicitly consider how the number of vacancies might limit the ability of the board to adjust board composition. This is with little loss of generality, since (i) only the proof of Proposition 6 depends on achieving an interior solution (i.e., one in which vacancy limits do not bind); and (ii) board size often changes (see Hermalin and Weisbach, 1988, for evidence).

[6] Alternatively, we could assume that the board always receives a signal, but its precision (i.e., s) is endogenous (we thank Canice Prendergast for this point). This alternative leads to similar results, except the comparative statics with respect to τ are ambiguous.

[7] First-stage profits, x_1, are sunk by the time the directors act, so we need not explicitly account for their impact on directors' utilities.

rectors' concerns for building reputations as competent managers may vary.

The variable p is the probability that the board obtains an additional signal, y, about the CEO. It reflects the intensity with which the board monitors the CEO. The disutility of monitoring is $\kappa_i d(p)$, where $d(\cdot)$ is a common, strictly increasing, strictly convex, and twice-differentiable function and κ_i is the director's distaste for monitoring. We imagine that directors' distastes for monitoring vary for three reasons. First, inside directors' careers are tied to the CEO's, so they rarely find it in their interest to monitor him. Second, the opportunity cost of the directors' time will vary among outside directors. Finally, directors who value the opportunity to serve on other boards could have an incentive to establish reputations for not "rocking the boat"; i.e., for not intensely monitoring the CEO.

Since utility functions are defined up to an affine transformation only, we can replace (1) with

$$x_2 - k_i d(p), \tag{2}$$

where $k_i = \kappa_i / \theta_i$. We interpret k_i as a measure of director i's *lack* of independence, at least in terms of the way he or she behaves.

We assume k_i is *fixed* for a given director i (at a specific firm and for a specific set of pecuniary incentives). In particular, it is invariant with respect to who the CEO is. We relax this assumption in Section III, subsection A, where we show it does not change the qualitative nature of our results. In addition, we discuss below the implications of basing individual director monitoring costs on the group level of monitoring.

C. *Updating Beliefs and Optimal Monitoring*

When new information is observed, either profits or a signal, the players update their beliefs about the CEO's ability. Specifically, if $\hat{\alpha}$ and τ are the prior estimates of the mean and precision of the distribution of the CEO's ability, then the posterior estimates are

$$\hat{\alpha}' = \frac{\tau\hat{\alpha} + tz}{\tau + t} \text{ and } \tau' = \tau + t, \tag{3}$$

where z is either x_1 or y and t is either r or s (see Morris H. DeGroot, 1970 p. 167). The posterior distribution is also normal.

From (3), the board has a more precise estimate of an *incumbent* CEO's ability at stage 3 than it would of any *replacement* CEO it hires. That is,

$$\tau > \tau_0, \tag{4}$$

where τ is the precision of its estimate of the incumbent CEO's ability. Intuitively, an incumbent is a "known entity," so there is less uncertainty about him than there would be about a new CEO.

The distribution of the signal y given the CEO's *true* ability, α, is normal with mean α and variance $1/s$; hence, the distribution of y given the CEO's *estimated* ability, $\hat{\alpha}$, is normal with mean $\hat{\alpha}$ and variance $1/s + 1/\tau$.[8] Define

$$H = \frac{s\tau}{s + \tau}$$

to be the precision of y given $\hat{\alpha}$.[9]

Observe that the board's posterior estimate of a CEO's ability is also the expected value of x_2. After fixing (sinking) the CEO's wage, it is also the expected value of profits.

The alternative to retaining a CEO is to hire a replacement. The expected earnings from a replacement are, by assumption, zero. Moreover, because all replacements are *ex ante* identical, they have no bargaining power. Hence, the directors can set a minimum wage, $w = 0$. The expected profit from a *replacement* CEO is, therefore, zero. Subsequent to obtaining a signal, y, the incumbent CEO will thus

[8] The random variable $y - \hat{\alpha}$ is the sum of two independently distributed normal variables: $y - \alpha$ and $\alpha - \hat{\alpha}$; hence $y - \hat{\alpha}$ is also normally distributed. Since the means of these two random variables are both zero, the mean of y given $\hat{\alpha}$ is, therefore, $\hat{\alpha}$. The variance of the two variables are $1/s$ and $1/\tau$ respectively, so the variance of $y - \hat{\alpha}$ and, thus, y given $\hat{\alpha}$ is $1/s + 1/\tau$.

[9] As a convention, we will denote functions of many variables, such as H, by capital letters. When we need to be explicit about an argument of such functions—for example, the function F evaluated at $x = x'$—we will write $F_{x=x'}$.

be dismissed if $\hat{\alpha}' < 0$. Using (3), we can restate the dismissal condition as

$$(5) \qquad -\frac{\tau\hat{\alpha}}{s} > y.$$

The firm's expected value *if* it will learn y is

$$V \equiv \int_{-\infty}^{\infty} \max\left\{0, \frac{\tau\hat{\alpha} + sy}{\tau + s}\right\} \sqrt{\frac{H}{2\pi}}\, e^{-(H/2)(y-\hat{\alpha})^2}\, dy.$$

Since the option to fire the CEO is a valuable option, it follows that $V > \hat{\alpha}$ for all τ.

Straightforward calculations reveal that V can be written as

$$(6) \quad V = \hat{\alpha}\Phi(-(Y_c - \hat{\alpha})\sqrt{H}) + \frac{\sqrt{H}}{\tau}\phi((Y_c - \hat{\alpha})\sqrt{H}),$$

where Y_c is the left-hand side of (5), $\Phi(\cdot)$ is the distribution function of a standard normal random variable (i.e., with mean zero and variance one), and $\phi(\cdot)$ is its corresponding density function. Note that

$$\Phi(-(Y_c - \hat{\alpha})\sqrt{H})$$

is also the probability that the CEO will be retained if evaluated.

A higher-ability CEO is always better, but the value of the option to fire him is decreasing in $\hat{\alpha}$:[10]

LEMMA 1: *V is increasing in $\hat{\alpha}$, while $V - \hat{\alpha}$ is decreasing in $\hat{\alpha}$.*

That is, the value of additional information about the CEO's ability is smaller the greater is the prior estimate of his ability.

Consider, now, the issue of how the board decides on the intensity (probability, p) with which to monitor the CEO. We assume the board chooses p to maximize:

$$(7) \quad \max_{p \in [0,1]} pV + (1-p)\max\{0, \hat{\alpha}\} - \bar{k}d(p),$$

where $\bar{k}$ reflects, in some way, the collective preferences of the board (i.e., $\partial\bar{k}/\partial k_i \geq 0$ for all i and strictly positive for at least one i). For instance, $\bar{k}$ could be the average of the k_i's. More consistent, perhaps, with theories of voting, $\bar{k}$ could be the median k_i. Note that the resulting p will be Pareto optimal from the perspective of the board members.

The first-order condition for (7) is

$$(8) \quad V - \max\{0, \hat{\alpha}\} - \bar{k}d'(p) = 0.$$

Expression (7) is concave in p, so (8) is sufficient as well as necessary. Define P^* to be the solution to (8). To keep the analysis straightforward, we consider only interior solutions (i.e., $P^* \in (0, 1)$). Corner solutions are a relatively simple extension. Properties of P^* are:

PROPOSITION 1: *The intensity with which the board monitors the CEO, P^*, is*

- *(i) decreasing with its prior estimate of his ability, $\hat{\alpha}$, if $\hat{\alpha} \geq 0$;*
- *(ii) decreasing with the precision of its prior estimate, τ;*
- *(iii) decreasing with its collective lack of independence, $\bar{k}$; but*
- *(iv) increasing with the precision of the signal (i.e., s).*

Intuitively, the more costly monitoring is to the board's members (or the less weight they place on the firm's profits), the greater is the marginal cost of monitoring, so they engage in less of it. The more able the board believes the CEO to be, the less valuable is the option to fire the CEO, so the board monitors less. The option to fire the CEO is similarly less valuable the less uncertainty there is in its prior estimate, so the board monitors less intensely when the CEO's ability is known more precisely. However, the option to fire the CEO is more valuable the greater is the precision of the signal, so the board

[10] All proofs are in the Appendix.

monitors more intensely when the signal is more informative.

Proposition 1 is consistent with the general perception that less-independent boards do less monitoring and that long-established CEOs (i.e., CEOs with high values of τ) receive less scrutiny. Being monitored increases the likelihood of being dismissed, so Proposition 1 is also consistent with the evidence in Weisbach, which suggests that outsider-dominated boards (which are presumably more independent) are more likely to fire a poorly performing CEO than insider-dominated (less-independent) boards.

D. *Negotiations Between the CEO and the Board*

When they enter into negotiations, the board brings

$$pV + (1 - p)\max\{0, \hat{\alpha}\} - \bar{k}d(p) + R$$

in surplus to the bargaining table, where R is the share of b the board can expect to capture from a replacement CEO. However, given the limited-liability assumption ($w \geq 0$), the board cannot capture any share of b from a replacement CEO. Consequently, $R = 0$. The incumbent CEO brings his *expected* benefit,

$$(p\Phi(-(Y_c - \hat{\alpha})\sqrt{H}) + 1 - p)b,$$

to the table. So their joint surplus is

$$(9) \quad pV + (1 - p)\max\{0, \hat{\alpha}\} - \bar{k}d(p) + (p\Phi(-(Y_c - \hat{\alpha})\sqrt{H}) + 1 - p)b.$$

Maximizing (9) with respect to p yields the first-order condition

$$(10) \quad V - \max\{0, \hat{\alpha}\} - \bar{k}d'(p) - (1 - \Phi)b = 0.$$

Comparing (10) to (8), we see that the marginal benefit of monitoring is lower in (10) by $(1 - \Phi)b$, which means that the level of monitoring that maximizes joint surplus (9) is lower than the level of monitoring that maximizes the board's expected utility (7). That is, if P^{**} is the solution to (10), then $P^{**} < P^{*}$.

It is worth considering why $P^{**} < P^{*}$. Part of the surplus that can be shared by the *incumbent* CEO and the board is the incumbent's chance of getting the control benefit, b. If he is fired, then this chance is lost; it goes to the *replacement* CEO. Moreover, limited liability prevents the board from recapturing it by setting a negative wage. Consequently, the marginal *joint* benefit of monitoring is reduced.[11]

We assume that the board and the CEO cannot contract *directly* on the probability that the board will evaluate the CEO (i.e., p). This assumption is consistent with the general perception that it is difficult for outside parties to verify how diligent the board is in its monitoring function (if it were easy for outside parties to verify the board's diligence, presumably the board would contract with the shareholders on this issue). This, however, creates a problem, because the board's private incentive is to choose a level of monitoring greater than that which maximizes *joint* surplus; i.e., the board would choose P^{*} instead of P^{**}.

The only way for the CEO and board to avoid this problem of too much monitoring is to lower the board's incentives to monitor by raising $\bar{k}$. We interpret the negotiations over $\bar{k}$ as decisions over factors likely to affect the independence of the board, such as board composition (e.g., proportion of insiders versus outsiders), board compensation, and so forth.

We assume that when the board negotiates with the CEO over $\bar{k}$ and w it cares about its utility only; that is, it does *not* consider the new (future) directors' utility in their negotiation.

Let $\bar{k}_0$ denote the collective lack of independence of the *continuing* directors.[12] If

[11] In many ways, the situation is similar to Philippe Aghion and Patrick Bolton's (1987) exclusive-dealing model. There, a retailer (our board) and a monopoly producer (our incumbent CEO) enter into an exclusive-dealing contract because of their concern that an entrant (our replacement CEO) will capture future surplus.

[12] Note the flexibility to change board composition comes from filling *exogenous* vacancies or *adding* directors to the board—no continuing director need leave to realize a change in board composition.

bargaining with the CEO yields a new board with a different lack-of-independence parameter, $\bar{k}_1$, then the *continuing* directors' expected utility is

$$(11)\quad P^*_{\bar{k}=\bar{k}_1}V + (1 - P^*_{\bar{k}=\bar{k}_1})\max\{0, \hat{\alpha}\} - \bar{k}_0 d(P^*_{\bar{k}=\bar{k}_1}) - w.$$

Observe that the equilibrium probability of obtaining a signal, P^*, is a function of the *new* board's lack of independence, $\bar{k}_1$, not the continuing directors' lack of independence, $\bar{k}_0$.

We model the negotiations between the CEO and the board as a Nash bargaining game: the CEO and board agree to the level of independence (i.e., $\bar{k}$) and wage that maximize the product of their surpluses from trade. Provided the limited-liability constraint does not bind, the resulting composition (i.e., $\bar{k}$) will also maximize their joint surplus.[13] Assuming that the CEO has bargaining power is consistent with the institutional literature on boards, which suggests that CEOs, both in the United States and abroad, have considerable say over who is nominated for board positions. It is also consistent with the view that a CEO who has proven himself to be more valuable (in expectation) than any potential replacement should have some degree of bargaining power.

The surplus of the players is the difference between what they expect to receive if an agreement is reached and what they expect to receive if no agreement is reached. If no agreement is reached, the CEO leaves the firm—in which case his utility is 0. The CEO's surplus is, therefore,

$$P^*\Phi(-(Y_c - \hat{\alpha})\sqrt{H})b + (1 - P^*)b + w.$$

If no agreement is reached, the board hires a replacement CEO. Let U_0 be the board's expected utility if it hires a replacement (we will derive its value shortly—see Lemma 2 below). The board's surplus is thus,[14]

$$P^*V + (1 - P^*)\hat{\alpha} - \bar{k}_0 d(P^*) - w - U_0.$$

Under Nash bargaining, the board and the CEO choose $\bar{k}$ and w to maximize

$$(12)\quad (P^*V(\hat{\alpha}, \tau) + (1 - P^*)\hat{\alpha} - \bar{k}_0 d(P^*) - w - U_0) \times (P^*\Phi(-(Y_c - \hat{\alpha})\sqrt{H})b + (1 - P^*)b + w).$$

To maximize (12), we need to know the value of U_0.

LEMMA 2: $U_0 = P_0 V_0 - \bar{k}_0 d(P_0)$, *where* V_0 *is V evaluated for a new CEO—i.e.,*

$$V_0 = \frac{\sqrt{H}}{\tau_0}\phi(0)$$

—and P_0 *solves the equation*

$$V_0 - \bar{k}_0 d'(p) = 0;$$

that is, P_0 *is the existing board's utility-maximizing level of monitoring of a new CEO. Moreover, the wage paid a replacement CEO is zero.*

Intuitively, new CEOs have no bargaining power, since they all have equal expected value. Consequently, the board can set a minimum wage and get its most preferred level of independence, which is to replicate its current level (i.e., $\bar{k}_0$).

Recall our assumption that the board can choose to fire the CEO *prior* to bargaining. It might, at first, seem that the board would fire the incumbent CEO if and only if his estimated ability were less than the estimated ability of

[13] Other bargaining games would yield qualitatively similar results provided the CEO's bargaining power increases with his perceived ability.

[14] The reader will note that we have replaced $\max\{\hat{\alpha}, 0\}$ with $\hat{\alpha}$. As we will show in Proposition 2, any *incumbent* CEO who is not fired prior to bargaining must have an estimated ability greater than zero.

a replacement (i.e., if and only if $\hat{\alpha} < 0$). This is not, however, true:

PROPOSITION 2: *A unique finite cutoff, $A_c > 0$, exists such that an incumbent CEO is fired prior to bargaining if and only if his estimated ability is less than A_c.*

Proposition 2 follows because the right to evaluate a CEO creates a valuable option. The value of this option increases with the prior uncertainty about the CEO (i.e., $1/\tau$). Consequently, its value is greater for a new CEO than for an incumbent CEO. A new CEO is, therefore, more desirable than an incumbent CEO ceteris paribus. So, an incumbent's estimated ability must be strictly greater than a new CEO's if he is to retain his job.

A natural question to ask is whether less-independent boards tolerate worse performance than do more-independent boards; that is, do greater values of $\bar{k}_0$ lead to lower values of A_c. The answer is yes:

PROPOSITION 3: *The minimum estimated ability for the incumbent CEO at which he will be retained, A_c, falls as the board becomes less independent; that is,*

$$\frac{\partial A_c}{\partial \bar{k}_0} < 0.$$

Remark 1: Since $\hat{\alpha}$ is a decreasing function of performance [recall (3)], Proposition 3 implies that CEO dismissals are more sensitive to (negative) firm performance when the board is more independent. As such, Proposition 3 is consistent with the evidence in Weisbach.

Proposition 3 holds because a replacement CEO must be monitored more than an incumbent CEO. The less independent the board (i.e., the greater the board's distaste for monitoring, $\bar{k}_0$), the greater is the cost to such a board from hiring a new CEO because he requires more monitoring. Hence, such a board is more willing to tolerate a mediocre CEO than is a more-independent board (i.e., one with less distaste for monitoring).

Consider, now, bargaining between the board and an incumbent CEO who will be retained (i.e., one for whom $\hat{\alpha} > A_c$). Maximizing (12) with respect to $\bar{k}$ and w yields first-order conditions that are equivalent to

$$(13) \quad (V - \hat{\alpha} - \bar{k}_0 d'(p)) \times (p\Phi b + (1-p)b + w) + (p(V-\hat{\alpha}) + \hat{\alpha} - \bar{k}_0 d(p) - w - U_0) \times (\Phi - 1)b = 0 \text{ and}$$

$$(14) \quad p(V-\hat{\alpha}) + \hat{\alpha} - \bar{k}_0 d(p) - w - U_0 - (p\Phi b + (1-p)b + w) \leq 0.$$

Since $\hat{\alpha} > A_c$, the board's expected utility exceeds U_0, so the second line of (13) is negative. The first line must, therefore, be positive, which implies

$$(15) \qquad V - \hat{\alpha} - \bar{k}_0 d'(p) > 0.$$

From the first-order condition for the board's optimal p (8), condition (15) implies that $p < P^*_{\bar{k}=\bar{k}_0}$, which, from Proposition 1, implies $\bar{k} > \bar{k}_0$. We have, thus, established:

PROPOSITION 4: *If the continuing directors choose to retain the CEO, then the new board will have less independence than did the continuing directors (i.e., $\bar{k} > \bar{k}_0$).*

We emphasize the word "continuing" because the new board is less independent only relative to those directors who continue to serve. The proposition does not compare the new board with the previous board (i.e., the continuing *and* departed directors).[15] If, on the

[15] To illustrate this point, consider a hypothetical board with ten directors: five outsiders and five insiders. Suppose that $k_i = k_{out}$ for the outsiders and $k_i = k_{in}$ for the insiders, $k_{out} < k_{in}$. Suppose, too, that $\bar{k}$ equals the board's average k. This board's average k is $\frac{1}{2}k_{in} + \frac{1}{2}k_{out}$. Suppose two insiders depart, then the average k of the *continuing*

other hand, "normal" attrition from the board leads to an average level of independence among the continuing directors that approximates the level of independence of the original board, then Proposition 4 suggests an explanation for the finding that boards become less independent over the career of the CEO (see Hermalin and Weisbach, 1988).

Proposition 4 suggests that corporate governance is subject to a stochastic form of "entropy": in the long run, boards will be relatively ineffective, consistent with the common complaint leveled against them. Proposition 4 is, however, subject to two caveats that potentially affect its interpretation. First, a key assumption behind this result is that the monitoring burden is shared equally by the directors (i.e., each must expend p). If the monitoring burden could be shared unequally—if for instance monitoring was a team production problem such as considered by Holmstrom (1982)—then this entropy result need not hold. Directors would have an incentive to free ride on the diligence of other directors. This in turn would give them an incentive to want new directors with strong proclivities for monitoring (i.e., low k_i's) rather than, as here, the same proclivity they have. In a richer model of board activity, entropy would, then, depend on the degree to which monitoring is a collective activity (as here) versus a private activity (as in a teams problem).

Second, we have assumed away any role for the shareholders, in keeping with the institutional evidence that they rarely play a direct role in either the "normal" selection of directors or the day-to-day operations of the company (see Mace, for example). Proposition 4 serves to emphasize the importance of those occasions when shareholders "break" the entropy through hostile takeovers, proxy fights, or direct negotiations between large shareholders and management.

directors is $^3/_8k_{in}$ + $^5/_8k_{out}$. Suppose, consistent with Proposition 4, bargaining results in the addition of one insider and one outsider. The new board's average k is $^2/_5k_{in}$ + $^3/_5k_{out}$. The new board is, therefore, less independent than the continuing directors, but is more independent than the original board.

Whether the bargaining maximizes the board and incumbent CEO's joint surplus depends on whether the limited-liability constraint binds. If it does not bind, then (14) is an equality. Using it, (13) becomes

$$V - \hat{\alpha} - \bar{k}_0 d'(p) - (1 - \Phi)b = 0,$$

which is the first-order condition for maximizing joint surplus (9). If the limited-liability constraint does bind, then (13) is equivalent to

$$V - \hat{\alpha} - \bar{k}_0 d'(p) - (1 - \Phi)\zeta b = 0,$$

where $\zeta < 1$. Consequently, the solution to the problem in which the limited-liability constraint is binding involves more monitoring and, hence, greater board independence than if the constraint is not binding. This establishes:

PROPOSITION 5: *Suppose that the incumbent CEO is retained. If the limited-liability constraint is not binding, then the level of monitoring will maximize the CEO and board's joint surplus. If it is binding, then the level of monitoring will exceed the joint-surplus-maximizing level. Correspondingly, board independence will be greater if the constraint is binding than if it is not binding.*

We also want to know how estimated ability affects the ultimate equilibrium level of scrutiny (the probability of being evaluated) that the CEO will face.

PROPOSITION 6: *The equilibrium probability that the future board evaluates an incumbent CEO who is retained is decreasing with the prior estimate of his ability.*

Remark 2: Given the monotonic relationships between monitoring and board independence and between first-period earnings performance and estimated ability, Proposition 6 implies that performance and the independence of additions to the board should be negatively correlated, which is consistent with Hermalin and Weisbach's (1988) findings.

Propositions 4 and 6 show that history matters in corporate governance; that is, we can expect some hysteresis. Strong, independent boards will beget stronger, more-independent boards than will weak boards. Consequently, if we follow two firms, A and B, over time, then there is a good probability that we will find A always has a stronger board than B if A initially has the stronger board. Moreover, this could still be true even if B's recent performance is better than A's; indeed, from Proposition 6, better performance by B (i.e., a higher estimate of $\hat{\alpha}$) could actually accentuate the difference between the two boards' relative strength. These results underscore the importance of considering endogeneity in empirical studies of corporate governance and they potentially explain the inconclusive results of MacAvoy et al. and others.

Finally, we consider the relationship between the wage, w, and estimated ability.

PROPOSITION 7: *There exists an* $\tilde{A}$, $A_c < \tilde{A}$, *such that an incumbent CEO with estimated ability in* $[A_c, \tilde{A}]$ *is paid a wage of zero. There also exists an* $\hat{A}$, $\tilde{A} < \hat{A} < \infty$, *such that an incumbent CEO's wage is increasing in his estimated ability for estimated abilities in* $[\hat{A}, \infty)$.

For a retained CEO, the relation between his wage and estimated ability (past performance) is initially flat (zero). When the wage is positive, it equals one-half times the difference between the surplus that the board brings to the table and the surplus that the CEO brings. Whether the wage is increasing in estimated ability depends on whose surplus is increasing faster in $\hat{\alpha}$. Since the board's surplus is unbounded but the CEO's is bounded, it must be that the wage is eventually increasing in estimated ability. What we have not been able to establish is how the wage varies with estimated ability between $\tilde{A}$ and $\hat{A}$.[16] Overall, Proposition 7 predicts that the level at which the *non*contingent portion of a CEO's compensation is set should be insensitive to past performance for relatively low levels of past performance, but sensitive at relatively high levels of past performance.

It is worth noting that even if the CEO's wage is nonincreasing in his estimated ability, his overall well-being, $w + (p\Phi + 1 - p)b$, is increasing in his estimated ability.

III. Extensions

A. *The Board Has a Preference for the Incumbent CEO*

It is easy to imagine that the board has a preference for keeping the incumbent CEO. This could be a result of personal loyalty to the CEO—after all, many a directorship is the result of close ties between the CEO and the director (see, e.g., Mace, 1971). Alternatively, an incumbent CEO may take actions to entrench himself.

Let m be the additional value that an incumbent CEO yields the board. If $\hat{\alpha}$ is the board's estimate of his ability, then the board will treat him *as if* his estimated ability were $\hat{\alpha} + m \equiv \tilde{\alpha}$. It follows that the results from the previous section continue to hold, except with $\tilde{\alpha}$ replacing $\hat{\alpha}$. In particular, the next proposition is an immediate corollary of our earlier results.

PROPOSITION 8: *As the additional value that the incumbent CEO yields the board,* m, *rises the following occur:*

- *(i) the intensity with which the current board monitors the CEO decreases;*
- *(ii) the independence of the future board decreases; and*
- *(iii) the minimum estimated ability for the incumbent CEO at which he will be retained prior to bargaining decreases.*

(The three results follow from Propositions 1, 6, and 2, respectively.)

In other words, Proposition 8 simply indicates that the more the board values the incumbent CEO independent of his ability, the less intensely he will be monitored by the board and the lower the standard to which he will held by the board. These results are consistent with the widely held belief that entrenched CEOs or CEOs who have cultivated personal loyalty are less scrutinized and face lower standards.

[16] We have been able to establish it, however, for specific examples. For instance, wage is strictly increasing in estimated ability (above $\tilde{A}$) if $d(p) = \frac{1}{2}p^2$, $\bar{k}_0 = 1$, $\tau = 1$, $\tau_0 = \frac{1}{2}$, $s = 1$, and $b = \frac{1}{4}$.

To the extent m is endogenous, Proposition 8 predicts that a CEO would undertake activities that raise m. An example of such an activity is given by Andrei Shleifer and Robert W. Vishny (1989). They argue that CEOs attempt to reduce the probability that they will be dismissed by making investments that are more profitable under them than any replacement CEO. Even if such investments decrease firm value, a CEO has an incentive to make them because they raise his value vis-à-vis a replacement.

Proposition 8 identifies another cost of entrenchment in addition to Shleifer and Vishny's investment-distortion cost: The more entrenched the CEO is, the less intensely he is monitored. Consequently, the board is less likely to identify problem CEOs who should be dismissed (even if the benefit m must be foregone), which further reduces expected firm value.

This analysis also shows that a CEO is better off with his friends on the board (i.e., people for whom m is positive). A CEO is, therefore, likely to use whatever influence he has to put directors who will be loyal to him on the board and to ensure the loyalty of those already on board.[17] Given this, it is not surprising that boards often become interlocked (see Hallock for evidence).

B. *Effects of Board Action on Share Price*

How is the value of the firm affected by the board's decision to fire or to retain the CEO? We consider the answer at two points: prior to when the board could obtain a signal and after it would have obtained a signal. Without loss of generality, we again assume the incumbent CEO offers no additional benefit to the board (i.e., $m = 0$).

Prior to monitoring, but after the first fire/retain decision, the value of the firm is[18]

$$P^*V + (1 - P^*)\hat{\alpha}. \tag{16}$$

Since P^* is decreasing in $\hat{\alpha}$ (recall Proposition 1), (16) need not be increasing in $\hat{\alpha}$. If, however, the disutility-of-effort function, $d(\cdot)$, is convex enough, then (16) will be increasing in $\hat{\alpha}$.

LEMMA 3: *If*

$$d(p) \le d(1) - \frac{d(1) - d(0)}{\log(2)} \log(2 - p) \quad \forall p \in [0, 1], \tag{17}$$

then (16) *is increasing in* $\hat{\alpha}$.

We will henceforth assume that (17) holds.[19]

Let FV equal (16) under an incumbent CEO and let FV_0 equal (16) under a replacement CEO. The probability of realizing a first-period profit such that the CEO is *dismissed* is

$$\Phi\left(\frac{\tau_0 + r}{r} A_c \sqrt{\frac{r\tau_0}{r + \tau_0}}\right),$$

where A_c is the cutoff ability level defined in Proposition 2. Consequently, at the beginning of the game the firm will be worth

$$\mathbb{E}_x\left\{\text{FV} \,\middle|\, x_1 \ge \frac{\tau_0 + r}{r} A_c\right\} \times \left(1 - \Phi\left(\frac{\tau_0 + r}{r} A_c \sqrt{\frac{r\tau_0}{r + \tau_0}}\right)\right) + \text{FV}_0 \Phi\left(\frac{\tau_0 + r}{r} A_c \sqrt{\frac{r\tau_0}{r + \tau_0}}\right).$$

[17] For an extreme example see Bryan Burrough and John Helyar's (1990) discussion of the board of RJR-Nabisco.

[18] Our analysis ignores the present discounted value of the firm *beyond* the period considered by our model. This is slightly problematic because, as we argued in Propositions 4 and 6, we should expect hysteresis across CEO regimes. Given, however, the relatively long tenure of CEOs (ten years on average—see, e.g. Hermalin and Weisbach, 1988), this future omitted part of firm value will generally represent a very small portion of the firm's value.

[19] If $d(\cdot)$ is not convex enough, then (16) may be decreasing in $\hat{\alpha}$ over some range of $\hat{\alpha}$. To see this, suppose $d(\cdot)$ were affine. Then there would exist an $\hat{\alpha}^*$ such that $P^* = 1$, for $\hat{\alpha} < \hat{\alpha}^*$ and $P^* = 0$, for $\hat{\alpha} > \hat{\alpha}^*$. Since $V > \hat{\alpha}$, this would imply that (16) must decrease as $\hat{\alpha}$ crosses $\hat{\alpha}^*$.

After the first realization of profits, x_1, the firm's value is

$$(18) \qquad x_1 + \chi \text{FV} + (1 - \chi)\text{FV}_0,$$

where

$$\chi = \begin{cases} 1 & \text{if } P^*V + (1 - P^*)\hat{\alpha} - \bar{k}_0 d(P^*) \\ & > U_0 \\ 0 & \text{otherwise} \end{cases}$$

indicates whether the incumbent CEO is retained or fired.

From Section II, subsection D,

$$\text{FV}_{\hat{\alpha}=A_c} - \bar{k}_0 d(P^*_{\hat{\alpha}=A_c})$$

$$= \text{FV}_0 - \bar{k}_0 d(P_0) \equiv U_0.$$

Moreover, from Proposition 1, $P^*_{\hat{\alpha}=A_c} < P_0$;[20] hence, $\text{FV}_{\hat{\alpha}=A_c} < \text{FV}_0$. There thus exists an interval of $\hat{\alpha}$'s starting at A_c such that investors would prefer that the CEO be fired, but such that the board would prefer to retain the CEO. Consequently, there is a discontinuous drop in the value of the firm at $\hat{\alpha} = A_c$. Since $\hat{\alpha}$ and x_1 are monotonically related, we can conclude that firm value, expression (18), is increasing for all values of x_1 *except* at

$$x_1 = \frac{\tau_0 + r}{r} A_c,$$

where there is a discontinuous drop in firm value.

We summarize the analysis so far.

PROPOSITION 9: *Higher first-stage profit is positively related to whether the CEO keeps his job. But higher firm value is not monotonically related to whether the CEO keeps his job. Moreover, there is a range of first-stage profits such that investors would prefer that the CEO be fired, while the board prefers to retain him.*

Remark 3: Proposition 9 suggests that earnings (i.e., x_1) should be a better predictor of CEO turnover than share price, which is consistent with the empirical literature (see, e.g., Weisbach or Murphy and Zimmerman).

Proposition 9 and the discussion preceding it indicates that a tension can exist between investors and directors over whether the CEO should be fired, with the investors preferring to fire and the directors preferring to retain. This provides an explanation for the common phenomenon of investors seeming more eager than the board to dismiss management. It can also explain why takeovers and other costly control contests can be worth mounting.

Now we turn to the stock reaction when the board bases its fire/retain decision on its private signal. If the board fires the CEO, then the expected value of *future* cash flows is zero. Prior to evaluation, the expected value of future cash flows is positive. It follows, therefore, that:

PROPOSITION 10: *The firm's stock price falls if the CEO is fired on the basis of the board's private information.*

Finally, suppose $\bar{k}$ is *not* known to investors. Ignorance of $\bar{k}$ does not change Proposition 10, so we will focus on what happens when the board fires the CEO based on public information. For any value of $\bar{k}$ if the board wants to fire the CEO, investors would also want the CEO fired. If we imagine a distribution over $\bar{k}$ such that it is uncertain whether the board will fire the CEO for a given level of first-stage profits, then firing the CEO will be considered good news by investors and will cause the stock price to rise. The stock price will also rise because firing the CEO signals that the board is relatively more independent than was anticipated and will, thus, monitor more intensely. This yields:

PROPOSITION 11: *Suppose that the board's independence is unknown to investors. Then the firm's stock price rises if the CEO is fired on the basis of public information.*

[20] Recall P_0 is the optimal intensity of monitoring for a replacement CEO.

Remark 4: Our result that the stock price reaction to a CEO dismissal differs depending on whether the board used public or private information is consistent with, and could even explain, the ambiguous relation between CEO dismissal and stock price reaction found in event studies of CEO turnover. See Warner et al. for a survey of these studies and a similar explanation for their inconclusive findings.

IV. A Nonbargaining Interpretation

A potential concern is the realism of the bargaining game and the extent to which our results depend on it. Hence, it is worth reinterpreting the model in a way that does not depend on bargaining.

In this interpretation, the timing is the same, except that the bargaining stage, stage 4, no longer exists. We also want to reinterpret stage 5: Let

$$p(V - \hat{\alpha}) + \hat{\alpha} - \bar{k}d(p)$$

be the firm's expected profit; where, now, $\bar{k}d(p)$ is the cost of monitoring We now interpret $\bar{k}$ to be a cost parameter known to the firm's decision makers, but possibly unknown to investors.

We assume, now, that a board's level of monitoring, p, is an intrinsic attribute of the board. In particular, it is invariant with respect to $\hat{\alpha}$ or other parameters. Boards that monitor more—have a higher p—are more costly for the firm than boards that monitor less—have a lower p. That is, $d'(p) > 0$. We assume, additionally, that this *marginal* cost is also increasing in p (i.e., $d''(p) > 0$).[21]

[21] For example, there could be benefits to having inside directors on the board (perhaps to groom them as potential successors to the CEO—see Richard F. Vancil [1987] on this point) or less-intensely-monitoring outside directors (perhaps because they bring needed expertise to the firm). These benefits are increasing in the number of such directors, but with diminishing marginal returns. When these directors are seen as the opportunity cost of more-intensely-monitoring outside directors, we have $d'(p) > 0$ and $d''(p) > 0$.

We can now reinterpret Proposition 1 as a statement about board composition and the underlying parameters.

COROLLARY 1: *Under the alternative interpretation of this section, the level of board independence, p, is*

(i) decreasing with the prior estimate of the CEO's ability, $\hat{\alpha}$;
(ii) decreasing with the precision of the prior estimate, τ; but
(iii) increasing with the precision of the signal, s.

Observe that Corollary 1(i) and (ii) are substitutes for Proposition 4 (surviving CEOs have easier boards), while Corollary 1(i) is a substitute for Proposition 6 (board independence is decreasing with estimated CEO ability).

Propositions 2 and 3 continue to hold under this alternative interpretation (although Proposition 3 has little economic meaning). The loyalty-entrenchment result, Proposition 8, continues to hold under this alternative interpretation. Likewise, provided $\bar{k}$ is unknown to investors, the share-price results, Propositions 9–11, also continue to hold under this alternative interpretation.

Most of our results are, therefore, not dependent on the existence of a bargaining stage. Rather they are driven by combining a matching model, similar to Jovanovic's, with endogenous monitoring. Bargaining enables us to address the central enigma, set forth by Berle and Means and others, of how a seemingly inefficient institution has survived. In particular, it serves to explain how, why, and when CEOs have a say over who serves on the board. It also serves to explain how, despite this say, the board can still provide a valuable monitoring role.

V. Policy Implications of the Model

As corporate governance has remained essentially the same since the days of Berle and Means, so too have the criticisms and proposed reforms of it. For example, Lipton and Lorsch call for a number of changes, including a smaller board (to reduce free-riding), for more outsiders, more meetings, director pay linked to stock performance, and appointment of a "lead" director (if not the chairman) who is separate from the CEO.[22] These policies, in Lipton and Lorsch's view, would lead to better monitoring of the CEO.

In the context of our model, each element of the Lipton and Lorsch proposal serves to reduce the $\bar{k}$ of the board. For example, stock-based incentives lower the k_i's of all directors, while replacing high-k insiders with lower-k outsiders lowers average k. At first glance, one might think that efforts to lower the board's $\bar{k}$ through regulation or political pressure would lead to more effective monitoring.

This argument, however, ignores the nature of the equilibrium in the model. The CEO and board bargain over the *effective* $\bar{k}$, which takes account of all incentives that potential directors will have while they are on the board. As long as the bargaining process is itself unaffected by reforms, the equilibrium $\bar{k}$ will be little affected.

It follows that we need to distinguish between those policies that will affect the bargaining process and those that will not. For instance, requiring a specified fraction of the board to be outsiders would result in an outsider-dominated board, but not necessarily one that is more independent than the insider-dominated board that would otherwise prevail—the CEO and board members will have latitude in the selection process to offset whatever benefits are created by exogenously imposed "independence."[23] On the other hand, the model suggests that requiring incentive pay for directors could have an effect: By lowering $\bar{k}_0$, this requirement would affect the bargaining, leading to more independent boards and greater monitoring (see Proposition 6). Moreover, because of hysteresis, these benefits can persist—although entropy could lead them to diminish over time.

Of course this analysis begs the question of why corporations do not voluntarily adopt effective reforms such as this. One answer is that just as the board and the CEO negotiate over board composition, they would also negotiate over the implementation of reforms. Provided his past success gave him sufficient bargaining power, the CEO would be able to block or blunt such reforms.[24]

VI. Concluding Remarks

A recent *Harvard Business Review* "Perspectives Section" provides some insight into the realism of our model (Smale et al.). John Smale, who became the nonexecutive chairman of General Motors following Robert Stempel's forced resignation, describes policies adopted by the GM board that have dramatically improved its effectiveness. In contrast, Alan Patricof, a leading venture capitalist, argues: "Deep down [CEOs] really wish they didn't have boards. That's why, at the end of the day, most independent directors get neutralized in one fashion or another (Smale et al., p. 8)." A model of corporate governance should be consistent with both perspectives; it should explain both how some boards are active monitors of management, yet how some CEOs are able to avoid scrutiny.

By studying the determinants of board composition as a bargaining process, our model is consistent with both active monitoring in some firms and CEO dominance in others. The process by which GM acquired a strong board is illustrative of the model's logic: The company had a crisis induced by poor profits and the

[22] This proposal is fairly representative of the many governance reforms that have been proposed by the business press, academics, and business people themselves (see American Law Institute, 1982; Jensen, 1993; John G. Smale et al., 1995). See, too, Brickley et al. (1997) for a discussion and evidence on one of these potential reforms, the separation of the CEO and chairman's positions.

[23] Since an outsider is simply someone with no other ties to the corporation, it is hard to imagine that high-k outsiders could not be found (e.g., through interlocking boards).

[24] An additional prediction of our analysis is that new firms or those with weak CEOs (i.e., firms less subject to the agency problems considered here) will be the first to adopt reforms.

board was forced to act. The new CEO had no bargaining power and, thus, had to contend with an active board. None of this would have happened had the previous managers performed better; they would have maintained their jobs and their control over the board. Subsequently, after a period of good performance, GM went back to a more traditional arrangement of have the CEO also serve as chairman (*Wall Street Journal,* December 5, 1995 p. B1).

The model is consistent with a number of empirical regularities: CEO turnover is negatively related to performance and this relation is stronger when the board is more independent. The probability that independent directors are added to the board increases following poor corporate performance. And boards tend to become less independent over the course of the CEO's career. The model also explains why management turnover is more related to earnings than to stock returns. Finally, the model provides insight into the effectiveness of various policies designed to enhance the board's monitoring.

Despite the model's consistency with existing empirical evidence, a number of directions for future research remain. One is to model the board's operation in greater detail. For instance, we have assumed that the board chooses a common intensity of monitoring, p. What we have not considered is how the board implements this choice. For instance, does p represent the collective output of the board (e.g., what it does at board meetings) or is it an aggregate of individual directors' efforts (e.g., carefully reading reports prior to board meetings)? If it is the second, to what extent is the board able to overcome the problem of free-riding endemic to team production (see, e.g., Holmstrom, 1982)? Once free-riding among directors is an issue, the dynamics of board composition become more complicated. For example, the continuing directors can reduce their own workloads by adding very independent directors (i.e., low-k directors) to the board. This, in turn, could offset the entropy prediction of Proposition 4.

For example, unlike most American companies, a German or Japanese company typically has strong ties to one particular bank and representatives of this bank usually serve on the company's board.[25] These representatives presumably have a strong interest in the company's well-being.[26] The diligence of the rest of the board is unclear; free-riding considerations would tend to reduce their effectiveness, while the bank representatives have incentives to ensure that directors be selected who will be less likely to free ride. Similar issues could be expected to arise in family-owned firms in the United States.

One limitation of our model is that it focuses solely on the monitoring role of boards. The institutional literature (see, e.g., Mace or Vancil) emphasizes that boards also play important roles providing information and advice to management, and serving as a training ground for future CEOs. A richer model of boards should take into account these roles as well. To the extent they represent opportunity costs of monitoring [make $d'(p) > 0$], these other roles complement our analysis.

Our model could also be extended to investigate the transition from an entrepreneurial firm to a managerial firm. In this transition, an entrepreneur (or his or her venture capital firm) has an incentive to maximize the value of the firm by minimizing the impact of the entropy problem.

A last topic for future research would be to consider noncorporate situations where boards play a monitoring role. For example, universities, trusts, and other nonprofit institutions all have bodies that function much like corporate boards of directors. Much of the analysis presented above would seem equally applicable to these boards, but as with international comparisons further work is worth pursuing.[27]

[25] See Kaplan (1994a, b) for recent evidence on the effects of these banking relationships on corporate governance in Germany and Japan.

[26] Although it should be remembered that such directors are themselves agents (of the bank), which could create a second set of agency problems. Despite this, it is still reasonable to expect these directors to be more concerned about the firm's profits than other directors.

[27] See William G. Bowen (1994) for a discussion of the differences between profit and nonprofit boards.

APPENDIX: PROOFS

PROOF OF LEMMA 1:

$$\frac{\partial V}{\partial \hat{\alpha}} = \Phi + \hat{\alpha}\phi\sqrt{H}$$

$$+ \frac{H}{\tau}(Y_c - \hat{\alpha})\phi\sqrt{H}\left(\text{note } \frac{\partial V}{\partial Y_c} = 0\right)$$

$$= \Phi > 0 \left(\text{recall } H = \frac{s\tau}{\tau + s} \quad \text{and} \quad Y_c - \hat{\alpha} = -\frac{\tau + s}{s}\hat{\alpha}\right).$$

Consequently,

$$\frac{\partial(V - \hat{\alpha})}{\partial \hat{\alpha}} = \Phi - 1 < 0.$$

PROOF OF PROPOSITION 1:

Let Ω be the expression to be maximized in (7). Consider (i), if $\hat{\alpha} \geq 0$, then:

$$\frac{\partial^2 \Omega}{\partial \hat{\alpha} \partial p} = \frac{\partial [V - \hat{\alpha}]}{\partial \hat{\alpha}} < 0 \text{ by Lemma 1,}$$

so, by the usual comparative statics, $\partial P^*/\partial \hat{\alpha} < 0$. Similarly,

$$\frac{\partial^2 \Omega}{\partial \bar{k} \partial p} = -d'(p) < 0; \text{ and } \frac{\partial^2 \Omega}{\partial \tau \partial p} = \frac{\partial V}{\partial \tau}$$

$$= \left(-1 + \frac{1}{2}\frac{s}{s + \tau}\right)\frac{\sqrt{H}}{\tau^2}\phi < 0$$

(where the second result uses the fact that $\partial V/\partial Y_c = 0$). Hence, $\partial P^*/\partial \bar{k} < 0$ and $\partial P^*/\partial \tau < 0$. Finally,

$$\frac{\partial^2 \Omega}{\partial s \partial p} = \frac{\partial V}{\partial s} = \frac{\tau}{2(\tau + s)^2\sqrt{H}}\phi > 0,$$

so, by the usual comparative statics, $\partial P/\partial s > 0$.

PROOF OF LEMMA 2:

Consider bargaining with a new CEO. If this bargaining is unsuccessful, the board can hire yet another CEO. Hence, from (12), bargaining entails maximizing

$$(P^*V_0 - \bar{k}_0 d(P^*) - w - U_0)$$
$$\times ((P^*\Phi + 1 - P^*)b + w)$$

with respect to $\bar{k}$ and w. Given the monotonic relationship between P^* and $\bar{k}$ (Proposition 1) we can equivalently maximize this product in P^* and w. The first-order conditions are

$$\text{(A1)} \quad (V_0 - \bar{k}_0 d'(P^*)) \times ((P^*\Phi + 1 - P^*)b + w) + (P^*V_0 - \bar{k}_0 d(P^*) - w - U_0) \times (\Phi - 1)b = 0 \quad \text{and}$$

$$\text{(A2)} \quad P^*V_0 - \bar{k}_0 d(P^*) - w - U_0 - ((P^*\Phi + 1 - P^*)b + w) \leq 0.$$

In equilibrium, $P^*V_0 - \bar{k}_0 d(P^*) - w = U_0$— one new CEO yields the board the same utility as another new CEO. It follows, then, from (A2) that $w = 0$. Plugging that back into (A1) yields

$$V_0 - \bar{k}_0 d'(P^*) = 0.$$

This is the first-order condition (8). Since P^* is monotonic in $\bar{k}$, the solution to the Nash bargaining game is therefore $\bar{k}_1 = \bar{k}_0$.

PROOF OF PROPOSITION 2:

Let U^E equal the equilibrium expected utility of the board if it bargains with the incumbent CEO. Since $P^*_{\bar{k}=\bar{k}_0}$ is the board's most preferred level of monitoring, we know

$$\text{(A3)} \quad U^E \leq P^*_{\bar{k}=\bar{k}_0}V + (1 - P^*_{\bar{k}=\bar{k}_0}) \times \max\{0, \hat{\alpha}\} - \bar{k}_0 d(P^*_{\bar{k}=\bar{k}_0}).$$

Using the envelope theorem, it is readily shown that the right-hand side of (A3) is increasing in $\hat{\alpha}$. Moreover, as $\hat{\alpha}$ goes to infinity, the right-hand side of (A3) also goes to infinity. Differentiating the right-hand side of (A3) with respect to τ using the envelope theorem yields

$$\text{(A4)} \quad P^*_{\bar{k}=\bar{k}_0}\left[-1+\frac{1}{2}\frac{s}{\tau+s}\right]\frac{\sqrt{H}}{\tau^2}\phi<0$$

(the option value is decreasing with the precision with which the CEO's ability is estimated). Suppose, now, that $\hat{\alpha}=0$. It follows from (4) and (A4) that

$$\text{(A5)} \quad P^*_{\bar{k}=\bar{k}_0}V-\bar{k}_0 d(P^*_{\bar{k}=\bar{k}_0}) < P_0V_0-\bar{k}_0 d(P_0)$$

$$\text{(A6)} \quad = U_0.$$

Combining (A3) and (A6) establishes that $A_c>0$. Since the right-hand side of (A3) is continuous and increasing without bound but is less than U_0 for an estimated ability of 0, it follows that A_c exists and is unique.

PROOF OF PROPOSITION 3:

In the proof of Proposition 2, we established that

$$\text{(A7)} \quad P^*_{\bar{k}=\bar{k}_0}(V_{\hat{\alpha}=A_c}-A_c)+A_c - \bar{k}_0 d(P^*_{\bar{k}=\bar{k}_0})-U_0=0$$

for all $\bar{k}_0$. Since (A7) holds for all $\bar{k}_0$, it is an identity. Differentiating (A7) with respect to $\bar{k}_0$ using the envelope theorem yields

$$\text{(A8)} \quad [P^*\Phi+1-P^*]\frac{\partial A_c}{\partial \bar{k}_0} - d(P^*_{\bar{k}=\bar{k}_0})+d(P_0)=0.$$

From Proposition 1, $P^*_{\bar{k}=\bar{k}_0}<P_0$. Hence, since $d(\cdot)$ is an increasing function, it follows from (A8) that $\partial A_c/\partial\bar{k}_0<0$.

PROOF OF PROPOSITION 6:

There are two cases to consider: (i) the limited-liability constraint is binding ($w=0$) and (ii) it is not binding. Begin with case (i): From Proposition 1, the probability that the CEO is monitored is monotonic in $\bar{k}$, so maximizing (12) with respect $\bar{k}$ is equivalent to maximizing

$$\text{(A9)} \quad (pV(\hat{\alpha},\tau)+(1-p)\hat{\alpha}-\bar{k}_0 d(p)-U_0) \times(p\Phi+1-p)$$

with respect to p (since the CEO will be retained, we know $\hat{\alpha}>0$). Define Ψ to equal (A9). By well-known comparative statics results, it is sufficient to show $\partial^2\Psi/\partial\hat{\alpha}\partial p$ is negative:

$$\text{(A10)} \quad \frac{\partial^2\Psi}{\partial\hat{\alpha}\partial p}=2p(\Phi-1)^2+2(\Phi-1) +\frac{\partial\Phi}{\partial\hat{\alpha}}p[V-\hat{\alpha}-\bar{k}_0 d'(p)] +\frac{\partial\Phi}{\partial\hat{\alpha}}[p(V-\hat{\alpha})+\hat{\alpha} -\bar{k}_0 d(p)-U_0].$$

Using the first-order condition for (A9), (A10) can be rewritten as

$$\frac{\partial^2\Psi}{\partial\hat{\alpha}\partial p}=2p(\Phi-1)^2+2(\Phi-1) +\frac{\partial\Phi}{\partial\hat{\alpha}}\frac{V-\hat{\alpha}-\bar{k}_0 d'(p)}{1-\Phi}.$$

Hence, we have

$$\text{(A11)} \quad \frac{\partial^2\Psi}{\partial\hat{\alpha}\partial p}<2(\Phi-1)^2+2(\Phi-1) +\frac{\partial\Phi}{\partial\hat{\alpha}}\frac{V-\hat{\alpha}}{1-\Phi}.$$

We will now show that the right-hand side of (A11) is negative. Note, first, that

$$\frac{\partial \Phi}{\partial \hat{\alpha}} = \sqrt{H}\left(\frac{\tau + s}{s}\right)\phi\left(\sqrt{H}\left(\frac{\tau + s}{s}\right)\hat{\alpha}\right).$$

Next, make the substitution

$$z = \sqrt{H}\left(\frac{\tau + s}{s}\right)\hat{\alpha} \tag{A12}$$

and use (6) to rewrite the right-hand side of (A11) as

$$2(\Phi(z) - 1)^2 + 2(\Phi(z) - 1) + \sqrt{H}\left(\frac{\tau + s}{s}\right)\phi(z)\left(-\frac{zs}{(\tau + s)\sqrt{H}} + \frac{\phi(z)\sqrt{H}}{(1 - \Phi(z))\tau}\right).$$

Simplifying, this reduces to

$$2(\Phi(z) - 1)^2 + 2(\Phi(z) - 1) - z\phi(z) + \frac{\phi(z)^2}{1 - \Phi(z)}. \tag{A13}$$

Straightforward calculations reveal that this last expression is negative for all $z \geq 0$ (and, hence, for all $\hat{\alpha} \geq 0$). So the right-hand side of (A11) is negative, which, from (A11), entails

$$\frac{\partial^2 \Psi}{\partial \hat{\alpha} \partial p} < 0.$$

Now consider case (ii). From Proposition 5, the level of monitoring satisfies (10):

$$V - \hat{\alpha} - \bar{k}_0 d'(p) - (1 - \Phi)b = 0. \tag{A14}$$

Let Ω be the left-hand side of (A14). The result follows if $\partial\Omega/\partial\hat{\alpha} < 0$.

$$\frac{\partial \Omega}{\partial \hat{\alpha}} = \Phi - 1 + b\frac{\partial \Phi}{\partial \hat{\alpha}}$$

$$= \Phi - 1 + \frac{\partial \Phi}{\partial \hat{\alpha}}\frac{V - \hat{\alpha} - \bar{k}_0 d'(p)}{1 - \Phi} \tag{A15}$$

$$< \Phi - 1 + \frac{\partial \Phi}{\partial \hat{\alpha}}\frac{V - \hat{\alpha}}{1 - \Phi}$$

where (A15) follows from (A14). Using the z-transformation, we have

$$\frac{\partial \Omega}{\partial \hat{\alpha}} < \Phi(z) - 1 - z\phi(z) + \frac{\phi(z)^2}{1 - \Phi(z)}.$$

Straightforward calculations reveal that this last expression is negative for all $z \geq 0$ (and, hence, for all $\hat{\alpha} \geq 0$).

PROOF OF PROPOSITION 7:

Consider $\tilde{A}$ first. From (14), $w = 0$ if

$$[p(V - \hat{\alpha}) + \hat{\alpha} - \bar{k}_0 d(p) - U_0] - [p\Phi b + (1 - p)b] < 0.$$

At $\hat{\alpha} = A_c$, the first bracketed term is zero, while the second is strictly positive. The existence of $\tilde{A}$ then follows from continuity.

Turn to $\hat{A}$. If $w > 0$, then

$$2w = [p(V - \hat{\alpha}) + \hat{\alpha} - \bar{k}_0 d(p) - U_0] - [p\Phi b + (1 - p)b].$$

The first bracketed term increases without limit in $\hat{\alpha}$, while the second has an upper bound of b. It follows then that beyond a certain level, $\hat{A}$, that w must be increasing in $\hat{\alpha}$.

PROOF OF LEMMA 3:

From Proposition 2, we know $\hat{\alpha} \geq A_c > 0$ or $\hat{\alpha} = 0$. Differentiate (16) with respect to $\hat{\alpha}$:

$$1 + P^*(\Phi - 1) + (V - \hat{\alpha})\frac{dP^*}{d\hat{\alpha}}.$$

From (8), this can be rewritten as

$$1 + P^*(\Phi - 1) + \bar{k}d'(P^*)\frac{dP^*}{d\hat{\alpha}}.$$

Also from (8), it is readily shown that

$$\frac{dP^*}{d\hat{\alpha}} = \frac{\Phi - 1}{\bar{k}d''(P^*)}.$$

So (16) is increasing in $\hat{\alpha}$ if

$$\text{(A16)} \quad 1 + (\Phi - 1)\left(P^* + \frac{d'(P^*)}{d''(P^*)}\right) \geq 0.$$

Since $\hat{\alpha} \geq 0$, $\Phi \geq {}^1/_2$, so (A16) holds if

$$\text{(A17)} \qquad 2 \geq P^* + \frac{d'(P^*)}{d''(P^*)}.$$

Define $\bar{d}(p)$ to equal the right-hand side of (17). It is readily shown that

$$p + \frac{\bar{d}'(p)}{\bar{d}''(p)} = 2,$$

so (A17) follows if $d'(p)/d''(p) \leq \bar{d}'(p)/\bar{d}''(p)$. By (17), $d(\cdot)$ is more convex than $\bar{d}(\cdot)$. By adapting a well-known result on when one individual will have a greater Arrow-Pratt measure of absolute risk aversion than another individual (see, e.g., Chi-fu Huang and Robert H. Litzenberger, 1988 p. 29), it readily follows that $d'(p)/d''(p) \leq \bar{d}'(p)/\bar{d}''(p)$ for all $p \in [0, 1]$.

REFERENCES

Aghion, Philippe and Bolton, Patrick. "Contracts as a Barrier to Entry." *American Economic Review*, June 1987, *77*(3), pp. 388–401.

Agrawal, Anup and Knoeber, Charles R. "Firm Performance and Mechanisms to Control Agency Problems between Managers and Shareholders." *Journal of Financial and Quantitative Analysis*, September 1996, *31*(3), pp. 377–97.

American Law Institute. *Principles of corporate governance and structure: Restatement and recommendations*. American Law Institute, Tenetative Draft No. 1, 1982.

Baysinger, Barry D. and Butler, Henry N. "Corporate Governance and the Board of Directors: Performance Effects of Changes in Board Composition." *Journal of Law, Economics and Organization*, Spring 1985, *1*(1), pp. 101–24.

Berle, Adolph A. and Means, Gardiner C. *The modern corporation and private property*. New York: MacMillan, 1932.

Bhagat, Sanjai and Black, Bernard. "Do Independent Directors Matter?" Working paper, Columbia University, 1996.

Booth, James R. and Deli, Daniel N. "Factors Affecting the Number of Outside Directorships Held by CEOs." *Journal of Financial Economics*, January 1996, *40*(1), pp. 81–104.

Borokhovich, Kenneth A.; Parrino, Robert P. and Trapani, Teresa. "Outside Directors and CEO Selection." *Journal of Financial and Quantitative Analysis*, September 1996, *31*(3), pp. 337–55.

Bowen, William G. *Inside the boardroom: Governance by directors and trustees*. New York: Wiley, 1994.

Brickley, James A.; Coles, Jeffrey L. and Jarrell, Gregg A. "The Leadership Structure of the Corporation: Separating the Positions of CEO and Chairman of the Board." *Journal of Corporate Finance*, June 1977, *3*(3), pp. 189–220.

Brickley, James A.; Coles, Jeffrey L. and Terry, Rory L. "Outside Directors and the Adoption of Poison Pills." *Journal of Financial Economics*, June 1994a, *35*(3), pp. 371–90.

______. "Appendix to Accompany 'Outside Directors and the Adoption of Poison Pills'." Working paper, Arizona State University, 1994b.

Brickley, James A. and James, Christopher M. "The Takeover Market, Corporate Board Composition, and Ownership Structure: The Case of Banking." *Journal of Law and Economics*, April 1987, *30*(1), pp. 161–80.

Brown, William and Maloney, Michael T. "Acquisition Performance and Corporate Board Composition." Working paper, Clemson University, 1992.

Burrough, Bryan and Helyar, John. *Barbarians at the gate*. New York: Harper and Row, 1990.

Byrd, John W. and Hickman, Kent A. "Do Outside Directors Monitor Managers? Evidence from Tender Offer Bids." *Journal of Fi-*

nancial Economics, October 1992, *32*(2), pp. 195–221.

Cotter, James F.; Shivdasani, Anil and Zenner, Marc. "Do Independent Directors Enhance Target Shareholder Wealth during Tender Offers?" *Journal of Financial Economics*, February 1997, *43*(2), pp. 195–218.

Coughlan, Anne T. and Schmidt, Ronald M. "Executive Compensation, Managerial Turnover, and Firm Performance: An Empirical Investigation." *Journal of Accounting and Economics*, April 1985, *7*(1/2/3), pp. 43–66.

DeAngelo, Harry and DeAngelo, Linda. "Proxy Contests and the Governance of Publicly Held Corporations." *Journal of Financial Economics*, June 1989, *23*(1), pp. 29–60.

DeGroot, Morris H. *Optimal statistical decisions*. New York: McGraw-Hill, 1970.

Demb, Ada and Neubauer, F.-Friedrich. *The corporate board*. Oxford: Oxford University Press, 1992.

Fama, Eugene F. "Agency Problems and the Theory of the Firm." *Journal of Political Economy*, April 1980, *88*(2), pp. 288–307.

Fama, Eugene F. and Jensen, Michael C. "Separation of Ownership and Control." *Journal of Law and Economics*, June 1983, *26*(2), pp. 301–26.

Gertner, Robert and Kaplan, Steven N. "The Value-Maximizing Board." Working paper, University of Chicago, 1997.

Hallock, Kevin. "Reciprocally Interlocking Boards of Directors and Executive Compensation." *Journal of Financial and Quantitative Analysis*, September 1997, *32*(3), pp. 331–44.

Hermalin, Benjamin E. and Weisbach, Michael S. "The Determinants of Board Composition." *Rand Journal of Economics*, Winter 1988, *19*(4), pp. 589–606.

______. "The Effects of Board Composition and Direct Incentives on Firm Performance." *Financial Management*, Winter 1991, *20*(4), pp. 101–12.

Hirshleifer, David and Thakor, Anjan V. "Managerial Performance, Boards of Directors, and Takeover Bidding." *Journal of Corporate Finance*, March 1994, *1*(1), pp. 63–90.

Holmstrom, Bengt. "Moral Hazard in Teams." *Bell Journal of Economics*, Autumn 1982, *13*(2), pp. 324–40.

______. "Managerial Incentive Problems—A Dynamic Perspective." Working paper, Northwestern University, 1993.

Huang, Chi-fu and Litzenberger, Robert H. *Foundations for financial economics*. Amsterdam: North-Holland, 1988.

Jensen, Michael C. "The Modern Industrial Revolution, Exit, and the Failure of Internal Control Systems." *Journal of Finance*, July 1993, *48*(3), pp. 831–80.

Jensen, Michael C. and Murphy, Kevin J. "Performance Pay and Top-Management Incentives." *Journal of Political Economy*, April 1990, *98*(2), pp. 225–64.

Jovanovic, Boyan. "Job Matching and the Theory of Turnover." *Journal of Political Economy*, October 1979, *87*(5), pp. 972–90.

Kaplan, Steven N. "Top Executives, Turnover, and Firm Performance in Germany." *Journal of Law, Economics and Organization*, April 1994a, *10*(1), pp. 142–59.

______. "Top Executive Rewards and Firm Performance: A Comparison of Japan and the United States." *Journal of Political Economy*, June 1994b, *102*(3), pp. 510–46.

Kaplan, Steven N. and Reishus, David. "Outside Directorships and Corporate Performance." *Journal of Financial Economics*, October 1990, *27*(2), pp. 389–410.

Kini, Omesh; Krakaw, William and Mian, Shehzad. "Corporate Takeovers, Firm Performance, and Board Composition." *Journal of Corporate Finance*, April 1994, *1*(3/4), pp. 383–412.

Klein, April. "Firm Productivity and Board Committee Structure." *Journal of Law and Economics*, 1998 (forthcoming).

Lipton, Martin and Lorsch, Jay W. "A Modest Proposal for Improved Corporate Governance." *Business Lawyer*, November 1992, *48*(1), pp. 59–77.

Lorsch, Jay W. and MacIver, Elizabeth. *Pawns or potentates: The reality of America's corporate boards*. Boston: Harvard Business School Press, 1989.

MacAvoy, Paul; Cantor, Scott, Jr.; Dana, James D. and Peck, Sarah. "ALI Proposals for Increased Control of the Corporation by the Board of

Directors: An Economic Analysis.'' *Statement of the business roundtable on the American Law Institute's proposed principles of corporate governance and structure: Restatement and recommendations*. New York: Business Roundtable, 1983.

Mace, Myles L. *Directors: Myth and reality*. Boston: Harvard Business School Press, 1971.

Mayers, David; Shivdasani, Anil and Smith, Clifford. ''Board Composition in the Life Insurance Industry.'' *Journal of Business*, January 1997, *70*(1), pp. 33–62.

Murphy, Kevin J. and Zimmerman, Jerold L. ''Financial Performance Surrounding CEO Turnover.'' *Journal of Accounting and Economics*, January/April/July 1993, *16*(1/2/3), pp. 273–315.

Noe, Thomas H. and Rebello, Michael. ''The Design of Corporate Boards: Composition, Factions, and Turnover.'' Working paper, Georgia State University, 1996.

Roe, Mark. *Strong managers, weak owners: The political roots of American corporate finance*. Princeton, NJ: Princeton University Press, 1994.

Rosenstein, Stuart and Wyatt, Jeffrey G. ''Outside Directors, Shareholder Independence, and Shareholder Wealth.'' *Journal of Financial Economics*, August 1990, *26*(2), pp. 175–92.

Shivdasani, Anil. ''Board Composition, Ownership Structure, and Hostile Takeovers.'' *Journal of Accounting and Economics*, January/April/July 1993, *16*(1/2/3), pp. 167–98.

Shleifer, Andrei and Vishny, Robert W. ''Management Entrenchment: The Case of Manager-Specific Investments.'' *Journal of Financial Economics*, November 1989, *25*(1), pp. 123–39.

Smale, John G.; Patricof, Alan J.; Henderson, Denys; Marcus, Bernard and Johnson, David W. ''Redraw the Line between the Board and the CEO.'' *Harvard Business Review*, March/April 1995, *73*(2), pp. 5–12.

Stigler, George J. and Friedland, Claire. ''The Literature of Economics: The Case of Berle and Means.'' *Journal of Law and Economics*, June 1983, *26*(2), pp. 237–68.

Vancil, Richard F. *Passing the baton: Managing the process of CEO succession*. Boston: Harvard Business School Press, 1987.

Wall St. Journal. ''GM Decides One Head Is Better Than Two.'' December 5, 1995, p. B1.

Warner, Jerold B.; Watts, Ross L. and Wruck, Karen H. ''Stock Prices and Top-Management Changes.'' *Journal of Financial Economics*, January/March 1988, *20*(1/2), pp. 461–92.

Warther, Vincent A. ''Board Effectiveness and Board Dissent: A Model of the Board's Relationship to Management and Shareholders.'' Working paper, University of Michigan, 1994.

Weisbach, Michael S. ''Outside Directors and CEO Turnover.'' *Journal of Financial Economics*, January/March 1988, *20*(1/2), pp. 431–60.

Yermack, David. ''Higher Valuation of Companies with a Small Board of Directors.'' *Journal of Financial Economics*, February 1996, *40*(2), pp. 185–212.

[10]

© *Academy of Management Review*, 1990, Vol. 15, No. 1, 72–87.

The Composition of Boards of Directors and Strategic Control: Effects on Corporate Strategy

BARRY BAYSINGER
ROBERT E. HOSKISSON
Texas A&M University

Boards of directors of large corporations provide a governance safeguard to both equity capital and managerial employment contracts. Thus, the board is a potentially important instrument of internal control. This article develops theory and propositions concerning (a) the relation among ownership, managerial control, and the composition of the boards of directors; (b) the relation between the composition of the boards and control strategies (strategic versus financial controls); and (c) the relation among choice of control, corporate strategy, and strategic choice.

Corporate law in the United States requires that the business of publicly traded corporations be conducted under the direction of a board of directors (Eisenberg, 1976). These laws also grant directors the formal authority to ratify management initiatives, to evaluate managerial performance, and to allocate rewards and penalties to management on the basis of criteria that are supposed to reflect shareholders' interests (Fama & Jensen, 1983a). Some organization theorists argue that through the possession of these powers, boards set the premises of managerial decision making (e.g., Mizruchi, 1983). That is, astute chief executive officers (CEOs) learn what the dispositions of the board are, conduct themselves in a manner compatible with these dispositions, and, thus, initiate and implement decisions that comport with the board's concept of strategy.

Economists also view the board as an important element in the governance structure of the large corporation (Fama & Jensen, 1983a). *Corporate governance* refers to the integrated set of internal and external controls that harmonize manager-shareholder (agency) conflicts of interest resulting from the separation of ownership and control (Berle & Means, 1968; Williamson, 1984). Without governance controls, managers are more likely to deviate from the interests of shareholders (Fama & Jensen, 1983a). Agency theorists argue that the board, with its legal authority to hire, fire, and compensate top management, safeguards invested capital and, thus, is an important element of corporate governance (Williamson, 1984).

An alternative perspective is that especially astute or opportunistic CEOs influence the inclinations of the board and, thus, set the premises for the board's deliberations and decisions. Many believe, for example, that managers dominate their boards by using their de facto power to select and compensate directors and by exploiting personal ties with them (Allen, 1974; Galbraith, 1967; Jones & Goldberg, 1982; Herman, 1981; Mace, 1971; Pfeffer, 1972; Vance, 1964). Not surprisingly, those who question the effectiveness of board governance also advocate reforms that would limit either all or a significant majority of directorships to truly independent outsiders (Eisenberg, 1976).

Perhaps in response to these concerns the Securities and Exchange Commission (SEC) proposed that the New York Stock Exchange (NYSE) require audit committees that are made up entirely of outside directors (Mautz & Neary, 1979). Therefore, in 1984, possibly to preempt formal legislation, the NYSE implemented the audit committee rule (Kesner, 1988). As a result, outsiders typically exceed insiders on the boards of large firms (Patton & Baker, 1987). Given the formal premise-setting power of the board, it may be useful to evaluate how this secular change in board composition may affect manager-shareholder relationships, the strategic decision-making process and, ultimately, strategic outcomes in large corporations.

Evaluating the strategic implications of the composition of boards of directors requires empirical analysis. To provide a foundation for that analysis, this article develops theory and propositions concerning the board's role in managing the relationship between corporate owners and managers; it also explains how recent changes in the composition of boards may have affected this system of internal controls. Because this effort requires synthesizing several literatures, the article begins with an organizing framework and a brief overview.

Corporate Governance and Corporate Strategy: An Interdisciplinary Model

Four distinct constructs are employed to develop the central concepts of this article. As Figure 1 shows, the constructs to the left of the dashed line are drawn primarily from agency theory and the corporate-governance literature, which use an organizational-economics perspective for analyzing corporate organizations. Constructs to the right of the dashed line are drawn primarily from the organizational-control and strategy-implementation literatures, which are grounded in organization theory. Researchers of these disciplines are concerned, at least in part, with the evolution and continued survival of large, widely held corporations in which ownership and control are specialized (Oviatt, 1988).

As noted, agency theorists view the board as a potentially effective element of corporate governance and, hence, internal control. Developments in agency-control theory suggest that the emphasis given to control system measures and rewards not only motivates the effort of the agent but, where the agent has decision-making responsibility, influences the nature (e.g., riskiness) of the decisions (Eisenhardt, 1985; Hambrick & Snow, 1988). Therefore, agency theory provides a partial basis for developing propositions about the relation between

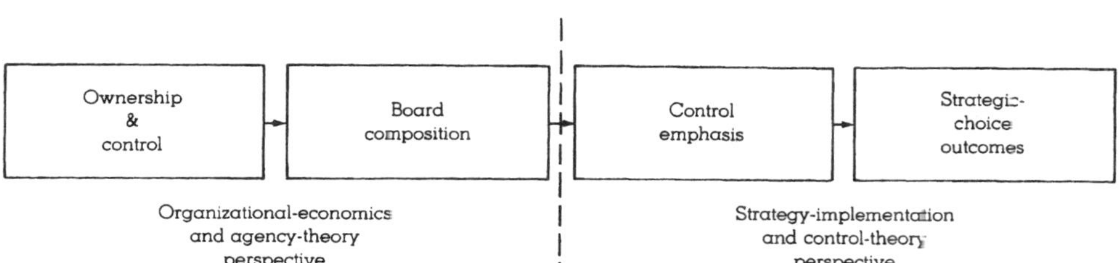

***Figure 1.* Model depicting the relation between board composition and corporate strategy.**

the control system emphasis resulting from the composition of the board and how changes in that composition may ultimately affect strategic choice.

Further development of these propositions benefits greatly from the strategy-implementation and control literatures, which provide a foundation for analyzing information processing within the board. Corporate law gives directors the right to evaluate and reward managers. Operationally, directors must draw inferences about the merits of top management on the basis of the financial performance of the firm or their direct observations of the decision-making process. A priori, the capacity to perform this function is not uniform across directors. More specifically, the amount and quality of information possessed by inside directors should be superior to that typically possessed by outside directors.

For example, outsiders usually serve as directors on several boards (Patton & Baker, 1987). Between managing their own businesses and serving on multiple boards, outside directors may not be able "to understand each business well enough to be truly effective" (Patton & Baker, 1987, p. 11). Consequently, outside directors may suffer a comparative disadvantage, relative to insiders, in discriminating accurately between the financial performances of the firm that are due to poor management and those that are due to forces beyond management control (Williamson, 1975). Top managers who face boards that are dominated by outside directors may be "evaluated in terms of the outcome of the adopted choice rather than in terms of the strategic desirability of the whole risk situation" (Luce & Raiffa, 1957, p. 76). Inside directors, who are part of the decision-making process, may be more likely to evaluate and reward top management through open and subjective evaluative processes.

Therefore, changes in board composition may change the relationship between top management and shareholders, as mediated by the board of directors, from an emphasis on open and subjective evaluative methods to an emphasis on more objective methods. A priori, such changes in corporate governance may be strategically important. For example, Baysinger and Hoskisson (1989) found evidence that the way internal controls are structured between top corporate and business-unit managers affects the choice of business-level strategy.

Of course, corporate governance and corporate strategic business unit (SBU) relations are conceptually and operationally distinct processes. Yet, the study of corporate governance may benefit from the application of other disciplines. For example, organizational-control theory, which traditionally has focused on the management of supervisor-worker relationships, suggests that the way those relationships are managed affects worker behavior (e.g., Eisenhardt, 1985; Ouchi, 1979). Additionally, control theory has been extended to problems involved in managing corporate-SBU relations (Baysinger & Hoskisson, 1989; Gupta, 1987). This article simply attempts to extend control theory to the management of relations between top management and shareholders via the board of directors. From this perspective, secular changes in board composition, through changes in the emphasis of control, may have important strategic implications for the corporation.

The remainder of this article synthesizes the agency-theory and strategy-implementation constructs used in developing this general proposition. The discussion is organized around (a) the relation between board composition and the allocation of risks between owners and managers, (b) the relation between board composition and control strategy, and (c) the behavioral and strategic-choice implications of the elements of corporate governance and control strategy.

Board Composition and the Separation of Ownership and Control

Corporations are both work-sharing and risk-sharing entities (Eisenhardt, 1985). Organized production involves parties who are responsible for formulating and implementing strategies and parties who contribute capital and are willing to bear the risk of losses (Alchian & Demsetz, 1972; Fama & Jensen, 1983a; Jensen & Meckling, 1976). Risk bearing is necessary because when strategic assets are deployed, it is not known whether the difference between stochastic cash flows and obligated production and distribution costs will be positive, negative, or zero. Although this so-called residual risk is experienced in all types of organizations, organizational forms may be differentiated on the basis of how risks are allocated among their constituents.

In large corporations, shareholders purchase and hold equity shares which, in return for bearing residual risk, entitle them to any positive residuals generated by the production and sale of output. In contrast, those who manage these firms usually receive fixed salaries plus bonus incentives tied to performance measures (Eaton & Rosen, 1983). The large, open corporation is thus distinguished from other organizations (e.g., closed corporations and partnerships) through the nearly complete separation of decision management and residual risk bearing. Agency theory suggests that this so-called separation of ownership and control is economically efficient, despite the noted potential for conflicts of interest.

Efficiency of Separating Ownership and Control

Shifting residual risk from managers to shareholders has many advantages that have facilitated the development of the large corporation (Alchian & Demsetz, 1972; Fama & Jensen, 1983b). Chief among these is that the separation of ownership and control specifically allocates residual risks to the parties who bear it at the lowest cost. Individual shareholders are able to minimize the effects of losses in a firm by holding a small number of stocks in many unrelated firms (Copeland & Weston, 1979). Managers, by contrast, cannot readily diversify their employment risks. If, for some reason, corporate managers were made to bear significant residual risks, they would likely seek much higher pecuniary rewards (Knoeber, 1986), or they would have to initiate otherwise unattractive corporate and business-level strategies, which would lessen the firm's residual risk (Amihud & Lev, 1981).

The central agency contracts of the large corporation are structured to avoid these inefficiencies. They allocate risks and responsibilities to the parties who are best able to bear and perform them, thus differentiating separation of ownership and control. To maintain this specialization, shareholder-manager relations must be managed in a discriminating way. Shareholders' interests must be safeguarded by controls on management, but controls must be implemented in order to avoid unduly shifting residual risks onto management. Efficiently managing shareholder-manager relations is an important function of the board of directors.

General Governance Role of the Board

According to agency theory, individual shareholders bear residual risk efficiently, but only to the extent that their collective interests are safeguarded by governance mechanisms. *Individually*, shareholders can protect themselves from mismanagement by selling their stocks through the organized securities exchanges. This option is not available to the entire group of shareholders, except through leveraged buyouts. Therefore, shareholders are viewed as "the only voluntary constituency whose relation with the corporation does not come up for periodic renewal" (Williamson, 1985, p. 304), and their interests must be protected by governance mechanisms such as the board of directors.

Both historically and within the individual corporation, the "separation of residual risk bearing from decision management leads to decision systems that separate decision management from decision control" (Fama & Jensen, 1983a, p. 304). That is, as firms grow large and management and ownership become specialized, conflicts of interest arise. These conflicts in turn give rise to the need to specialize further *decision management* (initiation and implementation) and *decision control* (ratification and monitoring) (Fama & Jensen, 1983a). Decision management is naturally the responsibility of senior management, whereas decision control becomes the responsibility of the board of directors.

Placing the responsibility for decision control with a board precludes managers from being the sole evaluators of their own performance and, thus, provides a safeguard to invested capital. Managerial performance usually is evaluated and rewarded by a combination of inside senior managers and independent outsiders who act as auditors (Herman, 1981). Because, as discussed previously, directors have the legal right to evaluate internal management, the board is believed to set the premises of managerial decision making.

As was noted, some researchers question the efficacy of including inside directors in the decision-control process. What purpose is served by giving managers a say in board deliberations? How can inside directors avoid conflicts of interest between loyalty to their superiors and the fiduciary obligations to shareholders? Clearly, the practice of including inside directors on the board seems inconsistent with the need to separate decision management from decision control. Yet, a closer examination of this issue reveals that inside directors play an important role both in maintaining the separation of ownership and control in large corporations and in preserving the efficiencies ascribed to this arrangement.

Special Governance Role of Inside Directors

In a growing body of organizational research, the performance implications of board composition and structure have been evaluated (Chaganti, Mahajan, & Sharma, 1985; Hill & Snell, 1988; Kesner, 1988; Kesner, Victor, & Lamont, 1986; Kohls, 1985; Mattar & Ball, 1985; Norburn, 1986; Vance, 1983). An important conclusion of this literature is that corporate governance mechanisms "bring the interests of managers *and* shareholders into congruence" (Oviatt, 1988, p. 216, emphasis added). As Williamson (1985) argued, "the board of directors should be regarded *primarily* as a governance structure safeguard between the firm and owners of equity capital and *secondarily* as a way by which to safeguard the contractual relation between the firm and its management" (p. 298, emphasis added). Inside directors are crucial to this secondary governance role of the board.

Effective control strategies, or governance structures, give boards high powers of inference: Through these control strategies directors are able to discriminate legitimate and illegitimate causes of financial misfortune. Thus, the board's methods of evaluation and reward allocation are effective only to the extent that through them strategic managers are responsible only for performance outcomes that result from opportunism or persistently incompetent decisions. That is, through effective internal controls, top management is protected either from the adverse personal consequences of outcomes over which they have no control or from short-term losses that are the result of investments in future cash flows. Such controls prevent a manager from being "penalized or rewarded for outcomes partially outside his/her control" (Eisenhardt, 1985, p. 136).

Top managers in complex corporations struggle against a variety of external and internal forces in order to accomplish the goals they set for the corporation. Managers in complex organizations thus have limited roles as "influencers of events rather than controllers of certain outcomes" (Bourgeois, 1987, p. 347). Under these circumstances, "good outcomes can occur despite poor efforts and poor outcomes can occur despite good efforts" (Eisenhardt, 1985, p. 136). Without an effective system to control decisions, managers are apt to behave in ways that reduce their exposure to risks. Unfortunately, implementing effective methods of internal control in complex organizations is difficult because information about the relation between managerial behavior and financial performance often is hidden in the "complex causality that determines any organizational outcome—including stock value" (Oviatt, 1988, p. 218). Insiders, because they are participants in the decision processes, have access to information that is relevant to assessing managerial competence and the strategic desirability of initiatives, regardless of their short-run or long-run performance outcomes. Outside directors may prefer to maintain an open and subjective relationship with top management, but they simply may lack the amount and quality of information upon which such relationships must be based. Including insiders on the board appears to represent an attempt to overcome problems of information processing and, hence, to improve the effectiveness of decision control.

Of course, some directors who are traditionally classified as outsiders may have more of this type of information than others. These would include, for example, outsiders who serve as top managers in organizations that operate in similar technological, regulatory, or competitive environments; former executives of the firm; personal associates of the top management; and so forth. Moreover, all outsiders may gain insights from inside directors concerning whether periodic losses either were the result of strategically appropriate actions of management that simply turned out poorly or were due to incompetence or opportunistic actions. Outside directors need this type of information to avoid confounding their decisions and risks (Williamson, 1985), and they may be expected to use such information when they draw inferences about the relation between observable performance and the quality of the decision-making process leading to it. Yet, such mitigating factors notwithstanding, the typical outside director will probably be far less able to evaluate top management on the basis of open and subjective evaluative methods than the typical insider.

By improving the chances that managers will be evaluated on the basis of the quality of their decisions, rather than periodic cash flow changes, inside directors preserve the separation of ownership and control. As Williamson observed, "To the extent that management participation (on the board) permits reviews on the merits to be done more responsibly (it) serves to safeguard an employment relation that would otherwise be exposed to excessive risk" (1984, p. 1220). As will be argued more fully, this secondary governance role of the board is strategically relevant because "restricting residual claims to agents in the decision process leads to decisions (for example, less investment in risky projects that lower the costs of outputs) that tend to penalize the organization in the competition for survival" (Fama & Jensen, 1983a, p. 306).

As for the conflict of interest issue, a number of writers have argued that inside directors' ties to the CEO can compromise their effectiveness as decision controllers in cases in which managerial opportunism is the cause of financial losses. A closely reasoned article by Mizruchi (1983), however, suggests that although this is a legitimate concern, it is somewhat overdrawn: The key issue is one of incentives.

Both inside and outside directors are legally liable for the outcomes of the strategic decision-making process, and these liabilities have grown in severity (American Law Institute, 1982). Because of this increased liability, few directors are likely to remain loyal to corrupt or incompetent CEOs, regardless of their personal or professional relationships. Moreover, agency theorists argue that because inside directors' reputations and economic well-being are tied directly to the financial success of the firm, their loyalty to top management is likely to be predicated on the CEO's competence (Fama, 1980; Fama & Jensen, 1983a). Thus, in general, both inside and outside directors should be motivated to safeguard investors' interests. The important difference is that outsiders, in and of themselves, often lack the type of information needed to be truly effective in controlling decisions.

Of course, insiders cannot be so dominant in

board deliberations that the control function of the board is compromised. Rather, "so long as the basic control relation of the board to the corporation is not upset, management's participation on the board . . . permits the board to observe and evaluate the process of decision making as well as the outcomes . . . an important function in view of the *inadequacy of formal procedures* for grievance" (Williamson, 1985, p. 317, emphasis added).

Board Composition and Decision-Control Emphasis

As noted, organizational control theory traditionally has been focused on the problems associated with managing relationships between workers and their supervisors, and it has been suggested that the quality of these relationships affects the behaviors of workers (e.g., Eisenhardt, 1985; Ouchi, 1979). Extending control theory to problems involved in managing corporate-SBU relations has been a more recent development, but the focus is on similar issues (Baysinger & Hoskisson, 1989; Gupta, 1987).

Strategic Versus Financial Control Strategies

Performance-based control strategies emphasize monitoring, evaluating, and rewarding an agent's performance (Eisenhardt, 1985) and, thus, focus on the information aspects of control. Evaluations of managerial performance can be based either on inferences concerning the quality of the decision-making process (behavior control) or on the measurable outcomes of decision-making processes (outcome control) (Eisenhardt, 1985; Ouchi, 1980; Thompson, 1967). Because senior-level corporate managers make decisions under conditions of uncertainty, their specific behaviors are not as programmable as other employee tasks. Therefore, although the terms *behavior control* and *outcome control* are useful in describing controls applied to nonmanagerial employees, in this article the terms *strategic controls* and *financial controls*, respectively, are used to convey these concepts in the context of controlling corporate managers.

Gupta (1987), in his discussion of corporate-SBU relations, characterized what is referred to here as *strategic control* in terms of (a) *openness* in the relationship between corporate-level managers and division managers, and (b) the willingness of management to rely on *subjective information* when evaluating division managers' performances. Under a system of strategic controls, division (SBU) managers are evaluated on the basis of how strategically desirable their decisions were before implementation (ex ante) and on the basis of the financial performance of the firm after the decisions were implemented (ex post). Under a system of financial controls, however, managers are evaluated and rewarded primarily, if not solely, on the basis of their success (ex post) in meeting performance criteria. Financial controls also have ex ante counterparts (e.g., budgets), but through them the emphasis is placed on ex post financial outcomes because managerial compensation incentives are most often tied to these measures (Hoskisson, Hitt, & Hill, 1989).

Board Composition and the Emphasis of Control Strategies

Because of the detailed nature of strategic controls, implementing them requires the controller to have much more information than is required for implementing financial controls. Because inside and outside directors usually differ in the type of relevant information they possess, there are likely to be differences in the decision-control strategies they employ.

As noted, inside directors, as part of the decision-making process, have relatively greater access to subjective information about top managers' performance. Because insiders and the CEO often interact in ways that are relevant to assessing the quality of the decision-making process, relations between these parties are more likely to be open as well as subjective. Therefore, in terms of information processing, it is expected that the inside part of any board will evaluate and reward top management on the basis of strategic controls.

The outside part of the board usually enjoys few of these informational advantages and this makes their use of strategic controls far less likely. By definition, outside directors have limited contact with the day-to-day decision processes of the firm. Their ability to evaluate the quality of top management's decision-making process is limited to board interactions, at which point the strategic plans may be at their final stage, needing only ratification by the board of goals and strategies. Consequently, outside directors lack the type of subjective information needed for evaluating and rewarding managers on the quality of their decision processes.

Drawing parallels from the strategy-implementation literature, outsider-dominated boards face the same types of information-processing problems faced by corporate-level managers of unrelated diversified firms. An outsider who spends a small amount of time on any one firm's business is little different from a corporate manager who must evaluate the performance of a large number of divisions (Baysinger & Hoskisson, 1989; Hoskisson & Hitt, 1988; Dundas & Richardson, 1982). Of course, outside directors may be able, through their experiences, to make detached judgments about the quality of the strategic decisions of top managers. Unfortunately, the very nature of strategic decisions makes them unique and unstructured (Mintzberg, Raisinghani, & Théorêt, 1976). Consequently, in order for outsiders to appreciate fully the quality of the decision, they may need supplemental experience with that firm's process, and it is this latter knowledge that is unavailable to the truly independent outside director.

Of course, many outsiders who are former executives of the firm will be well informed. Such directors are not truly independent, and those who advocate more outside directors in the composition of a board have independent outsiders in mind (Eisenberg, 1976). Thus, while relations between inside directors and top management may be open and subjective (strategic-control emphasis), relations between (truly) independent outside directors may be more objective and formulaic (financial-control emphasis).

As more outside directors are added to a board, there may come a point where their influence predominates. Of course, this influence is not simply a numbers game: the ratio of outsiders to insiders. As suggested above, some outsiders gain enough information to act like insider-controllers. However, to the extent that insiders are in control of the evaluation process, we may expect them to evaluate top management in an open and subjective manner, thereby exercising the high powers of inference required for effective strategic control. In terms of the ratio of outsiders to insiders, it is difficult to predict when this cross-over point will occur. Contingency factors such as the CEO's personal power and the characteristics of outside directors will come into play. Yet, when making discrete comparisons among corporations, or when comparing general tendencies across time periods, it is expected that the predominance of outside directors on boards will be associated with financial controls.

> *Proposition 1: All else being equal, when the choice of evaluation methods is in the hands of independent outside directors, top management is likely to be rewarded on the basis of objective financial performance criteria.*

> *Proposition 2: All else being equal, when the choice of evaluation methods is in the hands of inside directors, top management is likely to be rewarded on the basis of an open and subjective appraisal of the quality of the process leading to financial performance outcomes.*

Control Emphasis and the Allocation of Residual Risk

From the managers' perspectives, financial controls tend to correlate managerial rewards directly with short-term variations in the market value of the firm (Demski, 1987; Gupta, 1987).

Operationally, this is accomplished either by disciplinary practices that are highly sensitive to short-term cash flow, net profit, growth, or market share results or by compensation schemes that tie much of the pecuniary rewards to quarterly earnings. Such controls seem attractive because they are based on easily measured data and, therefore, little information about the complex decision-making process leading to performance outcomes is needed. Linking managerial rewards to agreed-upon performance outcomes also prevents opportunistic managers from attributing poor performance to the vagaries of the marketplace and other factors over which they have no control. Managers' incentives to expend exceptional effort are increased under these financial controls because they cannot shift the blame for poor performance.

Tying managers' rewards to financial performance thus remedies an important conflict of interest and can solve the problem of shirking. This may explain the rising popularity of stock options as a form of managerial compensation (Bhagat, Brickley, & Lease, 1985). Unfortunately, even though financial controls are simple to implement, "placing an employee's income from labor at risk, via some type of incentive arrangement, does not appear to be an efficient way to arrange the distribution of production risks; after all, we have an elaborate capital market for just this purpose" (Demski, 1987, p. 119). This action, which shifts the risk to managers, is likely to be inefficient because of the influence it has on managerial behavior and, ultimately, on the managers' strategic choices.

Control Emphasis and Strategic Choice

An important premise of control theory is that the type of control strategy chosen affects both the intensity of the managers' efforts and the direction of that effort (Hambrick & Snow, 1988). According to this view, "control system measures and rewards not only motivate behavior, but also alter risk sharing patterns" (Eisenhardt, 1985, p. 137). Thus, the concept of control in the agency and organizational economics literature differs from traditional organizational control theory because of this concern over the direction-of-effort issue (Eisenhardt, 1985).

As argued above, outsider-dominated boards may skew the direction of managerial effort away from the optimally risky strategies that many shareholders prefer and the long-term orientation that is required for competitive advantage. According to basic finance theory, shareholders who hold diversified portfolios of stocks prefer high average returns on each security in the portfolio, even at the cost of higher return variance, because their overall risk is reduced (Copeland & Weston, 1979). Moreover, research by Hoskisson and Hitt (1988) has shown that shareholders evaluate risky expenditures, such as R & D, more highly when strategic controls are emphasized. Conversely, they concluded that when financial controls are emphasized, long-term expenditures (R & D) are given a lower market evaluation.

Along the same lines, Fischel and Bradley (1986) discussed the behavioral implications of changes in corporate law, which increase management's liability for short-term performance declines. They noted that "risky projects can have poor outcomes; if managers are (penalized) whenever decisions that were optimal ex ante turn out poorly ex post; they will tend to avoid risky projects" (p. 266). Increasing managers' liability for financial performance in the short run may increase their diligence in maximizing short-term profits, but it also may reduce their incentives to take risks. Increases in the representation of outsiders to the board of directors may have the same effect because the insiders' influence in the decision-control process is reduced.

Proposition 3: To the extent that outsider-dominated boards emphasize financial controls in evaluating and rewarding top management, such boards increase the intensity of managerial effort in terms of maximizing short-run prof-

its, but they also direct that effort away from the high risk-return strategies shareholders prefer.

The Control Emphasis of the Board and Corporate Diversification Strategies

Given the premise-setting power of the board, an interesting implication is that the diversification strategies of firms may be influenced by the ratio of outside to inside directors. Corporate-level managers play a critical role in determining the domains, or the mix of businesses/industries (Bourgeois, 1980), within which the firm will compete (Child, 1972).

An economic analysis of the choice of corporate-level strategy suggests that "risk averse managers can be expected to diversify . . . employment risk by other means, such as engaging their firms in conglomerate mergers, which generally stabilize the firm's income stream and may even be used to avoid the disastrous effects bankruptcy has on managers" (Amihud & Lev, 1981, p. 606). In this context *employment risk* becomes the losses of income, tenure, or reputation associated with financial losses or bankruptcy. Therefore, from the manager's perspective, the selection of domains can be a useful dimension which goes beyond maximizing the value of the firm to shareholders.

The relation between managerial employment risk and corporate strategy may be depicted graphically, as in Figure 2. The ordinate in Figure 2 measures the financial performance of the firm that is expected from different patterns of diversification. The abscissa depicts differences in the degree to which the firm diversifies from its core business. Labeling the axis with the taxonomic classes developed by Rumelt (1974) is only a convenience; diversification could just as easily be measured as a continuous variable (Palepu, 1985). It is important to note, however, that movement to the right along the abscissa in Figure 2 represents *increasing*

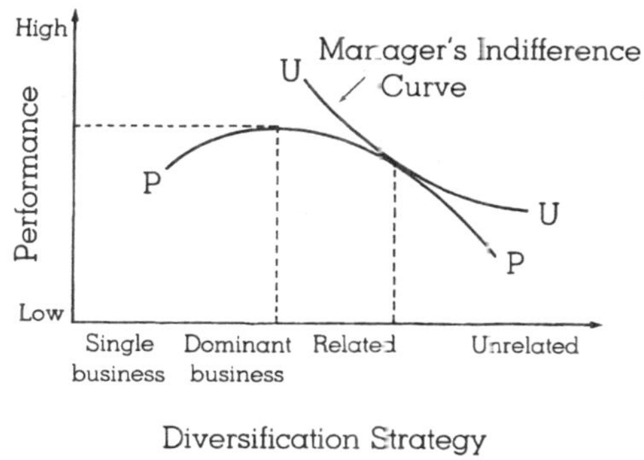

***Figure 2.* Potential conflict over diversification strategy.**

unrelatedness, in the conventional sense of the term (Rumelt, 1974).

Figure 2 also includes an indifference curve (UU) that depicts managers' trade-offs between returns to shareholders and levels of related and unrelated diversification. Managers value returns to shareholders because this is a primary indicator of their talent (Fama, 1980). Greater diversification, however, also directly increases managerial utility, that is, to the extent that overall risk of business failure is reduced by unrelated diversification, managerial employment risk is also reduced as long as profits are not sacrificed to such a degree that powerful shareholders or directors threaten to take hostile action (Amihud & Lev, 1981). Indifference curve UU shows the trade-off that managers perceive between these two choices.

Curve PP in Figure 2 also depicts what might be considered a reasonable estimate of the relation between diversification strategies and the economic performance of the firm (Porter, 1987; Rumelt, 1974, 1982). To the extent that SBUs transfer and share skills, related diversification may generate better corporate returns than could be obtained in undiversified firms; but diversification can be carried too far (Porter, 1987).

Although depicting a functional relation between level of diversification and corporate performances as convex from above may be controversial, evidence suggests that this is a close approximation (Varadarajan & Ramanujam, 1987). All that is required for the present discussion is the reasonable notion that, after some point, continued unrelated diversification will compromise economic performance.

All else being equal, risk-averse managers may invest resources in unrelated acquisitions beyond the point where the expected internal rate of return from the new business equals the estimated opportunity cost of capital, because this reduces managerial employment risk (Amihud & Lev, 1981). Because shareholders can diversify risk through the careful management of their stock portfolios, they would prefer that the management of any firm they owned invested resources in a new product or process, or related diversification, that yielded superior performance (Copeland & Weston, 1979). As long as managers perceive personal benefits from managing a diversified portfolio of firms, however, excessive unrelated diversification may be chosen.

Of course, managers do not select these domains in a vacuum. Boards in which inside directors play an important role in the decision-control process will reduce the employment risks associated with dominant and related business diversification strategies. Because, as previously argued, managers who operate under such controls are rewarded on the basis of the strategic relevance of their decisions, they should favor, or at least not disfavor, the higher performance profile associated with related or dominant business strategies. This is not to say that outside directors are indifferent to the choice of corporate strategy. However, Hill and Snell (1988) showed that greater outsider representation was associated with greater diversified scope and a lower concentration of diversified activities in related areas. Given the hypothesized correspondence between strategic controls and some threshold representation of insiders on the board overall and on key committees, this finding is not entirely surprising.

Proposition 4: To the extent that they emphasize financial controls, outsider-dominated boards will be associated with high levels of diversification.

Proposition 5: To the extent that they emphasize strategic controls, insider-controlled boards will be associated with lower levels of diversification.

The Control Emphasis of the Board and the Intensity of R & D

Using a sample of R & D-intensive firms, Hill and Snell (1988) also reported a significant negative relation between outside-director dominance and the intensity of the research and development. They suggested that this is the opposite of what would be expected if outsiders acted as guardians of the stockholders' welfare in a research-intensive environment. Along the lines of Lawrence and Lorsch's (1967) research, Hill and Snell suggested that because "innovation strategy requires a high degree of intra-firm integration, a firm involved in innovation brings more insiders onto the board in an attempt to integrate the functional activities of the firm around its strategy" (p. 588). Complementary to this idea is that inside directors safeguard the interests of management, which is especially important in highly uncertain environments.

R & D-intensive firms are continually subjected to technological uncertainty. For example, a leading pharmaceutical firm never knows when a competitor will discover a new drug that will displace its dominant product. Thus, while returns may be higher for such firms, corporate-level managers may be unwilling to provide impetus to R & D initiatives because of the greater residual risk. This problem may be overcome by including inside directors as important players in the decision-control process.

Managers who are evaluated by strategic controls are likely to assign higher utility values to the uncertain cash flows associated with positive spending decisions for R & D. Managers in R & D-intensive firms especially prefer this control because they have to bear more of the consequences of technological obsolescence than do shareholders who can diversify their risk. Therefore, managers should be more likely to support R & D initiatives generated at the operational level when insiders have an important place in making control decisions because through such processes insiders are better able to differentiate between decisions and risks. Thus, Hill and Snell's (1988) results are consistent with the notion that insider-dominated boards tend to preserve the separation of ownership and control.

Of course, strategic controls may provide greater opportunity for managerial opportunism. Despite this, shareholders of firms that compete in R & D-intensive industries may tacitly accept an emphasis on strategic control because of the high risk of *technological mugging* (Kay, 1982). On balance, then, strategic controls are congruent with the dominance of R & D spending as a critical success factor (Ettlie, Bridges, & O'Keefe, 1984; Hoskisson & Hitt, 1988). Hill and Snell's (1988) finding that the intensity of R & D is diminished in firms in which outsiders dominate the decision-control process is consistent with this notion.

Proposition 6: To the extent that they emphasize financial controls, outsider-dominated boards will be associated with a lower emphasis on research and development.

Proposition 7: To the extent that they emphasize strategic controls, insider-controlled boards will be associated with a higher emphasis on research and development.

Discussion and Research Implications

American managers have been increasingly criticized for their unwillingness to take risks and their well-noted short-term orientation (Hayes & Abernathy, 1980). Although these phenomena and changes in board composition may be unrelated, a possible relation suggests the value of an empirical analysis, especially in light of secular changes in this variable. For example, if the recent decline in the numbers of insiders who participate in the decision-control process affects managers' risk preferences and R & D spending, empirical analysis of the issues raised here may yield information relating to the recent competitive decline of the American economy (Hill, Hitt, & Hoskisson, 1988)

Changes in board composition toward outsider domination also have come during a period of increased levels of diversification (Michel & Shaked, 1985; Porter, 1987; Rumelt, 1974, 1982). Some have suggested that managerial preferences for unrelated diversification reflect either top management's efforts at empire building (Marris, 1964) or their willingness to sacrifice shareholder returns for personal security (Amihud & Lev, 1981). The theory and propositions developed here suggest that it is important to understand *why* managers may have developed these preferences. Reforms in board composition and governance may turn out to have been a causal factor in this process, despite the well-meaning attempts to control undesirable managerial behavior. Once again, although the correlation between increased diversification and the trend toward outsider-dominated boards may be coincidental, an investigation of possible causal relations seems worthwhile.

The potential of an empirical analysis of this possibility seems great. First, as Patton and Baker (1987) noted, large U.S. corporations have, from 1969 to 1984, been moving toward greater independence in their boards of directors. Second, rule changes promulgated by the New York Stock Exchange now require listed firms to create board committees (e.g., audit, compensation, planning) to protect shareholders' interests more effectively (Kesner, 1988). Consequently, the number of committees per board has been rising significantly during the past two decades (Braiotta & Sommer, 1987; Kesner, 1988; Waldo, 1985). If such changes are not uniform across major U.S. corporations, there may be enough *variability* in board composition, and changes in this variable, to support empirical research based on analysis of variance techniques using cross-sectional methods. However, because these reforms have resulted in changes on a case-by-case basis, a longitudinal test of these propositions may be necessary.

Besides examining the relation between diversification and board composition, changes in board composition also provide a number of interesting natural experiments that would be useful for testing the validity of the framework developed here. For instance, while agency theory suggests that stock options are employed according to ownership and control arrangements (Eaton & Rosen, 1983), large U.S. firms appear to have increased the use of stock options disproportionately (Oviatt, 1988). This comes at a time of growing evidence that directors are "using the signals of financial markets to adjust top managers' compensation" (Oviatt, 1988, p. 218). Perhaps this is due to the increased presence of outsiders on boards.

Moreover, in a time-series analysis Murphy (1984) found that salary and bonuses for top management in large U.S. corporations were significantly and positively related to a measure of total shareholder returns. Although these findings are equivocal (Kerr & Bettis, 1987), perhaps it is not a coincidence that the trend toward more independent boards mirrors the trend toward the higher levels of emphasis on financial controls and associated incentives. Hoskisson, Hitt, and Hill (1989) found that reliance on these financial controls and incentives is negatively associated with the intensity of R & D. Therefore, these issues merit further research, as does a contingency perspective on corporate governance.

An important conclusion drawn from research on strategy implementation and organization control is that organizational effectiveness depends, in part, on achieving a match between control strategies and the strategic context of the firm (Gupta, 1987; Hill & Hoskisson, 1987). Effective corporations implement risky business-level strategies by adopting internal controls that are informationally rich and that feature open and subjective corporate-SBU relations. Lower risk divisional strategies tend to be implemented using controls that are more formal and objective without compromising effectiveness. This research explicitly indicates that the match between internal controls and strategic choice can enhance organizational effectiveness.

It may be, for example, that in certain industries board composition should emphasize outsider dominance, whereas in other industries boards should emphasize either insider or mixed dominance. It would seem, given the theoretical justification presented, that outsider-dominated boards may work in situations in which high levels of diversification and low levels of R & D expenditure are acceptable. This is likely for unrelated diversified firms that focus on a portfolio of mature stable businesses, such as Hanson Trust. The opposite would be true for insider-dominated boards. Therefore, in smaller growth firms in R & D-intensive industries it is likely that insider-dominated boards would be appropriate. Of course, it must be assumed that whenever outsiders or insiders dominate there must be enough of the minority to monitor the contractual relations between owners and managers.

Conclusions

Discussions of corporate governance have tended to be the special preserve of economists and lawyers; yet, the strategic implications of governance structure also merit attention. Oviatt (1988), in concluding his very useful review of the agency and transaction cost literature, hoped that others would attempt to gain "not only a greater understanding of the relationship between shareholders and managers, but also a greater general understanding of organizational incentives and control" (p. 223).

This article has attempted to address Oviatt's challenge, proposing that in organizations in which agency relations exist and must be managed, attempts to regulate the intensity of agent behavior through financial controls may affect the direction of that behavior as well. A priori, corporate governance structure and strategic-choice processes would seem to be related.

In the strategy-implementation literature it is argued that the management of corporate-SBU relations is related to the firm's strategic context (Gupta, 1987). This article extends that argument by introducing relevant concepts from organizational economics and agency theory. The most general implication is that the boundaries of strategy-implementation theory and organizational-control theory should be extended to include the management of owner-manager relations in large business firms. Also, economic and legal discourse on corporate governance should be extended to include consideration of strategic implications of various forms of internal control.

This suggests the value of examining the strategic outcomes of changes in boards of directors as dictated by public policy reforms. For example, a growing number of directors are being threatened with legal action for malfeasance (Worthy & Neuschel, 1984). This increase in liability puts a premium on the control of management. Governance scholars implicitly argue that shareholder well-being is a monotonically increasing function of the proportion of independent outsiders serving on boards of directors (Eisenberg, 1976). Yet, the contingency theory developed here suggests the need to tailor corporate governance to the information-processing requirement of different strategies or industry settings. Thus, although this article is not directed at serving public-policy ends, it nontheless raises an issue that should be considered before new board reforms are implemented.

References

Alchian, A. A., & Demsetz, H. (1972) Production, information costs and economic organization. *American Economic Review*, 62, 777–795.

Allen, M. P. (1974) The structure of interorganizational elite cooptation. *American Sociological Review*, 39, 393–406.

American Law Institute (1982) *Principles of corporate governance and structure: Restatement and recommendations*. New York: American Law Institute.

Amihud, Y., & Lev, B. (1981) Risk reduction as a managerial motive for conglomerate mergers. *Bell Journal of Economics*, 12, 605–617.

Barton, S. L., & Gordon, P. J. (1987) Corporate strategy: Useful perspective for the study of capital structure? *Academy of Management Review*, 12, 67–75.

Baysinger, B., & Hoskisson, R. E. (1989) Diversification strategy and R & D intensity in large multiproduct firms. *Academy of Management Journal*, 32, 310–332.

Berle, A., & Means, G. (1968) *The modern corporation and private property*. New York: Macmillan.

Bhagat, S., Brickley, J. A., & Lease, R. C. (1985) Incentive effects of stock purchase plans. *Journal of Financial Economics*, 14, 195–215.

Bourgeois, J. (1980) Strategy and environment: A conceptual integration. *Academy of Management Review*, 5, 25–39.

Bourgeois, J. (1987) Strategic management: From concept to implementation. In G. E. Germane (Ed.), *The executive course* (pp. 347–391). Reading, MA: Addison-Wesley.

Braiotta, L., Jr., & Sommer, A. A., Jr. (1987) *The essential guide to effective corporate board committees*. Englewood Cliffs, NJ: Prentice-Hall.

Chaganti, R. S., Mahajan, V., & Sharma, S. (1985) Corporate board size, composition, and corporate failures in retailing industry. *Journal of Management Studies*, 22, 400–417.

Child, J. (1972) Organizational structure, environment, and performance: The role of strategic choice. *Sociology*, 6, 2–22.

Copeland, T., & Weston, J. F. (1979) *Financial theory and corporate policy*. Reading, MA: Addison-Wesley.

Demski, J. S. (1987) Managerial accounting. In G. E. Germane (Ed.), *The executive course* (pp. 101–122). Reading, MA: Addison-Wesley.

Dundas, K. N. M., & Richardson, P. R. (1982) Implementing

the unrelated product strategy. *Strategic Management Journal*, 3, 287–301.

Eaton, J., & Rosen, H. (1983) Agency, delayed compensation, and the structure of executive remuneration. *Journal of Finance*, 38, 1489–1505.

Eisenberg, M. (1976) *The structure of the corporation*. Boston: Little, Brown.

Eisenhardt, K. (1985) Control: Organizational and economic approaches. *Management Science*, 31, 134–149.

Ettlie, J. E., Bridges, W. P., & O'Keefe, R. D. (1984) Organization strategy and structural differences for radical versus incremental innovation. *Management Science*, 30, 682–695.

Fama, E. F. (1980) Agency problems and the theory of the firm. *Journal of Political Economy*, 88, 288–307.

Fama, E. F., & Jensen, M. C. (1983a) Agency problems and residual claims. *Journal of Law and Economics*, 26, 301–326.

Fama, E. F., & Jensen, M. C. (1983b) Separation of ownership and control. *Journal of Law and Economics*, 26, 327–349.

Fischel, D., & Bradley, M. (1986) The role of liability rules and the derivative suit in corporate law: A theoretical and empirical analysis. *Cornell Law Review*, 71, 261–283.

Galbraith, J. K. (1967) *The new industrial state*. New York: New American Library.

Gupta, A. K. (1987) SBU strategies, corporate-SBU relations, and SBU effectiveness in strategy implementation. *Academy of Management Journal*, 30, 477–500.

Hambrick, D. C., & Snow, C. C. (1988) Strategic reward systems. In C. C. Snow (Ed.), *Strategy, organization design, and human resource management* (pp. 333–368). Greenwich, CT: JAI Press.

Hayes, R. H., & Abernathy, W. J. (1980) Managing our way to economic decline. *Harvard Business Review*, 58(4), 67–77.

Herman, E. S. (1981) *Corporate control, corporate power*. New York: Cambridge University Press.

Hill, C. W. L., Hitt, M. A., & Hoskisson, R. E. (1988) Declining U.S. competitiveness: Innovation, the M-form structure and the capital markets. *Academy of Management Executive*, 2, 51–60.

Hill, C. W. L., & Hoskisson, R. E. (1987) Strategy and structure in the multiproduct firm. *Academy of Management Review*, 12, 331–341.

Hill, C. W. L., & Snell, S. A. (1988) External control, corporate strategy, and firm performance in research intensive industries. *Strategic Management Journal*, 9, 577–590.

Hoskisson, R. E., & Hitt, M. A. (1988) Strategic control systems and relative R & D investment in large multiproduct firms. *Strategic Management Journal*, 9, 605–621.

Hoskisson, R. E., Hitt, M. A., & Hill, C. W. L. (1989) *Managerial incentives and investment in R & D in large multiproduct firms*. Unpublished manuscript, Texas A&M University, Department of Management.

Jensen, M. C., & Meckling, W. C. (1976) Theory of the firm: Managerial behavior, agency costs, and ownership structure. *Journal of Financial Analysis*, 3, 305–360.

Jones, T. M., & Goldberg, L. D. (1982) Governing the large corporation: More arguments for public directors. *Academy of Management Review*, 7, 603–611.

Kay, N. M. (1982) *The evolving firm: Strategy and structure in industrial organization*. New York: St. Martin's Press.

Kerr, J., & Bettis, R. A. (1987) Boards of directors, top management compensation, and shareholder returns. *Academy of Management Journal*, 30, 645–664.

Kesner, I. F. (1988) Director characteristics and committee membership: An investigation of type, occupation, tenure, and gender. *Academy of Management Journal*, 31, 66–84.

Kesner, I. F., Victor, B., & Lamont B. (1986) Board composition and the commission of illegal acts: An investigation of Fortune 500 companies. *Academy of Management Journal*, 29, 789–799.

Knoeber, C. R. (1986) Golden parachutes, shark repellents, and hostile tender offers. *The American Economic Review*, 76(1), 155–167.

Kohls, J. (1985) Corporate board structure, social reporting, and social performance. In L. E. Preston (Ed.), *Research in corporate social performance and policy* (Vol. 7, pp. 165–189). Greenwich, CT: JAI Press.

Lawrence, P., & Lorsch, J. (1967) *Organization and environment*. Boston: Harvard University Press.

Luce, R. D., & Raiffa, H. (1957) *Games and decisions*. New York: Wiley.

Mace, M. L. (1971) *Directors: Myth and reality*. Cambridge, MA: Harvard University, Graduate School of Business Administration.

Marris, R. (1964) *The economic theory of managerial capitalism*. Glencoe, IL: Free Press.

Mattar, E., & Ball, M. (1985) *Handbook for corporate directors*. New York: McGraw-Hill.

Mautz, R. K., & Neary, R. D. (1979) Corporate audit committees—quo vadis? *Journal of Accountancy*, 148(4), 83–88.

Michel, A., & Shaked, I. (1985) Evaluating merger performance. *California Management Review*, 27(3), 109–118.

Mintzberg, H., Raisinghani, D., & Théorêt, A. (1976) The structure of "unstructured" decisions processes. *Administrative Science Quarterly*, 21, 246–275.

Mizruchi, M. (1983) Who controls whom? An examination of the relation between management and boards of directors in large American corporations. *Academy of Management Review*, 8, 426–435.

Murphy, K. J. (1984) *Corporate performance and managerial remuneration: An empirical analysis*. Working Paper No. MERC 84-10, University of Rochester, Managerial Economics Research Center, Graduate School of Management: Rochester, NY.

Norburn, D. (1986) Gogos, yoyos, and dodos: Company directors and industry performance. *Strategic Management Journal*, 7, 101–117.

Ouchi, W. (1979) A conceptual framework for the design of organization control mechanisms. *Management Science*, 25, 833–848.

Ouchi, W. (1980) Markets, bureaucracies and clans. *Administrative Science Quarterly*, 25, 124–141.

Oviatt, B. M. (1988) Agency and transaction cost perspectives on the manager-shareholder relationship: Incentives for congruent interests. *Academy of Management Review*, 13, 214–225.

Palepu, K. (1985) Diversification strategy, profit performance, and the entropy measure. *Strategic Management Journal*, 6, 239–255.

Patton, A., & Baker, J. C. (1987) Why won't directors rock the boat. *Harvard Business Review*, 65(6), 10–18.

Pfeffer, J. (1972) Size and composition of corporate boards of directors: The organization and its environment. *Administrative Science Quarterly*, 17, 218–228.

Porter, M. E. (1987) From competitive advantage to corporate strategy. *Harvard Business Review*, 65(3), 43–59.

Rumelt, R. P. (1974) *Strategy, structure, and economic performance*. Boston: Harvard Business School, Division of Research.

Rumelt, R. P. (1982) Diversification strategy and profitability. *Strategic Management Journal*, 3, 359–369.

Thompson, J. D. (1967) *Organizations in action*. New York: McGraw-Hill.

Vance, S. C. (1964) *Boards of directors: Structure and performance*. Eugene: University of Oregon Press.

Vance, S. C. (1983) *Corporate leadership: Boards, directors and strategy*. New York: McGraw-Hill.

Varadarajan, P., & Ramanujam, V. (1987) Diversification and performance: A reexamination using a new two-dimensional conceptualization of diversity in firms. *Academy of Management Journal*, 30, 380–393.

Waldo, C. H. (1985) *Boards of directors: Their changing roles, structure, and information needs*. Westport, CT: Quorum.

Williamson, O. E. (1975) *Markets and hierarchies: Analysis and antitrust implications*. New York: Free Press.

Williamson, O. E. (1984) Corporate governance. *Yale Law Journal*, 93, 1197–1230.

Williamson, O. E. (1985) *The economic institutions of capitalism: Firms, markets, and relational contracting*. New York: Macmillan.

Worthy, J. C., & Neuschel, R. P. (1984) *Emerging issues in corporate governance*. Evanston, IL: Northwestern University Press.

Barry Baysinger (Ph.D., Virginia Polytechnic Institute and State University) is an Associate Professor of Management and Director of the Center for Entrepreneurship, College of Business Administration, Texas A&M University. Correspondence regarding this article may be sent to him at the Department of Management, Texas A&M University, College Station, TX 77843-4221.

Robert E. Hoskisson (Ph.D., University of California, Irvine) is an Associate Professor in the Department of Management, College of Business Administration, at Texas A&M University.

We gratefully acknowledge the helpful comments of Robert Albanese, Jay Barney, Rita Kosnik, Don Hellriegel, Michael Hitt, Thomas Turk, and the doctoral students in the economics of corporate governance seminar at Texas A&M University.

[11]

Strategists on the Board

Terry McNulty, Andrew Pettigrew*

Terry McNulty
Centre for Creativity, Strategy and Change, Warwick Business School, University of Warwick, Coventry, UK

Andrew Pettigrew
Warwick Business School, University of Warwick, Coventry, UK

Abstract

The paper examines the contribution to strategy by chairmen and non-executive directors in large UK companies. The collective label of 'part-time board member' is used to refer to individuals performing these roles. The paper asks 'how, if at all, do part-time board members influence strategy in UK plc's'?. Using data gathered from interviews with 108 company directors, the paper suggests that part-time board members do not simply ratify decisions made by all-powerful executives. A conceptual model is developed to show that part-time board members are able to influence processes of strategic choice, change and control by shaping both the ideas that form the content of company strategy and the methodologies and processes by which those ideas evolve. Their involvement in strategy is conditioned by factors such as: changing norms about corporate governance; the history and performance of the company; the process and conduct of board meetings and informal dialogue amongst company directors between board meetings.

Descriptors: boards, directors, strategy, corporate governance, part-time board member

Introduction

To understand strategy, we need to know more about the strategists. To better understand boards, we need to know more about the behaviour of those who sit on boards. This paper brings together the subjects of boards and strategy by examining the contribution to strategy by chairmen and non-executive directors in large UK publicly quoted companies. Given the part-time responsibilities of many chairmen and all non-executive directors, the collective label of 'part-time board members' is used to refer to individuals performing these roles.

The 1990's has witnessed a surge of interest in boards of directors. Much of the interest, at least in the UK context, has been a reaction to governance irregularities and mismanagement in some UK companies. More is known now about board structure, board composition and director compensation than it was at the beginning of the decade. There is greater knowledge about who sits in UK boardrooms, whom they sit alongside, how much they are paid and how they are selected (Conyon 1994, 1995). However, less is known about what board members do. Behaviour in UK boardrooms is not nearly as transparent as the structure and composition of UK boards.

Organization Studies
1999, 20/1
47–74

0170–8406/99
0020–0003 $3.00

Prescriptive writing about boards and directors continues to afford part-time board members a role in strategy (Demb and Neubauer 1992; Institute of Directors 1995). Work in the managerial hegemony tradition suggests that part-time board members are barely involved in strategy (Mace 1971; Lorsch and MacIver 1989). This paper asks how, if at all, do part-time board members influence strategy in UK plc's?

The first half of the paper identifies choice, change and control as key aspects of firms' strategic conduct. In the second half of the paper, empirical interest turns to examining how part-time board members engage with these processes. Attention is given to the actions of part-time board members *vis-à-vis* executive directors, both inside and outside the boardroom. Data from interviews with 108 board members are used to construct a framework (Figure 1) which conceptualizes part-time board members' involvement in strategy as: 'taking strategic decisions', 'shaping strategic decisions' and 'shaping the content, context and conduct of strategy'. Each of the three levels of part-time board member involvement in strategy described in Figure 1 engage part-time board members in processes of choice, change and control in differing ways. Behaviour by part-time board members conveyed by the model challenge findings of previous research that part-time board members simply ratify decisions made by executives (Pahl and Winkler 1974; Lorsch and MacIver 1989). Rather, the framework reveals that part-time board members are able to shape both the ideas that form the content of firms' strategies and the methodologies and processes by which those ideas evolve. In so doing, part-time board members are capable of exerting control over management and influencing processes of strategic choice and change.

Not all part-time board members are equally involved in strategy. Empirical data show that the involvement of part-time board members in strategy is conditioned by factors such as public debate and policy making about corporate governance, the history and performance of a company, the conduct and process of a board and informal relations between board members. These factors are discussed in the paper in a manner intended both to explain the findings of this study and to motivate more processually and contextually attuned theorizing about the behaviour of boards and directors.

Literature Review

Boards and Directors in the UK

The legal framework which shapes board structure and conduct in the United Kingdom (UK) offers a light touch. The legal structure of corporate behaviour in the UK rests on the simple principle that the (owners) shareholders appoint agents (directors) to run the business and the directors report annually to shareholders on their stewardship. There are approximately 2000 Public Limited Companies (PLCs) quoted on the UK Stock

Exchange in which managers are accountable to directors and directors are accountable to shareholders. Companies registered after 1 November 1929 are legally required to have at least two directors. No distinction is made between classes of directors; for instance, between executive (full-time or inside) directors and non-executive (outside or part-time) directors. There is no requirement in UK law for companies to have a board of directors. However, directors do tend to meet in committees familiar to us as 'boards of directors' (Charkham 1994).

Out of practice rather than law, four main roles have evolved on boards of directors: chairman; chief executive officer; executive director and non-executive director. The chairman role is pivotal in the UK board context with or without the additional responsibilities of Chief Executive Officer. As a minimal requirement, chairmen are responsible for the composition and conduct of the board. Over 80 percent of the largest 1,000 UK Plc's now separate the role of chairman and chief executive officer, and the majority of chairmen perform the role on a part-time basis. During the 1980's and 1990's the numbers of non-executive directors on UK boards has increased (Conyon 1994) suggesting that, at least numerically, non-executive directors now play an increasingly important role in UK plc's. Non-executive directors can be current or retired chief executives or executive directors of PLC's, and a minority have political, military, academic or civil service backgrounds. The role of non-executive director is also part time. Chief executives usually carry the lead executive authority in the company and chair the executive team, which itself consists of executive directors and senior managers. Not all executive team members necessarily sit on the board as an executive director. The finance director would invariably do so, but the Personnel Director, for example, would not usually do so. In practice, all directors are appointed by the board and elected by the shareholders.

Boards and Strategy

Knowledge about the structure and composition of boards exceeds knowledge about their behavioural dynamics. Hill (1995) argued that the organizational sociology of boards, incorporating the boardroom role of the corporate elite, is a major missing link in analyses of boards and directors. With the exception of Spencer (1983), Pahl and Winkler (1974), Hill (1995) and Pettigrew and McNulty (1995), inadequate access to the corporate elite has resulted in us knowing little about the work and conduct of boards and directors. Consequently, normative models outlining the functions of boards and directors require greater empirical scrutiny. This is particularly true in relation to the role of boards and directors in company strategy.

It is widely argued in policy making, practitioner and some scholarly oriented writing that boards should be active in strategy (Andrews 1981; Demb and Neubauer 1992; Goodstein et al. 1994; Institute of Directors 1995). However, theoretical and empirical writing about boards and directors is inadequate in its treatment of strategy. For instance, control is a major theme in writing about boards. Agency theorists (Jensen and Meckling 1976; Kosnik 1987), view a board of directors as a mechanism to ensure that top management actions are in accord with shareholder interests. The purpose of a board of directors is to monitor top management and resist the opportunism and self-interested behaviour of managers. Performance incentives in the form of compensation and the ability to hire and fire managers are seen as means to ensure that managers' incentive structures accord with shareholder interests (Fama and Jensen 1983). However, little has been said by agency theorists about strategy as a means of control over managers.

Unlike agency theorists, resource dependency theorists do not assume that managers and owners have differing interests. They emphasize the institutional role of boards in helping to link the organization to its environment and to secure critical resources. Boards are viewed as a mechanism for reducing environmental uncertainty (Pfeffer 1972; Pearce and Zahra 1991). However, whilst resource dependency theorists direct attention to the role of boards in attaining resources, they do not consider the use of such resources (Finkelstein and Hambrick 1996; Stiles and Taylor 1996).

The strategic management literature is also largely silent on boards' involvement in strategy. Finkelstein and Hambrick (1996) recently criticized the strategy field for being populated by 'descriptive and prescriptive strategy frameworks', which omit attention to senior executives and boards of directors.

There is a significant gap between prescription that boards should be active in strategy, and empirical evidence that boards are indeed active in strategy. A review of US literature about boards concluded that there is a 'dearth of work on board involvement in strategic decision-making' (Finkelstein and Hambrick 1996). Those 'few studies' identified by Finkelstein and Hambrick (1996) about the effects of boards on strategy do not provide a conclusive set of findings about the impact of boards on the strategic behaviour of firms (Hill and Snell 1988; Pearce and Zahra 1991; Judge and Zeithaml 1992; Goodstein et al. 1994; Hoskisson et al. 1994). Empirical studies closer to boardroom behaviour also provide a mixed set of findings about the involvement of the board and part-time board members in strategy. Early work is sceptical about board involvement in strategy, concluding that boards are not involved in strategy formation (Mace 1971; Herman 1981; Lorsch and MacIver 1989). Lorsch and MacIver (1989) found that the primary role of boards in the strategy formation process was in advising and evaluating, rather than in initiating strategy. More recently, Demb and Neubauer's (1992) survey of directors from a number of European countries concluded that 'setting strategic direction' is one of the major duties of the board. However, they found a wide spectrum of opinion about the way boards should be involved in strategy. Amongst the sample of directors from the UK, opinions differed as to whether boards should have an initiating role, an approving role or a decision-making role in strategy. Grumbar and Kelly (1993), executive search consultants, surveyed over 200 chief executives and non-executive directors drawn from the top 500 UK plc's. They found that chief executives and directors differed in their understanding of the present role of non-executive directors and disagreed over what the role should be. Chief executives and non-executive directors disagreed about how much influence non-executive directors should have in decisions about mergers and acquisitions. Non-executive directors claimed a greater influence than chief executives believed them to have or wanted them to have.

Processes of Strategic Choice, Change and Control

The nature, extent, timing and behavioural dynamics of part-time board members' involvement in strategy are at the heart of the empirical contribution of this paper. Attention is focused on processes of choice, change and control as key aspects of the strategic conduct of firms. Empirical data are presented examining how part-time chairmen and non-executive directors on the boards of UK companies engage with those processes of choice, change and control and contribute to the strategy of the firm.

Attention to processes of choice and change is consistent with the view that strategic management is about processes of organizational renewal and growth (Schendel and Hofer 1979). The survival and competitive performance of firms has been found to be tied up with firms' capacity to deliver change in a high quality and timely fashion (Pettigrew and Whipp 1991). Therefore, as well as trying to identify whether part-time board members seek to influence the choices of firms about corporate goals and the means to achieve them, it is important to examine whether part-time board members also seek to shape the change processes which realise those means and goals.

Attention to control is consistent with the view of agency theorists that control is at the centre of board conduct (Fama and Jensen 1983). However, the particular theoretical orientation and data collection methods of agency theorists have not necessarily revealed the processes through which boards engage in control-related activities. Central to these control processes are attempts by boards to influence the nature and extent of strategic thinking in the firm, the criteria and mechanisms of performance measurement and financial control, the policies of reward and remuneration and, of course, the hiring and firing of the full and part-time members of the board.

Throughout these discussions of choice, change and control processes there is the crucial analytical requirement to study both the content and the process of board involvement in strategy. Chakravarthy and Doz (1992) and Pettigrew (1992a), contrary to much of the history of writing in this area, have taken the view that the content (the 'what' of strategic involvement) can only be effectively analyzed through its inseparable links with the process of strategy (the 'how' of strategic involvement).

There is also a crucial analytical requirement to capture the behaviour relating to part-time board members' involvement in processes of choice, change and control. How do part-time board members operate in these complex social institutions called 'boards' (Hill 1995) to impact on strategy? Part-time board members need power and influence to contribute to the exercise of directoral duties (Lorsch and MacIver 1989; Pettigrew and McNulty 1995). How do part-time board members overcome power discrepancies *vis-à-vis* executive directors to influence strategy? In rare studies of decision-making behaviour at board level, Pahl and Winkler (1974) and Hill (1995) reveal power discrepancy between full-time executive directors and non-executive directors. Pahl and Winkler (1974) distinguished between boards 'taking decisions' and 'making decisions' to argue that boards' formal authority to make decisions is undermined by the manipulative practices of managers below board level. Processes of 'manipulation', 'screening' and 'institutionalized pre-emption' were identified as behaviours used by managers to control the decision-making process, and leave boards merely as 'decision taking' and 'legitimating institutions' functioning to ratify decisions made elsewhere.

As 'outsiders' and 'part-timers', are part-time board members able to exert influence at critical stages of strategy-making and decision processes? Subsequent work on strategic decision-making has confirmed that making choices is simply the final part of the decision-making process. Important influencing activities earlier in decision processes include signalling the need for action (Nutt 1984) identifying, diagnosing and selling issues (Dutton and Ashford 1993) and generating alternatives. Eisenhardt and Zbaracki's (1992) review of the literature on strategic decision-making codifies and assesses much of the research on top-level choice behaviour. This research is thus guided by a view of choice behaviour which recognizes its boundedly rational, emotional and political character and which is also mindful of the complex, non-linear character of choice making with phases of identification, development and selection not necessarily following one another in any simple manner.

It is also crucial to examine decision processes as part of the broader set of behaviours in organizations. In examining the change aspects of board involvement in strategy, it is important to include what Pettigrew (1973) described as problem sensing and development of concern behaviour and what Dutton and Ashford (1993) characterized as the tactics of agenda building at the top of the firm. Boards can only act upon and make choices about that which they are prepared to recognize and thereby include as a legitimate part of their deliberations. So choice, change and control processes must include processes of mobilizing bias, the suppression of issues and decisions and non-decision-making behaviour.

Research Process and Study Sample

The rather distant character of much research on boards and directors means that greater attention needs to be given to behavioural dynamics in and around the boardroom (Pettigrew 1992). There is a need to get closer to boards and directors to collect primary data about processes of contribution, power and influence. The research process reported in this paper has been guided by these methodological concerns.

This paper is part of a larger project aimed at studying the contribution, power and influence of part-time chairmen and non-executive directors within and across the UK plcs they serve as part-time board members. Data presented in this paper are taken from interviews with 108 board members between 1994 and 1997. All interviews were taped. All interviewees accepted our offer of non-attributable conversations. With the exception of one individual, all interviewees agreed that their name could be listed in published output to indicate their participation in the study. A list of those individuals interviewed is attached to this paper as Appendix A. Ninety-two men and 16 women were interviewed.

For the purposes of this study, it was not practical to select respondents randomly. However, the project has been successful in negotiating access to a set of people previously thought by many to be too elusive and private for research interviews. This quality and quantity of access has never before been achieved in a UK field study of boards and directors. Fuller discussions of the research process used throughout the study are provided in Pettigrew and McNulty (1995, 1998).

Important points to note here are that board experiences of individuals making up the interview sample cover many organizations located in the largest 500 UK Plcs, excluding subsidiaries and investment trusts (The Times 1000 Survey 1997). The total of 108 individuals cover the four main roles on boards discussed above. Sixty-five part-time board members were interviewed, including 37 chairmen and 28 non-executive directors. Forty-three full-time board members were interviewed, 23 of these were chief executives, a further 14 were executive directors and 6 were company secretaries. Interviews with 'executives' have enhanced the reliability of the data gathered from the self-reports of the part-time chairmen and non-executive directors. Full-time executive board members observe part-time board members in action and thus are able to evaluate their contribution and influence. In some instances, the reliability of data was further enhanced by interviews with several members of the same board.

Part-time Board Members: Their Involvement in Strategy

Executives and non-executive directors interviewed for this study agree that part-time board members rarely initiate the substantive content of strategy. A chief executive, quoted below, distinguished between the role of part-time board members in the content of strategies adopted or the processes followed to achieve them:

> '[the board] can challenge as to whether the process is in place [and the] process is a good process...[that] will lead to an output which can be deemed by the board to be the strategy that we are following. I do not think the non-executive directors can easily propose what the strategy should be... I do not think the non-executive director can ever be in the position to create [the strategy].'

A very experienced chairman and non-executive director, who has also been a chief executive, supported the view expressed above:

'I do not think you can normally expect the non-executive directors to come forward with great wealth-creating ideas for the board..It would be marvellous for that to happen but I cannot think of an instance where I have seen that happen...there is a fine line, but a clear line — the non-executive must not do the executives' job. Otherwise, the board ceases to function, and the executive rightly resents that and then it becomes a disaster..It is not the non-executive directors' duty to devise a strategy, but it is to see that there is one in place.'

Interviews with both full-time executive and part-time non-executive members of the board, reveal only a small number of examples of part-time board members generating or initiating the content of strategy. Two non-executive directors reported having influenced the internationalization of firms' business activities. For example, one non-executive director recalled that:

'[name of country] I knew well ... it has enormous potential. I said "go there, acquire a good team of people and you will get in at a price which is sensible and attractive". That they have done.'

A part-time chairman described how, as a response to a changing business environment, he had tried to shape the attitude of executive directors towards managing the business.

'When I came onto the board there was considerable hostility to the introduction of competition. I decided that the right thing to do was embrace it .. Once we had decided to embrace it and commit to it, then we actually had a good deal more influence with the course of the legislation ... we started to define the framework. [I was saying] "the world is changing, and what are we going to do" ... I do not think they lacked the confidence that they could compete, but I think they saw accurately that it was a big complicated task to open up the market.'

Part-time board members were able to initiate strategic behaviour in these firms because they were 'low experience contexts'. Until recently, the firms had been state-owned and their executives had had little experience of conducting business outside the UK, or even of acting in a competitive context. Part-time board members, drawing on their own personal experience and knowledge of conducting business abroad and managing in a competitive business context, reported a direct influence on the strategy of these firms.

There are also two reports of part-time board members generating strategy in firms experiencing crisis or poor performance. One chief executive recalled:

'With [name of company] when I [the chief executive] arrived ... the non-execs were pretty determined that we needed to get out of certain businesses and consistently brought it up till we did so. So they can have a view and influence the board, but I have to say it is pretty rare to find that happening ...'

However, with the exception of circumstances such as those described above, the initiation and generation of strategy are much more likely to be led by executive directors. It is the executive board members, acting outside the boardroom, who tend to generate the content of strategy. The ability of part-time board members to shape that content comes through their influence over the context and conduct of the strategy process.

Figure 1 Levels of Part-time Board Member Involvement in Strategy

	Taking Strategic Decisions	Shaping Strategic Decisions	Shaping the Content, Context and Conduct of Strategy
Definition	Influence is exerted inside the boardroom at the end of the capital investment decision process	Influence occurs early in the decision process as part-time board members shape the preparation of capital investment proposals by executives	Influence is continuous and not confined to decision episodes
Board Behaviour	Inside the boardroom, boards take decisions to either accept, reject or refer capital investment proposals	Consultation with part-time board members by the executive, either formally or informally, whilst a capital investment proposal is being prepared enables board members to test ideas, raise issues, question assumptions, advise caution, and offer encouragement Executives 'sieve' capital investment proposals in anticipation of the need for board approval	The board develops the context for strategic debate, establishes a methodology for strategy development, monitors strategy content and alters the conduct of the executive in relation to strategy
Board Involvement	All boards take strategic decisions.	Some boards shape strategic decisions	A minority of boards shape the context, content and conduct of strategy.

The involvement of part-time board members in the content, context and conduct of strategy is conceptualized in Figure 1. In introducing the model, it is important to note the following methodological, conceptual and theoretical features. The model is based on rare primary data about the behaviour of boards and directors inside and outside the boardroom. The model describes a range of behaviour not identified in other studies of boards and directors. Three levels of part-time member involvement in strategy are identified: 'taking strategic decisions', 'shaping strategic decisions' and 'shaping the content, context and conduct of strategy'. Each level of involvement is distinguished conceptually by decision and non-decision behaviour, power relations between board members, and dialogue and social interaction between board members. Also, each level of involvement describes different effects on the content and process of adopted strategies — the greatest impact being achieved when the effects are simultaneous. For instance, part-time board members' ability to increase their influence on the strategy of firms, beyond simply approving executives' ideas and choices, is a function of them shaping the very process by which those strategic ideas and choices evolve.

The model shows that involvement in strategy varies between part-time board members and between boards. All part-time board members participate in 'taking strategic decisions' at board meetings. 'Shaping strategic decisions' analyses antecedents of decision-taking processes in the boardroom to uncover how some part-time board members shape strategic decisions before they reach the boardroom. 'Shaping the content and conduct of strategy' is the deepest form of part-time board member involvement in strategy. Here, the influence of some part-time board members extends beyond shaping and taking particular strategic decisions to creating conditions and methodologies for developing strategy. A later section of the paper examines variation in involvement in more detail.

The levels 'shaping strategic decisions' and 'shaping the content, context and conduct of strategy', reveal behaviour by part-time board members that challenges previous research findings about managerial hegemony on boards (Mace 1971; Pahl and Winkler 1974; Judge and Zeithaml 1992). In the context of broader debates about corporate control (Hill 1995) the model suggests that strategy is a sphere of activity in which part-time board members are capable of exercising control over management. The next section of the paper describes behaviours indicative of part-time board members' involvement in strategy at each level.

Taking Strategic Decisions

Boards have a decisional role (Mintzberg 1987) in the sphere of strategy. Boards take strategic decisions when part-time board members approve, disapprove or refer capital investment proposals brought to the board by the executive. Typically, proposals are about acquiring another firm, embarking on a joint venture, merging businesses or disposing of a business operation. Capital investment proposals may reflect broader strategic intentions relating to the growth and diversification of business activities. Alternatively, a proposal may reflect a strategic intention to consolidate business activities by re-focusing business activities and cutting costs. When taking strategic decisions, part-time board members exert influence at the end point in the decision process. Thus, having been presented with a proposal for capital investment by the executive, the board takes the decision either to accept or reject the proposal, or to refer it for modification.

The process by which a board takes strategic decisions starts from a base of control by the board over the executive. A board may set levels, typically in financial terms, which determine when executives have to seek approval for capital expenditure from the board before embarking on a course of action. An agenda for a board meeting will contain items about capital expenditure, for example a proposal to acquire another company. Typically, the executive prepare a paper to accompany the capital expenditure item on the agenda. At the board meeting, the prime objective of the executive is to gain board 'approval' for the proposed course of action. A board may ratify proposals developed by the executive, reject them, or ask for modification of a proposal. Here, boards are taking strategic decisions, and, in so doing, appear to exercise a degree of control over executives' discretion to make choices about the future direction of the company. However, how real is the control exercised by the board? Are they merely 'decision-taking', rather than 'decision-making' institutions (Pahl and Winkler 1974)?

Data collected for this study suggest that boards approve the majority of proposals put forward by executives. During the interviews, executives were asked 'What proportion of proposals which go to the board are approved?'. The typical response was 90–95 percent. The lowest figure quoted by an executive director was 80 percent. Some executives indicated a 100 percent approval rate. Responses by part-time board members to the same question also indicated a 90–95 percent approval rate. The rejection of proposals is rare when compared to the approval of capital expenditure proposals. In essence, boards find themselves saying 'yes' to executives more than they say 'no'. Similar findings have led other researchers to conclude that boards are doing little more than rubber stamping executive action (Mace 1971; Pahl and Winkler 1974). Some boards may indeed perform the ritualistic function of rubber-stamping executive action. However, data from this study suggest that all boards do not behave as 'rubber stamps' all the time. It is not appropriate to generalize that all boards function simply to give a final blessing to decisions effectively made elsewhere. This argument is supported by both critical incident data collected during this study and data about antecedents of strategic decisions taken in the boardroom.

Some boards do say 'no' to proposals of the executive. Using a critical incident methodology data collected for this study confirms a less than 100 percent rate of approval for executive proposals. From over 100 critical incidents reporting the contribution of part-time board members, there are 8 in-depth accounts of boards' ability to say 'no' to the specific proposals put to the board by executives (McNulty and Pettigrew 1996). In these instances, the proposals were either to diversify business activities, acquire a business or dispose of business operations. These examples of part-time board members' ability to say 'no' to executives have been provided by both the part-time board members themselves and by executive directors. One executive director described the board's rejection of a proposal by the executive to dispose of a business operation:

> 'the executive came up with a proposal to dispose of one of our operations ... the executive had lost patience with it ... It was taking up far too much time. It was in fact producing good money ... it was an executive team decision to get rid of it. The non-executive said "wait a minute I thought we had just had a strategy away-day six months ago and we decided we should be [doing certain things in certain areas of the world]. What are we doing getting rid of this operation?". The reply came "oh, it is taking far too much time to manage". The non-executives very politely, but very firmly, said "that is not a good enough reason for throwing away our shareholders" investment in [name of country]. Go away and find a way that you can run this organization ...'

Similarly, a chief executive described the board's response to an acquisition proposal:

> 'In my belief there are strong strategic reasons for [acquiring a business]. However, the board were particularly interested, correctly so, with regards to the balance

sheet and whether we should invest that money at all ... It was fairly clear that the board members were not keen to put the money into this ...'

Nevertheless, executives do enjoy a high success rate when they take capital investment proposals to the board. Does this high rate of success mean that boards are merely rubber stamps 90 percent of the time? Data quantifying the rate of board approval or disapproval for executive proposals are inadequate for answering this question. Restricting the analyses to the decision event in the boardroom provides only limited insight into the process by which capital expenditure proposals are generated by executives and decided upon by boards. The data reveal little about the influencing behaviour of board members before proposals get to the board. Analysis of the antecedents of particular decision episodes and behaviour outside the boardroom, shows the possibilities for part-time board members to influence strategy other than at the point of taking strategic decisions. Approval of a proposal by a board does not necessarily mean that the proposal is bereft of board influence. The next section of the paper presents data suggesting that part-time board members are capable of influencing capital investment proposals long before they are approved by the board.

Shaping Strategic Decisions

Literature about decision making in organizations suggests that making choices and taking decisions is the final episode in a continuous decision-making process in context (Pettigrew 1990). A whole range of behaviour earlier in the decision process may impact on the final decision that is taken. 'Taking strategic decisions' describes how boards may accept, reject or request modification of capital investment proposals. Taking strategic decisions focused on behavioural episodes of decision taking inside the boardroom. The second level of involvement in strategy, labelled 'shaping strategic decisions', considers the behaviour of both full-time executive directors and part-time board members before boards take capital investment decisions. A finding is that the influence of part-time board members is not, in all instances, confined to the point at which a decision is taken by the board, inside the boardroom, to approve or disapprove capital expenditure.

The majority of respondents who answered the question 'what proportion of proposals are accepted by the board?' qualified their answer to indicate that part-time board members may shape capital investment decisions before the point at which a decision is taken by the board to approve or disapprove capital expenditure. Capital investment is shaped by part-time board members through two kinds of process. First, by executives directly consulting part-time board members whilst preparing capital investment proposals. Executives may consult part-time board members inside the boardroom, using a 'preliminary' paper to test their ideas. Alternatively, executive directors may consult part-time board members informally, outside the boardroom. Second, executive directors may anticipate the response of the board and self-regulate those proposals that finally go to the board for approval.

Opportunities for part-time board members to shape capital expenditure proposals stem from the requirement that boards should formally approve capital investment plans. An individual, who holds positions of part-time chairman and non-executive director commented:

'It is like many of these things in decision-making...you have to get approval, but you always get it. So then people say "well what is the point, it is rubber stamp". But it is not, because the decision itself will be framed knowing that approval has to be obtained. If you did not have to have that, the decision could take a different form; it could be more capricious. You cannot be capricious in a decision, if, in the end, you have to explain it.'

A chief executive confirmed that boards draw influence from the process of approval:

'[the non-executive] act as a brake on the power of the chief executive. That is what they do. If you want to boil it down, that is what the non-executive does ... if I want to do something and decide that it is the right thing to do for the business ... the board is the ultimate obstacle which a proposal within the business has to pass ... we then have to sell it to the group of pretty intelligent and knowledgeable people who may come at the problem with a wider vision than the one we might employ.....'

Evidence from executive directors suggests that part-time board members frequently influence the preparation of capital investment proposals before formal submission to the board. The opportunity to influence strategic proposals may arise in different ways. A chief executive described how he used the board in a formal way whilst preparing a proposal for capital investment:

'When a chief executive feels that there is a reasonable chance that the non-execs would take another line ... then you should try and bring it to the board on two occasions. First of all get the non-execs' wisdom and intelligence on different ideas. Also, at the same time, you focus the board as a group with regards to its ideas and approach. So when you do a detailed paper you have a view whether it will go through.'

Executives draw part-time board members into the process of preparing capital investment proposals outside as well as inside the boardroom. In so doing, executives involve part-time board members informally at an early stage in the process of developing proposals. A chief executive said:

'... you take the initial soundings, you find out if anybody has any experience or if they have any views. That is taken at an early point in time so that the executive then know what they are working with and take that into account ... certainly if I were making an acquisition which perhaps was controversial, then I would seek their views beforehand.'

Part-time board members may also influence capital investment proposals without direct contact with the executive. In such instances, the process of influence happens in a more indirect and subtle way than described above. In essence, the need for approval and desire to avoid rejection of proposals by the board creates self-regulating behaviour by executives. One chief executive described such action by executives, using the analogy of a 'sieve' to describe the functions of the board:

> '... the fact that that sieve [the board] is there forces the consideration down the line anyway. You do not put up silly propositions because you know the sieve is there. They may get through if that sieve was not there... The sieve is working by being the hurdle that has to be crossed ...'

Interaction with part-time board members, initiated by executives outside the boardroom, at a pre-proposal stage, may be interpreted as manipulative behaviour by executives. Pahl and Winkler (1974) described pre-board meeting activity amongst executives as a 'screening operation' designed to control information to the board, rather than '... preparation for a testing occasion'. Theories of managerial hegemony would suggest that those really doing the influencing are the executives, and those being most influenced are the non-executive. Undoubtedly, the process of influence between executives and non-executives does work in this way in some instances. Faced with opposition to an idea or proposal, executives have recalled trying to 'knock-over' non-executives 'outside the board meeting'. Executives can also control the information flow to the board to eliminate 'discordant information' and develop a 'coherent case' for the actions they want approved (Pahl and Winkler 1974). One non-executive director, who is also a chief executive remarked:

> '... any non-exec is only as good as the executive will allow him to be. I will tell you now that any executive can kid any non-exec to do virtually anything. If he is really strong-willed, and he has all the facts, and so forth, it is jolly difficult for you to find-out as a non-exec. You receive papers and whether they have all the facts in, you do not know. You have to assume the executive, who are a team, support each other.'

However, there is a sufficient body of data collected during this study to suggest that the process of influence is not simply dominated by an all-powerful executive. Interviews reveal the possibilities for a more dynamic and fluid view of power and influence, inside and outside the boardroom, which enables part-time board members to shape the content of strategy proposals early in their gestation. In addition to those instances when boards reject executive proposals, there are numerous accounts of part-time board members challenging, dissenting, testing executives, both formally and informally, early in the process of building up strategy proposals. A chief executive described such an instance:

> 'We wanted to acquire [name of company] ... now I know a lot of people have some very strong views about [name of country] companies. So I talked with each of them individually, prior to that, to make sure they understood thoroughly how important their decision was and to really drag out their concerns, so that the paper that eventually went in to the board addressed many of those issues. The one thing you do not want is them throwing things out. If that is going to happen do not put papers in, [you would] test it out before.'

The most popular explanation amongst respondents for the high ratio of proposals approved by the board is not that boards are a rubber stamp.

Rather, that rejection of a capital investment proposal by the board is so undesirable for an executive, that self-regulating action is taken by the executive to prevent this. For example, executives screen proposals amongst themselves and filter out unpalatable options for part-time board members early in the process. The process of consultation enables part-time board members to 'test ideas', 'question the assumptions behind the ideas', 'raise issues and concerns', 'advise caution' and 'offer encouragement'.

The process of consultation is not always initiated by executives. Shaping behaviour is not simply a product of executive action and part-time board member reaction. A chief executive revealed that:

> 'We would try and get the papers out for a board meeting at least four days in advance. Now very often I will receive calls from non-execs prior to the board meeting, when they have got stuck into the papers. It is very often for clarity purposes, but occasionally it is "what do you want to do this for?".'

The preceding discussion has treated capital investment decisions as part of strategic behaviour within firms. Research has previously identified that part-time board members rubber-stamp executive proposals. However, data collected for this study suggest that this 'minimalist' behaviour is not the only behaviour of boards (Pettigrew and McNulty 1995). Rather, part-time board members contribute to the strategic behaviour of firms in two ways. First, by approving or disapproving capital investment proposals, boards take strategic decisions. Second, by influencing the strategic thinking of executives, part-time board members shape the content of capital investment proposals before they even enter the boardroom for formal approval by the board. Once inside the boardroom, this influence may continue as part-time board members debate, test, and challenge the proposal, to outcomes either of approval, modification or rejection.

When part-time board members influence strategy through the capital expenditure process, their influence is episodic, intermittent, and reactive. It is episodic because it is based around particular capital investment proposals, which, although comprising common items on board-meeting agendas, are basically rather self-contained episodes of decision-making. Influence is an intermittent process because the generation of capital investment proposals does not necessarily require continuous involvement of the board. Executives draw part-time board members into the process at various stages in the life-cycle of ideas and proposals. The influence process is reactive, rather than pro-active, because it is a process based on the need for executives to gain approval for their plans from the board. At best, the process may become consultative as executives attempt to minimize the possibilities of proposals being rejected in the boardroom. Finally, the influence process is largely about part-time board members checking and controlling executive choices, rather than initiating action. A chief executive commented:

> 'The non-executive director is there to ensure that something stupid is not being done, for example, somebody pursuing a major investment which clearly does not have a sensible financial return.'

The next section of the paper considers whether the influence of part-time board members goes beyond accepting and rejecting capital investment proposals. Do part-time board members contribute to strategy in ways other than taking and shaping decisions about capital expenditure?

Shaping the Context, Content and Conduct of Strategy

It is inadequate to focus purely on processes of choice and decision making to understand strategic behaviour (Mintzberg and Waters 1990; Pettigrew 1990). The third level of part-time board member involvement in strategy, described in Figure 1, is labelled 'shaping the context, content and conduct of strategy'. By contrast with the preceding discussion of 'taking strategic decisions' and 'shaping strategic decisions', part-time board member involvement in strategy is not conceptualized here purely in terms of choice and decision processes. Data from this study suggest that capital investment decisions do not fully capture the impact that some part-time board members have on strategy. Shaping the context, content and conduct of strategy conveys how part-time board members influence, not only the content of strategy, by taking and shaping strategic decisions, but also the processes and methodologies through which those ideas evolve.

Processes of strategic choice, change and control should not be abstracted from the contexts in which they occur. Those processes are crucially shaped by features of context, the content of actions and decisions contained within the processes, and the conduct of those who are active in these processes. Those part-time board members who have an involvement in strategy that is deeper than taking and shaping strategic decisions have been able to shape features of the context, conduct and content of strategy.

By shaping the context in which the strategy process occurs, part-time board members are able to influence the conditions within which the strategy process happens in firms. Part-time board members can shape the extent to which strategy is deliberately formulated as opposed to being left to emerge. Part-time board members are also able to influence where, when and how processes of strategic thinking occur within firms.

Mintzberg (1987) distinguished between deliberate and emergent strategy. The concept of emergent strategy introduced the idea that strategy can form in an organization without being consciously intended. Earlier in this paper, it was argued that part-time board members rarely formulate the content of strategy. However, data suggest that some part-time board members deliberately try to ensure that strategy is formulated by executive directors rather than just left to emerge. They do so by encouraging the executive directors to explicitly and intentionally think strategically. Part-time board members can shape the strategy process by creating a climate in and around the boardroom in which strategic thinking is perceived to be a legitimate and valued activity. At the most fundamental level, part-time board members 'prompt' and 'question' executives about the existence of a strategy and of processes for developing strategy within the firm. A part-time chairman remarked:

'It is the role of the non-executive to be satisfied that there is a proper strategy in place and that it is being adhered to. [Initiating strategy] is not a non-executive role, unless there isn't a strategy. If there is not a strategy, the non-executives are entitled to demand that there should be one. ...'

A chief executive confirmed that:

'Strategy is an area where the board pay a lot of attention, prompting us, in terms of the importance of having a clearly defined strategic vision, and the need to continuously go through the process of determining what our long-term strategy is.'

A part-time chairman recalled:

'[on joining the firm] one of the first things I said was "what about strategy and plans". At [name of another company] we have ten-year, three-year and one-year plans ... they do not have that. ... So next week at [name of company] we are going away for two days to a hotel down in the country and we are having senior executives put out as close to their first shot of a plan. Other companies I have joined have that good practice so you have got a lot more focusing there, not on the framework they have or do not have, but on the sensitivities and interrogation of the content within an acceptable framework.'

Part-time board members may encourage a greater and more open dialogue about strategy at board level by constructing contexts in which strategy is debated and even formulated. Several part-time chairmen have described how they used the position of chairman to develop time and space for boards to have a dialogue with the executive about strategy. One part-time chairman recalled:

'[the company] was run by a rather strong chief executive who had his own ideas about strategy and he did not consult his non-execs. When I became chairman, I insisted we had strategy conferences ... that had not happened before. They [the executive] were forced to bring their ideas out and there is no doubt that strategy was modified as a result. It was not overturned, but what happened was that we created an environment in which the executives felt that they needed to tell more to the non-execs and derive more help from the non-executive as a result. That was a change in the environment.'

When a board is unhappy with the level of information about strategy provided by the executive, changes may be instigated in the board process to increase its exposure to executives' strategic thinking and involvement in the strategy process. A chief executive recalled an earlier experience of his as an executive director in which a non-executive director challenged a chief executive at the board about the process by which strategic decisions were being brought to the board:

'[name of chief executive] at [name of company] used to bring to the board gargantuan things and used to look at the board and say "what are you going to do about it". [name of non-executive director] said to the chief executive "you must be joking, at [name of company] we would have papers to the board on this size of issue. Just turning up and expecting us to act on something you have only given us this morning — we know where you stand, but we have not had the chance to discuss it — that is not on" ... it taught me a lesson. I think it is very important to have papers to the board on issues that may well lead to investment and authorization issues in adequate time for the board to feel they have had a chance to discuss it or even call for the chief executive to get external advice. ...'

The vignette above was corroborated in an interview with the non-executive director involved. The above data reveals that some part-time board members are able to shape features of the climate and context of the strategy process. The extracts also reveal that part-time board members can shape the conduct of the strategy process and by so doing impact on the behaviours used to create and implement strategy within the firm. Part-time board members may also shape the strategic conduct of executives by establishing a methodology for forming strategy, and monitoring the execution of that methodology by executives. A chief executive commented that part-time board members in the firm have revealed:

'how people do [strategy] in other firms ... they are in facilitating mode in the sense of saying "this is what you need to do ... Based on our experience, you should be thinking about the following" ...'

Part-time board members also work with executive directors, agreeing methods for developing strategy, and time-scales for delivering strategic intentions. A chief executive described how he and the part-time board members introduced a strategic-planning process into a firm:

'The conversations we had at the time when I was developing the strategy were, "what I am going to do exactly? How I am going to do it? How long is it going to take? What resources am I going to apply to it"? And I said — "I shall deliver this within a certain timescale; it will have these elements; it will have done this work; it will have this resource analysis; it will have this data analysis; and I will come forward with what I think we should be trying to achieve" ...'

Part-time board members shape the conduct of the strategy process further by changing it in order to ensure that executive action occurs within a clear framework of strategic responsibility and accountability to the board. A chief executive described practices introduced by a newly appointed part-time chairman:

'We previously had what was called a strategy group which was chaired by the chairman, and an operations committee chaired by [the chief executive]. One of the good things about [name of new chairman] arriving is that he is quite clearly chairman of the board. His job is there to manage the board and ensure that the executive has got a clear direction as to what the board wants and then for the executive to get on and run it. The roles in the past were pretty muddled ... [at the level below the board] ... we now have a group executive committee.'

Data from this study suggest that part-time board members may introduce strategic controls on the executive. A chief executive commented that:

'What you have got to do is have the right control procedure, so that people do not go off the rails and the thing is contained and there is the right degree of oversight. In operational decisions, we do actually have a defined set of protocols of what we can and cannot do and delegated authorities, which is a delegated authority for all operational matters of the group to the chief executive, which is then devolved down to the executive directors.'

Part-time board members do not always rely on such formal mechanisms for exercising control over executives. Using the analogy of 'stakes in the ground' an executive director remarked that:

'On all strategic matters now, we have got to take the board with us now [that is] ... [the ex chief executive] would have said "we will just tell them". To an extent, some of the perameters of strategy are now are being influenced by non-executive directors. We put forward a variety of financing scenarios for our acquisition programme ... one of the directors enunciated a principle about the financing arrangements, which was immediately picked up by the chief executive who said "Yes, I think that is a good point. We will take that as one of our stakes in the ground".'

The suggestion here is that 'stakes in the ground' bound the discretion of the executive. Whereas previously in this firm, the executives controlled the decision-making process, the process is now being opened up, shared with and shaped by the board. The processes described impact upon the behavioural dynamics on the board. New behavioural norms and expectations are created, altering the preparation of strategic ideas and the presentation of information by the executive to the board. The executive director acknowledged that:

'[the process of questions, the stakes in the ground] ... does condition my thinking on stuff I am presenting to the board. I do actually think, "what is going to be the impact of this". I am anticipating and conditioning the task. ... One of the mental tests we now apply is "how will X react to that, how will Y react to that" ... We would often think "Why is he concerned in that respect?". You do not actually articulate it like that, but "yes" you do start to question yourself.'

The chief executive of the same organization corroborated the influence of the board on executive behaviour:

'[the board] colours how you approach things ... If you know what the issues are, and what their views are, you do not go and challenge them directly by putting things forward that they are going to say "no" to.'

Part-time board members' contribution to the strategy process does not necessarily stop with raising the awareness of executives of the need to think about strategy. Contribution does not stop with the introduction of models for planning strategy, or the construction of contexts in which strategy is formulated and debated. Where a strategy is in place, part-time board members evaluate its content and impact on it by asking executives to justify their strategic intentions and, by monitoring the actions taken by executives, who are asked to justify why certain courses of action have either been taken or are not being taken. A chief executive commented that:

'They [the board] are looking at strategic things in the sense of saying "What are we doing about this and that". They look at the business; they study the figures; they ask "Is this a growth business?; What has happened to our profits here?; Is this a business we should be in"?.'

At the same time as assessing executives' conduct, part-time board members are evaluating the content of strategy. A chief executive, who is also a non-executive commented:

'If the board is working, then you are actually in quite a good position as a non-exec to get a feel of what is going on. And of course you notice the kind of thing the chief executive brings to the board or wants to do or wants to discuss and you see him becoming besoddon with power. Or you see him becoming adversarial to all, or driving towards a particular personal line of business or you see him becoming particularly blinkered. ... A good chairman can get a situation where his non-execs and himself turn forcibly on the chief executive and say "this is just not on and you have to pay more attention to the Asia pacific market and stop being in love with the US". Obviously, the kid glove is better than the steel hand, but the right sorts of non-execs with the right sorts of experience make a pretty formidable force, if they choose to do so, for a chief executive good enough to listen.'

Finally, the ultimate act in shaping the context, content and conduct of strategy occurs when a board fires the chief executive. An individual recalled his own appointment to the position of chief executive.

'... There was a feeling that the company had lost its way a bit and that really a change was necessary. That is their [non-executive directors] role in my opinion. If they see the business is really going off the rails, their role is to change the senior management..They brought me in to sort it out and they have been very supportive of the sorting out. If they felt that I was not doing the right job, or whatever, then I think it is their role either to advise me of the fact or get rid of me.'

Contextual and Processual Influences on Strategy Involvement

Compared with findings of previous studies (Spencer 1983: Pahl and Winkler 1974) this study shows boards and their part-time members to be more actively involved in corporate strategy. The three categories of strategy involvement described by the model do however expose variation in part-time board members' involvement in strategy. Not all part-time board members are involved to the same degree in strategy in the ways described in Figure 1. All boards take strategic decisions as a matter of procedure. Thus, all part-time board members are involved in taking strategic decisions. On some boards, this may indeed mean that part-time board members play a minimal part in a ritual of collective decision taking. However, it is not accurate to generalize that all part-time board members' involvement in strategy is simply 'rubber-stamping' decisions taken by executives elsewhere. Rather, this paper provides evidence to suggest that part-time board members are capable of shaping both ideas that form the content of strategy as well as the methodologies and processes through which those ideas evolve.

What are the conditions that are encouraging greater levels of influence on strategy by part-time board members? What factors explain why some part-time board members are more involved in strategy than others? This section of the paper develops propositions based on contextual variables somewhat implicit in the preceding analysis to further examine the involvement of part-time board members in strategy. The propositions do not provide an exhaustive explanation of involvement. Rather, those made here are the ones the authors believe offer the most promising lines of enquiry for future research and have the greatest potential for building on existing models of board behaviour (Finkelstein and Hambrick 1996; Pettigrew and McNulty 1995). The propositions deliberately focus attention on factors other than board structure and composition (Finkelstein and Hambrick 1996) in order to encourage more contextually and processually sensitive studies of board and director conduct. The propositions relate to features of the 'outer and inner context' of the firm; and the process and conduct of the board. Furthermore, the propositions are presented to encourage multiple factor explanations of part-time board member behaviour. It is doubtful whether any one factor can fully explain part-time board members' involvement in strategy. Rather, it is the analytical interplay of several factors that is likely to provide the deepest understanding of the conditions that enable or constrain part-time board members' involvement in strategy.

Data from this study support the speculation that norms are changing about director involvement in strategy and that boards are being expected to be more involved in strategy (Finkelstein and Hambrick 1996). More active involvement in strategy by part-time board members is being encouraged by the heightened interest and debate about systems of corporate governance. In the UK, performance weaknesses, corporate scandal and increased shareholder activism are forces contributing to greater numbers of non-executive directors in UK firms, with seemingly greater legitimacy to exercise their duties as directors (Cadbury 1992; Hampel Report 1998).

However, the greater involvement of part-time board members in strategy cannot be explained purely by the increased attention being given to duties and responsibilities of boards and directors by corporate governance policy-makers and opinion-formers at national level. Rather, to explain the level of part-time board member involvement in strategy, it is also necessary to analyze factors closer to the settings of part-time board member behaviour, for instance, factors relating to the history and performance of the firm and the process and conduct of the board.

A number of studies link crises in business performance to the mobilization and use of power by part-time board members (Lorsch and MacIver 1989; Pettigrew and McNulty 1995). Data presented in this paper do not support the stereotype that part-time board members only have influence at times of corporate crisis. However, data in the paper do suggest that part-time board members' opportunities to challenge executives about both strategy and the methodologies for developing strategy increase at times of performance difficulty. Part-time board members' involvement in strategy is greater at those points in the life-cycle of firms that involve strategic transition (Zald 1969). Earlier in the paper, rare instances were described when board members generated or initiated the firms' movement into international markets. These instances are taken from newly-privatized firms, whose executives were open to learning from part-time board members about how to conduct business outside the UK. The greater the level of strategic decision activity, for instance, acquisitions, mergers, divestiture, the greater the opportunity for part-time board members to be take and shape strategic decisions (Zald 1969; Finkelstein and Hambrick 1996). In addition to the above features of the inner and outer context of the firm, any explanation of part-time board member behaviour must also examine the inner context of the board. The conduct and process of the board are crucial determinants of part-time board members' involvement in strategy. Greater attention needs to be given to how the contribution of part-time board members is conditioned by factors such as: the agenda for the board meeting; the process and conduct of the board meeting; strategy 'away-days'; and informal dialogue between board members, between board meetings. There is limited understanding of the importance of board process and conduct to the contribution of part-time board members, because research, distant from the phenomenon of boards and directors, has tended to rely on surrogate measures of board size, structure and composition to explain influence (Finkelstein and Hambrick 1996).

Part-time board members are limited in the time they have to perform the role. Their contact with the company is restricted to a small number of days per year, and, compared to executives, they are deficient in terms of their knowledge of the host company. For these reasons, it is vital that the contact they have with the firm maximizes rather than minimizes their opportunities to contribute to strategy. The conduct and process of the board, as well as external relationships between board members can either enable or constrain part-time board members' opportunities to influence strategy.

The involvement of part-time board members in strategy is greater in those organizations in which it is an important item on the board agenda. On some boards, the agenda consists of 'routine, procedural' items such as reports on business performance, board sub-committees and budget planning exercises; and the publication of company results and dividend policy. These items encourage only a review of past performance rather than discussion about critical strategy-related issues facing the firm in the future. This kind of board agenda restricts part-time board members' opportunities to question, probe and challenge executives about strategy, and indicates that part-time board members are not being consulted by executives, who perceive that the responsibility for strategy lies with them, to be dealt with away from the boardroom.

On the other hand, a board agenda treating strategy as the legitimate responsibility of the whole board, can be an important mechanism for drawing part-time board members into the strategy process. 'Real issues' are brought to the board for early discussion rather than confirmation so that part-time board members have a genuine opportunity to support or challenge executives as they deliberate on bold and risky decisions, and thereby to influence the resolution of these decisions. It is not perceived as a sign of weakness on the part of the executive for issues to be brought to the board for resolution. The agenda is planned carefully to ensure that issues are raised which may require future board decisions The board is given time to prepare their views and construct a decision. Indeed, such an agenda may allow an issue to proceed through several iterations over time, enabling a more continuous board-level dialogue about strategyl, allowing part-time board members more opportunity to shape the thinking of executives, and vice versa.

However, opportunities for board members to contribute to strategy are not assured simply by allotting time on the board agenda to discuss strategy. It is necessary that space on the board agenda for strategy is accompanied by processes of information sharing, challenge and open debate. Without these, the time allotted to strategy on the agenda may just lead to ritualistic and superficial consideration rather than to genuine debate.

Part-time board members' involvement in strategy is greatest in those firms where the board meeting is conducted in ways that ensure that executives bring information to the board as a precursor of debate. Presentations by executives to the board can be valuable mechanisms for bridging gaps between executives and part-time board members' knowledge and understanding of situations and issues. Presentations about firms' profitability, profitability levers, business trends and market share are valuable for increasing part-time board members' understanding of important issues facing firms. Whilst presentations open up the board process to the acquisition of information and debate, they are not the only tool needed to involve part-time board members in strategy. It is important that, within the board process, executives spend time listening as well as presenting and reporting to the board. The time spent at board meetings between presentation by executives and debate is an important indicator of board behaviour in this respect. Furthermore, it is important that presentation and debate involve the whole board and are not solely channelled through an overdominant chief executive. Boards do vary in the extent to which there is open debate during which executive directors, other than the chief executive, are allowed to speak their minds as directors of the company and members of the board. Where 'shades of opinion' amongst the executive are allowed to be revealed, part-time board members have a greater flow of information and wider perspective against which they can probe and question strategy.

Part-time board members' involvement in strategy increases in those firms in which special events, such as strategy 'away days', involve the whole board in strategy. Over and above the regular cycle of board meetings, some firms have special events once or twice a year specifically focused on strategy. Data suggests that these can provide all board members with a more informal setting for reviewing both the content and process of strategy. The events that appear to involve part-time board members the most in strategy are those that are deliberately structured to be more informal and relaxed than a regular board meeting and where the purpose is for executives to share their thinking with part-time board members rather than to justify or convince part-time board members of a particular course of action.

Construction of the board agenda and the conduct of the board meeting must be seen in the context of the behaviour of board members between board meetings. Opportunities for part-time board members to become involved in strategy are considerably enhanced in those firms where there is also an informal interim dialogue, via telephone conversations, etc., between executives and part-time board members. This is another mechanism for informing part-time board members about company affairs and drawing them into the strategy process. The number of times executives, including the chief executive, ask part-time board members for a view about a strategic issue is one indicator of executives' willingness to use and involve part-time board members in strategy formation. Informal dialogue between executive and non-executive directors is another sign that part-time board members are considered sufficiently important to make sharing information with them desirable. Informal dialogue allows board members to develop personal relationships. Part-time board members gain access to new information and a wider perspective which deepen their understanding of issues and place them in a better position to make judgements in the boardroom. Informal dialogue also allows part-time board members to exert influence without undermining individuals in 'public' view of the whole board.

Informal interim dialogue between part-time board members also conditions strategy involvement. One important mechanism for creating informal dialogue between part-time board members is the 'chairman's dinner with non-executive directors'. These events tend to be held once or twice year and vary in the extent to which they involve the chief executive. Not all chairmen and chief executives engage in this practice. Some believe such events to be divisive in terms of executive–non-executive relations. However, in those firms where dinners occur, part-time board members have an opportunity to talk openly, in a more private setting, about the calibre of the executive and the quality of strategic thinking. It is apparent from the preceding analysis that important strategic behaviour is often predicated on the basis of such informal dialogue. The extent and causes of the variation in informal dialogue between executive and non-executive directors in different firms are issues worthy of further research.

Conclusion

This paper has described and analyzed the contribution to strategy made by part-time board members. By revealing behavioural dynamics on boards, the study shows that boards and their part-time members are actively involved in corporate strategy. Whilst the influence of part-time board members on strategy is rarely expressed through their ability to initiate strategic plans and ideas, the findings of this study do not concur with the picture conveyed by managerial hegemony theorists (Mace 1971; Pahl and Winkler 1974; Kosnik 1987) that board members are hapless and manipulated.

Study findings about the active involvement of boards and directors in processes of strategic choice, change and control are relevant to agency and resource dependency theorists and strategic management scholars who need to theorize about boards. The involvement of part-time board members in strategy is consistent with agency perspectives which treat boards as important mechanisms of corporate control. All three levels of strategy involvement displayed in Figure 1 reveal strategy to be a means by which boards, through their part-time members, can exert a controlling influence over executive management. From a resourcing perspective, the attention given in this study to processes of strategic control and choice reveal boards and their directors to be central to both the use and acquisition of resources. From a strategic management perspective, findings are consistent with the view that, in theorizing about strategy, greater attention needs to be paid to the role of boards and directors in processes of strategic leadership and change (Finkelstein and Hambrick 1996).

Corporate governance has indisputably attracted attention in recent years. Internationally, norms and expectations are changing as boards and shareholders are encouraged to make corporate management more accountable for their performance and compensation. Greater public scrutiny of management is one contributory factor enabling boards and their part-time members to become more involved in strategy. The conceptual model of part-time board member involvement in strategy and propositions about the contextual and processual influences on strategy involvement offer a basis for examining the changing circumstances of boards and for testing the findings of this study beyond UK companies.

Appendix

Interview Sample

Lord Alexander of Weedon
*Sir Michael Angus
The Rt Hon, the Lord Armstrong of Ilminster
The Rt Hon Lord Ashburton
Dr Neville Bain
Mary Baker
*Sir John Banham
Nicholas Baring
Nicholas Barber
Bob Bauman
*Keith Bedell-Pearce
Sir Robin Biggam
Peter Birch
Sir Derek Birkin
Professor Sue Birley
Jonathan Bloomer
Lord Blyth of Rowington
Roger Boissier
John Bradley
John Browne
Ann Burdus
Sir Peter Carey
Sir John Carter
Sir Peter Cazalet
Sir Robert Clark
Neil Clarke
Alan Clements
Richard Clothier
Sir Alan Cockshaw
Janet Cohen
Sir Colin Corness
Professor Sir Frederick Crawford
Sir Peter Davis
June De Moller
Kenneth Dixon
Lady Eccles of Moulton
Sir John Egan
Sir Richard Evans
Sheila Forbes
Niall Fitzgerald
David Gilchrist

Mr Richard Giordano
General Sir James Glover
Sir Nicholas Goodison
Tony Hales
Jan Hall
*Sir Ronald Hampel
*Judith Hanratty
Sir Christopher Harding
Sir Timothy Harford
Sir Denys Henderson
Michael Hennessy
Derek Higgs
Sir Robert Horton
Lady Elspeth Howe of Aberavon
Sipko Huismans
Mike Jackson
Sir Martin Jacomb
Peter Jarvis
Sir Hugh Jenkins
Alan Jones
Richard Lapthorne
John Leighfield
Prue Leith
Roger Leverton
*Sir Richard Lloyd
Hugh McCoy
Robert Malpas
Luke March
Sir Colin Marshall
Sir Peter Middleton
Sir John Milne
Sir Nigel Mobbs
Sir Brian Moffat
Dr Janet Morgan
The Hon Sara Morrison
Ian Much
Sir Geoffrey Mulcahy
Dr Gerard Murphy
Roger Myddelton
Yve Newbold
Mick Newmarch
Sir Robin Nicholson
The Rt Hon, the Lord Nickson of Renagour
*Sir Edwin Nixon
Baroness O'Cathain of the Barbican
Keith Orrell-Jones
Joseph Palmer
Sir Bruce Pattullo
Sir Brian Pearse
Sir Eric Pountain
*The Rt Hon, the Lord Prior of Brampton
Sir Alick Rankin
Hubert Reid
Richard Reynolds
Sir Ralph Robins
Louis Sherwood
The Lord Simon of Highbury
Anthony Stenham
Anthony Stoughton-Harris
Jim Sutcliffe
Max Taylor
Howard Trust
The Lord Tugendhat of Widdington
The Rt Hon, the Lord Walker of Worcester
Sir Peter Walters
David Wellings

Note: One respondent preferred to keep their participation in the study anonymous.
* The respondent was interviewed on two separate occasions.

Note

* The authors wish to acknowledge the financial support of the Economic and Social Research Council, Grant No. R000236109.

References

Andrews, Kenneth
1981 'Corporate strategy as a vital function of the board'. *Harvard Business Review* (Nov./Dec.): 174–184.

Cadbury Report
1992 *Committee on the financial aspects of corporate governance*. London: Moorgate.

Chakravarthy, Balaji, and Yves Doz
1992 'Strategy process research: focusing on corporate self renewal'. *Strategic Management Journal* 13 (Summer): 5–14.

Charkham, Johnathan
1994 *Keeping good company: A study of corporate governance in five countries*. Oxford: Oxford University Press.

Conyon, Martin
1994 'Corporate governance changes in UK companies between 1988 and 1993'. *Corporate Governance, An International Review* 2/2: 97–109.

Conyon, Martin
1995 'Cadbury in the boardroom'. *Price Waterhouse, Corporate Register* (March): 4–14. Hemmington Scott Publishing.

Demb, Ada, and Friedrich Neubauer
1992 *The corporate board.* New York: Oxford University Press.

Dutton, Jane, and Susan Ashford
1993 'Selling issues to top management'. *Academy of Management Review* 18/3: 397–428.

Eisenhardt, Kathleen, and Mark Zbracki
1992 'Strategic decision-making'. *Strategic Management Journal* 13 (Winter): 17–37.

Fama, Eugene, and Michael Jensen
1983 'Separation of ownership and control'. *Journal of Law and Economics* 26 (June): 301–325.

Finkelstein, Sydney, and Donald Hambrick
1996 *Strategic leadership: top executives and their effects on organisations.* Minneapolis: West Publishing.

Goodstein, Jerry, Kanak Gautum, and Warren Boeker
1994 'The effects of board size and diversity on strategic change'. *Strategic Management Journal* 15: 241–250

Grumbar, J.J., and M.A.J Kelly
1993 *Corporate governance: the role of the non-executive director.* London: Egon Zehnder International and Executive Interim Management.

Hampel Report
1998 *Committee on corporate governance: Final report.* London: Gee Publishing.

Herman, Edward
1981 *Corporate control, corporate power.* New York: Cambridge University Press.

Hill, Stephen
1995 'The social organisation of boards and directors'. *British Journal of Sociology* 46/2: 245–278.

Hill, Charles, and Scott Snell
1988 'External control, corporate strategy and firm performance in research-intensive industries'. *Strategic Management Journal* 9: 577–590.

Institute of Directors
1995 *Good practice for directors: Standards for the board.* London: Institute of Directors.

Jensen, Michael, and William Meckling
1976 'Theory of the firm: managerial behaviour, agency costs and ownership structure'. *Journal of Financial Economics* 3: 305–360.

Johnson, Richard, Robert Hoskisson, and Michael Hitt
1994 *Downscoping: how to tame the diversified firm.* New York: Oxford University Press.

Judge, William, and Carl Zeithaml
1992 'Institutional and strategic choice perspectives on board involvement in strategic decision process'. *Academy of Management Journal* 35/4: 766–794.

Kosnik, Rita
1987 'Greenmail: a study of board performance in corporate governance'. *Administrative Science Quarterly* 32: 163–185.

Lorsch, Jay, with Elizabeth MacIver
1989 *Pawns or potentates.* Boston: Harvard Business School Press.

Mace, Myles
1971 *Directors: myth and reality.* Cambridge, MA: Harvard University Press.

McNulty, Terry, and Andrew Pettigrew
1996 'The contribution, power and influence of part-time board members'. *Corporate Governance: An International Review* 4/3: 160–179.

Mintzberg, Henry
1987 'Five P's for Strategy'. *California Management Review* (Fall): 11–24.

Mintzberg, Henry, and Jim Waters
1990 'Does decision get in the way'? *Organisation Studies* 11/1: 1–6.

Nutt, Paul
1984 'Types of organisation decision processes'. *Administrative Science Quarterly* 29: 414–450.

Pahl, Raymond, and J. Winkler
1974 'The economic elite: theory and practice' in *'Elites and power in British society'*. P. J. Stanworth and A. Giddens (eds.). Cambridge: Cambridge University Press.

Pearce, John, and Shakar Zahra
1991 'The relative power of CEO's and boards of directors: association with corporate performance'. *Strategic Management Journal* 12/2: 135–153.

Pettigrew, Andrew
1973 *The politics of organisational decision-making*. London: Tavistock.

Pettigrew, Andrew
1990 'Studying strategic choice and strategic change. A comment on Mintzberg and Waters: "Does decision get in the way"?'. *Organisation Studies* 11/1: 6–11.

Pettigrew, Andrew
1992 'On studying managerial elites'. *Strategic Management Journal* 13: 163–182.

Pettigrew, Andrew
1992a 'The character and significance of strategy process research'. *Strategic Management Journal* 13 (Winter): 5–16.

Pettigrew, Andrew, and Terry McNulty
1995 'Power and influence in and around the boardroom'. *Human Relations* 48/8: 845–873.

Pettigrew, Andrew, and Terry McNulty
1998 'Sources and uses of power in the boardroom'. *European Journal of Work and Organisational Psychology* (June).

Pettigrew, Andrew, and Richard Whipp
1991 *Managing change for competitive success*. Oxford: Blackwell.

Pfeffer, Jeffrey
1972 'Size and composition of corporate boards of directors: The organisation and its environment'. *Administrative Science Quarterly* 17: 218–228.

Schendel, Dan, and Charles Hofer
1979 *Strategic management: A new view of business policy and planning*. Boston, MA: Little, Brown.

Spencer, Anne
1983 *On the edge of the organisation. The role of the outside director*. Chichester: Wiley.

Stiles, Philip, and Bernard Taylor
1996 'The strategic role of the board'. *Corporate Governance, An International Review* 4/1: 3–10.

Times, The
1997 *The Times 1000*. London: Times Books.

Zald, Meyer
1969 'The power and functions of boards of directors'. *American Journal of Sociology* 5: 97–111.

[12]

© Academy of Management Journal
2001, Vol.44, No.4, 639—660

THE STRATEGIC CONTEXT OF EXTERNAL NETWORK TIES: EXAMINING THE IMPACT OF DIRECTOR APPOINTMENTS ON BOARD INVOLVEMENT IN STRATEGIC DECISION MAKING

MASON A. CARPENTER
University of Wisconsin—Madison

JAMES D. WESTPHAL
University of Texas at Austin

This study examines how external network ties determine a board's ability to contribute to the strategic decision making process. Although the simple number of director appointments to other boards does not affect board monitoring or advice on strategy, appointments that can provide directors with relevant strategic knowledge and perspective do predict such involvement. In effect, the strategic context of social network ties, not simply the number of ties, is an important influence on corporate governance.

Increased research attention is being devoted to the influence of corporate board members on important organizational outcomes. According to agency theorists, effective boards independently monitor strategic challenges facing a firm and evaluate management's performance in addressing them (Beatty & Zajac, 1994; Fama & Jensen, 1983). Directors may overturn poor decisions or replace "underperforming" managers as a result of such monitoring (Brudney, 1982). Moreover, agency theory also suggests that directors are motivated to engage in competent monitoring activity by the reputational effects of poor decisions (Fama, 1980). From this perspective, poor management decisions will be attributed, in part, to inadequate oversight by directors, which will ultimately hurt their prospects in the labor market for directors and managers.

In addition, although agency theorists emphasize the board's role as an independent control mechanism, the broader literature on boards suggests a second possible role for directors; specifically, in some cases they may provide ongoing advice to top managers on possible strategic changes or the implementation of existing strategies (Demb & Neubauer, 1992; Lorsch & MacIver, 1989). In such cases, boards serve as a strategic consultant to top managers, rather than (or in addition to) exercising independent control. This view was advanced by Pfeffer and Salancik (1978: 170), who identified the provision of advice and counsel and the exercise of control as two primary components of a board's internal administrative function (see also Westphal, 1999).

The governance literature also suggests that there is considerable variance in the degree to which directors make an actual impact on strategic decision making, with some boards unable to monitor or advise management effectively (Mace, 1971; Wade, O'Reilly, & Chandratat, 1990). Prior empirical studies have focused primarily on lack of board power as an explanation for limited board involvement. For example, it is often proposed that boards are less likely to exert control over strategic decision making on behalf of shareholders when they lack formal or social independence from management—as indicated by the percentage of outside or nonexecutive directors, or the prevalence of friendship ties or other social connections between managers and directors (Baliga, Moyer, & Rao, 1996; Boeker & Goodstein, 1993; Hill & Snell, 1988; Kesner, Victor, & Lamont, 1986; Mallette & Fowler, 1992; Wade et al., 1990). However, as Westphal's (1998: 530) recent review of the literature suggests, there is little consistent evidence that board independence or "structural power" increases board involvement in strategic decision making.

Several authors have noted the persistent challenges faced by directors in making meaningful contributions to corporate strategy, regardless of their power to do so (Demb & Neubauer, 1992; Lorsch & MacIver, 1989; Westphal, 1999; Westphal & Zajac, 1997). Such challenges have been held to stem in part from questions of whether many direc-

Both authors contributed equally and are listed in alphabetical order. We appreciate the helpful comments and suggestions of Andrew Henderson and Rakesh Khurana on an earlier version of this article. The article has also benefited from the contributions of Rita Kosnik, Gregory Northcraft, and three anonymous reviewers for the *Academy of Management Journal*.

tors have suitable knowledge or information to contribute meaningfully to strategy. For instance, it has been repeatedly suggested that outside directors are often inadequately prepared to participate in board discussions because their time and attention are divided and diluted by their other board appointments; serving on boards at multiple companies makes it difficult for them to gain an adequate understanding of the issues facing any one firm. For these reasons, proponents of governance reform have strongly advocated limits to the number of boards upon which directors may sit (*BusinessWeek*, 1997).

A number of empirical studies have examined how board power and independence affect policy outcomes, but very little research represents an attempt to identify factors that determine whether boards have adequate knowledge and information to make meaningful contributions to strategic decision making. Moreover, research has not addressed the specific question of how multiple board appointments affect directors' ability to contribute to strategy. To address these questions, we developed a sociocognitive perspective on how appointments to other boards affect the capability of the members of a firm's board to monitor and advise its management in the strategic decision making process. We tested our theoretical perspective with a unique data set that combines archival reports with primary behavioral data obtained through surveys of *Forbes* 1000 outside directors and CEOs. The theoretical perspective and empirical analysis presented here may help answer recent calls for research that examines the "substantive context" of board appointments (Nohria, 1992: 14) and moves our understanding beyond the simple number of such appointments or director independence as predictors of board influence and decision making (Mizruchi, 1996; Pettigrew, 1992; Stinchcombe, 1990).

THEORY AND HYPOTHESES

Director Appointments and Board Involvement in Strategic Decision Making

The sociocognitive perspective developed in this study suggests the importance of directors' networks of appointments to other boards in determining whether they have the appropriate strategic knowledge and perspective to monitor and advise management in the strategic decision making process. As noted above, critics of corporate governance have typically argued that directors' appointments to other boards reduce their ability to contribute to decision making at a focal board. Such an argument assumes that the knowledge and perspective gained on other boards are largely irrelevant to decision making at the focal firm. In contrast, our sociocognitive perspective indicates how experience on other boards can enhance or diminish directors' ability to contribute to strategy, by focusing their attention on relevant strategic issues.

The sociocognitive perspective on organizational decision making suggests that individuals cope with complex decision making tasks by relying upon the schemata or "knowledge structures" they have developed about their environment (Kiesler & Sproull, 1982; Walsh, 1995). In the absence of complete information, or given uncertainty regarding the relevance of different pieces of information, individuals tend to follow a top-down or theory-driven approach to decision making, rather than a bottom-up or data-driven approach based on present information (Abelson & Black, 1986; Nisbett & Ross, 1980; Ocasio, 1997). Given the extreme information complexity facing directors in evaluating strategic decisions (Lorsch & MacIver, 1989), they can be expected to rely heavily upon the implicit theories that they have developed regarding corporate strategy and the competitive environment. Moreover, from this perspective, the knowledge structures that individuals use to cope with information-processing demands are developed from experience in similar roles (Dearborn & Simon, 1958; Walsh, 1995).

In our framework, directors are likely to use knowledge structures developed from their experience on other boards. The literature on interlocking directorates supports this view. This work demonstrates how the involvement of directors on other boards provides an important source of information about business practices and policies (cf. Mizruchi, 1996; Palmer, Jennings, & Zhou, 1993). For example, Useem (1982) observed that executives use their board appointments as a way to scan the environment for timely and pertinent information. He quoted several executives who suggest that board appointments provide a vehicle for learning, making such statements as "Direct involvement in other companies' affairs replaces an awful lot of reading . . . it's a hell of a tool for top management education" (1982: 209–210). Similarly, directors can learn about the efficacy of different practices and how to implement them properly by observing the consequences of management decisions (Haunschild, 1993). Such learning is particularly vivid because directors observe the decision-making process firsthand in their monitoring role, participate actively by giving advice to management, and then witness the consequences of those decisions.

Directors also learn about business practices through their communication with other directors in board and committee meetings. Information acquired from fellow directors may be particularly influential because it often comes from a trusted source (Davis, 1991; Useem, 1982; Weick, 1995). This information is typically more timely and up-to-date than that derived from secondary sources, and it may also be more salient because of its recency (Kahneman, Slovic, & Tversky, 1982). Thus, a sociocognitive perspective on board involvement emphasizes how directors' social structural context, including their ties to other boards, provides direct strategic experience and indirect access to strategic information through social contact with other directors. Such experience and information can, in turn, critically inform the knowledge structures used to monitor decisions or give advice on a focal board. In the following section, we further develop our sociocognitive perspective to consider variation in the strategic context of director ties to other boards, in order to address whether and when those ties provide relevant strategic knowledge and perspective for monitoring and advising the management of a focal firm.

Environmental Stability and Director Involvement in Strategic Decision Making

Related board ties and involvement in stable environments. Environmental stability refers to the extent to which a firm's competitive environment is complex, uncertain, and prone to strategic change (Huber & McDaniel, 1986). It is emphasized here because such stability is a key determinant of the particular strategic issues facing a firm and its top management (Duncan, 1972; Wiersema & Bantel, 1993). Accordingly, environmental stability may be an important determinant of how directors can contribute to strategic decision making. Theory and research on environmental turbulence and strategic decision making distinguish between two basic strategic issues in the decision-making process—the development of new strategies and the implementation of existing strategies—and suggest that, in stable environments, the latter is more important. Specifically, if there is less change in an environment, there is less need to regularly identify new strategic alternatives in order to maintain fit with the environment, so firms in stable environments are more likely to compete primarily through the better implementation of existing strategies (Andrews, 1971; Fredrickson, 1984; Ginsberg, 1990; Tushman & Romanelli, 1985). Moreover, Fama and Jensen (1983) explicitly recognized board monitoring of strategy implementation as an important component of a board's obligation to protect shareholders.

How then might directors' ties to other boards enhance their ability to monitor and advise management on the implementation of existing strategies in a stable environment? We suggest that directors will be better able to contribute to strategy in such an environment when their other board ties are *strategically related* to the focal firm. Strategically related board ties refer to a director's appointments to the boards of other companies that follow similar corporate strategies and operate in similar product-market and international market contexts. A central tenet of the strategy literature is that the effectiveness of strategy implementation is contingent on strategy content (Barney & Zajac, 1994; Galbraith & Kazanjian, 1986). For instance, research suggests that a strategy of diversification requires different kinds of corporate reward systems and information systems than strategies that focus on a single market (Galbraith & Merrill, 1991; Gerhart & Milkovich, 1990; Gomez-Mejia, 1992). Thus, given that strategically related ties enable directors to observe firsthand the experiences of other firms in implementing similar strategies, they provide directors with a more sophisticated understanding of the combination of systems and structures needed for successful implementation of the firm's strategy. Moreover, strategically related board ties also help directors acquire relevant knowledge through social interaction with other directors in board and committee meetings, as board members evaluate management and raise ideas and suggestions for better strategy implementation.

From a sociocognitive perspective, these social connections and opportunities for vicarious learning can lead to more highly developed knowledge structures for implementing the focal firm's strategy. Research on sociocognition has shown that individuals who have experience concentrated in a related domain, rather than dispersed across different contexts, have more highly developed knowledge structures for that domain, with fewer schema categories and more information units per category (Day & Lord, 1992; Lurigio & Carroll, 1985; Sujan, Sujan, & Bettman, 1988). As a result, individuals engaging in problem solving for domains (such as strategy) where they have concentrated experience not only have more information at their disposal, but also have more efficiently structured information, and this leads to faster and more accurate information processing (Day & Lord, 1992).

Thus, to the extent that firms in stable environments compete primarily through better implementation of existing strategies (rather than identification of new strategies to fit a changing environment), strategically related board ties should enhance directors' ability to contribute to strategic decision making in stable environments through monitoring and advice interactions. This point suggests several related hypotheses. The first hypothesis addresses the effect of a director's appointments to other boards on his or her perceived ability to contribute to a focal board. Involvement with other firms following strategies similar to those of a focal firm better equips a director to monitor management decision making and provide relevant information and advice to managers on the focal board. Thus, such an individual may perceive him or herself to be better able to contribute to strategic decision making. In effect, a director's perceived ability to contribute to decision making is expected to mediate the effect of appointments to other boards on involvement in monitoring and advice interactions. The first hypothesis, which predicts that strategically related board appointments will increase a director's perceived ability to contribute to decision making, concerns one portion of this mediated relationship.

Two additional hypotheses address the overall, board-level relationship between the portfolio of all directors' appointments and actual board behavior. As discussed above, boards may contribute to strategic decision making by regularly monitoring the decision-making process, as suggested by agency theorists, or by providing advice to top managers on strategic issues. The theoretical perspective developed here suggests that in stable environments, board appointments to strategically related firms should enhance the capacity of a focal firm's board members to contribute to strategic decision making through increased monitoring activity or the provision of more advice to management on strategic issues. Thus,

Hypothesis 1a. In a stable environment, the appointment of a director to the boards of other firms that are strategically related to the focal firm will increase the director's perceived ability to contribute to board discussions of strategic issues.

Hypothesis 1b. In a stable environment, the appointment of a director to the boards of other firms that are strategically related to the focal firm will increase the level of board monitoring of strategic decision making.

Hypothesis 1c. In a stable environment, the appointment of a director to the boards of other firms that are strategically related to the focal firm will increase the level of board advice interactions on strategic issues.

Heterogeneous board ties and involvement in unstable environments. As noted above, unstable environments are characterized by a relatively high level of unpredictable change or volatility (Aldrich, 1979; Duncan, 1972; Sharfman & Dean, 1991), which places considerable information-processing demands on corporate leaders (Carpenter & Fredrickson, 2001; Fredrickson & Mitchell, 1984; Priem, 1990; Wiersema & Bantel, 1993). In such environments, organizational success often depends on the ability of top managers to identify new strategic alternatives that maintain an organization's fit with its changing environment (Haleblian & Finkelstein, 1993; Tushman & Anderson, 1986). Thus, leaders must not only attend to the current strategy, but must also recognize when and how that strategy should be changed.

Our sociocognitive perspective suggests that in turbulent environments, directors' ability to contribute to strategy is enhanced by a combination of strategically related board ties and ties to firms that follow different strategies than does a focal firm. As in stable environments, board involvement with similar companies provides information and knowledge that can enhance a director's ability to monitor the firm's current strategy. Moreover, board ties to similar companies can also help a director stay abreast of changes in the business environment.

However, board involvement with companies following different strategies and operating in different business environments typically provides directors with greater knowledge and insight about a broad range of potential strategic alternatives. As discussed above, our perspective suggests that board ties to firms with related strategies can provide firsthand experience and indirect information through social contact with other directors that leads to more highly developed knowledge structures related to implementing a firm's current strategy. Research has also shown that well-developed knowledge structures can hinder effective information processing outside an individual's area of expertise. For instance, individuals with more concentrated exposure to a particular problem-solving approach or strategy are less likely to notice or consider alternative approaches (Dutton & Duncan, 1987; Ocasio, 1997). Thus, when directors' other appointments are concentrated among similar companies, they are less likely to notice strategic alternatives emerging in other environments. In effect directors' schemata for major strategic alternatives are highly focused on a limited range of options.

Similarly, the social cohesion perspective on network ties suggests that if the appointments of the directors of a firm's board are highly concentrated among firms with very similar strategies, these individuals are more likely to become socialized into accepting the firm's current strategy (Burt, 1987; Palmer et al., 1993). Social network ties, including board interlock ties, channel social influence as well as information (Burt, 1987; Davis, 1991; Walker, 1985). Thus, through their participation in monitoring implementation of similar strategies at other firms, directors with strategically related board ties should tend to develop beliefs that justify those strategies and accept them as appropriate. As a result, when external appointments are largely concentrated among firms with strategies similar to the focal firm's, this similarity may reinforce existing managerial commitment to the current strategy and lead directors to ignore environmental changes that threaten its long-term viability (note that strategically related ties may not increase commitment to the current mode of strategy *implementation,* because such ties link the focal board with firms that have similar strategy *content,* but not necessarily similar implementation).

Thus, in turbulent environments, directors can benefit from interlocks that expose them to possible strategic alternatives. Such ties effectively broaden the schemata or knowledge structures that directors use in monitoring and advising management, so that boards are not only more likely to identify appropriate strategic alternatives to a current strategy, but are also more willing to change the current strategy in order to maintain the organization's fit with its changing environment. In effect, board ties to firms with different strategies can help prevent or counteract excessive managerial commitment to a firm's current strategy (Hambrick, Geletkanycz, & Fredrickson, 1993; Weick, 1995). Alternatively, when director appointments are concentrated among strategically dissimilar firms, with very few board ties to firms following similar strategies, a board may lack sufficient expertise to monitor the firm's current strategy or to assess the organizational implications of abandoning the strategy. Indeed, a common dilemma facing firms is how to develop new strategies while simultaneously implementing current strategies (Kazanjian & Drazin, 1987). Therefore, in unstable environments, an optimal portfolio of outsider board appointments may include a heterogeneous mix of ties to strategically similar and dissimilar firms (that is, both firms with strategies similar to those of the focal firm and those with dissimilar strategies). Such heterogeneity is likely to wed the knowledge and expertise requisite to monitor ongoing implementation of the current strategy with information and advice about possible strategic alternatives that would allow the firm to maintain fit with its changing environment (Ginsberg, 1990).

This perspective is consistent with the view, presented in the top management team literature, that exposure to different beliefs about means-ends relationships (different beliefs about what strategies lead to high performance) through greater diversity of backgrounds and experience can facilitate adaptation in turbulent environments by stimulating debate about the appropriateness of a current strategy and about the feasibility of strategic alternatives (Boeker, 1997; Bourgeois, 1980; Haleblian & Finkelstein, 1993; Hambrick & Mason, 1984). Moreover, the larger literature on demographic diversity suggests that diversity in job-related experience (in this case, experience in strategic decision making on other boards) tends to have beneficial effects on group process and performance. In contrast, diversity on visible, or non-job-related, characteristics (such as age) is less likely to have such beneficial outcomes (Carpenter & Fredrickson, 2001; Jehn, Chadwick, & Thatcher, 1997: 300; O'Reilly, Snyder, & Boothe, 1993; Pelled, 1996; Williams & O'Reilly, 1998). Research on small group decision making suggests that the positive effects of job-related diversity on group performance are mediated by task-related conflict, and the more negative effects of non-work-related diversity are mediated by affective or relationship conflict. In summarizing this literature, Jehn and colleagues stated that "visible individual demographic differences increase relationship conflict, while informational demographic differences increase task-focused conflict [and] conflict researchers . . . have recently found that while relationship conflicts based on personality clashes and interpersonal dislike are detrimental to group functioning, task conflicts based on disagreements regarding the specific task content are beneficial in many situations" (Jehn et al., 1997: 287–288). Similarly, Williams and O'Reilly stated that "In general, research shows that functional diversity [diversity on a job-related characteristic] has positive effects on group performance" (1998: 100), and they also attributed this overall finding to higher levels of task conflict in diverse groups.

Moreover, job-related diversity is particularly likely to enhance group functioning when individuals know each other (Pelled, Eisenhardt, & Xin, 1999; Williams & O'Reilly, 1998). According to Williams and O'Reilly, "Ironically, laboratory studies have shown that groups may be more able to use unique information when group members are familiar with one another instead of being strangers" (1998: 99). Pelled and colleagues (1999) showed that such familiarity reduces emotional conflict resulting from demographic diversity. For these reasons, heterogeneous experiences among board members may not enhance affective conflict, given abundant evidence that directors of *Forbes* 1000 firms are not only familiar with one another, but often form cohesive social bonds in board and committee meetings and through social interaction outside of formal meetings (Useem, 1982).

Thus, in our sociocognitive framework, diversity in the strategic experience of board members through network ties to other firms should enhance their ability to contribute in turbulent environments by engendering debate or task-related conflict about a firm's current strategy. Such interaction should facilitate adaptation to environmental changes (Wiersema & Bantel, 1992). Moreover, given the social cohesion characterizing most boards, the benefits of debate and task-related conflict among directors should not be overwhelmed by affective conflict. These benefits from diversity in strategy experience are less relevant in stable environments where there is less need to engage in strategic change to maintain fit with the environment.

This argument leads to a second set of hypotheses. Hypothesis 2a, which parallels Hypothesis 1a, addresses how an individual director's board appointments may enhance her or his perceived ability to contribute to decision making, given that such perceptions are expected to mediate the effect of appointments to other boards on involvement in monitoring and advice interactions. Our theoretical argument that heterogeneous board ties can enhance involvement in turbulent environments implies that, to the extent that an individual director's board ties complement the ties of other directors with respect to strategic relatedness, thus increasing board heterogeneity, the director should be better able to contribute to the board through monitoring and advice interactions. According to this logic, for instance, a director with many board appointments to strategically dissimilar firms is particularly valuable to a focal board if the ties of other directors are concentrated among strategically similar firms. Two additional hypotheses, 2b and 2c, which parallel Hypotheses 1b and 1c, address how board-level ties may affect actual board behaviors in unstable environments. The theoretical argument developed above would suggest that in such environments, boards with a heterogeneous mix of links to both strategically different and strategically similar firms should be better able to contribute to strategic decision making through either increased monitoring activity or more frequent advice to management on strategic issues.

Hypothesis 2a. In an unstable environment, the greater the extent to which a director's board appointments to other firms complement the appointments of other directors in their strategic relatedness to the focal firm, the greater the director's perceived ability to contribute to board discussions of strategic issues.

Hypothesis 2b. In an unstable environment, the greater the extent to which directors' board appointments are heterogeneous in their strategic relatedness to the focal firm, the higher the level of board monitoring of strategic decision making.

Hypothesis 2c. In an unstable environment, the greater the extent to which directors' board appointments are heterogeneous in their strategic relatedness to the focal firm, the higher the level of board advice interactions on strategic issues.

METHODS

Sample and Data Collection

The sample frame for this study consisted of 600 large and medium-sized companies randomly selected from the *Forbes* 1000 index of U.S. industrial and service firms. To gauge the behavioral processes that characterize board involvement in strategic decision making, we sent a questionnaire survey to all 600 CEOs from these companies. In addition, to assess directors' perceptions about their involvement, we sent a second survey to each individual serving as an outside director at a company whose CEO had responded to the first survey (n = 1,312). All surveys were distributed in April 1995.

Although surveys have been used frequently to measure behavioral processes at lower levels of organizations, surveys of top managers have often suffered from low response rates (less than 25 percent). To ensure the highest possible response in this case, we took the following steps (Fowler, 1993; Groves, Cialdini, & Couper, 1992): (1) An in-depth pretest was used to streamline the survey, making it easier and more appealing to complete (see further discussion below); (2) requests for participation linked the current study with an ongoing series of surveys on top management issues conducted by a major business school (to which hundreds of these CEOs' peers had responded), emphasized the need for research on CEO-board relations, and engaged respondents' natural interest in the topic (see Groves et al., 1992); and (3) about 21 days after the initial mailing, nonrespondents were sent a second letter with a new questionnaire. In total, 263 CEOs and 564 outside directors responded, representing response rates of 44 percent and 43 percent, respectively. These response rates are high in comparison to those of other top management surveys (cf. Pettigrew, 1992). Data on diversification, internationalization, or board interlocks were unavailable for 35 of the responding companies; thus, survey data from 228 CEOs and 492 outside directors are used in the analyses, numbers representing 38 percent of all CEOs and directors in the sample frame (that is, on the average, the final sample includes 2.2 directors per company in the CEO survey).

To check for nonresponse bias, we collected archival data for companies in the larger sample frame. For the 531 companies with complete data, we examined whether respondents and nonrespondents differed significantly on several different variables derived from archival sources using the Kolmogorov-Smirnov two-sample test (Siegel & Castellan, 1988). This test assesses whether significant differences exist in the distribution of respondents and nonrespondents for a given variable, including differences in central tendency, dispersion, skewness, and so forth. The results of this test provide consistent evidence across multiple variables that respondents and nonrespondents come from the same population. Moreover, separate analyses also showed that directors in the survey sample were representative of directors in the larger sample frame (all outside directors at the 531 companies for which complete archival data were available) with respect to (1) the independent variables (such as relatedness of individual directors' board ties), and (2) director characteristics included as control variables in the study (such as management experience, education level, board tenure, and functional background). Thus, it appears that sample selection bias was not present in the data.

Data on board interlocks, director characteristics, ownership, and board structure were obtained from the following sources: *Standard & Poor's Register of Corporations, Directors, and Executives,* the *Dun & Bradstreet Reference Book of Corporate Managements, Who's Who in Finance and Industry,* and corporate proxy statements. Data on firm diversification and international operations were obtained from the PC-COMPUSTAT Business Segment Database and from Compact Disclosure. Size and performance data were also obtained from PC-COMPUSTAT. All independent and control variables were gauged in the period $t - 1$, and dependent variables were gauged at time t.

Dependent Measures

Data for our three dependent variables, *directors' perceived ability to contribute to board discussions, board monitoring,* and *board advice interactions* were gathered through surveys. To enhance the construct validity of the survey measures, we conducted a pretest involving in-depth pilot interviews with 22 top managers and board members (cf. Fowler, 1993: 102). Following Judge and Zeithaml (1992), in the questionnaire we defined strategic issues as nonroutine, resource allocation decisions that should affect the performance of an organization. We further sought to develop survey questions that would assess a board's involvement in *either* the implementation or the consideration of new strategies. We used feedback from participants in the pretest to ensure that the items would capture both areas of strategic issue involvement and, in the survey, included additional questions that focus on each area of involvement. After completing the pilot questionnaire, each individual was asked to identify questions that were unclear, difficult to answer, or potentially subject to bias. These interviews were also used to ensure that questions were interpreted as expected, to identify improvements to the format of the survey, and to modify its length. Multiple response formats were used to reduce response bias, and items measuring each construct were scattered throughout the survey (DeVellis, 1991). Moreover, we carefully worded questions to minimize the likelihood of social desirability bias, using input from the pilot interviews.

Director's perceived ability to contribute to board discussions was measured with a multi-item scale in the director survey. Specific items in this scale assess the degree to which directors perceive that they have sufficient knowledge on relevant strategic issues to contribute to board discussions and the degree to which they feel adequately prepared to contribute. Cronbach's alpha for this scale was .88, suggesting acceptable interitem reliability (Nunnally, 1978). After a factor analysis was applied to the survey items using the iterated principal factors method, a scree test indicated one common factor, and promax rotation verified that all items loaded on the same factor as expected, with loadings for each item greater than .5. Thus, we estimated factor scores using the Bartlett method (Harman, 1976).

Board advice interactions and *board monitoring* were also assessed with multi-item scales. The wording of each question was developed from available qualitative research (Alderfer, 1986; Demb & Neubauer, 1992; Lorsch & MacIver, 1989) suggesting how top managers and directors describe CEO-board interaction and the board's role vis-à-vis management (for instance, as a sounding board on strategic issues); in addition, we used feedback from the pilot interviews to further improve the clarity and face validity of each question. For instance, questions about advice interactions asked about the extent to which the CEO solicited board input on corporate strategy and the frequency of advice and council discussions with board members, and monitoring questions asked about the extent to which the board monitored strategic decision making or evaluated CEO performance. The Appendix gives specific items. These measures assess monitoring and advice interactions at the board level. We also conducted separate analyses of individual director involvement in monitoring and advice interactions; the results of these analyses were consistent with those reported below for boards.

The iterated principal factors method was then again applied to the survey items. A scree test showed two common factors, and promax rotation indicated that the monitoring and advice items loaded on different factors as expected, with loadings for each item greater than .5 on one factor and less than .2 on the other. Furthermore, Cronbach's alpha was .92 for the monitoring scale and .89 for the advice interactions scale, again indicating acceptable reliability (Nunnally, 1978). Accordingly, given encouraging evidence regarding interitem reliability and discriminant validity (that is, the factor loadings suggesting that CEOs discriminated between the two constructs as expected), we also estimated the monitoring and advice factors using the Bartlett method (Harman, 1976)

Further analyses were conducted to assess the interrater reliability of these measures. Specifically, we compared CEO and outside director responses by calculating kappa coefficients for the monitoring and advice items. Kappa is a correlation coefficient that corrects for the expected level of correlation between raters (chance correlation). Values exceeding .75 are typically thought to indicate excellent agreement beyond chance, and values between .40 and .75 are considered indicative of fair to good agreement beyond chance (Fleiss, 1981; Landis & Koch, 1977). The sample for this analysis included companies with a responding CEO and at least one responding director ($n = 188$). Kappa coefficients exceed .75 for all survey items but one, which achieved .73, and the overall kappa is .82. Given these high levels of interrater reliability, it is perhaps not surprising that the hypothesized effects presented below were substantively unchanged when monitoring and advice interactions were measured with director responses rather than CEO responses, or vice-versa.

Independent Measures

Related board appointments in stable environments. Hypotheses 1a–1c predict the effects of individual directors' board appointments to other firms that are strategically related to a focal firm. In our measures of relatedness, inside and outside directors were combined, as separate analyses revealed no significant differences in results when we distinguished between the two.

We measured relatedness across four different strategic dimensions that have been studied extensively in the strategy literature (e.g., Kim, 1989; Porter, 1986, 1998; Rumelt, 1974): First, *board appointments related by product market* were measured as the number of a director's appointments to the boards of companies in a primary business similar (having the same four-digit Standard Industrial Classification [SIC] code) to that of a focal firm, divided by the director's total number of appointments. Second, *board appointments related by foreign market* were measured by counting appointments to the boards of companies with the same primary foreign market as a focal firm, normalized by the number of appointments. For example, two firms that reported France as their primary foreign market would exhibit a high degree of foreign market relatedness. In separate analyses, we weighted appointments according to the difference between a focal firm's presence in each of its markets (as a portion of total sales) and the appointed-to firm's presence. The results presented below were substantively unchanged, demonstrating that they were robust to different measures of foreign market relatedness.

For the third dimension of strategic relatedness, we assessed the *diversification* of a focal firm and of the other firms to which a director was connected using the entropy measure (Palepu, 1985). This measure takes into account the number of segments in which a firm operates and weights each segment according to its contribution to total sales. It is defined as follows: $\Sigma P_i \times \ln(1/P_i)$, where P is the sales (dollar value) attributed to segment i and $\ln(1/P_i)$ is the weight for each segment i, or the logarithm of the inverse of its sales. We calculated the absolute difference between the diversification of a focal firm and the diversification of each of the other firms to which a director was connected. The difference scores were then added and normalized by the total number of appointments. This figure was then subtracted from the highest value of diversification dissimilarity in the sample, so that higher values indicate greater relatedness. The reason for calculating relatedness as an average can be illustrated with the following example: say one firm's board (A) has 18 ties with firms that are relatively dissimilar to the focal firm (the relatedness is .1 for each tie), and another board (B) has three ties with firms that are very similar to the focal firm (the relatedness is .6 for each tie). Failing to normalize these measures would give each board a comparable relatedness score, when in fact B's directors have more related experience.

Appointments *related by degree of internationalization,* our fourth dimension, were measured with a variation of the *degree of internationalization* (*DOI*) composite measure validated by Sullivan (1994). This measure gauges internationalization in terms of three important and theoretically distinct characteristics. The first characteristic, foreign sales, is calculated as a ratio of foreign sales to total sales and reflects a firm's dependence on sales to foreign markets. The second characteristic, foreign production, reflects a firm's reliance on owned foreign asset stocks and is measured by foreign assets as a percentage of total assets. As in research on international business, here the sales and asset characteristics address a firm's dependence on foreign consumer markets and dependence on foreign production resources, respectively. The third characteristic, geographic dispersion, gauges a firm's number of country subsidiaries as a percentage of the highest number of country subsidiaries represented in our sample. Sullivan (1994) found that this characteristic provided a rough indication of the cultural variety associated with the previous two dimensions (Johansen & Vahlne, 1977). All three DOI variables range theoretically from 0 to 1.

Foreign sales, foreign production, and geographic dispersion are summed to form our composite measure of DOI, which therefore has a theoretical range of 0 to 3. Like Sullivan (1994), we found that these variables demonstrated high inter-item reliability ($\alpha = .86$) and loaded on one factor with a high eigenvalue and high explained variance and that the composite measure was normally distributed. There are several single-indicator measures of DOI, including number of foreign subsidiaries and ratios such as foreign sales to total sales, foreign assets to total assets, and number of foreign employees to total employees, but Sullivan showed that these other measures are highly correlated. To gauge relatedness on this dimension of strategy, we calculated the absolute difference between the DOI of a focal firm and the DOI of each of the other firms to which a director was connected. Again, the difference scores were added and normalized by the number of appointments. We then subtracted this figure from the highest value of DOI dissimilarity in the sample to create an index of relatedness.

Hypotheses 1b and 1c predict the effects of board-level appointments to other firms that are strategically related to a focal firm on board behavior. To test these hypotheses, we developed a set of aggregate variables for the relatedness of individual director appointments across all directors on a board. For instance, we calculated product market similarity by counting the number of companies to which the focal firm was connected by a board tie in a primary business (as reflected in a four-digit SIC code) similar to that of the focal firm, divided by the total number of appointments. For analyses conducted at the level of the individual director, predicting the director's perceived ability to contribute (Hypotheses 1a and 2a), the variables were calculated for the particular director.

Heterogeneous board appointments in unstable environments. To test Hypotheses 2a through 2c, we developed separate measures of the heterogeneity of board appointments. First, we assessed the extent to which an individual director's board appointments to other firms differed from the appointments of other directors in their strategic relatedness to a focal firm by calculating the absolute value of the difference between the director's relatedness score on a given strategic dimension and the average relatedness scores of other directors on the board (the measure of relatedness is defined above). High values indicated that a director's appointments differed from the appointments of other board members on a given dimension of relatedness. For example, if other directors had many appointments to firms with very similar international presences, a director with more appointments to firms with international strategy that differed from the focal firm's would have a relatively high heterogeneity score on that dimension.

Finally, we developed a set of variables measuring strategic heterogeneity at the board level to assess the effect of board appointments on involvement in turbulent environments. We measured the extent to which a board's portfolio of director appointments is heterogeneous in its relatedness on a given dimension as $(\Sigma|r_i - \bar{r}|)/n$, where r_i is the relatedness score for director i, $\bar{r}$ is the average relatedness for the board, and n is the number of board members (note that this board-level measure excludes duplicate ties to the same firm). Higher values indicated greater heterogeneity in strategic relatedness; conversely, smaller values indicated that a firm's appointments were concentrated among firms that were either relatively similar or relatively dissimilar to the focal firm on a given strategic dimension.

Other Measures

Environmental instability, the change rate of environmental factors relevant to strategic decision making (Duncan, 1972), is often a function of an industry's competitive dynamics (Chen, 1996; Wiersema & Bantel, 1993). Following Wiersema and Bantel (1993), we measured environmental instability as changes in the industry concentration ratio. This ratio is calculated as the percentage of an industry's sales, at the four-digit SIC level, accounted for by the four largest firms. Large absolute changes in the concentration ratio indicate high environmental instability. Such change reflects "shifts in market share due to new entrants, exits, consolidations, and erosion of market share, thus they capture the dynamic nature of a firm's industrial environment" (Wiersema & Bantel, 1993: 493). We observed change over the three-year period prior to the survey date (1992–94). Moreover, we used (monthly) stock price volatility as an alternative measure of instability (calculated as the average annual price coefficient of variation across all firms in the industry in a particular year [Haunschild & Miner, 1997]). The results presented below were substantively unchanged, demonstrating that they were robust to alternate measures of environmental instability.

Several control variables were also included in the models. Following Wiersema and Bantel's (1992) classification scheme for level of education, we controlled for directors' education level using number of years of schooling (cf. Kosnik, 1987). A director's years of higher-level education may indicate knowledge pertinent to strategic decision making, which may affect ability to contribute in potentially competing ways to appointment to other boards. Similarly, more extensive general management experience could also be associated with directors' ability to monitor and advise management. Therefore, we also controlled for *management experience,* measured as the number of years during which a director had previously worked on a top management team. In addition, we also controlled for the number of *functional areas* in which directors had prior experience, because their ability to contribute may be enhanced if they have a broader base of prior experience (see Finkelstein, 1992). Directors may acquire firm-specific expertise over time; therefore, their *tenure* may influence the ability of directors to monitor and advise management. Thus, we controlled for the number of years directors had served on a board. Each of these four variables was averaged across directors in the board-level models.

We also controlled for the *prior level of diversification* and *internationalization,* since the complexities involved in managing highly diversified and/or international firms may tend to require greater monitoring and/or advice capabilities (Sanders & Carpenter, 1998; Zajac & Westphal, 1994). For similar reasons, we controlled for firm size, measured as the natural logarithm of firm *sales.* In addition, we controlled for prior firm performance in models of board monitoring and advice interactions. An adaptation perspective would suggest that relatively poor firm performance could prompt CEOs to appoint directors with relevant appointments to other boards to enhance the board's capability to monitor and/or provide advice (Cyert & March, 1963). Two recent studies have provided evidence for a negative relationship between firm performance and board involvement in strategic decision making (Johnson, Hoskisson, & Hitt, 1993; Judge & Zeithaml, 1992). Accordingly, we included two measures of firm performance: *prior return on equity,* an accounting-based measure, and *prior market-to-book value,* a market-based measure.

Several studies contain the argument that CEOs co-opt boards, rendering them passive by appointing their friends as directors (e.g., Finkelstein & Hambrick, 1988). Some researchers have also suggested that a CEO secures the passivity of outside directors simply by appointing them to the board (Alderfer, 1986; Boeker, 1992; Wade et al., 1990). Moreover, recent research has shown that top managers' openness to board advice is largely determined by the portion of a board composed of a CEO's personal friends and the portion of the board composed of directors appointed after the CEO was appointed (Westphal, 1999). Thus, we controlled for these variables (*CEO-board friendship ties* and *appointments after the CEO*) in the analyses, measuring friendship ties with questions in the CEO survey. We also included *CEO ownership* as a control variable in the monitoring and advice models. Agency theorists have argued that incentives can provide an alternative or substitute for board monitoring, and incentives can also motivate top managers to seek advice from a board (Beatty & Zajac, 1994; Rediker & Seth, 1995). Moreover, incentives could motivate other directors to monitor strategic decision making more actively and to offer their expertise on strategic issues (Bergh, 1995). Thus, we controlled for *director ownership* in analyses of board monitoring and advice interactions. In addition, we controlled for *board size* in these models, given that large boards may be less cohesive and thus less able to monitor decision making effectively (Johnson et al., 1993). We also controlled for board size in models of directors' perceived ability to contribute to decision making because each director might see himself or herself as having less opportunity to contribute on a large board.

Prior studies have also examined whether a board's leadership structure is related to indicators of the board's ability to control management (e.g., Baliga et al., 1996; Finkelstein, 1992; Mallette & Fowler, 1992). Thus, we controlled for *leadership structure* in models of board monitoring, using a dichotomous variable coded 1 if the CEO and board chair positions were separate and 0 otherwise. Although we did not expect board centrality to independently affect board involvement, in separate analyses we included different measures of centrality, such as in-degree centrality and the Bonacich measure (Wasserman & Faust, 1994); these measures yielded consistently nonsignificant results, and the hypothesized effects on board monitoring and advice interactions were unchanged. We also did not expect the hypothesized effects on advice interactions to be affected by the level of monitoring, or vice-versa, because the dependent variables were lagged and negatively correlated; separate analyses confirmed that the results were unchanged when the monitoring was included in the advice models and advice was included in the monitoring models.

RESULTS

Table 1 provides the means, standard deviations, and bivariate correlations for all data used to analyze predictions of directors' perceived ability to contribute to board discussions. Table 2 provides these descriptive statistics for all data used to analyze predictions of board monitoring and advice interactions. Given that all our dependent variables were continuous and that the independent variables were continuous or categorical, multiple ordinary least squares (OLS) regression analysis was the primary statistical technique employed. The entire sample was dichotomized at the median of the environmental stability measure, with those firms falling below the median accordingly classified as in relatively stable industries and those falling above it classified as in relatively unstable industries. Thus, we ran separate sets of regressions for each subsample (stable and unstable) and another set using the product-term approach to test interaction effects. Analyses of directors' ability to contribute to board discussions were conducted for the sample of responding directors, and analyses of board monitoring and advice interactions were conducted for all companies in the survey sample. Tables 3 and 4 present regression results.

Results of the multiple regression analysis testing Hypothesis 1a support the prediction that related appointments will be positively associated with directors' perceptions of their ability to contribute to board discussions in stable environments (Table 3). For example, the coefficients for product-market, diversification, and internationalization relatedness were all positive and significant. And,

TABLE 1
Descriptive Statistics and Pearson Correlation Coefficients for Analyses of Directors' Perceived Ability to Contribute to Board Discussions[a]

Variable	Mean	s.d.	1a	1b	1c	1d	2a	2b	2c	2d	3	4	5	6	7	8	9	10	11
Board ties weighted by:																			
1a. Product-market relatedness	0.39	0.29																	
1b. Foreign market relatedness	0.51	0.28	.16																
1c. Diversification relatedness	0.52	0.25	.19	.10															
1d. Internationalization relatedness	0.46	0.31	.23	.16	.09														
Board ties weighted by complementarity in:																			
2a. Product-market relatedness	0.32	0.28	−.09	.05	.04	−.10													
2b. Foreign market relatedness	0.30	0.24	.11	.22	.02	.07	.16												
2c. Diversification relatedness	0.28	0.21	.03	.01	−.10	.04	.16	.14											
2d. Internationalization relatedness	0.35	0.26	.06	−.12	.06	.03	.21	.16	.07										
3. Education level	15.96	1.30	.07	.05	.05	.12	.04	.04	−.07	−.03									
4. Tenure on the board	9.68	7.72	.13	.07	.07	.05	.07	.11	.03	−.04	.08								
5. Functional areas	1.29	0.91	.03	.16	.12	.03	.05	.08	−.04	.02	.07	−.02							
6. Management experience	21.32	12.99	.01	.16	.09	.05	.01	.04	.16	.06	.02	.15	.19						
7. Focal firm diversification	0.76	0.52	.18	.12	.20	.08	.01	.08	.20	.07	−.01	.07	.09	.07					
8. Focal firm internationalization	0.68	0.48	.12	.15	.15	.19	.09	.07	.02	.18	.17	.04	.05	.06	.27				
9. Logarithm of sales	7.62	1.50	.04	−.03	−.15	−.08	−.01	.03	.01	.02	.01	.09	−.01	.08	.25	.16			
10. Board size	12.41	3.54	.06	.09	.02	.03	−.05	.06	−.04	.08	−.01	.04	.03	−.02	.13	.10	.11		
11. Perceived ability to contribute	0.00	0.89	.16	.09	.19	.16	.15	.10	.17	.19	.07	.26	.16	.04	−.16	−.12	.05	−.13	

[a] $n = 492$ directors; for correlations greater than .13, $p < .05$.

TABLE 2

Descriptive Statistics and Pearson Correlation Coefficients for Analyses of Board Monitoring and Advice Interactions[a]

Variable	Mean	s.d.	1a	1b	1c	1d	2a	2b	2c	2d	3	4	5	6	7	8	9	10	11	12	13	14	15	16	17	18
Board ties weighted by:																										
1a. Product-market relatedness	0.41	0.23																								
1b. Foreign market relatedness	0.53	0.21	.16																							
1c. Diversification relatedness	0.46	0.20	.19	.07																						
1d. Internationalization relatedness	0.44	0.25	.23	.16	.08																					
Board ties weighted by heterogeneity in:																										
2a. Product-market relatedness	0.29	0.25	−.12	.03	.04	−.07																				
2b. Foreign market relatedness	0.24	0.22	.13	.23	.02	.06	.13																			
2c. Diversification relatedness	0.24	0.19	−.04	.01	−.07	.06	.13	.08																		
2d. Internationalization relatedness	0.31	0.22	.05	−.10	−.03	−.03	.20	.17	.07																	
3. Education level	15.98	0.76	.05	−.03	.05	.09	.04	.03	−.07	−.04																
4. Tenure on the board	9.88	5.84	.09	.02	.04	.04	.08	.06	.09	−.05	.07															
5. Functional areas	1.31	0.71	.03	.13	.07	.03	.04	.12	−.07	.02	.02	−.02														
6. Management experience	21.20	8.09	.00	.10	.08	.05	.01	.00	.19	.04	−.05	.03	.21													
7. CEO ownership	0.05	0.06	.04	.06	.03	.08	.13	.08	.06	.06	.04	.01	−.02	.05												
8. CEO-board friendship ties	0.39	0.35	.02	.09	.01	.06	.01	.12	.11	.03	.03	.04	−.05	.01	.04											
9. Appointments after the CEO	0.31	0.25	.04	.17	.02	.11	.13	.12	.04	−.01	−.01	−.13	−.02	.07	.02	.27										
10. Director ownership	0.06	0.08	.02	−.01	.05	.11	.05	−.02	.00	.08	.03	.12	.07	.06	.14	−.03	.01									
11. Prior return on equity	0.13	0.11	.12	.03	−.01	.04	.03	.05	.03	.04	.09	−.16	.03	−.01	.03	−.07	−.05	.08								
12. Prior market-to-book value	1.63	1.07	.12	.02	.05	.05	.04	.06	.02	−.02	.07	−.07	.05	−.03	.11	−.07	−.01	.11	.26							
13. Focal firm diversification	0.72	0.53	.16	.12	.24	.06	.11	.03	.25	.04	−.01	.06	.09	.07	−.10	.04	.03	−.04	−.07	−.10						
14. Focal firm internationalization	0.67	0.49	.12	.20	.09	.20	.08	.23	.03	.19	.15	.04	.05	.07	−.08	−.15	.05	.07	.06	.04	.26					
15. Logarithm of sales	7.60	1.52	.04	−.02	−.11	−.10	−.01	.02	.04	−.09	.01	.10	−.01	.09	−.04	−.05	.14	−.13	.02	.03	.25	.16				
16. Board size	12.33	3.47	.03	.08	.04	.03	−.10	.09	−.07	.03	−.02	.05	.03	−.01	−.02	−.04	−.01	.12	−.01	.02	.11	.08	.10			
17. Board leadership structure	0.29	0.46	.15	.08	.01	.17	.09	.05	.20	.11	.02	−.07	.01	.01	.12	−.25	−.26	.01	.09	−.02	−.06	−.10	.13	.02		
18. Board monitoring	0.00	0.87	.20	.16	.28	.16	.21	.17	.23	.24	.11	.17	.15	.08	−.16	−.26	−.10	.25	.12	−.10	−.18	−.22	−.04	.02	.32	
19. Board advice interactions	0.00	0.80	.21	.15	.20	.19	.16	.12	.27	.20	.10	.19	.15	.04	.13	.22	.27	.14	−.10	−.07	−.14	−.17	−.06	.01	−.05	−.15

[a] $n = 228$ firms; for correlations greater than .13, $p < .05$.

TABLE 3
Results of Multiple Regression Analysis for Stable Environments[a]

	Hypothesis 1a: Director Contribution		Hypothesis 1b: Board Monitoring		Hypothesis 1c: Board Advice Interactions	
Independent Variable	**Model 1**	**Model 2**	**Model 1**	**Model 2**	**Model 1**	**Model 2**
1. Board ties weighted by:						
Product-market relatedness		0.44 (0.17)**		0.57 (0.28)*		0.71 (0.29)**
Foreign market relatedness		0.07 (0.18)		0.07 (0.33)		0.44 (0.34)
Diversification relatedness		0.66 (0.21)**		1.98 (0.59)***		2.27 (0.61)***
Internationalization relatedness		0.33 (0.15)*		0.78 (0.25)***		0.87 (0.25)***
2. Board ties weighted by complementarity/ heterogeneity in:						
Product-market relatedness		0.18 (0.14)		0.36 (0.28)		−0.04 (0.30)
Foreign market relatedness		0.26 (0.17)		0.49 (0.32)		0.07 (0.34)
Diversification relatedness		0.12 (0.36)		0.15 (0.32)		0.55 (0.34)
Internationalization relatedness		0.13 (0.15)		−0.00 (0.27)		−0.30 (0.28)
3. Education level	0.07 (0.03)*	0.07 (0.03)*	0.10 (0.09)	0.10 (0.09)	0.12 (0.09)	0.11 (0.09)
4. Tenure on the board	0.02 (0.01)*	0.02 (0.05)*	0.02 (0.01)*	0.03 (0.01)*	0.03 (0.01)**	0.03 (0.01)*
5. Functional areas	0.05 (0.04)	0.05 (0.05)	0.20 (0.09)*	0.20 (0.09)*	0.11 (0.09)	0.11 (0.10)
6. Management experience	0.00 (0.00)	0.00 (0.00)	0.00 (0.01)	0.00 (0.01)	0.00 (0.01)	0.00 (0.01)
7. Focal firm diversification	−0.11 (0.07)	−0.13 (0.07)	−0.31 (0.13)*	−0.31 (0.13)*	−0.28 (0.13)	−0.28 (0.13)*
8. Focal firm internationalization	−0.13 (0.08)	−0.12 (0.08)	−0.37 (0.14)**	−0.35 (0.13)**	−0.27 (0.14)	−0.27 (0.14)
9. Logarithm of sales	−0.03 (0.02)	−0.03 (0.03)	−0.01 (0.05)	−0.01 (0.05)	−0.01 (0.05)	−0.02 (0.05)
10. Board size	−0.02 (0.01)	−0.02 (0.01)	−0.03 (0.03)	−0.02 (0.03)	−0.04 (0.02)	−0.05 (0.03)
11. CEO ownership			−1.33 (0.77)	−1.32 (0.77)	0.84 (0.76)	0.86 (0.77)
12. CEO-board friendship ties			−0.09 (0.17)	−0.09 (0.17)	0.38 (0.16)	0.38 (0.16)*
13. Appointments after the CEO			−0.31 (0.27)	−0.29 (0.27)	0.73 (0.25)**	0.73 (0.25)**
14. Director ownership			2.19 (0.85)*	2.13 (0.84)*	0.81 (0.88)	0.77 (0.89)
15. Prior return on equity			−1.03 (0.60)	−1.03 (0.60)	−1.04 (0.58)	−1.04 (0.58)
16. Prior market-to-book value			0.07 (0.07)	−0.07 (0.07)	−0.01 (0.06)	−0.01 (0.06)
17. Board leadership structure			0.46 (0.16)**	0.45 (0.16)**		
Constant	1.33 (0.53)*	1.38 (0.53)**	−1.26 (1.44)	−1.56 (1.51)	0.07 (1.46)	0.25 (1.59)
F	5.17***	10.70***	4.59***	6.22***	5.34***	7.36***
R^2	.16	.47	.21	.39	.22	.42
ΔR^2		.31***		.18***		.20***

[a] Unstandardized coefficients are reported with standard errors in parentheses; $n = 250$ for directors' perceived ability to contribute, and $n = 114$ for board monitoring and advice interactions.
* $p < .05$
** $p < .01$
*** $p < .001$
T-tests were one-tailed for hypothesized effects, two-tailed for control variables.

although the coefficient for foreign market relatedness was not significant, it was positive, as hypothesized. Conversely, the results indicate that having more board appointments to firms with *different* strategies tends to *reduce* directors' perceived ability to contribute to board discussions. These results held after we controlled for complementarity in strategic relatedness, which is consistently unrelated to directors' perceived ability to contribute in stable environments. Several control variables significantly predicted the ability to contribute, including a director's education level and tenure on the board and the number of functional areas in which the director had prior experience; board size was negatively related, as expected.

A similar pattern of results provided robust support for Hypotheses 1b and 1c (Table 3). Hypothesis 1b predicts that, in stable environments, board appointments to other strategically related firms will be positively associated with the level of board monitor-

TABLE 4
Results of Multiple Regression Analysis for Unstable Environments[a]

Independent Variable	Hypothesis 1a: Director Contribution		Hypothesis 1b: Board Monitoring		Hypothesis 1c: Board Advice Interactions	
	Model 1	Model 2	Model 1	Model 2	Model 1	Model 2
1. Board ties weighted by:						
Product-market relatedness		0.14 (0.18)		0.11 (0.27)		0.33 (0.26)
Foreign market relatedness		−0.10 (0.21)		−0.08 (0.32)		0.34 (0.31)
Diversification relatedness		0.25 (0.22)		1.38 (0.58)*		0.33 (0.56)
Internationalization relatedness		0.23 (0.15)		0.13 (0.24)		0.29 (0.23)
2. Board ties weighted by complementarity/ heterogeneity in:						
Product-market relatedness		0.39 (0.15)**		0.96 (0.31)**		0.67 (0.30)*
Foreign market relatedness		0.44 (0.18)**		0.64 (0.33)*		0.66 (0.32)*
Diversification relatedness		1.30 (0.38)***		1.11 (0.32)***		1.05 (0.32)***
Internationalization relatedness		0.59 (0.16)***		0.59 (0.26)*		0.34 (0.26)***
3. Education level	0.01 (0.03)	0.01 (0.03)	0.09 (0.08)	0.11 (0.09)	0.04 (0.09)	0.04 (0.09)
4. Tenure on the board	0.02 (0.01)**	0.02 (0.01)**	0.02 (0.01)	0.02 (0.01)	0.02 (0.01)	0.03 (0.01)*
5. Functional areas	0.06 (0.04)	0.06 (0.04)	0.20 (0.09)*	0.20 (0.09)*	0.17 (0.09)	0.17 (0.09)
6. Management experience	0.00 (0.00)	0.00 (0.00)	0.01 (0.01)	0.01 (0.01)	0.01 (0.01)	0.01 (0.01)
7. Focal firm diversification	−0.06 (0.08)	−0.16 (0.08)*	−0.92 (0.41)*	−0.91 (0.41)*	−0.73 (0.39)	−0.71 (0.40)
8. Focal firm internationalization	−0.14 (0.08)	−0.15 (0.08)	−0.29 (0.14)*	−0.28 (0.14)*	−0.27 (0.13)*	−0.27 (0.13)*
9. Logarithm of sales	−0.01 (0.03)	−0.01 (0.03)	−0.02 (0.04)	−0.02 (0.04)	−0.01 (0.04)	−0.01 (0.04)
10. Board size	−0.02 (0.01)	−0.02 (0.01)	−0.01 (0.03)	−0.01 (0.03)	−0.04 (0.02)	−0.04 (0.03)
11. CEO ownership			−1.37 (0.73)	−1.36 (0.73)	1.21 (0.70)	1.13 (0.71)
12. CEO-board friendship ties			−0.05 (0.19)	−0.05 (0.19)	0.41 (0.19)*	0.41 (0.19)*
13. Appointments after the CEO			−0.46 (0.30)	−0.46 (0.30)	0.74 (0.30)*	0.73 (0.30)*
14. Director ownership			1.89 (0.83)*	1.88 (0.82)*	0.83 (0.80)	0.81 (0.80)
15. Prior return on equity			−1.14 (0.61)	−1.13 (0.61)	−1.07 (0.60)	−1.06 (0.60)
17. Prior market-to-book value			−0.07 (0.07)	−0.07 (0.07)	−0.02 (0.07)	−0.02 (0.07)
18. Board leadership structure			0.45 (0.18)*	0.45 (0.18)*		
Constant	−1.20 (0.57)*	−1.05 (0.56)	−1.59 (1.44)	−2.75 (1.47)	0.13 (1.36)	0.13 (1.47)
F	5.08***	13.36***	4.05***	5.59***	4.61***	6.49***
R^2	.15	.59	.19	.36	.21	.41
ΔR^2		.44***		.17***		.20***

[a] Unstandardized coefficients are reported with standard errors in parentheses; $n = 242$ for directors' perceived ability to contribute, and $n = 114$ for board monitoring and advice interactions.

* $p < .05$

** $p < .01$

*** $p < .001$

T-tests were one-tailed for hypothesized effects, two-tailed for control variables.

ing of strategic decision making. Hypothesis 1c predicts that such appointments will be positively associated with the level of advice interactions on strategic issues. Three different kinds of strategic relatedness (product-market, diversification, and internationalization relatedness) were positively associated with both monitoring and advice interactions. Conversely, having more board appointments to firms with *unrelated* strategies was *negatively* associated with both kinds of involvement. A separate analysis provided evidence that directors' perceived ability to contribute effectively mediated these relationships: when ability to contribute is added to models of monitoring and advice interactions, the effects of the relatedness variables become nonsignificant, and the coefficient for ability to contribute is strongly and positively significant in both models (Baron & Kenny, 1986). Again, as shown in the table, we found that the hypothesized effects were significant even after controlling for heterogeneity in strategic relatedness, which is consistently unrelated to either form of board involvement.

Hypothesis 2a is the first test of our theoretical framework in unstable competitive environments. Specifically, in such environments we predicted that the more a director's board appointments complemented the appointments of other directors in their strategic relatedness to the focal firm, the greater would be the director's perceived ability to contribute to board discussions. Table 4 shows the results of regression analyses predicting directors' perceived ability to contribute in unstable environments. Complementarity in strategic relatedness is positively related to directors' perceived ability to contribute for all four dimensions of corporate strategy, supporting Hypothesis 2a. At the same time, the results show that simple relatedness does not predict the ability to contribute.

The results for tests of Hypotheses 2b and 2c are also presented in Table 4. Consistent with our predictions for unstable environments, the greater the heterogeneity of directors' board appointments in terms of product-market, diversification, and internationalization relatedness, the higher the level of board monitoring and advice interactions. Heterogeneity in foreign market relatedness was also marginally associated with advice interactions in such environments. These results held after the simple relatedness of board ties was controlled for; simple relatedness was generally unrelated to either kind of involvement. Moreover, separate analyses again suggested that directors' perceived ability to contribute to board discussions mediated the effects of complementary appointments on director monitoring and advice interactions. Thus, the results consistently show that the strategic relatedness of board ties increases director involvement in stable environments but does not do so in unstable environments. The opposite pattern emerges in unstable environments. We also conducted separate analyses using the product term approach to test interactions between environmental stability and the independent variables, and the interactions were significant, consistent with the split-sample findings.

To supplement the primary analyses of overall board involvement presented above, we conducted further analyses that focused on board involvement in either strategy implementation or the consideration of new strategies using additional survey items (such as "To what extent does the board monitor the implementation of strategic decisions?"). In general, the relatedness of board ties was positively associated with reported involvement in implementation, and it was negatively associated with advice on new strategic alternatives in turbulent environments (this effect was not significant in stable environments). These results appear to further support our theoretical arguments, as we would expect directors who have experience with related strategies to be more capable of contributing insight on implementation of a firm's current strategy. In contrast, directors who have experience with different strategies should be more capable of contributing insight about alternatives. Also, the nonsignificant effect of relatedness on advice about new strategic alternatives in stable environments is consistent with the view that strategic change is relatively less important in stable environments than in turbulent environments. The implications of our combined results are discussed below.

DISCUSSION

Overview of Findings

Overall, the findings provided strong support for our theoretical framework. Empirical analyses yielded a consistent pattern of results suggesting that the monitoring and advising behavior of directors depends on the strategic perspective and base of expertise provided by their appointments to other boards. For example, strategically related board ties were found to enhance board involvement in firms facing relatively stable environments, and strategically heterogeneous board ties were found to enhance involvement in firms facing relatively unstable environments. Therefore, it would appear that the strategic context of director appointments, not simply the presence or number of such appointments, is an important influence on corporate governance.

A growing body of research on boards recognizes corporate director appointments as an indicator of access to information network flows (Mizruchi, 1996; Palmer et al., 1993), but much of it has emphasized a firm's number of interlocks (centrality) as indicative of the extent to which it is integrated into a community of information. Critics of interlock research have emphasized the need to examine the "substantive context" of interlock appointments if their consequences are to be understood (Nohria, 1992: 14; Pettigrew, 1992; Stinchcombe, 1990). Our findings address this issue by showing how board interlock ties affect a firm's corporate governance to the degree that such ties are aligned with the strategic needs of the firm. Thus, although the literature on interlocking directorates has tended to emphasize a firm's *social* context as an important determinant of organizational behavior, the findings of this study suggest that the effects of a firm's social structural context are moderated by its *strategic* context.

Accordingly, this study extends network theories of corporate governance. The findings are consistent with a sociocognitive perspective on board involvement in which director ties to other boards provide direct strategic experience and indirect access to strategic information through social contact with other directors, which in turn can critically inform the knowledge structures used to monitor decisions or give advice on a focal board. Those knowledge structures can enhance board capability to contribute to strategic decision making if they address the primary strategic issues facing firms, such as implementation of existing strategies in stable environments versus the development of new strategies *and* implementation in turbulent environments. Conversely, knowledge structures conditioned by board ties to other firms can reduce a board's capability to contribute to strategy if these structures do not match the strategic contingencies facing the firm. This view is consistent with Granovetter's (1992) and Weick's (1995) social network embeddedness perspectives on organizational behavior, which suggest that individual action is conditioned by information spread through social structural relations, rather than strictly by an individual's personal decision-making capabilities or by widespread social norms. In extending this perspective to explain board involvement in strategic decision making, our study pinpoints the specific kinds of network ties that can influence behavior.

Moreover, research on board power and control has typically focused on structural board independence as a critical determinant of a board's ability to protect shareholder interests. Such research has not addressed whether and when directors have the appropriate strategic perspective and knowledge to exercise control effectively. In the behavioral literature on boards, low levels of director involvement have typically been attributed to the social and political influence of top managers over outside directors (cf. Finkelstein & Hambrick, 1996); the findings of this study suggest that directors may also abstain from monitoring and advising management to the extent that they lack relevant strategic information and knowledge needed to contribute to the decision-making process. As more boards acquire the structural power needed to influence organizations (Useem, 1993; Westphal & Zajac, 1997), it becomes increasingly important to develop models of board effectiveness that predict whether boards also have the ability to exercise their influence.

Although agency-based views on boards of directors attribute lower levels of director involvement to the significant costs associated with monitoring activities, such as the time required to prepare for meetings (Beatty & Zajac, 1994), the perspective developed in this study suggests how and when the information and expertise directors gain from serving on other boards can permit them to economize on governance costs, by raising the "returns" from investing a given amount of time and attention in the monitoring and advising of management at a particular firm. Our findings are consistent with the view that if directors' appointments to other boards provide them with relevant strategic information and expertise and focus their attention on relevant strategic issues (such as strategic change versus implementation), then directors are likely to realize *positive* sociocognitive "externalities" from their appointments to other boards. That is, investments in monitoring and advising at one firm provide directors with knowledge and perspective that raise the quality of their contributions at other firms with similar strategic priorities. Such externalities permit economies of monitoring and advising across firms. Conversely, directors' appointments may provide them with inappropriate strategic information and focus their attention away from critical strategic issues facing a focal firm. Under those conditions, directors may instead experience *negative* sociocognitive externalities from their other board memberships, thus leading to *dis*economies of monitoring and advising.

Finally, some prior research on the diffusion of innovations has distinguished between a director's experience as an inside board member—at her or his home company—and experience as an outside director, at another company; these statuses are sometimes referred to as "directional" and "nondirectional," respectively (Palmer et al., 1993). For instance, Palmer and his colleagues suggested that inside director ties may have stronger effects on the diffusion of innovations than outside director ties, because insiders are likely to devote more time than outsiders to implementing innovations, leading to greater psychological commitment to them (Palmer, Barber, Zhou, & Soysal, 1995; Palmer et al., 1993). Similarly, directors' beliefs about corporate strategy might be influenced more by their experience as top managers at their home companies than by their experience as outside directors at other firms. In order to test this possibility empirically, we conducted separate analyses in which the relatedness of manager-director ties was measured separately from the relatedness of outside director ties. The hypothesized effects were supported for both sources of experience, and the effects of manager-director ties were not consistently stronger than the effects of outside director ties.

Limitations, Implications, and Conclusion

Limitations. Although the findings of this study are consistent with a sociocognitive perspective on board involvement in which board ties to other firms help determine whether directors have the appropriate knowledge and perspective to contribute to strategic decision making, our empirical approach does not permit a direct examination of the cognitions that mediate these relationships. This limitation is shared by most empirical research in the top management team literature, which is also largely rooted in a sociocognitive perspective (Finkelstein & Hambrick, 1996; Hambrick & Mason, 1984). In addition, although we did measure the degree to which directors advised and monitored management, we were unable to assess the quality of the advice given or the extent to which it ultimately improved firm performance. Finally, the findings of this study may be less applicable to relatively small firms, whose directors tend to have fewer board appointments at other companies.

Future research directions. These limitations suggest several directions for future research. Perhaps most importantly, research is still needed that goes beyond our relatively direct measures of board behavior to gauge the strategic expertise and perspectives of corporate board members, assessing how cognitions mediate the effects of board ties on strategic decision making. For instance, researchers could examine whether directors who have strategically related board ties demonstrate more nuanced understanding of the requirements for implementing that strategy. Content analysis might be used to measure the complexity of director recommendations regarding information systems, reward systems, and other systems and structures needed to implement strategies effectively. This approach has been used in research on group decision making to measure the complexity of group member cognitions (e.g., Tetlock, Peterson, McGuire, Chang, & Feld, 1992).

In addition, to the extent that the strategic relatedness or heterogeneity of board ties predicts director behaviors, such behaviors may have particular implications for firm performance. For instance, our theoretical argument would suggest that heterogeneous board ties could enhance performance for firms operating in turbulent environments. In partial support of this view, Uzzi (1996) found that firms in the highly turbulent women's fashion industry were most likely to survive when they possessed a combination of strong and diverse ties to other organizations. Thus, future research should study whether or not the congruence of environmental stability and director appointments similarly affects performance differentials among firms.

Research might also examine whether firms with appropriate board appointments rely less on alternative control mechanisms. For example, Johnson and colleagues (1993) observed that boards influence firms either through strategic controls (such as board monitoring) or through financial mechanisms (such as managerial incentives). Therefore, in future studies, researchers might examine whether the addition of board appointments that provide relevant strategic expertise lead firms to reduce their reliance on financial controls, thus minimizing the costs associated with such controls (that is, the costs resulting from imposition of firm-specific risk on decision makers [Jensen & Meckling, 1976]). Conversely, firms may rely more heavily on such financial controls where directors' appointments to other boards do not provide them with the relevant strategic perspective and knowledge base.

Finally, it should be noted that reciprocal board appointments are common in many countries (Demb & Neubauer, 1992). However, because research in non-U.S. settings has emphasized the social rather than the strategic nature of reciprocal board appointments (e.g., Stokman, Zeigler, & Scott, 1985), there is an opportunity to extend the social psychological perspective developed in this study to research on corporate governance outside of the United States. For instance, given that there are markedly fewer restrictions on the types of board connections and the contents of communication flows between managers of different firms in European countries, the strategic context of board appointments may be even more influential there.

Managerial implications. In addition to their theoretical importance, the results of this research, have significant implications for both public policy and business practice. For example, there is growing external stakeholder pressure for the U.S. government to legislate constraints on board member appointments that go beyond the existing Clayton Act (Section 8) prohibition of certain kinds of interlocking directorates among direct competitors (*BusinessWeek,* 1997). Indeed, the results presented here confirm that boards are less likely to be effective advisors and monitors when their members are appointed to the boards of other firms that are strategically irrelevant to the needs of a focal firm. Therefore, to the extent that firms are prevented from realizing benefits from the relatedness or the heterogeneity of appointments discussed in this research, additional legislated board constraints may have unintended negative consequences for the corporate governance of public U.S. firms.

Similarly, there is evidence that corporate leaders give considerable weight to the number of other board memberships held by director candidates when selecting new outside directors for their boards (Davis, 1993). However, the results of this study suggest the need to consider whether a director will connect a firm with other organizations that can furnish relevant strategic knowledge and perspective, rather than simply focus on the number of board seats the candidate already holds. For example, if a firm in a turbulent industry has a board composed primarily of directors who sit on the boards of other firms with similar strategies, such a board's ability to monitor and advise may be considerably enhanced by appointing directors who sit on the boards of other firms that follow different diversification and internationalization strategies in different product and geographic markets.

In conclusion, the findings of this study suggest the value of developing sociocognitive theories that address whether and when corporate leaders have the appropriate strategic knowledge and perspective to contribute to corporate governance. Moreover, although little rigorous empirical research has directly examined behavioral processes in CEO-board relationships, our findings also show the potential power of models that link the broader sociostructural context in which boards are embedded, as well as the environmental conditions that surround them, with the microbehavioral processes that occur inside the "black box" of corporate boards.

REFERENCES

Abelson, R. P., & Black, J. B. 1986. Introduction. In R. P. Abelson & J. B. Black (Eds.), ***Knowledge structures:*** 1–18. Hillsdale, NJ: Erlbaum.

Alderfer, C. P. 1986. The invisible director on corporate boards. ***Harvard Business Review,*** 64(6): 38–52.

Aldrich, H. 1979. ***Organizations and environments.*** Englewood Cliffs, NJ: Prentice-Hall.

Andrews, K. 1971. ***The concept of corporate strategy.*** Illinois: Dow-Jones-Irwin.

Baliga, B. R., Moyer, C., & Rao, R. S. 1996. CEO duality and firm performance: What's the fuss? ***Strategic Management Journal,*** 17: 41–53.

Barney, J., & Zajac, E. 1994. Competitive organizational behavior: Toward an organizationally-based theory of competitive advantage. ***Strategic Management Journal,*** 15(winter special issue): 5–9.

Baron, R., & Kenny, D. 1986. The moderator-mediator variable distinction in social psychological research: Conceptual, strategic, and statistical considerations. ***Journal of Personality and Social Psychology,*** 51: 1173–1182.

Beatty, R., & Zajac, E. 1994. Managerial incentives, monitoring, and risk-bearing: A study of executive compensation, ownership, and board structure in initial public offerings. ***Administrative Science Quarterly,*** 39: 313–335.

Bergh, D. D. 1995. Size and relatedness of units sold: An agency theory and resource-based perspective. ***Strategic Management Journal,*** 16: 221–239.

Boeker, W. 1992. Power and managerial dismissal: Scapegoating at the top. ***Administrative Science Quarterly,*** 27: 538–547.

Boeker, W. 1997. Strategic change: The influence of managerial characteristics and organizational growth. ***Academy of Management Journal,*** 40: 152–170.

Boeker, W., & Goodstein, J. 1993. Performance and successor choice: The moderating effects of governance and ownership. ***Academy of Management Journal,*** 36: 172–186.

Bourgeois, L. 1980. Performance and consensus. ***Strategic Management Journal,*** 1: 227–248.

Brudney, V. 1982. The independent director—Heavenly city or potemkin village? ***Harvard Law Review,*** 95: 597–659.

Burt, R. S. 1987. Social contagion and innovation: Cohesion versus structural equivalence. ***American Journal of Sociology,*** 92: 1287–1335.

BusinessWeek. 1997. The best and worst boards. December 8: 90–98.

Carpenter, M. A., & Fredrickson, J. W. 2001. Top management teams, global strategic posture, and the moderating role of uncertainty. ***Academy of Management Journal,*** 44: 533–545.

Chen, M. 1996. Competitor analysis and interfirm rivalry: Toward a theoretical integration. ***Academy of Management Review,*** 21: 100–135.

Cyert, R. M., & March, J. G. 1963. ***A behavioral theory of the firm.*** Englewood Cliffs, NJ: Prentice-Hall.

Davis, G. F. 1991. Agents without principles? The spread of the poison pill through the intercorporate network. ***Administrative Science Quarterly,*** 36: 583–613.

Davis, G. F. 1996. ***Who gets ahead in the market for corporate directors: The political economy of multiple board memberships.*** Paper presented at the annual meeting of the Academy of Management, Cincinnati.

Day, D., & Lord, R. 1992. Expertise and problem categorization: The role of expert processing in organizational sensemaking. ***Journal of Management Studies,*** 29: 35–47.

Dearborn, D., & Simon, H. 1958. Selective perception: A note on the departmental identifications of executives. ***Sociometry,*** 21: 140–144

Demb, A., & Neubauer, F. 1992. ***The corporate board.*** New York: Oxford University Press.

DeVellis, R. F. 1991. ***Scale development: Theory and applications.*** Newbury Park, CA: Sage.

Duncan, R. 1972. Characteristics of organizational environments and perceived environmental uncertainty. ***Administrative Science Quarterly,*** 17: 313–327.

Dutton, J., & Duncan, R. 1987. The creation of momentum for change through the process of strategic issue diagnosis. ***Strategic Management Journal,*** 8: 279–296.

Fama, E. 1980. Agency problems and the theory of the firm. ***Journal of Political Economy,*** 88: 288–307.

Fama, E., & Jensen, M. 1983. Separation of ownership and control. ***Journal of Law and Economics,*** 26: 301–325.

Finkelstein, S. 1992. Power in top management teams: Dimensions, measurement, and validation. ***Academy of Management Journal,*** 35: 505–538.

Finkelstein, S., & Hambrick, D. 1988. Chief executive compensation: A synthesis and reconciliation. ***Strategic Management Journal,*** 10: 543–558.

Finkelstein, S., & Hambrick, D. 1996. ***Strategic leadership: Top executives and their effects on organizations.*** St. Paul: West.

Fleiss, J. L. 1981. ***Statistical methods for rates and proportions,*** New York: Wiley.

Fowler, F. J. 1993. ***Survey research methods.*** Newbury Park, CA: Sage.

Fredrickson, J. W. 1984. The comprehensiveness of strategic decision processes: Extension, observation, future direction. ***Academy of Management Journal,*** 27: 399–424.

Fredrickson, J. W., & Mitchell, T. R. 1984. Strategic decision processes: Comprehensiveness and performance in an industry with an unstable environment. ***Academy of Management Journal,*** 27: 399–423.

Galbraith, C., & Merrill, G. 1991. The effect of compensation program and structure on SBU competitive strategy: A study of technology-intensive firms. ***Strategic Management Journal,*** 12: 353–370.

Galbraith, J., & Kanzanjian, R. 1986. ***Strategy implementation: Structure, systems, and processes.*** St. Paul: West.

Gerhart, B., & Milkovich, G. 1990. Organizational differences in managerial compensation and financial performance. ***Academy of Management Journal,*** 33: 663–691.

Ginsberg, A. 1990. Connecting diversification to performance: A sociocognitive approach. ***Academy of Management Review,*** 15: 514–535.

Gomez-Mejia, L. 1992. Structure and the process of diversification. ***Strategic Management Journal,*** 13: 381–397.

Granovetter, M. 1992. Problems of explanation in economic sociology. In N. Nohria & R. Eccles (Eds.), ***Networks and organizations: Structure, form and action:*** 25–56. Boston: Harvard Business School Press.

Groves, R. M., Cialdini, R. B., & Couper, M. P. 1992. Understanding the decision to participate in a survey. ***Public Opinion Quarterly,*** 56: 475–495.

Haleblian, J., & Finkelstein, S. 1993. Top-management team size, CEO dominance, and firm performance: The moderating roles of environmental turbulence and discretion. ***Academy of Management Journal,*** 36: 844–863.

Hambrick, D., & Mason, P. 1984. Upper echelons: The organization as a function of its top managers. ***Academy of Management Journal,*** 15: 514–535.

Hambrick, D., Geletkanycz, M., & Fredrickson, J. 1993. Top executive commitment to the status quo: Some tests of its determinants. ***Strategic Management Journal,*** 14: 401–418.

Harman, H. H. 1976. ***Modern factor analysis*** (3rd ed.). Chicago: University of Chicago Press.

Haunschild, P. 1993. Interorganizational imitation: The impact of interlocks on corporate acquisition activity. ***Administrative Science Quarterly,*** 38: 564–592.

Haunschild, P., & Miner, A. 1997. Modes of interorganizational imitation: The effects of outcome salience and uncertainty. ***Administrative Science Quarterly,*** 42: 472–500.

Hill, C., & Snell, S. 1988. External control, corporate strategy, and firm performance in research-intensive industries. ***Strategic Management Journal,*** 9: 577–590.

Huber, G., & McDaniel, R. 1986. The decision making paradigm of organizational design. ***Management Science,*** 32: 572–589.

Jehn, K. A., Chadwick, C., & Thatcher, S. M. B. 1997. To agree or not to agree: The effects of value congruence, individual demographic dissimilarity, and conflict on workgroup outcomes. ***International Journal of Conflict Management,*** 8: 287–305.

Jensen, M. C., & Meckling, W. H. 1976. Theory of the firm: Managerial behavior, agency costs, and ownership structure. ***Journal of Financial Economics,*** 3: 305–350.

Johansen, J., & Vahlne, J. 1977. The internationalization process of the firm—A model of knowledge development and increasing foreign market commitments. ***Journal of International Business Studies,*** 8: 23–32.

Johnson, R., Hoskisson, R., & Hitt, M. 1993. Board of director involvement in restructuring: The effects of board versus managerial controls and characteristics. ***Strategic Management Journal,*** 14(summer special issue): 14: 33–50.

Judge, W., & Zeithaml, C. 1992. Institutional and strategic choice perspectives on board involvement in the strategic decision process. ***Academy of Management Journal,*** 35: 766–794.

Kahneman, D., Slovic, P., & Tversky, A. 1982. ***Judgment under uncertainty: Heuristics and biases.*** Cambridge, England: Cambridge University Press.

Kazanjian, R., & Drazin, R. 1987. Implementing internal diversification: Contingency factors for organization design choices. ***Academy of Management Review,*** 12: 342–354.

Kesner, I. F., Victor, B., & Lamont, B. T. 1986. Board composition and the commission of illegal acts: An investigation of *Fortune* 500 companies. ***Academy of Management Journal,*** 29: 789–799.

Kiesler, S., & Sproull, L. 1982. Managerial response to changing environments: Perspectives on problem sensing from social cognition. ***Administrative Science Quarterly,*** 27: 548–570.

Kim, W. 1989. Developing a global diversification measure. ***Management Science,*** 25: 376–383.

Kosnik, R. 1987. Greenmail: A study of board performance in corporate governance. ***Administrative Science Quarterly,*** 32: 163–185.

Landis, J. R., & Koch, G. G. 1977. The measurement of observer agreement for categorical data. ***Biometrics,*** 33: 671–679.

Lorsch, J., & MacIver, E. 1989. ***Pawns and potentates: The reality of America's corporate boards.*** Boston: Harvard Business School Press.

Lurigio, A. J., & Carroll, J. S. 1985. Probation officers' schemata of offenders: Content, development, and impact on treatment decisions. ***Journal of Personality and Social Psychology,*** 48: 1112–1126.

Mace, M. 1971. ***Directors: Myth and reality.*** Boston: Harvard Business School Press.

Mallette, P., & Fowler, K. 1992. Effects of board composition and stock ownership on the adoption of poison pills. ***Academy of Management Journal,*** 35: 1010–1035.

Mizruchi, M. 1996. What do interlocks do? An analysis, critique, and assessment of research on interlocking directorates. In J. Hagan & K. Cook (Eds.), ***Annual review of sociology,*** vol. 22: 271–298. Palo Alto, CA: Annual Reviews.

Nisbett, R., & Ross, L. 1980. ***Human inference: Strategies and shortcomings of social judgment.*** Englewood Cliffs, NJ: Prentice-Hall.

Nohria, N. 1992. Introduction: Is a network perspective a useful way of studying organizations? In N. Nohria & R. Eccles (Eds.), ***Networks and organizations: Structure, form, and action:*** 1–22. Boston: Harvard Business School Press.

Nunnally, J. 1978. ***Psychometric theory*** (2nd ed.). New York: McGraw-Hill.

Ocasio, W. 1997. Toward an attention-based view of the firm. ***Strategic Management Journal,*** 18(summer special issue): 187–206.

O'Reilly, C., R. Snyder, & Boothe, J. 1993. Effects of executive team demography on organizational change. In G. Huber & W. Glick (Eds.), ***Organizational change and redesign:*** 147–175. New York: Oxford University Press.

Palepu, K. 1985. Diversification strategy, profit performance, and the entropy measure. ***Strategic Management Journal,*** 6: 239–255

Palmer, D., Barber, B. M., Zhou, X., & Soysal, Y. 1995. The friendly and predatory acquisition of large U.S. corporations in the 1960s: The other contested terrain. ***American Sociological Review,*** 60: 469–499.

Palmer, D., Jennings, P., & Zhou, X. 1993. Late adoption of the multidivisional form by large U.S. corporations: Institutional, political, and economic accounts. ***Administrative Science Quarterly,*** 38: 100–131.

Pelled, L. H. 1996. Demographic diversity, conflict and work group outcomes: An intervening process theory. ***Organization Science,*** 7: 615–631.

Pelled, L. H., Eisenhardt, K. M., & Xin, K. R. 1999. Exploring the black box: An analysis of work group diversity, conflict, and performance. ***Administrative Science Quarterly,*** 44: 1–28.

Pettigrew, A. 1992. On studying managerial elites. ***Strategic Management Journal,*** 13: 163–182.

Pfeffer, J., & Salancik, G. 1978. ***The external control of organizations: A resource dependence perspective.*** New York: Harper & Row.

Porter, M. E. 1986. ***Competition in global industries.*** Boston: Harvard Business School Press.

Porter, M. E. 1998. ***Competitive strategy*** (2nd ed.). New York: Free Press.

Priem, R. 1990. Top management team factors, consensus, and firm performance. ***Strategic Management Journal,*** 11: 469–478.

Rediker, K., & Seth, A. 1995. Boards of directors and substitution effects of alternative governance mechanisms. ***Strategic Management Journal,*** 16: 85–100.

Rumelt, R. 1974. ***Strategy, structure, and economic performance.*** Cambridge, MA: Harvard University Press.

Sanders, W. G., & Carpenter, M. A. 1998. Internationalization and firm governance: The roles of CEO compensation, top team composition, and board structure. ***Academy of Management Journal,*** 41: 158–178.

Sharfman, M., & Dean, J. 1991. Conceptualizing and measuring the organizational environment: A multidimensional approach. ***Journal of Management,*** 17: 681–700.

Siegel, S., & Castellan, N. J. 1988. ***Nonparametric statistics for the behavioral sciences*** (2nd ed.). New York: McGraw-Hill.

Stinchcombe, A. 1990. Weak structural data. ***Contemporary Sociology,*** 19: 380–382.

Stokman, F., Ziegler, R., & Scott, J. (Eds.). 1985. ***Networks of corporate power.*** New York: Polity Press and Blackwell.

Sujan, H., Sujan, M., & Bettman, J. 1988. Knowledge structure differences between more effective and less effective salespeople. ***Journal of Marketing Research,*** 25: 81–86.

Sullivan, D. 1994. Measuring the degree of internationalization of a firm. ***Journal of International Business Studies,*** 25: 325–342.

Tetlock, P. E., Peterson, R. S., McGuire, C., Chang, S., & Feld, P. 1992. Assessing political group dynamics: A test of the groupthink model. ***Journal of Personality and Social Psychology,*** 63: 403–425.

Tushman, M., & Anderson, P. 1986. Technological discontinuities and organizational environments. ***Administrative Science Quarterly,*** 31: 439–465.

Tushman, M., & Romanelli, E. 1985. Organizational evolution: A metamorphosis model of convergence and reorientation. L. L. Cummings & B. M. Staw (Eds.), ***Research in organizational behavior,*** vol. 7: 171–222. Greenwich, CT: JAI Press.

Useem, M. 1982. Classwide rationality in the politics of managers and directors of large corporations in the United States and Great Britain. ***Administrative Science Quarterly,*** 27: 199–226.

Useem, M. 1993. ***Executive defense: Shareholder power and corporate reorganization.*** Cambridge, MA: Harvard University Press.

Uzzi, B. 1996. Embeddedness and economic performance: The network effect. ***American Sociological Review,*** 61: 4: 674–698.

Wade, J., O'Reilly, C. A., & Chandratat, I. 1990. Golden parachutes: CEOs and the exercise of social influence. ***Administrative Science Quarterly,*** 35: 587–603.

Walker, G. 1985. Network position and cognition in a computer software firm. ***Administrative Science Quarterly,*** 30: 103–130.

Walsh, J. 1995. Managerial and organizational cognition: Notes from a trip down memory lane. ***Organization Science,*** 6: 280–321.

Wasserman, S., & Faust, K. 1994. ***Social network analysis: Methods and applications.*** Cambridge, England: Cambridge University Press.

Weick, K. 1995. ***Sensemaking in organizations.*** Thousand Oaks, CA: Sage.

Westphal, J. D. 1998. Board games: How CEOs adapt to increases in structural board independence from management. ***Administrative Science Quarterly,*** 43: 511–537.

Westphal, J. D. 1999. Collaboration in the boardroom: The consequences of social ties in the CEO/board relationship. ***Academy of Management Journal,*** 42: 7–24.

Westphal, J. D., & Zajac, E. 1997. Defections from the inner circle: Social exchange, reciprocity, and the diffusion of board independence in U.S. corporations. ***Administrative Science Quarterly,*** 42: 161–183.

Wiersema, M., & Bantel, K. 1992. Top management team demography and corporate strategic change. ***Academy of Management Journal,*** 35: 91–121.

Wiersema, M., & Bantel, K. 1993. Top management team turnover as an adaptation mechanism: The role of the environment. ***Strategic Management Journal,*** 14: 485–504.

Williams, K. Y., & O'Reilly, C. A. 1998. Demography and diversity in organizations: A review of 40 years of research. In L. L. Cummings & B. M. Staw (Eds.), ***Research in organizational behavior,*** vol. 20: 77–140. Greenwich, CT: JAI Press.

Zajac, E., & Westphal, J. 1994. The costs and benefits of managerial incentives and monitoring in large U.S. corporations: When is more not better? ***Strategic Management Journal,*** 15: 121–142.

APPENDIX

Survey Items and Factor Loadings

Perceived Ability to Contribute

1. To what extent are you capable of contributing to board discussions on strategic issues? ("not at all," 1; "moderately," 3; "very much so," 5) .83
2. To what extent do you have sufficient knowledge on relevant strategic issues to contribute to board discussions? ("not at all," 1; "to some extent," 3; "very much so," 5) .78
3. To what extent are you able to add valuable insight to the board on strategic issues? ("not at all," 1; "to some extent," 3; "very much so," 5) .87
4. I am capable of making important contributions to the strategic decision making process. ("strongly disagree," 1; "neither agree nor disagree," 3; "strongly agree," 5) .76

For all the monitoring and advice items except for the last one, the response scale was "minimally," 1; "moderately," 3; "very much so," 5.

Board Monitoring

1. To what extent does the board monitor top management strategic decision making? .81
2. To what extent does the board formally evaluate [the CEO's] performance? .80

APPENDIX
(continued)

3. To what extent does the board defer to [the CEO's] judgment on final strategic decisions? .85

Board Advice Interactions

1. To what extent does [the CEO] solicit board assistance in the formulation of corporate strategy? .84
2. To what extent are outside directors a "sounding board" on strategic issues? .87
3. [In the past twelve months:] How often have you provided advice and counsel to the CEO on strategic issues? (____ times) .81

Mason A. Carpenter is an assistant professor in the School of Business and an associate of the Weinert Center for Entrepreneurship at the University of Wisconsin—Madison. He received his Ph.D. from the University of Texas at Austin. His research concerns corporate governance, top management teams, the strategic management of global firms, and global new ventures.

James D. Westphal is a professor of management in the McCombs School of Business at the University of Texas at Austin. He received his Ph.D. from Northwestern University. His current research interests include boards of directors and executive compensation, institutional processes, and interorganizational networks.

[13]

Greenmail: A Study of Board Performance in Corporate Governance

Rita D. Kosnik
Texas A&M University

Based on predictions from agency theory and a theory of managerial hegemony, this study compares the board structure of 53 companies that privately repurchased stock at a premium above the market place—i.e., paid greenmail—and 57 companies that resisted greenmail. The decision to pay greenmail is used as a proxy for the board's ineffectiveness, which is defined as the inability of the board's outside directors to prevent management from making decisions—such as paying greenmail—that are in conflict with stockholders' interests. Boards that effectively resisted greenmail were found to have more outside directors, more directors with executive experience, and more directors who represented interorganizational transactions than boards of companies that paid greenmail.•

According to corporate state laws, a corporate board of directors is the formal representative of the company's stockholders whose task it is to supervise management's performance and protect stockholders' interests (Henn, 1974). In the last few decades, this legal governing role of boards has been actively promoted by corporate governance reformers, who have introduced proposals for new board conditions and for procedures that should promote the board's effectiveness in monitoring management on behalf of stockholders (Eisenberg, 1976; Schwartz, 1979; American Law Institute, 1982).

The New York Stock Exchange (NYSE) and federal regulatory agencies such as the Securities and Exchange Commission (SEC) have been active proponents of this movement. For example, since 1965 the New York Stock Exchange has required all registered companies to have at least three outside directors on their boards. Since mid-1978, the NYSE has also reinforced a practice suggested by Roderick Hills, former chairman of the SEC, to exclude executive directors from a board's audit committee. Other proposals have emphasized the need for more open and systematic selection procedures in which potential board members are screened on the basis of their ability to ratify management's decisions and monitor their implementation rather than on the basis of their social status or external connections (Bacon and Brown, 1975). Little is known, however, about the degree to which such reforms have actually contributed to the board's governing effectiveness (Business Roundtable, 1978); the governing performance of boards is still part of a mystique that surrounds the board and its members.

Although the performance of boards of directors has been studied extensively from a resource-dependency perspective (e.g., Zald, 1967; Pfeffer, 1972; Pfeffer and Salancik, 1978), little empirical research is available on the governing performance of boards within the company. Of the few studies that are available (e.g., Vance, 1964; Baysinger and Butler, 1985; Chaganti, Mahajan, and Sharma, 1985), most measure board performance by the company's financial performance. This practice, which is reinforced by the limited availability of readily accessible data on board governance, limits the interpretability of the studies' findings, since most studies fail to control for the multitude of endogenous and exogenous factors that influence a company's financial performance. In

0001-8392/87/3202-0163/$1.00.

•
The author thanks David Larcker for his assistance and support in designing this study, and the following people for their constructive comments on earlier versions of this manuscript: Barry Baysinger, Robert Dewar, Robert Duncan, Gareth Jones, and the associate editor and anonymous reviewers of *ASQ*.

addition, the impact of the board's governance on corporate performance is likely to be indirect and confined to particular incidents in which the board actively intervenes in the company's strategic decision making in order to prevent management from making decisions that are in conflict with stockholders' interests. Given that the board's governing role is oversight, it follows that as long as management's decisions and actions are consistent with stockholders' interests and promote the long-term performance of the firm any type of board—even a passive one—will appear effective as a corporate governance institution (Mizruchi, 1983).

Therefore, more accurate insights into the antecedents of effective board governance might be gained by studying the governing performance of boards in situations in which the board is faced with acute governance problems. It is in decision situations that involve a conflict of interest between corporate management and stockholders that the effectiveness of the board's intervention becomes a critical determinant for the decision outcome. Greenmail—a company's private repurchase of a block of its stock from a minority stockholder at a premium above the market price—presents the board with such a governance dilemma. While greenmail allows corporate management to secure its control position when faced with a challenging raider, the transaction also discriminates among corporate stockholders and may have a negative effect on the wealth of residual stockholders who were not part of the deal. Hence, because management and stockholders have conflicting interests in the payment of greenmail, the board's effectiveness in protecting all stockholders' interests becomes a decisive factor in the company's decision whether or not to pay greenmail at stockholders' expense.

This study then, seeks to identify the board characteristics that discriminate boards that effectively resisted a greenmail offer from boards that allowed greenmail to be paid at the cost of stockholders' wealth. By limiting the scope of the study and concentrating on the board's reaction to a greenmail proposal, rather than its governance performance in general, the observation of the board's governing impact and the identification of relevant exogenous influences become more straightforward than in studies of annual performance. The study's findings will allow us to identify structural contingency factors that are likely to affect the governing effectiveness of boards in general and which therefore provide direction for future research.

GREENMAIL: A MEASURE OF BOARD INEFFECTIVENESS

The private repurchase of company stock at a premium above the market price became quite popular in the period between 1979 and 1984 when firms spent about five and one-half billion dollars to repurchase their shares in private transactions, at an aggregate premium of over one billion dollars (Securities and Exchange Commission, 1984). For blocks of stock that ranged in size from 5 to 20 percent, companies paid prices that were on average 5 to 50 percent higher than the market price (Bradley and Wakeman, 1983).

Greenmail transactions generally occur under the explicit or rumored threat that a substantial stockholder will challenge the incumbent management in a takeover or a proxy fight. In

Greenmail

exchange for a premium above the market price, management could thwart the threat and protect its own control position by buying back the stockholder's stake in a private transaction. "Raiders" like David Murdock, Carl Icahn, and Victor Posner are known to systematically screen for potential greenmail targets among companies that are temporarily undervalued due to managerial inefficiency or cyclical market effects (*Business Week,* 1985).

Private repurchases of stock are in conflict with stockholders' interests for several reasons. First, greenmail allows the incumbent management to consolidate its control position and to shield itself from the disciplining influence of the market for corporate control, because it eliminates a minority stockholder who is a potential threat to management's control of the company. Such a repurchase renders ineffective an important incentive for efficient managerial performance and could induce more opportunistic and self-indulgent managerial behavior at stockholders' expense (Bradley and Wakeman, 1983; Dann and DeAngelo, 1983). Second, private stock repurchases discriminate against small corporate stockholders: only substantial stockholders who can create credible threats to management's control position are able to extract the favorable conditions of a greenmail transaction. Third, if the company finances the stock repurchase and the premium payment through debt, then the greenmail payment transfers wealth away from the company's residual stockholders. This wealth transfer may become reflected in reduced dividend payments or in the higher risk of corporate default, which lowers the market value of the firm's securities and decreases the value of future investment opportunities for stockholders (Brealey and Myers, 1981:391).

Empirical research evidence further demonstrates that greenmail transactions that terminate potential takeover attempts negatively affect the value of the firm, because the average private stock repurchase is followed by a significant drop in the target company's average abnormal returns[1] (Bradley and Wakeman, 1983; Dann and DeAngelo, 1983; Securities and Exchange Commission, 1984). For instance, for a total sample of 61 private stock repurchases between 1974 and 1980, Bradley and Wakeman (1984) reported that the companies' average abnormal returns dropped significantly, with 3.8 percent in the 30-day period beginning the day before the repurchase was announced. For the same time period, the authors reported an average drop in average abnormal returns of 12.5 percent for the 21 repurchases that terminated an explicit takeover bid. This average drop in stockholders' return also tends to eliminate the initial rise in the company's stock that occurs at the time that the prospective raider acquires his stake in the company and elicits expectations of an upcoming takeover bid. An SEC study on 89 greenmail transactions between 1979 and 1983, for instance, reported a total decline in average abnormal returns of 3.6 percent from the day of the raider's stock acquisition up to five days after the repurchase (Securities and Exchange Commission, 1984).

It should be recognized, however, that greenmail has also been defended as being favorable to stockholders' interests because it informs the market of the firm's present value and disciplines inefficient managements (Macey and McChesney,

1
A company's abnormal return is the difference between the recorded rate of return for the company's stock on a particular trading day and the company's normal rate of return. The normal rate of return is an estimate of the typical return for a company's stock; the single-factor market model defines it as a function of the company's specific risk factors (α, β) and the rate of return for the total market (R_m), or [$\alpha + \beta R_m$]. A drop in a company's abnormal return represents a negative-wealth effect for stockholders.

1985). However, the evidence in support of this view is not conclusive so far (Holderness and Sheehan, 1984; Mickelson and Ruback, 1984; Securities and Exchange Commission, 1984). Moreover, there is no systematic evidence available at this point on the long-term effects of greenmail on corporate performance and the value of the firm.

Therefore, based on the available evidence, one can conclude that, by depriving stockholders of a potential takeover bid for the sake of management's prolonged control, the private repurchase of stock leaves residual stockholders with a net loss in wealth. Hence, it follows that boards of directors that allow management to secure its own control position by paying greenmail at stockholders' expense prove ineffective in governing management's performance and in protecting stockholders' interests. From this observation the following research question emerges: What structural attributes distinguish boards that were ineffective in preventing management from paying greenmail at stockholders' expense from boards that effectively resisted greenmail?

THEORETICAL BACKGROUND

The organization and management literature provides only limited insight into this question. Although boards of directors have been studied quite extensively by sociologists and organization theorists, most of the research focuses on the board's external role within the global society, within the industry or the interorganizational network, rather than on the board's internal governing role. For instance, in their class-hegemony model of boards, Marxist sociologists have identified the board as a vehicle used by the American upper class to enhance and consolidate its ruling position in modern society (Mills, 1956; Domhoff, 1969; Ratcliff, 1980). Likewise, theories of interlocking directorates have depicted boards as the focal points in interorganizational networks, where directors with multiple board memberships promote the informal coordination of corporate activities and transactions (e.g., Dooley, 1969; Allen, 1974; Burt, 1979; Pennings, 1980). Resource-dependency theorists have studied the implications of these interorganizational linkages for the interlocked company and have emphasized the instrumental, boundary-spanning role of boards and their outside directors in managing the company's dependence on external suppliers of resources (Zald, 1967; Pfeffer, 1972; Pfeffer and Salancik, 1978). Within the field of organization and management theory, the internal governance performance of boards is only addressed as part of a general theory of managerial hegemony.

A Theory of Managerial Hegemony

The theory of managerial hegemony describes the board as a legal fiction: a co-opted appendage institution that, despite its formal governing power over management, is in fact dominated by corporate managements and, hence, ineffective in alleviating conflicts of interests between management and stockholders (Galbraith, 1967; Mace, 1971; Herman, 1981; Vance, 1983; Wolfson, 1984). As a result, the board's role in corporate governance is confined to being "another management [-dominated] tool" (Pfeffer, 1972:219), a passive and compliant "rubber stamp" for management's proposals and decisions (Herman, 1981). This instrumental view of corporate boards is consistent with the traditional managerialist theory of corporate control, which emphasizes managements' growing control of corporate affairs as corporate ownership becomes more dispersed among many small stockholders (Berle and Means, 1932; Williamson, 1964; Winter, 1964).

According to the managerial hegemony theory, the board's lack of detachment is a result of management's control over the selection of outside board members (Mace, 1971; Williams, 1979), which is said to induce the co-optation of compliant directors, who are expected to rubber-stamp management's policies (Herman, 1981; Wolfson, 1984). The directors' passive board behavior is further attributed to their relative lack of knowledge about the company's affairs (Estes, 1980), their dependence on information and insights that are provided by the company's top executives (Bacon and Brown, 1975; Wolfson, 1984), and the directors' interests in the benefits that accrue from their mere board membership but that are unaffected by the board's actual governing effectiveness: board compensation, the prestige and status that are associated with board memberships, and the reciprocation of favors among executives and directors (Mills, 1981; Hirsch, 1982; Vance, 1983). Directors, therefore, are expected to refrain from overt criticism of management's behavior in order not to jeopardize their board seat and its associated benefits. The theory of managerial hegemony thus depicts the board as an ineffective governing institution and attributes its ineffectiveness to the outside directors' lack of independence from the incumbent management.

The empirical evidence in support of this theory is scarce. The managerial hegemony perspective on boards is commonly illustrated by single case studies and anecdotes of companies whose failing performance is explained in terms of the preponderance of outside directors on their boards and those directors' passive board behavior (e.g., Koontz, 1967; Mace, 1971; Louden, 1982). Only a few studies have empirically tested the board's governing performance for a larger sample of companies (e.g., Vance, 1964; Pfeffer, 1972; Chaganti, Mahajan, and Sharma, 1985). Their results provide mixed support for the claim that boards are ineffective monitors of managerial performance and that corporate performance is negatively affected by the board's outside directors. The most interesting findings from the managerialist perspective have been provided by recent survey studies, designed to explore the profile of directors and their perspectives on their legal governance role (Drieghe, 1982; Hirsch, 1982; Spencer, 1983; Whisler, 1984). For instance, participating directors emphasized how prestige and the reciprocation of mutual favors among directors and executives were more powerful incentives for joining boards than the financial benefits that accrue from board memberships. Also, top executives described the accumulation of multiple board memberships as a normal extension of their corporate career (Hirsch, 1982).

Agency Theory

Outside organization and management theory, the board's governance performance is studied in agency theory. Agency theory is a theory of the firm that analyzes the managerial incentive problems that are induced by the separation of corporate ownership and corporate decision making (Alchian and Demsetz, 1972; Jensen and Meckling, 1976; Fama and Jensen, 1983). The theory defines the relationship between management and stockholders as a contract between agents and principals in which the agent's behavior is conditioned by the incentive structures that are implicitly or explicitly incorporated in the contract. Agency problems arise in corporations because the agents (i.e., professional managers) stop bearing the full wealth effects of their own decisions if they do not own a substantial part of the corporation's equity. Under those conditions, the agents are likely to engage in behavior that benefits their personal wealth or power but that is opportunistic and inefficient from the principals' (i.e., stockholders') point of view (Jensen and Meckling, 1976). Examples of such inefficient managerial behavior are the excessive use of company resources for managerial "perks," which may range from free lunches to private jets (Jensen and Meckling, 1976), the adoption of a short-term, risk-aversive attitude in strategic investment decisions for the sake of stability and the protection of management's own control position (Lambert and Larcker, 1985), or the excessive pursuit of diversification as a strategy to increase the firm's size and the managers' associated prestige and status (Amihud and Lev, 1981).

Assuming that such agency problems are prevalent in corporations, agency theorists concentrate their research on identifying the optimal structure and the relative effectiveness of monitoring mechanisms that discipline management's opportunistic inclinations and reduce the negative effects on wealth for stockholders. Potential monitoring devices include executive compensation programs with incentive systems or stock-option plans (Harris and Raviv, 1979; Lambert and Larcker, 1985), the disciplining impact of competitive forces in the product market (Williamson, 1964) and in the managerial labor market (Fama, 1980), and the threat of takeovers in the market for corporate control (e.g., Manne, 1965; Walkling and Long, 1984). For example, the competition in the market for corporate control disciplines management's opportunism because prolonged managerial inefficiency is most likely to initiate a downward trend in the firm's stock price. The resulting undervaluation of the company's shares makes the company an attractive target for takeovers and, hence, jeopardizes management's control position. In addition, excessively self-indulgent management behavior could damage the executives' career prospects and lower the value of their human capital in the managerial labor market (Fama, 1980).

It is within this framework that agency theorists have identified the board as an alternative monitoring device that helps control the corporate agency problem by governing management's decisions and assessing their impact on stockholders' wealth (Alchian and Demsetz, 1972; Fama and Jensen, 1983). While the board's internal monitoring role complements external monitoring devices like the competition in the markets for corporate control and managerial labor, board governance also has advantages over the discipline of such global market forces; the board's interventions can be proactive, more fine-tuned, and more cost efficient than, for example, a change in control due to a takeover (Alchian and Demsetz, 1972; Fama and Jensen, 1983).

Agency theorists perceive the board's effectiveness in monitoring management as being critical for the survival of all corporations that are characterized by the separation of ownership and decision making (Fama and Jensen, 1983). Within this framework, the effectiveness of the board will largely depend on the directors' identification with stockholders' interests and their expertise and experience in strategic decision making and control.

Agency research on boards was initiated only recently (Baysinger and Butler, 1985; Baysinger and Zeithaml, 1985; Lambert, Larcker, and Lys, 1985). Baysinger and Butler (1985), for instance, compared the financial performance of 266 major U.S. business corporations over a 10-year period and found that the relative independence of boards, measured by the proportion of outside directors, had a positive yet lagged effect on the firms' average return on equity, relative to the industry's average return. Their findings suggest a more complex relationship between a board's relative independence and a company's financial performance.

A synthesis. The above review illustrates how managerial hegemony theory and agency theory share a similar focus: both concentrate on the board's relationship to corporate management and its stockholders. Both theories also assume the prevalence of a corporate control problem that induces conflicts of interest between corporate managers and stockholders and that surfaces in inefficient managerial behavior, with negative consequences for stockholders' wealth. The theories seem to digress on the issue of the board's actual governing performance. Managerial hegemony theory rejects the board of directors as a possible effective governing force in corporate control problems; agency theory underscores the governing potential of boards, along with alternative internal and external disciplinary forces. However, a thorough analysis of the theories indicates that the managerial hegemony theory is not as radical in rejecting board governance as a first reading might suggest. Rather, imbedded in each theory is a qualified perspective on the governing performance of boards that, with varying degrees of explicitness, identifies the conditions and attributes believed to lead to either effective or ineffective board governance. For managerial hegemony theorists, the board's failing performance is a result of the directors' lack of independence vis-à-vis corporate management. For agency theorists, critical conditions for effective board monitoring are the board's identification with stockholders' interests and the board's expertise in strategic decision making and control. So, although both theories draw on different disciplinary frameworks and although the agency perspective on boards is integrated in a better developed and structured model of corporate control, both theories are complementary in identifying the structural contingencies that might affect a board's performance in acute problems of corporate governance, such as the greenmail attempts that are the focus of this study.

Hypotheses

The managerial hegemony perspective on board governance

suggests that the board's ineffectiveness in resisting greenmail will be induced by the outside directors' dependence on management. This dependence will be most acute in situations in which exogenous relationships exist between outside directors and managers. Family ties, contractual transactions, or informal reciprocity arrangements may consolidate the directors' dependency by making their board membership and their board behavior subordinate to the terms and the continuation of their external interactions with the company's management. For instance, outside board members who are related to the company's managers, and who might have been selected for this reason, may feel more inclined to support publicly the proposals of their family-member executives than would unrelated directors. Outside directors may also experience this pressure when their board position is subject to an informal arrangement in which executives and outside directors reciprocate favors by sitting on each others' boards (Hirsch, 1982; Whisler, 1984). In order to ensure the executives' support on their own board, these outside directors may easily fall victim to a code of mutual deference and forbearance that impels them to comply with management's policies according to the norm that "I won't stir up dust at your board if you don't stir up dust at my board" (Bacon and Brown, 1975; Vance, 1983). A third factor in compliance is the existence of contractual connections. Outside directors who have established transactions with the company or who represent external contractors may consider their board membership as an instrument for securing their own contract rather than for promoting stockholders' interests in the value of the firm. Hence, these directors are likely to engage in compliant, opportunistic board behavior in order to ensure management's continued support for the contract (Eisenberg, 1975; Smith, 1977).

The above discussion leads to the following hypotheses:

Hypothesis 1: Boards of directors that paid greenmail at stockholders' expense will have more members of the company executives' families among their outside directors than boards that successfully resisted paying greenmail.

Hypothesis 2: Boards of directors that paid greenmail at stockholders' expense will have relatively more outside directors who acquired their board seat through an informal reciprocity arrangement with the company's management than do boards who successfully resisted paying greenmail.

Hypothesis 3: Boards of directors that paid greenmail at stockholders' expense will have more outside directors who are contractually linked to the company, be it directly or through affiliated organizations, than do boards that successfully resisted paying greenmail.

The agency definition of boards as effective governing institutions is contingent upon the outside directors' skills and expertise in decision control and their identification with stockholders' interests. A first critical factor for the board's effective governing performance when faced with paying greenmail would be the board's relative independence, or the proportion of outside board members. Effective board governance presumes that board members engage in a critical assessment of management's performance and that they take a dispassionate stand vis-à-vis management's interests and values. Only outside directors can effectively fulfill this monitoring role, since the inside directors' objectivity will be impaired by their dual role as full-time managers (Weidenbaum, 1984). Hence, the higher the relative number of outsiders on the board, the lower the probability that the board will be dominated by the company's management and that it will tolerate managerial opportunism at stockholders' expense:

Hypothesis 4: Boards that successfully resisted paying greenmail will have a higher proportion of outside directors than boards that paid greenmail at stockholders' expense.

The agency definition of board monitoring further presumes that the board's outside directors identify with the interests of the company's stockholders and that they have the skills to assess accurately the performance of its management. Agency theorists have extensively studied the conditions that promote executives' identification with stockholders' interests. They agree that executives with high-equity interests in the company—relative to their income from fixed compensation—are less likely to engage in decisions that have negative consequences for stockholders' wealth (Larcker and Balkcom, 1984; Walkling and Long, 1984). Similarly, one can expect outside directors' stockholdings in the company to promote their identification with stockholders' interests and to reinforce the directors' critical assessment of management's performance:

Hypothesis 5: The outside directors of boards that successfully resisted paying greenmail will, on average, own a higher value of company equity than the outside directors of boards that paid greenmail.

Also critical for the board's governing effectiveness are the directors' skills and experience in assessing the implications of strategic decisions on future corporate performance and stockholders' wealth (Smith, 1977). Outside directors who hold executive positions in other companies could be important contributors to a board's governing performance, since they can draw on their own expertise and experience as strategic decision makers:

Hypothesis 6: Boards that resisted paying greenmail will have a higher proportion of outside directors who have executive experience in other companies than do boards that paid greenmail.

The above hypotheses were tested in a comparative analysis of the 53 boards of all U.S. companies that were publicly identified as having paid greenmail between 1979 and 1983 and a sample of 57 boards of U.S. companies that resisted greenmail in the same time period, although they faced the same threat for corporate control as the greenmail-paying companies.

METHOD

Sample

The companies studied were identified in a nonrandom process and were selected on the basis of their exposure to greenmail, to allow a juxtaposition of boards that were positioned at opposite ends of the performance continuum: boards that allowed greenmail payment versus boards that resisted the greenmail option. Boards of companies that never faced a challenge for control by a minority stockholder were not considered for the analysis, because it would have been impossible to judge their relative effectiveness in protecting stockholders' interests in a greenmail attempt.

For the period 1979–1983, 53 boards were identified as having allowed greenmail payment amidst reported rumors or explicit threats for a takeover or a proxy fight by a minority stockholder. Only those repurchases that involved 5 percent or more of the company's outstanding equity were included, in order to ensure that the minority stockholder involved represented a credible takeover threat that induced an acute agency conflict for the incumbent management. All reported private repurchases that occurred between 1979 and 1983 were identified by screening the section of "Reacquired Shares" in the *Wall Street Journal Index,* an annual listing of all the companies that were reported by the *Wall Street Journal* as buying back stock in open or private transactions. In order to distinguish the greenmail transactions from other open stock repurchases, the actual terms of each repurchase and the prevalence of rumored or explicit takeover threats were verified through extensive readings of the original *Wall Street Journal* articles that reported the transactions.

All 53 greenmail-paying companies that were thus selected were listed on the New York Stock Exchange or the American Stock Exchange. The size of the stock repurchases ranged from 5 to 38 percent of the company's outstanding stock, with an average of 13 percent. The companies in the sample paid an average premium of 55 percent over the stock price.[2] Nine of them paid more than twice the stock price, or a premium of over 100 percent. A second set of 57 boards was identified that had resisted paying greenmail under the same circumstances that characterized the greenmail transactions in the first sample during the same time period. Companies were selected if (1) one of eight notorious corporate raiders (the Bass brothers, the Belzberg family, Carl Icahn, Irwin Jacobs, Carl Lindner, David Murdock, Victor Posner, and Saul Steinberg) had acquired 5 percent or more of the company's stock between 1979 and 1983, and (2) if the raider had increased his stockholdings within one year following the original acquisition, (3) amidst reported rumors or explicit threats of a control battle. The raiders were selected on the basis of their reported reputations as "aggressive greenmail hunters" in the popular business press (*Business Week; Fortune;* the *Wall Street Journal*). Because each of them had also triggered at least one of the greenmail transactions that had been selected for study in the first sample, their challenge was judged to be credible enough to induce a greenmail transaction, ceteris paribus. However, the other selection criteria were included to underline the credibility of this challenge for control.

As a first step in the sample definition, the investment activities of each of the eight raiders between 1979 and 1983 were reconstructed from reports in the *Wall Street Journal* and the "General Section" of the *Wall Street Journal Index.* Included under each raider's investments were all stock transactions made by companies that were either affiliated with the raider or controlled by him during the observation period. The raiders' affiliated companies were identified by extensive screening of articles in the *Wall Street Journal, Barron's, Dow*

2
The premium was defined as the relative difference between the repurchase price per share and the stock price 30 days before the minority stockholder had acquired his stake in the company. The date of the initial acquisition is reported in 13D reports, which a new stockholder has to file with the SEC when he acquires 5 percent or more of a company's outstanding securities.

Jones News Service, and *Mergers and Acquisitions*. A list of all companies in which the raider had acquired 5 percent or more of the outstanding equity was derived from each raider's investment activities. The size and the terms of the acquisition were verified in the 13D reports, which are periodically published in the *SEC News Digest* and *Insiders' Chronicle*. Subsequent changes in the raider's stockholdings up to January 1985 were recorded, to verify that the raider had increased his stockholdings at least once within one year after the initial acquisition and had publicly challenged management's control position. The *Wall Street Journal, Business Week, Fortune,* and *Insiders' Chronicle* were the main sources for this verification. The one-year period was selected as a cut-off time because one year was the average period between the raiders' initial stock acquisition and the greenmail transaction for the 53 companies in the first sample.

Among the companies that met these selection criteria, 57 were found to have resisted paying greenmail despite the presence of a notorious raider among their stockholders. Of the 57 companies thus selected, 17 companies were taken over by January 1985, only five of them by a raider. The fact that almost half of the other acquisitions occurred within one year after the raider's stock acquisition suggests that many companies resorted to a "white knight" to fight the raider's takeover attempt.

Different industries were reoresented in both samples of greenmail-paying and greenmail-resisting companies, as shown in Table 1. Compared to the greenmail-resisting companies, significantly more greenmail-paying companies belonged to the oil industry or were into consumer products, but fewer of them belonged to the financial sector. A first plausible explanation is that oil companies were relatively undervalued as a result of the lower oil prices and their production overcapacity, due to vigorous exploitation programs (*Business Week,* 1985). Another plausible explanatory factor is company size: a raider would need access to enormous sources of funds to create a credible takeover threat to a big company. In this sample, the average greenmail-paying company was indeed smaller than the average greenmail-resisting company, yet the difference was only significant in terms of firm value (Table 1). The significant differences in industry and firm value between the samples of greenmail-paying and greenmail-resisting companies had no further implications for the study's design, as neither variable was significantly correlated to any of the independent board variables.

Measures

For each of the 110 greenmail-paying and greenmail-resisting companies, data were collected on the six board attributes that were predicted to be relevant for the boards' governing performance in the greenmail decision: the proportion of outsiders; the proportion of outside directors with executive experience; the proportion of outside directors who were family of management, who had contracts with the company, or who had reciprocity arrangements with the company's management; and the average proportion of company equity that was held by the boards' outside directors. The measures, described in Table 2, were aggregated per board from the indi-

Table 1

Sample Characteristics of 53 Greenmail-Paying Companies and 57 Companies That Resisted Greenmail between 1979 and 1983

	Resisted greenmail	Paid greenmail
Industry (%)*		
Heavy industry	19	17
Petroleum	3	9
Consumer products	33	49
Services	19	17
Finance	26	6
X^2 (5df) = 11.57 ($p \leq .05$)		
Size (Means)		
No. of employees	12,003	8,103 (n.s.)
Sales (in dollars)	1,212,393	842,696 (n.s.)
No. of stockholders	13,520	10,442 (n.s.)
Firm value†	.4682E+10	.9026E+09‡

* Heavy industry includes mining, steel production, steel processing, and construction. Finance includes banking, insurance, and real estate.
† Firm value = (number of shares outstanding) × (stock price 30 days before 13D).
‡ $F(1,109) = 5.12 (p \leq .05)$.

Table 2

Measures of Independent and Control Variables

Variables	Measures
Board	
Family	Percentage of board's outside directors who are family of one of the company's executives.
Reciprocity	Percentage of board's outside directors who have one or more of the company's executives on their own board.
Contracts	Percentage of board's outside directors who have any of the following contracts with the company (directly or through the director's employer): trusteeship (5% or more of the company's equity); investment services; financial services; legal services; consulting services; or supply or purchase of materials/products.
Outsiders	Percentage of outside directors on board; i.e., directors not employed by the company and not retired from the company.
Executives	Percentage of board's outside directors who hold executive positions in other companies or organizations.
Equity	Average dollar value of company stock held by board's outside directors, relative to the total value of the company's outstanding equity.
Control	
Management resistance	[(No. of shares owned by top 3 executives) × (stockprice)] + [(No. of unexercised options held by top 3 executives) × (excess option value)] / ($ annual salary and bonuses for top 3 executives)*
Institutional investors	Percentage of company's outstanding equity held by institutional investors.†
Stock concentration	The average dollar value of corporate equity per stockholder (excluding the stock held by institutional investors, executives, and board members).

* Stock price was recorded 30 days before the raider or greenmail-seeking stockholder filed his acquisition of the company's stock in a 13D report with the SEC. Excess option value = [stock price—the option's exercise value] if stock price > exercise value, 0 if stock price ≤ exercise value. The top three executives are the three officers with the highest annual reported income from salary and bonuses.
† Source: *Standard and Poor's Stock Guide.*

vidual data that were collected for the companies' 759 outside directors (which is 62.7 percent of the sample's total population of both inside and outside directors). Only outside board members were included in the analysis because it was

Greenmail

presumed that only outsiders could effectively monitor corporate management. Outside directors were defined as all directors who were not employed full-time by the company or who had not retired from employment with the company. The profiles of the average board and the average outside director in the sample are described in the Appendix. The correlation matrix for the independent variables is reported in Table 3.

Table 3

Pearson Product-Moment Correlations among Board Variables (N = 110)

Variables (%)	Means	S.D.	1	2	3	4	5
1. Outsiders	62.66	15.67					
2. Executives	45.52	22.67	.11				
3. Reciprocity	3.49	8.32	−.36	.27••			
4. Family	5.00	12.04	−.28••	−.16	−.06		
5. Contracts	13.36	12.45	.07	−.23•	.04	.26••	
6. Equity	27,958.22	69,795.23	−.01	.18	−.05	−.49•	.06

•$p \le .05$; ••$p \le .01$.

Also included in the analysis were two control variables: management's own resistance to greenmail and the stockholders' control position. Both control variables were introduced because they represent factors that are likely to have influenced the company's decision whether or not to pay greenmail and the board's governing role in that decision. The impact of the board's governing performance on the greenmail decision is contingent on management's disposition toward greenmail. If management itself resists the private repurchase of company stock, then the board's governing intervention to protect stockholders' interests by rejecting greenmail is clearly less critical for the outcome of the decision. In addition, stockholders with a substantial stake in the company's equity are often actively involved in the company's decision making, and they may affect a company's resistance to greenmail.

The measure of management's resistance to greenmail was derived from the agency research on managerial resistance to takeovers. This literature provides consistent evidence that managements' opposition to a takeover is a positive function of their relative income from fixed salary and a negative function of the value of their equity holdings in the company (Hannan and Mavinga, 1980; Larcker and Balkcom, 1984; Walkling and Long, 1984). Given the protective effect of greenmail transactions for incumbent managements, managements that resist takeovers will also be interested in paying greenmail as a way to thwart unwanted challengers. Hence, managements are most likely to resist greenmail if they do not oppose a takeover, i.e., if their equity holdings in the company are high relative to their income from fixed compensation. The extent of stockholders' control was measured separately for the company's institutional investors and its residual stockholders by the relative concentration of their stockholdings (Table 2).

Data Collection

Except for the measures of director reciprocity and the control position of institutional investors, data for all measures were collected from the companies' proxy materials. Since proxies seek to solicit stockholders' approval for the annual reelection of directors and officers, they provide extensive information about the company's top management and board members as well as the latest developments in the company's strategies and performance. They further inform stockholders about managers' and directors' special interests in the company, such as stockholdings, existence of family ties among managers and directors, and any remunerated services that were provided by board members. Where possible, data from the proxies were cross-validated against information provided by *Standard and Poor's* and *Moody's Industrial Manual.* Data for the reciprocity variable were recorded from *Standard and Poor's Industrial Guide:* for each of the 759 outside directors, the board composition of the directors' principal company was examined to identify whether members of the target company's management were among the board members. Information about the percentage of equity that was controlled by institutional investors was recorded from *Standard and Poor's Stock Guide.*

The measures of the board variables and the control variables were observed for the year in which the greenmail transaction was announced. For the control sample, the variables were measured for the year following the raider's acquisition of stock, as reported in the 13D report. The board's governing performance and the impact of its composition were expected to be most critical during this one-year period, which corresponded to the average interval between the 13D filing and the greenmail transaction in the greenmail-paying sample.

Analysis

Linear discriminant analysis (LDA) was used to test the predicted effect of the six board characteristics on the outcome of the greenmail decision. Discriminant analysis was judged the proper technique because it provides a test of the differences between the average score profiles of two or more a priori defined groups in terms of a set of multiple predictor variables (Klecka, 1980). The technique also allows an evaluation of each variable's contribution to the discrimination, based on the relative magnitude of its coefficient in the discriminant function.

The analysis was done in two steps. First, LDA (direct method) was applied to the full sample to identify the relative impact of management's resistance and stockholders' control over the outcome of the greenmail decision. Next, in order to identify the discriminating profiles of effective and ineffective boards, LDA (direct method) was applied to a subsample of companies in which management's resistance to greenmail was low. A company's resistance to greenmail is an accurate proxy for a board's effectiveness in protecting stockholders' interests only if management is inclined to pay greenmail at stockholders' expense. If management would oppose paying greenmail to a threatening stockholder, then the board's monitoring performance would be less critical for the final decision. The company's rejection of greenmail could then be due either to management's own resistance to greenmail or the board's effectiveness in protecting stockholders' interests. The subsample of companies with low managerial

Greenmail

resistance to greenmail consisted of all greenmail-paying and greenmail-resisting companies for which the measure of management's resistance to greenmail was below the measure's median value for the total sample. Out of the total sample, 59 companies were thus identified as having management teams with low resistance to greenmail, 32 of which paid greenmail.

RESULTS

The goal of the first LDA was to evaluate the relative impact of the management, stockholders, and board variables on the outcome of the greenmail decision. The discriminant function of independent and control variables for the total sample of companies significantly separated the greenmail-paying and greenmail-resisting companies ($F(12,97) = 2.312$, $p \leq .001$). As shown in Table 4, the function's accuracy in distinguishing greenmail-paying from greenmail-resisting companies was significantly better than the outcome of classification by chance ($z = 5.13$, $p \leq .001$).

Table 4

Discriminant Function and Coefficients for 110 Companies

Discriminant function

Eigenvalue: .28663	
Group centroids:	Greenmail ($n_1 = 53$): −.55014 No greenmail ($n_2 = 57$): +.51154 $F(12,97) = 2.3169$ ($p \leq .01$)
Hit ratio: 74.55%	
Classification accuracy*:	$z = 5.1342$ ($p \leq .001$*)

Discriminant coefficients

Independent variables	Standardized discriminant weights	Rank	Structure correlations (loadings)	Predicted effect on the probability of "no greenmail"
Management resistance	.620	1	.527	+
Institutional investors	.487	3	.353	+
Stock concentration	.004	9	−.092	+
Outsiders	.286	5	.087	+
Executives	.258	6	.106	+
Reciprocity	.018	8	.181	−
Family	.451	4	.201	−
Contracts	.154	7	.188	−
Equity	−.561	2	−.580	+

$$*\ z = \frac{Y - \pi}{\sqrt{\frac{\pi(1 - \pi)}{n}}},$$

where Y = the proportion of correct classifications by the discriminant function; π = the outcome of classification by chance, and n = the total number of observations. π was determined by the proportional chance criterion $[\pi = (n_1/n)^2 + (n_2/n)^2]$ where n_i = the number of observations in group i (Joy and Tollefson, 1975).

The relative effect of each variable on the occurrence of greenmail was judged based on the absolute value of the variable's discriminant coefficient. Standardized discriminant coefficients were preferred over structure correlations because the coefficients' magnitudes reflect better the relative contribution of the individual predictor variables to the discriminant function (Klecka, 1980). The fact that discriminant coefficients are sensitive to a high level of multicollinearity among the predictor variables was not problematic for the present analysis because the intercorrelations among the independent variables (Table 3) were very low (Cochran, 1964; Eisenbeis, 1977). The direction of each variable's effect on the greenmail outcome was reflected in the sign of its discriminant coefficient: a positive discriminant coefficient indicated that the variable was positively related to the company's resistance to greenmail (the greenmail-resisting group had a positive centroid); a negative discriminant coefficient indicated that the variable was positively related to the payment of greenmail (the greenmail-paying group had a negative centroid).

Accordingly, management's own resistance to greenmail was the most powerful factor in explaining a company's payment of or resistance to greenmail. Whether or not the companies in the sample paid greenmail was mostly dependent on management's own incentives for resisting greenmail: the higher managers' stockholdings in the company, relative to their income from salary and bonuses, the lower the probability that the company paid greenmail.

The companies' resistance to greenmail was further determined by the percentage of company stock that was held by institutional investors. As expected, companies that resisted paying greenmail had a higher proportion of their equity controlled by institutional investors than did companies that paid greenmail. Both management's resistance and the control position of institutional investors were more relevant for a company's resistance to paying greenmail than any of the board characteristics, except for the average amount of equity that was held by the board's outside directors. The concentration of stock among the company's residual stockholders contributed little to the outcome of the greenmail decision.

Linear discriminant analysis was repeated for the subsample of 59 companies with low management resistance to greenmail, in order to assess the performance effect of the different board attributes. Table 5 shows that the discriminant function of board variables did not significantly separate greenmail-paying from greenmail-resisting companies [$F(11,47) = 1.727$]. Yet the function's hit ratio of successful classifications (75 percent) was significantly better than the outcome of random classification ($z = 3.72$, $p \leq .001$). of the greenmail-paying companies with low management resistance, 81 percent were correctly classified (compared to 55 percent by chance), as were 66 percent of the companies that had resisted paying greenmail despite management's low resistance (compared to 45 percent by chance).

The discriminant weights for most characteristics in the second analysis were considerably higher than their corresponding weights in the unsegmented sample. In other words, more board characteristics were found relevant for the outcome of the greenmail decision after having controlled for the impact of management's resistance. This finding is consistent with the presumption that board composition and the outside directors' profile would be most relevant for the outcome of the greenmail decision when management's resistance to paying greenmail was low and management's and stockholders' interests were in acute conflict.

Greenmail

Table 5

Discriminant Function and Coefficients for 59 Companies with Low Managerial Resistance to Greenmail

Discriminant function

Eigenvalue: .40420	
Group centroids:	Greenmail (n_1 = 32): −.57401
	No greenmail (n_2 = 27): +.68030
	F(11,47) = 1.7270 (n.s.)
Hit ratio: 75%	
Classification accuracy:	$z = 3.72$ ($p \leq .001$)

Discriminant coefficients

Independent variables	Standardized discriminant weights	Rank	Structure correlations (loadings)	Predicted effect on the probability of "no greenmail"
Institutional investors	.241	7	.195	+
Stock concentration	.390	5	−.075	+
Outsiders	.584	1	.087	+
Reciprocity	−.180	8	.029	−
Family	−.267	6	−.103	−
Contracts	.502	3	.384	−
Equity	−.478	4	−.181	+
Executives	.545	2	.277	+

The most relevant positive discriminators between the boards of greenmail-paying and greenmail-resisting companies were the proportion of outside directors and the proportion of outside directors with executive jobs. As predicted by the agency model, boards of companies that resisted greenmail had a higher proportion of outside directors and a higher proportion of outside director-executives. The outside directors' equity holdings had a negative effect on the company's resistance to paying greenmail. This finding was inconsistent with the agency prediction that directors' equity holdings would promote their identification with stockholders' interest and hence lower the probability of paying greenmail.

Boards of companies that paid greenmail also counted more family members of management among their outside directors, as well as a higher proportion of directors whose board position was reciprocated by external board seats for one or more of the company's executives. These findings were consistent with the hypotheses of the managerial hegemony model that kinship relationships and reciprocity arrangements would promote the board's compliance with corporate managements, even when management is in favor of paying greenmail. A similar prediction for boards whose outside directors had contracts with the company was not supported: boards of companies that effectively resisted paying greenmail had significantly more outside directors who were contractually linked to the company than did the greenmail-paying companies.

DISCUSSION

This study identifies a number of board characteristics that were significantly related to the boards' effectiveness in preventing management from paying greenmail at stockholders' expense: the proportion of outside directors, the proportion of outsiders with executive experience, and the proportion of outsiders with contractual interests in the company. A negative performance effect was found for the presence of management's family members and directors with reciprocity arrangements among the board members and for the outside directors' average equity holdings in the company. Because the study was based on a selected sample that focused on greenmail problems only, no predictions can be made about the role of these respective board attributes for a board's global governing performance. Yet, at the same time, the narrow focus of the study allowed a more accurate definition of board performance than is possible in studies using corporate financial performance as a dependent variable. Therefore, the board attributes that were here found to distinguish the boards of greenmail-paying and greenmail-resisting companies could represent meaningful variables in the explanation of differential board performance and are therefore directive for future research.

For instance, the higher proportion of outside directors that was found on the boards of greenmail-resisting companies could reflect the superior governing performance of independent outsiders compared to inside directors, as is suggested by a number of research studies (Baysinger and Butler, 1985; Lambert, Larcker, and Lys, 1985). However, several other studies have failed to find a significant direct relationship between the presence of outside directors and board and company performance (Schmidt, 1977; Chaganti, Mahajan, and Sharma, 1985; Waldo, 1985). A plausible explanation for this lack of significant results is that the contribution of outside directors to the board's governing performance is contingent on the characteristics of the company and its environment (Drieche and Baysinger, 1986) and on the outside directors' qualifications and performance incentives.

Among the latter group of factors, a first category of potential contingencies that is suggested by the findings of the present study concerns the directors' social and professional relations with corporate management. The theory of managerial hegemony emphasizes the detrimental effect of such external links on the board's governing performance. The argument is consistent with the traditional class-hegemony theory of boards, which argues that family ties and friendship relationships between directors and management promote the directors' compliance with management because they make the board part of the social network that supports the internal cohesion of America's upper class (Mills, 1956; Domhoff, 1969; Koenig and Gogel, 1981). Also, survey results suggest that reciprocity arrangements through which directors and executives exchange board seats induce a similar compliance effect, because it makes directors and executives dependent on each others' support for their respective proposals and decisions (Leech and Mundheim, 1976; Hirsch, 1982).

However, the finding that companies that resisted paying greenmail had relatively more contracts with their outside directors than companies that paid greenmail would suggest that the "old-boy network" of executives and directors is not supported by contractual relationships between outside directors and the company (Vance, 1983). Possibly, the directors' explicit stake in the company's performance could promote their scrutiny of management's performance more than their compliance with management's proposals.

Greenmail

A second category of potential contingency factors that was identified by the present findings concerns the directors' professional qualifications. An effective governing board requires the input of directors who are "experts in decision control," based on their experience in other organizations (Fama and Jensen, 1983: 315). Corporate governance reformers underscore this view as they advocate the need to select outside directors on the basis of their integrity and their ability to ratify and monitor managerial decisions (Eisenberg, 1975; Smith, 1977). Accordingly, outside directors who have executive experience in other companies might be better-performing board members. However, this does not necessarily explain the fact that the greenmail-resisting companies in this sample had more outside directors with executive experience than the greenmail-paying companies. Alternatively, directors with executive jobs may have had a personal stake in the company's rejection of greenmail: their resistance to greenmail may have been induced by the fear of developing a reputation as being lenient toward greenmail, which would have made their own company a potential target for subsequent greenmail raids.

A third category of contingency factors that was here identified concerns the outside directors' performance incentives. So far, there is no clear evidence available about the motivating impact of directors' stockholdings in the company, aside from speculations and incidental evidence (Bacon and Brown, 1975; Vance, 1983). Agency research has shown that management's relative equity ownership in the company motivates managers to promote stockholders' interests when making strategic decisions (Amihud and Lev, 1981; Larcker and Balkcom, 1984; Walkling and Long, 1984). Possibly, equity ownership does not have the same motivational effect on directors' performance because their equity interests in the company are too small. In the current sample, for instance, outside directors' equity holdings were significantly smaller than the equity holdings by the companies' top three executives ($p \leq .05$).

Of all three types of contingencies that have here been identified as potentially relevant for the governing performance of boards, the impact of equity ownership, combined with the effect of other incentives such as board compensation, the directors' social network and their reputation, seems the most promising topic for future research. For, as corporate directors face increasing charges on their legal liabilities and as boards become more actively involved in strategic decision making, the effective performance of boards and their outside directors could become more critically dependent on the right incentive structure.

The design of future research to study the performance effect of these contingencies will involve a trade-off between the meaningfulness of the findings and their generalizability. For instance, the current study was designed to overcome the limited interpretability of studies that equate board performance with corporate financial performance without controlling for the effect of multiple endogenous and exogenous factors. Yet, when studying the board's performance for a specific governance problem such as greenmail, the interpretation of the findings cannot be extended beyond the greenmail problem, and the definition of the critical incident becomes critical for the validity of the results. The problem that is at the core of this design dilemma is the relationship between board performance and corporate (financial) performance. Studying the impact of board composition and board performance on corporate performance requires a comprehensive contingency model that incorporates the strategic factors that determine the fit between the organization's structure and leadership or between its strategy and its environment; or, a trend analysis could be developed that measures board and company performance over time. Other designs, such as the one developed in this study, cannot validly examine the extent to which board attributes have an impact on the company's financial performance; neither do they allow an extrapolation of the findings on board performance to the company's financial performance.

Although this study focused on the role of structural contingencies in a board's governance performance, a thorough understanding of the role and performance of boards of directors also requires that a number of new areas be explored. A first important issue for future research concerns the dynamics of board governance, including the processes and procedures of board decision making and decision control, and the formation of power coalitions among directors and executives. In addition, more research is needed about the extent to which boards can effectively combine different functions within an organization (Mintzberg, 1985; Drieghe and Baysinger, 1986). For instance, although outside directors who represent vertically interdependent organizations are commonly depicted as "common messengers" (Pennings, 1980: 23) who assist management in controlling a company's resource dependency, the present findings suggest that these directors may also play a role in the governance of managerial decisions. Other studies have emphasized the board's support function in the company's strategy formulation and implementation (Baysinger and Zeithaml, 1985) and its role in coping with the company's dependence on external resources (Zald, 1967; Pfeffer, 1972; Pfeffer and Salancik, 1978)

Finally, the hypotheses of this study were derived from a confrontation of two different approaches to board governance: a managerial hegemony model and agency theory. The fact that both frameworks were found to offer relevant insights into the contingencies that might affect board performance in corporate governance illustrates how the integration of different research traditions can provide new insights into the functioning and performance of corporate boards of directors.

REFERENCES

Alchian, Armen A., and Harold Demsetz
1972 "Production, information costs and economic organization." American Economic Review, 62: 777–795.

Allen, Michael P.
1974 "The structure of interorganizational elite cooptation: Interlocking directorates." American Sociological Review, 39: 393–406.

American Law Institute
1982 Principles of Corporate Governance and Structure: Restatement and Recommendations. New York: American Law Institute.

Greenmail

Amihud, Yakow, and Baruch Lev
1981 "Risk reduction as a managerial motive for conglomerate mergers." Bell Journal of Economics, 12: 650–667.

Bacon, Jeremy, and James K. Brown
1975 Corporate Directorship Practices: Role, Selection and Legal Status of the Board. New York: Conference Board.

Baysinger, Barry D., and Henry D. Butler
1985 "Corporate governance and the board of directors: Performance effects of changes in board composition." Journal of Law, Economics and Organizations, 1: 101–124.

Baysinger, Barry D., and Carl P. Zeithaml
1985 "A contingency approach to diversification and board composition: Theory and empirical evidence." Paper presented at the Annual Meetings of the Academy of Management, San Diego, August.

Berle, Adolph A., Jr., and Gardiner C. Means
1932 The Modern Corporation and Private Property. New York: Macmillan.

Bradley, Michael, and L. Macdonald Wakeman
1983 "The wealth effects of targeted share repurchases." Journal of Financial Economics, 11: 366–373.

Brealey, Richard, and Stewart Myers
1981 Principles of Corporate Finance. New York: McGraw-Hill.

Burt, R. S.
1979 "A structural theory of interlocking corporate directorates." Social Networks, 1: 415–435.

Business Roundtable
1978 The Role and Composition of the Board of Directors of the Large Publicly Held Corporation. New York: Business Roundtable.

Business Week
1985 "The raiders: They are really breaking the vise of the managing class." March 4: 80–91.

Chaganti, Rajeswararao S., Vijay Mahajan, and Subhash Sharma
1985 "Corporate board size, composition and corporate failures in retailing industry." Journal of Management Studies, 22: 400–416.

Cochran, William G.
1964 "On the performance of the linear discriminant function." Technometrics, 6: 179–190.

Dann, Larry Y., and Harry DeAngelo
1983 "Standstill agreements, privately negotiated stock purchases and the market for corporate control." Journal of Financial Economics, 11: 275–300.

Domhoff, William G.
1969 Who Rules America? Englewood Cliffs, NJ: Prentice-Hall.

Dooley, Peter D.
1969 "The interlocking directorate." American Economic Review, 59: 314–323.

Drieghe, Rita H.
1982 "External directorships and interlocking directorates: A survey of corporate directors." Unpublished manuscript, Texas A&M University.

Drieghe, Rita H., and Barry D. Baysinger
1986 "Boards of directors and corporate governance: Is board independence a fallacy?" Paper presented at the Annual Meetings of the Academy of Management, Chicago, August.

Eisenbeis, Robert A.
1977 "Pitfalls in the application of discriminant analysis in business, finance, and economics." Journal of Finance, 32: 875–900.

Eisenberg, Melvin
1975 "Legal models of management structure in the modern corporation: Officers, directors and accountants." California Law Review, 63: 375–386.
1976 The Structure of the Corporation. Boston: Little, Brown.

Estes, Robert M.
1980 "Corporate governance in the courts." Harvard Business Review, 58 (July–August): 50–58.

Fama, Eugene F.
1980 "Agency problems and the theory of the firm." Journal of Political Economy, 88: 288–307.

Fama, Eugene F., and Michael C. Jensen
1983 "Separation of ownership and control." Journal of Law and Economics, 26: 301–325.

Galbraith, John K.
1967 The New Industrial State. New York: New American Library.

Hannan, Timothy, and Ferdinand Mavinga
1980 "Expense preference and managerial control: The case of the banking firm." Bell Journal of Economics, 11: 671–682.

Harris, Milton, and Artur Raviv
1979 "Optimal incentive contracts with imperfect information." Journal of Economic Theory, 20: 231–259.

Henn, Harry G.
1974 Corporation Law. St. Paul, MN: West Publishing.

Herman, Edward S.
1981 Corporate Control, Corporate Power. New York: Cambridge University Press.

Hirsch, Paul M.
1982 "The view from the boardroom: Fortune 500 directors' response to research and models about them." Unpublished manuscript, Graduate School of Business, University of Chicago.

Holderness, Clifford G., and Dennis P. Sheehan
1984 "Raiders or saviors? The evidence on six controversial investors." Unpublished manuscript, No. MERC 84-06, Graduate School of Management, University of Rochester.

Jensen, Michael C., and William H. Meckling
1976 "Theory of the firm: Managerial behavior, agency costs and ownership structure." Journal of Financial Economics, 3: 305–360.

Joy, O. Maurice, and John D. Tollefson
1975 "On the financial applications of discriminant analysis." Journal of Financial and Quantitative Analysis, 10: 723–739.

Klecka, William R.
1980 Discriminant Analysis. Beverly Hills, CA: Sage.

Koenig, Thomas, and Robert Gogel
1981 "Interlocking corporate directorates as a social network." American Journal of Economics and Sociology, 40: 37–50.

Koontz, Harold
1967 The Board of Directors and Effective Management. New York: McGraw-Hill.

Lambert, Richard A., and David F. Larcker
1985 "Executive compensation, corporate decision-making and shareholder wealth: A review of the evidence." Midland Corporate Finance Journal, 2: 6–22.

Lambert, Richard A., David F. Larcker, and Thomas Lys
1985 "Takeover resistance, managerial incentives, and shareholder wealth." Unpublished manuscript, The Wharton School, University of Pennsylvania.

Larcker, David F., and John E. Balkcom
1984 "Executive compensation contracts and investment behavior: An analysis of mergers." Unpublished manuscript, The Wharton School, University of Pennsylvania.

Leech, Noyes, and Robert H. Mundheim
1976 "The outside director of the publicly held corporation." Business Lawyer, 31: 1799–1810.

Louden, J. Keith
1982 The Director: A Professional's Guide to Effective Board Work. New York: American Management Association.

Mace, Miles LaGrange
1971 Directors: Myth and Reality. Boston: Harvard University Press.

Macey, Jonathon R., and Fred S. McChesney
1985 "The theoretical analysis of corporate greenmail." Yale Law Journal, 95: 13–26.

Manne, Henry G.
1965 "Mergers and the market for corporate control." Journal of Political Economy, 73: 110–120.

Mickelson, Wayne H., and Richard S. Ruback
1984 "Corporate investments in common stock." Unpublished manuscript, Sloan School of Management, Massachusetts Institute of Technology.

Mills, C. Wright
1956 The Power Elite. London: Oxford University Press.

Mills, Geoffrey
1981 On the Board. Hampshire, England: Wiley.

Mintzberg, Henry
1983 Power In and Around Organizations. Englewood Cliffs, NJ: Prentice-Hall.

Mizruchi, Mark S.
1983 "Who controls whom? An examination of the relation between management and boards of directors in large American corporations." Academy of Management Review, 8: 426–435.

Pennings, Johannes M.
1980 Interlocking Directorates. San Francisco: Jossey-Bass.

Pfeffer, Jeffrey
1972 "Size and composition of corporate boards of directors." Administrative Science Quarterly, 17: 221–228.

Pfeffer, Jeffrey, and Gerald R. Salancik
1978 The External Control of Organizations: A Resource-Dependence Perspective. New York: Harper and Row.

Ratcliff, Richard E.
1980 "Banks and corporate lending: An analysis of the impact of the internal structure of the capitalist class on the lending behavior of banks." American Sociological Review, 45: 553–570.

Schmidt, Richard
1977 "The board of directors and financial interest." Academy of Management Journal, 20: 677–682.

Schwartz, Donald E. (ed.)
1979 Commentaries on Corporate Structure and Governance. New York: ALI-ABA.

Securities and Exchange Commission
1984 "The impact of targeted share repurchases and stock prices." Information Memorandum, 84–100. New York: SEC, Office of the Chief Economist.

Smith, Bryan F.
1977 "The TI board: Pioneering reforms." Directors and Boards, 2: 4–23.

Spencer, Arne
1983 On the Edge of the Organization: The Role of the Outside Director. New York: Wiley.

Vance, Stanley C.
1964 Boards of Directors: Structure and Performance. Eugene, OR: University of Oregon Press.
1983 Corporate Leadership: Boards, Directors and Strategy. New York: McGraw-Hill.

Waldo, Charles N.
1985 Boards of Directors: Their Changing Roles, Structure, and Information Needs. Westport, CT: Quorum Books.

Walkling, Ralph A., and Michael S. Long
1984 "Agency theory, managerial welfare and takeover bid resistance." Rand Journal of Economics, 15: 54–68.

Weidenbaum, Murray L.
1984 "The director as cultivator of management." Directors and Boards, 9: 27–30.

Whisler, Thomas L.
1984 Rules of the Game: Inside the Boardroom. New York: Dow Jones-Irwin.

Williams, Harold Marvin
1979 Power and Accountability: The Changing Role of the Corporate Board of Directors. The 1979 Benjamin F. Fairless Memorial Lecture. Pittsburgh: Carnegie-Mellon University Press.

Williamson, Oliver E.
1964 The Economics of Discretionary Behavior: Managerial Objectives in a Theory of the Firm. Englewood Cliffs, NJ: Prentice-Hall.

Winter, Sidney G.
1964 "Economic natural selection and the theory of the firm." Yale Economic Essays, 4: 225–231.

Wolfson, Nicholas
1984 The Modern Corporation: Free Market versus Regulation. New York: McGraw-Hill.

Zald, Mayer N.
1967 "Urban differentiation, characteristics of boards of directors and organizational effectiveness." American Journal of Sociology, 73: 261–272.

Greenmail

APPENDIX: Sample Characteristics of 110 Boards and 759 Outside Directors

Board characteristics	Mean	Range
Total no. of directors	11	4–21
No. of board meetings per year	8	4–28
No. of board committees	3	1–8
Proportion of outside directors	63%	22–92%
Board compensation*	$12,093	$2,400–$30,000
% of outside directors with		
Executive jobs	46%	0–100%
Reciprocity relations with management	3.4%	0–50%
Family relations with management	4.9%	0–80%
Contracts with the company	13.3%	0–71%
Characteristics of outside directors		
Age	5	33–88
No. of years on the board	8	0–48
No. of committee memberships	1	0–6
No. of board memberships	3	1–13
Distribution of outside directors' functional backgrounds		
Executives	45.1%	
Retired executives	13.3%	
Lawyers	12.3%	
Bankers	11.3%	
Consultants/CPAs	5.9%	
Business professors	3.6%	
Private investors	2.6%	
Non-business professors	2.6%	
Politicians and celebrities	2.2%	
Professional directors	1.1%	

* Board compensation based on annual retainer and attendance fees for board meetings only. Full attendance is assumed.

Part III
Board Characteristics and Organisational Performance

[14]

ELSEVIER Journal of Financial Economics 40 (1996) 185–211

JOURNAL OF Financial ECONOMICS

Higher market valuation of companies with a small board of directors

David Yermack

Stern School of Business, New York University, New York, NY 10012, USA

(Received November 1994; final version received July 1995)

Abstract

I present evidence consistent with theories that small boards of directors are more effective. Using Tobin's Q as an approximation of market valuation, I find an inverse association between board size and firm value in a sample of 452 large U.S. industrial corporations between 1984 and 1991. The result is robust to numerous controls for company size, industry membership, inside stock ownership, growth opportunities, and alternative corporate governance structures. Companies with small boards also exhibit more favorable values for financial ratios, and provide stronger CEO performance incentives from compensation and the threat of dismissal.

Key words: Boards of directors; Corporate governance
JEL classification: G30; G32; K22

1. Introduction

A growing body of empirical research examines the structure and effectiveness of corporate governance systems. An important insight from this literature is that top managers' decisions appear to be influenced by executive compensation, takeover threats, monitoring by boards of directors, and other control

I have benefited from helpful comments by Rita Maldonado-Bear, Wayne Mikkelson (the editor), Eli Ofek, participants in the NYU finance seminar, and an anonymous referee. I thank Eli Ofek for the use of company diversification data, and Andrei Shleifer for arranging financial support. Data collection for this paper would not have been possible without the help of research assistants Jason Barro and Melissa McSherry, the staff of the Cole Room at Harvard Business School's Baker Library, and more than 100 companies that kindly responded to data inquiries.

SSDI 0304405X9500844 5

mechanisms. I contribute to this literature by evaluating a proposal for limiting the size of boards of directors in order to improve their effectiveness. My evidence supports this proposal, as I find an inverse association between firm value and board size in a panel of major U.S. companies.

Lipton and Lorsch (1992) state that '. . . the norms of behavior in most boardrooms are dysfunctional', because directors rarely criticize the policies of top managers or hold candid discussions about corporate performance. Believing that these problems increase with the number of directors, Lipton and Lorsch recommend limiting the membership of boards to ten people, with a preferred size of eight or nine. The proposal amounts to a conjecture that even if boards' capacities for monitoring increase with board size, the benefits are outweighed by such costs as slower decision-making, less-candid discussions of managerial performance, and biases against risk-taking. Jensen (1993) takes up this theme, pointing out the 'great emphasis on politeness and courtesy at the expense of truth and frankness in boardrooms' and stating that 'when boards get beyond seven or eight people they are less likely to function effectively and are easier for the CEO to control'.

Some evidence shows that reducing board size has become a priority for institutional investors, dissident directors, and corporate raiders seeking to improve troubled companies. Kini et al. (1995) present evidence that board size shrinks after successful tender offers for under-performing firms. At American Express, the outside director who in 1993 organized the removal of the company's CEO cited the 'unwieldy' 19-person board as an obstacle to change, stating that the 'size of the board does make a difference', according to Monks and Minow (1995). Smaller boards have emerged recently during overhauls of corporate governance at such prominent companies as General Motors, IBM, Occidental Petroleum, Scott Paper, W.R. Grace, Time Warner, and Westinghouse Electric. Institutional investor pressure reportedly contributed to many of these changes, such as the 1995 reduction in Grace's board from 22 directors to 12.

In a sample of 452 large U.S. public corporations observed over the period 1984 to 1991, I find an inverse relation between firm market value, as represented by Tobin's Q, and the size of the board of directors. The association appears in both cross-sectional analyses of the variation among firms and in time-series analyses of the variation within individual companies. The negative relation between board size and firm value attenuates as boards become large, implying that the greatest incremental costs arise as boards grow from in size from small to medium. The loss in firm value when boards grow from six to 12 members, for example, is estimated to be equal to the value lost when boards grow from 12 to 24. Very few boards have fewer than six or more than 24 directors.

A range of additional evidence is consistent with the finding that companies achieve the highest market value when boards are small. Several measures of operating efficiency and profitability are negatively related over time to board size within firms. Smaller boards are more likely to dismiss CEOs following periods of poor performance. Similarly, evidence shows that CEO compensation exhibits greater sensitivity to performance in companies with small boards. Stock returns for a sample of companies announcing significant changes in board size show that investors react positively when boards shrink and negatively when board size increases.

The inverse association between board size and firm value proves robust to a variety of tests for alternative explanations. I introduce variables to control for firm size, industry, board composition, inside stock ownership, the presence of growth opportunities, diversification, company age, and different corporate governance structures. None of these modifications changes the conclusion that companies with small boards are valued more highly in the capital markets.

An alternative interpretation of the results is that board size arises from prior company performance, with troubled firms adding directors to increase monitoring capacity. I conduct a range of tests to obtain insight into the direction of causation between board size and firm value. The tests show that while the rate of director turnover increases following poor performance, board size remains quite stable over time with little sensitivity to performance.

The remainder of this paper is organized as follows. Section 2 reviews prior research on board structure and firm performance. Section 3 presents the main result of an inverse association between board size and firm value, and illustrates the result's robustness to controls for firm size, growth opportunities, diversification, board composition, and other variables. Section 4 presents evidence about the direction of causation between board size and firm value. Section 5 provides supporting evidence that smaller boards oversee managers more effectively, showing that financial ratios and CEO incentives are stronger when boards are small and that investors react favorably to large reductions in board size. Section 6 concludes the paper.

2. Prior research on board structure

Criticisms and proposals for the reform of boards of directors have proliferated in recent years. Monks and Minow (1995) present a lengthy summary of this literature, which relies upon a premise that monitoring by the board can improve the quality of managers' decisions. Many commentators urge that boards have a large fraction of outside directors, that directors own large amounts of company stock, that CEOs have only limited power to set board agendas and appoint new directors, and that rigorous CEO performance reviews take place regularly. As noted above, limiting board size has begun appearing on some agendas for reform, although only Lipton and Lorsch (1992) and Jensen (1993) identify board size as a high priority.

Much empirical research has examined whether board structure is related to company performance, but these studies have largely overlooked board size. Instead, investigators have most frequently examined the importance of outside directors and directors' equity ownership.

Studying board composition, Hermalin and Weisbach (1991) find no relation between firm performance and the fraction of outside directors. However, this conclusion is not supported by Baysinger and Butler (1985), who find some evidence that companies perform better if boards include more outsiders. Other studies find that boards dominated by outsiders are more likely to behave in shareholders' interest. See, for example, Weisbach (1988) (CEO turnover), Byrd and Hickman (1992) (tender offer bids), and Brickley, Coles, and Terry (1994) (poison pill adoptions and control auctions). Rosenstein and Wyatt (1990) find positive investor reactions to appointments of outside directors.

With respect to board stock ownership, Mørck, Shleifer, and Vishny (1988) find significant, though nonmonotonic, associations between different levels of director stock ownership and Tobin's Q, suggesting that some levels of board stock ownership have systematic advantages. McConnell and Servaes (1990) and Hermalin and Weisbach (1991) report similar results, while Bagnani, Milonas, Saunders, and Travlos (1994) find that bondholder returns also exhibit a nonmonotonic association with board stock ownership.

Lipton and Lorsch (1992), Jensen (1993), and other advocates of small boards contend that board size affects corporate governance independent of other board attributes. As noted above, their arguments focus on the productivity losses that arise when work groups grow large, an insight borrowed from organizational behavior research such as Steiner (1972) and Hackman (1990). According to Jensen (1993), '. . . as groups increase in size they become less effective because the coordination and process problems overwhelm the advantages from having more people to draw on'.

Empirical research on the importance of board size is thin. Holthausen and Larcker (1993a, b) consider board size among a range of variables that might influence executive compensation and company performance. Holthausen and Larcker (1993a) present results indicating a positive association between board size and the value of CEO compensation. Holthausen and Larcker (1993b) fail to find consistent evidence of an association between board size and company performance.

A clear problem in studying board size is that the number of directors might arise endogenously as a function of other variables, such as company size, performance, or the CEO's preferences. Along these lines, the managerial quality hypothesis of Byrd and Hickman (1992) argues that high-caliber CEOs may '. . . dress up their firms' boards with independent directors' to please shareholders with an illusion of active monitoring; a similar argument could be made about the willingness of good CEOs to surround themselves with small boards. Because many intangible forces of this type might influence board size, we cannot accept at face value an association between board size and firm value without considering alternative explanations. I investigate many of these possible explanations in Section 3.3, after presenting my main finding of a negative relation between firm value and board size.

3. Board size and firm value

The main hypothesis of this paper is that firm value depends on the quality of monitoring and decision-making by the board of directors, and that the board's size represents an important determinant of its performance. Below I estimate a straightforward model of the relation between firm value and board size. I follow the methods of several recent related studies, such as Morck, Shleifer, and Vishny (1988), Hermalin and Weisbach (1991), and Lang and Stulz (1994), by regressing a set of explanatory variables against an estimate of Tobin's Q, which measures the ratio of a firm's market value divided by the replacement cost of its assets. I include controls for such variables as firm size, industry membership, board composition, and past company performance. After presenting the main result, I illustrate its robustness to a variety of alternative specifications and evaluate whether alternative theories can account for the observed inverse relation between board size and firm value.

3.1. Data description

My analysis uses a panel of firms drawn from the annual *Forbes* magazine rankings of the 500 largest U.S. public corporations based on sales, total assets, market capitalization, and net income. I use a sample selection rule that requires each company to qualify for any of these *Forbes* lists during at least four years of the eight-year period between 1984 and 1991. I also require each company to have four or more consecutive fiscal years of stock market and financial statement data between 1984 and 1991. The four-year requirement represents an attempt to balance two sampling issues: collecting several observations for each company so that econometric panel data techniques can be used, and limiting survivorship bias by allowing companies to enter and exit the panel over time. I omit utility and financial companies because of concerns that government regulation leads to different, more limited roles for their boards of directors. I obtain a final sample of 3,438 observations for 452 companies across eight years.[1]

[1] Three sample firms began 1984 as public companies, remained public at least until 1988, were delisted in going-private transactions, and became public again by 1991. In these cases, the data set does not include the firms' second incarnations. Approximately 20 firms changed the timing of their fiscal years during the sample period; in these cases, 'flow' variables, such as sales, are normalized to 12-month equivalents for the transition fiscal years which were not 12 months long.

Table 1 presents characteristics of the board of directors for the sample observations, including mean and median values for key variables, and sample correlations of other board attributes with board size. Board sizes range between four and 34 for sample firms, with a mean of 12.25 and a median of 12.

The sample correlations between board size and other variables do not give a consistent indication of whether smaller boards should be expected to monitor top managers more effectively than larger boards. While numerous studies have found positive links between firm performance and the presence of independent or expert board members, these types of directors are less likely to appear on small boards. Board size is negatively correlated with the fraction of directors who are corporate insiders or who have conflicts-of-interest due to their 'gray' status (signifying directors who are relatives of company officers and those who benefit from personal business ties to the firm), and positively correlated with the fraction of directors who serve as CEOs of other firms. Further, smaller boards are more likely to have CEOs who either founded the company or belong to the founding family, a quality that Johnson et al. (1985) found was associated with low firm value. However, directors on small boards tend to have greater levels of stock ownership and are more likely to receive performance-based director fees in the form of stock options. Each of these characteristics suggests that small boards may have better incentives to monitor, though Mørck, Shleifer, and Vishny (1988) and others have found that board equity ownership has ambiguous associations with firm value. Small boards are also likelier to include active monitors in the form of major stockholder-directors and non-CEO chairmen. Smaller boards have lower rates of director turnover than other boards, probably due to the better performance of companies with small boards documented herein.

From the evidence in Table 1, I conclude that number of directors is but one of many board attributes that might contribute to firm value, and that the complex associations between board size and other variables do not suggest clearly whether firms with small boards should have high or low market values.

3.2. Regression analysis

To investigate whether board size has a significant association with firm value, I estimate least-squares regressions, using Tobin's Q as the dependent variable and board size as one of many explanatory variables. The dependent variable, measured for each company at the close of each fiscal year ending in calendar 1984 through 1991, is defined as

$$Tobin's\ Q = \frac{Market\ value\ of\ assets}{Replacement\ cost\ of\ assets}. \qquad (1)$$

Table 1
Board of directors characteristics

Descriptive statistics for characteristics of boards of directors. The sample consists of 3,433 annual observations for 452 companies between 1984 and 1991. Companies are included in the sample if they are ranked by *Forbes* magazine as one of the 500 largest U.S. public corporations at least four times during the eight-year sample period. Utility and financial companies are excluded. The table presents the mean, median, and standard deviation for each variable, as well as Pearson sample correlation coefficients between the board-size variable and all others.

Board size represents the number of members of the board of directors as of the annual meeting date during each fiscal year. The percentage of inside directors is the fraction of board members who are current or former officers of each company. Gray directors are those who have substantial business relationships with the company, either personally or through their main employers, and also relatives of corporate officers. Outside directors are those who have neither inside nor gray status. Director fees include annual retainers and fees paid for regular and special board meetings during the fiscal year. The dummy variable for director stock option plan equals one if the company has a plan in place for awarding stock options to outside directors. Director turnover is the fraction of board members who leave before the next annual meeting. The CEO-from-founding-family dummy variable equals 1 if the CEO is from a family which either founded the company or acquired control during a takeover. The dummy variable for 5% stockholder-directors equals 1 if one or more members of the board beneficially own at least 5% of the common stock or serve as representatives of an outside 5% holder (not including employee stock ownership plans).

	Mean	Median	Std. dev.	Correlation with board size
Board size	12.25	12	0.43	1.00
Board composition				
Inside directors	0.36	0.33	0.16	− 0.09
Gray directors	0.10	0.08	0.12	− 0.16
Outside directors	0.54	0.56	0.19	0.17
Directors who are CEOs of other firms	0.14	0.13	0.12	0.14
Compensation and turnover				
Director fees (1991 dollars)	$29,539	$29,601	$10,657	0.33
Director stock option plan (dummy variable)	0.09	0	0.29	− 0.09
Director turnover (% of board per year)	8.3%	7.1%	10.2%	0.15
Governance structure and stock ownership				
CEO from founding family (dummy variable)	0.24	0	0.42	− 0.26
Non-CEO chairman of board (dummy variable)	0.17	0	0.38	− 0.06
Presence of 5% stockholder-director (dummy variable)	0.24	0	0.43	− 0.14
Director and officer stock ownership (% of common)	9.1%	2.8%	14.3%	− 0.27

Last column: All correlations with board size are significant at the 1% level.

I estimate the market value of assets by adding together estimated values of the components of total liabilities and stockholders' equity. The market value of common stock is obtained directly from the CRSP database. I estimate the market value of preferred stock by taking the ratio of preferred dividends over the prevailing yield on Moody's index of high-grade industrial preferred stocks. The market value of long-term debt is estimated from a recursive algorithm that infers the maturity structure of each firm's debt and takes account of changes in the prevailing yield on Moody's index of A-rated industrial bonds. I assume other liabilities have market value equal to book value. The replacement costs of inventories and fixed assets are estimated by recursive algorithms that take account of inflation, real depreciation rates, capital expenditures, and the method of inventory valuation used by each company. Other assets are assumed to have market value equal to book value. The recursive methods for valuing debt, inventory, and fixed assets closely follow those of Perfect and Wiles (1994) in their q_{PW} estimator of Tobin's Q.[2]

Fig. 1 illustrates mean and median values of Tobin's Q for companies sorted by board size. The number of directors for each company was obtained from proxy statements for firms' annual meetings, which usually occur in the fifth or sixth month of each fiscal year. Mean and median Tobin's Q values decline almost monotonically over the range of board sizes. For companies with between four and eight directors, mean Q values range between 1.5 and 2, while the mean Q value falls to slightly above 1 for companies with 20 or more directors.

In addition to board size, my regressions include controls for other variables that I expect either to affect Tobin's Q directly or to affect each board's incentives and ability to monitor managers.

A company's profitability has a significant impact upon its market value, so I include return on assets (*ROA*) in the regression model as an explanatory variable. I calculate *ROA* as operating income divided by total assets (measured at the start of each year) and compound the ratio continuously. The regression model includes *ROA* for the most recent year and two years of lagged values.

In addition to current and past profitability, many theorists including Myers (1977) and Smith and Watts (1992) argue that firm value depends on future investment opportunities. Like others, I use the ratio of capital expenditures over sales as a proxy for investment opportunities. Below, I consider whether other possible measures of investment opportunities lead to differences in the model's estimates.

During the 1984–91 period of this study, diversified firms were valued less highly in the capital markets than stand-alone businesses, as shown by Lang and

[2] The lone difference between my methodology and the q_{PW} estimator of Perfect and Wiles (1994) is that my estimate of the replacement cost of property, plant, and equipment uses a slightly different method for estimating real rates of economic depreciation and cost-reducing technical progress.

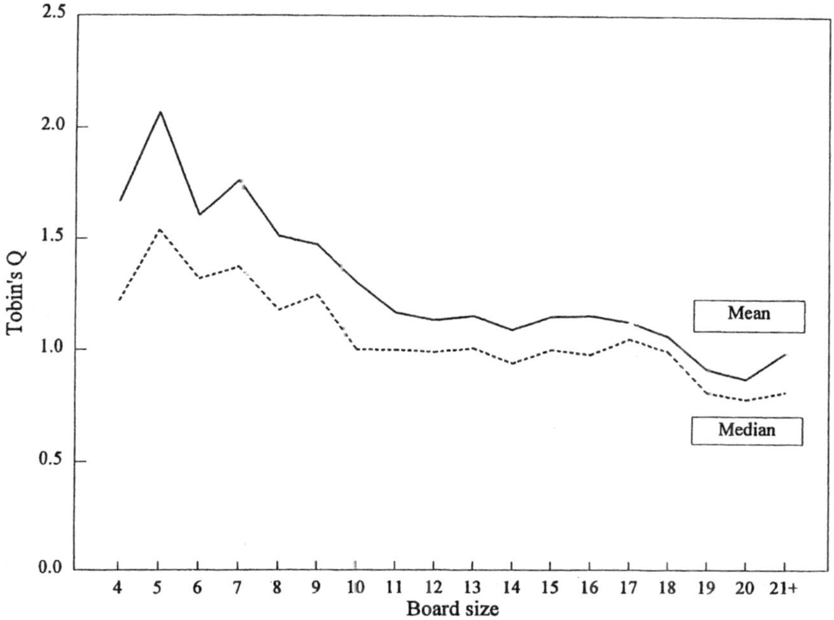

Fig. 1. Board size and Tobin's Q: Sample means and medians.

Sample means and medians of Tobin's Q for different sizes of boards of directors. The sample consists of 3,438 annual observations for 452 firms between 1984 and 1991. Companies are included in the sample if they are ranked by *Forbes* magazine as one of the 500 largest U.S. public corporations at least four times during the eight-year sample period. Utility and financial companies are excluded. Data for board size is gathered from proxy statements filed by companies near the start of each fiscal year. Tobin's Q is estimated at the end of each fiscal year as *Market value of assets/Replacement cost of assets*. The estimation of Q follows the q_{PW} specification of Perfect and Wiles (1994), which is described more fully in the text.

Stulz (1994) and Berger and Ofek (1995). Moreover, diversified companies are likely to have larger boards, because many boards grow in size when companies make acquisitions and because boards of conglomerates may seek outside expertise for a greater number of industries. To control for diversification, I include a variable that counts the number of business segments for which firms report audited financial statement data in each fiscal year's annual report.

As discussed in Section 2, many investigators have suggested that boards with high stock ownership and a majority of outside directors monitor managers more effectively. I include measures of these two variables in the regression model: the percentage of common stock owned by directors and officers and the percentage of outside directors on each company's board. Outside directors exclude current and former officers of the firm, and nonemployee directors who have personal or business relationships with the company. These directors, often referred to as 'gray', include such groups as lawyers, bankers, consultants, major suppliers, and relatives of corporate officers.

I control for firm size with the log of total capital, measured in millions of 1991 dollars. Total capital equals the market value of equity at the end of the year, plus the estimated values of long-term debt and preferred stock, calculated as described above. Below, I consider alternative measures of company size in Section 3.3.2.

Finally, I include in the regressions dummy variables for individual years and two-digit SIC industries. I use a log specification for the board-size variable, based upon the convex association between board size and market value suggested by Fig. 1. I obtained the financial statement data used in regressions from Compustat, except for a handful of observations for which data were hand-collected. Data for board size, board composition, and inside stock ownership were obtained from annual meeting proxy statements.

Because unobservable characteristics are likely to affect each company's market value, I estimate both ordinary least squares (OLS) regressions and fixed-effects models. The OLS model includes two-digit SIC dummy variables that allow a different intercept for firms in each industry, while the fixed-effects estimator assigns a unique intercept to each company. Hausman and Taylor (1981) state that the fixed-effects framework represents a common, unbiased method of controlling for omitted variables in a panel data set. Table 2 presents coefficient estimates for the OLS and fixed-effects models, with White (1980) robust standard errors accompanying the OLS estimates.

The regression estimates for both models show an inverse and significant association between firm value and board size. This downward slope is consistent with an interpretation that coordination, communication, and decision-making problems increasingly hinder board performance when the number of directors increases. Further, the convex relation implied by the log form of the board-size variable suggests that costs accumulate at a decreasing rate as board size grows. A convex relation also emerges from estimates of different functional forms, including piecewise linear models and regressions of Tobin's Q against board size and board size squared. For clarity, in the remainder of the paper, I concentrate on results using the board-size log, and I generally report fixed-effects estimates to control for unobservable company characteristics.

The fixed-effects estimate for the board-size log coefficient of -0.337 implies that Tobin's Q falls by about 0.23 if board size doubles and by about 0.13 if board size rises 50%. Expanding an eight-person board by one member implies a reduction in Q of about 0.04, while adding one director to a 15-person board implies a fall in Q of about 0.02. These changes in value are economically significant. Since the median firm in my sample has a market value of just under \$2.6 billion (equity and long-term debt, in 1991 dollars), and since most firms' values of Tobin's Q are close to one (see Fig. 1), a change

Table 2
Regression coefficient estimates: Board size and market valuation

Regression coefficient estimates of the association between Tobin's *Q* and the number of directors sitting on company boards. The sample consists of 3,438 annual observations for 452 firms between 1984 and 1991. Companies are included in the sample if they are ranked by *Forbes* magazine as one of the 500 largest U.S. public corporations at least four times during the eight-year sample period. Utility and financial companies are excluded. The dependent variable is an estimate of Tobin's *Q* at the end of each fiscal year. The log of board size is the natural log of the number of directors sitting on each company's board as of the annual meeting date each year, as reported in company proxy statements. The first column presents OLS estimates with White (1980) robust standard errors. The second column presents estimates from a fixed-effects model, which assigns a unique intercept to each company.

The model includes control variables for company performance (return on assets in the current year and two lags), firm size (the log of total capital, in 1991 dollars), growth opportunities (capital expenditures over sales), diversification (the number of business segments for which financial statement data is reported), board composition (the percentage of outside directors on the board), and inside stock ownership (director and officer beneficial ownership, in percent). *ROA* equals operating income over total assets (start of year) and is compounded continuously. Total capital equals the market value of common stock at the end of the year, plus estimates of the market values of long-term debt and preferred stock. Both models include dummy variables for years, and the OLS model includes two-digit SIC industry dummy variables.

Dependent variable: *Tobin's Q*

Variable	OLS estimates	Fixed-effects estimates
Log of board size	− 0.428***	− 0.337***
	(0.043)	(0.056)
Return on assets (current year)	3.856***	2.048***
	(0.403)	(0.147)
Return on assets (prior year)	0.502	− 0.093
	(0.536)	(0.151)
Return on assets (two years prior)	1.039**	0.450***
	(0.451)	(0.130)
Firm size (log of total capital)	0.119***	0.413***
	(0.012)	(0.020)
Capital expenditures/Sales	− 0.116	0.176
	(0.209)	(0.123)
Number of business segments	− 0.042***	− 0.049***
	(0.006)	(0.009)
Board composition (% outside directors)	− 0.213***	0.172*
	(0.067)	(0.088)
Officer and director stock ownership (%)	0.279***	0.310***
	(0.096)	(0.108)
Sample size	3,400	3,400
F-statistic	68.1	2.7
(*P*-value)	(0.00)	(0.00)
R-squared	0.5459	0.3021

Significant at 1% (***), 5% (**), and 10% (*) levels.

in Q of 0.01 reduces firm value by about 1%, or approximately $25 million for the median firm.

While the results suggest a monotonic relation between smaller board size and higher firm value, we should be cautious about concluding that the association holds at very small levels of board size. This conjecture is difficult to test, since few companies in my sample have board size below six (only 87 observations out of 3,438), and every board has at least four members. Fig. 1's display of mean and median values of Tobin's Q suggests that no consistent association between board size and firm value exists over the lowest range of board sizes, as the values of Q decline steadily only after board size grows beyond seven. Re-estimating Table 2's OLS regression for the subset of observations with board size of seven or less yields a negative but insignificant estimate for the board-size log coefficient.

Coefficient estimates for other variables in Table 2 are generally significant in the expected direction. Current and past levels of profitability, measured by return on assets, have positive associations with Tobin's Q. Diversified firms appear to be valued less highly than other companies. Board stock ownership has a positive association with firm value. The effect of the board composition variable is ambiguous and appears sensitive to the inclusion of firm effects in the model. Capital expenditures over sales, the variable I use to measure investment opportunities, does not have significant coefficient estimates, though in the fixed-effects model the estimate is positive as expected, with a p-value of 0.15. Firm size, when measured by the log of the market value of total capital, is positively associated by construction with Tobin's Q. Other measures of firm size are discussed below.

The finding of an inverse association between board size and firm value appears insensitive to the method of estimation. A between-firms estimator, which considers only cross-sectional averages of the variables across companies, produces an estimate of -0.396 for the board-size log (significant at the 1% level). A random-effects model, which represents a minimum-variance weighted average of the within- and between-firms estimators (Hausman and Taylor, 1981), yields an estimate of -0.450 for the board-size coefficient (p-value below 1%). An OLS estimate based on first differences of the variables produces an estimate of -0.239 for the board-size log (p-value below 5%). Year-by-year cross-sectional estimates of the OLS model in Table 2 yield negative and significant coefficients for the board-size log variable in every year. While the estimate is closest to zero in 1990 and 1991, it is difficult to spot a time trend, as the two most negative estimates occur for 1987 and 1989.

3.3. Further controls

Several plausible explanations could account for the negative association between board size and firm value. Regression results in Table 2 are consistent with the hypotheses of Lipton and Lorsch (1992) and Jensen (1993), that small boards operate more effectively, but board size could be associated with other corporate attributes that affect firm value. Moreover, my results imply, somewhat counterintuitively, that many companies have bypassed a simple, inexpensive way of improving corporate performance. For these reasons, I conduct additional tests of the robustness of my basic finding and discuss the results in the following sections.

3.3.1. Growth opportunities

Tobin's Q is an ambiguous measure of value-added by management, since the Q- ratio can also capture the value of future investment opportunities. While the model controls for growth opportunities by using capital expenditures over sales, Smith and Watts (1992) and other authors have used additional proxies, including research and development (R&D) expense over sales, depreciation expense over sales, the earnings–price ratio, and the variance of common stock returns. I re-estimate the fixed-effects model of Table 2 with each of these growth opportunity measures substituted for capital expenditures over sales, but the key coefficient on the board-size log exhibits virtually no change. Board size itself does not appear to have any systematic association with the presence of growth opportunities; regressions of the five growth-opportunity variables against the board-size log yield only one statistically significant estimate and no consistent pattern of signs.

3.3.2. Firm size

Company size, board size, and firm value can be correlated in complicated ways, so I check the robustness of my results to different definitions and functional forms of the firm size variable. I estimate a total of 12 fixed-effects models, based upon three different measures of size: total capital (market value of equity and long-term debt), total assets (book value), and net sales during the prior fiscal year. I use four different specifications for each size variable: log terms, linear terms, linear and squared terms, and linear, squared, and cubed terms. The estimated coefficient for the board-size log is negative and significant in every specification (nine estimates have p-values below 1%, two have p-values of 3%, and one has a p-value of 8%).

3.3.3. Active monitors

The correlations in Table 1 suggest that small boards have a higher incidence of active monitors. I re-estimate the model after adding dummy variables for the presence of a non-CEO chairman, a non-CEO company president who also sits on the board, and a 5% stockholder-director. The fixed-effects estimate for the board-size log remains virtually unchanged. Of the new variables, only the dummy for non-CEO chairman has an interesting estimate: The coefficient is

0.039 and significant at the 11% level, implying that firms are valued more highly when the CEO and chairman positions are separated. Numerous alternative specifications of the stockholder-director variable do not change the main conclusion.

3.3.4. Close ownership structures

Table 1 suggests that small boards are more common in companies controlled by founding families. These firms could have tighter ownership structures and turn over assets more slowly, leading to low book values of assets, which imply high values of Tobin's Q. I add to the model a dummy variable equal to one if the CEO belongs to the company's founding family, but the fixed-effects estimate for the board-size log exhibits little change. The founding-family variable has a negative and significant estimate of -0.11, suggesting that firm value increases once the founding family surrenders control. Company age could also be closely associated with ownership structure, since firms probably become more widely held over time. I re-estimate the model with a variable equal to the number of years since each firm's original incorporation; again, the board-size estimate remains nearly the same as in Table 2.

4. Past performance and current board size

The analysis above shows that companies with small boards of directors attain higher values in the capital markets than do their counterparts with large boards. However, we might interpret these findings in two ways. Small boards could contribute to better performance, or companies might adjust board size in response to past performance. If companies expand their boards in the aftermath of poor performance, the causation of the board size-firm value relation may run in the opposite direction from the Lipton–Lorsch (1992) and Jensen (1993) hypotheses.

Prior studies by Hermalin and Weisbach (1988) and Gilson (1990) examine the interplay between company performance and changes in boards of directors. Hermalin and Weisbach (1988) find that poor performance leads to both more departures of board members and more appointments to the board. While Hermalin and Weisbach are silent on the net effect of these two forces, they estimate similar magnitudes for each, suggesting that director turnover increases after poor performance, but board size does not. Gilson (1990), in a study limited to financially distressed companies, also finds that board turnover increases after poor performance; moreover, Gilson finds that firms reduce board sizes during distressed periods. If this pattern held for all companies, one would observe smaller boards in low-valued companies, contrary to the findings of this paper. However, it is not clear that Gilson's results apply to the majority of companies, since the median firm in his sample is small and performs very poorly.

I examine the question of causation by estimating regression models of the association between past performance and changes in board size. Following Hermalin and Weisbach (1988), I estimate maximum-likelihood Poisson models of the number of directors leaving and joining each company's board each year.

Table 3
Regression coefficient estimates: Effect of company performance on director appointments, departures, and changes in board size

Coefficient estimates for regression models of changes in board size. The first two columns present maximum-likelihood Poisson models of the number of directors joining and leaving each company's board. The third column presents OLS estimates of the net change in board size, equal to director additions minus director departures. All variables are measured annually, based upon the membership of companies' boards as reported in proxy statements for annual shareholder meetings.

The sample consists of 3,438 annual observations for 452 firms between 1984 and 1991. Companies are included in the sample if they are ranked by *Forbes* magazine as one of the 500 largest U.S. public corporations at least four times during the eight-year sample period. Utility and financial companies are excluded. The key explanatory variable for all three models is the firm's abnormal stock return during the fiscal year, defined as the raw return minus the return predicted by the CAPM. Other explanatory variables are similar to those used by Hermalin and Weisbach (1988). CEO at retirement age is a dummy variable equal to one if the company's CEO is between the ages of 62 and 66. New CEO is a dummy equal to one if the CEO has four years of tenure or less. All models include two-digit SIC industry dummy variables. The text discusses assumptions used in calculating abnormal stock returns. Each coefficient estimate appears with robust standard errors.

Dependent variable	Director appointments	Director departures	Change in board size
Estimation	Poisson ML	Poisson ML	OLS
	Estimate	Estimate	Estimate
Abnormal stock return (fiscal year)	– 0.238** (0.093)	– 0.238*** (0.084)	– 0.005 (0.106)
Abnormal stock return (prior fiscal year)	– 0.087 (0.088)	– 0.126 (0.084)	0.039 (0.091)
Change in firm size [log(sales)]	0.419*** (0.163)	– 0.347* (0.185)	0.770*** (0.198)
CEO at retirement age (dummy for ages 62 to 66)	0.129** (0.054)	0.133** (0.055)	– 0.015 (0.062)
New CEO (dummy for 4 years' tenure or less)	0.148*** (0.048)	0.273*** (0.050)	– 0.156*** (0.055)
SIC industry dummies	2-digit	2-digit	2-digit
Sample size	2,943	2,943	2,943
F-statistic			1.9
(*P*-value)			(0.00)
R-squared			0.0313

Significant at 1% (***), 5% (**), and 10% (*) levels.

As a further check, I estimate a least squares model in which the dependent variable is equal to the total annual change in board size (director additions minus departures). Key explanatory variables for all models are abnormal stock returns, the change in company size (measured by the log of net sales), and dummy variables for whether the company's CEO is nearing retirement (between the ages of 62 and 66) or new (appointed within the last four years). Abnormal stock returns equal the firm's raw stock return during the fiscal year, minus the return predicted by the capital asset pricing model (CAPM). The CAPM calculations use β estimates calculated over the last 120 trading days of the prior fiscal year, and risk-free rates equal to the yield on ten-year U.S. Treasury bonds.

Table 3 displays the results. The models provide no evidence that boards either expand or contract in response to performance. Like Hermalin and Weisbach, I find that poor performance is associated with higher levels of both director appointments and departures. The effects are similar, suggesting that more directors are replaced when companies perform poorly, but that total board size does not change. The same conclusion emerges from the OLS model of the net annual change in board size. I obtain qualitatively similar results from re-estimating all three equations, using seven-year aggregate totals of all variables between 1984 and 1991 for each company. The OLS model does show that boards tend to grow larger in response to changes in company size, as opposed to performance, but the effect appears weak; a firm almost needs to quadruple in size before it can be expected to add one director.

I conduct additional tests of whether the link between board size and firm value can be attributed to adjustments in board size due to past performance. I re-estimate the basic model of firm value and board size in an instrumental variables framework, using lagged values of the board-size log as instruments for the current value. The new estimates are virtually indistinguishable from the original model's OLS estimate in Table 2. I also regress Tobin's Q against long lags of board size and compare the results with regressions of current levels of board size against long lags of Tobin's Q. I use a fixed-effects framework similar to that in Table 2. I find that up to three years' lagged values of board size have significant associations with subsequent values of Tobin's Q, while no corresponding association exists between lagged values of Tobin's Q and subsequent values of board size. I conclude that the evidence supports the interpretation that past board size influences current firm value, rather than the opposite – that past performance influences current choices of board size.

5. Additional evidence of small boards' effectiveness

Further evidence about the performance of small boards is reflected in patterns of company operating performance, CEO turnover, and executive compensation, as well as shareholder reactions to board size changes. The analysis in the following sections illustrates that key financial ratios exhibit an inverse association with board size, and that CEO incentives – from compensation and the threat of dismissal – diminish in strength as board size increases. I also identify six sample companies that announce significant reductions in board size for corporate governance reasons. These firms realize positive abnormal stock returns around the announcement date, while a parallel sample of four companies announcing large expansions in board size realize negative abnormal returns.

5.1. Board size and financial ratios

If corporate governance becomes less effective as board size increases, I expect lower profitability in companies with large boards, and I also expect less efficient use of assets. I estimate fixed-effects models of board size and three key financial ratios: sales over assets, return on assets, and return on sales. I define return on assets as operating income over total assets at the start of the year, and return on sales as operating income over net sales, and compound both ratios continuously. I regress all three variables against the board-size log and control variables similar to those in the model for Tobin's Q: firm size (the log of total capital), board stock ownership, board composition, the number of business segments, and dummy variables for individual years. I do not include controls for investment opportunities, since it is not obvious why their presence should influence current operating performance.

Table 4 presents the fixed-effects estimates. Consistent with the finding for Tobin's Q, all three dependent variables have negative and significant associations with the board-size log. Companies with large boards appear to use assets less efficiently and earn lower profits.

However, the favorable evidence of an association between board size and financial ratios does not extend to models using less aggregate measures of profitability and efficiency. I estimate three further regressions that have dependent variables equal to sales per employee; the cost of goods sold over sales; and selling, general, and administrative expenses over sales. The board-size log coefficient is not significant in any of these models when they are estimated in a fixed-effects framework.

5.2. Board size and CEO turnover

Selecting, evaluating, and dismissing a company's top managers represents a central responsibility of boards of directors. If large board size contributes to behavioral norms that inhibit candid discussions of managerial performance, as argued by Lipton and Lorsch (1992) and Jensen (1993), we should expect weaker links between performance and turnover for CEOs in companies with large boards.

Table 4
Fixed-effects estimates: Board size and financial ratios

Coefficient estimates for fixed-effects regression models of financial ratios. Standard errors appears below each estimate. The sample consists of 3,438 annual observations for 452 firms between 1984 and 1991. Companies are included in the sample if they are ranked by *Forbes* magazine as one of the 500 largest U.S. public corporations at least four times during the eight-year sample period. Utility and financial companies are excluded.

The dependent variables are three standard measures of operating efficiency and profitability. *ROS* and *ROA* are based on operating income and are compounded continuously. The main explanatory variable for each model is the natural log of board size, which represents the number of directors sitting on each company's board as of the annual meeting for each fiscal year. In addition to the other controls listed, each model includes dummy variables for individual years.

Dependent variable	Sale/ assets	Return on assets	Return on sales
	Estimate	Estimate	Estimate
Log of board size	– 0.163**	– 0.037***	– 0.025***
	(0.079)	(0.008)	(0.006)
Board composition (% outside directors)	– 0.187	0.005	– 0.009
	(0.126)	(0.012)	(0.009)
Officer and director stock ownership (%)	0.287*	0.022	– 0.029***
	(0.153)	(0.015)	(0.011)
Number of business segments	0.006	– 0.0026**	– 0.0020**
	(0.013)	(0.0013)	(0.0009)
Firm size (log of total capital)	0.083***	0.045***	0.031***
	(0.026)	(0.003)	(0.002)
Sample size	3,428	3,425	3,425
F-statistic	23.6	66.3	44.3
(*P*-value)	(0.00)	(0.00)	(0.00)
R-squared	0.0647	0.1627	0.1148

Significant at 1% (***), 5% (**), and 10% (*) levels.

I estimate a probit model of CEO turnover, similar to the model of Warner, Watts, and Wruck (1988). The (0, 1) dependent variable equals one if the CEO leaves his position before the end of the current fiscal year or during the first half of the subsequent fiscal year. The main explanatory variable is the firm's cumulative abnormal stock return over the current fiscal year and two prior years. The use of a relatively long interval for the abnormal stock return is consistent with other studies. For example, Warner et al. (1988) use four years of performance data in their turnover model. I construct the abnormal stock returns described in Section 4. I include controls for CEO age (which should be positively related to turnover) and CEO stock ownership (which should affect turnover negatively, if high stock ownership represents a form of CEO entrenchment). I also include dummy variables for industries and CEO ages 64, 65, and

Table 5
Probit coefficient estimates Board size and CEO dismissal incentives

Regression coefficient estimates for a binary probit model of CEO turnover. The dependent variable equals one if a CEO leaves his position during the second half of the current fiscal year or the first half of the subsequent fiscal year. The main explanatory variable is the firm's cumulative abnormal stock return for the current year and two prior years. The abnormal stock return is defined as the raw stock return minus the return predicted by the CAPM. The sample consists of 3,438 annual observations for 452 firms between 1984 and 1991. Companies are included in the sample if they are ranked by *Forbes* magazine as one of the 500 largest U.S. public corporations at least four times during the eight-year sample period. Utility and financial companies are excluded. Coefficient estimates appear with White (1982) robust standard errors. Missing values occur for companies that do not have a three-year history of common stock returns.

To illustrate how CEO incentives from the threat of dismissal are affected by different characteristics of boards of directors, the second column presents estimates for a model that includes an interaction term between the abnormal stock return and the log of board size. Both models also include variables for the fraction of common stock owned by the CEO, CEO age, dummy variables for CEO ages 64, 65, and 66, and dummies for one-digit SIC industries.

Dependent variable: *CEO leaves position (0, 1)*	Estimate	Estimate
CEO age	0.043***	0.043***
	(0.006)	(0.006)
CEO stock ownership (%)	− 2.022***	− 2.027***
	(0.755)	(0.746)
Cumulative abnormal stock return (current year and two prior years)	− 0.358***	− 1.496***
	(0.071)	(0.581)
Interaction term: Abnormal stock return × log (board size)		0.471**
		(0.239)
Sample size	3,305	3,305

Significant at 1% (***), 5% (**), and 10% (*) levels.

66, since much of the CEO turnover at these ages represents regular planned retirements. Table 5 presents coefficient estimates with White (1982) robust standard errors. In the first column, variables for abnormal stock performance, CEO age, and CEO stock ownership all have expected signs with high significance.

To test for the importance of board size in the link between performance and CEO turnover, I add to the model an interaction term equal to the abnormal stock return times the board-size log. As shown in the second column of Table 5, the augmented model has a more negative estimated association between performance and turnover, coupled with a positive and significant estimate for the interaction term. I interpret these estimates as evidence that smaller boards are more likely to dismiss CEOs for poor performance, and that this threat of dismissal declines as board size increases.

A sampling issue arises when considering whether to exclude CEOs who have served less than three years, since the main explanatory variable is a three-year abnormal stock return. Even if part of this return occurred under a prior CEO, it is likely that boards will hold new CEOs responsible for several years of past performance, since most are promoted from within the firm. Deleting from the sample CEOs in their first and second years (19% of the observations) only enhances the strength of the conclusions. The estimates change little, and the t-statistics increase for both the abnormal stock return and its interaction with the board-size log (results not reported).

The analysis of CEO turnover in Weisbach (1988) shows that boards dominated by outside directors are more likely to dismiss CEOs for underperformance. I control for this effect by adding an interaction term between the abnormal stock return and the fraction of outside directors on each board. This variable's estimate is insignificant. I obtain similar results for an interaction term between board stock ownership (excluding the CEO's shares) and the abnormal stock return. When all three interaction terms appear in the same model, only board size has a significant association with the strength of CEO dismissal incentives; when board size is dropped and the other two interaction terms remain in the model, neither is significant. I conclude that CEO dismissal incentives weaken as board size increases, and I am unable to reach similar conclusions about the importance of the other board attributes.

5.3. Board size and CEO compensation incentives

Establishing managerial incentives through compensation contracts represents another important board responsibility. I study the interplay between CEOs' compensation incentives and board size to see whether small boards perform this task more effectively. I use Jensen and Murphy's (1990) model for studying the pay–performance sensitivity of CEO compensation. The authors define pay–performance sensitivity as the dollar change in CEO compensation per dollar change in stockholder wealth; they estimate this coefficient with linear regressions, using first differences of annual variables. Following their approach, I regress one-year changes in CEO salary plus bonus (obtained from corporate proxy statements) against one-year changes in stockholder wealth for each firm-year in the sample.[3] To capture the importance of board size in the pay–performance relation, I repeat the approach followed in my model of CEO

[3] All dollar values are adjusted for inflation. The change in stockholder wealth is calculated as the return to common stockholders during the fiscal year times market capitalization at the start of the year, all as reported by CRSP. For firms with more than one class of common stock, I add changes in the value of all classes. The analysis omits CEOs who do not serve 12-month fiscal years. Missing values occur during CEO transition periods, since first differences cannot be calculated.

Table 6
OLS estimates: Board size and CEO compensation incentives

OLS estimates for a model of CEO performance incentives from compensation. The dependent variable is the annual change in the CEO's salary and bonus. The main explanatory variable is the annual change in stockholder wealth. To illustrate how performance incentives are affected as board size increases, the model in the right column includes an interaction term between the change in stockholder wealth and the log of board size.

The sample consists of 3,438 annual observations for 452 firms between 1984 and 1991. Companies are included in the sample if they are ranked by *Forbes* magazine as one of the 500 largest U.S. public corporations at least four times during the eight-year sample period. Utility and financial companies are excluded. Coefficient estimates appear with White (1980) robust standard errors. A large number of missing values occur due to the first-differencing framework (which eliminates one year of data) and episodes of CEO turnover (each of which eliminate two first-difference observations).

Dependent variable: *Change in CEO's salary + bonus*	Estimate	Estimate
Constant	39,348*** (11,842)	35,668*** (12,750)
Change in stockholder wealth (per $1,000)	0.015** (0.007)	0.139** (0.065)
Interaction term: Change in stockholder wealth × log (board size)		– 0.045** (0.023)
Sample size	2,412	2,412
F-statistic	8.0	6.6
(*P*-value)	(0.00)	(0.00)
R-squared	0.0033	0.0055

Significant at 1% (***), 5% (**), and 10% (*) levels.

turnover, adding to the model interaction terms between board size and the change in stockholder wealth.

Table 6 presents the results. In the first column, I estimate the pay–performance sensitivity of CEO salaries and bonuses as $0.015 per $1,000 change in stockholder wealth, which is quite close to Jensen and Murphy's (1990) estimate. The second column in Table 5 presents estimates for a model that includes an interaction term between the change in stockholder wealth and the board-size log. The negative and significant coefficient for this interaction term, coupled with the increased estimate for the stockholder wealth coefficient, suggests that CEOs receive stronger compensation incentives in companies with smaller boards. The results change little when the analysis is repeated using abnormal changes in stockholder wealth, calculated with the CAPM assumptions used above.

I add to the model interaction terms between the change in stockholder wealth/percentage of outside directors and the change in stockholder

Table 7
Reactions to announcements of significant board size changes

Investor reactions to announcements by ten sample companies of significant changes in board size. Companies were identified by searches of the Nexis database and the Wall Street Journal Index. The analysis includes firms that announced changes in board size of at least four members on an event date in 1984 or later. Events are excluded if board size changes were related to mergers, CEO transitions, or corporate control contests.

Abnormal stock returns around the announcement dates are calculated by three methods: raw returns minus market returns, raw returns minus market model expected returns, and excess returns extracted from the CRSP database. The market return used in calculations is the CRSP value-weighted index, and market model parameters are estimated from one year of daily trading data prior to the event period. T-statistics for market model abnormal returns are based on standardized prediction errors (Dodd and Warner, 1983).

Companies decreasing board size	Number of directors		% outside directors		Abnormal stock returns 1 day before to 1 day after announcement		
	Before	After	Before	After	Net-of-market	Market model	CRSP excess return
Chrysler (1991)	20	13	70%	77%	5.1%	5.4%	5.5%
Control Data (1985)	18	14	61%	36%	5.9%	7.2%	6.4%
Adolph Coors (1988)	10	5	0%	0%	0.6%	0.7%	n.a.
W.R. Grace (1991)	33	26	36%	54%	− 0.7%	− 1.8%	0.3%
Perkin–Elmer (1991)	13	9	85%	89%	2.1%	2.1%	1.6%
Time Warner (1992)	21	15	48%	67%	0.7%	0.2%	0.5%
Mean					2.3%*	2.3%	2.9%*
T-statistic					2.10	1.67	2.24
P-value					0.09	0.17	0.09

Companies increasing board size	Number of directors		% outside directors		Net-of-market	Market model	CRSP excess return
	Before	After	Before	After			
Cummins Engine (1985)	14	18	50%	50%	– 1.1%	– 0.7%	– 1.2%
Lafarge (1985)	10	16	30%	50%	– 7.9%	– 7.5%	– 7.0%
Squibb (1984)	17	22	35%	45%	– 0.5%	– 0.3%	– 1.2%
Xerox (1987)	14	18	50%	50%	– 1.5%	– 1.3%	– 1.7%
Mean					– 2.8%	2.5%	– 2.8%
T-statistic					– 1.59	– 1.44	– 1.94
P-value					0.21	0.25	0.15
Difference in means					5.0%**	4.8%*	5.6%**
T-statistic					2.46	2.17	2.95
P-value					0.04	0.06	0.02
					Abnormal stock returns 10 days before to 10 days after announcement		
Difference in means					17.6%***	17.7%***	14.9%**
T-statistic					3.77	3.41	3.31
P-value					0.01	0.01	0.01

Significant at 1% (***), 5% (**), and 10% (*) levels.

wealth/level of board stock ownership. The additional interaction terms allow me to check whether these board attributes also affect the level of CEO incentives. Neither variable has a statistically significant estimate, and a likelihood ratio test shows that they do not have joint significance.

5.4. Reactions to significant changes in board size

Investor reactions to changes in board size should provide additional evidence of links between board size and market valuation. Within my 452 firms, I analyze those companies that have changed board size by at least four directors at one time since 1984. I base my choice (changes of four or more as the cutoff point) upon the relative lack of observations for greater changes and my subjective judgment that board-size changes of two or three members are not substantial. From my candidate sample of 195 board-size changes of four or more, I eliminate those changes occurring gradually during the fiscal year and those for which no event date could be identified in press reports or proxy statements. I also exclude changes made in the aftermath of mergers and acquisitions and changes that occur around CEO transitions or as tactical moves in a corporate control contest. The resulting sample for analysis, listed in Table 7, includes ten cases of companies changing board size by four or more on one date, explicitly or apparently for corporate governance reasons.[4] Six of these companies reduced board size by four or more members, while four companies increased board size by at least four.

I study company stock returns around announcement dates of board-size changes. I obtain abnormal stock returns by three methods: subtracting the return for the CRSP market-wide index, subtracting market model expected returns (with α and β parameters estimated from one year of trading data prior to the event period), and extracting excess daily returns from CRSP's NYSE/AMEX file. I use CRSP's value-weighted, dividend-inclusive market index as the market return. Table 7 presents the abnormal stock return in the three right-hand columns, covering an event period beginning one day before each announcement and ending one day after.

Investors appear to welcome decreases in board size and to disapprove of board expansions. Abnormal stock returns are positive around five of six

[4] For two of the ten companies, simultaneous announcements of other news might contaminate the events for purposes of study. When Chrysler reduced the size of its board in 1991, the change attracted attention because of the exclusion from the new board of United Auto Workers President Owen Bieber. Time Warner's 1992 reduction in board size occurred within days of the death of co-CEO Steven Ross. In both cases, the companies denied any connection between the reductions in board size and the other news. It is not clear that either event should have affected the firms' market values, as Bieber's role in Chrysler was described as marginal and Ross's illness had led to a well-publicized withdrawal from day-to-day management six months before.

announcements of board-size reductions and negative around all four announcements of board-size increases. The average magnitude of each effect is approximately 2.5%. The difference in means between the two subgroups, which equals approximately 5%, has statistical significance at levels between 2% and 6%, depending on which type of abnormal return is analyzed.

Inspection of the data suggests that some information leakage takes place before public announcement dates, as abnormal daily returns cumulate gradually for approximately two weeks prior to announcements. If the event window is widened to encompass ten trading days before until ten trading days after each announcement, the results become dramatic, with a difference in mean abnormal returns of approximately 15% (p-value below 1%).

Though this analysis involves a small sample, the ten observations show that investors react favorably to significant reductions in board size and react unfavorably to board expansions. It is not likely that the results reflect changes in board composition; Table 7 shows that although three of the sample companies that reduced their boards simultaneously increased the role of outside directors (including Adolph Coors, according to its announcement), one company did the opposite, and the remaining two essentially left board composition unchanged. Two of four companies expanding their boards increased the fraction of outside directors, but nevertheless experienced negative abnormal returns.

Despite shareholders' apparently favorable reactions to announcements of smaller board size, subsequent changes in firm value over long periods do not provide further support for the hypothesis that smaller boards manage companies better. I calculate average changes in the value of Tobin's Q over one, two, and three year periods following the announcements of board size changes shown in Table 7. Average Q values exhibit a slight upward pattern for both the six companies reducing their boards and the four firms that added directors. Differences between the two groups are not statistically significant.

6. Summary and conclusions

This paper evaluates a recent proposal in the legal and finance literature for reducing the size of corporate boards of directors. Lipton and Lorsch (1992) and Jensen (1993) have criticized the performance of large boards, stating that problems of poor communication and decision-making overwhelm the effectiveness of such groups. I find evidence consistent with this theory. Using a variety of regression models with data from 1984–91 for 452 large public corporations, I find an inverse association between board size and firm value. The association appears to have a convex shape, suggesting that the largest fraction of lost value occurs as boards grow from small to medium size.

The basic result proves robust to a variety of controls for company size, the presence of growth opportunities, and alternative corporate governance and ownership structures. No evidence is consistent with conjectures that companies change board size as a result of past performance.

A range of supporting evidence is consistent with the main finding of an inverse association between board size and firm value. Financial ratios related to profitability and operating efficiency appear to decline as board size grows. CEO performance incentives provided by the board through compensation and the threat of dismissal operate less strongly as board size increases. A small group of sample companies that announce significant reductions in board size realize substantial excess stock returns around the announcement dates, while the opposite occurs for companies that announce board expansions.

References

Bagnani, Elizabeth Strock, Nikolaos T. Milonas, Anthony Saunders, and Nickolaos G. Travlos, 1994, Managers, owners, and the pricing of risky debt: An empirical analysis, Journal of Finance 49, 453–477.

Baysinger, Robert D. and Henry N. Butler, 1985, Corporate governance and the board of directors: Performance effects of changes in board composition, Journal of Law, Economics and Organization 1, 101–124.

Berger, Philip G. and Eli Ofek, 1995, Diversification's effect on firm value, Journal of Financial Economics 37, 39–65.

Brickley, James A., Jeffrey L. Coles, and Rory L. Terry, 1994, Outside directors and the adoption of poison pills, Journal of Financial Economics 35, 371–390.

Byrd, John W. and Kent A. Hickman, 1992, Do outside directors monitor managers?, Journal of Financial Economics 32, 195–221.

Dodd, Peter and Jerold B. Warner, 1983, On corporate governance, Journal of Financial Economics 11, 401–438.

Gilson, Stuart, 1990, Bankruptcy, boards, banks, and blockholders: Evidence on changes in corporate ownership and control when firms default, Journal of Financial Economics 27, 355–387.

Hackman, J. Richard, ed., 1990, Groups that work (Jossey-Bass, San Francisco, CA).

Hausman, Jerry A. and William E. Taylor, 1981, Panel data and unobservable individual effects, Econometrica 49, 1377–1398.

Hermalin, Benjamin and Michael Weisbach, 1988, The determinants of board composition, Rand Journal of Economics 19, 589–606.

Hermalin, Benjamin and Michael Weisbach, 1991, The effects of board composition and direct incentives on firm performance, Financial Management 20, 101–112.

Holthausen, Robert W. and David F. Larcker, 1993a, Boards of directors, ownership structure and CEO compensation, Unpublished manuscript (Wharton School, University of Pennsylvania, Philadelphia, PA).

Holthausen, Robert W. and David F. Larcker, 1993b, Organizational structure and financial performance, Unpublished manuscript (Wharton School, University of Pennsylvania, Philadelphia, PA).

Jensen, Michael C., 1993, The modern industrial revolution, exit, and the failure of internal control systems, Journal of Finance 48, 831–880.

Jensen, Michael C. and Kevin J. Murphy, 1990, Performance pay and top-management incentives, Journal of Political Economy 98, 225–264.

Johnson, W. Bruce, Robert P. Magee, Nandu J. Nagarajan, and Harry A. Newman, 1985, An analysis of the stock price reaction to sudden executive deaths, Journal of Accounting and Economics 7, 151–174.

Kini, Omesh, William Kracaw, and Shehzad Mian, 1995, Corporate takeovers, firm performance, and board composition, Journal of Corporate Finance 1, 383–412.

Lang, Larry H.P. and René M. Stulz, 1994, Tobin's Q, corporate diversification, and firm performance, Journal of Political Economy 102, 1248–1280.

Lipton, Martin and Jay W. Lorsch, 1992, A modest proposal for improved corporate governance, Business Lawyer 48, no. 1, 59–77.

McConnell, John J. and Henri Servaes, 1990, Additional evidence on equity ownership and corporate value, Journal of Financial Economics 27, 595–612.

Monks, Robert A.G. and Nell Minow, 1995, Corporate governance (Basil Blackwell, Cambridge).

Mørck, Randall, Andrei Shleifer, and Robert Vishny, 1988, Management ownership and market valuation: An empirical analysis, Journal of Financial Economics 20, 293–315.

Myers, Stewart C., 1977, Determinants of corporate borrowing, Journal of Financial Economics 5, 147–175.

Perfect, Steven B. and Kenneth W. Wiles, 1994, Alternative constructions of Tobin s Q: An empirical comparison, Journal of Empirical Finance 1, 313–341.

Rosenstein, Stuart and Jeffrey G. Wyatt, 1990, Outside directors, board independence, and shareholder wealth, Journal of Financial Economics 26, 175–191.

Smith, Clifford W., Jr. and Ross L. Watts, 1992, The investment opportunity set and corporate financing, dividend, and compensation policies, Journal of Financial Economics 32, 263–292.

Steiner, I.D., 1972, Group process and productivity (Academic Press, New York, NY).

Warner, Jerold B., Ross L. Watts, and Karen H. Wruck, 1988, Stock prices and top management changes, Journal of Financial Economics 20, 461–492.

Weisbach, Michael, 1988, Outside directors and CEO turnover, Journal of Financial Economics 20, 431–460.

White, Halbert, 1980, A heteroskedasticity-consistent covariance matrix estimator and a direct test for heteroskedasticity, Econometrica 48, 817–838.

White, Halbert, 1982, Maximum likelihood estimation of misspecified models, Econometrica 50, 1–26.

[15]

© Academy of Management Journal
1999, Vol. 42, No. 6, 674–686.

NUMBER OF DIRECTORS AND FINANCIAL PERFORMANCE: A META-ANALYSIS

DAN R. DALTON
CATHERINE M. DAILY
Indiana University

JONATHAN L. JOHNSON
University of Arkansas

ALAN E. ELLSTRAND
California State University, Long Beach

Although a host of theory-driven rationales suggest a relationship between board of directors size and firm performance, the literature provides no consensus about the direction of that relationship. A meta-analysis of 131 samples (N = 20,620) provided systematic evidence of nonzero, positive, true population estimates of board size–performance relationships.

Narrative reviews describe board composition–performance links as "vexing," "contradictory," "mixed," and "inconsistent" (e.g., Finkelstein & Hambrick, 1996; Johnson, Daily, & Ellstrand, 1996; Zahra & Pearce, 1989). In a recent meta-analysis, however, we found no evidence of substantive relationships between board composition and financial performance (Dalton, Daily, Ellstrand, & Johnson, 1998). This finding was invariant across multiple performance indicators, firm size, and multiple measurements of board composition.

Research attention to board composition has been indirect. The composition of a firm's board is typically a surrogate for the extent to which the board is independent of the firm's CEO (e.g., Daily, Johnson, & Dalton, 1999; Dalton et al., 1998; Seward & Walsh, 1996). Although more than 20 measurements of board composition can be found in relevant research—for example, the proportion of inside directors, outside directors, affiliated directors, or interdependent directors (Daily et al., 1999)—these measures are all designed to capture some aspect of board independence.

This focus on board independence is grounded in agency theory, which addresses inefficiencies that arise from the separation of companies' ownership and control (Eisenhardt, 1989; Fama & Jensen, 1983; Jensen & Meckling, 1976; Shleifer & Vishny, 1997). Berle and Means's (1932) seminal work suggested that managers did not have sufficient equity in the firms they managed to give them the incentive to turn their full attention to profit maximization. Instead, managers may pursue self-interested initiatives at the expense of shareholders. One monitoring mechanism that may temper that tendency is oversight by the board of directors; this oversight, or control, function of a board is often described as the most critical of directors' roles (Fama, 1980; Mizruchi, 1983; Zahra & Pearce, 1989). Consistent with agency theory, then, a board comprised of members with dependent relationships with a firm (that is, inside directors, affiliated directors, and/or interdependent directors) is less likely to provide a dispassionate assessment of the firm's CEO.

Board independence, however, may not be the only aspect of contemporary boards associated with firm performance. Another factor of interest to observers of corporate governance is the literal size of a board of directors. There has been less empirical attention paid to this aspect of boards; it is interesting that there has also been no consensus regarding the direction of the performance relationship one would expect as a function of board size.

BOARD OF DIRECTORS SIZE AND FINANCIAL PERFORMANCE

Advantages Associated with Larger Boards

Resource dependence theory has been the primary foundation for the perspective that larger boards will be associated with higher levels of firm performance (e.g., Alexander, Fennell, & Halpern, 1993; Goodstein, Gautam, & Boeker, 1994; Mintzberg, 1983; Pfeffer, 1972, 1973; Pfeffer & Salancik, 1978; Provan, 1980). In this view, board size may be a measure of an organization's ability to form environmental links to secure critical resources (Goodstein et al., 1994). According to Pfeffer and

Salancik, "The greater the need for effective external linkage, the larger the board should be" (1978: 172).

Pfeffer (1972, 1973) and Provan (1980), for example, demonstrated that board size was associated with a firm's ability to extract critical resources such as amount of budget, external funding and leverage from an environment. Birnbaum (1984), in a finding also consistent with the tenets of resource dependence, reported that environmental uncertainty (lack of information and volatility) led to increased board size. Booth and Deli (1996), too, noted that the size of a board would reflect the extent of a firm's contracting environments.

Research on board interlocks may also provide a rationale for expecting larger boards to be associated with positive corporate outcomes (e.g., Bazerman & Schoorman, 1983; Burt, 1980). There is some evidence, for example, that board interlocks are associated with effective capital acquisition (e.g., Burt, 1983; Mizruchi & Stearns, 1988; Stearns & Mizruchi, 1993). It may be that larger boards provide more possibilities for such interactions.

The expertise-counsel account of board service suggests that directors may provide CEOs with advice of a quality unobtainable from other corporate staff (e.g., Zahra & Pearce, 1989). Lorsch and MacIver reported that many directors are themselves CEOs: "CEOs have the most relevant experience and expertise to be effective directors. CEOs understand the complex problems of running a major enterprise and, it is argued, provide the best counsel and advice" (1989: 174). This view is consistent with the finding that directors consider "their key normal duty" to be that of advising the CEO of the company on whose board they sit (Lorsch & MacIver, 1989: 64). A larger board with more CEO members, then, may offer an exceptional level of high-quality advice and counsel to a CEO.

Advantages Associated with Smaller Boards

Researchers have not achieved consensus on the idea that larger boards will be associated with better performance. Jensen, for example, suggested that "When boards get beyond seven or eight people they are less likely to function effectively and are easier for the CEO to control" (1993: 865). This view is consistent with that of Firstenberg and Malkiel, who argued that a board with eight or fewer members "engenders greater focus, participation, and genuine interaction and debate" (1994: 34; cf. Kameda, Stasson, David, Parks, & Zimmerman, 1992; Lipton & Lorsch, 1992).

Although we are unaware of research specifically addressing group dynamics and boards, there is extensive work that may inform concerns about large board size (reviews include Ellis and Fisher [1994], Guzzo and Dickson [1996], and Guzzo and Salas [1995]). Social loafing for example, refers to a decrease in the effort exerted by individuals in a group as the total number of people in the group increases (e.g., Kidwell & Bennett, 1993; Latane, Williams, & Harkins, 1979; Sheppard, 1993).

Group cohesiveness is another construct that may have application for boards of directors. Cohesiveness, which may be facilitated by having fewer group members, has been related to performance. Evans and Dion (1991), for example, relying on a meta-analysis, reported a positive association between group cohesion and performance. Arguably, smaller boards would, on average, have more group cohesiveness (Lipton & Lorsch, 1992; cf. Jensen, 1993).

Also, largeness can significantly inhibit a board's ability to initiate strategic actions (Goodstein et al., 1994). This idea is consistent with the more general view that larger boards may be less participative, less cohesive, and less able to reach consensus. Judge and Zeithaml (1992), for example, reported that larger boards were less likely to become involved in strategic decision making. Goodstein and colleagues (1994) reported that board size inhibited strategic change through reorganization. Yermack (1996; cf. Lin, 1996) demonstrated that board smallness was associated with higher market evaluations as well as higher returns on assets (ROA) and returns on sales (ROS). He concluded that whatever benefits may be associated with board largeness may be overwhelmed by poor communication and decision-making processes.

Mintzberg (1983) suggested that board members' assessments of top management are more easily manipulated when boards are large and diverse. It might be reasonably expected, then, that large boards would tend to be more diverse, more contentious, and more fragmented than small boards. In such cases, CEOs may gain advantage in power relations with board members through tactics like "coalition building, selective channeling of information, and dividing and conquering" (Alexander, Fennell, & Halpern 1993: 79). In fairness, however, others have expressed diametrically opposed opinions of the likely power relationship between CEOs and large boards. Ocasio, for example, suggested this:

> The stability and cohesiveness of the governing coalition under the CEO can best be contested when the number of directors on the board is large. A large board is more likely than a small one to generate alternative political coalitions that challenge the CEO and take control over the firm. A large board also limits the possibility of the CEO exerting social influence to maintain his power. (1994: 291)

This perspective is consistent with that of Zahra and Pearce, who concluded that "larger boards are not as susceptible to managerial domination as their smaller counterpart" (1989: 309).

It has also been suggested that larger boards develop factions and coalitions that lead to group conflict; such dynamics may embitter the process of reaching consensus (Goodstein et al., 1994). Notably, some observers have suggested that a tendency to react slowly or indecisively in a crisis—a tendency likely associated with group conflict—might jeopardize the very existence of a firm (e.g., Daily & Dalton, 1994a, 1994b; Sutton & Callahan, 1987).

A host of theory-driven rationales thus suggest a relationship between board size and firm performance, but the literature provides no consensus about the direction of that relationship.

METHODS

Meta-Analytic Procedures

This meta-analysis was conducted according to the guidelines provided by Hunter and Schmidt (1990). Meta-analysis allows researchers to correct for various statistical artifacts and to aggregate results across studies to obtain an estimate of the true relationship between two variables. Meta-analytic procedures require that each correlation observed in a given study be weighted by the study's sample size; thus, a mean weighted correlation across studies can be calculated. Then the researchers can calculate the standard deviation of the observed correlations to estimate the variability in the relationship between the variables of interest. The total variability across studies is comprised of the true variation in the population, variation due to sampling error, and variation due to other artifacts, such as reliability and range restriction.

To correct for such artifacts, we relied on MetaDos (Stauffer, 1994), software that employs Hunter and Schmidt's (1990) artifact distribution formulas. Since all variables in our meta-analysis were objective, we relied on a conservative .80 reliability estimate (e.g., Bommer, Johnson, Rich, Podsakoff, & MacKenzie, 1995; Dalton et al., 1988; Hunter & Schmidt, 1990).

With corrected standard deviation estimates and the standard errors of the mean-corrected effect sizes established, credibility and confidence intervals can be calculated (e.g., Whitener, 1990). The credibility interval provides diagnostics regarding the potential for moderating variables. Also, a 95 percent confidence interval that does not include zero is an indicator that there is a true relationship between the variables of interest (e.g., Finkelstein, Burke, & Raju, 1995).

Sample

We used several search techniques to identify relevant studies. It was unnecessary that board size–financial performance relationships be the main focus of a study, only that a correlation between these variables be available. Through computer-aided and manual searches, we obtained the applicable research reports. We also contacted authors whose work, although not directly examining board size and financial performance, included indexes of board composition. As total directors is the denominator for such proportions, we requested the correlations between numbers of directors and the measures of financial performance on which they relied.

This process yielded 27 studies with a total of 131 samples drawn from an aggregate 20,620 companies. For the meta-analysis and the moderating analyses that follow, this overall "N" is a necessary element by which significance distributions are calculated. The relatively large sample-to-study ratio is a function of the common reliance, in governance research, on multiple indicators of financial performance.

RESULTS

The results for board size and financial performance indicate a systematic relationship. The corrected mean correlation estimate is .16, and the 95 percent confidence interval does not include zero. Notably, the overall results have a 90 percent credibility interval of .38, a value over three times the guideline (.11) Kowlowsky and Sagie (1993; cf. Whitener, 1990) suggested for identifying moderating variables.

Moderating Variables for the Board Size–Financial Performance Meta-Analysis

In any meta-analysis, there are two requirements for potential moderating variables (Dalton et al., 1998). First, the literature should provide some theoretical rationale for a given variable's moderating the relationship of interest. Also, the studies on which the meta-analysis is based, or a reasonable subset of them, must include the variable.

Firm size. As we have noted in earlier research (Dalton et al., 1998), an obvious assumption made when any board structure–performance relationship is posited is that the choice of various governance options *could* be associated with changes in organizational strategy and firm performance. Several aspects of firm size may influence the governance of organizations in ways that temper boards' ability to affect change.

It has been observed that CEOs and directors are less constrained by organizational systems and structures in smaller firms (Daily & Dalton, 1992, 1993; Eisenhardt & Schoonhoven, 1990; Hoskisson, Johnson, & Moesel, 1994). Cyert and March (1963) provided an early expression of this view in their notion of the dominant coalition. In this view, organizations are comprised of coalitions, groups of individuals and constituencies pursuing certain, and often disparate, interests. It may be that as the scale and complexity of an organization and its environment grow, such coalitions proliferate. In that case, there may be an attendant lack of stability and cohesiveness within these groups (e.g., Finkelstein & Hambrick, 1996; Ocasio, 1994; Thompson, 1967). Mintzberg (1983) noted that as the number of influential constituencies in an organization increases, goal consistency is lost.

Finkelstein and Hambrick's (1996) work in the area of managerial discretion leads to a similar conclusion. They also underscored the impact of a firm's scale and environment on the discretion of its officers. Hambrick and Finkelstein suggested that officers' latitude is a "function of the degree to which the environment allows variety and change" (1987: 379). These authors also directly discussed firm size, noting specifically that officers are more likely to be influential in smaller firms (Finkelstein & Hambrick, 1996). Smaller firms may facilitate power and more narrowly focus firms' planning, core knowledge, and environmental scanning processes (Baysinger & Hoskisson, 1990).

Hannan and Freeman (1989) argued that smaller firms change more readily and that larger firms inhibit creativity and innovation. Although we would not argue that change is universally associated with positive outcomes it would seem that the relatively early adoption of relevant innovation can be an important aspect of organizational progress and renewal (e.g., Rogers, 1995).

Largeness may be associated with advantages as well. Pfeffer and Salancik (1978), for example, argued that larger firms have far more influence over their environments than do smaller firms and are concomitantly more likely to enlist the support of critical constituencies. Haveman (1993) suggested that having control over such resources makes it easier to initiate and sustain change.

We conducted moderator analyses by forming relevant subgroups and computing separate meta-analyses for each. Our subgroups were (1) samples composed of *Fortune* 500 and Standard & Poor's 500 companies and (2) those composed of smaller organizations. Specifically, we classified firms with $300 million or more in sales as large and firms with less than $300 million as small. A critical ratio (essentially a *Z*-score for which a value of 1.96 or greater indicates a statistically significant difference) was calculated to differentiate between the moderator subgroups (Quinones, Ford, & Teachout, 1995). As can be seen in Table 1, the relationship between board size and financial performance is greater for smaller firms. The critical ratio (−2.19) indicates that the population correlation estimates for the large (r = .12) compared to the

TABLE 1
Board of Directors Size and Financial Performance

Variable	Sample Size for Meta-Analysis	Number of Samples from Studies	Observed r	Corrected r	Observed Variance	Corrected Variance	90 Percent Credibility Interval	95 Percent Confidence Interval	Critical Ratio[a]
Overall analysis (all samples)	20,620	131	.13	.16	.02	.02	−.03: .35	.10: .16	
Firm size as moderator									
Large firms	15,412	113	.09	.12	.02	.02	−.05: .28	.06: .12	
Small firms	5,208	18	.17	.21	.02	.02	.04: .39	.11: .24	−2.19
Board composition as moderator									
Boards with low independence	10,578	66	.12	.15	.02	.03	−.05: .36	.08: .17	
Boards with high independence	10,042	65	.14	.17	.02	.02	.01: .34	.10: .18	−0.46
Performance comparison									
Market performance indicators	2,278	10	.08	.10	.00	.00	−.09: .12	.02: .14	
Accounting performance indicators	18,342	121	.14	.17	.02	.03	−.03: .37	.11: .17	−1.59

[a] The critical ratio is essentially a *Z*-score. A value of 1.96 or greater indicates a statistically significant difference, in this case between the corrected correlations for large firms and small firms.

small (r = .21) companies are statistically significant. The magnitude of the relationship is greater for the smaller firms.

Board composition. The association between board composition and financial performance has been the subject of many studies (for compendiums, see Finkelstein and Hambrick [1996], Johnson et al. [1996], and Zahra and Pearce [1989]), including a meta-analysis (Dalton et al., 1998). As noted earlier, board composition is a surrogate for board independence, or the extent to which a board is likely to dispassionately evaluate a CEO. Moreover, independence implies a board is able or willing to provide guidance that does not necessarily mirror the will of the CEO.

We have argued that larger boards may offer several advantages associated with firm financial performance. Among these are advantages posited in resource dependence theory. Specifically, a large board may increase the organization's ability to form environmental links that help it secure critical resources (e.g., Pfeffer & Salancik, 1978). It may be possible, however, to extract both the advantages of a larger board with regard to resources and the advantages that have been argued to accrue to independent boards. A moderating effect of board composition would suggest, for example, that a larger board with greater relative independence (that is, a high proportion of outside directors) would be associated with higher levels of financial performance than a larger board with less independence.

To test this proposition, we divided the sample into two categories, those above and those below the median for board composition, defined as the proportion of outside board members. Board independence did not moderate the board size–financial performance relationship (Table 1). The critical ratio of −.46 indicates that the population correlation estimate for the low-independence group (r = .12) is not statistically different from that for the high-independence group (r = .14).

Comparison of performance indicators. It may also be instructive to example differences in performance indicators. Governance structure and financial performance research has relied on accounting-based indicators (e.g., Buchholtz & Ribbins, 1994; Finkelstein & D'Aveni, 1994; Ocasio, 1994), market-based indicators, or combinations of both (e.g., Hoskisson et al., 1994; Johnson, Hoskisson, & Hitt, 1993). In the finance literature, differential influences of these indicator types on financial performance variables have been discussed. Market-based indicators, for example, are said to be often subject to forces beyond management's control (Grossman & Hoskisson, 1998; Hambrick & Finkelstein, 1995; Joskow, Rose, & Shepard, 1993). Moreover, it has been suggested that boards find that accounting measures provide convenient targets for CEOs to reach (Joskow et al., 1993). It may be, then, that results differ depending on whether an accounting or a market measure gauges financial performance.

For this analysis, samples were dichotomized into those relying on accounting-based indicators of financial performance, like ROA, ROE, or ROS, and indicators based on market returns, like Jensen's alpha, the Treynor measure, or the Sharpe measure. There was no evidence that the type of measure used affected board size–performance relationships. The critical ratio (−1.59) illustrates that the population correlation estimate for the market-based measures (r = .10) is not statistically different from that for the accounting indicators (r = .17). This result should be cautiously interpreted, as only ten samples relied on market-based performance measures.

DISCUSSION

Meta-analysis is an effective means of establishing the best estimate for a true population relationship between two variables from multiple studies. In this case, the results for our overall meta-analysis of the board size–financial performance association strongly suggest a nonzero, positive relationship. Moreover, moderator analyses gave some evidence that, although this relationship can be demonstrated for large and small firms, the effect is greater for the latter. Also, these relationships are consistent for market-based and accounting-based firm performance measures. Likewise, board composition does not moderate the board size–financial performance relationship.

Meta-analysis can demonstrate the existence of a relationship, but it does not isolate the cause of the connection. Meta-analytical procedures do not help researchers determine whether the demonstrated relationship is a function of resource dependence, board interlocks, the expertise and counsel role of boards, the monitoring and control role of boards, or of some combination of these elements. A comparison of the results we reported in earlier work (Dalton et al., 1998) with those reported here, however, may underscore an interesting aspect of corporate governance research.

Dalton and colleagues (1998) focused on board independence and financial performance. As previously noted, research interest in board independence has been largely grounded in agency theory (e.g., Fama & Jensen, 1983; Jensen & Meckling, 1976; Shleifer & Vishny, 1997). As managers may pursue self-interested initiatives at the expense of shareholders, monitoring mechanisms, including boards of directors, are essential (Fama & Jensen, 1983; Jensen & Meckling, 1976). A major prescription of agency theory, then, is that effective boards will be largely comprised of independent, outside directors. Examination of this control-monitoring role has dominated the corporate governance literature (e.g., Dalton et al., 1998; Finkelstein & Hambrick, 1996; Johnson et al., 1996).

Control, however, is one of several critical board tasks. Others include providing resources and expertise and counsel (e.g., Daily et al., 1999; Johnson et al., 1996; Pfeffer & Salancik, 1978; Zahra & Pearce, 1989). Interestingly, these multiple roles may be neither complementary nor fungible. Inside directors, for example, are considered valuable for their service in the expertise-counsel role (e.g., Baysinger & Hoskisson, 1990; Hoskisson et al., 1994), but they are routinely criticized for their lack of independence from CEOs. Similarly, affiliated directors (outside directors with business or personal relationships with a firm) may be outstanding in a resource role but will also be criticized for their lack of independence.

It appears, then, that extant measurements of board independence relying on the proportions of board members who are inside, outside, affiliated, or independent/interdependent (cf. Daily et al., 1999; Dalton et al., 1998) may not capture the dynamics of directors' multiple roles. With board size held constant, as the proportion of one category of board members increases, the proportions of other categories necessarily decrease. Even the most ardent advocate for resource dependence would not endorse a board comprised entirely of affiliated directors. In addition to compromising board independence, that approach would dissolve the local knowledge, training, and succession patterns facilitated by service on the board by inside officers.

In our earlier meta-analysis (Dalton et al., 1998), which relies on various proportions of board member types, we did not consider this perspective. We assumed that a higher proportion of one category of director or another was superior and would be associated with higher financial performance. An alternative view would be that it is not representation of one or another board member type that is key, but rather, the ability of a board to leverage all these roles. Larger boards can seat inside directors (offering local expertise, training, and succession), affiliated directors (resource dependence links), and other outside and/or independent/interdependent directors (independence). It may be, then, that a board should ideally be of sufficient size to be comprised of members who do, in concert, fill all these often separate roles.

It should be acknowledged that our board size–financial performance meta-analysis, although entirely consistent with this proposition, does not constitute a strong test of it. It is true that board largeness *could* facilitate filling the full range of board roles. It is not true, however, that large boards will routinely do so. In many ways, the present meta-analysis is similar to much of the research in the general area of board composition. Typical board independence measures identify boards that *could* be more independent. Clearly, no measurement based on the proportion of director types will definitively determine if given boards are, in fact, more independent. Even so, the implications of a reliance on agency theory as compared to resource dependence theory, for example, extend well beyond a measurement issue.

There is a contemporary example of a tactical choice that might be based on a theoretical choice. Reducing board size has become a priority in the institutional investment community, particularly for troubled companies (Yermack, 1996). Curiously, organizational failure is the very circumstance in which a reliance on resource dependence theory would suggest the opposite strategy, board expansion (Daily & Dalton, 1994b; Pfeffer & Salancik, 1978; Sutton & Callahan, 1987). Perhaps the institutional investment community is more inclined to rely on agency perspectives than on those of resource dependence. This remains an empirical question, but in general it could also be that the choice of agency theory or resource dependence theory is contingent on other factors. Still, it is interesting that, in the case of organizational crisis, agency and resource dependence do seem to prescribe different approaches for corporate governance structures.

Our moderation analysis indicates that firm size moderates the board size–corporate financial performance relationship. Although that relationship is statistically significant for the large- and small-firm groups, the magnitude of the board size–performance relationship is greater for smaller firms. As noted before, meta-analysis provides no rationale for this finding. We suspect, however, that results can best be interpreted in terms of the dominant coalition (Cyert & March, 1963) and managerial discretion perspectives (Finkelstein & Hambrick, 1996). It may be that smaller firms do not have as many competing coalitions as their larger counterparts. If so, stability and cohesiveness among constituent groups may be higher (e.g., Ocasio, 1994; Thompson, 1967) and goal consistency stronger. Also, Finkelstein and Hambrick (1996) would argue that firm smallness enhances the discretion of officers and directors.

Limitations of the Study

In interpreting these results, we must be attentive to the limitations of meta-analytical approaches. The direction of the demonstrated relationship between board size and financial performance, for example, could be misspecified. Perhaps firms with outstanding performance at one time are subsequently predisposed to increase the sizes of their boards. Retrospective meta-analyses relying on bivariate relationships cannot demonstrate causality.

The board size–financial performance relationship could be further assessed in at least four ways, which are outlined below. The best test, of course, would be a direct empirical examination. A second type of empirical investigation is possible, but it is derivative in the sense that studies not directly examining the relationship of interest may bear reasonably on the question. Some evidence might also be garnered from research on public policy, particularly governmental or administrative policies driven by assumptions of causality. Lastly, the perspectives and policies of nongovernmental corporate constituencies—in this case, the institutional investment community—may also have some probative value with regard to the causality question.

An empirical examination. We were able, relying on the same data with which the meta-analysis was conducted, to conduct a "weak" test to provide some perspective on the issue of the direction of the relationship of interest. In the overall sample, there were no studies examining board size–performance relationships that were truly lagged, with measurements at time 1 for board size and at times 1, 2, 3, and so forth for performance. Similarly, there were no studies with measurements of performance at time 1 and of board size at times 1, 2, 3, and so forth. However, in 14 studies multiyear performance measures were aggregated. Board size was measured once (in year 1), but performance was a three-year average of measures for year 1, year −1, and year −2.

It is possible, then, to compare these 14 samples with the 117 samples that were wholly cross-sectional. The corrected correlation for the cross-sectional samples was .16, and it was .17 for the lagged samples. The critical ratio was .34, well below statistical significance. Although not robust, this test does suggest that a composite of prior years' performance does not better inform the board size–financial performance relationship than a contemporaneous performance measure.

Derivative empirical research. Other research studies not directly addressing board size and financial performance may provide some derivative evidence about this relationship. Interestingly, the available data mostly concern firms at the lower extreme of corporate performance, those performing poorly and those in crisis. There are fewer relevant examples for firms characterized by better performance.

Hambrick and D'Aveni (1992), for example, noted an inability of firms in financial distress—in the five years prior to a formal bankruptcy filing—to obtain and retain outside directors (cf. Daily, 1996; Gales & Kesner, 1994). It has been suggested that this is a critical deficiency for distressed firms as this is the period when outside directors who might offer resource links are essential for the firms' survival (Hambrick & D'Aveni, 1992; Sutton & Callahan, 1987).

Gilson (1990) also noted smaller boards in poorly performing companies. He speculated that prospective directors might not wish to associate with declining firms. Small board size in such firms may also be related to a structural reduction in the board monitoring role. In a formal bankruptcy filing, federal courts often intervene and become a—perhaps *the*—active monitor for firm affairs, supplanting the control role of the directors (e.g., Daily, 1996; Gales & Kesner, 1994; Gilson, 1990).

Gilson (1990) also reported that average board size declines after bankruptcy filings and major debt restructurings. This result is consistent with a finding of Hermalin and Weisbach (1988), who reported that poorly performing companies have smaller boards after an outside executive succession. The dynamics for such a change are unclear. It could be, for example, that inside board members leave a company—and its board, of course—because they have been passed over for promotion to CEO.

There is also some evidence that suggests higher-performing companies have larger boards. Daily and Johnson (1997) suggested, for example, that the CEOs of such firms are granted wider discretion, not only as to the number of directors they are allowed to choose, but also as to their type. They found, for example, that firms with higher performance in one period actually had a lower proportion of independent directors in a subsequent period. They concluded that "CEOs of firms that are performing well use their discretion to appoint directors" (Daily & Johnson, 1997: 113).

Other research, too, may inform board size–performance relationships. Yermack (1996), for example, noted that more diversified firms are likely to have larger boards of directors because boards tend to increase in size when companies make acquisitions. This association is suggestive, but a better test requires a demonstration that acquiring firms are, on average, better performers. In general, however, the Yermack (1996) finding is consistent with Johnson and colleagues' (1993) report that firm size is strongly related to board size.

Public policy. The general issue of board governance structure relationships and corporate financial performance has engaged a number of influential agencies. Although the academic community has been an active participant and advisor, others have translated opinion to action. The Securities and Exchange Commission (SEC), the New York Stock Exchange, the American Stock Exchange, and the National Association of Securities Dealers all have specific guidelines related to corporate governance structures (e.g., Daily et al., 1999; Kesner, 1988). Also, the SEC has specific guidelines regarding the proxy reporting of affiliated directors (Daily & Dalton, 1994a; Daily, Johnson, Ellstrand, & Dalton, 1998).

Other forums, too, have recommended board governance structures. These include the American Law Institute Principles of Corporate Governance, the Buffett Symposium, the Business Roundtable, the Cadbury Report (United Kingdom), the General Motors Board of Directors Corporate Governance Guidelines, the Hilmer Report (Australia), the National Association of Corporate Directors Blue Ribbon Report on Director Professionalism, and the SEC Staff Report on Corporate Accountability. The product of each of these forums has been specific recommendations concerning "appropriate" board structures. Notably, in every case the prescription is that better board governance structure will improve corporate financial performance (e.g., Biggs, 1995; Dalton & Daily, 1998; Fisch, 1997; Millstein & MacAvoy, 1998).

The institutional investment community. The institutional investment community, particularly pension funds, can be an enormously influential corporate constituency (see Davis and Thompson [1994] for an overview of institutional investor activism and also see Grundfest [1993]). The scale of institutional investment underscores its potential influence. The Council of Institutional Investors, for example, represents some 100 pension funds with combined assets of $1 trillion (Schultz & Warren, 1998). Institutional investors, primarily private and public pension funds, control in excess of 50 percent of corporate equity (Davis & Thompson, 1994). Many of these funds are substantially more active than others in their attempts to influence—if not dictate—corporate policy.

One could quibble about what constitutes an activist institution, but such a list would certainly include the California Public Employee Retirement System, the California State Teachers Retirement System, the Colorado Public Employee Retirement System, the Council of Institutional Investors, the Florida State Board of Administration, the International Brotherhood of Teamsters Pension Fund, Lens, the New York City Pension System, the New York State Common Retirement System, the Pennsylvania Public School Employee Retirement System, the State of Wisconsin Investment Board, and the College Retirement Equities Fund (e.g., Wahal, 1996). These groups have routinely targeted board structure issues as platforms for their efforts to improve board performance. The premise by which these investor groups operate is that board governance structure has a direct and significant impact on firm value (e.g., Biggs, 1995; Black, 1998; Fromson, 1990; Schellhardt, 1991).

It should be acknowledged that the apparently consistent conviction of public policy agencies and the institutional investment community regarding the link between board structures and improved corporate financial performance does not establish the existence of such a link. It is interesting, however, that these constituencies speak in concert on this matter. As noted earlier, a study relying on multiperiod, structural equations modeling will be necessary to more clearly document the direction of the board size–corporate financial performance relationship.

Other aspects of the current study should be interpreted with caution. We found no evidence of a moderating influence of board composition on the board size–firm financial performance relationship. The measure of board composition on which we relied—the only common measure available from the studies—was the proportion of outside directors. This is a coarse measure that may poorly capture the multiple aspects of board independence (Daily et al., 1999). It could be, then, that a moderating analysis relying on the proportion of affiliated directors (e.g., Daily et al., 1999) or the proportion of interdependent/independent directors (Boeker, 1992; Wade, O'Reilly, & Chandratat, 1990) would be more fruitful. Also, we relied on the total number of directors on a board. Future research may extend this work by considering a finer cut—the number of affiliated directors or of interdependent/independent directors.

Another of our moderation analyses, the one for firm size, was also relatively coarse-grained. The preponderance of studies (113 of 131) used for the meta-analysis relied on samples of *Fortune* 500 or Standard & Poor's 500 companies. Other sample companies were varied but in all cases much smaller. Still, the over $300 million/less than $300 million dichotomy on which we relied does not provide a fine gradation.

Future Research

Future research can contribute on a number of dimensions. Longitudinal designs may establish the direction of causality for board size–financial performance links. Additionally, finer-grained examinations may provide much more guidance on the dynamics of the relationships of interest here.

Another potentially interesting extension may include board committees. Lorsch and MacIver (1989; cf. Bilimoria & Piderit, 1994; Daily, 1994, 1996; Harrison, 1987; Kesner, 1988) explained that many critical processes and decisions do not derive from boards-at-large, but rather, from board committees (such as audit, compensation, nominating, executive, pension-retirement, and strategic planning): "Clearly, committees enable directors to cope with two of the most important problems they face—the limited time they have available, and the complexity of the information with which they must deal" (Lorsch & MacIver, 1989: 59).

Research conducted in the area of CEO compensation may provide an intriguing insight into some subtleties of board committee and corporate outcome relationships. Singh and Harianto (1989), for example, reported that the numbers of insiders on compensation subcommittees were related, not to the dollar value of golden parachute programs, but to the numbers of officers who would receive compensation under such programs. It has also been reported that the amount of CEO compensation is related to the makeup of compensation committees (O'Reilly, Main, & Crystal, 1988; cf. Tosi & Gomez-Mejia, 1989).

Paying attention to boards of directors at the committee level may provide other benefits as well. It is appropriate to consider a board committee to be a small group (e.g., Guzzo & Dickson, 1996). Although we are aware of no research specifically addressing group size dynamics and board committees, a distinguished tradition of research addresses small group and team effectiveness (outstanding compendiums include Ellis and Fisher [1994], Guzzo and Dickson [1996], Guzzo and Salas [1995], and Guzzo and Shea [1992]). It may be, for example, that board committees are more cohesive and less likely to break into coalitions than full boards (Evans & Dion, 1991).

Board committees may also be less subject to social loafing (e.g., Latane et al., 1979). We would also expect more efficient communications generally and, if committee assignments have been made carefully, a more focused use of director expertise in committees then in whole boards (Ellis & Fisher, 1994; Guzzo & Salas, 1995; Lorsch & MacIver, 1989).

Research should also be designed to directly examine the potential "disconnect" between the major governance theories to which we have referred. Whether one prefers to rely on the prescriptions of agency theory or on those of resource dependence would seem to be fundamental to one's notion of optimal board size.

Given the increasing activism targeted on corporate governance structure issues, future research facilitating some convergence of these disparate views might be useful to the academic and practitioner communities. We hope that the research reported here is a modest step toward understanding some of these relationships, as well as a stimulus for future research in this area.

REFERENCES

Alexander, J. A, Fennell, M. L., & Halpern, M. T. 1993. Leadership instability in hospitals: The influence of board-CEO relations and organizational growth and decline. ***Administrative Science Quarterly,*** 38: 74–99.

Baysinger, B. D., & Hoskisson, R. E. 1990. The composition of boards of directors and strategic control. ***Academy of Management Review,*** 15: 72–87.

Bazerman, M. H., & Schoorman, F. D. 1983. A limited rationality model of interlocking directorates. ***Academy of Management Review,*** 8: 206–217.

Berle, A., & Means, G. 1932. ***The modern corporation and private property.*** New York: Macmillan.

Biggs, J. 1995. Why TIAA-CREF is active in corporate governance. ***The Participant,*** November: 2.

Bilimoria, D., & Piderit, S. K. 1994. Board committee membership: Effects of sex-based bias. ***Academy of Management Journal,*** 37: 1453–1477.

Birnbaum, P. H. 1984. The choice of strategic alternatives under increasing regulation in high technology industries. ***Academy of Management Journal,*** 27: 489–510.

Black, B. S. 1998. Does shareholder activism improve company performance? ***Corporate Governance,*** 19(3): 1–6.

*Boeker, W. 1992. Power and managerial dismissal: Scapegoating at the top. ***Administrative Science Quarterly,*** 37: 400–421.

Bommer, W. H., Johnson, L. J., Rich, G. A., Podsakoff, P. M., & MacKenzie, S. B. 1995. On the interchangeability of objective and subjective measures of employee performance: A meta-analysis. ***Personnel Psychology,*** 48: 587–605.

Booth, J. R., & Deli, D. N. 1996. Factors affecting the number of outside directorships held by CEOs. ***Journal of Financial Economics,*** 40: 81–104.

*Buchholtz, A. K., & Ribbins, B. A. 1994. Role of chief executive officers in takeover resistance: Effects of

CEO incentives and individual characteristics. *Academy of Management Journal*, 37: 554–579.

Burt, R. S. 1980. Cooptive corporate actor networks: A reconsideration of interlocking directorates involving American manufacturing. *Administrative Science Quarterly*, 25: 557–581.

Burt, R. S. 1983. *Corporate profits and cooptation.* New York: Academic Press.

Cyert, R. M., & March, J. G. 1963. *A behavioral theory of the firm.* Englewood Cliffs, NJ Prentice-Hall.

Daily, C. M. 1994. Bankruptcy in strategic studies: Past and promise. *Journal of Management*, 20: 263–295.

*Daily, C. M. 1995. The relationship between board composition and leadership structure and bankruptcy reorganization outcomes. *Journal of Management*, 21: 1041–1056.

*Daily, C. M. 1996. Governance patterns in bankruptcy reorganizations. *Strategic Management Journal*, 17: 355–375.

*Daily, C. M., & Dalton, D. R. 1992. The relationship between governance structure and corporate performance in entrepreneurial firms. *Journal of Business Venturing*, 7: 375–386.

*Daily, C. M., & Dalton, D. R. 1993. Board of directors leadership and structure: Control and performance implications. *Entrepreneurship Theory and Practice*, 17: 65–81.

*Daily, C. M., & Dalton, D. R. 1994a. Bankruptcy and corporate governance: The impact of board composition and structure. *Academy of Management Journal*, 37: 1603–1617.

*Daily, C. M., & Dalton, D. R. 1994b. Corporate governance and the bankrupt firm: An empirical assessment. *Strategic Management Journal*, 15: 643–654.

*Daily, C. M., & Dalton, D. R. 1995. CEO and director turnover in failing firms: The illusion of change. *Strategic Management Journal*, 16: 393–401.

*Daily, C. M., & Dalton, D. R. 1994. Outside directors revisited: Prescriptions for CEOs and directors. *Journal of Small Business Strategy*, 5: 57–68.

*Daily, C. M., & Dalton, D. R. 1997. The urge to merge: The role of governance structures in mergers and acquisitions. *Journal of Business Strategies*, 13: 151–166.

*Daily, C. M., & Johnson, J. L. 1997. Sources of CEO power and performance implications: A longitudinal assessment. *Journal of Management*, 23: 97–117.

Daily, C. M., Johnson, J. L., Ellstrand, A. E., & Dalton, D. R. 1998. Compensation committee composition as a determinant of CEO compensation. *Academy of Management Journal*, 41: 209–220.

Daily, C. M., Johnson, J. L., & Dalton, D. R. 1999. On the measurements of board composition: If you have seen one, you certainly have not seen them all. *Decision Science*, 30: 83–106.

Dalton, D. R., & Daily, C. M. 1998. Board independence: So what? *Corporate Board*, 19(113): 15–19.

Dalton, D. R., Daily, C. M., Ellstrand, A. E., & Johnson, J. L. 1998. Meta-analytic reviews of board composition, leadership structure, and financial performance. *Strategic Management Journal*, 19: 269–290.

*Davis, G. F. 1991. Agents without principles? The spread of the poison pill through the intercorporate network. *Administrative Science Quarterly*, 36: 583–613.

Davis, G. F., & Thompson, T. A. 1994. A social movement perspective on corporate control. *Administrative Science Quarterly*, 39: 141–173.

Eisenhardt, K. M. 1989. Agency theory An assessment and review. *Academy of Management Review*, 14: 57–74.

Eisenhardt, K. M., & Schoonhoven, C. B. 1990. Organizational growth: Linking founding team, strategy, environment, and growth among U.S. semiconductor ventures, 1978–1988. *Administrative Science Quarterly*, 35: 504–529.

Ellis, D. G., & Fisher, B. A. 1994. *Small group decision making.* New York: McGraw-Hill.

Evans, C. R., & Dion, K. L. 1991. Group cohesion and performance: A meta-analysis. *Small Group Research*, 22: 175–186.

Fama, E. F. 1980. Agency problems and the theory of the firm. *Journal of Political Economy*, 88: 288–307.

Fama, E. F., & Jensen, M. C. 1983. Separation of ownership and control. *Journal of Law and Economics*, 26: 301–325.

Finkelstein, L. M., Burke, M. J, & Raju, N. 1995. Age discrimination in simulated employment contexts: An integrative analysis. *Journal of Applied Psychology*, 80: 652–663.

*Finkelstein, S., & D'Aveni, R. A. 1994. CEO duality as a double-edged sword: How boards of directors balance entrenchment avoidance and unity of command. *Academy of Management Journal*, 37: 1079–1108.

Finkelstein, S., & Hambrick, D. C. 1996. *Strategic leadership: Top executives and their effects on organizations.* Minneapolis/St. Paul: West.

Firstenberg, P. B., & Malkiel, B. G 1994. The twenty-first century boardroom: Who will be in charge? *Sloan Management Review*, 36(1): 27–35.

Fisch, J. E. 1997. Taking boards seriously. *Cardozo Law Review*, 19: 265–290.

*Fizell, J. L., & Louie, K. K. T. 1990. CEO retention, firm performance, and corporate governance. *Managerial and Decision Economics* 11: 167–176.

Fromson, B. D. 1990. The big owners roar. *Fortune*, July 30: 66–78.

Gales, L. M., & Kesner, I. F. 1994. An analysis of board of director size and composition in bankrupt organizations. ***Journal of Business Research,*** 30: 27–39.

Gilson, S. C. 1990. Bankruptcy, boards, banks, and bondholders. ***Journal of Financial Economics,*** 27: 355–387.

*Goodstein, J., Gautam, K., & Boeker, W. 1994. The effects of board size and diversity on strategic change. ***Strategic Management Journal,*** 15: 241–250.

Grossman, W., & Hoskisson, R. E. 1998. CEO pay at the crossroads of Wall Street and Main: Toward the strategic design of executive compensation. ***Academy of Management Executive,*** 12(1): 43–57.

Grundfest, J. A. 1993. Just vote no: A minimalist strategy for dealing with barbarians inside the gate. ***Stanford Law Review,*** 45: 857–937.

Guzzo, R. A., & Dickson, M. W. 1996. Teams in organizations: Recent research on performance and effectiveness. In J. T. Spence, J. M. Darley, & D. J. Foss (Eds.), ***Annual review of psychology:*** 307–338. Palo Alto, CA: Annual Reviews.

Guzzo, R. A., & Salas, E. 1995. ***Team effectiveness and decision making in organizations.*** San Francisco: Jossey-Bass.

Guzzo, R. A., & Shea, G. P. 1992. Group performance and intergroup relations in organizations. In M. D. Dunnette & L. M. Hough (Eds.), ***Handbook of industrial and organizational psychology:*** 269–313. Palo Alto, CA: Consulting Psychologists Press.

Hambrick, D. C., & D'Aveni, R. A. 1992. Top team deterioration as part of the downward spiral of large corporate bankruptcies. ***Management Science,*** 38: 1445–1466.

Hambrick, D. C., & Finkelstein, S. 1987. Managerial discretion: A bridge between polar views of organizations. In L. L. Cummings & B. W. Staw (Eds.), ***Research in organizational behavior:*** 369–406. Greenwich, CT: JAI Press.

Hambrick, D. C., & Finkelstein, S. 1995. The effects of ownership structure on conditions at the top: The case of CEO pay raises. ***Strategic Management Journal,*** 16: 175–193.

Hannan, M. T., & Freeman, J. H. 1989. ***Organizational ecology.*** Cambridge, MA: Harvard University Press.

Harrison, J. R. 1987. The strategic use of corporate board committees. ***California Management Review,*** 30(1): 109–125.

Haveman, H. A. 1993. Organizational size and change: Diversification in the savings and loan industry after deregulation. ***Administrative Science Quarterly,*** 38: 20–50.

Hermalin, B. E., & Weisbach, M. S. 1988. The determinants of board composition. ***RAND Journal of Economics,*** 19: 589–606.

*Hoskisson, R. E., Johnson, R. A., & Moesel, D. D. 1994. Corporate divestiture intensity in restructuring firms: Effects of governance, strategy, and performance. ***Academy of Management Journal,*** 37: 1207–1251.

Hunter, J. E., & Schmidt, F. L. 1990. ***Methods of meta-analysis: Correcting error and bias in research findings.*** Newbury Park, CA: Sage.

Jensen, M. C. 1993. The modern industrial revolution, exit, and the failure of internal control systems. ***Journal of Finance,*** 48: 831–880.

Jensen, M. C., & Meckling, W. H. 1976. Theory of the firm: Managerial behavior, agency costs, and ownership structure. ***Journal of Financial Economics,*** 3: 305–350.

Johnson, J. L., Daily, C. M., & Ellstrand, A. E. 1996. Boards of directors: A review and research agenda. ***Journal of Management,*** 22: 409–438.

*Johnson, R. A., Hoskisson, R. E., & Hitt, M. A. 1993. Board of director involvement in restructuring: The effects of board versus managerial controls and characteristics. ***Strategic Management Journal,*** 14 (summer special issue): 33–50.

Joskow, P., Rose, N., & Shepard, A. 1993. Regulatory constraints on CEO compensation. ***Brookings papers on economic activity: Microeconomics:*** 158: 70–72.

Judge, W. Q., & Zeithaml, C. P. 1992. Institutional and strategic choice perspectives on board involvement in the strategic decision process. ***Academy of Management Journal,*** 35: 766–794.

Kameda, T., Stasson, M. F., David, J. H., Parks, C., & Zimmerman, S. 1992. Social dilemmas, subgroups, and motivational loss in task-oriented groups: In search of an "optimal" team size. ***Social Psychology Quarterly,*** 55: 47–56.

Kesner, I. F. 1988. Directors' characteristics and committee membership: An investigation of type, occupation, tenure, and gender. ***Academy of Management Journal,*** 31: 66–84.

Kidwell, R. E., & Bennett, N. 1993. Employee propensity to withhold effort: A conceptual model to intersect three avenues of research. ***Academy of Management Review,*** 18: 429–456.

Kowlowsky, M., & Sagie, A. 1993. On the efficacy of credibility intervals as indicators of moderator effects in meta-analytic research. ***Journal of Organizational Behavior,*** 14: 695–699.

Latane, B., Williams, K., & Harkins, S. 1979. Many hands make light work: The causes and consequences of social loafing. ***Journal of Personality and Social Psychology,*** 37: 822–832.

Lin, L. 1996. The effectiveness of outside directors as a corporate governance mechanism: Theories and evidence. ***Northwestern University Law Review,*** 90: 898–976.

Lipton, M., & Lorsch, J. W. 1992. A modest proposal for

improved corporate governance. ***Business Lawyer,*** 48: 59–77.

Lorsch, J. W., & MacIver, E. 1989. ***Pawns and potentates: The reality of America's corporate boards.*** Boston: Harvard University Press.

March, J. G. 1962. The business firm as a political coalition. ***Journal of Politics,*** 24: 662–678.

Millstein, R. M., & MacAvoy, P. W. 1998. The active board of directors and performance of the large publicly traded corporation. ***Columbia Law Review,*** 98: 1283–1321.

Mintzberg, H. 1983. ***Power in and around organizations.*** Englewood Cliffs, NJ: Prentice-Hall.

Mizruchi, M. S. 1983. Who controls whom? An examination of the relation between management and boards of directors in large American corporations. ***Academy of Management Review,*** 8: 426–435.

Mizruchi, M. S., & Stearns, L. B. 1988. A longitudinal study of the formation of interlocking directorates. ***Administrative Science Quarterly,*** 33: 194–210.

*Mizruchi, M. S., & Stearns, L. B. 1994. A longitudinal study of borrowing by large American corporations. ***Administrative Science Quarterly,*** 39: 118–140.

*Ocasio, W. 1994. Political dynamics and the circulation of power: CEO succession in U.S. industrial corporations, 1960–1990. ***Administrative Science Quarterly,*** 39: 285–312.

O'Reilly, C. A., Main, B. G., & Crystal, G. S. 1988. CEO compensation as tournament and social comparison: A tale of two theories. ***Administrative Science Quarterly,*** 33: 257–274.

*Pearce, J. A., & Zahra, S. A. 1992. Board compensation from a strategic contingency perspective. ***Journal of Management Studies,*** 29: 411–438.

*Pfeffer, J. 1972. Size and composition of corporate boards of directors: The organization and its environment. ***Administrative Science Quarterly,*** 17: 218–229.

*Pfeffer, J. 1973. Size, composition, and function of hospital boards of directors: The organization and its environment. ***Administrative Science Quarterly,*** 18: 349–364.

Pfeffer, J., & Salancik, G. R. 1978. ***The external control of organizations: A resource-dependence perspective.*** New York: Harper & Row.

*Provan, K. G. 1980. Board power and organizational effectiveness among human service agencies. ***Academy of Management Journal,*** 23: 221–236.

Quinones, M. A., Ford, J. K., & Teachout, M. S. 1995. The relationship between work experience and job performance: A conceptual and meta-analytic review. ***Personnel Psychology,*** 48: 887–910.

Rogers, E. M. 1995. ***Diffusion of innovations.*** New York: Free Press.

Schellhardt, T. D. 1991. More directors are recruited from outside. ***Wall Street Journal,*** March 20: B1.

Schultz, E. E., & Warren, S. 1998. Pension system ousts company's board in big victory for institutional investors. ***Wall Street Journal,*** May 29: A2.

Seward, J. K., & Walsh, J. P. 1996. The governance and control of voluntary spin-offs. ***Strategic Management Journal,*** 17: 25–39.

Sheppard, J. A. 1993. Productivity loss in performance groups: A motivation analysis. ***Psychological Bulletin,*** 113: 67–81.

Shleifer, A., & Vishny, R. W. 1997. A survey of corporate governance. ***Journal of Finance,*** 52: 737–783.

Singh, H., & Harianto, F. 1989. Management board relationships, takeover risk, and the adoption of golden parachutes. ***Academy of Management Journal,*** 32: 7–24.

Stauffer, J. M. 1994. ***MetaDos: Psychometric meta-analysis program.*** Terre Haute: Indiana State University.

Stearns, L. B., & Mizruchi, M. S. 1993. Board composition and corporate financing: The impact of financial institution representation on borrowing. ***Academy of Management Journal,*** 36: 603–618.

Sutton, R. I., & Callahan, A. L. 1987. The stigma of bankruptcy: Spoiled organizational image and its management. ***Academy of Management Journal,*** 30: 405–436.

Thompson, J. D. 1967. ***Organizations in action.*** New York: McGraw-Hill.

Tosi, H. L., & Gomez-Mejia, L. R. 1989. The decoupling of CEO pay and performance: An agency theory perspective. ***Administrative Science Quarterly,*** 34: 169–190.

*Wade, J., O'Reilly, C. A., & Chandratat, I. 1990. Golden parachutes: CEOs and the exercise of social influences. ***Administrative Science Quarterly,*** 35: 587–603.

Wahal, S. 1996. Pension fund activism and firm performance. ***Journal of Financial and Quantitative Analysis,*** 21: 1–23.

*Westphal, J. D., & Zajac, E. J. 1995. Who shall govern? CEO/board power, demographic similarity, and new director selection. ***Administrative Science Quarterly,*** 40: 60–83.

Whitener, E. M. 1990. Confusion of confidence intervals and credibility intervals in meta-analysis. ***Journal of Applied Psychology,*** 75: 315–321.

Yermack, D. 1996. Higher market evaluation of companies with a small board of directors. ***Journal of Financial Economics,*** 40: 185–211.

Zahra, S. A., & Pearce, J. A. 1989. Boards of directors and corporate financial performance: A review and integrative model. ***Journal of Management,*** 15: 291–334.

*Zahra, S. A., & Stanton, W. W. 1988. The implications of board of directors composition for corporate strategy and performance. ***International Journal of Management,*** 5: 229–236.

[a] References marked with an asterisk indicate studies included in the board-size meta-analysis.

Dan R. Dalton is the dean of the Kelley School of Business, Indiana University, and the Harold A. Poling Chair of Strategic Management. He received his Ph.D. from the University of California. His research interests include corporate governance and corporate social responsibility.

Catherine M. Daily is an associate professor of strategic management in the Kelley School of Business, Indiana University. She received her Ph.D. from Indiana University. Her research interests include corporate governance, strategic leadership, the dynamics of bankruptcy and business failure, and entrepreneurship.

Jonathan L. Johnson is an assistant professor in the department of management, University of Arkansas. He received his Ph.D. from Indiana University. His research interests include social networks within and between organizations and corporate governance.

Alan E. Ellstrand is an assistant professor in the department of management/HRM, California State University, Long Beach. He received his Ph.D. from Indiana University. His research interests include top management teams and corporate governance.

[16]

Strategic Management Journal, Vol. 12, 135–153 (1991)

THE RELATIVE POWER OF CEOs AND BOARDS OF DIRECTORS: ASSOCIATIONS WITH CORPORATE PERFORMANCE

JOHN A. PEARCE II and SHAKER A. ZAHRA
School of Business Administration, George Mason University, Fairfax, Virginia, U.S.A.

A typology of the relative powers of the chief executive officer and the board of directors was derived based on the literature, highlighting four situations: Caretaker, Statutory, Proactive and Participative boards. Data collected from Fortune *500 Industrial and* Fortune *500 Service corporations supported the typology. The results showed significant differences among the four board types in their characteristics, internal process, decision-making styles, board effectiveness, and contribution to company performance. Powerful boards were associated with superior corporate financial performance.*

INTRODUCTION

Suggestions to reform corporate boards of directors are most frequently directed at strengthening their powers relative to that of the chief executive officers (CEOs). These suggestions are predicted on the assumption that counterproductive managerial domination of boards is widespread (Geneen, 1984; Fama and Jensen, 1983; Mizruchi, 1983; Nader, 1984). As evidence of such domination, it has been observed that over 85 percent of *Fortune* 500 industrial companies have chairs who also serve as their own corporations' CEOs (*The Changing Board*, 1983–1986). Moreover, the CEO is identified as the central figure in director recruitment and selection, despite the prevalence of nominating committees (Foster, 1982). Even when the board is staffed by a majority of outside directors, the board functions on information provided by the CEO (Aram and Cowan, 1983). The CEO also plays a principal role in determining the remuneration and tenure of outside directors (Geneen, 1984). Individually and in combination, these factors weaken the board as a crucial instrument of corporate governance (Brown, 1976; Vance, 1983).

Understandably, most reform efforts have been based on the premise that a healthy balance between CEO and board powers is required to ensure effective company performance (Vance, 1983; Pearce and Robinson, 1987). Power is the capability of one social actor to overcome resistance in achieving a desired objective or result (Pfeffer, 1980). Power reflects the capacity of directors or CEOs to 'bring about the outcomes they desire' through both formal and informal means (Salancik and Pfeffer, 1977: 3).

As social network research has convincingly demonstrated, the exercise of power can take place through formal authority or informal influence (Tichy, Tushman, and Fombrun, 1979; Pearce and David, 1983). In the case of boards, corporate bylaws give directors the authority to disapprove managerial recommendations or actions. Of course, directors do not rely solely on their formal authority to carry out their duties to the firm. Directors are likely to use informal forums to indicate their viewpoints to executives (Mueller, 1979).

Powerful boards are considered necessary for organizational effectiveness for four reasons. First, powerful boards provide useful business

0143–2095/91/020135–19$09.50

Received 16 January 1989
Revised 15 September 1990

contacts, thus strengthening the link between corporations and their environments (Bazerman and Schoorman, 1983; Castaldi and Wortman, 1984; Pfeffer, 1972, 1973; Provan, 1980; Zald, 1967, 1969). Second, powerful boards actively contribute to the development of the organization's mission and goals (Pearce, 1982; Pearce and David, 1987), and evaluate CEO and company performance (Andrews, 1987). Further, these boards provide competent counsel and advice regarding strategic options that firms may consider. Third, powerful boards are necessary for effective 'checks and balances' in corporate governance (Dalton and Kesner, 1985). Such boards monitor and evaluate CEO and company performance, and take appropriate actions to ensure organizational effectiveness. By performing this role, directors protect the interests of shareholders.

Finally, powerful boards play a crucial role in creating corporate identity. They establish and monitor compliance with codes of ethics (Andrews, 1984; Nader, 1984; Purcell, 1978). Powerful boards imprint their firms with their unique 'world view' that sets the tone for definition of expectations of executives and employees, and guides development of policies throughout the firm. In essence, they function as the brain and soul of the organization (Mueller, 1979), as well as the guardian of shareholders' interests. The pervasive influence of these boards throughout many aspects of organizational life is widely believed to enrich their firms even though their contributions cannot be fully captured in financial terms (Mintzberg, 1983; Zahra and Pearce, 1989).

LITERATURE REVIEW

A typology of CEO–board power relations

Much of the literature on CEO–board interaction is anecdotal in nature. It highlights the existence of distinct functional and dysfunctional patterns of interaction between the CEO and board. An examination of the several typologies that exist shows that four types of boards are considered particularly important and deserving of attention. They are: Caretaker, Statutory, Proactive, and Participative boards. These four types integrate different models present in the literature. As Figure 1 shows, the four board types have been highlighted in a growing body of literature in strategic management and organization theory.

The board types reflect four important board attributes: composition, characteristics, internal process, and decision-making styles. Variations across these attributes are believed to result in differences in the contribution of board types to company performance. The current understanding of these differences and their effects on performance is presented below in the form of board profiles.

Caretaker boards are characterized by low board power and low CEO power. In essence, the board is viewed as a legal necessity and, as a result, it is incapable of commanding decision-making power (Molz, 1985). This board weakness is coupled with a near void in corporate leadership either because of organizational stagnation or because of a shift in power distribution among the CEO and other key executives. In this case the board is able only to meet the letter, but not the spirit, of the law. Caretaker boards lack the appropriate mix of desirable director qualities and organization to serve as a credible element of corporate governance. For example, Caretaker boards are usually dominated by company executives and their associates. Hence, outsiders' representation may be limited. As a result, board proceedings and deliberations tend to be informal and superficial. In fact, the decision-making process can become largely ceremonial, with its sole purpose being to approve CEO choices. Consequently, these boards do not contribute significantly to effective company performance.

Statutory boards reflect the prototypical image of ineffective boards in the literature (Aram and Cowan, 1984; Vance, 1968, 1983; Wood, 1983). As suggested in Figure 1, Statutory boards differ from Caretakers in that a powerful CEO is the central figure in organizational decision-making but the board is still considered a legal necessity. Many Statutory boards often function as 'rubber stamps' of managerial decisions, and do not thoroughly examine managerial decisions because of the lack of expertise or interest. Since directors are principally chosen and retained through the influence of the CEO, the board pays little attention to defining its roles and responsibilities. Given the inherently weak position of Statutory boards, CEOs do not consider directors true partners in shaping the strategic posture of the

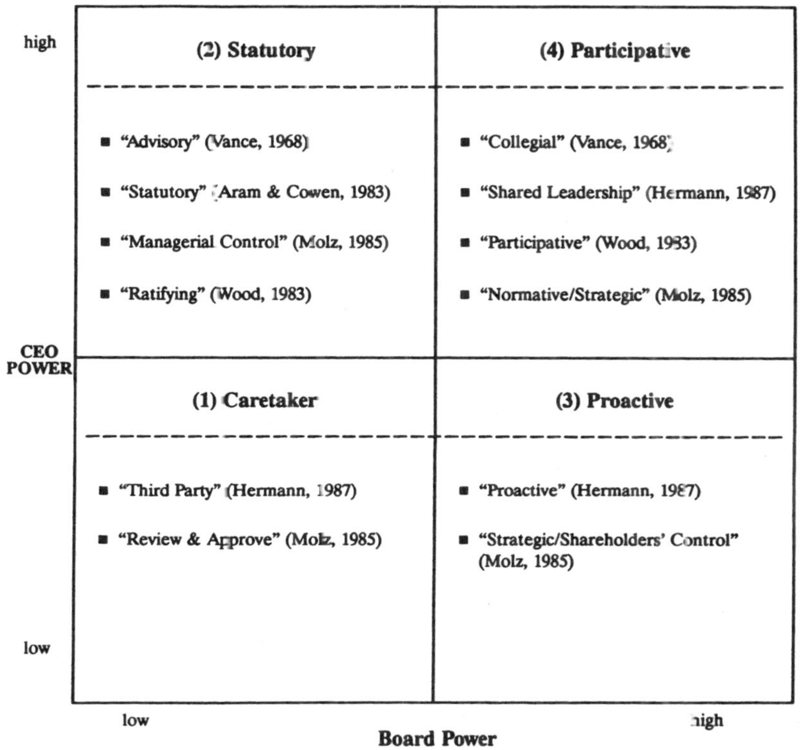

Figure 1. Board of director typology

corporation. Board powers are, therefore, limited to the ceremonial approval of managerial choices, which falsely adds an appearance of legitimacy to executives' actions.

Proactive boards: awakened to their legal responsibilities by shareholder activism (Vogel, 1983) and increased director liability (*Business Week*, 8 September 1986; Kesner and Johnson, 1990), Proactive boards are a true instrument of corporate governance, enjoying much more power than the Caretakers and Statutory types. Proactive boards command powers that surpass those of their CEOs (Herman, 1981; Molz, 1985), as depicted in Figure 1.

Specifically, for Proactive boards to exist, they must usually be composed primarily of outside directors to enhance their independence of management, to increase the level of expertise presented among directors, to enhance objectivity in board proceedings and decisions, and to ensure the effective representation of important constituents in society.

In Proactive boards, directors' responsibilities are divided among established committees. Indeed, attention is give to the appropriate flow of information among these committees. Further, Proactive boards meet frequently to ensure timely dissemination of information and effective decision-making. Given their expertise, visible involvement in their tasks, and efficient decision-making process, Proactive boards contribute positively to company performance.

Participative boards are 'characterized by discussion, debate, and disagreement. Differences of opinion are resolved by a vote, a majority vote prevailing' (Vance, 1983: 9). In this case the leadership of the firm is most likely to be separated from that of the board with outside directors constituting a majority of board membership.

There are two major differences between the Participative and Proactive types. The first relates to the process the boards follow in making decisions. In the Participative mode, emphasis is on building and reaching consensus among directors and the top management team. Thus, extensive negotiations take place in board deliberations, using formal and informal channels of communications. However, when disagreements arise, the Proactive board relies on its formal powers to resolve these disputes. This reliance on formal powers by Proactive boards can hinder the quality of the dialogue between directors and the CEO. It can also create rival factions on the board. A second difference between these Participative and Proactive boards pertains to the relative powers of the CEO and directors. In the Proactive mode, directors possess more formal powers than the CEO, and may use this power to bring about fundamental changes in corporate governance. In contrast, directors in the Participative mode have powers equal to those of the CEO; hence, negotiation and compromise are often viewed as essential for effective governance.

Despite the wide recognition of the four power modes depicted in Figure 2, little effort has been made to validate their existence empirically. Further, although these modes may manifest themselves in board composition, characteristics, process, and style (Vance, 1968), suspected differences owing to these attributes have not been studied systemically. Finally, the implications of power modes for corporate performance have not been examined, even though the literature suggests that when CEOs and boards share strategic powers about equally, organizational performance will improve (Herman, 1981; Vance, 1968; Wood, 1983). Consequently, concrete evidence on this and other assertions about the effect of board type on company performance does not exist.

Although corporate laws vest considerable formal powers in the board, the CEO is widely recognized in the literature as the real power broker (Geneen, 1984; Mace, 1971; Mintzberg, 1983; Mueller, 1979). Boards are often constructed in accordance with CEO preferences. In recent years, however, reform advocates have suggested that managerially dominated boards are weak and do not contribute positively to effective company performance (Nader, 1984). These advocates also propose that both CEOs and companies would benefit greatly from designing and maintaining powerful boards. Because evidence on the effectiveness of strong boards is lacking, CEOs should be assisted in determining the relative merits of strong boards. In addition, because CEO decision criteria are considered to be the principal basis of board member selection (Vance, 1983), changes or adjustments in these criteria should begin with a thorough understanding of how these executives assessed their own boards. Therefore, by surveying CEOs, useful guidelines can be developed to help executives use their powers constructively.

STUDY OBJECTIVES

This study had three objectives. The first was to present an attempt to empirically validate a typology of CEO–board relative powers. Such a typology was needed to integrate several fragmented views of CEO–board powers. While intuitively appealing, these views had not been studied systematically in the literature. Thus, it is not clear which types of CEO–board power relationships were associated with effective company performance. The second objective was to examine differences in the overall effectiveness among board types (modes) in order to pinpoint functional and dysfunctional types. Differences among the four board types regarding corporate financial performance formed an important dimension of this relationship that needed to be explored. The third objective was to examine differences in board attributes (composition, characteristics, processes, and decision styles) among boards in alternative relationships with CEOs. Disclosed differences could then be used

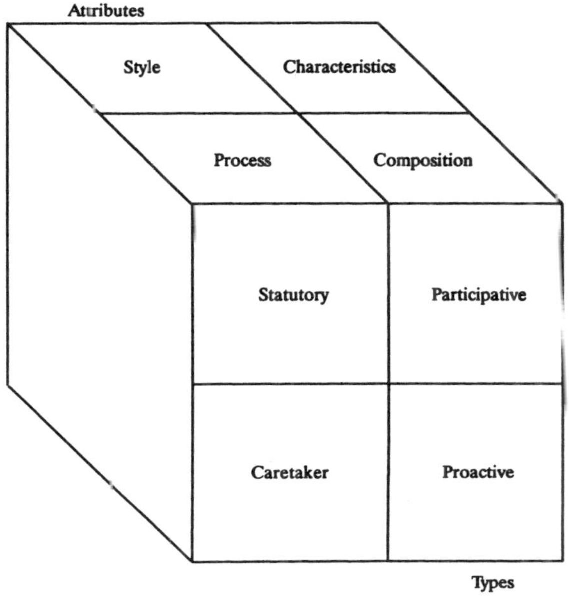

Figure 2 Four board types and their underlying attributes

to help explain variations among board types associated with varied levels of organizational performance.

Three interrelated propositions guided this study. The first was that four unique board modes would be distinguishable based on the relative powers the CEO and the board possess, as depicted in Figure 2. These power modes represent unique configurations of four board attributes: composition, characteristics, process, and style (Zahra and Pearce, 1989). Composition denoted the overall size of the board (total number of directors), the representation of certain classes of directors (e.g. females and minorities), and the number of outsiders. Outside directors were not members of the current or immediate past top management team, were not key officers of the company divisions or subsidiaries, and were not relatives of the aforementioned groups. Characteristics referred to the attributes that distinguished the board as a group. Examples include directors' independence from the top management, competence and expertise, their devotion to and involvement in their tasks, their representation of multiple constituent groups, and ethical conduct. Process referred to board internal proceedings. Finally, decision style referred to the approach a board takes in making its decisions.

As suggested in Figure 2, each of the board types is expected to be associated with a distinct combination (gestalt) of four attributes: composition, characteristics, process, and decision style. This means that the board types are expected to vary significantly in their relative emphasis on the four dimensions. Consequently, by identifying these combinations, the results of this study can assist executives in taking actions to strengthen their boards and improve organizational effectiveness.

The second proposition that guided this study was that the four power modes would differ significantly in their associations with board and company performance. Proponents of board reform have long argued that strengthening the board *vis-à-vis* the CEO was essential to superior company performance (Nader, 1984; Geneen, 1984). The assertion stood in contrast to the suggestion that managerially dominated boards are associated with higher financial performance (for a review see Molz, 1988). This debate, however, has made little progress toward resolution because most past research on 'managerial domination' has not incorporated specific measures of CEO and board power. Instead, nearly all research used the traditional dichotomy of inside versus outside directors as a measure of domination. As a result, prior research has yielded almost predictably contradictory findings (Kesner, 1987; Molz, 1988; Schmidt, 1975; Vance, 1955, 1968). This situation was made complicated because some executives viewed their boards as being effective, despite the fact that these boards contributed little to company performance. Thus, the approach taken in this study was to examine variations among the four modes and levels of board and company performance, as a refined means to identify successful and unsuccessful CEO–board relations.

The final proposition that guided this study was that CEO input would be an essential ingredient for successful board reform. If the CEO is the true power broker depicted in the literature, CEO views concerning strengthening board power should be systematically examined and carefully incorporated into suggestions for reform.

RESEARCH QUESTIONS

The proposed typology depicts potentially dysfunctional and effective board power modes. To better understand how the four board types differ as models of corporate governance, six research questions (RQ) are emphasized in this study:

RQI: How do CEO–board powers relate to board characteristics?
RQ2: How do CEO–board powers relate to board composition?
RQ3: How do CEO–board powers relate to board internal process?
RQ4: How do CEO–board powers relate to board decision-making styles?
RQ5: How do CEO–board powers relate to board effectiveness?
RQ6: How do CEO–board powers relate to organizational performance?
RQ7: Are Participative boards associated with superior financial performance?

In brief, the objective of this study was to validate the existence of the four board types and to examine their association with corporate performance.

METHODOLOGY

Sample

The development of the research instrument started with in-depth telephone interviews with executives in 15 *Fortune* 500 industrial companies, supplemented by in-person interviews with the CEOs and one or more outside board members of 72 manufacturing companies. These semi-structured discussions probed for the sources and impact of board and CEO powers and, for example, of how relative powers manifested themselves in strategic decisions. The results of these interviews were used to construct a questionnaire that served as the primary data collection instrument for the current study.

Surveys of *Fortune* 500 firms present a special problem; namely, that corporate policies in several of these firms prohibit executives from participating in various types of mail surveys. In order to determine the real size of the population from which participants in our study might actually be drawn, it was necessary to learn which *Fortune* 500 firms would permit their executives to consider responding to a survey.

Therefore, a letter was sent to each of *Fortune*'s largest 500 industrial and largest 500 service firms asking if they had a corporate prohibition against executives participating in university-sponsored survey research. Of the 898 firms that responded, 305 stated that their CEO could not or would not participate for organizational or publicly stated personal reasons. The remaining 695 companies, which represented non-respondents to the letter (87 corporations) as well as firms that stated no *a priori* basis for non-participation, represented the pool from which the survey sample might be elicited.

The questionnaire was mailed to the 400 manufacturing and 295 service corporations from the *Fortune* 500 and the *Service* 500 lists which had not reported a corporate or CEO policy of unwillingness to participate in academic research conducted by mail. Companies that participated in the initial telephone interviews were also excluded from the mailing list.

The questionnaire was directed to the CEO (or the highest-ranking corporate officer) and was accompanied by a letter explaining the objective of the investigation and assuring respondents of the confidentiality of their answers. The letter stated that the purpose of the study was to better understand what boards actually did, and how they were organized to carry out their tasks. Before mailing the survey, the letter was edited by three reviewers; one was a former general manager in a *Fortune* 500 corporation and two were research colleagues, to avoid misleading or prejudicial language.

A total of 69 manufacturing and 70 service firms returned completed questionnaires, for an overall response rate of 20.0 percent. The response pattern was similar to that achieved by others who recently studied *Fortune* boards (e.g. Henke, 1986). In addition, responding and non-responding firms were compared on size (measured by their assets), earnings per share, dividends per share, stock financial strength, and *Value Line*'s evaluations of the predictability of their earnings. No significant differences were found between the two sets of companies on these criteria at $p < 0.05$, thus supporting the representativeness of the sample.

The respondents were asked to state their exact current, formal title. Analysis of the 139 surveys showed that 98 percent of the respondents indicated their title, and that 60 percent held the title CEO and board Chairman, 10 percent served as CEOs, 10 percent served as Chair, 5 percent were presidents and board Chairs, and the remaining 15 percent were either senior executive vice-presidents (8 percent) or board secretaries (7 percent). This figure suggests that the respondents were among the key top executives of their corporations.

Measurement of the variables

Respondents were asked to rate CEO power, board power, and five characteristics of the boards. These include independence, expertise, role involvement, representation, and ethical conduct. In addition, respondents provided data on board composition and process, as described below.

CEO–board powers

The executives were asked to 'rate the amount of formal authority or power' they and their boards had regarding each of the following 15 areas: changing company by-laws; approving changes in capital structure; decisions about capital expenditures; decisions about future divestments; decisions about future acquisitions; establishing long-term goals; policy formation; planning for top leadership succession; selecting a new CEO; evaluating the performance of key executives (other than CEOs); selection of corporate strategy; decisions to adopt new technologies; decisions regarding top executives' compensation; decisions regarding charitable contributions; and dealing with external groups. These items were based on the responses provided through the series of CEO and board member interviews. In many instances they were found to be similar to the observations of prior descriptive studies (Andrews, 1987; Boulton, 1978; Henke, 1986; Louden, 1975; Mace, 1971; Mintzberg, 1983; Mueller, 1979). By investigating the power each group had in these 15 areas, the feasibility of determining their relative positions through the proposed typology became apparent.

In view of the recognition of formal authority and informal influence as a means to exercise board powers, two evaluations were requested of each respondent, one for the CEO and the other for the board. A six-point scale was used as the basis for rating each governance area: 'A great deal of authority' (coded 5); 'Above average' (coded 4); 'Moderate' (coded 3); 'Some' (coded 2); 'Very little' (coded 1); and 'No authority' (coded 0). To minimize ambiguity or bias about scale anchors, numerical values accompanied a point along the scale. The first set of responses was used to create a 'CEO power score' ($\alpha = 0.86$) which was plotted on the x-axis of a matrix, as shown in Figure 1. The second set of responses was plotted on the y-axis as the 'Board power score' (α = 0.79). By dichotomizing CEO and board scores at the median (low vs. high), a 2×2 matrix was created that depicted four categories of boards.

The fact that the same items were used to gauge respondents' views of power raised the issue of the independence of the two indexes. As expected, a test of correlation found a significant correlation, $r = 0.31$. This coefficient was modest in view of the relatively large sample size and the fact that data were collected from the same source. Because the data were based on self-report, there was a possibility that respondents might tend to overestimate CEO powers. Although this possibility was counterbalanced by CEOs' growing awareness of public concern over their domination of boards, a limitation of this study was that some type of self-serving bias could not be totally dismissed in any interpretation of the results. That is, the fact that the respondents rated both CEO and board power may have magnified response bias.

In deriving the typology, four special precautions were taken. First, the 15 governance items were included based on the frequency of their appearance on authoritative lists of board responsibilities (Andrews, 1981; Aram and Cowen, 1983; Boulton, 1978; Brown, 1976; Juran and Louden, 1975; Koontz, 1971; Louden, 1975; Mace, 1971; Mintzberg, 1983; Vance, 1983). Second, items were chosen to cover the traditional and strategic definition of the role of the board. The traditional definition focused primarily on the responsibility of the board in representing shareholders, evaluating CEO performance, and approving changes in corporate by-laws. The strategic perspective broadened the role of the board to include contributions to setting corporate direction and goals, evaluating company mission, and appraising decision-making on acquisitions or divestments. Third, as Lehmann (1979) suggested, the appropriate solution was within the $n/30$ to $n/50$ region, where n was the sample size. Fourth, the proosed typology was built on strong support from previous classifications, as shown by the references cited in Figure 1.

In combination, Caretaker and Statutory boards represented 55.5 percent of the sample, thereby providing support for the widespread notion that a substantial number of boards are relatively weak. On the other hand, Proactive boards which were characterized by low CEO and high board powers, represented 21.9 percent of the participating firms. Finally, Participative boards, which represented the remaining 22.6 percent of the sample, exhibited high powers for both the CEOs and their boards.

Board characteristics

A comprehensive review of board of directors' research over the past 25 years highlighted five board characteristics (Zahra and Pearce, 1989). These characteristics were chosen for investigation in this study: (1) independence from top management (Geneen, 1984); (2) expertise (Vance, 1978); (3) role involvement (Vance, 1983; Zahra and Pearce, 1990); (4) representation of diverse interests (Koontz, 1971; Pearce, 1983); and (5) ethical conduct (Mueller, 1979; Vance, 1983). Respondents were asked to report on these five board characteristics.

Independence (α = 0.64). An index of the sum of the respondents' ratings on three items was used to measure board independence from CEO and members of the top management team, following a seven-point semantic differential scale developed for this study. The items were (a) dependent vs. independent; (b) follower vs. leader; and (c) ceremonial vs. real. An example item was:

In making decisions, your board is usually

Dependent on the CEO	1 : 2 : 3 : 4 : 5 : 6 : 7	Independent in action

Expertise (α = 0.77). Respondents were asked to rate three items along a five-point scale (1 = poor to 5 = excellent). The items included: overall competence in two relevant areas of expertise, familiarity with company operations, and familiarity with industry conditions. These items were extracted from previous theoretical work on board expertise (Vance, 1983; Zahra and Pearce, 1989). These items gauged respondents' experience with companies' business and operations.

Role involvement (α = 0.60). This variable measured the extent to which directors were actively involved in performing their roles. Respondents were asked to rate their boards on two seven-point semantic differential items. The items were: passive vs. active, and uninvolved vs. involved. An illustrative item was:

Your board is:
Passive 1 : 2 : 3 : 4 : 5 : 6 : 7 Active

Ratings were summed to produce an overall index. This response format made it possible to avoid overlap among the items used to derive the typology and those measuring role involvement. These items were based on descriptions provided by Geneen (1984).

Representation ($\alpha = 0.76$). This was measured using a scale consisting of the sum of two items: representing shareholders' interests and representing different groups in society. Respondents were asked to rate their boards using a five-point response scale (1 = poor to 5 = excellent). The items were developed based on past research by Carpenter (1988) and Epstein (1986).

Ethical conduct ($\alpha = 0.83$). This was measured using the sum of scores on two seven-point semantic differentials developed for this study based on the work of Carpenter (1988) and Vance (1983): dishonest vs. honest and immoral vs. moral. An example item was:

In making decisions, members of your board are:
Dishonest 1 : 2 : 3 : 4 : 5 : 6 : 7 Honest

An overall scale of the board's apparent adherence to ethical conduct was created by adding responses to the two items.

A note of caution about the scale on ethical conduct is in order. Ethical conduct is a complex concept (Kesner and Johnson, 1990), and the two-item semantic differential scale used to gauge it is unlikely to have fully captured its full nature. Future reseachers may endeavor to employ a comprehensive measure of this variable.

Note that the Cronbach alpha scores (which measure scale internal consistency) associated with independence and role involvement exceed 0.60, the level which is considered acceptable for exploratory research such as this study (Nunnally, 1959; Bagozzi, 1978). Nevertheless, care should be exercised in interpreting the results of these two scales since a more conservative criterion would require an even higher alpha level.

Board composition

Respondents were asked to report on four board composition variables: overall board size, number of female directors, number of minority directors, and number of outside directors (Lang and Lockhart, 1990).

Overall board size was defined as the total number of directors on a board. Similarly, respondents provided data on the number of female directors on the board, the number of non-Caucasian directors, and the number of outside directors. The definition of outside directors was provided to the respondents in the questionnaire. It read as follows: 'Outside directors are those members of the board who are not employed as part of the company's management team, their subordinates, relatives, or managers of the firm's subsidiaries. Also, these directors are not members of the firm's immediate past management team.'

Board process and style

Respondents provided data on two measures that gauged board process and style. The first, the efficiency of board process, referred to the approaches that directors followed in making decisions and undertaking their responsibilities (Vance, 1983). It was measured by a composite index ($\alpha = 0.78$) that was derived by summing respondents' ratings on three questionnaire items: thoroughness of deliberations, frequency of meetings, and board organization. These items were developed based on Vance's (1983) work. Responses followed a five-point scale (coded: 1 = poor to 5 = excellent).

The second measure of board process was based on three items measured by seven-point semantic differential scales: slow vs. quick decision-making, uninformed vs. informed decision-making, and impulsive vs. deliberate decision-making. For example,

In making decisions, your board is:
Slow 1 : 2 : 3 : 4 : 5 : 6 : 7 Quick

These items were developed for this study based on the work by Ross (1988). Respondents' ratings on these three items were summed to produce an overall index labeled 'quality of internal process' (α = 0.81). The individual item topics are presented in Table 1.

Board decision style

Respondents rated five seven-point semantic differential items that examined board decision-making style. The five scores were summed to produce an overall index (α = 0.77). The items were regressive vs. progressive, timid vs. aggressive, hostile vs. friendly, discouraging vs. encouraging, and supportive vs. nonsupportive. The items followed the theoretical work by Ross (1988). An example item was,

In dealing with directors, your board is:
Hostile 1 : 2 : 3 : 4 : 5 : 6 : 7 Friendly

Board effectiveness

Four items were used to measure respondents' perceptions of their boards' effectiveness. These items employed two different scaling techniques (Likert scales and semantic differentials) to gauge and then reconfirm the respondents' judgement of their boards' overall performance and effectiveness *per se*. Because these questionnaire items varied in response format to ensure reliable results, their scores were standardized ($x = 0$; S.D. = 1) and their intercorrelations were examined. The average intercorrelation was 0.79, which suggested that the items overlapped a great deal. Consequently, the four items standardized scores were summed to produce an overall board performance index (α = 0.83).

Two approaches were used in this study to examine the relationship between board type and company performance. The first centered on respondents' subjective evaluations of company performance. The second approach utilized secondary data pertaining to objective criteria of corporate performance.

Objective measures. Corporate financial measures included the most recent 3-year average earnings per share (EPS) and evaluation of the stock financial strength of the company as judged by *Value Line*. EPS is among the most widely used measures of performance in board research, and by investors in making their judgements concerning the future of the corporation. Company financial strength (stock performance ratings) provides an independent, external expert evaluation of the company's financial position. Data concerning these two measures were gathered from company documents provided in *Standard and Poor*'s and *Value Line*'s reports.

Subjective ratings. Respondents' evaluations of perceived company performance employed three items: company competitive position, overall company performance, and overall company profitability. In each case, the respondents were asked to rate their company performance by assigning a score ranging from 0 (poor) to 100 (outstanding). Because of the theoretical overlap and the high correlations among the three items, their scores were standardized and summed to produce an overall index labeled 'perceived company performance' (α = 0.86).

Controlling for industry variations in corporate performance

Past research suggests that industries vary significantly in their performance. Therefore, to control for variations in company performance, we followed the procedure suggested by Sousa De Vasconcellos e Sá and Hambrick (1989). For objective performance criteria, the difference between each company's own performance and its industry average (defined at the two-digit SIC) was computed, then divided by the industry average; which was then multiplied by 100. Data on industry average were collected from *Fortune*, *Business Week*, *Forbes*, and *Moody's*.

A similar procedure was followed regarding subjective performance data. First, average scores for each industry group in the sample were computed on the overall subjective performance index. Second, a firm's score was then subtracted from the mean, and the difference was then divided by the mean; all then were multiplied by 100.

ANALYSIS

Having classified boards into appropriate power types, we proceeded to examine the study's six research questions. The purpose was to examine the significance of differences among the four board types concerning their characteristics, composition, process, decision-making styles, effectiveness, and corporate financial performance.

The first step in the analysis entailed performing multivariate analysis of variance (MANOVA) on the components of each set of attributes and performance. In this analysis the four board types were treated as the predictor ('main effect'). Six MANOVA runs were performed using different dependent variables: one for each set of board attributes (characteristics, composition, process, and style), one for board performance, and one for company financial performance. In the six MANOVA analyses the main effect (board type) was significant. Finally, given the fact that board type was significant, univariate analysis of variance (ANOVA) was conducted (Spector, 1977). In the final step of the analysis significant ANOVAs were followed by the Duncan's range test in order to pinpoint significant differences in the means of pairs of board types.

RESULTS

Power relations and board characteristics

The first research question (RQ1) probed possible differences in board characteristics as a function of relative CEO–board powers. Multivariate analysis of variance (MANOVA) was used to test the significance of differences among the four types. In this analysis, the four power types were treated as the predictor and the characteristics as the dependent variables. The results of MANOVA were significant ($p < 0.001$). Therefore, univariate analysis of variance (ANOVA) followed MANOVA to examine patterns of variations in board characteristics. The results are presented in Table 1.

ANOVA results of the independence scale were significant ($p < 0.001$). A progression was observed (from low–low to high–high) among the scores of the four types, with Caretaker boards having the lowest scores and Participative having the highest. As Table 1 shows, Duncan's range test of differences among groups means suggested that Caretakers and Participative types were statistically different ($p < 0.05$).

Expertise was treated as a dependent variable and board types as the predictors. ANOVA results of differences in the means of the four groups were significant at $p < 0.01$. The Duncan's range test showed that Caretaker boards had significantly lower scores than the other three types. The same test also showed that the Statutory types had lower scores than Proactive and Participative boards.

In performing ANOVA, role involvement was considered a dependent variable whereas board types were the predictors. ANOVA results showed that group means were significantly different at $p < 0.01$. As shown in Table 1, Duncan's range test indicated that group mean scores for Caretaker and Statutory boards were significantly lower than their Participative counterparts.

Focusing on representation as a dependent variable, ANOVA results were significant at $p < 0.001$ (Table 1). The four board types differed significantly in their scores on this variable. Caretaker boards had significantly lower scores than the other three types. According to Duncan's test, Caretaker boards had significantly lower scores than the other three types.

Referring to ethical conduct ANOVA indicated that the four board types differed significantly in their scores on this variable ($p < 0.05$). According to Duncan's test results, Caretaker boards had the lowest scores among the four board types.

It is appropriate to point out here that, for this and other research questions, caution is advised in interpreting the results of comparisons among pairs of board types. While significant in the statistical sense, the results suggest, but do not assure, that the distinctiveness of the group was large and clear enough to have value for practicing managers. Future research with improved measures is needed to establish that meaningful differences exist.

Power relations and board composition

The second research question (RQ2) was: Do the four types of boards differ in their composition? To answer this question, four board composition variables that have been highlighted in the literature were considered: overall size, number of female directors, black and minority directors (other than females), and number of outside directors.

Table 1. Relative powers, and board characteristics and composition: ANOVA results

Dimensions	Board types: Caretakers (C) (n = 21)	Statutory (S) (n = 57)	Proactive (PR) (n = 30)	Participative (P) (n = 31)	F-value	Significant Duncan's range test results*
Characteristics						
1. Independence	15.00	16.51	17.17	19.32	11.67***	P>C
2. Expertise	10.35	11.42	12.03	12.45	5.67**	S>C;PR>C;P>C; PR>S;P>S
3. Role involvement	11.21	11.81	12.24	13.10	3.97**	P>C;P>S
4. Representation	7.20	8.10	8.10	8.90	9.14***	S>C;PR>C;P>C
5. Ethical conduct	13.11	13.50	13.50	13.97	3.28*	S>C;PR>C;P>C
Composition						
1. Overall size	13.11	12.96	12.58	14.27	1.09	—
2. Number of females	0.41	0.64	0.67	0.99	2.97*	P>C
3. Blacks; minorities	0.39	0.19	0.50	0.46	1.48	—
4. Outsiders	8.57	9.56	8.42	10.59	1.86	—

*d.f. = 3,134; $p < 0.05$; **d.f. = 3,134; $p < 0.01$; ***d.f. = 3,134; $p < 0.00$.

MANOVA indicated that the four board types (modes) did not vary significantly in the four measures of composition. When ANOVAs were conducted—using the four composition measures as dependent variables and the four board types (modes) as predictors—some interesting results emerged.

As Table 1 shows, ANOVA results indicated that there were no significant differences among the four types concerning size, number of outsiders, and number of blacks and other minority directors. Significant differences were found only in the number of female directors, with Participtive boards leading others in this regard. They were followed by Proactive, Statutory and Caretaker boards, respectively. Participative boards also had a significantly higher number of females as directors than Caretakers, as judged by the Duncan's range test. It appeared that as the power of the board increased relative to the CEO, female representation increased. An explanation of this finding was the desire of these boards to be responsive to the social changes taking place in our society, thus moving away from the established interpersonal networks.

Power relations and internal process

The third research question (RQ3) probed the possibility that the four board types (modes) varied significantly in their internal processes. As shown in Table 2, the measures emphasized two areas: overall efficiency and quality. MANOVA was run, employing board types (modes) as predictor and board process (efficiency and quality) as the dependent variable. MANOVA results were significant ($p < 0.001$). ANOVAs were run as a follow-up test of significant MANOVA. The results are presented in Table 2.

ANOVA of group mean differences, based on the overall index of board process efficiency, was significant ($p < 0.001$). As Table 2 shows, Participative boards were viewed as the most efficient followed by Proactive, Statutory, and Caretaker boards, respectively. When pairs of group means were contrasted, only Caretakers were found to be lower than other board types on their overall internal efficiency. This observation was corroborated by the scores of individual items reported in Table 2.

As presented in Table 2, ANOVA of group

Table 2. Power relations and board process and style: ANOVA results

Board variables	Board types: Caretakers (C) (n = 21)	Statutory (S) (n = 57)	Proactive (PR) (n = 30)	Participative (P) (n = 31)	F-value	Significant Duncan's range test results*
Process						
Internal efficiency scale	10.51	11.28	11.89	12.58	7.01***	
Deliberations	3.81	4.01	4.29	4.70	4.42**	PR>C;P>C
Meeting frequency	4.48	4.72	4.80	4.88	1.99	P>C
Organization	3.90	4.41	4.48	4.70	12.16***	S>C;PR>C;C>P
Quality of process	16.26	17.22	18.18	18.86	3.94*	P>C;P>PR
Slow vs. quick	5.47	5.85	6.17	6.06	2.02	PR>C;P>C
Uninformed vs. informed	5.74	5.85	6.17	6.39	2.21	—
Impulsive vs. deliberate	5.05	5.54	5.86	6.45	7.65***	P>C;P>PR
Decision style						
Overall scale	29.22	30.22	31.54	32.64	4.19*	PR>C;P>C
Regressive vs. progressive	5.21	5.73	6.17	6.67	11.28***	PR>C;P>C;P>S
Timid vs. aggressive	5.51	5.79	5.83	5.96	2.50	—
Hostile vs. friendly	6.11	6.11	6.55	6.42	1.75	—
Discouraging vs. encouraging	6.05	6.20	6.32	6.65	2.39	—
Not supportive vs. supportive	6.37	6.35	6.59	6.90	3.11*	P>C;P>S

*d.f. = 3,134; $p < 0.05$; **d.f. = 3,134; $p < 0.01$; ***d.f. = 3,134; $p < 0.001$.

mean differences on the quality of board process were significantly different ($p < 0.05$). Duncan's test showed that Caretaker boards had a significantly lower mean score than their Participative counterparts. Also, ANOVA was conducted on individual items. Significant differences were found in the case of the impulsive vs. deliberate scale ($p < 0.01$); Participative boards had the highest score followed by Proactive, Statutory and Caretaker boards, respectively. Participative boards had significantly higher scores than Proactive and Caretaker types. In contrast, ANOVA analysis of the scale items showed that no significant differences were found on either the slow vs. quick or uninformed vs. informed decision making.

Power relations and decision style

The fourth research question (RQ4) probed the possibility that the four board types differed significantly in their decision-making styles. Hence, ANOVA was run based on the four board types as predictors and decision style as the dependent variable. ANOVA showed that the four board types differed significantly on the index of group style ($p < 0.05$). As Table 2 shows, both Proactive and Participative boards had significantly higher scores than Caretakers. ANOVA also indicated that significant differences existed in two of the five items. As we moved away from Caretakers, the boards were viewed as progressive (item 1) and generally more supportive of CEO efforts (item 5). Table 2 also displayed areas where different board types surpassed one another on the dimensions of decision style. Proactive and Participative boards were viewed as more progressive than their Caretaker and Statutory counterparts. Also, Participative boards were viewed as more supportive of the CEOs than Caretakers and Statutory boards.

Power relations and board performance

The fifth research question (RQ5) probed the link between board type and board effectiveness. To address this question, ANOVA was used in conjunction with the Duncan's range test. As shown in Table 3, the results disclosed that the four types had significantly different mean board performance scores ($p < 0.01$). Of particular interest was the fact that CEOs viewed both the Proactive and Participative types as significantly more effective than either the Caretaker or Statutory types. This indicated that powerful boards (e.g. Proactive and Participative) were perceived as being more effective than their weaker counterparts.

Power relations and corporate performance

The sixth research question (RQ6) probed the possibility that the association between the four board types and performance, and subjective and objective measures of company performance, would be different. To answer this question, both subjective and objective corporate performance measures were used.

Subjective performance. Table 4 presents the results of ANOVA in which the four board types were the predictor variable and the subjective performance index was the dependent variable. ANOVA was significant ($p < 0.001$). Caretaker boards were associated with the lowest level of performance among the four groups ($p < 0.05$). Table 4 also shows that all group pair comparisons were significant; as we moved toward more powerful (e.g. Participative) boards, each type was more highly associated significantly with perceived company performance.

Objective performance. As Table 4 shows, ANOVA revealed that the four board types were different on EPS ($p < 0.05$) and financial strength ($p < 0.05$). In both cases, Caretakers were associated with the lowest performance and Participative boards had the highest performance levels. Duncan's test results showed that Caretaker and Statutory boards did not differ significantly in their performance. In addition, these two board types had significantly lower performance than the Proactive and Participative types ($p < 0.05$). Finally, Participative boards surpassed their Proactive counterpart in both EPS and financial strength.

DISCUSSION

A typology of four CEO–board powers was presented and empirically supported. Consistent with the theoretical discussion summarized in Figure 1, the results showed that significant differences existed among the four board types

Table 3. Power relations and board effectiveness: ANOVA results

	Board types					
Performance	Caretakers (C) ($n = 21$)	Statutory (S) ($n = 57$)	Proactive (PR) ($n = 30$)	Participative (P) ($n = 31$)	F-value	Significant Duncan's range test results*
Index	0.17	0.42	0.88	1.65	5.21**	PR>C;PR>S; P>C;P>S

*d.f. = 3,134; $p < 0.05$; **d.f. = 3,134; $p < 0.01$.

Table 4. Board power relations and company performance

Company performance	Caretakers (C) (n = 21)	Statutory (S) (n = 57)	Proactive (PR) (n = 30)	Participative (P) (n = 31)	F-value	Significant Duncan's range test results*
	Board types					
Subjective						
Company performance (%)	−34.2	−23.1	28.1	50.2	8.31**	S>C;PR>C;P>C; PR>S;P>S;P>PR
Objective						
Earnings per share (%)	−23.3	−19.3	19.2	33.0	4.11*	PR>C;PR>S; P>PR
Financial strength (%)	−16.3	− 9.2	10.0	21.2	3.21*	PR>C;PR>S; P>S;P>PR

*d.f. = 3,134; $p < 0.05$; **d.f. = 3,134; $p < 0.01$.

concerning their characteristics, process and style, effectiveness, and association with organizational performance.

Regarding characteristics, less powerful boards (Caretaker and Statutory) tended to lack independence and necessary expertise. They were also viewed as less involved in understanding their responsibilities than their powerful counterparts.

Only one difference was found among the four boards on member composition; powerful boards had higher numbers of female directors. We speculated that powerful boards were more sensitive than their weaker counterparts to the changes in society, especially the active participation of females in corporate governance.

The four board modes were also significantly different in their internal processes. Boards that had power equal to or more than the CEO (e.g. Proactive and Participative) were described by the CEO as being more efficient, better informed, and more careful yet quicker in making decisions than weaker boards (Caretaker and Statutory).

As Table 2 shows, more powerful board types were viewed by the CEOs as being more progressive and more encouraging and supportive of CEO efforts. These qualities, along with well-developed internal processes, may have made CEOs disposed to view powerful boards as more effective than weaker boards (Table 3). These results raised a question about the widespread belief that CEOs desired weaker boards that rubber stamp their decisions.

An important finding from this study was that Participative boards were associated with the highest level of company financial performance. This finding supported normative assertions in the literature that the increased strategic power of boards, coupled with a similar power position by the CEO, were instrumental in effective organization performance. Incorporating relative CEO–board positions into the analysis offered a basis on which to resolve contradictory results on the long-suspected association between board and company performance (Molz, 1988).

Another possibility is that the results may reflect a changing sentiment on the part of CEOs regarding the desirable board qualities and activities. If this is the case, some may ask: Why do weak boards still exist? One explanation is that the evolution of the corporate system has been accompanied by dispersion of ownership and increased powers of senior executives. This represents a paradox; separation of ownership and managerial control was expected to strengthen the board, making it a true representative of shareholders. Instead, dispersion of ownership may have resulted in a widespread lack of accountability of directors and executives alike, resulting in a near-universal decline of the role of boards. In addition, because legal and public expectations of boards have been vague, some boards may have seen it appropriate to perform only a perfunctory, ceremonial role. This attitude, coupled with lack of accountability of directors (Brown, 1976; Nader, 1984), may have contributed to the existence of some passive boards.

The present study has two implications for senior executives. First, CEOs with Participative boards view them as being associated with superior organizational financial performance. Thus, CEOs might be generally well advised to seek ways to share power with directors in an effort to achieve more favorable financial results. Implementation of this suggestion would require that CEOs and boards join in determining appropriate areas of interest to both parties, and delineating the desired manner of board participation.

Consistent with the spirit of our findings, executives should view the development of powerful boards as a means to enhance organizational vitality. Powerful boards are desirable because of their potential influence on the life of the organization. In general, powerful boards are in a position to influence the creation and maintenance of viable organizations that are disposed to contribute well to the social mission of the firm.

In addition, our study highlights the need for directors and CEOs to develop an explicit strategy for board development. Targets of such efforts could include developing appropriate criteria for director selection, reviewing board committee structure and decision-making styles, evaluating board proceedings as well as the frequency and quality of meetings, evaluating the flow of information between the CEO and board, and establishing appropriate means for directors to evaluate board performance and areas needing additional improvement.

Finally, our results suggest a need to re-examine the widespread notion that self-interested CEOs stifle board reform efforts. Too many factors indicate that they do not or cannot. First, shareholders' activism has risen, pressuring CEOs, directors, and courts to reform corporate governance structure. An astute CEO will consider a powerful board to be critical in shielding the CEO and the firm against potential shareholders' activism arising from perceptions of abuses of power by the top management team. Powerful boards convey to shareholders at large an image of effective checks and balances that helps to assure shareholders that their interests are well protected.

Second, as the competitive pressures mount, board input into the strategic process becomes more desirable. Executives need information about potential competitors' activities, potential entrants into the industry, and customer response to the firm's strategy. In addition to this role in scanning the environment, directors may share their experience with the CEO regarding certain strategies. Hence, CEO's insights and suggestions are complemented by directors' ideas. The CEO's self-interest, therefore, is served by soliciting and incorporating directors' views.

Third, recent research suggests that corporate performance is a major factor in determining CEO's compensation (DeKop, 1987; Gomez-Mejia, Tosi, and Hinkin, 1987). Our results show that the highest financial results are associated with the Participative mode. Therefore, CEOs have an incentive to strengthen their boards: namely, to heighten organizational performance that will result in improved CEO compensation.

The study also has implications for strategic management scholars. The results underscore the importance of understanding CEOs' views as a means to improve efforts on board reform. Most reform efforts have been predicated on the assumption that the CEO's self-interest is an obstacle to having an effective board. The results of the present study question this view and highlight the need to better incorporate CEOs' opinions into board reform efforts for them to be fruitful.

The study also opens a line of inquiry on the influence of boards on company performance by identifying a potentially important contingency: CEO–board relative power positions, as summarized in Figure 2. Given the observed pattern of variations among board characteristics and process variables based on these power positions, this contingency should be recognized in future investigations. Different patterns of associations between board variables and performance may exist in different board types (e.g. Caretaker vs. Proactive). As a result, the search for universal associations may need to be abandoned in favor of examining specific relationships within particular CEO–board power types.

A question remains regarding the antecedents of the board–CEO power positions identified in this paper. The literature points out that external environmental forces and internal organizational factors may play important roles in this regard. A fruitful future research avenue may be to assess the relative impact of environmental forces and internal factors (e.g. company age, size, life cycle phase, organizational culture, and norms associated with participative management) on these power positions. Do boards become more powerful when the firm's environment becomes more complex or volatile? Is there an appropriate match between board type and internal factors? What is the effect of a mismatch between board type and internal factors on company performance?

To answer the above questions, a longitudinal perspective is necessary. Board–CEO power positions may shift over time. Therefore, two questions deserve attention: (1) What are the external environmental and internal factors that precipitate changes in board–CEO powers? and (2) How are changes in CEO–board power modes (e.g. from Caretaker to Proactive) associated with company performance? Are certain changes (e.g. from Caretaker to Participative) associated more with high corporate financial performance than others (e.g. Statutory to Proactive)? Answers to these questions can be useful in introducing successful board reforms.

Finally, there is a need to replicate our findings using different populations and measures. For example, different measures of board characteristics can be developed to provide higher reliability coefficients for independence and role involvement. Data could be collected from directors and CEOs to corroborate our findings. Different measures of CEO–board powers could be developed by observing the weight of CEO and board views in making critical strategy decisions. By using such multiple indicators of board and CEO relative powers, future reseachers could more accurately classify board types to study their distinguishing qualities and processes.

In conclusion, the current study suggests that there is a significant association between powerful boards of directors and superior corporate financial performance. This finding will hopefully accelerate the search for an equitable power balance between executives and boards of directors, with a goal of enhancing the strength of boards so that they can optimally serve as integral components of effective governance.

REFERENCES

Andrews, K. R. 'Corporate strategy as a vital function of the board', *Harvard Business Review*, **59**(6), 1981, pp. 174–188.

Andrews, K. R. 'Difficulties in overseeing ethical policy', *California Management Review*, **26**(4), 1984, pp. 133–137.

Andrews, K. R. *The Concept of Corporate Strategy*, 3rd edn, Richard D. Irwin, Homewood, IL, 1987

Aram, J. D. and S. A. Cowen. *Information for Corporate Directors. The Role of the Board in the Management Process*, NAA Press, New York, 1983.

Bagozzi, R. P. 'Sales force performance and satisfaction as a function of individual difference, interpersonal, and situation factors', *Journal of Marketing Research*, **15**, 1978, pp. 524–538.

Bazerman, M. H. and F. D. Schoorman. 'A limited rationality model of interlocking directorates', *Academy of Management Review*, **8**, 1983, pp. 206–217.

Boulton, W. R. 'The evolving board: A new look at the board's changing roles and information needs', *Academy of Management Review*, **3**, 1978, pp. 827–836.

Brown, D. D. *Putting Corporate Boards to Work*, Macmillan, New York, 1976.

Business Week. 'The job nobody wants', 8 September 1986, pp. 56–61.

Carpenter, R. N. 'Corporate governanace; Part II: Directors' responsibilities', *Directors and Boards*, **29**(3), 1988, pp. 3–6.

Castaldi, R. and M. S. Wortman. 'Board of directors in small corporations: An untapped resource', *American Journal of Small Business*, **11**, 1984, pp. 1–11.

Dalton, D. R. and I. F. Kesner 'Organizational performance as an antecedent. Inside/outside chief executive succession: an empirical assessment', *Academy of Management Journal*, **28**, 1985, pp. 749–762.

DeKop, J. 'Top executive compensation and pay for performance'. In D. B. Balkin and L. R. Gomez-Mejia (eds), *New Perspectives in Compensation*, Prentice Hall, Englewood Cliffs, NJ, 1987, pp. 285–293.

Drucker, P. *Management: Tasks, Responsibilities, Practices*, Harper & Row, New York, 1974.

Epstein, E. J. *Who Owns the Corporation? Management vs. Shareholders*, Priority Press Publications, New York, 1986.

Fama, E. F. and M. Jensen. 'Separation of ownership and control'. *Journal of Law and Economics*, **26**, 1983, pp. 301–325.

Foster, W. G. 'Board and room', *Forbes*, **130**, 1982, pp. 219–227.

Geneen, H. S. 'Why directors can't protect the shareholders', *Fortune*, 17 September 1984. pp. 28–32.

Gomez-Mejia, L. R., H. Tosi, and T. Hinkin. 'Managerial control, performance, and executive compensation', *Academy of Management Journal*, **30**, 1987, pp. 51–70.

Henke, J. W., Jr. 'Involving the board of directors in strategic planning', *Journal of Business Strategy*, **7**(2), 1986, pp. 87–95.

Herman, E. S. *Corporate Control. Corporate Power*, Cambridge University Press, Cambridge, 1981.

Hermann, M. 'The executive's lament: On structuring CEO–Board relations in the public and non-profit sectors', *Ohio State University's Quarterly Report*, **11**(3), 1987, pp. 1–10.

Juran, J. M. and J. K. Louden. *The Corporate Director*, American Management Association, New York, 1966.

Kesner, I. F. 'Directors' stock ownership and organizational performance: An investigation of *Fortune* 500 companies', *Journal of Management*, **13**, 1987, pp. 499–508.

Kesner, I. F. and R. B. Johnson. 'Boardroom crisis: fiction or fact', *Academy of Management Executive*, **3**(1), 1990, pp. 23–35.

Koontz, H. *The Board of Directors and Effective Management*, McGraw-Hill, New York, 1971.

Kosnik, R. D. 'Effects of board demography and directors' incentives on corporate greenmail decisions', *Academy of Management Journal*, **33**, 1990, pp. 129–150.

Lang, J. R. and D. E. Lockhart. 'Increased environmental uncertainty and changes in board linkage patterns', *Academy of Management Journal*, **33**, 1990, pp. 106–128.

Lehmann, D. R. *Market Research and Analysis*, Richard D. Irwin, Homewood, IL, 1979.

Louden, J. K. *The Effective Director in Action*, Amacom, New York, 1975.

Mace, M. L. *Directors: Myth and Reality*, Harvard University Press, Boston, MA, 1971.

Mintzberg, H. *Power In and Around Organizations*, Prentice-Hall, Englewood Cliffs, NJ, 1983.

Mizruchi, M. S. 'Who controls whom? An examination of the relation between and board of directors in large American corporation', *Academy of Management Review*, **8**(3), 1983, pp. 426–435.

Molz, R. 'The role of the board of directors: Typologies of interaction', *Journal of Business Strategy*, 1985 (Spring), pp. 86–93.

Molz, R. 'Managerial domination of boards of directors and financial performance', *Journal of Business Research*, **16**, 1988, pp. 235–250.

Mueller, R. K. *Board Compass: What It Means To Be a Director in a Changing World*, D. C. Heath, Lexington, MA, 1979.

Nader, R. 'Reforming corporate governance', *California Management Review*, **26**(4), 1984, pp. 126–132.

Nunnally, J., Jr. *Tests and Measurements: Assessment and Prediction*, McGraw-Hill, New York, 1959.

Pearce, J. A., II. 'The company mission as a strategic tool', *Sloan Management Review*, **23**(3), 1982, pp. 15–24.

Pearce, J. A., II. 'The relationship of internal versus external orientations to financial measures of strategic performance', *Strategic Management Journal*, **4**(4), 1983, pp. 297–306.

Pearce, J. A., II and F. R. David. 'A social network approach to organizational design-performance', *Academy of Management Review*, **8**(3), 1983, pp. 436–444.

Pearce, J. A., II and F. R. David. 'The bottom-line on corporate mission statements', *Academy of Management Executive*, **1**(2), 1987, pp. 109–116.

Pearce, J. A., II and R. B. Robinson, Jr. 'A measure of CEO social power in strategic decision making', *Strategic Management Journal*, **8**(3), 1987, pp. 297–304.

Pfeffer, J. 'Size and composition of corporate boards of directors: The organization and its environment', *Administrative Science Quarterly*, **17**, 1972, pp. 218–229.

Pfeffer, J. 'Size, composition, and function of hospital boards of directors: A study of organization–environment linkage', *Administrative Science Quarterly*, 1973, pp. 349–364.

Pfeffer, J. *Power of Organizations*, Pitman, Boston, MA, 1980.

Provan, J. G. 'Board power and organizational effectiveness among human service agencies', *Academy of Management Journal*, **23**, 1980, pp. 221–236.

Purcell, T. V. 'Institutionalizing ethics on corporate boards', *Review of Social Economy*, **26**(1), 1978, pp. 41–53.

Ross, R. S. *Small Groups in Organizational Settings*, Prentice-Hall, Englewood Cliffs, NJ, 1988.

Salancik, G. R. and J. Pfeffer. 'What gets power—and how they hold on to it: A strategic contingency model of power', *Organizational Dynamics*, **5**, 1977, pp. 3–21.

Schmidt, R. 'Does board composition really make a difference?', *Conference Board Record*, **12**(10), 1975, pp. 38–41.

Sousa De Vasconcellos e Sá, J. A. and D. C. Hambrick. 'Key success factors: Test of a general theory in the mature industrial sector', *Strategic Management Journal*, **10**(4), 1989, pp. 367–383.

Spector, P. E. 'What to do with significant multivariate effects in multivariate analyses of variance', *Journal of Applied Psychology*, **62**, 1977, pp. 158–163.

The Changing Board. Heidrick & Struggles, Chicago, IL, 1983–1986.

Tichy, N. M., M. Tushman, and C. Fombrun. 'Network analysis in organizational settings', *Academy of Management Review*, **4**, 1979, pp. 507–519.

Vance, S. C. *Functional Control and Corporate Performance in Large Scale Industrial Enterprise*, University of Massachusetts, Amherst, MA, 1955.

Vance, S. C. *The Corporate Directors: Structure and Performance*, University of Oregon Press, Eugene, OR, 1968.

Vance, S. C. 'Corporate governance: assessing corporate performance by boardroom attributes', *Journal of Business Research*, **6**, 1978, pp. 203–220.

Vance, S. C. *Corporate Leadership: Boards, Directors, and Strategy*, McGraw-Hill, New York, 1983.

Vogel, D. 'Trends in shareholders activism: 1970–1982', *California Management Review*, **25**, 1983, pp. 68–87.

Wood, M. M. 'From the boardroom: What role for college trustees?', *Harvard Business Review*, **61**(3), 1983, pp. 52–62.

Zahra, S. A. and J. A. Pearce II. 'Board of directors and corporate financial performance'. *Journal of Management*, **15**(2), 1989, pp. 291–334.

Zahra, S. A. and J. A. Pearce II. 'Determinants of board of directors' strategic involvement', *European Management Journal*, **8**(2), 1990, pp. 164–173.

Zald, M. N. 'Urban differentiation, characteristics of boards of directors, and organizational effectiveness', *American Journal of Sociology*, **73**, 1967, pp. 261–272.

Zald, M. N. 'The power and functions of boards of directors: A theoretical synthesis'. *American Journal of Sociology*, **75**, 1969, pp. 97–111.

[17]

© Academy of Management Journal
1999, Vol. 42, No. 1, 7–24.

COLLABORATION IN THE BOARDROOM: BEHAVIORAL AND PERFORMANCE CONSEQUENCES OF CEO-BOARD SOCIAL TIES

JAMES D. WESTPHAL
University of Texas at Austin

Empirical research has typically rested on the assumption that board independence from management enhances board effectiveness in administering firms. The present study shows how and when a *lack* of social independence can increase board involvement and firm performance by raising the frequency of advice and counsel interactions between CEOs and outside directors. Hypotheses were tested with original survey data from 243 CEOs and 564 outside directors on behavioral processes and dynamics in management-board relationships.

In recent years, corporate stakeholders have expressed increased concern about the influence of boards of directors over corporate affairs. Large institutional investors, for instance, have strongly criticized the relationships that are thought to exist between top managers and outside directors in many corporations. In particular, advocates of board reform have commonly suggested that boards lack independence from top management and that their dependence fosters board passivity in the decision-making process. This perspective is reflected in the popular media, where it is frequently assumed that social ties between top managers and outside directors (e.g., friendships) diminish board effectiveness; such relationships are often described in pejorative terms as "chummy" or even "collusive" (*Wall Street Journal,* 1993: B1; 1995, 1996).

Academic research on boards has also devoted increased attention to how CEO-board relationships influence board effectiveness. Empirical researchers have often assumed that a lack of social independence from management can compromise board effectiveness in the strategy-making process. It has been proposed, for instance, that CEOs keep their boards largely passive and uninvolved in strategic decision making through cooptation, or packing boards with their supporters (e.g., Herman, 1981; Mace, 1986; Wade, O'Reilly, & Chandratat, 1990). Outside directors are thought to engage in less vigilant monitoring and to exert less control over top managers with whom they have close personal ties (e.g., Fredrickson, Hambrick, & Baumrin, 1988; Spencer, 1983; Walsh & Seward, 1990).

The present study departs from this dominant view of how a lack of board social independence from management affects a board's contribution to strategic decision making. The perspective developed in this study first builds on prior literature in which a board's role in an organization has been broadly conceived as including two different forms of administration: the provision of advice and counsel and the exercise of oversight and control (cf. Pfeffer & Salancik, 1978). I then develop a theoretical framework that draws from the literatures on advice seeking and social ties in organizations to consider how social factors such as trust and perceived social obligations in CEO-board relationships may promote rather than hinder board involvement and effectiveness in administering a firm. In particular, although existing perspectives tend to suggest that a *lack* of independence should reduce a board's involvement and effectiveness in firm administration, this study examines how social ties between top managers and outside directors may facilitate board involvement by encouraging the provision of advice and counsel in the strategy-making process.

The theoretical framework developed in this study also addresses the issue of when this alternative model of board social independence and involvement is more or less applicable than the more

This study was generously funded by the State Farm Companies Foundation. I am also indebted to Edward Zajac for providing financial support and assistance on this project. Thanks also to Gautam Ahuja, Mason Carpenter, Jennifer Chatman, Alison Davis-Blake, James Fredrickson, Ranjay Gulati, Paul Hirsch, Robert Hoskisson, Herminia Ibarra, Fiona Lee, Priti Shah, Mark Shanley, Ann Tenbrunsel, Brian Uzzi, and seminar participants at the Massachusetts Institute of Technology, the University of Michigan, the University of North Carolina at Chapel Hill, the University of Notre Dame, the University of Texas at Austin, the University of Washington, and Washington University for their helpful comments on an earlier version of this article. Mike Frandsen and Dennis Zhang provided valuable assistance in data collection.

traditional empirical model that focuses primarily on how board independence affects control. In particular, I explore how managerial incentive alignment may affect whether social ties between a CEO and board enhance involvement by encouraging CEO-board collaboration rather than reduce board involvement by hindering vigilant control. The proposed theoretical framework was tested with a comprehensive data set that combines longitudinal archival data on board structure, CEO compensation, and performance with primary survey data from a large sample of both top managers and outside directors regarding processes and dynamics in CEO-board relationships. The following section first describes the traditional perspective on how social ties in CEO-board relationships affect board involvement in strategic decision making and then develops an alternative "collaboration model" of the relationship between CEO-board social ties and board involvement in firm administration.

CEO-BOARD SOCIAL TIES AND BOARD INVOLVEMENT

The Independent Board Model

Much of the empirical literature examining how CEO-board relationships influence board involvement in firm governance is predicated on the assumption that effective boards influence corporate strategy and performance primarily by monitoring management on behalf of shareholders. For instance, Walsh and Seward (1990) described the board as an internal control mechanism, and Kosnik (1987, 1990) emphasized the role of outside directors in disciplining managerial decision making. Moreover, governance researchers have stressed that effective corporate directors serve shareholders by actively evaluating managerial performance (Boyd, 1994; Rechner & Dalton, 1991; Westphal & Zajac, 1995).

Theoretical support for the importance of board monitoring as a form of involvement is rooted in agency theory (Jensen & Meckling, 1976). According to this perspective, the function of boards is to reduce agency costs resulting from the delegation of strategic decision making, or "decision management," to top executives by exercising "decision control," which involves monitoring managerial decision making and performance (Fama & Jensen, 1983: 303). In doing so, boards rely crucially upon outside directors, who are considered less likely than insiders to "collude with managers to expropriate residual claimants" (Fama & Jensen, 1983: 315). The formal independence possessed by outsiders is assumed to permit more objective evaluation. Several studies have examined the influence of board independence on director involvement in strategic decision making. Johnson, Hoskisson, and Hitt (1993) and Judge and Zeithaml (1992) provided evidence that including more outside directors on a board increased board involvement (cf. Pearce & Zahra, 1991). These studies have suggested that the presence of more outside directors might promote involvement by raising the level of monitoring and control.

Researchers have also recognized variation in the extent to which outside directors are truly independent. Although outside board members are formally independent of top management, powerful social and psychological factors are thought to compromise their willingness and ability to objectively monitor managerial performance. From this perspective, CEOs use their influence over director selection to render boards passive by favoring the appointment of personal friends and other individuals with whom they share close social ties (Finkelstein & Hambrick, 1988; Johnson et al., 1993; Kimberly & Zajac, 1988). Researchers have also theorized that social ties are created through the appointment process itself. Board appointments confer prestige and status, as well as financial rewards and perquisites. Thus, given norms of reciprocity, outside directors should feel socially obligated to support CEOs who favored their appointment (Johnson et al., 1993; Wade et al., 1990). Overall, the dominant perspective in prior research on CEO-board relations suggests that personal social ties and obligations between managers and directors critically impair a board's capacity to monitor and control management decision making and performance, thus diminishing effective board involvement in the strategy-making process.

The Collaborative Board Model

Although much of the empirical literature on board involvement is based on the assumption that boards contribute to strategy primarily by monitoring management, the larger literature on boards suggests an additional way in which directors can influence strategy. Pfeffer and Salancik's (1978: 170) influential discussion of the different possible functions performed by outside directors distinguished between a board's role as an administrative body and its role in linking an organization with its environment. They further identified two distinct functions within the broader administrative role: the provision of expert advice and counsel and the exercise of oversight and control.

Several other scholars have also suggested that boards can extend their involvement beyond monitoring to the provision of ongoing advice and counsel on strategic issues (e.g., Baysinger & Butler, 1985; Gomez-Mejia & Wiseman, 1997; Johnson, Daily, & Ellstrand, 1996; Whisler, 1984; Zahra & Pearce, 1989). Bacon and Brown (1975: 18) and Lorsch (1989) described how directors may serve as a sounding board for management in addition to exercising control, and Alderfer (1986) suggested that the best CEO-board relationships included ongoing collaboration in the decision-making process (cf. Spencer, 1983). Although several prior studies have thus considered the board role in providing advice, there is some disagreement about the role of outside directors in exercising this function. Baysinger and Butler (1985) suggested that outside directors serve primarily to exercise control and that inside directors are the main source of advice on strategic issues. Daily and Dalton (1994) argued, however, that outside directors can provide access to valuable information—about, for instance, how to secure needed resources from the environment—in addition to exercising control (cf. Judge & Zeithaml, 1992; Pearce & Zahra, 1991; Pfeffer & Salancik, 1978).

Thus, the provision of advice has been recognized as a potentially important form of board involvement, but empirical researchers have neither explicitly modeled advisory relations nor examined how social factors may enhance a board's ability to exercise this function. Whereas the independent board model focuses on how social ties in the CEO-board relationship may diminish board involvement in firm decision making by reducing monitoring activity, it is suggested here that boards may provide advice and counsel as well as engage in control and that social ties may increase the prominence of advisory interactions as a form of involvement. Social ties with outside directors should enhance the propensity of top managers to solicit their advice on strategic issues while also increasing the outside directors' tendency to offer such advice. According to the larger literature on advice seeking, a primary inhibitor to seeking advice is the *perceived* effect it could have on the advice seeker's status. Employees tend to believe that others will view their need for assistance as an admission of uncertainty or dependency and as an indication that they are less than fully competent or self-reliant (Blau, 1955; Rosen, 1983). Moreover, individuals seeking advice from a superior may need to disclose the existence of problems and to admit their own limitations in solving them—implicitly or explicitly—thus relinquishing power derived from information asymmetry in the agency relationship (Jensen & Meckling, 1976).

This concern about losing status has been shown to inhibit a variety of different kinds of advice seeking. Allen (1977) showed that engineers sought relatively few technical ideas from others because they feared that such requests would engender skepticism about their competence. Ashford and Northcraft (1992) found evidence that feedback seeking by managers was impeded by impression management concerns, or a fear of appearing uncertain or dependent, and these concerns were particularly salient in an evaluative context, when the information providers (e.g., directors) were in a position to evaluate the person seeking information (e.g., a CEO). Studies have shown, however, that personal relationships increase employees' tendency to seek advice from either friends or others in their work units by creating a sense of social security that reduces the perceived risk (Anderson & Williams, 1996; Fischer, 1982; Rosen, 1983). Personal ties encourage advice seeking by enhancing mutual trust. Trust has been described as the willingness to take risks, or to make oneself vulnerable (cf. Mayer, Davis, & Schoorman, 1995). Thus, social ties should encourage CEO advice seeking by increasing a CEO's willingness to take the perceived social and professional risks associated with such behavior. Much research in organizational behavior has shown that interpersonal trust promotes cooperative problem-solving activity in groups (Zand, 1972) and enhances upward communication in superior-subordinate dyads (Roberts & O'Reilly, 1974).

The literature on helping behavior also suggests that people feel more comfortable offering advice to individuals with whom they have a social relationship, and research on friendship has shown that people feel socially obligated to give advice to friends who appear in need of assistance (Shah & Jehn, 1993). Moreover, dyadic social ties may have additional, board-level effects. The small-groups literature suggests that as the proportion of individuals offering advice increases, social conformity pressures may increase the likelihood that remaining group members will engage in similar behavior (Hackman, 1992).

Thus, the perspective developed in this study suggests that although boards may engage in both monitoring and advice giving, CEO-board social relations can determine the relative emphases they place on these roles; according to the independent board model, social ties should decrease involvement by reducing monitoring activity; in contrast, according to the collaboration model, such relations should increase involvement by encouraging the provision of advice and counsel on strategic issues. I next develop specific hypotheses.

CEO-board friendship ties. Silver characterized friendship as "protypical [of] personal relations that are normatively free of instrumental and calculative orientations" (1990: 1474). Krackhardt (1992) noted that friendship implies trust, or the expectation of personal loyalty. Similarly, Segal (1979) noted that certain social obligations are normatively part of the friendship relationship: for instance, a friend is expected to come to one's aid or defense when needed. The friendship relation is governed by communal norms, whereby individuals are obligated to care for each other's welfare, rather than exchange-based norms, whereby individuals are concerned with reciprocation of benefits (Clark & Mills, 1982; Jehn & Shaw, 1997). Thus, friendship ties between a CEO and outside directors should increase a board's loyalty to the CEO. Although the independent board model suggests that such loyalty should diminish board monitoring activity, the collaboration model discussed above suggests that perceived friendship ties may increase a CEO's advice-seeking behavior by enhancing his or her trust in the board's support, while also enhancing the board's perceived social obligation to provide assistance. Thus,

Hypothesis 1a. Friendship ties between a CEO and a board will be negatively associated with the board's monitoring of the CEO.

Hypothesis 2a. Friendship ties between a CEO and a board will be positively associated with interactions between them involving advice and counsel on strategic issues.

Director appointment by a CEO. As discussed above, norms of reciprocity may cause outside board members to feel socially obligated to support the CEO who was responsible for nominating them to a board (Boeker, 1992; Daily & Dalton, 1995). In fact, several empirical studies have provided evidence that the portion of a board appointed by a CEO can enhance the board's support for the CEO's leadership. Studies have linked the percentage of CEO appointments to the size of CEO compensation packages and explanations for CEO incentive compensation as well as to the adoption of antitakeover provisions (Lambert, Larcker, & Weigelt, 1993; Main, O'Reilly, & Wade, 1995; Zajac & Westphal, 1995). Thus, the conventional independent board model would suggest that boards comprised largely of a CEO's appointees would be less likely to engage in vigilant monitoring of CEO performance, because most of the directors feel socially obligated to return the favor of appointment by supporting the CEO's leadership. According to the collaboration model, however, a high proportion of outside directors appointed by a CEO may engender a closer, more collaborative working relationship by enhancing the CEO's trust in the support of his or her directors. Thus,

Hypothesis 1b. The portion of outside directors appointed after a given CEO's appointment will be negatively associated with board monitoring of the CEO.

Hypothesis 2b. The portion of outside directors appointed after a given CEO's appointment will be positively associated with interactions between the CEO and board involving advice and counsel on strategic issues.

Incentive Alignment and Board Involvement

The discussion thus far has developed two models of how CEO-board relations affect board involvement in managerial decision making. This section considers how normative agency theory might help determine when each model is most applicable. On the one hand, the costs of lower levels of board control may depend on whether partial substitutes for monitoring are available. Although some level of board monitoring is necessary and valuable, agency theorists recognize financial incentives as a partial substitute for monitoring activities, suggesting that the need for monitoring declines as agent incentives are aligned more closely with the interests of principals (Gomez-Mejia & Balkin, 1992; Gomez-Mejia & Wiseman, 1997; Kosnik, 1990). Empirical evidence suggests that relatively large reductions in agency costs are derived from the mere introduction of financial incentives, or from relatively small levels of incentive alignment (Rediker & Seth, 1995; Zajac & Westphal, 1994). Thus, when CEO incentives have been introduced, the agency costs associated with CEO-board social ties should be relatively small.

Further, CEO financial incentives should not only reduce the costs of CEO-board social ties, but should also *enhance* the *benefits* of such ties. From an agency perspective, incentive alignment motivates a CEO to use corporate resources to the advantage of shareholders (Jensen & Murphy, 1990). Several studies in the small groups literature have shown that when mechanisms are in place to motivate groups' members to pursue stakeholder objectives, social cohesion facilitates productive group interaction; the absence of such mechanisms, however, can lead to a negative relationship between cohesion and productive interaction (Guzzo & Shea, 1992; Schachter, Ellerston, McBride, & Gregory, 1951; Seashore, 1954). Thus, incentive alignment should motivate CEOs to use their social capital as a resource in developing more effective policies for shareholders. Accordingly, financial incentive alignment should moderate the effects of CEO-board social ties on board involvement: when incentive alignment is present, the collaboration model is more applicable, and when incentive alignment is absent, the independent board model is more germane. Thus,

Hypothesis 3. The higher the level of CEO incentive alignment, the weaker the negative relationship between (a) CEO-board friendship ties and board monitoring of a CEO and (b) the portion of outside directors appointed after the CEO and board monitoring of the CEO.

Hypothesis 4. The higher the level of CEO incentive alignment, the stronger the positive relationship between (a) CEO-board friendship ties and interactions between the CEO and board involving advice and counsel on strategic issues and (b) the portion of outside directors appointed after the CEO and these interactions.

Board Involvement and Firm Performance

Prior evidence regarding the ultimate performance consequences of board independence from management has been inconsistent (cf. Finkelstein & Hambrick, 1996). This inconsistency can be resolved, in part, by specifying the different behavioral processes (that is, forms of board involvement in strategic decision making) that could mediate this relationship (Cook & Campbell, 1979). According to the collaboration model, social ties may ultimately enhance firm performance by enabling boards to extend their involvement beyond decision control to decision management (Fama & Jensen, 1983: 303). From this perspective, board advice and counsel complement board monitoring as a form of involvement: when involvement extends beyond control to include advisory interactions, directors participate in formulating strategic decisions as well as in evaluating them (through periodic CEO performance reviews, for instance), so that boards influence each major phase of the decision-making process.

Several researchers have recognized the potential value of outside director advice and counsel in generating strategic proposals. Johnson, Daily, and Ellstrand (1996) suggested that advice and counsel interactions may enable top managers to tap the breadth of knowledge possessed by outside directors, thus complementing the depth of firm-specific knowledge held by insiders. Pfeffer and Salancik (1978) also discussed how advice and counsel from outside directors can broaden the range of strategic options considered by management, and Judge and Zeithaml (1992) suggested that fresh perspectives and new information provided by outside directors can help managers identify promising strategic opportunities. This view is consistent with the larger literature on group decision making, which has shown that a closed leadership style characterized by a failure to incorporate outside perspectives in making decisions can lead to truncated consideration of alternatives and adherence to faulty or obsolete assumptions (Janis, 1982; Tetlock, Peterson, McGuire, Chang, & Feld, 1992). Conversely, the solicitation of outside opinions can help expose unrealistic assumptions or alternatives and prevent premature conclusions.

Moreover, as agency theorists have acknowledged, although board monitoring can help partially resolve the agency problem between managers and shareholders, its effectiveness is limited by information asymmetries in the CEO-board relationship (Jensen & Meckling, 1976). Outside directors may not become aware of organizational problems in a timely fashion (cf. Baker, Jensen, & Murphy, 1988). To the extent that CEOs must often disclose information about organizational problems in seeking advice from outside directors, advice seeking reduces this information asymmetry and results in more informed board involvement. This formulation is consistent with prior research on leader-member exchange showing that superior-subordinate relationships characterized by frequent advisory interactions (in addition to supervisory control interactions) yield the highest performance (Bauer & Green, 1996). Thus, the quality of board involvement may be higher where monitoring activity is complemented by relatively high levels of director advice and counsel.

This discussion suggests two additional hypotheses. In the first, a positive relationship between board monitoring and subsequent firm performance is predicted; this hypothesis, together with Hypotheses 1a and 1b, addresses whether social ties ultimately reduce firm performance by lowering the level of board monitoring, as suggested by the independent board model. The second hypothesis, together with Hypotheses 2a and 2b, addresses whether social ties ultimately enhance firm performance by raising the level of board advice and counsel, as the collaboration model suggests.

Hypothesis 5. Board monitoring of CEOs will be positively associated with subsequent firm performance.

Hypothesis 6. CEO-board interactions involving advice and counsel on strategic issues will be positively associated with subsequent firm performance.

Incentive Alignment, Board Involvement, and Firm Performance

Finally, agency theory also suggests that CEO incentive alignment moderates the effects of board involvement on firm performance. To the extent that CEO incentives can partially substitute for board monitoring as a solution to the agency problem (Jensen & Meckling, 1976), higher incentive alignment should lessen the need for monitoring activity, reducing the relationship between monitoring and performance. In effect, where CEO interests are already well aligned with shareholder interests, there is less incremental benefit from a marginal increase in monitoring activity. In addition, incentives should also increase the relationship between CEO advice seeking and performance. From an agency perspective, incentive alignment should focus managerial attention and effort toward using corporate resources in a way that benefits shareholders. Thus, incentives should motivate managers not only to seek advice from outside directors (as argued above), but also to follow through and incorporate useful information and perspectives gained from those interactions into strategic decisions. Thus,

Hypothesis 7. The higher the level of CEO incentive alignment, the weaker the positive relationship between board monitoring of a CEO and subsequent firm performance.

Hypothesis 8. The higher the level of CEO incentive alignment, the stronger the positive relationship between CEO-board interactions involving advice and counsel on strategic issues and subsequent firm performance.

Overall, then, incentive alignment was expected to moderate relationships between CEO-board social ties, board involvement, and firm performance. As incentive alignment increases, the behavioral and ultimate performance consequences of CEO-board social ties should become more consistent with the collaborative board model and less consistent with the independent board model.

METHODS

Sample and Data Collection

The sample frame for this study consisted of 600 companies randomly selected from the *Forbes* 1,000 index of U.S. industrial and service firms. I sent a questionnaire to all 600 CEOs from these companies and, to permit interrater reliability assessments, sent a second survey to the outside directors of each company whose CEO responded to the first survey (N = 1,312). Directors who sat on more than one board in the survey sample were asked to respond for only one company (the company was randomly selected and specified in the cover letter); similarly, CEOs who sat on another board in the survey sample were not surveyed twice. The surveys were distributed in April 1995.

Surveys of corporate top managers have often suffered from response rates of less than 25 percent, and response rates above 40 percent are exceptional (Judge & Dobbins, 1995). To ensure the highest possible number of responses in this case, I took the following steps (Forsythe, 1977; Fowler, 1993; Groves, Cialdini, & Couper, 1992): (1) an in-depth pretest (described below) was used to streamline the survey, making it easier and more appealing to complete, (2) requests for participation linked the current study with an ongoing series of surveys on top management issues conducted by a major business school to which hundreds of the surveyed CEOs' and directors' peers had responded, and (3) nonrespondents were sent a new questionnaire about 21 days after the initial mailing. The response rate for CEOs was 44 percent (N = 263), and for directors, it was 43 percent (N = 564). Data on incentive alignment and ownership were obtained from proxy statements, and data on board composition and board structure were obtained from proxies, *Standard and Poor's Register*, the *Dun and Bradstreet Reference*, and *Who's Who in Finance and Industry*. I used the COMPUSTAT and CRSP (Center for Research on Securities Prices) databases to obtain performance, size, and industry data. Archival data were unavailable for 20 of the companies with responding CEOs, leaving a final sample of 243 CEOs and an effective response rate of 41 percent.[1] Firms in the final sample represented 27 different two-digit Standard Industrial Classification (SIC) categories in both the manufacturing and service sectors, including financial services firms and electric utilities, and ranged from single-product firms to highly diversified conglomerates. In addition, these firms ranged from 260 million to 58 billion in sales, from 500 to 200,000 employees, and from 500 million to 195 billion in assets.

For the 543 companies for which complete archival data were available, I examined whether respondents and nonrespondents differed significantly on variables derived from archival sources using the Kolmogorov-Smirnov test (Siegel & Castel-

[1] On average, 2.14 directors responded per firm (minimum of 0, maximum of 5).

lan, 1988).[2] This test assesses whether significant differences exist in the distribution of respondents and nonrespondents for a given variable. This is a stringent test, because if the sample distributions differ significantly at any point, it is concluded that the samples come from different populations. The results of this test provided consistent evidence across multiple variables that respondents and nonrespondents came from the same population; the variables were incentive alignment, firm performance, size, and the number of a firm's directors appointed after its CEO (p = .32–.77).

Dependent Measures

To enhance the construct validity of the survey measures, I conducted a pretest involving in-depth pilot interviews with 22 top managers and board members (cf. Fowler, 1993: 102). After each individual had completed the pilot questionnaire, I asked him or her to identify questions that were unclear, difficult to answer, or potentially subject to bias. I also used these interviews to ensure that questions were interpreted as expected, to identify improvements to the format of the survey, and to modify its length. To reduce response bias, multiple response formats were used, and items measuring each construct were scattered throughout the survey (DeVellis, 1991). Moreover, drawing on input from the pilot interviews, I carefully worded the final questions to minimize the likelihood of social desirability bias.

Advice and counsel interactions and *board monitoring* were assessed with two multi-item scales in the CEO survey (see Appendix A for the texts of these scales). In developing the wording of the questions, I drew from available qualitative research suggesting how top managers and directors describe CEO-board interaction and a board's role vis-à-vis management; feedback from the pilot interviews was used to further improve the clarity and face validity of each question. The items were factor-analyzed with the iterated principal factors method. A "scree" test indicated two common factors, and "promax" rotation verified that the advice and monitoring items loaded on different factors as expected, with loadings for each item greater than .5 on one factor and less than .2 on the other. Cronbach's alpha was .88 for the advice and counsel scale and .92 for the monitoring scale, suggesting acceptable interitem reliabilities (Nunnally, 1978). I estimated advice and monitoring factors using the Bartlett method.

I examined interrater reliability by comparing CEO and outside director responses for the monitoring and advice items, calculating kappa coefficients for each item. Kappa is a correlation coefficient that corrects for the expected level of correlation between raters. The sample included companies with a responding CEO and at least one responding outside director (n = 188). As shown in Table 1, kappa coefficients exceeded .75 for all but one survey item, and the overall kappa was .82, which represents an exceptional level of agreement according to criteria set forth by Fleiss (1981).[3]

Two measures of firm performance were used: *return on equity* (an accounting-based measure) and the *market-to-book value of equity* (a market-based measure). The latter measure gauges a firm's effectiveness in creating value for shareholders by comparing its market value with the cost of capital contributed by shareholders. Following Johnson and colleagues (1993) and Judge and Dobbins (1995), I adjusted each measure for industry differences by subtracting the average value for the firm's primary industry. Performance was measured two years after the survey date ($year_{t+2}$). In other analyses, I measured performance in $year_{t+1}$, and the results reported below were substantively unchanged.

Independent Measures

The *portion of a board appointed after a CEO* was calculated as the number of outside directors appointed during a CEO's tenure divided by the total number of outside board members. To assess the level of *CEO-board friendship ties*, CEOs were asked to consider their personal relationships with outside board members and to indicate (1) how

[2] Although this test could not be applied to board leadership structure, a difference of proportions test showed that respondents and nonrespondents did not differ significantly on the proportion of firms with separate CEO and board chair positions (.29 versus .27, p = .37). Respondents and nonrespondents were also not significantly different with respect to the number of board memberships they held (p = .69), and separate analyses confirmed that the subset of firms with a responding CEO and at least one responding outside director (n = 188) was also not significantly different from other firms in the sample frame on the independent and dependent variables measured with archival data.

[3] Correlations between the monitoring variable and several control variables provided further evidence for construct validity. The monitoring measure was positively associated with archival variables that have been used in prior studies as causal indicators of monitoring, including CEO–board chair separation (p = .34), director stock ownership (p = .27), blockholder ownership (p = .17), and institutional ownership (p = .20).

TABLE 1
Results of Interrater Reliability Assessment[a]

Item[b]	Agreement Observed	Agreement Expected	κ	Z^c
Board monitoring				
1. To what extent does the board monitor top management strategic decision making?	86.50%	24.86%	.82	24.80
2. To what extent does the board formally evaluate your performance?	85.65	21.16	.82	24.97
3. To what extent does the board defer to your judgment on final strategic decisions?	87.76	25.82	.84	25.47
Advice and counsel interactions				
1. To what extent do you solicit board assistance in the formulation of corporate strategy?[d]	79.32	24 00	.73	21.75
2. To what extent are outside directors a "sounding board" on strategic issues?	85.73	21.11	.81	24.65
3. How often have directors provided advice and counsel in discussions outside of board/committee meetings (by telephone *or* in person)?	87.09	24.55	.83	25.14
Overall κ			.82	24.98

[a] $N = 188$. Where multiple outside directors responded for the same company, director responses were averaged. This procedure helped to ensure that reliability estimates were not inflated by common perspectives derived from respondents' holding the same position.

[b] The phrasing of each item is taken from the CEO survey; most items were altered appropriately for the director survey. For purposes of comparison across items, I calculated kappas for continuous-scale items by converting them into categorical variables (i.e., dividing into quartiles).

[c] Z-statistics for all kappas are highly significant.

[d] Although this item restricts advice and counsel to CEO-initiated interactions, the results reported for the regression analyses were substantively unchanged when this item was excluded.

many they considered to be acquaintances but not friends and (2) how many they considered to be friends. Excluding mere acquaintances allowed a more precise measure of perceived friendship (cf. Chatman & Brown, 1995). The number of perceived friends was then divided by the total number of outside board members. This approach to measuring friendship is commonly used in organizational research (e.g., Brass, 1984; Krackhardt, 1992). It was not necessary to validate the survey measure of friendship ties against some alternative, behavioral measure, because the theoretical arguments regarding advice seeking required only that CEOs *perceived* the presence of friendship. Moreover, a separate analysis of interrater reliability showed a high level of agreement between CEOs and responding board members about the number of outsider directors who were friends of the CEO (κ = .76).[4]

I used two measures of CEO incentive alignment commonly used in the governance literature (e.g., Bergh, 1995; Kosnik, 1990; Johnson et al., 1993). First, *CEO ownership* was measured as the number of common shares owned by the CEO divided by the total amount of common stock outstanding. This definition captures the extent to which an agency problem exists by measuring the extent to which ownership and control are separated. It also reflects evidence in social psychology and organizational behavior for the "mere ownership effect" (Beggan, 1992: 229), which suggests that individuals feel more motivated to protect property as their ownership stake increases, independent of the property's financial value. Second, *long-term incentive plan compensation* indicated the extent to which CEO compensation was contingent upon the achievement of specific performance goals. Goal specificity has been identified as a critical determinant of motivation (Locke, Shaw, Saari, & Latham, 1981), and Larcker (1983) and Jarrell (1993) both discussed how incentives can lengthen executives' time horizons and focus their attention on creating shareholder value. Long-term incentive plan compensation was calculated as the total value of long-term incentive grants made in the year prior to the

[4] Although high interrater reliability should allay concerns about response bias, I also conducted an analysis in which friendship was measured with the CEO survey and advice was measured with the director survey; the results were unchanged. Since the advice items preceded the friendship items on the director survey, these relationships cannot be attributed to response bias. I also conducted an analysis in which friendship ties excluded relationships formed after the director(s) joined the boards and, again, the results were unchanged; this finding rules out the possibility that advice interactions encouraged the formation of friendship, rather than the reverse.

survey date divided by total compensation in that year (cf. Westphal & Zajac, 1995).

Control Variables

Several control variables were included in the analyses. First, "problemistic" search could lead firms' leaders to react to poor performance with higher levels of monitoring or advice interactions (Cyert & March, 1963). Prior studies have offered mixed evidence on the relationship between firm performance and changes in board composition thought to increase monitoring capacity (Daily & Dalton, 1995; Hermalin & Weisbach, 1988), but two recent studies have provided evidence for a negative relationship between firm performance and overall board involvement (Johnson et al., 1993; Judge & Zeithaml, 1992). Thus, I controlled for firm performance in the year prior to the time the survey was administered in models of board monitoring and advice. I also controlled for the prior value of firm performance in models predicting subsequent performance, consistent with prior research (e.g., Haveman, 1992).

Although prior evidence regarding the effect of firm size on board decision making is also mixed (Finkelstein & Hambrick, 1996), one might expect the greater complexity involved in governing large organizations to make directors at such firms more inclined to delegate decision-making responsibility, reducing their involvement (Zajac & Westphal, 1994). Thus, I controlled for *sales* (measured as a logarithm) in all models. Prior research has suggested that directors lack the structural power to control management decisions when the CEO also serves as board chair, and some evidence links board leadership structure to responsible decision making (Mallette & Fowler, 1992; Westphal & Zajac, 1995); thus, a variable indicating *separation of the CEO and board chair positions* was included in the monitoring models (this variable was not necessarily expected to influence advice interactions, and separate analyses confirmed that it was unrelated to advice and did not affect the hypothesized results). I also controlled for *CEO tenure.* CEOs are most likely to consider major strategic changes early in their tenures (Gabarro, 1985), so length of tenure may be related to board involvement in strategy making. Daily (1996) suggested that directors who are affiliated with a focal firm through a family or business relationship may have access to valuable sources of information, raising the possibility that director affiliations could influence the level of board involvement. Thus, I controlled for the percentage of outside directors who were affiliated with a focal firm using two measures: *affiliated directors: family ties* and *affiliated directors: business ties.* The measures were based on the Securities and Exchange Commission's definitions of the relevant relationships.

Given some prior evidence that ownership by outside directors or other external blockholders may increase a board's motivation and/or power to exercise control, I included both ownership measures in the analyses (Bergh, 1995). *Director ownership* was measured as the percentage of total common equity held by outside directors, and *blockholder ownership* was measured as the percentage held by owners of 5 percent or more of a firm's common voting shares, *excluding* managers, directors, and institutions (e.g., Bergh, 1995). Although prior evidence is mixed (e.g., Bethel & Liebeskind, 1993; Black, 1998; Wahal, 1996), some authors have suggested that institutional owners, in particular, are active in compelling higher levels of board control (Davis & Thompson, 1994). Thus, I controlled for *institutional ownership,* measured as the percentage of total common stock held by pension funds, banks and trust companies, savings and loans, mutual fund managers, and labor union funds (Kochhar & David, 1996; Hill & Hansen, 1991; Kochhar & David, 1996).[5] Given that powerful owners could also affect management decision making independent of their influence over board involvement, these variables were included in the models of performance calculated for this study, as well as in the models of board monitoring and advice. Finally, I controlled for change in corporate strategy in the models of performance, given that strategic change can disrupt organizations in a way that impairs performance or can facilitate adaptation that enhances performance (cf. Hannan & Freeman, 1989; Zajac & Shortell, 1989). Finally, I measured *change in corporate strategy* as the change in the entropy measure of diversification over the two-year period prior to survey administration.

Analysis

Since the proposed relationships between CEO-board social ties, monitoring, and advice interactions were recursive, I used ordinary least squares (OLS) multiple regression analysis to estimate models of monitoring and advice (Johnston, 1984). The performance models were estimated using two-stage least squares regression. To the extent

[5] In separate analyses, I restricted this measure to ownership by institutions classified as "pressure-resistant" by Kochhar and David (1996), including public pension funds, mutual funds, and foundations. The results were substantively unchanged from results presented below.

that the models of board monitoring, advice, and performance encompassed a larger system of equations in which some variables that predict board monitoring and/or advice might be independently related to performance, OLS regression could yield biased estimates in modeling performance (Johnston, 1984). Two-stage least squares regression corrects for this bias by generating reduced-form estimates of monitoring, advice, and prior performance and then including predicted values from these equations as instruments in a second-stage equation estimating subsequent firm performance.

RESULTS

Descriptive statistics and bivariate correlations are displayed in Table 2. The results of multiple regression analyses of board monitoring and advice and counsel interactions are provided in Table 3. The first set of results was inconsistent with the independent board model. Neither the level of CEO-board friendship ties nor the portion of a firm's board appointed after its CEO was significantly related to the level of board monitoring activity. The main effects did support the collaborative board model, however. Consistent with Hypothesis 2, friendship ties and subsequent board appointments were both positively related to the level of advice and counsel interactions on strategic issues.

The results also generally supported the hypothesized effect of the interaction between social ties and incentive alignment on board monitoring and advice interactions (Hypotheses 3–4). As CEO ownership or long-term incentive plan compensation increased, the negative effect of friendship ties on board monitoring grew weaker (i.e., more positive), and the positive effect of such ties on advice interactions grew stronger. Similarly, for two of the interaction terms, as incentives increased the negative effect of subsequent board appointments on monitoring grew weaker, and the positive effect of subsequent board appointments on advice interactions grew stronger.

A further analysis of simple effects (Jaccard, Turrisi, & Wan, 1990) indicated that both social tie variables were insignificant in predicting advice interactions at low levels of CEO ownership or long-term incentive plan compensation (for example, at zero), and the significant effects in model 3 indicate that social ties were positively related to advice and counsel interactions at *average levels* of each incentive variable. Conversely, although the effects of social ties on board monitoring were insignificant at average levels of CEO ownership and long-term incentive plan compensation, they became significant at low levels of incentive alignment. In general, these results support the proposition that incentive alignment moderates the effects of CEO-board social ties on board involvement. When incentive alignment is absent, the independent board model is more appropriate in predicting

TABLE 2
Descriptive Statistics and Pearson Correlation Coefficients[a]

Variable	Mean	s.d.	1	2	3	4	5	6	7	8	9	10	11	12	13	14	15	16
1. CEO-board friendship ties	0.39	0.35																
2. Portion of board appointed after CEO	0.31	0.26	.23															
3. Sales[b]	7.59	1.52	−.05	.15														
4. CEO ownership	0.05	0.06	.04	.02	−.04													
5. Long-term incentive plan compensation	0.33	0.27	−.16	.03	.09	.09												
6. Director ownership	0.02	0.06	−.03	.00	−.14	.13	.10											
7. Blockholder ownership	0.17	0.22	.01	−.04	.18	−.11	−.09	−.08										
8. Institutional ownership	0.29	0.16	−.06	.04	.16	−.07	−.12	−.11	−.22									
9. CEO tenure	6.99	6.02	.08	.27	.06	−.22	−.15	−.17	−.03	−.02								
10. Affiliated directors: Family ties	0.08	0.11	.12	.01	−.03	−.05	−.09	.03	.02	−.04	.11							
11. Affiliated directors: Business ties	0.35	0.24	.09	.01	.14	−.07	−.06	−.18	−.11	−.05	.04	−.03						
12. Separation of CEO and board chair positions	0.29	0.46	−.27	−.26	.13	.15	.13	.02	−.01	.05	−.22	.02	.01					
13. Change in corporate strategy	0.01	0.65	.02	−.03	−.05	.03	.01	−.04	.06	.09	−.08	−.05	.02	.04				
14. Board monitoring	0.00	0.87	−.10	−.08	−.04	−.16	−.19	.27	.17	.20	−.08	−.12	−.09	.34	.03			
15. Advice and counsel interactions	0.00	0.81	.24	.26	−.06	.14	.06	.12	.06	.07	−.13	.11	.19	−.05	.05	−.14		
16. Return on equity	0.00	0.07	.14	.11	−.06	.05	.02	.08	.07	.14	.01	.03	.04	.02	.05	.22	.25	
17. Market-to-book value of equity	0.03	0.76	.20	.13	−.03	.08	.04	.10	.12	.08	−.02	.06	.01	.03	.07	.18	.33	.19

[a] $N = 243$. Correlations greater than .13 are significant at $p < .05$.
[b] Logarithm.

TABLE 3
Results of OLS Regression Models[a]

Variable	Monitoring			Advice and Counsel Interactions		
	Model 1	Model 2	Model 3	Model 4	Model 5	Model 6
1. CEO-board friendship ties		−0.15 (0.16)	−0.15 (0.16)		0.36 (0.15)**	0.37 (0.15)**
2. Portion of board appointed after CEO		−0.27 (0.21)	−0.26 (0.21)		0.41 (0.20)*	0.41 (0.20)*
3. Prior return on equity	−0.77 (0.50)	−0.76 (0.50)	−0.75 (0.50)	−0.94 (0.45)	−0.86 (0.45)	−0.72 (0.44)
4. Prior market-to-book value of equity	−0.06 (0.05)	−0.06 (0.05)	−0.60 (0.05)	−0.03 (0.05)	−0.03 (0.05)	−0.02 (0.05)
5. Sales[b]	−0.01 (0.04)	−0.01 (0.04)	−0.01 (0.04)	−0.06 (0.04)	−0.05 (0.03)	−0.05 (0.03)
6. CEO ownership	−1.47 (0.65)*	−1.46 (0.65)	−1.41 (0.64)*	0.57 (0.58)	0.55 (0.58)	0.54 (0.57)
7. Long-term incentive plan[c] compensation	−0.47 (0.22)*	−0.46 (0.22)*	−0.45 (0.21)*	0.26 (0.20)	0.24 (0.19)	0.23 (0.19)
8. Director ownership	2.46 (1.00)*	2.43 (1.00)*	2.33 (1.00)*	1.29 (0.89)	1.21 (0.88)	1.41 (0.88)
9. Blockholder ownership	0.46 (0.26)	0.36 (0.26)	0.34 (0.25)	0.09 (0.23)	0.08 (0.23)	0.08 (0.22)
10. Institutional ownership	0.55 (0.33)	0.56 (0.33)	0.56 (0.33)	0.16 (0.28)	0.16 (0.28)	0.16 (0.27)
11. CEO tenure	−0.01 (0.01)	−0.01 (0.01)	−0.00 (0.01)	−0.01 (0.01)	−0.01 (0.01)	−0.01 (0.01)
12. Affiliated directors: Family ties	−1.05 (0.56)	−1.00 (0.54)	−1.00 (0.54)	0.64 (0.51)	0.59 (0.50)	0.58 (0.49)
13. Affiliated directors: Business ties	−0.40 (0.28)	−0.36 (0.27)	−0.36 (0.26)	0.55 (0.24)*	0.52 (0.24)*	0.50 (0.24)*
14. Separation of CEO and board chair positions	0.50 (0.13)***	0.50 (0.13)***	0.49 (0.13)***			
15. Friendship ties × CEO ownership			7.32 (2.34)***			5.36 (2.12)**
16. Friendship ties × LTIP compensation			1.29 (0.61)*			1.58 (0.55)**
17. Portion of board appointed after CEO × CEO ownership			7.02 (3.63)*			4.36 (3.37)
18. Portion of board appointed after CEO × LTIP compensation			1.26 (0.82)			2.00 (0.72)**
Constant	0.20 (0.37)	0.24 (0.38)	0.30 (0.36)	−0.04 (0.32)	−0.05 (0.31)	−0.04 (0.30)
F	5.19***	5.04***	9.27***	2.56*	4.32***	10.04***
R^2	.18	.19	.38	.08	.16	.40
ΔR^2		.01	.19***		.08**	.14***

[a] N = 243. Standard errors are in parentheses. T-tests were one-tailed for hypothesized effects and two-tailed for control variables.
[b] Logarithm.
[c] Abbreviated below as "LTIP."
* $p \leq .05$
** $p \leq .01$
*** $p \leq .001$

board involvement, and when incentive alignment is average to high, the collaborative board model fits better.

The results of a two-stage least squares regression analysis of firm performance are presented in Table 4. Hypothesis 5 predicted a positive relationship between board monitoring of CEOs and subsequent firm performance. The results support this hypothesis for both return on equity and market-to-book value. Hypothesis 6 is also supported: the level of advice and counsel interactions was positively related to each measure of subsequent firm performance. Hypotheses 7–8 predicted that incentive alignment would determine when each kind of involvement is most effective. Neither kind of incentive alignment interacted with board monitoring to influence firm performance, but the results do support Hypothesis 8: The relationship between advice interactions and subsequent firm performance became stronger as the level of CEO ownership or the level of CEO long-term incentive plan compensation increased for both measures of performance.[6]

DISCUSSION

The findings of this study appear to have important implications for the corporate governance literature. The first set of results showed not only that social ties typically fail to reduce the level of board

[6] I also conducted separate analyses of board advice, monitoring, and performance for the smaller sample of firms with a responding CEO and at least one responding outside director (N = 188). Results for the hypothesized effects were substantively the same as the results reported in Tables 3 and 4. Results were also unchanged when friendship ties, advice, and/or monitoring were measured with responses to the director survey, which reflects the high levels of interrater reliability reported above.

TABLE 4
Results of Two-Stage Least Squares Regression Models of Firm Performance[a]

	Return on Equity			Market-to-Book Value of Equity		
Variable	**Model 1**	**Model 2**	**Model 3**	**Model 4**	**Model 5**	**Model 6**
1. Advice and counsel interactions		0.01 (0.01)**	0.01 (0.01)**		0.19 (0.06)***	0.20 (0.06)***
2. Board monitoring		0.01 (0.01)**	0.01 (0.01)**		0.12 (0.05)*	0.12 (0.06)*
3. Prior return on equity	0.43 (0.03)***	0.43 (0.03)***	0.44 (0.03)***			
4. Prior market-to-book value of equity				0.62 (0.04)***	0.62 (0.04)***	0.46 (0.04)***
5. Sales[b]	−0.00 (0.00)	−0.00 (0.00)	−0.00 (0.00)	−0.01 (0.03)	−0.03 (0.03)	−0.02 (0.03)
6. CEO ownership	0.03 (0.04)	0.03 (0.05)	0.04 (0.05)	0.80 (0.52)	0.79 (0.78)	0.78 (0.53)
7. Long-term incentive plan[c] compensation	0.01 (0.02)	0.01 (0.02)	0.02 (0.02)	0.19 (0.17)	0.19 (0.17)	0.18 (0.18)
8. Director ownership	0.11 (0.07)	0.11 (0.07)	0.11 (0.07)	1.13 (0.80)	1.11 (0.80)	1.16 (0.81)
9. Blockholder ownership	0.02 (0.02)	0.02 (0.02)	0.02 (0.02)	0.29 (0.20)	0.28 (0.20)	0.28 (0.21)
10. Institutional ownership	0.04 (0.02)	0.04 (0.02)	0.04 (0.02)	0.34 (0.26)	0.34 (0.26)	0.34 (0.26)
11. Change in corporate strategy	0.00 (0.01)	0.00 (0.01)	0.00 (0.01)	0.07 (0.07)	0.07 (0.07)	0.07 (0.08)
12. Advice interactions × CEO ownership			0.17 (0.06)**			1.56 (0.77)*
13. Advice interactions × LTIP compensation			0.05 (0.02)**			0.70 (0.22)***
14. Board monitoring × CEO ownership			−0.10 (0.06)			−0.71 (0.72)
15. Board monitoring × LTIP compensation			−0.03 (0.02)			−0.37 (0.22)
Constant	0.05 (0.03)*	0.05 (0.03)*	0.04 (0.03)	0.03 (0.29)	0.02 (0.35)	0.03 (0.38)
F	17.07***	20.26***	25.74***	19.33***	22.69***	29.37***
R^2	.36	.47	.63	.39	.50	.65
ΔR^2		.11**	.16***		.11***	.15***

[a] $N = 243$. Standard errors are in parentheses. T-tests are one-tailed for hypothesized effects, two-tailed for control variables.
[b] Logarithm.
[c] Abbreviated below as "LTIP."
* $p \leq .05$
** $p \leq .01$
*** $p \leq .001$

monitoring activity, but also that such ties enhance the provision of advice and counsel from outside directors on strategic issues. These results offer perhaps the first large-sample empirical evidence that addresses how boards can extend their involvement in corporate governance beyond monitoring to provide ongoing advice and counsel to management on strategic issues (Baysinger & Butler, 1985; Johnson et al., 1996; Zahra & Pearce, 1989). Much of the empirical literature on boards of directors has proceeded from the assumption that social ties in CEO-board relationships diminish the involvement and effectiveness of outside directors by reducing their tendency to control management decision making (e.g., Johnson et al., 1993; Tosi & Gomez-Mejia, 1989; Wade et al., 1990). The findings of this study suggest instead that such ties, rather than promoting a passive board role, may increase board involvement by encouraging collaboration between top managers and outside directors in strategic decision making.

The findings are also consistent with results of behavioral research on advice seeking at lower levels of organizations. This literature has shown that personal relationships between colleagues in a work unit increase the level of advice-seeking behavior by alleviating impression management concerns, such as the fear of appearing uncertain or dependent, and concerns about revealing sensitive information, especially when the colleagues are in a position to evaluate the advice seekers' performance. The results support the view that CEOs are more willing to take the social and professional risks associated with advice-seeking behavior when they can rely on the loyalty of their boards. Similarly, the results are also consistent with research on friendship in organizations, which has shown that friendship ties among group members lead to higher levels of task-related communication and mutual assistance by enhancing interpersonal trust.

Further results showed that CEO incentive alignment moderated relationships between social ties and board involvement: Higher levels of CEO ownership or long-term incentive compensation further enhanced the positive relationship between social ties and board advice while reducing the negative relationship between social ties and board monitoring. This moderation is consistent with the view that management incentives decrease the need for board monitoring as a control mechanism and also motivate CEOs to use their social capital (their social ties to directors) as a resource in strategic decision making. Although some prior research has linked management incentives to corporate strategy and overall firm performance (e.g., Abowd, 1990; Gibbs, 1993), the present study extends this literature by addressing how incentives affect behavioral processes (here, advice seeking) that may mediate these relationships.

The last set of results addresses the ultimate performance consequences of each kind of board involvement, showing that CEO-board collaboration and control are independently and positively related to subsequent firm performance. These findings provide systematic empirical support for the view that boards can contribute to strategy not only by independently evaluating managements, but also by serving as sounding boards for top managers who are in the process of formulating strategy (Bacon & Brown, 1975: 18; Johnson et al., 1996; Lorsch, 1989). Together with the first set of results, these findings challenge the dominant assumptions that underlie most empirical research on boards and that characterize social ties narrowly as frictions that reduce the efficiency of corporate governance (Fama & Jensen, 1983; Hirsch, Michaels, & Friedman, 1987). Rather than impairing corporate governance by reducing the vigilance of board monitoring, social ties can ultimately contribute to board effectiveness and firm performance by fostering collaboration between CEOs and directors in the strategy-making process without reducing board control.

It might be suggested that CEOs are more comfortable seeking advice from their friends and appointees because those individuals may be less experienced or knowledgeable than themselves, and thus less capable of challenging them. To explore the validity of this interpretation, I analyzed the effect of director expertise and experience on the observed relationships. I used four indicators of expertise, averaged across directors (Finkelstein, 1992; Wiersema & Bantel, 1992): the number of different management positions a director had held, the number of different functional areas the director had worked in, the number of years the director had served as a top manager, and the director's level of education. Factor analysis confirmed that all four indicators loaded on the same factor. A separate regression analysis showed that the effects of social ties on advice and counsel interactions were unchanged when director expertise and experience were controlled for. Also, as shown in Appendix B, the interaction between director expertise and social ties had a positive effect on advice interactions, indicating that social ties were especially likely to increase advice when the level of director expertise was relatively high. These results are inconsistent with the view that social ties increase advice seeking because boards that have more social ties with CEOs are populated by less experienced or knowledgeable directors whose input might be less threatening to the CEOs.

Future Research Directions

Although this study focused on the administrative role of boards, future research should examine how CEO-board cooperation and control affect a board's ability to exercise its other major functions, including its role in managing resource dependence and enhancing organizational legitimacy. One could investigate, for instance, whether advice and counsel interactions between CEOs and manager-directors (outside directors who serve as top managers at another firm) might help managers to identify opportunities for interorganizational cooperation (for instance, strategic alliances) that secure needed resources and resolve interdependencies between firms. Conversely, CEO-board relationships characterized only by independent board control might reduce the likelihood that CEOs and manager-directors will identify and pursue such opportunities. Similarly, although in prior research on interlocking directorates the assumption has been that managers use outside directors to secure needed resources from the environment (for a review, see Mizruchi [1996]), the effectiveness of this cooptation mechanism may hinge on the particular content of CEO-board relationships.

Studies are also needed that examine how different kinds of CEO-board relationships are perceived by internal and external stakeholders and the consequences of these relationships for organizational legitimacy. There is evidence that institutional investors respond positively to changes in board structure that are thought to increase a board's monitoring capacity (for a review, see Westphal and Zajac [1998]). It is uncertain, however, whether external constituents also assess the actual behavioral processes occurring in CEO-board relationships (for example, monitoring and advice giving) in evaluating corporate governance. Given the potential decoupling of formal board structure and actual behavior (Meyer & Rowan, 1977; Westphal & Zajac, 1994), it is important to examine the depth at which external stakeholders evaluate corporate boards. According to an institutional perspective, firms with strong CEO-board social ties could satisfy external constituents by adopting formal structures that implied independent control (the socially legitimate CEO-board relationship) but could decouple these structures from actual board processes.

The findings of this study may also suggest new directions for research on management incentives. The confirmed interactions between incentive alignment and social ties suggest that incentives can be more effective in raising performance when managers have more social connections to draw upon for information and advice. Compensation researchers should further explore the role of social capital as an important contingency factor in the effectiveness of incentive compensation plans. Researchers investigating management incentives in particular might explicitly consider how managers are either constrained or enabled in responding to economic incentives by the social relationships in which they are embedded. Research is also needed that explores in more detail how incentives affect CEO behavior such as advice seeking. Stewardship theory suggests that managers are motivated by the intrinsic satisfaction their work provides rather than by extrinsic rewards (Davis, Schoorman, & Donaldson, 1997). This view might appear inconsistent with evidence that incentive compensation increases the tendency for CEOs to draw on their social ties for advice. However, it is possible that incentives influence CEOs' behavior primarily by communicating goals and directing the CEOs' attention toward them, and not strictly by motivating the CEOs to increase their financial compensation. Future studies should examine the psychological mechanisms that mediate the effects of incentives on CEO behavior toward boards.

Limitations and Managerial Implications

Several limitations of the study should be acknowledged. First, this research focused on advice interactions initiated by CEOs. A somewhat different set of social and economic factors may lead directors to initiate such interactions. Separate questions in the survey indicated that a large portion of such advice interactions (approximately 92 percent, on the average) were initiated by the CEOs, a finding that is consistent with prior descriptive surveys suggesting that such interactions are typically CEO initiated (Alderfer, 1986; Bacon & Brown, 1975; Demb & Neubauer, 1992). Nevertheless, board-initiated advice giving does occur, and it could become a more significant form of involvement in the future. Second, this study did not address the specific content or quality of board advice—for instance, I did not examine whether and when directors furnished information about developments in the external environment, as opposed to giving opinions about strategic options for coping with them. In this study, I did not seek to explain variation in the value or quality of advice or the accuracy of information furnished by outside directors, qualities that could moderate the effects of collaboration on performance; unique information or experience provided by outsiders could represent an especially valuable resource (Pfeffer & Salancik, 1978). Finally, as noted above, in this research I did not investigate how board collaboration and control affected a board's ability to perform certain external roles, such as managing resource dependence or building organizational legitimacy.

The present findings may have important normative implications for corporate boards. Institutional investors, management consultants, and the popular press have all strongly advocated greater board independence from management. Directors with close ties to management are routinely characterized in cynical terms as "pals of the CEO" or "hand-picked appointees," and their relationships to CEOs are described as overly "chummy" (e.g., *Wall Street Journal*, 1993: B1; 1995: B1; 1996). This study suggests that in fact board effectiveness and ultimately, firm performance may be enhanced by close, trusting CEO-board relationships combined with moderate to high levels of CEO incentive alignment. Thus, rather than dividing top managers and outside directors into independent groups, a firm might profit by using team development techniques that unify managers and directors into a single, cohesive team. Interestingly, although such interventions are commonly used to develop teamwork among lower-level employees, they have not been applied at the highest levels of organizations.

Overall, this study contributes to the corporate governance literature by providing empirical evidence on how CEOs and outside directors collaborate in the strategic decision making process and then demonstrating that such collaboration independently and positively contributes to firm performance. The results challenge dominant assumptions in the prior empirical literature on boards by showing how social ties in CEO-board relationships can enhance rather than diminish board involvement and firm performance by encouraging advice seeking in the strategic decision making process. More generally, the findings suggest the value of conducting rigorous empirical research that examines the behavioral processes and dynamics that underlie corporate governance.

REFERENCES

Abowd, J. M. 1990. Does performance-based managerial compensation affect subsequent corporate performance? ***Industrial and Labor Relations Review,*** 43: 552–573.

Alderfer, C. P. 1986. The invisible director on corporate boards. ***Harvard Business Review,*** 64: 38–52.

Allen, T. J. 1977. ***Managing the flow of technology: Technology transfer and the dissemination of technology information within the R&D organization.*** Cambridge, MA: MIT Press.

Anderson, S. E., & Williams, L. J. 1996. Interpersonal, job, and individual factors related to helping processes at work. ***Journal of Applied Psychology,*** 81: 282–296.

Ashford, S. J., & Northcraft, G. B. 1992. Conveying more (or less) than we realize: The role of impression-management in feedback-seeking. ***Organizational Behavior and Human Decision Processes,*** 53: 310–334.

Bacon, J., & Brown, J. K. 1975. ***Corporate directorship practices: Role, selection and legal status of the board.*** New York: Conference Board.

Baker, G. P., Jensen, M. C., & Murphy, K. J. 1988. Compensation and incentives: Practice vs. theory. ***Journal of Finance,*** 43: 593–616.

Bauer, T. N., & Green, S. G. 1996. Development of leader-member exchange: A longitudinal test. ***Academy of Management Journal,*** 39: 1538–1567.

Baysinger, B., & Butler, H. N. 1985. Corporate governance and the board of directors: Performance effects of changes in board composition. ***Journal of Law, Economics, and Organization,*** 1: 101–124.

Beggan, J. K. 1992. On the social nature of nonsocial perception: The mere ownership effect. ***Journal of Personality and Social Psychology,*** 62: 229–237.

Bergh, D. D. 1995. Size and relatedness of units sold: An agency theory and resource-based perspective. ***Strategic Management Journal,*** 16: 221–239.

Bethel, J. E., & Liebeskind, J. 1993. The effects of ownership structure on corporate restructuring. ***Strategic Management Journal,*** 14: 15–32.

Black, B. S. 1998. Shareholder activism and corporate governance in the United States. In P. Newman (Ed.), ***The new Palgrave dictionary of economics and the law:*** Forthcoming.

Blau, P. M. 1955. ***The dynamics of bureaucracy.*** Chicago: University of Chicago Press.

Boeker, W. 1992. Power and managerial dismissal: Scapegoating at the top. ***Administrative Science Quarterly,*** 37: 400–421.

Boyd, B. K. 1994. Board control and CEO compensation. ***Strategic Management Journal,*** 15: 335–344.

Brass, D. J. 1984. Being in the right place: A structural analysis of individual influence in an organization. ***Administrative Science Quarterly,*** 29: 518–539.

Chatman, J. A., & Brown, R. A. 1995. ***It takes two to tango: Understanding the personal and situational antecedents of friendship at the individual and dyadic levels.*** Paper presented at the annual meeting of the Academy of Management, Vancouver.

Clark, M. S., & Mills, J. R. 1982. Communal and exchange relationships. In L. Wheeler (Ed.), ***Review of personality and social psychology.*** Beverly Hills, CA: Sage.

Cook, T. D., & Campbell, D. T. 1979. ***Quasi-experimentation: Design and analysis issues for field settings.*** Chicago: Rand McNally.

Cyert, R. M., & March, J. G. 1963. ***A behavioral theory of the firm.*** Englewood Cliffs, NJ: Prentice-Hall.

Daily, C. M. 1996. Governance patterns in bankruptcy reorganizations. ***Strategic Management Journal,*** 17: 355–375.

Daily, C. M., & Dalton, D. R. 1994. Bankruptcy and corporate governance: The impact of board composition and structure. ***Academy of Management Journal,*** 37: 1603–1617.

Daily, C. M., & Dalton, D. R. 1995. CEO and director turnover in failing firms: An illusion of change? ***Strategic Management Journal,*** 16: 393–400.

Davis, J. H., Schoorman, F. D., & Donaldson, L. 1997. Toward a stewardship theory of management. ***Academy of Management Review,*** 22: 20–47.

Davis, G. F., & Thompson, T. A. 1994. A social movement perspective on corporate control. ***Administrative Science Quarterly,*** 39: 141–173.

Demb, A., & Neubauer, F. 1992. ***The corporate board: Confronting the paradoxes.*** Oxford: Oxford University Press.

DeVellis, R. F. 1991. ***Scale development: Theory and applications.*** Newbury Park, CA: Sage.

Fama, E. F., & Jensen, M. C. 1983. The separation of ownership and control. ***Journal of Law and Economics,*** 26: 301–325.

Finkelstein, S. 1992. Power in top management teams: Dimensions, measurement, and validation. ***Academy of Management Journal,*** 35: 505–538.

Finkelstein, S., & Hambrick, D. C. 1988. Chief executive compensation: A synthesis and reconciliation. ***Strategic Management Journal,*** 9: 543–558.

Finkelstein, S., & Hambrick, D. C. 1996. ***Strategic leadership: Top executives and their effects on organizations.*** St. Paul: West.

Fischer, C. S. 1982. What do we mean by "friend"? An inductive study. ***Social Networks,*** 3: 287–306.

Fleiss, J. L. 1981. ***Statistical methods for rates and proportions.*** New York: Wiley.

Forsythe, J. B. 1977. Obtaining cooperation in a survey of business executives. ***Journal of Marketing Research,*** 14: 370–373.

Fowler, F. J. 1993. ***Survey research methods.*** Newbury Park, CA: Sage.

Fredrickson, J. W., Hambrick, D. C., & Baumrin, S. 1988. A model of CEO dismissal. ***Academy of Management Review,*** 13: 255–270.

Gabarro, J. G. 1985. When a new manager takes charge. ***Harvard Business Review,*** 63(3): 110–123.

Gibbs, P. A. 1993. Determinants of corporate restructuring: The relative importance of corporate governance, takeover threat, and free cash flow. ***Strategic Management Journal,*** 14: 51–68.

Gomez-Mejia, L. R., & Balkin, D. B. 1992. Determinants of faculty pay: An agency theory perspective. ***Academy of Management Journal,*** 35: 921–955.

Gomez-Mejia, L. R., & Wiseman, R. M. 1997. Reframing executive compensation: An assessment and outlook. ***Journal of Management,*** 23: 291–374.

Groves, R. M., Cialdini, R. B., & Couper, M. P. 1992. Understanding the decision to participate in a survey. ***Public Opinion Quarterly,*** 56: 475–495.

Guzzo, R. A., & Shea, G. P. 1992. Group performance and intergroup relations in organizations. In M. D. Dunnette & L. M. Hough (Eds.), ***Handbook of industrial and organizational psychology,*** vol. 3: 271–313. Palo Alto, CA: Consulting Psychologists Press.

Hackman, J. R. 1992. Group influences on individuals in organizations. In M. D. Dunnette & L. M. Hough (Eds.), ***Handbook of industrial and organizational psychology,*** vol. 3: 199–267. Palo Alto, CA: Consulting Psychologists Press.

Hannan, M. T., & Freeman, J. 1989. ***Organizational ecology.*** Cambridge, MA: Harvard University Press.

Harman, H. H. 1976. ***Modern factor analysis*** (3rd ed.). Chicago: University of Chicago Press.

Haveman, H. A. 1992. Between a rock and a hard place: Organizational change and performance under conditions of fundamental environmental transformation. ***Administrative Science Quarterly,*** 37: 48–75.

Hermalin, B. E., & Weisbach, M. S. 1988. The determinants of board composition. ***Rand Journal of Economics,*** 19: 589–606.

Hill, C. W. L., & Hansen, G. 1991. A longitudinal study of the causes and consequences of changes in diversification in the U.S. pharmaceutical industry 1977–1986. ***Strategic Management Journal,*** 12: 187–199.

Herman, E. S. 1981. ***Corporate control, corporate power.*** New York: Cambridge University Press.

Hirsch, P. M., Michaels, S., & Friedman, R. 1987. "Dirty hands" versus "clean models": Is sociology in danger of being seduced by economics? ***Theory and Society,*** 16: 317–336.

Jaccard, J., Turrisi, R., & Wan, C. K. 1990. ***Interaction effects in multiple regression.*** Newbury Park, CA Sage.

Janis, I. L. 1982. ***Victims of groupthink.*** Boston: Houghton Mifflin.

Jarrell, G. A. 1993. An overview of the executive compensation debate. ***Journal of Applied Corporate Finance,*** 5(1): 76–82.

Jehn, K. A., & Shah, P. P. 1996. ***Interpersonal relationships and task performance: An examination of mediating processes in friendship and acquaintance groups.*** Paper presented at the annual meeting of the Academy of Management, Cincinnati.

Jehn, K. A., & Shah, P. P. 1997. ***Interpersonal relationships and task performance: An examination of mediating processes in friendship and acquaintance groups.*** Working paper, University of Pennsylvania.

Jensen, M. C., & Meckling, W. H. 1976. Theory of the firm: Managerial behavior, agency costs, and ownership structure. ***Journal of Financial Economics,*** 3: 305–350.

Jensen, M. C., & Murphy, K. J. 1990. Performance pay and top-management incentives. ***Journal of Political Economy,*** 98: 225–263.

Johnson, J. L., Daily, C. M., & Ellstrand A. E. 1996. Boards of directors: A review and research agenda. ***Journal of Management,*** 22: 409–438.

Johnson, R. A., Hoskisson, R. E., & Hitt, M. A. 1993. Board of director involvement in restructuring: The effects of board versus managerial controls and characteristics. ***Strategic Management Journal,*** 14 (special issue): 33–50.

Johnston, J. 1984. ***Econometric methods.*** New York: McGraw Hill.

Judge, W. Q., Jr., & Dobbins, G. H. 1995. Antecedents and effects of outside director's awareness of CEO decision style. ***Journal of Management,*** 21: 43–64.

Judge, W. Q., Jr., & Zeithaml, C. P. 1992. Institutional and strategic choice perspectives on board involvement in the strategic decision process. ***Academy of Management Journal,*** 35: 766–794.

Kimberly, J., & Zajac, E. J. 1988. The dynamics of CEO-board relationships. In D. C. Hambrick (Ed.), ***The executive effect: Concepts and methods for studying top managers:*** 179–204. Greenwich, CT: JAI Press.

Kochhar, R., & David, P. 1996. Institutional investors and firm innovation: A test of competing hypotheses. ***Strategic Management Journal,*** 17: 73–84.

Kosnik, R. D. 1987. Greenmail: A study of board performance in corporate governance. ***Administrative Science Quarterly,*** 32: 163–185.

Kosnik, R. D. 1990. Effects of board demography and directors' incentives on corporate greenmail decisions. ***Academy of Management Journal,*** 33: 129–150.

Krackhardt, D. 1992. The strength of strong ties: The importance of philos in organizations. In N. Nohria & R. G. Eccles (Eds.), ***Networks and organizations: Structure, form, and action:*** 216–239. Boston: Harvard Business School Press.

Lambert, R. A., Larcker, D. F., & Weigelt, K. 1993. The structure of organizational incentives. ***Administrative Science Quarterly,*** 38: 438–461.

Larcker, D. F. 1983. The association between performance plan adoption and corporate capital investment. ***Journal of Accounting and Economics,*** 5: 3–30.

Locke, E. A., Shaw, K. N., Saari, L. M., & Latham, G. P. 1981. Goal setting and task performance: 1969–1980. ***Psychological Bulletin,*** 90: 125–152.

Lorsch, J. W. 1989. ***Pawns or potentates: The reality of America's corporate boards.*** Boston: Harvard Business School Press.

Mace, M. L. 1986. ***Directors: Myth and reality*** (2nd ed.). Boston: Harvard Business School Press.

Main, B. G. M., O'Reilly, C. A. III, & Wade, J. 1995. The CEO, the board of directors and executive compensation: Economic and psychological perspectives. ***Industrial and Corporate Change,*** 4: 293–332.

Mallette, P., & Fowler, K. L. 1992. Effects of board composition and stock ownership on the adoption of "poison pills." ***Academy of Management Journal,*** 35: 1010–1035.

Mayer, R. C., Davis, J. H., & Schoorman, F. D. 1995. An integrative model of organizational trust. ***Academy of Management Review,*** 20: 709–734.

Meyer, J. W., & Rowan, B. 1977. Institutional organizations: Formal structure as myth and ceremony. ***American Journal of Sociology,*** 83: 340–363.

Mizruchi, M. S. 1996. What do interlocks do? An analysis, critique, and assessment of research on interlocking directorates. In ***Annual review of sociology,*** vol. 22: 271–298. Palo Alto, CA: Annual Reviews.

Nunnally, J. C. 1978. ***Psychometric theory.*** New York: McGraw Hill.

Pearce, J. A., & Zahra, S. A. 1991. The relative power of CEOs and boards of directors: Associations with corporate performance. ***Strategic Management Journal,*** 12: 135–153.

Pfeffer, J., & Salancik, G. R. 1978. ***The external control of organizations.*** New York: Harper & Row.

Rechner, P. L., & Dalton, D. R. 1991. CEO duality and organizational performance: A longitudinal analysis. ***Strategic Management Journal,*** 12: 155–160.

Rediker, K., & Seth, A. 1995. Boards of directors and substitution effects of alternative governance mechanisms. ***Strategic Management Journal,*** 16: 85–100.

Roberts, K. H., & O'Reilly, C. A. 1974. Failures in upward communication in organizations: Three possible culprits. ***Academy of Management Journal,*** 17: 205–215.

Rosen, S. 1983. Perceived inadequacy and help-seeking. In B. DePaulo, A. Nadler, & J. Fisher (Eds.), ***New directions in helping,*** vol. 2: 3–12. New York: Academic Press.

Schachter, S., Ellerston, N., McBride, D., & Gregory, D. 1951. An experimental study of cohesiveness and productivity. ***Human Relations,*** 4: 229–238.

Seashore, S. E. 1954. ***Group cohesiveness in the industrial work group.*** Ann Arbor: University of Michigan Press.

Segal, M. W. 1979. Varieties of interpersonal attraction and their interrelationships in natural groups. ***Social Psychology Quarterly,*** 42: 253–261.

Shah, P. P., & Jehn, K. A. 1993. Do friends perform better than acquaintances? The interaction of friendship, conflict, and task. ***Group Decision and Negotiation,*** 2: 149–165.

Siegel, S., & Castellan, N. J., Jr. 1988. ***Nonparametric statistics for the behavioral sciences*** (2nd ed.). New York: McGraw-Hill.

Silver, A. 1990. Friendship in commercial society: Eighteenth-century social theory and modern sociology. ***American Journal of Sociology,*** 95: 1474–1504.

Spencer, A. 1983. ***On the edge of the organization.*** New York: Wiley.

Sundaramurthy, C. 1996. Corporate governance within the context of antitakeover provisions. ***Strategic Management Journal,*** 17: 377–394.

Tetlock, P. E., Peterson, R. S., McGuire, C., Chang, S., & Feld, P. 1992. Assessing political group dynamics: A test of the groupthink model. ***Journal of Personality and Social Psychology,*** 63: 403–425.

Tosi, H. L., & Gomez-Mejia, L. R. 1989. The decoupling of CEO pay and performance: An agency theory perspective. ***Administrative Science Quarterly,*** 34: 169–189.

Wade, J. B., O'Reilly, C. A., & Chandratat, I. 1990. Golden parachutes: CEOs and the exercise of social influence. ***Administrative Science Quarterly,*** 35: 587–603.

Wahal, S. 1996. Pension fund activism and firm performance. ***Journal of Financial and Quantitative Analysis,*** 31: 1–23.

Wall Street Journal. 1993. Less-than-watchful eyes didn't oversee expenses of a utility's chairman. June 6: B1.

Wall Street Journal. 1995. How do you fire a CEO? Very, very slowly. January 20: B1.

Wall Street Journal. 1996. Beware of the Trojan horse in the boardroom. March 7: B1.

Walsh, J. P., & Seward, J. K. 1990. On the efficiency of internal and external corporate control mechanisms. ***Academy of Management Review,*** 15: 421–458.

Westphal, J. D., & Zajac, E. J. 1994. Substance and symbolism in CEOs' long-term incentive plans. ***Administrative Science Quarterly,*** 39: 367–390.

Westphal, J. D., & Zajac, E. J. 1995. Who shall govern? CEO/board power, demographic similarity, and new director selection. ***Administrative Science Quarterly,*** 40: 60–83.

Westphal, J. D., & Zajac, E. J. 1998. The symbolic management of stockholders: Corporate governance reforms and shareholder reactions. ***Administrative Science Quarterly,*** 43: 127–153.

Whisler, T. L. 1984. ***The rules of the game: Inside the corporate board room.*** Homewood, IL: Dow Jones-Irwin.

Wiersema, M. F., & Bantel, K. A. 1992. Top management team demography and corporate strategic change. ***Academy of Management Journal,*** 35: 91–121.

Zahra, S. A., & Pearce, J. A. 1989. Boards of directors and corporate financial performance: A review and integrative model. ***Journal of Management,*** 15: 291–334.

Zajac, E. J., & Shortell, S. M. 1989. Changing generic strategies: Likelihood, direction, and performance implications. ***Strategic Management Journal,*** 10: 413–430.

Zajac, E. J., & Westphal, J. D. 1994. The costs and benefits of incentives and monitoring in the largest U.S. corporations: When is more not better? ***Strategic Management Journal,*** 15 (special issue): 121–142.

Zajac, E. J., & Westphal, J. D. 1995. Accounting for the explanations of CEO compensation: Substance and symbolism. ***Administrative Science Quarterly,*** 40: 283–308.

Zand, D. E. 1972. Trust and managerial problem solving. ***Administrative Science Quarterly,*** 17: 229–240

APPENDIX A

Survey Scales

Possible responses for the board monitoring and advice and counsel items were 1, "minimally"; 2; 3, "moderately"; 4; and 5, "very much so."

Board Monitoring

1. To what extent does the board monitor top management strategic decision making?
2. To what extent does the board formally evaluate your performance?
3. To what extent does the board defer to your judgment on final strategic decisions?

Advice and Counsel Interactions

1. To what extent do you solicit board assistance in the formulation of corporate strategy?
2. To what extent are outside directors a "sounding board" on strategic issues?
3. How often have directors provided advice and counsel in discussions outside of board/committee meetings (by telephone *or* in person)? ______ Times

Friendship Ties

How many of the *outside* directors would you consider to be acquaintances or friends?
Acquaintances but not friends: ______ (number of directors).
Friends: ______ (number of directors).

APPENDIX B

Results of Supplementary OLS Regression Model[a]

Independent Variable	Advice and Counsel Interactions
1. CEO-board friendship ties	0.36 (0.15)**
2. Portion of board appointed after CEO	0.42 (0.20)*
3. Prior return on equity	−0.83 (0.43)
4. Prior market-to-book value of equity	−0.03 (0.05)
5. Sales[b]	−0.05 (0.03)
6. CEO ownership	0.55 (0.57)
7. Long-term incentive plan compensation	0.24 (0.19)
8. Director ownership	1.20 (0.88)
9. Blockholder ownership	0.08 (0.22)
10. Institutional ownership	0.16 (0.28)
11. CEO tenure	−0.01 (0.01)
12. Affiliated directors: Family ties	0.58 (0.50)
13. Affiliated directors: Business ties	0.51 (0.24)*
14. Director expertise and experience	0.10 (0.05)
15. Director expertise and experience × friendship ties	0.44 (0.15)**
16. Director expertise and experience × appointments after CEO	0.51 (0.21)*
17. Constant	−0.06 (0.30)
F	7.65***
R^2	.27

[a] $N = 243$. Standard errors are in parentheses.
[b] Logarithm.
* $p \leq .05$
** $p \leq .01$
*** $p \leq .001$

James D. Westphal is an assistant professor of management in the Graduate School of Business at the University of Texas at Austin. He received his Ph.D. from Northwestern University. His current research interests include boards of directors and executive compensation, with a focus on social processes in corporate governance.

[18]

The Influence of Top Management Team Heterogeneity on Firms' Competitive Moves

Donald C. Hambrick, Theresa S. Cho, and Ming-Jer Chen
Columbia University

This paper explores the executive origins of firms' competitive moves by focusing on top management team characteristics, specifically on team heterogeneity, rather than on the more often studied environmental and organizational determinants of such behaviors. Arguing that competitive actions and responses represent different decision situations, we develop propositions about how heterogeneity may enhance some competitive behaviors but impair others. With a large sample of actions and responses of 32 U.S. airlines over eight years, we find results that largely conform to our propositions. The top management teams that were diverse, in terms of functional backgrounds, education, and company tenure, exhibited a relatively great propensity for action, and both their actions and responses were of substantial magnitude. Heterogeneous teams, by contrast, were slower in their actions and responses and less likely than homogeneous teams to respond to competitors' initiatives. Thus, although team heterogeneity is a double-edged sword, its overall net effect on airline performance, in terms of changes in market share and profits, was positive.•

In recent years, strategy researchers have directed attention to the specific moves and countermoves made by rivals within industries (e.g., Chen and MacMillan, 1992; Smith, Grimm, and Gannon, 1992), recognizing that organizational vitality may depend more on the quantity, quality, and speed of a firm's and its adversaries' on-going actions and responses in the competitive arena than on the traditional concept of sustainable advantage (D'Aveni, 1994). Studies have shown some important effects of firms' competitive behaviors on company performance, indicating, for instance, that quick responders gain market share at the expense of slow responders (Chen and MacMillan, 1992). Research also has shed light on the determinants, or antecedents, of firms' competitive action and response tendencies. For example, Chen and Hambrick (1995) demonstrated that small and large firms differ markedly in their competitive behaviors; for example, small firms were shown to be more active and faster in initiating competitive challenges than large firms.

This paper, like Chen and Hambrick (1995), is one of a series of studies drawn from an extensive and progressively developed database that represents a comprehensive longitudinal study of domestic airline competition during the 1980s. In contrast to previous strategy research, which had tended to infer competition from more static and aggregate firm attributes or from structural properties of the industry, this program of research has examined some fundamental competitive issues through the systematic analysis of concrete, tangible market-oriented actions taken by firms. The research program falls into three distinct but highly related streams. The first stream, focusing on competitive dynamics or the action/response dyad, has shown that competitive response can be predicted by the attributes of the attack, the attacker, and the defender (Chen and MacMillan, 1992; Chen, Smith, and Grimm, 1992; Miller and Chen, 1994). The second stream, of which the present study is a part, has investigated strategic competitive behavior at the firm level—its human and organizational origins as well as performance

0001-8392/96/4104-0659/$1.00.

•
The authors acknowledge support from Columbia University's Management Institute. Warren Boeker, Sara Keck, John Michel, Peter Murmann, Michael Tushman, and Ruth Wageman made helpful suggestions on earlier drafts. We are grateful for access to the airline data base jointly assembled by the third author, Martin J. Gannon, Curtis M. Grimm, and Ken G. Smith.

implications (Smith et al., 1991; Chen and Hambrick, 1995). The third stream, conceptualizing a firm's strategy as the entire repertoire of its competitive moves, has examined the antecedents and performance implications of competitive inertia (Miller and Chen, 1994), simplicity of competitive moves (Miller and Chen, 1996a), and nonconformity in competitive repertoires (Miller and Chen, 1996b).

The cumulative goal of this research program has been to develop a coherent predictive theory of competitive behavior, which has so far been lacking in the field of strategic management. Such a theory should ultimately be more reliable if it is based on a common set of empirical observations. This research approach, akin to the PIMS studies (e.g., Hambrick, MacMillan, and Day, 1982) and the Aston studies (e.g., Pugh and Hickson, 1972), is somewhat unusual in the field of strategic management but should be an effective and efficient way to accumulate knowledge in this field. The multiple studies—warranted because of the scale, detail, and evidences of reliability of the data set—have been complementary, yielding integrated insights into the complex topic of competitive dynamics.

This stream of research is still embryonic, however, and far more needs to be known. In particular, theorists of competitive dynamics can benefit, we believe, by expanding their attention from environmental and organizational determinants of behavior to include the characteristics of the decision makers, in particular the company's top management team. Such an upper-echelons approach (Hambrick and Mason, 1984) would acknowledge that human and social biases, filters, and idiosyncratic processes at the top of the organization substantially influence competitive behaviors. This line of thought has been consistently supported in examinations of a wide array of organizational outcomes (summarized in Hambrick, 1994), but with limited exceptions (Smith et al., 1991), it has not yet been considered as a way to improve explanations of microcompetitive action and response behaviors.

Taking the upper-echelons perspective, this paper examines the effects of top management team heterogeneity on firms' competitive behaviors and ensuing organizational performance. We expected that heterogeneity, a central construct in the literature on top management, would be important in competitive decision making, conferring breadth of perspective, on one hand, but with the potential for team dissensus and inefficiency, on the other hand (Jackson, 1992). With a large sample of specific competitive actions and responses of 32 U.S. airlines over eight years, we examine the associations between team heterogeneity and (a) the firm's propensity to act, the magnitude of these actions, and the speed with which they are executed, and (b) the firm's propensity to respond to adversaries' actions, the magnitudes of responses, and the speed of responses.

BACKGROUND

Competitive Behaviors

Contrary to a model of sustainable advantage, Schumpeter and other theorists of the Austrian school (Jacobson, 1992) contended that competition is fluid and that a firm advances by continually taking action and responding to the actions of its adversaries. One stream of strategy research has adopted this framework by focusing on the microcompetitive behaviors of firms and the determinants and consequences of those moves. In this view, firm performance can be seen as an outcome of a series of competitive actions that may be rapidly nullified by opponents' incessant competitive challenges (D'Aveni, 1994).

Because of the importance of competitive behaviors to overall firm strategy and performance, an understanding of the determinants, or influencers, of those behaviors is essential. Several studies have already contributed to this understanding. MacMillan, McCaffery, and Van Wijk (1985) showed that competitors' response times to new products were a function of whether the products had major organizational significance for these firms. And a series of studies, using some of the same airline data we are using, has revealed additional determinants of competitive behaviors. First, using the action/response dyad as its analytical level, research has demonstrated that competitive response (likelihood, timing, etc.) can be predicted by the attributes of the actions (Chen, Smith, and Grimm, 1992; Miller and Chen, 1994) as well as those of the initiators and of the defenders (Chen and MacMillan, 1992). Second, distilling the properties of a firm's actions and responses to capture its competitive behavior at the firm level, research has further shown the significance of such behavioral antecedents as firm size (Chen and Hambrick, 1995), information-processing capacity (Smith et al., 1991), and market growth (Miller and Chen, 1994).

The research to date has focused almost solely on environmental and organizational explanations for competitive behaviors. Except for Smith et al. (1991), whose study of the impact of top management teams' educational and industry experience focused exclusively on competitive responses, no attention has been paid to the decision makers behind the observed market behaviors. Because research focusing on top management team characteristics has greatly aided understanding of other organizational phenomena (e.g., Bantel and Jackson, 1989; Finkelstein and Hambrick, 1990), we believe such a focus will also increase our understanding of competitive behaviors of firms, which represent instances of specific decisions or bounded sets of decisions in rivalrous arenas. Attention to decision makers can provide an important new vantage for researchers of competitive interaction, with possibly important theoretical and practical implications. Thus, with newly collected information about top executive characteristics added to the database of competitive interactions used in the prior studies, the current research delves into the largely unexplored terrain of the human origins of competitive decision making and behavior.

Although other characteristics of top management teams might also fruitfully be examined, we restrict our theoretical focus here to heterogeneity, first, to elaborate on the complex effects of this important construct and, second, because the fundamental differences between a firm's competitive actions and its responses to competitors' actions provide a unique arena for studying the potentially divergent effects of heterogeneity and possibly understanding conflicting results in the literature on top management teams.

Heterogeneity of Top Management Teams

Theoretical interest in top management teams can be traced to March and Simon's behavioral theory of the firm (March and Simon, 1958; Cyert and March, 1963). According to this theory, decision makers are often unable to make economically rational decisions because they are boundedly rational and must act in a social context of multiple and conflicting goals. Hambrick and Mason (1984) extended these ideas in their upper-echelons perspective. In their view, (1) the organization becomes a reflection of its top executives, and (2) the characteristics and functioning of the top management team have far greater potential for predicting organizational outcomes than do the characteristics of the chief executive officer (CEO).

Numerous studies over the last ten years have found significant associations between the demographic composition of the top management team and organizational characteristics. Studies have documented the tendency for young, short-tenure, highly educated teams to be relatively innovative, even after controlling for the type of industry (Bantel and Jackson, 1989; O'Reilly and Flatt, 1989). Organizational tenure of top management team members was found to be strongly associated with strategic persistence, or absence of change (Finkelstein and Hambrick, 1990; Grimm and Smith, 1991; Wiersema and Bantel, 1992). Other studies have found organizational effects arising from the mix of functional backgrounds (e.g., Thomas, Litschert, and Ramaswamy, 1991), industry experience (Eisenhardt and Schoonhoven, 1990), and turnover of top management teams (Virany, Tushman, and Romanelli, 1992). Moreover, top management team characteristics consistently predict organizational outcomes better than do CEOs' characteristics alone (summarized in Hambrick, 1994). Scholars of top teams have become particularly interested in the effects of the team's heterogeneity, the variation in team members' characteristics, which has been called a theoretical fulcrum for research on groups and top management teams (Jackson, 1992).

Although many investigations have been conducted on the effects of heterogeneity in groups in general (reviewed by Jackson, 1992) and several on top management teams in particular (reviewed by Hambrick, 1994), the conclusions have been contradictory. Beneficial effects have been observed in some studies. Bantel and Jackson (1989) found that top management team heterogeneity in educational level and functional background was positively associated with innovativeness in a large sample of banks. Eisenhardt and Schoonhoven (1990) showed that growth rates of semiconductor companies were positively related to the top team's heterogeneity in industry tenure. The imputed logic for these positive effects has been the same as originally proposed by Hoffman and Maier (1961): diversity enhances the breadth of perspective, cognitive resources, and overall problem-solving capacity of the group.

Team Heterogeneity

Other studies have found negative effects from top team heterogeneity. O'Reilly and Flatt (1989) showed that company innovation was negatively related to team heterogeneity in firm tenure in a wide cross section of firms. O'Reilly, Snyder, and Boothe (1993) similarly found that team heterogeneity in firm tenure was negatively related to adaptive change in a sample of electronics firms. Although heterogeneity may provide wider cognitive resources, it may also create gulfs or schisms that make the exchange of information difficult (Ancona and Caldwell, 1992). In some instances, heterogeneity may engender outright distrust and acrimony, as widely dissimilar group members may have different vocabularies, paradigms, and even objectives. Thus their aggregate cognitive endowment can become a net liability, with organizational innovation and performance suffering. Further supporting this latter logic, Wagner, Pfeffer, and O'Reilly (1984) found that heterogeneity in firm tenure was associated with higher turnover in top management teams, and the more distant an individual executive was from the average of the other group members, the more likely he or she was to depart. Jackson et al. (1991) obtained the same result in a sample of banks, further suggesting that demographic diversity may lessen the social integration of the top team. Measuring top team processes more directly, O'Reilly, Snyder, and Boothe (1993) found that heterogeneity in tenure was negatively associated with a multi-item measure of team rapport. Similarly, Smith et al. (1994) found that heterogeneity in tenure was negatively associated with informal communication within the team but had no association with social integration or communication frequency. Their study thus illustrates the potentially complex implications of top team heterogeneity.

Direct psychological measures of heterogeneity, although often used in research on work groups (e.g., Hoffman and Maier, 1961), are very difficult to obtain for senior executives in major firms and are unavailable for past, disbanded top management teams. Thus, in line with almost all prior research on top management team heterogeneity, we rely on demographic conceptions of the group, according to which the executives' functional backgrounds, educational experiences, and firm tenures serve as proxies for their perspectives, beliefs systems, and networks and affiliations (Jackson, 1992; Hambrick, 1994).

While distinctions might be drawn between different types of demographic heterogeneity, no established theory for doing so presents itself. Jackson (1992) noted the need to distinguish between different types of heterogeneity, drawing a distinction between heterogeneity of "personal attributes" (e.g., race, gender, and personality) and "task-related attributes" (the specific skills and abilities needed to perform the job). This is a promising line of thought but may have limited application for most research on top management teams, since the major dimensions for describing team members reflect a combination of skill-based and personal attributes. For instance, an executive's primary functional background reflects his or her domain of professional expertise, but it may also greatly reflect the person's personality, cognitive style, values, and other factors. The same could be said for educational background and tenure.

We expect each of the three forms of demographic heterogeneity we examine to contribute independently to dispersion in the group's perspective and that each will tap an amalgam of differences in professional orientations, values, cognitive styles, business and life experiences, and networks (Jackson, 1992). Although the three dimensions are common in prior research on top team heterogeneity, they have not heretofore been examined simultaneously.

Heterogeneity and Competitive Behaviors

A firm's competitive behaviors consist of its moves and countermoves, or its actions and responses to adversaries' actions. Each move represents an instance of a decision, or a bounded set of decisions, in which multiple senior executives are typically involved. This is not to say that every competitive move involves all members of the top management group. A decision about a geographic expansion may involve all the firm's senior executives, whereas a decision about a new sales force structure may involve only a subset of the top team. But even in decisions involving only a part of the firm, a number of executives would likely have input to the decision, especially in single-business firms like airlines, in which the activities of the senior-most executives are highly interdependent. Thus, even though some of the top groups we studied may not have had all the qualities needed to be called "teams," as discussed by Hambrick (1994), their members can be expected to interact, negotiate, and influence each other extensively, a conception that is in line with prior upper-echelons research.

The top team can thus be considered as the aggregate informational and decisional entity through which competitive moves are made. These moves depend on the team's scanning of the environment; recognizing problems and opportunities and interpreting other external stimuli; developing potential moves; negotiating, refining, and selecting moves; and implementing decisions (Mintzberg, Raisinghani, and Théorêt, 1976; Fredrickson and Iaquinto, 1989). Because top management team heterogeneity can be expected to influence these internal processes in ways that substantially affect competitive behaviors, we examine the relationships between top management team heterogeneity and three major dimensions of a firm's actions and responses: (1) its competitive propensity, or its relative tendency to undertake actions and respond to competitors' actions, (2) the competitive magnitude, or the relative scale and significance of the firm's actions and responses, and (3) competitive speed, or how quickly the firm implements its actions and responds to others' actions. In doing this, we distinguish between actions and responses as qualitatively different types of decision situations that are affected in different ways by top management team heterogeneity.

Competitive actions as creative initiatives. To undertake a competitive action, not directly prompted by an adversary's prior move, a firm must initiate and invent to "create" the move (MacMillan, 1982). Some actions are unequivocally novel, such as American Airlines' initial frequent-flyer program. Other competitive actions, such as expanding into new geographic markets, are less innovative but are still acts of initiative. In the context of competitive interplay, actions—compared with responses—can be considered creative initiatives. It is in creative, unstructured tasks that top management team heterogeneity is expected to have its most positive effects (Jackson, 1992). A diverse team has broader cognitive resources, encompassing a wider field of vision and more extensive external contacts, than does a homogeneous team (Hoffman and Maier, 1961; Jackson, 1992). With multifaceted backgrounds and orientations, heterogeneous top management team members can observe more opportunities, threats, and overall stimuli on multiple fronts and thus have a broader potential repertoire for generating actions.

At the same time, because of its diversity, the heterogeneous team may experience internal conflict and strains, which could result in slow decisions. It might further be expected that the conflict that often accompanies diversity would impair the firm's ability to launch actions at all. Overall, however, the heterogeneous team has access to such wide-ranging stimuli and has such a broad potential repertoire that its ability to conceive and launch actions on many fronts should outweigh the dampening effects of internal strains. Undertaking competitive actions is foremost a function of being able to create, or generate, those actions, particularly in very turbulent industries like the airline industry that lack clear models of competitive behavior. The top management team's ability to agree on certain actions, while not unimportant, is a secondary determinant of the firm's action propensity. Therefore, compared with homogeneous teams, which have relatively restricted, redundant scanning and action-design capabilities, the heterogeneous team can be expected to engage in quantitatively more actions than homogeneous teams. Thus, we propose:

Proposition 1: Top management team heterogeneity is positively related to the firm's action propensity.

The magnitude, or significance, of an action is also important. Some moves are relatively substantial in scale and boldness, while others are incremental and routine (MacMillan, McCafferey, and Van Wijk, 1985). The magnitude of an action can be characterized by its strategic significance, its noteworthiness, and its scope. The strategic significance of a firm's actions can be gauged by the firm's relative use of strategic rather than tactical initiatives. Strategic moves involve large outlays, long time-horizons, great departures from the status quo, and are difficult to reverse (Ghemawat, 1991; Chen, Smith, and Grimm, 1992). Tactical moves, such as price changes and sales force redeployments, tend to be incremental and limited in their implications. Competitive actions similarly vary in their noteworthiness, or the amount of attention they receive from industry observers and analysts (Porter, 1980; Chen and Hambrick, 1995). Some moves receive a great deal of attention in an industry, often because they are radical, creative, or complex, while others receive bare mention, often because they are conventional, limited, and predictable. Finally, a firm's actions can be considered in terms of their scope, or the extent of the firm's operations that are affected by the moves (Chen and MacMillan, 1992). Initiatives taken only in one product line or one region are relatively narrow in scope, while others affect the company's full range of operations, all of its products and markets (Porter, 1980). We expect that these three elements of competitive magnitude—strategic significance, noteworthiness, and scope—will reflect the firm's degree of boldness and, indirectly, innovation in its competitive initiatives. The firm that undertakes strategic and highly noteworthy moves of broad scope is behaving differently from a firm that takes primarily tactical, little-noted, and narrowly restricted moves.

We expect top management team heterogeneity to contribute substantially to these differences. As a source of broad cognitive resources, team heterogeneity has long been thought to enhance creativity and innovation (Hoffman and Maier, 1961; Bantel and Jackson, 1989; Jackson, 1992). Marketing innovations, such as American Airlines' introduction of a frequent-flyer program in the early 1980s, have been attributed to top management team diversity (Labich, 1990). Chaganti and Sambharya (1987) similarly observed an association between the functional diversity of top management teams in tobacco companies and strategic adaptation. With a broad array of information and experience, diverse teams can generate a wider range of options that synergistically combine the members' orientations while avoiding groupthink and behavioral inertia (Janis, 1972; Hambrick, 1994). Thus, we propose the following:

Proposition 2a: Top management team heterogeneity is positively related to the strategic significance of the firm's actions.

Proposition 2b: Top management team heterogeneity is positively related to the noteworthiness of the firm's actions.

Proposition 2c: Top management team heterogeneity is positively related to the scope of the firm's actions.

The speed of organizational moves has also received increasing attention (Smith and Grimm, 1991; D'Aveni, 1994), because the firm's speed in making its moves allows it to achieve early advantages in its initiatives, often putting its competition on the defensive (Stalk, 1988; Eisenhardt, 1989). Although we expect top management team heterogeneity to have positive effects on action propensity and magnitude, we expect that it will slow an organization's speed in executing its actions. Communications and decision making in a heterogeneous team are cumbersome because of the disparate perspectives and vocabularies (O'Reilly, Caldwell, and Barnett, 1989). Heterogeneity can even be a source of outright information blockage and conflict (Zenger and Lawrence, 1989; O'Reilly, Snyder, and Boothe, 1993). At a minimum, the wide-ranging information and opinions available in a heterogeneous team require time to process (Jackson, 1992). In contrast, the homogeneous top management team may take fewer actions, but when it does—when potential actions fall within the team's field of vision, preferences, and repertoire—it can act very quickly. We particularly expect that top management team heterogeneity will affect the amount of time taken to implement an action:

Proposition 3: Top management team heterogeneity is negatively related to the firm's action execution speed.

Overall, then, we expect the diverse, abundant cognitive resources of heterogeneous top management teams to be manifested in a propensity to launch competitive actions with relatively great magnitude, but not quickly. Conversely, homogeneous top management teams will undertake fewer, less substantial, but faster actions than heterogeneous teams. It is also possible that heterogeneity would increase the amount of time required to formulate an action, but we do not have data to test this idea.

Competitive responses as induced counterplay. Compared with launching initial actions, responding to an adversary's act does not require as much ability to scan broadly and create wide-ranging alternatives. When the adversary has taken an action, providing a distinct and usually obvious stimulus, the primary question becomes, "Should we respond?" For two reasons, we expect management team heterogeneity to have negligible effects in determining the firm's tendency to respond. First, the stimuli are relatively clear. Drawing on Mischel's (1968) concept of "situational strength," when the situation is "weak"—complex, ambiguous, and open to many interpretations—the characteristics of the actor greatly affect his or her behavior, just as top management team heterogeneity is expected to affect taking action. But when the situation is "strong"—unambiguous, with few and clear-cut stimuli—as in responding to a competitor, then the stimuli prevail in determining behavior. Even though there are instances of secretive competitive actions (Prescott and Smith, 1987), in an industry with an active business press and strong trade associations, competitors' actions can be assumed to be universally known to all top teams. Because the stimuli are generally unambiguous and overt, then, a firm's tendency to respond will be more a function of its resources and other characteristics (Smith et al., 1991) than of the cognitive limits and biases of the top management team.

Second, top management team heterogeneity will have little effect on a firm's propensity to respond because there is little need to create. The adversary's action provides a template, minimizing the degree to which responding requires idiosyncratic design capabilities. In its action, the initiator has already handed the potential responder a possible response. Even a homogeneous top management team, with limited cognitive breadth and repertoire, can, at a minimum, often simply imitate the action. Thus, we propose:

Proposition 4: Top management team heterogeneity is unrelated to the firm's response propensity.

We see a qualitative difference between the decision to respond and the characteristics of the response itself. Although situational strength may prevail in a firm's decision to respond, once the decision has been made, we expect top management team characteristics to affect the design and execution of the particular response. Heterogeneous top management teams should draw on their broader cognitive resources in designing more significant, bolder responses than homogeneous teams, who could be expected to undertake more incremental, measured, and conventional responses—perhaps simply imitating the action—reflecting the group's narrow and redundant cognitive endowment. Thus, we expect heterogeneous top management teams to engage in relatively high-magnitude responses. In assessing response magnitude, noteworthiness and scope are the important indicators. Significance, or the proportion of responses that are strategic rather than tactical, is not useful in the way it is for actions, because strategic actions tend to engender strategic responses, and tactical actions tend to engender tactical responses. Thus, we propose:

Proposition 5a: Top management team heterogeneity is positively related to the noteworthiness of the firm's responses.

Proposition 5b: Top management team heterogeneity is positively related to the scope of the firm's responses.

As with actions, responses by a heterogeneous team are likely to be slower than those of a homogeneous top management team. The design, negotiation, and elaboration of high-magnitude responses from heterogeneous teams take time. Added to the time such teams lose as a result of diversity and considering different points of view is the time that accrues strictly because the team often opts to design a special response from its wide-ranging cognitive resources rather than to counter with a narrow, marginal, or imitative response. In this study, we focus on two dimensions of response speed: response generation speed, or the time taken to formulate and announce a response to a competitor's action; and response execution speed, or the amount of time taken to implement an announced response. We propose:

Proposition 6a: Top management team heterogeneity is negatively related to the firm's response generation speed.

Proposition 6b: Top management team heterogeneity is negatively related to the firm's response execution speed.

Thus, we expect heterogeneity to exert the same effects on responses taken as on actions, increasing their magnitude but slowing their development and execution. In contrast to prior studies that have sought primarily to determine the overall advantages or disadvantages of top management team heterogeneity, we argue that heterogeneity may benefit some particular behavioral outcomes but impair others. The next question is whether the benefits outweigh the costs.

Heterogeneity and Organizational Performance

Researchers have found inconsistent evidence about the effects of top management team heterogeneity on organizational performance: positive effects (Eisenhardt and Schoonhoven, 1990), negative effects (Murray, 1989), and no effects (Michel and Hambrick, 1992). It is clear from our own propositions that heterogeneity may be a double-edged sword. On the one hand, we expect heterogeneity to enhance a firm's action propensity and its action and response magnitudes, potentially benefiting company performance (Chen and MacMillan, 1992). On the other hand we expect heterogeneity to reduce the firm's speed, both in acting and responding, possibly leading to lower performance (Eisenhardt, 1989; Chen and MacMillan, 1992).

Some theorists have incorporated contingency factors as potential moderators of the heterogeneity-performance link Jackson (1992), following Steiner (1972), proposed that heterogeneity has benefits for unstructured, novel tasks, but homogeneity is better for routine tasks. Another distinction, drawn by Hambrick and Mason (1984), was between stable and turbulent environments. In their view, heterogeneity yields benefits in turbulent environments; homogeneity is beneficial in stable environments. The U.S. airline industry in the period immediately following deregulation experienced exactly the conditions under which these theorists expect top management team heterogeneity to be advantageous. There was a high level of uncertainty and turbulence, no clear role models to be imitated, and extremely rivalrous conditions (Levine, 1987). Breadth of perspective, creativity, and a willingness to undertake unprecedented action were required under these conditions, and a heterogeneous top management should have been able to meet those needs. Thus, we propose:

Proposition 7: Top management team heterogeneity is positively related to overall performance improvements in a turbulent industry.

RESEARCH METHODS

Sample

Data were gathered from *Aviation Daily*, the major industry publication, on competitive moves by 32 major airlines, those noted by the Department of Transportation as having annual operating revenues of $100 million or more, for the post-deregulation years of 1979 to 1986.

Aviation Daily, a 50-year-old industry journal, offered complete and detailed information on airline competition. The journal aims at objectively reporting airlines' announcements and actions, which minimizes any concerns over post hoc rationalization of competitive moves and bias toward covering only certain airlines' activities. An extensive survey of 57 senior airline executives and industry experts (e.g., consultants and analysts) indicated that the respondents considered *Aviation Daily* comprehensive, accurate, and a significant source of information for the airlines themselves.

The method used in collecting the data was similar to Miller and Friesen's (1977), which has been labeled "structured content analysis" (Jauch, Osborn, and Martin, 1980). The methodology is unique in that competitive interactions of sample firms were directly identified from an extensive review of public information. A specially designed, structured coding schedule was used to perform the content analysis.

Dependent Variables

A competitive move has the potential effect of acquiring rivals' market shares or reducing their anticipated returns. To identify such moves, an extensive review of every issue of *Aviation Daily* was undertaken to discover all of the competitive moves in this industry, such as promotional activities or market expansions, as suggested by Levine (1987). To identify the actions that met with responses, a researcher then identified all entries in *Aviation Daily* that were responses by searching for the following key words: "in responding to," "following," "match," "under pressure of," or other words that indicated a move was a response to a competitor's action. The identification of responses was straightforward and involved little judgment.

Next, three researchers carefully traced streams of actions and responses back to the initial action. First, the researchers read all *Aviation Daily* issues in chronological order to find all competitive moves. Second, using the above keywords, the coders first identified responses and then worked back to find the report of the initial action, thereby tracing every initial action and all of the announced responses to it. In total, 1,445 moves (1,027 actions and 418 responses) over the eight years were identified. They were classified into 21 types (e.g., price cut, promotion, route entry) to allow statistical controls for types of moves taken.

Action propensity was calculated as the total number of actions a firm launched in a given year. *Response propensity* was measured by the total number of responses a firm executed in a year, given that it was identified as a competitor affected by an action. To define the response opportunities, the researchers first identified all airports affected by the initial action and defined the airlines that competed via those airports as affected and, hence, as potential responders. They then calculated response propensity as the percentage of response opportunities that the firm actually took in each year.

Five measures were used for the *competitive magnitude* of actions and responses: strategic significance, noteworthiness, and scope of a firm's actions; and noteworthiness and scope of responses.

Action significance was measured as the number of strategic actions the firm took in a year, divided by its total number of actions. Strategic actions involve substantial investments in fixed assets, people or structure, while tactical ones involve smaller investments, without large-scale or irreversible commitment (Miller and Chen, 1994). Three raters working independently classified actions as strategic (e.g., mergers and acquisitions, hub creations) or tactical (e.g., price cuts). There was total agreement among the raters in classifying the various types of moves as strategic or tactical.

Action noteworthiness was measured by the amount of industry attention accorded a move. We first counted the number of lines *Aviation Daily* devoted to reporting the action, but, because press attention differs inherently by type of move, we standardized the noteworthiness scores for each of the 21 types over all years and all airlines to have a mean of zero and standard deviation of one. Similarly, we measured *response noteworthiness* by the number of lines *Aviation Daily* devoted to the response, standardized for each type of response. We assume that *Aviation Daily*, a longstanding, well-respected industry publication, allocates space in proportion to newsworthiness and that on average, items commanding more attention are viewed as relatively innovative, bold, unexpected, or complex.

Action scope, or the extent to which the action affects the full breadth of the firm's operations, was measured as the proportion of the firm's revenue base potentially affected by the action. After identifying the airports affected by a firm's action, we divided the firm's annual number of passengers at these airports by the firm's total number of passengers in that year. For example, an airline's decision to initiate a nationwide price discount would be greater in scope, affecting all of its domestic market, than a discount at a specific airport. *Response scope* was similarly measured as the percentage of the firm's revenue base affected by its response.

For *competitive speed,* we used three measures: action execution speed, response generation speed, and response execution speed. *Action execution speed* is the amount of time a firm took to execute an announced action. First, we measured the time between the date the firm publicly announced or acknowledged the intended action and the date that action began to be executed, as both were reported in *Aviation Daily.* We then controlled for the different types of actions by standardizing the time lag across all years and firms (mean of zero and a standard deviation of one). To represent speed rather than time lag, the signs of the scores were reversed so that a large value indicates great speed. *Response generation speed* was measured as the amount of time a firm took to generate a response if it did so. Relying on the reports in *Aviation Daily,* we calculated the time lag between the day that a competitor announced its initial action and the day that the focal firm announced its response. This was again standardized by response type and reverse-scored to indicate speed. *Response execution speed* was the amount of time that a firm took to execute an announced response. Because a firm's response execution speed depends on the type of the initial action and other features that may have affected the execution time of that initial action, we regressed response execution time on type of action and action execution time for all years and airlines to control for these effects. We then used the average residual scores of the above regression results across all the responses made by an airline in a given year as its response execution time for that year. The signs of scores were again reversed so that a large value implies great speed.

To explore effects on organizational performance, we used two measures. The first was the firm's market share change during the year, calculated as the percentage change from the previous year in market share in those markets in which the airline was present (this year's market share minus last year's, divided by last year's). The second was the firm's change in profits during the year, calculated as the percentage change in dollar profits between this year and the previous year.

Independent and Control Variables

Each top management team was defined as all executives above the vice-president level (e.g., senior vice president, vice chairman, chief executive officer). This operationalization, used in prior top management team studies (e.g., Chaganti and Sambharya, 1987; Murray, 1989; Michel and Hambrick, 1992), yields a more complete group than if only executives who are inside directors are included (e.g., Finkelstein and Hambrick, 1990) but a more restrictive group than if all officers are included (e.g., Wagner, Pfeffer, and

O'Reilly, 1984). The chosen operationalization is intended to include all major line and staff executives, encompassing all the key activities of the firm at the senior-most level. This definition yielded a mean top management team size of 8.6 (standard deviation of 3.4) executives. All information pertaining to management characteristics was obtained from each year's *Dun and Bradstreet Directory of Corporate Management.*

We examined three types of top management team heterogeneity: functional heterogeneity, educational curriculum heterogeneity, and company tenure heterogeneity. Each of these three types of heterogeneity has been used in prior studies, but typically not together. The three types are complementary, reflecting diversity on somewhat different dimensions. To the extent that results are consistent across the three types, we can have greater confidence in the effects of heterogeneity on competitive behavior. Functional backgrounds represent executives' primary professional orientations, including their implicit causal models, vocabularies, and internal and external networks (e.g., Hambrick and Mason, 1984; Walsh, 1988). Educational curriculum similarly reflects professional orientations but also taps some fundamental formative qualities such as cognitive style, values, and early upbringing (Smart and Pascarella, 1986). Company tenure, which is strongly correlated with industry tenure and age in our sample, indicates an executive's cohort, frame of reference for viewing the history of the firm, and internal network (Wagner, Pfeffer, and O'Reilly, 1984). We did not measure tenure on the team, because we viewed it as a less fundamental reflection of an executive's orientation than tenure in the company. Since top management team boundaries are permeable, membership on the top management team, as we defined it, may or may not have been an important factor in an executive's point of view and internal social network, at least not when compared with the importance of membership in the firm.

Functional heterogeneity was measured by a variation of the Herfindal-Hirschman index,

$$H = 1 - \sum_{i=1}^{16} p_i^2,$$

where H is the heterogeneity measure and p the percentage of top management team members in each of 16 functional background categories listed in the Appendix. In almost all cases, coding executives' functional backgrounds was straightforward. In those few cases in which an executive had substantial experiences in more than one category, we selected as the primary category the one in which the executive spent the most time. In a validity test, Barbosa (1985) found that 82 percent of executives indicated their primary function as the same one he had coded from the *Dun and Bradstreet Directory.*

For *educational background heterogeneity,* we used eight different disciplines, listed in the Appendix, to code each executive's educational background. For executives with graduate degrees, we coded the corresponding graduate disciplines; for those without graduate degrees, we coded their

Team Heterogeneity

undergraduate disciplines. We then calculated the Herfindal-Hirschman index for educational background heterogeneity.

Company tenure heterogeneity was calculated as the standard deviation of the number of years the executives on the top management team had spent in the firm. We did not use the coefficient of variation, since one of our control variables was the top management team's mean company tenure.

We also included as control variables top management team size, average educational level (mean number of years of higher education), and firm size (measured by annual revenue-passenger miles). Firm size is a particularly important control variable, because a number of our dependent variables are inherently a function of company scale (Chen and Hambrick, 1995). Also, because competitive behaviors may depend on resource availability (Smith et al., 1991), we included three measures of organizational slack: equity/long-term debt, current assets/current liabilities, and prior profits (all lagged by one year). These data were collected from COMPUSTAT tapes. Finally, the years 1980–86 were included as dummy variables, with 1979 as the omitted category. The control variables are those identified as most essential in the competitive interaction and top management team literatures.

Analysis

In analyzing the data, we pooled the observations cross sectionally for all years. Although this approach produces more precise estimates, two potential problems exist: First, slope coefficients may be inconsistent over time, making the pooled techniques inappropriate. Second, the ordinary least squares (OLS) estimates may be biased, since neglected firm-specific characteristics would lead to violating assumptions about the independence of observations (Pindyck and Rubinfeld, 1991). Because a number of tests, including the Durbin-Watson test and Bartlett's test, indicated serial correlation and heteroskedasticity, we used a generalized-least-squares technique for analysis (Harrigan, 1982; Smith et al., 1991).

We used Kmenta's (1986) autoregressive heteroskedastic model to correct for serial correlation and heteroskedasticity. To correct for first-order serial correlation we applied the Cochrane-Orcutt transformation to each individual firm and corrected for heteroskedasticity by dividing dependent and independent variables by the firm-specific error variance obtained from the regressions on the serial-correlation-corrected data. After these transformations, the data were pooled and analyzed using OLS regression techniques. This approach was used in a number of recent related studies such as Miller and Chen (1994), Smith et al. (1991), and Finkelstein and Hambrick (1990).

RESULTS

Descriptive statistics and correlation coefficients for all variables are presented in Table 1.

Table 1

Means, Standard Deviations, and Correlations

Variable	Mean	s.d.	1	2	3	4	5	6	7	8	9
1. Firm size	798270	10586605									
2. Slack (E/LTD)	.63	1.12	.33***								
3. Slack (CA/CL)	1.15	.64	−.15	−.12							
4. Slack (Profit)	11300	102433	.28***	.11	.04						
5. TMT size	8.61	3.71	.15**	−.1	−.09	.03					
6. Average education	4.13	.93	.04	.20**	.09	.02	−.12*				
7. Average tenure	14.32	7.85	.38***	.49****	−.14	.16**	.14**	.00			
8. Functional heterogeneity	.84	.12	−.19***	−.27***	.18*	−.08	.24****	−.08	−.16***		
9. Educational background heterogeneity	.55	.25	.28****	.33****	−.22**	.08	.41****	.06	.15**	−.11	
10. Tenure heterogeneity	8.57	4.48	.29****	.01	−.13	−.02	.07	−.07	.55****	−.27****	.13
11. Action propensity	5.02	5.32	.61****	.06	.00	.11*	.02	−.02	.17**	−.11	−.02
12. Response propensity	.05	.06	.41****	04	.07*	−.07	−.07	.17****	.04	−.13***	.19****
13. Action significance	.17	.37	−.08	.03	−.08	.02	.08	−.04	.05	.09	.06
14. Action noteworthiness	0	.94	−.01	.02	−.06	.60	−.07	−.01	.07	−.04	−.07
15. Response noteworthiness	0	.98	−.03	−.03	.04	.04	−.11	−.05	−.56	−.06	−.09*
16. Action scope	.62	.22	−.15**	−.06	.02	−.02	−.09	−.17**	−.17**	.08	−.08
17. Response scope	.68	.25	−.35****	−.08	−.02	−.05	−.01	−.24	.06	.11	−.12
18. Action execution speed	0	.99	−.03	−.06	−.02	−.03	−.03	.02	.00	−.06	.00
19. Response generation speed	0	.99	−.21****	−.04	−.05	.00	.00	−.19****	.00	.09**	−.03
20. Response execution speed	0	.98	−.07	−.01	−.04	−.08	−.09+	−.05	.06	−.01	−.02
21. Growth in market share	−.0007	.11	.01	.01	−.01	.04	−.10	−.09	.10	−.04	−.03
22. Growth in profitability	−.14	.65	−.04	−.04	.02	−.02	.05	−.09	−.06	.04	.09

Variable	10	11	12	13	14	15	16	17	18	19	20	21
11. Action propensity	.19**											
12. Response propensity	−.08	−.16**										
13. Action significance	.01	.08	−.13**									
14. Action noteworthiness	.03	−.01	.05	.01								
15. Response noteworthiness	.01	.01	−.06	−.11**	.31***							
16. Action scope	−.11	−.17**	−.14*	.23***	.27**	.01						
17. Response scope	.20	−.21**	−.11	.07	.01	.12	−.02					
18. Action execution speed	−.02	−.06	.04	.09	.20****	−.05	.11**	.12**				
19. Response generation speed	−.01	−.11**	−.20****	.00	.07	−.02	.19***	.17***	.26***			
20. Response execution speed	.01	.03	−.04	.06	.11**	−.05	.08	.09*	.56**	−.08*		
21. Growth in market share	.20****	.03	−.27****	.10	−.08	.08	.02	.25	−.01	.05	.16	
22. Growth in profitability	.01	−.06	−.02	−.03	.15	.06	.13	.04	−.03	.10	.13	.01

* $p < .10$; ** $p < .05$; *** $p < .01$; **** $p < .001$.

Team Heterogeneity

Competitive Behaviors

Table 2 presents GLS regression results, with action characteristics as the dependent variables. Turning to the top management team heterogeneity variables, the results for action propensity generally supported proposition 1. Both education heterogeneity and tenure heterogeneity were significantly positively related to action propensity.

Table 2

Regression Results of Top Management Team Characteristics and Control Variables on Action Characteristics*

Variable	Action Characteristics: Propensity	Significance	Noteworthiness	Scope	Execution speed
Functional heterogeneity	.122	.063•••	.114••	.076••	−.010•••
	(.482)	(.024)	(.054)	(.037)	(.003)
Educational background heterogeneity	.355••••	−.053	.133••	.022••	−.144•••
	(.051)	(.192)	(.060)	(.011)	(.055)
Tenure heterogeneity	.084••	.012	.234	−.237	−.122
	(.040)	(.051)	(1.347)	(.942)	(.582)
Firm size	.832••••	.231••••	−.133••••	−.132	−.042
	(.124)	(.021)	(.030)	(.562)	(.159)
Slack (E/LTD)	−.053	−.012	−.424	−.073	.124
	(.623)	(.248)	(1.542)	(.442)	(.562)
Slack (CA/CL)	−.275••	.044•••	.093	−.044	.221•
	(.132)	(.017)	(.454)	(.257)	(.133)
Slack (Profit)	.054••••	.022••••	−.123••	.084	.023
	(.015)	(.005)	(.051)	(.281)	(.245)
TMT size	−.022	−.123••	−.132••	−.326•	−.122
	(.162)	(.058)	(.052)	(.181)	(.468)
Average education	.022•••	.134••	−.424•	−.314•••	−.143
	(.008)	(.066)	(.242)	(.116)	(.649)
Average tenure	−.321••	.064	.643••	.233	.334
	(.152)	(.242)	(.298)	(2.154)	(1.382)
N	156	153	642	642	603
F	124	164	142	180	165

• $p < .10$; •• $p < .05$; ••• $p < .01$; •••• $p < .001$.

* Because generalized-least-squares regression equations corrected for serial correlation are used, R^2 statistics are not reported. Standardized regression coefficients are listed, with standard errors in parentheses. Because no systematic pattern existed, the statistics for the dummy variables for the years 1980–86 are not shown.

Propositions 2a–2c linking top management team heterogeneity with action magnitude received substantial support. Functional heterogeneity was significantly positively related to action significance, partially supporting proposition 2a. Proposition 2b was more strongly supported, with both functional heterogeneity and educational heterogeneity significantly positively associated with action noteworthiness. Proposition 2c also received general support; the signs for both functional heterogeneity and educational heterogeneity were both positive and significant. Thus, the more diverse the top management team, the greater the overall magnitude of the firm's competitive actions.

Providing general support for proposition 3, both functional heterogeneity and educational heterogeneity were significantly negatively related to action execution speed. Tenure heterogeneity, however, did not have a significant effect.

The control variables showed highly significant associations with the action characteristics, as they did in all the results we will present. To maintain our focus, we will not comment here on the control variables but will note the most significant results below.

Table 3 presents GLS results for the response characteristics. In contrast to proposition 4, which predicted no relationship, all three types of top management team heterogeneity were significantly negatively associated with response propensity. Thus, the more heterogeneous the top management team, the less likely the firm was to respond to a competitor's action.

Table 3

Regression Results of Top Management Team Characteristics and Control Variables on Response Characteristics*

	Response Characteristics				
Variable	Propensity	Noteworthiness	Scope	Generation speed	Execution speed
Functional heterogeneity	−.015•••	.184••	.032••	−.542•••	−.322••
	(.006)	(.089)	(.015)	(.180)	(.159)
Educational background heterogeneity	−.054••	.154	.125	−.245•	−.025••
	(.027)	(.649)	(.632)	(.146)	(.012)
Tenure heterogeneity	−.155••	−.045	.342•	−.386••	−.132
	(.079)	(.371)	(.182)	(.192)	(.449)
Firm size	.664••••	−.123	−.320••	.465•••	−.524••••
	(.154)	(.554)	(.150)	(.156)	(.075)
Slack (E/LTD)	−.214••••	.132	.234	.362•	−.213
	(.041)	(.848)	(.944)	(.211)	(.792)
Slack (CA/CL)	−.012••••	−.032	−.222	.186	.211
	(.002)	(.250)	(1.325)	(.577)	(1.078)
Slack (Profit)	−.063•••	.244	.086	−.285••	−.233•
	(.025)	(.911)	(.641)	(.143)	(.138)
TMT size	−.126•••	−.034	−.081	.225	−.053
	(.042)	(.152)	(.365)	(.762)	(.792)
Average education	.204••	−.122	−.323	−.153	.053
	(.081)	(.494)	(1.597)	(.706)	(.782)
Average tenure	.144••••	−.243	−.224	.534••	.124
	(.032)	(1.066)	(.885)	(.265)	(.712)
N	139	286	286	263	263
F	723	484	155	401	112

• $p < .10$; •• $p < .05$; ••• $p < .01$; •••• $p < .001$

* Because generalized-least-squares regression equations corrected for serial correlation are used, R^2 statistics are not reported. Standardized regression coefficients are listed, with standard errors in parentheses. Because no systematic pattern existed, the statistics for the dummy variables for the years 1980–86 are not shown.

Propositions 5a and 5b, on response magnitude, were partially supported. Functional heterogeneity was significantly positively related to response noteworthiness and response scope. Tenure heterogeneity was also positively associated with response scope, but with marginal significance ($p < .10$). Overall, though, the results tend to support the premise that heterogeneous top management teams engage in relatively significant, bold competitive responses.

Propositions 6a and 6b posited that heterogeneous top management teams would be slower than homogeneous teams in their competitive responses. Results show consistent sup-

Team Heterogeneity

port for these ideas. All three types of heterogeneity were significantly and negatively associated with response generation speed. Similarly, both functional heterogeneity and educational heterogeneity were significantly negatively related to response execution speed. In the aggregate, there is evidence that the heterogeneous teams were slower than homogeneous teams in their competitive responses.

Performance

We proposed that in the turbulent industry we are studying that the advantages of top management team heterogeneity would outweigh the disadvantages and that the effects on overall corporate performance would be positive. The results, shown in Table 4, strikingly conform to these expectations. The dependent variables are the two performance measures, growth in market share and growth in profits. Performance for the prior year is included as a control variable, to assure that the analysis is capturing strictly change in performance in the focal year.

Table 4

Regression Results of Top Management Team Characteristics and Control Variables on Performance[*]

Variable	Growth in market share	Growth in profits
Functional heterogeneity	.332****	.623**
	(.042)	(.298)
Educational background heterogeneity	.064**	.323**
	(.029)	(.150)
Tenure heterogeneity	.093*	.323***
	(.058)	(.095)
Firm size	.232	−.312**
	(.594)	(.142)
Slack (E/LTD)	.144	.332
	(.561)	(1.389)
Slack (CA/CL)	.561**	.084
	(.224)	(.334)
Slack (Profit)	.524*	.124
	(.280)	(.541)
Previous year's performance (growth in market share or profit)	−.052**	-.134
	(.025)	(.492)
TMT size	.353	-.212
	(1.272)	(.721)
Average education	.230**	.454*
	(.115)	(.252)
Average tenure	.083	.304
	(.342)	(1.492)
N	139	138
F	54	43

$^{*}p < .10$; $^{**}p < .05$; $^{***}p < .01$; $^{****}p < .001$.

[*] Because generalized-least-squares regression equations corrected for serial correlation are used, R^2 statistics are not reported. Standardized regression coefficients are listed, with standard errors in parentheses. Because no systematic pattern existed, the statistics for the dummy variables for the years 1980–86 are not shown.

The results reveal a clear pattern: All three types of heterogeneity were positively associated with performance improvement, both in market share and profitability. Thus, despite the low response propensity and slowness of the heterogeneous top management team, its other benefits appear to more than compensate, and in general the airlines with diverse top management teams advanced in their competitive arena. These results show that top management team heterogeneity is of considerable consequence not only to the firm's competitive behaviors but also to its performance.

Effects from Control Variables

A brief review of the effects of the control variables is warranted, particularly since they showed some strong associations with both competitive behaviors and performance (as seen in Tables 2, 3, and 4). Because the four variables representing firm size and slack have been included in prior studies using the airline data, we will not comment on them. Instead, we will note briefly the effects of the top management team control variables.

Top management team size was negatively related to response propensity and to three measures of competitive magnitude (action significance, action noteworthiness, and action scope). This consistent pattern may suggest that large teams tend to be restrained in their competitive initiatives. Team size was positively related to growth in market share, however, indicating that, overall, there may be some benefits from large teams. Team members' average education level was positively related to action propensity, action significance, and response propensity but negatively related to action noteworthiness and action scope. The average education level of the top management team was positively related to both performance measures, however, indicating overall benefits from top management team education levels. Finally, the average tenure of the team showed limited effects, with little pattern. Average tenure was negatively related to action propensity, but positively related to action noteworthiness, response propensity, and response generation speed. These results indicate that the top management team characteristics we controlled for may have substantial implications for competitive behaviors and firm performance and may thus merit further study.

DISCUSSION

Both longstanding theory (Schumpeter, 1950) and more recent empirical evidence (e.g., Chen and MacMillan, 1992) indicate that firm performance depends greatly on the ongoing competitive behaviors of the firm and its adversaries. It is thus important to improve understanding of the determinants of those behaviors. This paper complements previous work emphasizing the environmental and organizational determinants of firms' microcompetitive behavior by incorporating the composition of the top management team as an important influence in such outcomes. Seeking to explore in depth the effects of one centrally important upper-echelon construct, top management team heterogeneity, we found broad and significant associations with both the firm's competitive behaviors and performance.

Team Heterogeneity

Top Management Team Heterogeneity and Competitive Behavior

The effects of top management team heterogeneity on the firm's competitive actions conformed to our propositions. First, heterogeneity was positively related to action propensity, or the basic tendency to undertake competitive initiatives. Second, it was positively related to the magnitude of competitive actions. Across multiple measures, gauging the significance, noteworthiness, and scale of actions, we found consistent evidence that heterogeneous top management teams were bolder in competitive actions than homogeneous teams. Finally, we found the heterogeneous teams were slower in their action execution than homogeneous teams. These findings fully align with prior theory positing several consequences of group heterogeneity: broad gathering of information, decision creativity and boldness, but friction and slowness in decision making and action.

Results for the firm's response characteristics were partly in line with expectations but diverged in one important way. Whereas we proposed that there would be no association between top management team heterogeneity and response propensity, we found a negative relationship for all three measures of heterogeneity. Thus there was broadly consistent evidence that homogeneous teams were most likely to respond to their adversaries' initiatives. Our logic in proposing no relationship was based on the premise that competitors' actions are usually so clear-cut and unambiguous that they amount to "strong situations" (Mischel, 1977) for the potential responder, and top management team characteristics will not influence the likelihood of a response. The finding of a negative relationship between heterogeneity and response propensity causes us to conclude that we were perhaps considering only the scanning element of the response decision-making process and ignoring other elements of the process (Mintzberg, Raisinghani, and Théorêt, 1976).

It may be that initiators' actions are generally unambiguous in their occurrence, and homogeneous and heterogeneous top management teams are equally aware of such events, but actions may be open to varying interpretations (Porter, 1980). Perhaps, then, heterogeneous teams experience dissensus about issues ranging from the meaning of the competitor's action to the design of an appropriate response. Conversely, the homogeneous team may have an advantage in this respect. Its internal similarity, shared vocabulary, and relatively fluid exchange properties enhance its ability to interpret the competitor's move and decide to make a countermove.

When acting, a top management team must develop a move from its repertoire; as our results suggest, the broader the repertoire, the greater the number of actions that can be created. In responding, however, the team becomes anchored to the nature of the initial action and does not have to create anything to respond. Simple imitation is commonly a possibility. The negative association between heterogeneity and response propensity suggests that the diverse orientations in heterogeneous teams may lead them to engage in more interpretation, negotiation, and creative formulation of responses, which lessens their likelihood of responding at all, compared with the more straightforward, reflexive response behaviors of homogeneous teams. Such a portrayal is further supported by our other findings on response characteristics. When heterogeneous top management teams did respond, their responses were of greater magnitude but slower than those of homogeneous teams. These findings were consistent with our propositions and add to the overall indication that heterogeneous top management teams are cognitively rich.

It might be said that heterogeneous teams are good (but slow) at creating, but that homogeneous teams are good at deciding (Jackson, 1992). Self-initiated actions involve creating competitive moves, and top management team heterogeneity will aid in this. Responding to another's actions, however, involves little creating; it is primarily a matter of deciding, and top management team homogeneity may enhance this competitive tendency. In this sense, our findings are consonant with Eisenhardt and Schoonhoven's (1990) more general conclusion that heterogeneity of industry experience brought helpful diversity to the top teams they studied, but that long tenures helped group processes. In our study, average team tenure, which is generally seen as a contributor to fluid group processes, had a very strong positive effect on response propensity, supporting the notion that top management groups with shared experiences and perspectives are most able to react to clear-cut stimuli. An additional reason that top management team heterogeneity dampens response propensity may be that diverse teams draw on their cognitive breadth to develop highly elaborate, multidimensional offensive strategies, which in turn restrict their flexibility in responding to others' initiatives. Moreover, such top management teams might become highly committed to their elaborate, creative offensive strategies and unwilling to move into a reactive mode.

Heterogeneity and Organizational Performance

Our results indicate that top management team heterogeneity may have potential benefits and drawbacks to the firm's competitive behaviors. It is understandable, then, that prior research has produced mixed results on the influence of top management team heterogeneity on overall organizational performance. In this study of the airline industry, the advantages of heterogeneity exceeded the disadvantages. All three types of heterogeneity examined were independently and positively associated with performance, measured both as change in market share and change in profits. And each type of heterogeneity contributed in its own way to overall airline performance.

We would not assert that top management team heterogeneity is always beneficial. The U.S. airline industry in the period studied was exceedingly turbulent and lacked clear competitive role models, precisely the conditions under which theorists expect top management team heterogeneity to be advantageous (Hambrick and Mason, 1984; Jackson, 1992). It may be that a more stable industry, with more widely accepted models or recipes for behavior (Spender, 1989) and less intense rivalry would have favored top management team homogeneity. It is also possible that after the period we studied, the airline industry became more orderly and programmed, yielding diminished benefits of top management team heterogeneity. But our results indicate that in a highly turbulent setting, diverse top management teams, despite their drawbacks, have superior competitive and adaptive capabilities.

It is also important to note that the three types of heterogeneity examined showed considerable consistency in their effects on competitive behaviors and performance. Among the 12 models presented in Tables 2, 3, and 4, two or three of the heterogeneity measures were significant in the same direction for 10 of the models. There were no instances of opposing significant effects. Moreover, for those criterion constructs for which we have multiple measures (such as competitive magnitude, speed, and performance), the effects of heterogeneity were highly consistent in their signs across those indicators. Thus, even though we have examined three different dimensions of heterogeneity—so different that they are not correlated among themselves and hence do not warrant being combined into an index—they exhibit strikingly consistent effects on corporate outcomes. These three forms of top management team dispersion may differ in their subtleties and the specific conduits by which they affect outcomes, but at the broadest level they can be considered complementary and corroborative of the importance of top management team heterogeneity as a robust construct.

Because our data were archival, we were unable to gain an in-depth understanding of the actual processes of competitive decision making in the firms we studied. For instance, it is possible that some of the actions and responses we studied were not a result of interactions among the entire executive group but, rather, involved a small subset of those managers. Additionally, some decisions, such as tactical pricing responses, may have been formulated in a routine, even automated way that minimally involved the senior executives. The strong and consistent results we obtained, however, suggest that these conditions did not prevail and that the composition of the top management team is of substantial importance to the competitive functioning of the firm. Insights about the actual team dynamics and processes involved in competitive moves will require field methods such as those used by Eisenhardt and Bourgeois (1988), Gersick (1989), and Smith et al. (1994). Our results suggest that field work, directed at understanding the actual processes of competitive decision making engaged in by homogeneous and heterogeneous top management teams, could bear fruit.

Our findings illuminate the importance of focusing on executive characteristics and processes as major influences on competitive dynamics. This conclusion is perhaps not so surprising, considering that these microcompetitive actions and responses, often the building blocks of sustainable advantage, tend to occur in a limited time span and with imperfect information. The cognitive and social processes and biases of the decision makers themselves will almost invariably become manifested in their strategic choices in such situations.

In addition to highlighting the "human factor" in interfirm competitive behavior, our study may have important practical implications. For instance, our results suggest that companies whose main focus is to launch innovative actions in an effort to gain competitive advantage may wish to ensure that their top management teams comprise executives with diverse backgrounds. Conversely, firms that strive to be promptly reactive to others' attacks may want to configure their top teams with greater homogeneity so that maximum efficiency in decision-making responsiveness and speed can be achieved. Depending on the environmental context and the firm's overarching strategic repertoire, the profile of the top management team can be modified to make it more congruent with the firm's objectives. Overall, our findings indicate the need to incorporate the composition of the top decision makers in attempts to understand and enhance competitive advantage.

REFERENCES

Ancona, Deborah G., and David F. Caldwell
1992 "Bridging the boundary: External activity and performance in organizational teams." Administrative Science Quarterly, 37: 634–665.

Bantel, Karen, and Susan E. Jackson
1989 "Top management and innovations in banking: Does the composition of the top team make a difference?" Strategic Management Journal, 10: 107–124.

Barbosa, Ricardo R.
1985 "Innovation in a mature industry." Unpublished doctoral dissertation, Columbia University.

Chaganti, Rajeswararao, and Rakesh Sambharya
1987 "Strategic orientation and characteristics of upper management." Strategic Management Journal, 8: 393–401.

Chen, Ming-Jer, and Donald C. Hambrick
1995 "Speed, stealth, and selective attack: How small firms differ from large firms in competitive behavior." Academy of Management Journal, 38: 453–482.

Chen, Ming-Jer, and Ian C. MacMillan
1992 "Nonresponse and delayed response to competitive moves: The roles of competitor dependence and action irreversibility." Academy of Management Journal, 35: 359–370.

Chen, Ming-Jer, Ken G. Smith, and Curtis M. Grimm
1992 "Action characteristics as predictors of competitive responses." Management Science, 38: 439–455.

Cyert, Richard M., and James G. March
1963 A Behavioral Theory of the Firm. Englewood Cliffs, NJ: Prentice-Hall.

D'Aveni, Richard A.
1994 Hypercompetition. New York: Free Press.

Eisenhardt, Kathleen M.
1989 "Speed and strategic choice: How managers accelerate decision making." California Management Review, 32: 533–576.

Eisenhardt, Kathleen M., and L. J. Bourgeois, III
1988 "Politics of strategic decision making in high velocity environments: Toward a midrange theory." Academy of Management Journal, 31: 737–770.

Eisenhardt, Kathleen M., and Claudia B. Schoonhoven
1990 "Organizational growth: Linking founding team, strategy, environment, and growth among U.S. semi-conductor ventures, 1978–1988." Administrative Science Quarterly, 35: 504–529.

Finkelstein, Sydney, and Donald C. Hambrick
1990 "Top management team tenure and organizational outcomes: The moderating role of managerial discretion." Administrative Science Quarterly, 35: 484–503.

Fredrickson, James W., and Anthony L. Iaquinto
1989 "Inertia and creeping rationality in strategic decision processes." Academy of Management Journal, 32: 516–542.

Gersick, Connie J. G.
1989 "Marking time: Predictable transitions in task groups." Academy of Management Journal, 32: 274–309.

Ghemawat, Pankaj
1991 Commitment: The Dynamic of Strategy. New York: Wiley.

Grimm, Curtis M., and Ken G. Smith
1991 "Management and organizational change: A note on the railroad industry." Strategic Management Journal, 12: 557–562.

Hambrick, Donald C.
1994 "Top management groups: A conceptual integration and reconsideration of the 'team' label." In B. M. Staw and L. L. Cummings (eds.), Research in Organizational Behavior, 16: 171–214. Greenwich, CT: JAI Press.

Hambrick, Donald C., Ian C. MacMillan, and Diana L. Day
1982 "Strategic attributes and performance in the BCG matrix—A PIMS-based analysis of industrial product businesses." Academy of Management Journal, 25: 510–531.

Hambrick, Donald C., and Phyllis A. Mason
1984 "Upper echelon: The organization as a reflection of its top managers." Academy of Management Review, 9: 193–206.

Team Heterogeneity

Harrigan, Katherine R.
1982 "Exit decisions in mature industries." Academy of Management Journal, 25: 707–732.

Hoffman, L. Richard, and Norman R. F. Maier
1961 "Quality and acceptance of problem solutions by members of homogeneous and heterogeneous groups." Journal of Abnormal and Social Psychology, 62: 401–407.

Jacobson, Robert
1992 "The 'Austrian' school of strategy." Academy of Management Review, 17: 782–807.

Jackson, Susan E.
1992 "Consequences of group composition for the interpersonal dynamics of strategic issue processing. In P. Shrivastava, A. Huff, and J. Dutton (eds.), Advances in Strategic Management, 8: 345–382. Greenwich, CT: JAI Press.

Jackson, Susan E., Joan F. Brett, Valerie I. Sessa, Dawn M. Cooper, J. A. Julin, and K. Peyronnin
1991 "Some differences make a difference: Individual dissimilarity and group heterogeneity as correlates of recruitment, promotions, and turnover." Journal of Applied Psychology, 76: 675–689.

Janis, Irving L.
1972 Victims of Groupthink. Boston: Houghton-Mifflin.

Jauch, Lawrence R., Richard N. Osborn, and Thomas N. Martin
1980 "Structured content analysis of cases: A complementary method for organizational research." Academy of Management Review, 5: 517–526.

Kmenta, Jan
1986 Elements of Econometrics, 2nd ed. New York: Macmillan.

Labich, Kenneth
1990 "American takes on the world." Fortune, 122: 40–48.

Levine, Michael E.
1987 "Airline competition in deregulated markets: Theory, firm strategy and public policy." Yale Journal on Regulation, 4: 393–494.

MacMillan, Ian C.
1982 "Seizing competitive initiative." Journal of Business Strategy, 2: 43–57.

MacMillan, Ian C., Mary L. McCaffery, and Gilles Van Wijk
1985 "Competitors' responses to easily imitated new products—Exploring commercial banking product introductions." Strategic Management Journal, 6: 75–86.

March, James G., and Herbert A. Simon
1958 Organizations. New York: Wiley.

Michel, John G., and Donald C. Hambrick
1992 "Diversification posture and top management characteristics." Academy of Management Journal, 35: 9–37.

Miller, Danny, and Ming-Jer Chen
1994 "Sources and consequences of competitive inertia: A study of the U.S. airline industry." Administrative Science Quarterly, 39: 1–23.

1996a "The simplicity of competitive repertoires: An empirical analysis." Strategic Management Journal, 17: 419–439.

1996b "Nonconformity in competitive repertoires: A sociological view of markets." Social Forces, 74: 1209–1234.

Miller, Danny, and Peter H. Friesen
1977 "Strategy-making in context: Ten empirical archetypes." Journal of Management Studies, 14: 253–280.

Mintzberg, Henry, Duru Raisinghani, and André Théorêt
1976 "The structure of 'unstructured' decision processes." Administrative Science Quarterly, 21: 246–275.

Mischel, Walter
1968 Personality and Assessment. New York: Wiley.

1977 "The interaction of person and situation." In D. Magnusson and N. S. Endler (eds.), Personality at the Crossroads: Current Issues in Interactional Psychology. Hillsdale, NJ: Erlbaum.

Murray, Alan I.
1989 "Top management group heterogeneity and firm performance." Strategic Management Journal, 10: 125–141.

O'Reilly, Charles A., III, David F. Caldwell, and William P. Barnett
1989 "Work group demography, social integration, and turnover." Administrative Science Quarterly, 34: 21–37.

O'Reilly, Charles A., III, and Sylvia Flatt
1989 "Executive team demography, organizational innovation, and firm performance." Working paper, University of California, Berkeley.

O'Reilly, Charles A., III, Richard C. Snyder, and Joan N. Boothe
1993 "Executive team demography and organizational change." In G. P. Huber and W. H. Glick (eds.), Organizational Change and Redesign: 147–175. New York: Oxford University Press.

Pindyck, Robert S., and Daniel L. Rubinfeld
1991 Econometric Models and Economic Forecasts. New York: McGraw-Hill.

Porter, Michael E.
1980 Competitive Strategy: Techniques for Analyzing Industries and Competitors. New York: Free Press.

Prescott, John E., and Daniel C. Smith
1987 "A project-based approach to competitive analysis." Strategic Management Journal, 8: 411–423.

Pugh, S. Douglas, and David J. Hickson
1972 "Causal inference and the Aston studies." Administrative Science Quarterly, 17: 273–276.

Schumpeter, Joseph A.
1950 Capitalism, Socialism, and Democracy, 3rd ed. New York: Harper.

Smart, John C., and Ernest T. Pascarella
1986 "Self-concept development and educational degree attainment." Higher Education, 15: 3–15.

Smith, Ken G., and Curtis M. Grimm
1991 "A communication-information model of competitive response timing." Journal of Management, 17: 5–23.

Smith, Ken G., Curtis M. Grimm, and Martin J. Gannon
1992 Dynamics of Competitive Strategy. Newbury Park, CA: Sage.

Smith, Ken G., Curtis M. Grimm, Martin J. Gannon, and Ming-Jer Chen
1991 "Organizational information processing, competitive responses, and performance in the U.S. domestic airline industry." Academy of Management Journal, 34: 60–85.

Smith, Ken G., Ken A. Smith, J. D. Olian, and H. P. Sims, Jr.
1994 "Top management team demography and process: The role of social integration and communication." Administrative Science Quarterly, 39: 412–438.

Spender, J. C.
1989 Industry Recipes: The Nature and Source of Managerial Judgment. Cambridge: Basil Blackwell.

Stalk, George, Jr.
1988 "Time—The next source of competitive advantage." Harvard Business Review, 88: 41–51.

Steiner, Ivan D.
1972 Group Process and Productivity. New York: Academic Press.

Thomas, Anisya S., Robert J. Litschert, and Kannan Ramaswamy
1991 "The performance impact of strategy-manager coalignment: An empirical examination." Strategic Management Journal, 12: 509–522.

Virany, Beverly, Michael Tushman, and Elaine Romanelli
1992 "Executive succession and organization outcomes in turbulent environments: An organization learning approach." Organization Science, 3: 72–91.

Wagner, W. Gary, Jeffrey Pfeffer, and Charles A. O'Reilly, III.
1984 "Organizational demography and turnover in top-management groups." Administrative Science Quarterly, 29: 74–92.

Walsh, James P.
1988 "Top management turnover following mergers and acquisitions." Strategic Management Journal, 9: 173–183.

Wiersema, Margarethe F., and Karen A. Bantel
1992 "Top management team demography and corporate strategic change." Academy of Management Journal, 35: 91–121.

Zenger, Todd R., and Barbara S. Lawrence
1989 "Organizational demography: The differential effects of age and tenure distributions on technical communication." Academy of Management Journal, 32: 353–376.

APPENDIX: Coding Categories for Executives' Backgrounds

Functional Background

1. CEO (Chief Executive Officer)
2. COO (Chief Operations Officer)
3. Finance/Treasurer
4. Planning
5. Personnel
6. Public Affairs
7. General Counsel/Secretary
8. Operations/Field Service
9. Marketing/Sales/Customer Service
10. Information Systems
11. International
12. Maintenance/Field Service
13. General Management
14. Other Corporate Staff
15. Accounting/Controller
16. Other

Educational Background

1. Engineering
2. Science
3. Business Administration
4. Economics
5. Liberal Arts
6. Law (LL.B./J.D.)
7. Business (other than administration, e.g., accounting, finance)
8. Other

Part IV
Board Characteristics and CEO Compensation

[19]

Charles J. Hadlock
University of Florida

Gerald B. Lumer
U.S. Department of Justice

Compensation, Turnover, and Top Management Incentives: Historical Evidence*

We find that the rate of top management turnover and the sensitivity of turnover to stock returns for a sample of large industrial firms from 1933 to 1941 was significantly smaller than estimates reported for modern panels. We present evidence that management compensation has become more sensitive to firm performance since the 1930s. In contrast to the conclusions of Jensen and Murphy and others, our findings indicate that management incentives under control of the board have become stronger rather than weaker over the past half century. These findings are consistent with internal and external control mechanisms functioning as complements.

I. Introduction

Several recent studies argue that regulatory and political constraints can have a significant effect on top management incentives and corporate governance. Important regulations that may affect corporate governance include rules concerning institutional ownership (Roe 1990, 1994), proxy contests (Pound 1991), and the market for corporate control (Jarrell and Bradley 1980). The papers in this literature suggest that these regulations tend to weaken the incentives of shareholders and outsiders to discipline effectively top managers of large publicly held corporations. In addition to explicit regulations, Jensen and Murphy (1990) hypothesize that political forces may constrain the set of feasible contracts that shareholders can offer to top managers, further weakening managers' incentives to maximize share-

* Joseph Bender, LeaAnn Collins, Ted Fee, Kristen Nummidor, and Sue Sullivan provided excellent research assistance. We thank Daron Acemoglu, Chunrong Ai, Ernie Berndt, David T. Brown, Douglas Diamond (the editor), Joel Houston, Chris James, Randall Kroszner, Ken Lehn, Mark Roe, Michael Ryngaert, Peter Temin, Henry Tosi, Michael Weisbach (the referee), and seminar participants at the Department of Justice and Ohio State University for helpful comments and suggestions. We thank Kevin J. Murphy for providing us with his compensation data. All errors remain our own. The views expressed are the authors' and do not necessarily reflect the views of the Department of Justice.

(*Journal of Business,* 1997, vol. 70, no. 2)

0021-9398/97/7002-0001$02.50

holder value. Jensen (1993)suggests that these regulatory and political forces have contributed to the large-scale failure of modern firms' internal control systems.[1]

Examining the effect of the regulatory and political environment on top management incentives and corporate governance is a difficult empirical task. Surprisingly, comparisons between the United States and countries that have dramatically different regulatory and political environments do not reveal particularly large differences in observed top management incentives (Kaplan 1994*a*, 1994*b*; Kang and Shivdasani 1995). However, comparisons across industries and between regulated and unregulated industries do suggest the possible importance of regulatory and political forces in corporate governance and management incentives (Joskow, Rose, and Shepard 1993; Parrino 1993; Hubbard and Palia 1995; Joskow, Rose, and Wolfram 1996). Perhaps the most dramatic contrast to observed modern U.S. top management incentive contracts is reported by Jensen and Murphy (1990). They find that pay-performance sensitivities in the 1930s were on the order of 10 times larger than in the 1970s and 1980s. This finding suggests that some important lessons can be learned by examining management incentives during this period, which was a time before many of the burdensome regulations on corporate governance were instituted.[2]

In this article we examine an important dimension of corporate governance and management incentives by investigating the determinants of top management turnover on a unique panel of 231 large industrial firms from 1933 to 1941.[3] We find that the rate of top management changes during this time period was on the order of one-half the rate researchers have found on modern data. Furthermore, we find that top management changes were much less sensitive to firm performance than estimates for modern firms. This finding is robust even after controlling for potential changes over time in board composition, ownership structure, firm size, firm age, the frequency of founder-run firms, and the variability of stock returns. In marked contrast with previous studies, our estimates imply that a firm's stock returns had no predictive

1. Grundfest (1990) and Jensen (1993) provide evidence consistent with the widespread failure of these control systems.

2. Pound (1991) illustrates that most of the important proxy regulations were instituted after 1942, with the 1956 revisions being the most significant. Important federal and state regulations of tender offers began in 1968 (Jarrell and Bradley 1980). Roe (1990) finds that several of the rules governing institutional ownership were put in place before and during the 1930s, but he also identifies many important regulatory restrictions put in place after the 1930s. A study of incentive contracts for any period preceding the 1930s would be extremely difficult because of the limited availability of public data on pay, ownership, and stock returns.

3. There is a large literature on the determinants of top management turnover for modern firms. See, e.g., Coughlan and Schmidt (1985), Warner, Watts, and Wruck (1988), and Weisbach (1988).

power in explaining top management changes in our sample. These results are inconsistent with changes in the regulatory and political environment since the 1930s being the sole explanation for the supposed weak link between performance and top management turnover observed today.[4]

The turnover results we present contrast sharply with the findings of Jensen and Murphy (1990) that pay-performance sensitivities for 1934–38 were much higher than for 1974–86. One explanation for these findings is that the high-powered incentive compensation employed during the period we examine successfully solved most incentive problems, so there was little need to replace poorly performing managers. An alternative explanation is that for some reason it was difficult to fire poorly performing managers during this period, so the board was forced to use a high degree of incentive compensation to provide substitute incentives.

To investigate, we examine the available compensation data for our panel of firms. We confirm Jensen and Murphy's (1990) finding that arithmetic pay-performance sensitivities measured as the change in a top manager's pay for a given change in shareholder wealth were on average higher in the 1930s compared to the modern era. However, when we regress the change in the logarithm of pay on stock returns as suggested by Rosen (1990), we find that the semielasticity of compensation with respect to stock returns was relatively low in the 1930s. Since modern firms are, on average, larger than firms in the 1930s, and arithmetic sensitivities tend to decline with firm size, these findings suggest the possibility that the Jensen and Murphy (1990) results on changes in pay-performance sensitivities over time may be driven by size effects.

This suspicion is confirmed when we directly compare compensation data for modern firms to our panel and add controls for size in the regression analysis. We find that once size effects are controlled for, there is no evidence for the assertions made by Jensen and Murphy (1990) that pay-performance sensitivities have decreased dramatically over the past 60 years. The data indicate that for larger firms pay-performance sensitivities have not changed significantly over time and for smaller firms pay-performance sensitivities have increased significantly over time. These findings coupled with our turnover results indicate that, on average, the incentives set by the board of directors have become stronger since the 1930s.

One explanation for the results we present is that they reflect the fact that there was little need to give top managers strong incentives

4. Furthermore, our results provide the first systematic empirical support for some of the assertions made by Berle and Means (1932), which Stigler and Friedland (1983) assert have never been rigorously empirically examined.

to maximize shareholder value during the period we examine. Alternatively, it could be that investors at the time did not understand the effects of incentive schemes. These explanations seem unlikely for several reasons. Christie and Nanda (1994) have presented evidence from the undistributed profits tax of 1936 that is consistent with agency problems being severe during this era. They find that a tax increase that gave managers an incentive to increase dividends raised the average market value of the firms they examine, which is consistent with managers' investing earnings in unprofitable projects. Holderness, Kroszner, and Sheehan (1996) report that for a large panel of firms in 1935, Tobin's q systematically varied with insider holdings in a similar way to the pattern for modern firms first identified by Morck, Shleifer, and Vishny (1988). This result is consistent with managerial incentives affecting firm value and the market recognizing the value created by these incentives. Taken together, these results suggest that agency problems were present during this period and the market was aware that incentive schemes could help alleviate these problems.[5]

What was different about the 1933–41 time period that could explain the presence of weaker management incentive contracts? One possibility is that because of the macroeconomic events of the time, boards did not blame managers for poor performance.[6] Another possibility is that boards did not have much knowledge or practice concerning how to structure managerial incentive schemes. Finally, it is possible that information on firm performance was less widely disseminated and more costly to assess and analyze, resulting in less shareholder oversight.[7] If these explanations are correct, our results would suggest that these factors have outweighed any political or regulatory changes in directing corporate governance and managerial incentives over time. If, as many have argued, current incentives or control mechanisms are too weak, the evidence we report would imply that things are moving in the right direction.

5. Additionally, our reading of the literature of the time suggests that there was widespread recognition that managers of large corporations had little incentive to act in shareholders' interest. As discussed by Stigler and Friedland (1983), the rapid rise to popularity of the writings of Berle and Means (1932) indicates an environment during this time period where managers were believed to be too insulated from outside discipline. An economist of this period, Robert Gordon, wrote extensively on this issue (Gordon 1938, 1940, 1945). He observes (1945, p. 277): "The chief executive is in a sense his own employer. Within broad limits he frequently sets his own compensation." He goes on to state (1945, p. 311): "Top management, usually securely in control of the proxy machinery, seldom has to worry about retaining its position." In addition, Hawley (1966), Roe (1990), and Pound (1991) all discuss the widespread distrust of big business and concentrated financial power in the 1930s.

6. Although the previous discussion indicates that the market was aware of the presence of poorly performing managers, it is still possible that the board was not able to detect poor performance or did not blame managers for poor performance.

7. For example, the availability of broad-based indexes to benchmark managers against managers of similar firms may have been less widely available.

The explanation for our results that appears to be most consistent with findings from the modern corporate governance literature is that there is a link between decisions by the board to remove managers and corporate control activity. A closer investigation of the period we study reveals that it was a time when there were extremely few corporate control transactions. Cash tender offers were rare (Jarrell and Bradley 1980), and it appears that almost all openly hostile control transactions were waged through proxy battles.[8] Friendly control transactions, which could serve to replace inefficient managers (Manne 1965), were at an all-time low during the period we study.[9] This low level of corporate control activity is reflected in the remarkable stability of our sample; only six of the 231 firms we examine leave the sample over an 8-year period, and only one of these was acquired.

Given that external control markets were almost completely inactive during the time period we examine, the evidence we present is strongly consistent with the findings of Denis and Denis (1995) that there is a strong link between decisions by the board to remove top managers and corporate control activity. Denis and Denis (1995) find that for 70% of the cases where there is a forced departure of a top manager, the firm experiences some form of corporate control activity between 1 year prior to the departure and 2 years after the departure. Furthermore, they characterize many of the top executive dismissals in their sample as a response to the threat of a control change. Additionally, Agrawal and Walkling (1994) find that turnover rates following failed and rumored takeover bids are higher than for a control sample with no takeover activity.[10]

Our results show that at a time when the threat of an external control change was very low, the internal mechanism for removing managers was extremely weak by historical standards. A similar finding has been obtained by Mikkelson and Partch (1995), who compare management

8. Jensen (1993) makes this observation. The authors of a leading legal textbook on control contests wrote in their preface in 1977: "In our first treatise, *Proxy Contests for Corporate Control* [New York: Columbia University Press, 1957], we made no mention of the tender offer or takeover bids. At that time, contests for control of publicly held corporations were generally waged through competing solicitation of proxies. . . . In the 1960's, however, tender offers, which had been used in England, appeared with increasing frequency on the American scene" (Aranow, Einhorn, and Berlstein 1977).

9. In a widely cited book on mergers Nelson (1959) begins a section on the 1932–42 time period by writing, "this eleven year period was noted for the absence of merger activity." To illustrate further, Golbe and White (1988, 1993) analyze a consistent series of the number of mergers in the United States from 1919 to 1979. The number of mergers per year from 1933 through 1942 never exceeded 140. As a comparison, in 1928 and 1929 there were over 1,000 mergers per year, and from 1960 to 1969 the average number of mergers per year exceeded 1,000.

10. Martin and McConnell (1991) document that turnover is extremely high following successful control changes, illustrating their disciplinary role. The evidence reported by Denis and Denis (1995) and Agrawal and Walkling (1994) suggests that just the threat of a control change may affect top management turnover.

turnover between an active takeover period (1984–88) and a less active period (1989–93). They find less turnover and smaller turnover-performance sensitivities in the less active period.[11] Taken as a whole, these results suggest that internal and external control mechanisms function as complements rather than substitutes in the removal of poorly performing top managers.

The rest of the paper is organized as follows. In Section II we describe our sample of firms and top management changes. In Section III we present baseline results concerning the effect of stock returns on management turnover. In Section IV we control for other variables that may affect the turnover-performance relationship such as founder status, board structure, and ownership structure. In Section V we present pay-performance estimates for our sample. In Section VI we offer concluding remarks.

II. Sample Description and Selection

A. *The Sample*

We draw our sample from the universe of firms with returns data for May 31, 1933, on the Center for Research in Security Prices (CRSP) New York Stock Exchange (NYSE) monthly tape. To minimize some of the heterogeneity between firms and to economize on data collection costs, we further limited ourselves to U.S. firms that were listed in the *Moody's Industrial Manual* for 1933 and that had a book value of assets above $20 million. This left us with a sample of 259 firms. From this sample we used the details provided by *Moody's* to eliminate all firms that as of May 1933 either were controlled by other industrial companies; were in the process of reorganization, receivership, or liquidation; or had no board of directors. These criteria eliminated 28 additional firms, leaving us with a final sample of 231 industrials. The median (mean) book value of assets for the firms in our sample as of 1933 was $49 ($118) million, or $412 ($999) million expressed in 1986 dollars.

Over the 8-year period we study, only six of the 231 firms depart from the sample. Of these three were liquidated, one was acquired, and two were delisted during reorganization proceedings. As a comparison, in the sample studied by Warner, Watts, and Wruck (1988), the average annual survival rate is 95.9%, which would imply 59 firms departing from our sample over the period we examine. The extremely low rate of exit in our sample is consistent with our earlier observation that there

11. A related finding is reported by Hubbard and Palia (1995), who find that CEO turnover increases following regulatory changes that open the external control markets in the banking industry.

appear to have been very few acquisitions and mergers during this time period.

B. Identifying Top Management Changes

We coded the names of all officers and directors for our panel of firms from the *Moody's* volumes for the years 1933–41. The *Moody's* data on officers and directors is accurate as of May 31 of each year, so our sample period is May 31, 1933–May 31, 1941, consisting of 7,308 firm-quarters where a turnover event may have occurred.[12] Following Warner, Watts, and Wruck (1988), we define the top management team to be the set of individuals holding the title of either chairman or president. If an individual is listed by *Moody's* as both a president and chairman, they are coded in the sample as a president. In our sample every firm has a president, while in 44.3% of the firm-quarters the firm has both a chairman and a president.

Using the *Moody's* data, we identified all instances where the set of individuals comprising the top management team changed between two successive *Moody's* listings. Using the *Commercial and Financial Chronicle* and the *New York Times,* we searched for the date and details of these changes. From these sources, we were able to obtain articles containing the date of the top management change for 92% of all cases. Using *Who's Who in Commerce and Industry,* several obituary indexes, and articles about the firms in the business press, we assessed for all of the remaining cases the smallest time window over which the change occurred. We assigned the date for these top management changes to be the midpoint of this window, which was usually substantially smaller than 1 year. Furthermore, in all but one of these cases we were able to determine whether the change was due to a death or illness. The one turnover event for which we cannot find this information occurred between 1933 and 1934.[13] This event and year for this company are not included in any of the analysis or tables and reduce our sample size to 7,304 firm-quarters.

We identified 244 changes in the set of individuals comprising the top management team occurring in 240 different firm-quarters. Of the 244 changes, 76 involve the death of either the president or the chairman. In table 1 we present summary statistics on the rate of nondeath top management changes. The data indicate a strikingly low rate of management turnover during the period we examine. The annual rate of

12. Because of the timing of the *Moody's* data, quarters were defined so that December 1–February 28 is the first quarter of a year.

13. W. Ferguson, chairman of Beatrice Creamery, left the firm between May 31, 1933, and May 31, 1934. A book on the history of Beatrice indicates that he was an absentee chairman during his tenure, but no source states whether he died in office.

TABLE 1 Summary Statistics for Top Management Changes

	All Observations	Nonfounder Observations	Founder Observations
Average annual number of nondeath changes in the top management team (%)	9.20	8.82	10.86
Average annual number of nondeath CEO changes (%)	3.83	3.88	3.58
Average annual number of nondeath president changes (%)	6.57	6.07	12.46
Mean age of departing top executive (years)	60.92	60.45	63.79
Median age of departing top executive (years)	61	61	67
Mean tenure of departing CEO (years)	12.66	11.14	20.82
Median tenure of departing CEO (years)	11	11	16

NOTE.—The entire sample consists of 7,304 firm-quarters. The ages of five individuals in the sample are missing. A change in the top management team is defined to be any change in the set of individuals holding the title of chairman or president. For these management changes, the founder calculations are for all observations where either the president or the chairman was a founder during the quarter. A CEO change is defined to be any change in the top management team where the firm's CEO leaves the top management team, where the CEO is defined to be the chairman if there is one and the president otherwise. A president change is defined to be any change in the top management team where the individual holding the title of president changes. For CEO (president) changes, the founder calculations are for all observations with a founder CEO (president). A departing top executive (CEO) is any president or chairman (CEO) who leaves the top management team. Tenure is calculated as the time in years since the CEO first took a job on the top management team.

nondeath changes in the top management team of 9.20% is substantially smaller than the 17.69% rate implied by the figures reported by Warner, Watts, and Wruck (1988).[14] Even if we adjust upward the rate of management changes to reflect the fact that in our sample top management teams are likely to be on average slightly smaller than in the Warner, Watts, and Wruck (1988) sample, the difference in the rate of top management changes is still substantial.[15]

The CEO title was not widely used in the 1930s, and *Moody's* does not use the CEO designation in its listing of officers. To proxy for CEO

14. We calculate the Warner, Watts, and Wruck (1988) figure by subtracting deaths from all changes and dividing by the sample size. Warner, Watts, and Wruck (1988) report figures for all changes and for changes reported in the *Wall Street Journal* (*WSJ*). Our figure is most comparable to the all changes category reported by Warner, Watts, and Wruck (1988), but even compared to the *WSJ* changes our firms exhibit less nondeath turnover.

15. In a 1963–78 sample Warner, Watts, and Wruck report that 65.7% of their sample had two top managers in 1978 but that prior to 1967 the majority of these firms had only one top manager. Using 65.7% as an upper bound would imply that the top management teams in their sample were, on average, 14.8% larger than the management teams in our sample. This is far too small to explain the 92% larger frequency of top management changes in their sample relative to ours.

changes, we define the firm's CEO to be the chairman if the firm had one and the president otherwise. Using this definition, the annual rate of nondeath CEO changes in our sample was 3.83%, which is significantly smaller than the comparable figure of 10.35% reported by Kaplan (1994*a*).[16] Again, the data indicate a very low rate of unconditional top management turnover during this time period.

Over 30% of the nondeath top management changes in our sample entailed the president taking the newly created chairman's job and a new individual taking over the presidency. This suggests that many of the chairmen of firms that had two top managers may have been effectively retired. Thus, we also consider changes in the individual who holds the title of president as a proxy for CEO changes. The annual rate of president changes in our sample is 6.57%.

C. *Reasons for Top Management Changes*

For each top management change we examined the details of the articles concerning the change and recorded the reason for the change. As other authors have noted, the reported reasons for top management turnover should be viewed with some skepticism. Of the 168 nondeath top management changes in our sample, 44 involved the president leaving the top management team, 45 involved the chairman leaving, and six involved both the chairman and president leaving. A large fraction (.40) of the changes that involve managers leaving the top management team have no reason reported for why the departure took place. This has been noted by Warner, Watts, and Wruck (1988) and Weisbach (1988) but is even more prevalent in our sample. The second leading category of reported reasons for top management departures was retirements and voluntary or amicable departures, which comprised 38.1% of all cases.[17] No other reported reason for a top management departure was given for more than 5% of all cases.

16. Kaplan's (1994*a*) figure is the most comparable in that he reports nondeath changes. Figures reported by Weisbach (1988), Jensen and Murphy (1990), and Houston and James (1995), imply similar large differences in the rate of CEO changes between the firms in our sample and modern firms. Using a definition of a CEO similar to ours, Denis, Denis, and Sarin (1995) find an 8.05% annual rate of CEO changes. Given that modern panels have very low rates of top management death, this would imply a large difference in the rate of turnover between our sample and theirs.

17. To be recorded as a retirement the article on the departure had to use the word "retire." Many articles did not use the word "retire" but contained statements such as this one by C. Wooley, chairman of American Radiator: "The time has come when I desire to be relieved from the duties and responsibilities of office, that they may turned over to younger men." We coded these statements as voluntary or amicable departures and treat them as similar to retirements. Warner, Watts, and Wruck (1988) report that 57 of their departures are categorized as "assume other position in firm," a categorization we do not use. In our sample when a manager assumed another position in the firm the reason for the change is coded as the reason given for why the manager takes the other position. The majority of these cases in our data are categorized as "no reason given" and could largely account for the difference in reported reasons for departure between the two samples.

While some of the retirements in our sample were described as mandatory retirements, empirically the institution of mandatory retirement appears to have been less prevalent than for modern firms. To illustrate, the annual rate of management departures for top managers aged 63, 64, and 65 was 2.0%, 3.1%, and 3.4%, respectively, while for managers under age 63 the rate was 3.06%. In contrast, Coughlan and Schmidt (1985) report annual rates of CEO turnover for CEOs aged 63, 64, and 65 of 19.0%, 54.1%, and 28.6%, respectively, and a rate for CEOs under the age of 63 of only 8.0%. Furthermore, only 9.0% of the managers that leave the top management team in our sample are aged 64–66, which contrasts sharply with higher figures reported for modern panels.

Pound's (1991) documentation that proxy fights during the period we examine were less costly than the modern era suggests the possibility that top management turnover in our sample was related to proxy contests for control. To assess the importance of proxy contests for control in our sample, we examined all firm-years where the number of new directors as a fraction of the total number of directors was greater than .5. There were 10 such firm-years. In three of these cases there was no management change in the year preceding or following the *Moody's* issue where the new directors first appear. In one case a firm in our sample completed a major merger with another firm and the boards were combined. In two cases the new board arose from the resolution of reorganization proceedings and a top management change occurred within a year of the new board appointments. One company generated three of the 10 cases. Initially, a controlling interest was purchased and the purchaser placed himself as chairman and replaced most of the board. Three years later this individual resigned as chairman after he was indicted on fraud charges, and both the board and top management changed in each of the subsequent 2 years. In the remaining single case, the year the board changed is the year a new president took office.

Based on this evidence, it appears that proxy contests for control accompanied by wholesale changes in the board and top management could be responsible for only one management change in our sample. While there were a few celebrated proxy cases for control before 1956, we have been unable to find any studies that systematically examine data on proxy contests before 1956. Our finding of the relative lack of importance of proxy contests in top management turnover is consistent with Williamson's (1983) assertion that the role of proxy contests in replacing ineffective managers was weak even before the most burdensome regulatory changes regarding proxy contests were put in place.

III. Estimation Results

Following previous research in this area, our approach is to perform logit regressions where the dependent variable takes a value of one when there is a management change and zero otherwise, and the independent variables include performance measures. We define the binary variable TOPCHANGE to take a value of one when there is a change in the set of individuals comprising the top management team. TOPCHANGE has the advantage that it is completely equivalent to the definition used by Warner, Watts, and Wruck (1988). In addition, we define the variable CEOCHANGE to take a value of one if the individual we define as the CEO leaves the top management team and zero otherwise, and the variable PRESCHANGE to take a value of one if the individual holding the title of president changes. As in Weisbach (1988), we use firm-quarters as the basic unit of observation.[18]

We regress the binary dependent variables indicating top management changes on performance measures constructed from the firm's annual stock returns. As other authors have pointed out, the board of directors should filter out marketwide movements in stock prices that do not reflect a manager's ability or effort when evaluating a manager's performance. To account for this, we include terms for the annual return on the CRSP equally weighted index. If the board makes top management changes because of poor performance, we expect a negative estimated coefficient on the firm's own stock return variables and a positive estimated coefficient on the market return variables.

A. *Baseline Results*

In table 2 we present the basic logit estimation results where we use changes in the top management team as our dependent variable. In column 1 we present estimates where we include return variables for the 3 years prior to the quarter. The coefficients on the firm's own stock return are all small, positive, and insignificantly different from zero. The coefficients on the market return variables are all small in magnitude and insignificantly different from zero. Since the standard errors on the returns coefficients are comparable to previous studies that have employed similar sized panels, it appears not that our results are just the reflection of very imprecise estimates but rather that these returns coefficients are individually estimated to be close to zero.

Previous authors have suggested that a manager's age could be an important explanator of top management changes. In column 1 we include a variable for the age of the oldest manager in the top management team and a binary variable that takes a value of one if any top manager is in the range of 64–66 years old at the start of the quarter. The coefficient on the age of the oldest manager of .021 is significant

18. This seems preferable to using years as the annual unit of observation, since performance measures included in the regressions will reflect the most recent performance measures observable by the board of directors with a short time lag. When we estimate the logit models presented in tables 2 and 3 using years as the basic unit of observation, our findings are qualitatively unchanged.

TABLE 2 Logit Estimates Predicting Top Management Changes

	(1)	(2)	(3)
Constant	−5.34***	−5.36***	−5.39***
	(.60)	(.59)	(.58)
$Return_{-1}$	.05		
	(.12)		
$Return_{-2}$	.04		
	(.10)		
$Return_{-3}$	.02		
	(.13)		
$Mktret_{-1}$	−.14		
	(.17)		
$Mktret_{-2}$	.04		
	(.14)		
$Mktret_{-3}$	−.10		
	(.16)		
Adj. $Return_{-1}$		.06	.06
		(.11)	(.11)
Adj. $Return_{-2}$		.03	
		(.12)	
Adj. $Return_{-3}$		.03	
		(.12)	
Dummy for two top managers	.39**	.39**	.40**
	(.18)	(.18)	(.18)
Dummy for top manager ages 64–66	.16	.16	
	(.22)	(.22)	
Maximum age of top managers	.021**	.021**	.022**
	(.010)	(.010)	(.010)
Number of observations	7,160	7,160	7,172
Number of observations where the dependent variable equals one	148	148	148
Log likelihood	−711.09	−712.21	−712.80
Significance of model, *p*-value	.0258	.0104	.0011

NOTE.—Asymptotic standard errors are reported in parentheses. The dependent variable TOPCHANGE is set equal to one if the set of individuals holding the title of president or chairman changes in a given quarter. In all specifications quarters where a top management change occurs due to a death, illness, control change, merger, or scandal are omitted. The difference in the number of observations across specifications is a result of missing 3-year lagged return data for 12 firm-quarters. $Return_{-1}$ is the firm's annual return for the year immediately preceding the quarter. $Mktret_{-1}$ is the annual return on the equally weighted index from Center for Research in Security Prices (CRSP) for the year preceding the quarter. Adj. $Return_{-1}$ is defined as $Return_{-1} - Mktret_{-1}$.

** Significant at the 5% level.

*** Significant at the 1% level.

at the 5% level. The variable for a manager being in the 64–66-year-old category is not significant. Additionally, in column 1 we include a binary variable that takes a value of one if the top management team has two people. The estimate on this coefficient is significant at the 1% level and indicates, not surprisingly, that larger management teams are more likely to experience a top management change.

Since the data do not reject equality in the magnitude of the coefficients on the firm's return and the market return, in all subsequent specifications we choose to use market-adjusted returns as our basic performance variable, where we define market-adjusted returns to be the firm's return minus the market return. In column 2 of table 2 we present estimates where we have included 3 years lagged annual market adjusted returns as the performance explanatory variables. Again, the coefficients on the returns variables are all small, positive, and insignificant.

Since previous studies indicate that returns more than 1 year prior to the unit of observation are not a significant explanator of turnover, and we find no evidence to the contrary in our data, we drop these lagged values from all subsequent specifications. This has the added practical advantage of limiting ourselves to a single performance measure when we consider the effects of factors such as founder status and ownership on the turnover-performance sensitivities. Additionally, in subsequent specifications we do not independently control for managers in the 64–66 age category by using a dummy variable, as this variable is insignificant after we control for age.

In column 3 of table 2 we present estimates where we have made these modifications. We consider this our baseline specification. Again, the estimated coefficient of .06 on adjusted returns is positive, small, and insignificantly different from zero. In contrast to almost all other studies of management turnover that find negative and significant coefficients on these types of performance variables, our data indicate that there was no relationship between stock performance and management turnover during the period we examine.

To check the conclusions from the logit model, we constructed performance deciles based on adjusted returns. Firm-quarters with the lowest adjusted returns were assigned to decile 1. The annual rate of nondeath top management changes for decile 1 was .073. This is lower than the rate of .089 for the best performers (decile 10). We then ranked the performance deciles from 1 to 10 according to the rate of nondeath management turnover within the decile, with a rank of 1 going to the decile with the lowest rate of turnover. The correlation between the performance rank of a decile and its turnover rank is positive (.55) and marginally significant (t = 1.87). This confirms the findings from the logit regressions that there is no evidence that poor stock performance led to changes in the top management team in our panel.

B. *Alternative Dependent Variables*

In table 3 we present estimation results for several alternative dependent variables. The coefficient on adjusted return in column 1 for the dependent variable corresponding to CEO changes is positive (.16) and insignificant, while for president changes the corresponding coefficient reported in column 2 is negative (−.06) but small and insignificant. As a comparison, in a similar specification Weisbach (1988) reports a significant negative coefficient for the effect of adjusted returns on CEO changes of −.64.

To capture top management changes that are most likely to reflect

TABLE 3 Logit Estimates Predicting Top Management Changes Using Alternative Dependent Variables

	Dependent Variable				
	CEO-CHANGE (1)	PRES-CHANGE (2)	OUTSIDE (3)	LEAVE (4)	FORCED (5)
Constant	−5.71***	−7.05***	−3.87***	−6.06***	−5.53***
	(.83)	(.65)	(1.13)	(.79)	(1.08)
Adj. Return$_{-1}$	.16	−.06	.02	.10	.08
	(.12)	(.16)	(.25)	(.12)	(.17)
Dummy for two top managers			.44	1.83***	2.16***
			(.38)	(.31)	(.46)
President's age		.049***			
		(.011)			
CEO's age	.016				
	(.013)				
Maximum age of top managers			−.029	.007	−.017
			(.020)	(.013)	(.018)
Number of observations	7,193	7,172	7,172	7,172	7,172
Number of observations where dependent variable equals one	61	107	32	85	42
Log likelihood	−350.46	−545.56	−203.83	−432.56	−241.45
Significance of model, p-value	.2853	.0000	.4618	.0627	.0000

NOTE.—Asymptotic standard errors are reported in parentheses. In all specifications quarters were a top management change occurs because of a death, illness, control change, merger, or scandal are omitted. The difference in the number of observations across specifications is a result of missing data on the ages of five of the 546 executives in the sample. We define the CEO to be the chairman if there is one and the president otherwise. CEOCHANGE is set equal to one if the individual who is the CEO leaves the top management team during the quarter. PRESCHANGE is set equal to one for all top management changes where the individual holding the title of president changes during the quarter. OUTSIDE is set equal to one if a top management change includes adding an outsider to the top management team during the quarter. LEAVE is set equal to one if the president or chairman leaves the top management team during the quarter. FORCED is set equal to one if the president or chairman leaves the top management team in a given quarter and the stated reason for the departure is not retirement, voluntary departure, taking an honorary position, or taking a government or prestigious position elsewhere.

*** Significant at the 1% level.

decisions by the board to replace suboptimal top managers, we create three additional dependent variables. The variable OUTSIDE takes a value of one when an outsider joins the top management team, the variable LEAVE takes a value of one if a top manager leaves the top management team,[19] and the variable FORCED is coded as one if a top manager leaves the top management team and the stated reason

19. In a few cases a president becomes vice chairman or chairman of the executive committee. Since in some cases when this happens this individual eventually becomes chairman, we do not code LEAVE as one for these departures from the top management

for departure is not retirement, voluntarily leaving, taking an honorary position, or taking a government or prestigious position elsewhere.[20] The results for these three dependent variables are presented in columns 3, 4, and 5 of table 3. In all three cases the coefficient on adjusted returns is small, insignificantly different from zero and opposite of the expected sign.

The results we report above employ what we consider to be the most appropriate specifications given the data available to us. The estimates we report differ sharply from the negative and significant coefficients on stock return performance variables reported by authors examining top management turnover for modern panels. Previous studies of management turnover use a variety of different specifications, largely due to different types of data availability in each study. Because of small differences in specifications across studies, it is hard to compare statistically our estimates to those in previously published studies. In results not reported here, we estimate an annual logit model of top management changes that is identical to the specification reported by Warner, Watts, and Wruck (1988). The estimated coefficients on the firm's contemporaneous and lagged returns in our sample are positive and significantly different from the negative coefficients reported by Warner, Watts, and Wruck (1988) at the 1% and 6% levels, respectively.[21] This provides additional evidence that turnover was less sensitive to stock returns during the period we examine compared to the modern era.

IV. Other Factors Influencing Turnover

Several papers on executive turnover have suggested that there may be substantial cross-sectional variation in the sensitivity of executive turnover to firm performance that can be explained by observable characteristics. These include age (Jensen and Murphy 1990), founder status of the executive (Denis, Denis, and Sarin 1995), the composition of the board (Weisbach 1988), and the ownership structure of the firm

---

team. These changes are included in the top management change dependent variable. They are similar to when a president becomes chairman and a new individual becomes president.

20. Because of differences in data availability, it is difficult to construct a variable representing forced departures that is exactly comparable to other samples. These variables are used as a rough attempt to capture the management changes that are most likely to reflect replacement of suboptimal managers.

21. While we use their exact specification, a difference remains in that Warner, Watts, and Wruck (1988) use the subset of top management changes reported in the *Wall Street Journal* as their dependent variable. Elsewhere in their paper they indicate that the results are similar when they use all top management changes as the dependent variable. The significance levels we report are for the asymptotic *t*-statistic of the difference between the coefficients we estimate and the coefficients reported by Warner, Watts, and Wruck (1988).

TABLE 4 Summary Statistics of Age, Tenure, Founder Status, Ownership Characteristics, and Board Composition

Variable	Mean	Median
Chairman's age (years)	63.2	63
Chairman's tenure (years)	13.7	11
CEO's age (years)	60.0	60
CEO's tenure (years)	12.4	10
Chairman is founder	.250	0
Chairman is member of founding family	.073	0
CEO is founder	.168	0
CEO member of founding family	.075	0
Holdings of chairman (%)	3.53	1.20
Holdings of CEO (%)	3.23	.98
Holdings of chairman and president (%)	3.91	1.17
Holdings of all officers and directors (%)	10.29	5.85
Holdings of inside directors excluding the chairman and president (%)	3.54	.81
Holdings of outside directors (%)	2.66	.91
Holdings of independent outside blockholders (%)	19.54	16.02
Fraction of outsiders on the board of directors (%)	52.4	55.56

NOTE.—The age, tenure, founder, and board composition statistics are calculated over the population of all firm-quarters with the relevant data available. The figures for chairmen are calculated over the population of quarters where the firm has a chairman who is not also president. The CEO is defined to be the chairman if there is one and the president otherwise. The tenure figures are calculated as the amount of time in years that had passed from the first date the individual took any top management job (either as president or chairman). The ownership figures are the total direct and indirect holdings of common stock as of December 31, 1935, for the 225 firms with complete data available. Details as to how indirect holdings were attributed to individuals are available from the authors. The chairman ownership statistics are for all individuals holding the title of chairman but not president. Of the 225 firms with ownership data, 96 have a chairman who is not president as of December 31, 1935. Forty-two companies have outside block holders who are apparently independent of top management and that hold common stock. The block holder figures in the table pertain to these 42 companies.

(Denis, Denis, and Sarin 1995). This raises the question as to whether the results we present above are driven by large changes in these variables since the 1930s.

A. *Founder Status and Tenure*

Using *Who's Who in Commerce and Industry,* obituaries, and the *Moody's* manuals published before 1933, we were able to assess for all 546 top managers in the sample the first year they became a member of the top management team and whether they were a founder or member of a founding family. The summary statistics for these variables are presented in table 4. As one might expect, there is a fairly high incidence of top managers who are founders in our sample. In 16.8% of the firm-quarters in our sample the individual we define to be the CEO is a founder and an additional 7.5% are not founders but are members of founding families. As a comparison, using a definition of CEO similar to ours, Denis, Denis, and Sarin (1995) report that only 6.1% of their panel of 1,394 modern firms have a CEO who is a founder.

TABLE 5 Logit Estimates of the Effect of Founder and Tenure Status on Top Management Changes

	Dependent Variable			
	TOPCHANGE (1)	CEOCHANGE (2)	PRESCHANGE (3)	FORCED (4)
Constant	−5.18***	−5.67***	−6.71***	−5.85***
	(.60)	(.85)	(.68)	(1.12)
FOUNDER	−.19	−.20	.52*	−1.02*
	(.23)	(.40)	(.29)	(.54)
TENURE	.020**	.007	.014	−.000
	(.009)	(.015)	(.012)	(.021)
Adj. Return$_{-1}$	−.20	−.04	−.18	−.58
	(.22)	(.28)	(.25)	(.39)
Adj. Return$_{-1}$ *FOUNDER	−.42	−.63	−.27	−.85
	(.37)	(.60)	(.42)	(.78)
Adj. Return$_{-1}$ *TENURE	.028	.022	.017	.067**
	(.017)	(.025)	(.021)	(.034)
Dummy for two top managers	.42**			2.26***
	(.18)			(.46)
AGE	.014	.014	.040***	−.011
	(.010)	(.014)	(.012)	(.019)
Number of observations	7,172	7,193	7,172	7,172
Log likelihood	−709.53	−349.65	−542.01	−236.98
Significance of model, p-value	.0020	.6616	.0000	.0000

NOTE.—Asymptotic standard errors are reported in parentheses. FOUNDER is a dummy variable that takes a value of one if either of the top managers are founders for the dependent variables TOPCHANGE and FORCED and a value of one if the CEO (president) is a founder for the dependent variable CEOCHANGE (PRESCHANGE). TENURE is the maximum of the president and chairman's tenure as a top manager for the dependent variables TOPCHANGE and FORCED and the CEO's (president's) tenure for the dependent variable CEOCHANGE (PRESCHANGE). AGE is the maximum of the president and chairman's age for the dependent variables TOPCHANGE and FORCED and the CEO's (president's) age for the dependent variable CEOCHANGE (PRESCHANGE). All other variables are defined as in tables 2 and 3.

* Significant at the 10% level.
** Significant at the 5% level.
*** Significant at the 1% level.

Since it is possible that individuals who are founders have a special status within their firms and are particularly hard to remove, it would appear to be particularly important to see if our results are driven by the high proportion of founders in our sample.

The figures presented in the right two columns of table 1 suggest that the unconditional rate of top management changes in our sample is not significantly lower for firms with top managers who are founders. We present in table 5 estimates of our basic specification for four of the dependent variables, where we have included terms related to the founder status of top managers.[22] The insignificant coefficient on the founder variable in column 1 provides no evidence that the low unconditional rate of top management changes in our sample arises from the relatively high proportion of founders in the sample. The positive and significant (t = 1.79) coefficient on founder variable in column 3 indicates that presidents who are founders appear more likely to be replaced, but the corresponding negative coefficient on forced departures (t = 1.89) suggests that founders are less likely to be forced out. All the coefficients of the interaction of the founder variable with the performance measure are negative, and none are significant. Thus it does not appear that top management changes are less sensitive to performance for firms with founders as top managers.[23]

If a manager has been in office a long time, he may have more control over the board and thus may be harder to remove. Alternatively, managers who have been in place a long time may have established that they are high-quality managers, and the incremental information in a single year's stock return may be discounted given the board's prior information on the manager. In either case, a top manager's tenure could be an important determinant of turnover, and omitting it from our regressions could result in an important misspecification. To control for this, we include terms in table 5 for the tenure of the top manager(s) and the interaction of tenure with returns. The coefficient on the tenure variable is significant only in the top management changes regression, where it enters with a positive sign (.020). Thus we have limited evidence that longer tenure increased the probability of a top management change. The coefficient on the interaction of tenure with returns is positive and significant only for the dependent variable representing forced departures.

B. *The Composition of the Board of Directors*

Weisbach (1988) finds empirical evidence that the structure of the board of directors influences executive turnover. To examine if the composition of the board has changed significantly over time, we define an outside director to be any director who is not an officer, a retired officer, general counsel to the firm, or has the same last name as an officer. Our median firm has 55.56% outsiders compared to a median in the 45%–50% range for Weisbach (1988). We are not able to obtain systematic data on all directors whom Weisbach (1988) classifies as

22. Since the dependent variables for outsider changes, departures, and forced departures are all intended to capture the same types of turnover events, we economize on space by using only forced departures in all subsequent specifications.

23. When we run our baseline specifications on the restricted subsample of nonfounder firm-quarters, the results are qualitatively unchanged from those reported above in tables 2 and 3.

"greys," for example, directors who are also investment bankers for a firm. Since these directors would usually end up in our sample classified as outsiders, the difference in the median firm's fraction of outside directors between the two samples is likely even smaller than the 5%–10% range indicated. Based on this data, it appears that the basic composition of the board of directors since the 1930s has remained fairly constant, and it is unlikely that our results are a reflection of major changes in board composition over time.

In results not reported here, we use Weisbach's (1988) methodology and categorize firm-quarters based on whether the firm's board had less than 40% outsiders, 40%–60% outsiders, or over 60% outsiders. When we add dummy variables for these board composition variables and the interaction of the board composition variables with adjusted returns, none of the estimated interaction coefficients is significant. Thus board composition does not appear to be a significant explanator of the turnover-performance sensitivities in our sample.

We do not interpret these results as evidence that board composition does not matter as a determinant of top management changes. Outside representation on the board may in general increase the sensitivity of management changes to performance. However, in our sample the relationship between management changes and performance is essentially nonexistent, and increased outside representation on the board is likely to be a second-order effect relative to other factors underlying our basic findings.

C. *Ownership Structure*

The ownership structure of firms could have an important effect on the mechanism governing the removal of top managers. The findings of Morck, Shleifer, and Vishny (1988) and Denis, Denis, and Sarin (1995) suggest that large holdings by insiders may entrench managers. At the same time, high ownership by outside board members and blockholders may result in more efficient removal decisions, as outsiders have a larger economic incentive to remove suboptimal managers.

We use data from the Securities and Exchange Commission's (SEC's) *Official Summary of Holdings of Officers, Directors, and Principal Stockholders* to construct variables related to a firm's ownership structure.[24] All but four of the firms in our sample have ownership data included in this document, which reports the direct and indirect holdings of all officers, directors, and 10% blockholders as of December 31, 1935. Since the identity of the source of indirect holdings are usually identified for each individual, we are able to divide indirect holdings

24. In a few cases we fill in missing ownership data of top managers with data from SEC filings.

held by multiple individuals between them to avoid double counting problems.

The ownership data is a cross section as of December 31, 1935. We construct quarterly ownership variables assuming that the ownership of any individual does not change substantially from this date until the end of our sample. We adjust all quarterly ownership figures to reflect changes in the set of individuals holding the title of president or chairman that occur after December 31, 1935. When an individual who takes the position of president or chairman after December 31, 1935, did not have an ownership position recorded in the *Official Summary* document, we find their first reported holdings in subsequent Form 5 and Form 6 SEC filings and use this figure for their ownership interest.

The basic summary statistics for the ownership data as of December 31, 1935, are contained in table 4. Most of the mean holdings we report are similar to figures reported by researchers on modern panels, while the median holdings we report tend to be somewhat higher, suggesting less variation in the dispersion of ownership in the 1930s.[25] The mean holdings by all officers and directors in our sample is 10.29% while the median is 5.85%. As a comparison, Morck, Shleifer, and Vishny (1988) report a 10.6% mean holdings for the entire board for a panel of 371 Fortune 500 firms and a median of 3.4%. Denis, Denis, and Sarin (1995) report a similar figure of 10.8% for the mean holdings of all officers and directors in their sample of *Valueline* firms.

Turning to the holdings of the top management team, Morck, Shleifer, and Vishny (1988) report mean (median) holdings of 6.3% (.5%) for the chairman and president, where the corresponding figure for our sample is 3.91% (1.17%).[26] The mean holdings for the individual we define to be the CEO in our sample is 3.23%, which is higher than the 2.42% figure reported by Jensen and Murphy (1990) for a panel of 746 CEOs and smaller than the 4.5% figure reported by Denis, Denis, and Sarin (1995). While the mean holdings for the top managers in our sample appear similar to modern firms, the medians are clearly higher. To illustrate, the median holdings for the individual we define to be the CEO is .98%, which is substantially higher than the median figure reported by both Jensen and Murphy (1990) (.25%), and Denis, Denis, and Sarin (1995) (less than .1%).

25. Gordon (1938) presents summary statistics for the total direct plus indirect holdings of 88 large industrials using the same SEC data source as we do and arrives at figures comparable to those we present. In a recent study Holderness, Kroszner, and Sheehan (1996) examine these SEC data and arrive at comparable figures for a much larger sample.

26. Noting that our firms exhibit slightly fewer two-person top management teams than modern firms would tend to make the holdings of the two top managers slightly smaller for our panel, all else being equal. Weisbach (1988) reports a mean holding of 3.71% for the top two officers of a 208-firm subsample of Morck, Shleifer, and Vishny's (1988) sample.

Holdings by outside board members appear to be higher in our sample relative to modern firms, while holdings by outside blockholders appear to be lower. Denis, Denis, and Sarin (1995) report a mean holding of 6.3% for all officers and directors except the CEO, where the corresponding figure in our sample is only slightly higher with a mean of 7.02%. The main difference is that Denis, Denis, and Sarin (1995) attribute most of these board holdings to inside directors, where we find close to an even division of these board holdings between inside and outside directors. Finally, our firms appear to have substantially lower institutional ownership and unaffiliated blockholder holdings. We find that for only 18.7% of our firms is there a blockholder that is unaffiliated with a board member compared to 45.2% reported by Denis, Denis, and Sarin (1995).[27]

Denis, Denis, and Sarin (1995) consider directly the role of ownership in top management turnover and find evidence that higher levels of holdings by top managers decrease the sensitivity of turnover to performance. Since ownership by the top management team for the median firm in our sample is somewhat higher than for modern firms, it is possible that our results are driven by this difference. In particular we have fewer firms with top managers holding very low fractions of the firm's equity.

We construct a binary variable TOPHOLD-1/5, which takes a value of one when the holdings of the top management team are between 1% and 5% and a variable TOPHOLD-5/100, which takes a value of one when these holdings are greater than 5%. In table 6 we present estimates where we add these variables and the interaction of these variables with adjusted returns to our baseline specification. These regressions are for the reduced subsample of firm-quarters for which we have ownership data and thus begin with the first quarter of 1936.

The coefficients on the ownership binary variables are significant only in the forced departure regression in column 4 of table 6. In this regression the estimates on the ownership variables are negative and significant at the 10% level, indicating that forced departures were less likely when the top management team owned over 1% of outstanding equity. In all specifications, none of the coefficients interacting returns with the ownership variables is significant. For the dependent variable representing CEO changes, the positive coefficient of .75 on adjusted returns is of the opposite of expected sign and is significant at the 10% level (t = 1.92). None of the other adjusted returns variables is significant. Thus there is little evidence that ownership effects are driving the low turnover-performance sensitivities in our sample.

27. We called a block unaffiliated if no officer or director listed the blockholder in his/her indirect interest holdings with above a 5% interest and if the name of the blockholder did not contain the last name of an officer or director. All other block holdings are attributed to the parties with which they are affiliated.

TABLE 6 Logit Estimates of the Effect of Ownership on Top Management Changes

	Dependent Variable			
	TOP-CHANGE (1)	CEO-CHANGE (2)	PRES-CHANGE (3)	FORCED (4)
Constant	−5.58***	−5.59***	−7.39***	−5.69***
	(.71)	(1.04)	(.75)	(1.37)
TOPHOLD-1/5	−.20	−.62	.13	−.78*
	(.23)	(.39)	(.27)	(.44)
TOPHOLD-5/100	−.11	−.55	.06	−.94*
	(.27)	(.53)	(.37)	(.56)
Adj. Return_{-1}	.10	.75*	.01	−.59
	(.37)	(.39)	(.38)	(.60)
Adj. Return_{-1} * TOPHOLD-1/5	.42	−.12	.37	.14
	(.53)	(.72)	(.63)	(.93)
Adj. Return_{-1} * TOPHOLD-5/100	.35	−1.52	.58	−.22
	(.58)	(1.33)	(.70)	(1.17)
Dummy for two top managers	.49**			2.13***
	(.22)			(.52)
AGE	.026**	.018	.056***	−.006
	(.012)	(.017)	(.012)	(.023)
Number of observations	4,787	4,787	4,787	4,787
Number of observations where dependent variable equals one	107	49	86	31
Log likelihood	−503.23	−241.28	−395.44	−173.25
Significance of model, *p*-value	.0098	.2159	.0010	.0002

NOTE.—Asymptotic standard errors are reported in parentheses. TOPHOLD-1/5 is a dummy variable that takes a value of one when the total holdings of common stock by the top management team are between 1% and 5% in the regressions with the dependent variables TOPCHANGE and FORCED and takes a value of one when the holdings of the CEO (president) are between 1% and 5% in the regressions using the dependent variable CEOCHANGE (PRESCHANGE). TOPHOLD-5/100 is defined similarly where the ownership range is between 5% and 100%. All other variables are defined as in the previous tables.

* Significant at the 10% level.
** Significant at the 5% level.
*** Significant at the 1% level.

In results not reported here, we experiment with specifications where instead of using binary variables we include the holdings by the top management team and its interaction with adjusted returns as explanatory variables. In all these specifications, none of the ownership variables, the adjusted returns variables, or the interaction of ownership with adjusted returns is significant at even the 10% level. When we add additional terms for holdings by other inside directors, holdings by outside directors, and holdings by blockholders, all of the estimated coefficients on these ownership variables are insignificant.[28] We con-

28. In a previous draft we created dummy variables indicating whether the total holdings by all inside board members including the chairman and president was in the less than 1%, 1%–5%, or greater than 5% range. We find some evidence that the greater than 1%

clude that there is little evidence that ownership effects explain the difference between the turnover-performance sensitivities we estimate and those presented by others for modern firms.

D. Other Potential Factors

Firm Size. Warner, Watts, and Wruck (1988) suggest that the rate of top management changes may be higher for the larger firms in their sample. Given their sampling technique, our sample is likely to be composed of, on average, larger firms than theirs, which would predict a higher turnover rate in our sample, the opposite of what we find. To explore further the importance of size, in results not reported here we run the baseline specification of column 3 of table 2 where we include the log of the firm's size as an additional independent variable. We estimate insignificant coefficients on this size variable when we use either the log of the firm's 1933 book value or the log of the firm's 1933 market value as our size measure. We divide our sample into subsamples according to whether the firm was above or below the median based on these size measures. The coefficients on adjusted returns do not differ significantly between size classes. Thus, within our sample, size does not seem to be an important explanator of the mechanism governing top management changes.

Firm Age. If firms in the 1930s were, on average, younger than modern firms, and if the pool of replacement managers is smaller for younger firms, our results could be due to this age difference. In results not reported here, we divide our sample in half, based on whether the firm's date of incorporation is above or below the median. We find no significant difference in the rate of top management changes between the two groups of firms, and the coefficient on adjusted returns in our baseline specification of column 3 of table 2 is positive and insignificant for both subsamples.

Quality of Managers. It is possible that the rapid economic downturn from 1929 to 1933 resulted in a widespread purging of poor managers. If this were true, the turnover results we present above may simply reflect a historically above-average pool of top managers in our sample. The data do not confirm this possible explanation. Using the 1929 *Moody's* we find that 48.5% of our firms experienced changes in the top management team for May 1929–May 1933.[29] The corresponding figure for May 1933–May 1937 is 41.1% and for May 1937–May 1941 is 45.8%. These figures suggest that turnover rates from 1929 to

firms have a higher turnover-performance sensitivity than the less than 1% firms. Although this indicates that ownership may affect turnover performance sensitivities in the expected way, it is of limited importance in making historical comparisons since the median firm in almost all studies of ownership has total insider holdings of above 1%.

29. This figure will include all top management changes including deaths. More detailed data concerning turnover between 1929 and 1933 are very costly to obtain.

1933 were only slightly higher than those during the time period we examine, and it does not appear that there was a dramatic change in the pool of top executives during the rapid economic decline from 1929 to 1933.

Information Content of Returns. A final potential explanation for our findings is that the signal-to-noise ratio of stock performance was much lower during the period we study than in more recent years. If this were true, the information content in poor stock performance would be smaller and we might expect to see a smaller sensitivity of management changes to stock performance.[30] It is well known (Fama 1973) that the 1930s were a time of historically high return variability, which would appear consistent with a smaller information content in returns data.

To investigate this explanation, we compare the variability of returns in our sample to the set of firms with returns data as of December 31, 1962, on the CRSP NYSE/AMEX monthly tape. We examine the returns variability for this set of firms from 1963 to 1978, the time period examined by Warner, Watts, and Wruck (1988). For each firm-quarter from the first quarter of 1963 to the fourth quarter of 1978 we calculate the prior year's return on a given stock and subtract the annual return on the equally weighted CRSP index. The distribution of the absolute value of this market-adjusted return is used as our measure of return variability.

For our sample from 1963 to 1978, the median and mean values of the return variability measure were .2067 and .2830, respectively. For our sample for June 1, 1933, to June 1, 1941, the median and mean values were .2237 and .3699, respectively, suggesting somewhat more variability in returns even after adjusting for market-wide effects. Examination of the data for 1933–41 reveals that much of the high variability arises from the first year of the sample when the annual return on the equally weighted index was over 300% for the year preceding June 1, 1933. If we eliminate the first 4 quarters from our 1933–41 sample we find that the median and mean values of the return variability measure were .1988 and .2711, respectively. These figures are smaller than the corresponding figures for 1963–78, and a Wilcoxon rank-sum test indicates the medians are different at the 10% level. We reestimated all of the basic regressions for the specifications employed in tables 2 and 3 with the first 4 quarters of the sample excluded, and all the results are qualitatively unchanged from what we report above. Thus it does not appear that our results are driven by higher variability of returns during the 1933–41 time period.

V. Compensation of Top Managers

The low rate of top management turnover and the weak sensitivity of turnover to stock returns that we report above are particularly surprising

30. This would still not explain the low unconditional turnover rates in our sample.

in light of the results presented by Jensen and Murphy (1990). Their results suggest that pay-performance sensitivities have declined by a factor of almost 10 since the 1930s. An interesting potential explanation for both sets of findings is that incentives generated by turnover policies and compensation policies have functioned as substitutes over time.

A. *Baseline Results*

To investigate this matter further, we collected all available compensation data for our panel of firms for the fiscal years 1934–40 from the Works Progress Administration study *Survey of American Listed Corporations,* as well as supplemental reports to this study. This source does not explicitly identify the pay of the chairman or the president, so we use the highest reported remuneration as our measure of top manager compensation.[31] Since our sample should include virtually all the industrials in the top quartile of the NYSE, there should be substantial overlap between our sample and the 1934–38 sample used by Jensen and Murphy (1990). For comparison purposes, we construct a panel of modern firms to compare to our 1934–40 sample. We identify all firms in the 1980 *Forbes* executive compensation survey that are listed on the CRSP NYSE monthly tape. From this initial set of firms we construct a panel using all available compensation for these firms from the 1974–86 *Forbes* surveys.[32]

After eliminating years with management changes, constructing first differences, and constructing returns data from the CRSP NYSE monthly tape, our 1934–40 sample consists of 739 observations representing 189 firms and our 1974–86 sample consists of 5,600 observations representing 632 firms. Our 1934–40 sample is larger than the 1934–38 sample employed by Jensen and Murphy (1990), and additionally we are able to exclude from the sample years where annual changes in compensation could reflect management changes. To maintain comparability with the results reported by Jensen and Murphy (1990), all monetary variables are converted to 1986 dollars using the consumer price index (CPI). The mean (median) top manager compensation was \$673,907 (\$579,064) in the 1934–40 sample and \$611,242 (\$556,876) in the 1974–86 sample.

Following Jensen and Murphy (1990), we regress annual changes in pay on the annual change in shareholder wealth and its 1-year lag. These estimates are reported in table 7. The sum of the coefficients on contemporaneous and lagged changes in shareholder wealth reported in column 1 imply a 9.9 cent (t = 7.86) total pay revision for each

31. Two firms in our sample are in the movie production and distribution industry. Since these firms have some very highly paid employees who are not managers, we exclude these two firms from the compensation regressions.

32. We thank Kevin J. Murphy for providing us with the *Forbes* compensation data. The compensation data are for fiscal years, so for each firm we calculate returns on a fiscal year basis.

TABLE 7 OLS Estimates of Top Management Pay-Performance Sensitivities for 1934–40 and 1974–86

	Dependent Variables					
Independent Variables	ΔPAY (1)	ΔPAY (2)	ΔLOGPAY (3)	ΔLOGPAY (4)	ΔLOGPAY (5)	ΔLOGPAY (6)
Constant	24.38***	28.52***	.045***	.051***	.032***	.047***
	(6.47)	(2.56)	(.008)	(.003)	(.008)	(.003)
ΔShareholder Wealth	.000048***	.0000124***				
	(.000009)	(.0000019)				
ΔShareholder Wealth$_{-1}$	.000051***	.0000065***				
	(.000009)	(.0000016)				
Return			.094***	.172***	.103***	.169***
			(.028)	(.009)	(.028)	(.009)
Return$_{-1}$					.053**	.040***
					(.026)	(.009)
Market Return			−.128***	−.121***	−.092**	−.125***
			(.043)	(.015)	(.043)	(.015)
Market Return$_{-1}$					.073*	.044***
					(.043)	(.013)
Number of observations	739	5,600	739	5,600	739	5,600
Adjusted R^2	.075	.011	.013	.058	.046	.070
Time period	1934–40	1974–86	1934–40	1974–86	1934–40	1974–86

NOTE.—Standard errors are in parentheses. ΔPAY is $PAY_t - PAY_{t-1}$, where for 1934–40 PAY_t is the highest reported pay of any executive of the firm for fiscal year t in thousands of 1986 dollars as reported by the *Survey of American Listed Corporations*. For the 1974–86 sample PAY_t is fiscal year salary and bonus for the CEO of the firm in thousands of 1986 dollars as reported by *Forbes*. ΔLOGPAY is the corresponding change in the natural logarithm of PAY. ΔShareholder Wealth is the start-of-fiscal-year market value in thousands of 1986 dollars multiplied by $r_t - i_t$, where r_t is the return for fiscal year t from Center for Research in Security Prices (CRSP) and i_t is the corresponding inflation rate. Return is defined to be $\ln(1 + r_t - i_t)$. Market Return is defined as $\ln(1 + v_t - i_t)$, where v_t is the annual return on the CRSP value-weighted index. All firm-years where a management change occurs during fiscal year $t - 1$ or t are excluded, as this invalidates the variables ΔPAY and ΔLOGPAY. OLS = ordinary least squares.

* Significant at the 10% level.
** Significant at the 5% level.
*** Significant at the 1% level.

$1,000 change in shareholder wealth for the 1934–40 sample. For the 1974–86 sample the corresponding estimate from column 2 is 1.89 cents (t = 8.24). The two estimates are different at the 1% level (t = 6.26). These results confirm the findings of Jensen and Murphy (1990) that pay-performance sensitivities estimated using an arithmetic specification have declined substantially since the 1930s.[33]

It is unclear, however, whether these results reflect real changes in compensation policies over time. Jensen and Murphy (1990) document that larger firms have smaller arithmetic pay-performance sensitivities.[34] Since modern firms tend to be larger than firms in the 1930s, the historical differences in estimated arithmetic pay-performance sensitivities could simply be a reflection of these size differences.

An additional shortcoming of using the arithmetic specification to make comparisons over time is that the results can be very sensitive to a few large firms when the size distribution of firms is skewed. To illustrate, if we eliminate the three observations for General Motors, the largest firm in our 1934–40 sample ranked by market value, the results change substantially (estimates not reported). The coefficient on the contemporaneous change in shareholder wealth falls to .000016 (t = 1.59), a third of its size when General Motors is included in the sample. This estimate is no longer different from zero or from the corresponding estimate for modern firms. The estimated total pay-performance sensitivity for the 1934–40 sample falls to 5.25 cents (t = 3.27) for each $1,000 change in shareholder wealth, and the magnitude of the difference in sensitivities over time is much smaller, though still significant at the 5% level (t = 2.07).

An alternative specification of the pay-performance relation utilizes changes in the logarithm of pay as the dependent variable and stock returns as the independent variable. Rosen (1990) argues that this type of semielasticity specification is less sensitive to size effects. In columns 3 and 4 of table 7 we present estimates for our 1934–40 sample and 1974–86 sample using a simple semielasticity specification. The estimated coefficient on the firm's stock return of .094 (t = 3.35) for the 1934–40 sample is smaller than the corresponding estimate of .172 (t = 18.3) for the 1974–86 sample, and the differences are significant at the 1% level.[35] Thus the semielasticity specification, which may better

33. Our estimates imply that pay-performance sensitivities have declined by a factor of approximately 5 since the 1930s, where Jensen and Murphy (1990) estimate a decline by a factor of almost 10. When we ignore management changes and restrict the sample to 1934–38, our estimates also imply a decline by a factor of approximately 10. Note that the total pay-performance sensitivity of 1.89 cents for the 1974–86 sample is very similar to the 2.19 cent estimate for 1974–86 reported in the identical specification by Jensen and Murphy (1990, table 1, col. 2).

34. This relationship between firm size and arithmetic pay-performance sensitivities is consistent with optimal contracting (Haubrich 1994).

35. Note that this semielasticity specification is identical to the specification used by Gibbons and Murphy (1990, table 1, col. 3) for their 1974–86 *Forbes* sample, except that we use a CRSP value-weighted index and they use a COMPUSTAT value-weighted

control for size effects, seems to indicate that incentives generated by compensation have increased significantly since the 1930s, opposite to the findings using the arithmetic specification.[36]

There are no lagged returns measures in columns 3 and 4 of table 7 in order to maintain comparability with previously published studies. The arithmetic specifications suggest that lagged firm performance has explanatory power in the pay-performance relationship, so we report in columns 5 and 6 of table 7 estimates where we add lagged returns and lagged market returns as explanatory variables to the basic semi-elasticity specification. The estimate on contemporaneous returns remains significantly greater for the 1974–86 period compared to the 1934–40 period at the 5% level (t = 2.24) and confirms the previous finding that pay-performance sensitivities estimated as semielasticities have increased over time. There are no significant differences over time in the estimated coefficients on lagged returns, contemporaneous market returns, or lagged market returns.

B. Controls for Firm Size

Given the different findings from the two types of specifications, it is difficult to assess how incentives generated by compensation policies have changed over time. It appears likely that the arithmetic results are purely a reflection of size effects, but we have no direct evidence for this assertion. If arithmetic pay-performance sensitivities are declining in firm size, then we should be able to control for size effects by modifying the arithmetic specification. A simple way to control for firm size in these regressions is to add terms that interact the change in shareholder wealth variables with $1/\text{MKT}_{t-1}$, where MKT_{t-1} is the market value of the firm's equity at the beginning of fiscal year t. If larger firms have smaller arithmetic pay-performance sensitivities, the coefficient on this term should be positive. Additionally, since we expect there to be substantial heteroscedasticity in the arithmetic regressions due to size effects, in all of the following regressions we correct the standard errors for heteroscedasticity using White's (1980) method.

The results for the two time periods with these simple size controls added to the basic arithmetic specification are reported in columns 1

index. Our estimates for the 1974–86 period are very similar to the corresponding Gibbons and Murphy (1990) estimates.

36. To ensure that ownership differences over time are not driving this finding, we divide the 1934–40 sample in half according to whether the maximum of the president's holding and the chairman's holding for each firm as of December 31, 1935, was above or below the median for the sample. The estimated semielasticity of pay with respect to returns between these two subsamples are almost identical. This indicates that our results are not a reflection of ownership substituting for incentive compensation. Additionally, when we restrict the modern sample to only include firms with the same one-digit Standard Industrial Classification codes as the 1934–40 panel, the semielasticity estimate for the modern period increases slightly, and the differences over time remains significant at the 1% level.

TABLE 8 OLS Estimates of Top Management Pay-Performance Sensitivities for 1934–40 and 1974–86

	Dependent Variables			
Independent Variables	ΔPAY (1)	ΔPAY (2)	ΔPAY (3)	ΔPAY (4)
Constant	25.89***	22.14***	10.70	89.46***
	(6.57)	(2.38)	(16.49)	(33.59)
PAY_{t-1}			.019	−.130**
			(.030)	(.055)
ΔShareholder Wealth	.0000484*	.0000048**	.0000559***	−.0000016
	(.0000247)	(.0000023)	(.0000248)	(.0000027)
ΔShareholder Wealth * $(1/MKT_{t-1})$	2.50	70.56***		
	(13.40)	(8.55)		
ΔShareholder Wealth * (PAY_{t-1}/MKT_{t-1})			−.042	.195***
			(.032)	(.036)
ΔShareholder $Wealth_{-1}$	.0000430*	.0000042***	.0000327	.0000053
	(.0000253)	(.0000015)	(.0000238)	(.0000041)
ΔShareholder $Wealth_{-1}$ * $(1/MKT_{t-1})$	34.84***	26.70***		
	(12.52)	(5.53)		
ΔShareholder $Wealth_{-1}$ * (PAY_{t-1}/MKT_{t-2})			.062**	.057
			(.029)	(.048)
Number of observations	739	5,600	739	5,600
Adjusted R^2	.082	.030	.091	.081
Time period	1934–40	1974–86	1934–40	1974–86

NOTE.—White (1980) heteroscedasticity-consistent standard errors are in parentheses. All variables are defined as in table 7. MKT_t is defined to be the firm's end-of-fiscal-year market value of equity in thousands of 1986 dollars. In all columns we exclude firm-years where a management change occurs during fiscal year $t-1$ or t. OLS = ordinary least squares.
* Significant at the 10% level.
** Significant at the 5% level.
*** Significant at the 1% level.

and 2 of table 8. The estimates in column 2 for 1974–86 indicate a strong negative relationship between size and the arithmetic sensitivity of pay to changes in shareholder wealth and lagged changes in shareholder wealth. The coefficients on the terms interacting changes in shareholder wealth with $1/MKT_{t-1}$ are positive and significant at the 1% level. The estimates in column 1 for the 1934–40 time period indicate a smaller role for firm size in arithmetic pay-performance sensitivities during this period. While the coefficients on the terms interacting changes in shareholder wealth with $1/MKT_{t-1}$ are positive, only the coefficient on lagged changes is significant ($t = 2.78$)

We can use the estimates from columns 1 and 2 of table 8 to compare the estimated arithmetic pay-performance sensitivities for similar size firms across time periods. The median beginning of period market value for firms in the 1934–40 sample is $286.7 million in 1986 dollars. The estimates from the 1974–86 time period given in column 2 of table 8 imply that a firm of this size would have an estimated total change in pay of 34.83 cents (t = 9.48) for each \$1,000 change in shareholder wealth. The estimates for 1934–40 reported in column 1 of table 8 imply a 22.16 cent (t = 4.30) pay revision for the same size firm following the same change in shareholder wealth. The difference between the two time periods of 12.67 cents is significant at the 5% level (t = 2.01). This finding indicates that smaller firms, as indicated by the median 1934–40 size, tended to have lower pay-performance sensitivities in the 1930s compared to the modern era. The median market value of firms in the 1974–86 sample is \$1,131.9 million (1986 dollars). For a firm of this size the 1974–86 estimates imply a total pay revision of 9.49 cents (t = 8.74), and the 1934–40 estimates imply a total pay revision of 12.43 cents (t = 1.60). These differences are not significant at conventional levels.

This simple control for size helps explain the differences between the arithmetic and semielasticity specifications of the pay-performance relationship. The low estimated pay-performance sensitivities for modern firms using an arithmetic specification without size controls reflects their relatively large size compared to 1930s firms, along with the fact that size decreases arithmetic sensitivities. This size effect appears to be particularly large in the modern era. Given these results, it is apparent that an arithmetic specification that does not control for size will be misspecified, and any inferences based on testing differences in these arithmetic sensitivities without controlling for firm size will be invalid. Once we control for size, the only statistically significant difference across time is that smaller firms have higher sensitivities in the modern era.

The finding that smaller firms have higher sensitivities in the modern era is consistent with our earlier findings using the semielasticity specifications. We note that the semielasticity specifications used in table 7 implicitly control for size in a manner similar to the direct controls for size employed above. To see this, note that the semielasticity specification (without lags) is approximately the same as

$$\frac{\Delta \text{Pay}}{\text{Pay}} = \alpha + \beta \frac{\Delta \text{ Shareholder Wealth}}{\text{Shareholder Wealth}} + \varepsilon, \tag{1}$$

where we have used the approximations $\Delta\log(\text{Pay}) \approx \Delta\text{Pay}/\text{Pay}$ and $\log(1 + r - i) \approx r - i$. This can be rewritten as

$$\Delta \text{Pay} = \alpha \text{Pay} + \beta \, \Delta \text{ Shareholder Wealth} \left(\frac{\text{Pay}}{\text{Shareholder Wealth}} \right) + \tilde{\varepsilon}. \tag{2}$$

Additionally, the basic arithmetic specification (without lags) can be written as

$$\Delta\text{Pay} = \alpha + \beta\ \Delta\ \text{Shareholder Wealth} + \varepsilon. \quad (3)$$

Comparing equations (2) and (3), the basic difference between specifications in measuring firm performance is that the semielasticity specification adjusts the change in shareholder wealth variables by the beginning-of-period pay-to-market-value ratio (PAY_{t-1}/MKT_{t-1}). This ratio is highly negatively correlated with firm size and positively correlated with the $1/MKT_{t-1}$ size control variable used above.

If we add terms for PAY_{t-1} and the interaction of the change in shareholder wealth variables with PAY_{t-1}/MKT_{t-1} to the arithmetic specification, we have a model that includes the arithmetic specification and the (approximate) semielasticity specification as restrictions.[37] The regression results for this specification are presented in columns 3 and 4 of table 8. For the 1974–86 time period the coefficients on the change in shareholder wealth and its lag become insignificant. The coefficient on contemporaneous changes in shareholder wealth interacted with the pay-to-market-value ratio is positive and highly significant, while the lagged interaction coefficient is insignificant. For the 1934–40 time period the coefficient on contemporaneous changes in shareholder wealth remains positive and significant, while the interaction of this variable with the pay-to-market-value ratio is not significant. The coefficient on lagged changes in shareholder wealth is not significant, while the coefficient on the interaction term is significant.

Although these results cannot conclusively indicate what the correct specification of the pay-performance relationship is, they do indicate that the performance terms corresponding to the semielasticity specification have significant explanatory power. What is most important for our purposes is that we can use these estimates to compare arithmetic pay-performance sensitivities over time for firms with the same pay-to-market-value ratio. The median pay-to-market-value ratio for the 1934–40 sample is .001817. At this ratio the estimates in columns 3 and 4 of table 8 imply a total pay revision of 12.42 cents (t = 1.63) for each \$1,000 change in shareholder wealth for the 1934–40 firms, and a total pay revision of 46.1 cents (t = 3.89) for the 1974–86 firms. The estimate for the modern firms is significantly higher at the 5% level (t = 2.39). At the 1974–86 median ratio of .000436 the 1934–40 estimates imply a total pay revision of 9.72 cents (t = 2.85) and the 1974–86 estimates imply a revision of 11.35 cents (t = 4.52). While the modern pay revision is estimated to be slightly higher, the differences are not significant (t = .38).

37. Note that this model does not include market benchmarks such as the market returns and lagged market returns variables used in the semielasticity specifications of table 7. When we add terms interacting these market returns variables with PAY_{t-1}, the reported coefficients in the tables change very little and the tests of differences in pay-performance sensitivities across time periods are significant at the same levels as reported above.

Since the pay-to-market-value ratio is strongly negatively correlated with firm size, these results are similar to our earlier findings that arithmetic pay-performance sensitivities have not changed significantly for larger firms but have increased significantly over time for smaller firms. We conclude that once size effects are controlled for by either examining semielasticity specifications or modifying arithmetic specifications to include size variables, there is no evidence for the assertions made by Jensen and Murphy (1990) concerning the decline in incentive compensation over time. For smaller firms the opposite result appears to be true. This finding, coupled with our results on top management turnover, indicates that the incentives set by the board of directors have, on average, become stronger since the 1930s.

VI. Conclusion

The results we present above indicate that the frequency of top management turnover for a panel of large industrial firms for 1933–41 was very low by historical standards. Furthermore, we estimate the sensitivity of top management turnover to stock returns to be close to zero. The data indicate that this result is not just a reflection of secular changes in variables thought to affect management turnover, including the founder status of top executives, board composition, and the ownership characteristics of firms. We interpret these findings as strong evidence that changes in the regulatory and political environment since the 1930s cannot explain the supposed weak relationship between performance and top management turnover observed today.

Our direct comparison of compensation policies between the 1934–40 time period and the 1974–86 time period indicates that the sensitivity of pay to the stock market performance of firms has not changed significantly for the largest firms and has actually increased significantly over time for smaller firms. In particular, our estimates imply that for firms at or below the median size of our 1934–40 sample, pay-performance sensitivities were significantly higher for 1974–86 than they were for 1934–40. Since even the median-sized firm in the 1934–40 sample was a very large firm by most standards, this evidence suggests there has been a widespread increase in the use of incentive compensation since the 1930s. This conclusion contrasts sharply with the findings of Jensen and Murphy (1990).

Taken as a whole, the evidence we present on compensation and turnover indicates that the internal incentive mechanisms under the control of the board of directors have become more sensitive to firm performance over the past half century. A related finding by Holderness, Kroszner, and Sheehan (1996) derived from a very large sample of firms from this period indicates that insider holdings have, on average, increased since this period. Additionally, corporate control transactions were at historically low levels from 1932 to 1942. Based on this evidence, it appears that management incentives in the 1930s were substantially weaker than they are today.

We have no conclusive explanation for why management incentives were so weak during this period. In fact, our results suggest some puzzles for future research that may help in our understanding of what determines management incentives. Based on the evidence presented here, it is apparent that regulatory and political constraints are not the only factors in the determination of the strength of internal control mechanisms. One possible explanation for our results is that we are observing a ''survival-of-the-fittest''-type outcome, with stronger incentive mechanisms winning out over time. At this stage, however, any such conclusion is largely speculation.

Our results are highly consistent with a finding from the modern corporate governance literature that there is a strong link between internal and external control mechanisms. We find very little top management turnover during a time period when there was very little external control activity by historical standards. A similar correlation between the level of activity in the corporate control market and the strength of internal control mechanisms has been documented by Mikkelson and Partch (1995).[38] These findings coupled with the findings of Denis and Denis (1995) suggest that further research is needed to identify conclusively and understand the link between these control mechanisms. If the threat of external control activity facilitates internal control mechanisms by either generating information on management performance or altering the board's incentive to monitor managers, the efficiency gains to an active market for corporate control may be even larger than previously thought.

38. As noted by Mikkelson and Partch (1995), in interpreting these results it would be informative to know the causes of intertemporal variation in corporate control activity. For our sample, regulatory and antitrust treatment of control transactions does not appear to be the sole explanation. Hawley (1966) explains that until at least 1938 the antitrust division of the Department of Justice had been ineffective because of lack of personnel and financial resources. Additionally, there were many fewer explicit regulations on tender offers, mergers, and proxy contests than in the modern era. A potential explanation is that there were severe financing constraints at the time. The difficulty financial intermediaries had in the deflationary environment of the 1930s may have hampered their ability to facilitate large control transactions (see Carosso [1970] on investment banking during this period). Furthermore, Bernanke (1983), Mishkin (1991), Calomiris (1993), and Calomiris and Hubbard (1995) present evidence that the costs of external finance for many firms were high during this time period; this could have made financing large control transactions difficult. Comment and Schwert (1995) similarly suggest that the change in takeover activity in the late 1980s may have been driven by financing constraints rather than regulatory forces.

References

Agrawal, Anup, and Walkling, Ralph. 1994. Executive careers and compensation surrounding takeover bids. *Journal of Finance* 49 (July): 985–1014.

Aranow, Edward; Einhorn, H.A.; and Berlstein, G. 1977. *Developments in Tender Offers for Corporate Control.* New York: Columbia University Press.

Berle, A., and Means, G. 1932. *The Modern Corporation and Private Property.* New York: Macmillan.

Bernanke, Ben. 1983. Nonmonetary effects of the financial crisis in the propagation of the Great Depression. *American Economic Review* 73 (June): 257–76.

Calomiris, Charles. 1993. Financial factors in the Great Depression. *Journal of Economic Perspectives* 7 (Spring): 61–85.

Calomiris, Charles, and Hubbard, R. Glenn. 1995. Internal finance and investment: Evidence from the undistributed profits tax of 1936–1937. *Journal of Business* 68 (October): 443–82.

Carosso, Vincent. 1970. *Investment Banking in America.* Cambridge, Mass.: Harvard University Press.

Christie, William G., and Nanda, Vikram. 1994. Free cash flow, shareholder value, and the undistributed profits tax of 1936 and 1937. *Journal of Finance* 49 (December): 1727–54.

Comment, Robert, and Schwert, G. William. 1995. Poison or placebo? Evidence on the deterrence and wealth effects of modern antitakeover measures. *Journal of Financial Economics* 39 (September): 3–44.

Coughlan, Anne T., and Schmidt, Ronald M. 1985. Executive compensation, management turnover, and firm performance: An empirical investigation. *Journal of Accounting and Economics* 7 (April): 43–66.

Denis, David J., and Denis, Diane K. 1995. Performance changes following top management dismissals. *Journal of Finance* 50 (September): 1029–57.

Denis, David J.; Denis, Diane K.; and Sarin, Atulya. 1995. Ownership structure and top management turnover. Working paper. West Lafayette, Ind.: Purdue University.

Fama, Eugene. 1973. *Foundations of Finance.* New York: Basic Books.

Gibbons, Robert, and Murphy, Kevin J. 1990. Relative performance evaluation for chief executive officers. *Industrial and Labor Relations Review* 43 (February): S30–S51.

Golbe, Devra L., and White, Lawrence J. 1988. Mergers and acquisitions in the U.S. economy: An aggregate and historical overview. In A. J. Auerbach (ed.), *Mergers and Acquisitions.* Cambridge, Mass.: National Bureau of Economic Research.

Golbe, Devra L., and White, Lawrence J. 1993. Catch a wave: The time series behavior of mergers. *Review of Economics and Statistics* 75 (August): 493–99.

Gordon, Robert A. 1938. Ownership by management and control groups in the large corporation. *Quarterly Journal of Economics* 52 (May): 367–79.

Gordon, Robert A. 1940. Ownership and compensation as incentives to corporate executives. *Quarterly Journal of Economics* 54 (May): 455–66.

Gordon, Robert A. 1945. *Business leadership in the large corporation.* Washington, D.C.: Brookings Institution.

Grundfest, Joseph. 1990. Subordination of American capital. *Journal of Financial Economics* 27 (September): 89–117.

Haubrich, Joseph G. 1994. Risk aversion, performance pay, and the principal-agent problem. *Journal of Political Economy* 102 (April): 258–76.

Hawley, Ellis W. 1966. *The New Deal and the Problem of Monopoly.* Princeton, N.J.: Princeton University Press.

Holderness, Clifford; Kroszner, Randall; and Sheehan, Dennis. 1996. Were the good old days that good? Evolution of manager stock ownership and corporate governance since the Great Depression. Working paper. Chicago: University of Chicago.

Houston, Joel, and James, Christopher. 1995. CEO compensation and bank risk. *Journal of Monetary Economics* 36 (November): 405–32.

Hubbard, R. Glenn, and Palia, Darius. 1995. Executive pay and performance: Evidence from the U.S. banking industry. *Journal of Financial Economics* 39 (September): 105–30.

Jarrell, Gregg, and Bradley, Michael. 1980. The economic effects of federal and state regulations of cash tender offers. *Journal of Law and Economics* 23 (October): 371–407.

Jensen, Michael C. 1993. The modern industrial revolution, exit, and the failure of internal control systems. *Journal of Finance* 48 (July): 831–80.
Jensen, Michael C., and Murphy, Kevin J. 1990. Performance pay and top management incentives. *Journal of Political Economy* 98 (April): 225–64.
Joskow, Paul; Rose, Nancy; and Shepard, Andrea. 1993. Regulatory constraints on CEO compensation. *Brookings Papers on Economic Activity: Microeconomics,* pp. 1–58.
Joskow, Paul; Rose, Nancy; and Wolfram, Catherine. 1996. Political constraints on executive compensation: Evidence from the electric utility industry. *Rand Journal of Economics* 27 (Spring): 165–82.
Kang, Jun-Koo, and Shivdasani, Anil. 1995. Firm performance, corporate governance, and top executive turnover in Japan. *Journal of Financial Economics* 38 (May): 29–58.
Kaplan, Steven. 1994*a*. Top executive rewards and firm performance: A comparison of Japan and the United States. *Journal of Political Economy* 102 (June): 510–46.
Kaplan, Steven. 1994*b*. Top executive, turnover, and firm performance in Germany. *Journal of Law, Economics, and Organization* 10 (January): 142–59.
Manne, Henry G. 1965. Mergers and the market for corporate control. *Journal of Political Economy* 73 (April): 110–20.
Martin, Kenneth J., and McConnell, John J. 1991. Corporate performance, corporate takeovers, and management turnover. *Journal of Finance* 46:671–87.
Mikkelson, Wayne H., and Partch, M. Megan. 1995. The decline of takeovers and disciplinary managerial turnover. Working paper. Eugene: University of Oregon.
Mishkin, Frederic S. 1991. Asymmetric information and financial crises: A historical perspective. In R. Glenn Hubbard (ed.), *Financial Markets and Financial Crises.* Chicago: University of Chicago Press.
Morck, Randall; Shleifer, Andrei; and Vishny, Robert. 1988. Management ownership and market valuation: An empirical analysis. *Journal of Financial Economics* 20 (January): 293–316.
Nelson, Ralph L. 1959. *Merger movements in American industry, 1895–1956* Princeton, N.J: Princeton University Press.
Parrino, Robert. 1993. Regulatory human capital and CEO turnover in the gas and electric utility industry. Working paper. Austin: University of Texas.
Pound, John. 1991. Proxy voting and the SEC. *Journal of Financial Economics* 29 (October): 241–85.
Roe, Mark J. 1990. Political and legal restraints on ownership and control of public companies. *Journal of Financial Economics* 27 (September): 7–42.
Roe, Mark J. 1994. *Strong Managers, Weak Owners.* Princeton, N.J.: Princeton University Press.
Rosen, Sherwin. 1990. Contracts and the market for executives. Working Paper no. 3542. Cambridge, Mass.: National Bureau of Economic Research.
Stigler, George, and Friedland, Claire. 1983. The literature of economics: The case of Berle and Means. *Journal of Law and Economics* 26 (June): 237–68.
Warner, Jerold; Watts, Ross L.; and Wruck, Karen H. 1988. Stock prices and top management changes. *Journal of Financial Economics* 20 (January): 461–92.
Weisbach, Michael S. 1988. Outside directors and CEO turnover. *Journal of Financial Economics* 20 (January): 431–60.
White, Halbert. 1980. A heteroscedasticity-consistent covariance matrix estimator and a direct test for heteroscedasticity. *Econometrica* 48 (May): 817–38.
Williamson, Oliver E. 1983. Organization form, residual claimants, and corporate control. *Journal of Law and Economics* 26 (June): 351–66.

Strategic Management Journal, Vol. 15, 335–344 (1994)

BOARD CONTROL AND CEO COMPENSATION

BRIAN K. BOYD
College of Business and Public Administration, Old Dominion University, Norfolk, Virginia, U.S.A.

The board of directors has been identified as a key internal control mechanism for setting CEO compensation. Theory suggests that CEOs will attempt to circumvent board control in an effort to maximize salary. This hypothesis was tested using a sample of 193 firms in a cross-section of industries. Corporate governance literature was reviewed to develop a multiple indicator measure of board control. Although, as hypothesized, CEO salaries were greater in firms with lower levels of control, CEO compensation was not significantly related to firm size or profitability.

A dozen chief executive officers of U.S. firms accompanied George Bush on his trade mission to Japan in 1992. The combined salaries of these CEOs exceeded $25 million, and received extensive criticism by both the domestic and international press. Executives of nonprofit organizations have also come under attack: rapid growth of hospital CEO salaries has prompted reform proposals in several states, and probes by the Internal Revenue Service (*The Wall Street Journal*, 1992a).

Subsequently, the Securities and Exchange Commission proposed a set of new rules designed to facilitate disclosure of executive compensation, and to describe better the criteria used to set compensation (*The Wall Street Journal*, 1992b). CEO salaries have shown limited correlation to firm size or performance, and have grown at a much faster rate than salaries for production workers (*Fortune*, 1985). Total CEO compensation (including cash, stock options, benefits, and perks) is substantially higher for U.S. executives than their counterparts in Europe or Asia—in 1992, for example, the U.S. CEO of a mid-sized firm had an average total compensation of $717,237. CEOs of similar sized firms averaged $439,441 in Britain, and $390,723 in Japan (*The Wall Street Journal*, 1992c). One trend in recent research is to examine the relationship of the board with CEO compensation.

While several studies have addressed the role of the board in setting CEO compensation, these have usually been as part of a larger analysis. Consequently, the unique effect of the board in setting compensation is still unclear. Additionally, studies have used very different measures to operationalize board control, thus limiting generalizability. The following sections develop a conceptual model for measuring board control, and relate that model to levels of CEO compensation. Data on board composition and CEO compensation were collected from 193 firms in a cross-section of industries. Hypothesis testing is followed by implications for future research.

LITERATURE REVIEW AND THEORY DEVELOPMENT

Research on executive compensation has only recently extended to the field of strategic manage-

Key words: Boards of directors, executive compensation, agency theory, strategy implementation

CCC 0143–2095/94/050335–10

Received 13 July 1992
Final revision received 11 November 1993

ment. Initial research on the topic focused on the role of firm performance, with disappointing results. While both profitability (Deckop, 1988) and sales growth (Baker, Jensen, and Murphy, 1988) have been linked to CEO compensation, the levels of explained variance have been relatively low. Studies of compensation and stock returns have been equally mixed. Benston (1985), and Kerr and Bettis (1987) both reported no relationship for these variables, while other studies have reported positive effects (Coughlan and Schmidt, 1985; Jensen and Murphy, 1990; Murphy, 1985, 1986). Similarly, studies linking CEO compensation to firm size have yielded conflicting results (Cicsel and Carroll, 1980; Lambert, Larcker and Weigelt, 1991). Other studies have taken a wider focus, and developed frameworks for explaining differences in CEO compensation across firms (e.g., Finkelstein and Hambrick, 1989; Rajagopalan and Prescott, 1990; Zajac, 1990). A recurrent theme in these studies is the role of the board of directors. Agency theory offers a framework for evaluating the effect of CEO/board relations on levels of executive compensation.

The role of the board under agency theory

Agency theory evolved from risk sharing research in economics. The unit of analysis is the relationship between a principal and agent, and the theory addresses causes and consequences of goal divergence between the two parties. Consequently, agency theory is a particularly useful framework for addressing CEO/board relations.

An agency problem exists when an agent (e.g., a CEO) has established goals which conflict with those of a principal (e.g., the board). Such problems are likely to occur when a key decision maker has no financial interest in the outcome of his decisions (Fama and Jensen, 1983). A CEO with no or minimal equity ownership, for example, is expected to have substantively different goals than stockholders or a CEO entrepreneur. Carl Ichan (1986: 101), for example, observed that 'The top man. . .usually finds expanding his power more important than rewarding owners (stockholders).' Specifically, the absence of ownership creates 'an incentive to consume more on the job than is agreed in his contract' (Fama, 1980: 295). Thus, the CEO may focus on maximizing his own wealth vs. that of the firm. The first step in pursuit of this strategy is to 'engineer a large fixed salary' (Walsh and Seward, 1990: 432). The net effect is for the CEO to pursue a salary which is higher than would be preferred by stockholders (Hill and Phan, 1991).

The agency problem can be alleviated by separating responsibilities for decision *management* vs. decision *control* (Fama and Jensen, 1983). Control mechanisms can be both internal and external. External controls would include market-based measures such as failure of the firm, or a takeover attempt. The board serves as the representative for stockholders (Fama and Jensen, 1983; Zald, 1969), and is the primary internal control mechanism to better align the different interests of shareholders and top management (Mizruchi, 1983; Walsh and Seward, 1990). A spate of recent shareholder suits has underscored the board's role as ultimate legal responsibility for policy decisions (*Business Week*, 1989). One responsibility of the board is to monitor CEO performance and determine compensation levels accordingly (Lorsch, 1989). The board of directors of at least one firm, Fairchild, has been sued by stockholders for allegedly overpaying its CEO.

Effective salary maximization requires that the CEO be able to circumvent these control mechanisms—i.e., be able to dominate or co-opt the board (Eisenhardt, 1989; Fama, 1980). Walsh and Seward noted that CEOs have 'no choice but to tamper with the board's ability to monitor and control their performance' (1990: 431) in the pursuit of job security. This rationale suggests that the board of directors plays a major role in setting CEO compensation.

Several studies have begun to explore the role of the board in setting CEO compensation. Tosi and Gomez-Mejia (1989) developed measures of compensation monitoring and influence. They found that monitoring reduced the CEO's influence in the pay process. Hill and Phan (1991) found that CEOs were better able to circumvent board monitoring and incentive mechanisms as CEO influence increased. Finkelstein and Hambrick (1989) reported similar findings, but also observed that extremely long CEO tenure (over 18 years) had a negative effect on compensation. In comparison, Deckop (1988) found compensation to have only a minimal relationship with CEO tenure. Finkelstein and Hambrick also reported that board vigilance, as measured by stock ownership, was unrelated to total compensation.

It is also important to recognize the overlap of the agency framework with related work on power. Over two decades ago, Zald (1969: 100) observed that boards have many responsibilities, including the selection and compensation of the chief executive. He noted that board effectiveness in the completion of these tasks depended on several factors, including 'sources of board member power *vis-à-vis* executives.' While board power facilitates protection of shareholder interests (Pearce and Zahra, 1991), CEO power can be used to limit and undermine board control (Hill and Phan, 1991; Kimberly and Zajac, 1988). Thus, the subsequent hypothesis (and, in fact, many of the individual variables) could be equally justified from a power perspective.[1]

The control model of CEO/board relations is also consistent with corporate governance research: The broad range of CEO salaries (Conference Board, 1991a) may simply be a function of the highly uneven levels of board control across firms. While there are numerous instances of inert, 'rubber stamp' boards (e.g., Business Roundtable, 1978; Mace, 1971; *The Los Angeles Times*, 1986), evidence would suggest that many boards are playing a more active role in corporate Americca (e.g., Boyd, 1990; Weidenbaum, 1986). Consequently, CEO compensation levels may substantially vary across firms, simply as a function of how well a board fulfils its control responsibilities.

In summary, CEO compensation appears to be only partially driven by firm size or performance. Control models attempt to explain this discrepancy with the following propositions: (1) The CEO will strive to maximize his own self-interest in regards to compensation; (2) His success at maximization is a function of an ability to circumvent or minimize board control. Thus, one would expect that the CEO could command a larger salary when he dominates the board of directors. Stated formally:

Hypothesis 1: CEO compensation will be inversely related to levels of board control.

[1] I am indebted to an anonymous SMJ reviewer for this insight.

METHOD

Sample

Data were collected from 193 firms in 12 industry groups as part of a larger research project. All data were collected for the year 1980. Industry groups were selected to represent a broad range of market conditions, as measured by Dess and Beard's (1984) environmental dimensions. The sample included most SIC industrial classes, including manufacturing, transportation, minerals, financial services, and retail trade. Industries included in the study are listed in Table 1, along with their respective 4-digit SIC codes, and the number of firms sampled in each industry.

A list of firms in each industry was generated using *Moody*'s manuals. Sample firms were publicly held in 1980, and headquartered in the U.S. Heavily diversified and subsidiary firms were excluded. In smaller industry groups, all firms meeting the selection criteria were included in the sample. In larger industry groups, however, the *N* was sufficient to permit stratified sampling based on size. This sampling design helps avoid limitations identified in other studies of CEO compensation, such as sampling a single industry, or sampling only the largest publicly held firms.

Measurement

CEO compensation. CEO compensation is composed of three elements: base salary, bonus, and long-term or deferred income. Total cash compensation is the sum of salary and bonus, and is the measure used by most studies of CEO compensation. Therefore, total cash compensation was used as the dependent variable in this study. Total cash compensation has been found to be an effective proxy for measures which include deferred income (Lewellen and Huntsman, 1970). Salary and bonus were not coded separately, since less than one-third of the sample reported separate data. As recommended by Finkelstein and Hambrick (1989), the logarithm of compensation was used to reduce heteroscedasticity.

Board control. There are several prerequisites for a board to be able to fulfil its control responsibilities adequately. Fama and Jensen (1983) argued that effective control requires that directors have sufficient incentive and are free from collusion or domination by the CEO. Given

Table 1. Descriptive information for sample

Industry	SIC	*N*	Mean CEO Compensation
Crude oil and natural gas	1311	18	$149,951
Paper products	2621	15	$262,450
Book publishing	2731	13	$158,859
Oil refining	2911	13	$262,915
Hydraulic cement	3241	15	$229,368
Steel	3312	14	$234,403
Electronic computing equipment	3573	12	$254,061
Semiconductors	3674	12	$201,215
Certified air transportation	4511	20	$250,005
Electrical power utilities	4911	21	$138,584
Department stores	5311	18	$297,344
National banks	6025	22	$188,869

the many nuances of board control, Eisenhardt (1989) recommended the use of multiple measures in operationalizing this construct. Statistically, multiple measurements are desirable when a construct can be measured in several ways, or in the face of measurement error (James, Mulaik, and Brett, 1982). Thus, a structural model which incorporates multiple measures of board control would offer a more powerful test of the control-compensation model. A review of corporate governance literature suggests several measures of the degree of board control:

First, *CEO duality* exists when a firm's CEO also serves as chairman of the board of directors. Holding the highly symbolic position of board chair would provide the CEO with a wider power base and locus of control (Hambrick and Finkelstein, 1987; Harrison, Torres, and Kukalis, 1988; Patton and Baker, 1987). In contrast, an independent board chair will facilitate objective assessment of CEO and top management team performance (Weidenbaum, 1986). Therefore, CEO duality is expected to have a negative relationship with the degree of board control (Morck, Shleifer, and Vishny, 1989). Data for all board variables were collected from proxy statements and annual reports. A dummy variable was coded as '1' if the CEO also served as board chair, and '0' otherwise.

The *ratio of insiders* on the board has been suggested as a second mechanism to weaken or nullify board control (Alderfer, 1986; Beatty and Zajac, 1990; Schellenger, Wood and Tashakori, 1989), thereby increasing the feasibility of board domination by the CEO (Patton and Baker, 1987). Fama (1980: 293), for example, proposed that inclusion of outside directors would help prevent top management from deciding 'that collusion and expropriation of security holder wealth are better than competition among themselves.' Similarly, Weisbach (1988) found that CEOs of poorly performing firms were more likely to be removed in companies with outsider-dominated than insider-dominated boards. Thus, the ratio of insiders is expected to have a negative relationship with board control. Insiders were defined as directors who are also members of a firm's management. The number of insiders was divided by the total number of board members.

Many critics of corporate governance recommend that outside directors acquire stock of the firms they advise (e.g., *Fortune*, 1991; *Business Week*, 1991). That recommendation is consistent with agency theory, which proposes that *board stock ownership* is a powerful incentive for fulfilling control responsibilities (Beatty and Zajac, 1990; Holderness and Sheehan, 1988; Patton and Baker, 1987; Shleifer and Vishny, 1986; Zald, 1969). Consequently, board stock ownership is expected to have a positive relationship with board control. This variable was measured as the percentage of common stock owned by the board of directors. Stock owned by the CEO was excluded from this measure.

Trends in institutional ownership are also related to board control. One survey found that 20 percent of *Fortune* 500 firms had large-block shareholding by pension and profit-sharing funds, and an additional 26 percent had large-block shareholding by financial firms (Shleifer and Vishny, 1986). As the magnitude of these large-block holdings increase, it becomes proportionately more difficult to withdraw or transfer holdings across firms. Consequently, institutional owners have assumed more active roles in their investments, often by obtaining seats on the board of directors (Holderness and Sheehan, 1988; *The Wall Street Journal*, 1991). Thus, the *number of directors representing ownership groups* is expected to have a positive relationship with board control (Zald, 1969). The SEC requires disclosure of all sources which own 5 percent or more of a firm's stock. This variable was coded as the number of these owners (or their agents) who sit on the board of directors.

A final variable proposed by agency theory is the *level of director compensation*. Fama and Jensen (1983) argued that the true value of a directorship is the opportunity to develop a reputation as an expert in decision control, thereby increasing the value of an individual's human capital. This perspective has been echoed by numerous writers (e.g., *Business Month*, 1990; Mace, 1971). Fama and Jensen also propose that this reputation building is most credible 'when the direct payments to outside directors are small (1983: 315).' Alternately, high levels of director compensation are thought to undermine the independence and credibility of outside directors (*Business Week*, 1991; Kosnik, 1990; *The Wall Street Journal*, 1991a, 1992d). For example, Baysinger and Hoskisson (1990: 72) commented on a common belief that chief executives 'dominate their boards by using their *de facto* power to select and compensate directors.' This rationale is also supported by anecdotal evidence. F. Ross Johnson, former CEO of RJR Nabisco, for example, justified high levels of director support by stating 'If I'm there for them, they'll be there for me' (*Business Week*, 1991: 94). Similarly, the CEO and Chair of Morton International argued that high levels of compensation compromise a director, with the net result of having 'destroyed his effectiveness' (*The Wall Street Journal*, 1991: B2). Therefore, director compensation is expected to have a negative relationship with board control.

Director compensation is composed of three elements: an annual retainer, per-meeting fees, and committee pay. Director compensation is unique in that levels for individual directors may vary, depending on attendance and committee service. Since not all directors will serve on board committees, most comparisons (e.g., *Business Week*, 1991; *Fortune* 1991; Kosnik, 1987) exclude committee pay when estimating compensation for an 'average' director. In 1990, committee pay comprised a relatively small portion (13%) of total director compensation in manufacturing and service firms (Conference Board, 1991b). Therefore, director compensation was measured in this study as the sum of annual retainer plus per-meeting fees. As with CEO compensation, stock options, insurance, and other benefits were excluded from this measure.

Firm size. This variable was measured by the logarithm of net sales. Financial data were taken from the Compustat data base, and supplemented by annual reports as needed.

Profitability. This variable was measured by return on equity.

Statistical methods

The model was tested using LISREL VII (Joreskog and Sorbom, 1988). This methodology is appropriate when studying variables which imperfectly represent latent constructs (Saris and Stronkhorst, 1984). By using multiple indicators, LISREL estimates are free from the biases imposed by measurement error or unreliability (Herting, 1985). The LISREL analysis combined both theoretical and measurement models. It is recommended that multiple criteria be used to evaluate the overall fit of a LISREL model (Bollen, 1989). The overall fit of the hypothesis to the observed correlations was assessed through five methods. First, the significance of the chi-square statistic was examined. Chi-square measures the overall fit of a given model, with a smaller value indicating a better fit. Second, a variant of chi-square which adjusts for degrees of freedom was examined. Third, the goodness-of-fit index (GFI) offers a measure of fit which is independent of sample size, and robust against nonnormality. Fourth, the root mean square residual was examined to estimate the average magnitude of the fitted residuals. Finally, the magnitude of the coefficient of determination for compensation was assessed. The significance of individual paths was assessed using t-ratios.

Statistical controls

As noted previously, studies have reported mixed results for relationships of CEO compensation with firm size and profitability. However, the pervasiveness of this research suggests that these variables should be included in any study of CEO compensation, if only for purposes of replication and control.

RESULTS

Descriptive statistics and intercorrelations for all variables are shown in Table 2. Point biserial correlations were used to estimate relations involving the dichotomous duality variable. These data indicate that the sample represents a broad range on different board control measures. For example, the average insider ratio was 30 percent, and ranged between 5 percent and 100 percent. Similarly, the proportion of stock ownership by directors ranged from 0 to 71 percent, with a mean of 5 percent. A 'typical' board would also meet seven to eight times yearly, have three board committees, and have one director representing an ownership group. Average CEO compensation was $215,914 and ranged between $56,050 and $654,253.

Results of measurement submodel

As proposed, CEO duality and total director compensation loaded negatively on board control, and board stock ownership and board representation by ownership groups loaded positively on board control. Contrary to expectations, the insider ratio loaded positively on the board control dimension. A separate confirmatory factor analysis for the board control submodel is reported in Table 3. As expected, the indicators do load very strongly on a single factor: χ^2 adjusted for degrees of freedom is 2.26, and the root mean square residual is 0.05. Overall coefficient of determination for the submodel is 0.80. Of course, the fit statistics do not reflect that, while the insider ratio loaded significantly on this dimension, the direction of loading was counter to expectations. Similar findings have been reported in a replication of the board control submodel in a different sample (Boyd and Carroll, 1993).

Model summary statistics

The LISREL model used to test the effect of board control on compensation is shown in Figure 1. The χ^2 statistic for the model is 66.82. This statistic is highly sensitive to sample size (Joreskog and Sorbom, 1988), and a recommended alternative is the χ^2/d.f. ratio (Carmines and McIver, 1981). This adjusted ratio is 3.93, and indicates that the model is an adequate fit to the data. The goodness-of-fit index (0.91) and root mean square residual (0.14) also indicate an adequate model. The coefficient of determination, or R^2, is 0.63 for CEO compensation. Summary statistics for all models are shown in Table 3.

Table 2. Descriptive statistics for variables

	(1)	(2)	(3)	(4)	(5)	(6)	(7)	(8)
	1.000							
	0.187	1.000						
	−0.118	−0.031	1.000					
	−0.287	0.190	0.337	1.000				
	−0.024	−0.184	0.201	0.164	1.000			
	0.601	0.081	−0.163	−0.302	−0.121	1.00		
	0.618	0.152	−0.207	−0.267	−0.173	0.64	1.000	
	0.196	−0.047	−0.049	−0.197	0.065	0.13	−0.193	1.000
Mean	12.6	0.48	0.30	4.87	0.89	8536.72	5.73	0.17
S.D.	0.53	0.50	0.16	10.68	1.28	5668.49	1.82	0.60

Variable list: 1. CEO compensation (logarithm), 2. CEO duality, 3. Insider ratio, 4. Percent of stock owned by directors, 5. Number of directors representing ownership groups, 6. Director compensation, 7. Firm size (logarithm), 8. Return on equity.

Table 3. Summary statistics for LISREL models

Model	χ^2	χ^2/d.f.	GFI	GFI_a	RMSR	CED
Structural model (17 d.f.)	66.82 (p = 0.0001)	3.93	0.91	0.82	0.14	0.63
Confirmatory factor model for board control (5 d.f.)	11.31 (p = 0.046)	2.26	0.98	0.93	0.05	0.80

GFI: Goodness of fit index, GFI_a: Goodness of fit index, adjusted for degrees of freedom, RMSR: Root mean square residual, CED: Coefficient of determination.

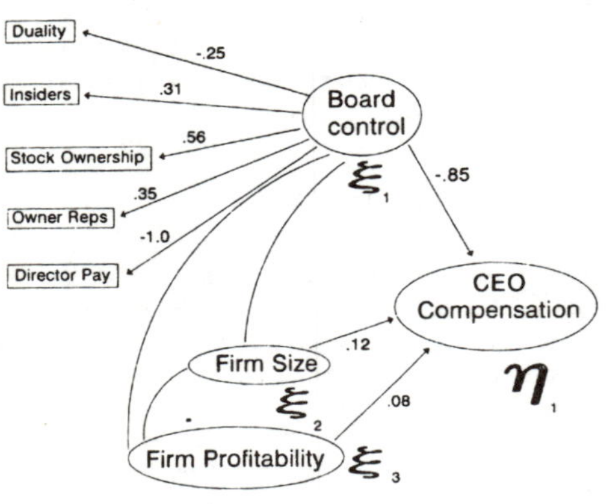

Figure 1. Simplified structural model
Note: Certain parameters (e.g., phi and theta-delta matrices) are excluded from the diagram

The coefficients for control, firm size, and profitability can be interpreted as effect sizes relative to CEO compensation (Hayduk, 1987)—a coefficient nearing 1 means a very large effect size, while a coefficient nearing 0 means a very weak effect. Thus, as shown in Figure 1, board control had the largest effect on compensation with a standardized coefficient of −0.85. Firm size had the next largest effect (0.12), followed by profitability (0.08). The standard errors of parameter estimates for size and profitability were relatively large and resulted in t-values of less than 2. Therefore, parameter estimates for these control variables were not statistically significant.

Hypothesis testing

Hypothesis 1 stated that CEO compensation will be inversely related to levels of board control. As shown in Figure 1, this hypothesis was supported with a $gamma_{11}$ coefficient of −0.85.

DISCUSSION

Board control has been included as one component in several models of CEO compensation. This paper proposed that multiple indicators are useful for operationalizing board control. Our model provided a more detailed understanding of board control, and explained a significant proportion of variance in CEO pay. These results support previous analysis describing the board as a key internal control mechanism (Walsh and Seward, 1990). Consequently, management teams may wish to consider strong boards as a 'lesser evil' to the risk of harsher, market-based controls.

Results of the measurement submodel for control also cause us to rethink some assumptions regarding board functions. Contrary to expectations, the ratio of insiders was negatively associated with compensation. The bulk of previous research argued that inside directors were essentially pawns of the CEO. Research presented here supports the work by Mizruchi (1983) and others who argued for a very different role of inside directors. Mizruchi suggested that inside directors will feel as if they are being evaluated by the outside directors. Inside directors, particularly those considered as possible successors to the CEO, may fear the appearance of siding with the CEO, and alienating outside board members. Baysinger and Hoskisson (1990) also argued that legal obligations and concern for professional reputation will cause inside directors to limit their support for their CEO. Additionally, since salaries of the top management team are often closely linked to that of the

CEO, the presence of inside directors may drive down CEO salaries simply to avoid the perception of impropriety or self-serving behavior.

Our analysis is subject to several limitations. As with other studies, only a minority of firms reported separate data for base salary vs. bonus. While the majority of studies use total cash compensation as the dependent variable, this does raise several questions. Finkelstein and Hambrick (1989) reported a significant link between bonus pay and ROE. How does the board moderate this relationship, if at all? Also, agency theory suggests that CEOs will attempt to reduce their own risk via larger base salaries; yet, such a pay structure may be dysfunctional for the organization and shareholders (Walsh and Seward, 1990). One might therefore expect that the ratio of bonus pay to total compensation would increase significantly as does board control. Since only a small subset of firms disaggregate compensation data, future studies on this topic will require a substantially larger sample size to address these kinds of questions.

One direction for future research focuses on the role of the board in the link between CEO pay and performance. Previous agency studies have taken contrary positions on this issue. Eisenhardt (1989: 65) argued that board which fulfils its control responsibilities will have superior information resources. Such information would enable the board to compensate CEOs for 'taking well-conceived actions whose outcomes may be unsuccessful.' Thus, Eisenhardt proposed that active boards would compensate CEOs based on their behavior rather than on balance sheets, thus diluting the pay/performance relationship. In contrast, empirical studies (Hill and Phan, 1991; Tosi and Gomez-Mejia, 1989) suggest that board control would strengthen the pay/performance relationship. An alternate explanation is that board control may qualitatively alter the nature of this linkage: superior board information on CEO abilities may lead to a weakened relationship of CEO pay with short-term performance, but a strengthened relationship with long-term performance.

Additionally, it would be worthwhile to replicate this analysis using CEO long-term compensation as the dependent variable. While Lewellen and Huntsman (1970) reported that cash compensation is an effective proxy for long-term compensation, long-term compensation has become a proportionately more important aspect of executive compensation over the last two decades. Recent changes in the reporting of executive compensation imposed by the Securities and Exchange Commission will substantially improve the feasibility of such research.

The results of the confirmatory factor model support the argument that board control be measured with multiple indicators. As such, it may be overly optimistic to measure board control with single indicators such as stock ownership or the ratio of insiders. Thus, a promising avenue for future research is further effort in conceptualizing and measuring this important variable. Comparison of perceptions of board control with archival measures used here would be an important test of validity, and may also offer some insights regarding potential self-report biases in surveys of senior managers.

Other research may identify additional applications of board control for strategic management research. For example, what are the implications of board control for corporate performance? While greater board involvement may increase the quality of management decisions, it may also complicate and lengthen the decision process. Consequently, board control may be advantageous under certain conditions (e.g., assessing possible actions of competitors) but a hindrance in other conditions (e.g., decisionmaking in high volatility environments).

A final agenda for future research is additional theory building on CEO/board relations. The present study drew primarily from agency theory to build a model of board control. Still, numerous other labels have been used to characterize CEO/board relations, including board vigilance, involvement, monitoring, and influence. Do these different terms draw on the same construct, several overlapping constructs, or entirely different dimensions? For example, as noted earlier, there are many parallels between agency and power perspectives in studying board control and executive compensation. Thus, while power and control would seem to be separate constructs, one can identify many indicators (e.g., duality) which may represent both dimensions. Integration of these diverse approaches to conceptualizing CEO—board relations would be invaluable in future studies of executive compensation.

ACKNOWLEDGEMENTS

I would like to acknowledge the helpful comments of Greg Dess, Ed Zajac, and members of Old Dominion's Corporate Governance Group. The insightful and constructive comments of two SMJ reviewers played a substantial role in guiding the evolution of this manuscript. An earlier version of this paper was presented at the 1993 Academy of Management Annual Conference in Atlanta.

REFERENCES

Alderfer, C. P. (1986). 'The invisible director on corporate boards', *Harvard Business Review*, **64**(6), pp. 38–52.

Baker, G. P., M. C. Jensen and K. J. Murphy (1988). 'Compensation and incentives: Practice vs. theory', *Journal of Finance*, **43**, pp. 593–616.

Baysinger, B. and R. E. Hoskisson (1990). 'The composition of boards of directors and strategic control: Effects on corporate strategy', *Academy of Management Review*, **15**, pp. 72–87.

Beatty, R. P. and E. J. Zajac (1990). 'Top management incentives, monitoring, and risk-bearing: A study of executive compensation, ownership, and board structure in initial public offerings', Best Paper Proceedings, Academy of Management, pp. 7–11.

Benston, G. J. (1985). 'The self-serving management hypothesis: Some evidence', *Journal of Accounting and Economics*, **7**, pp. 67–84.

Bollen, K. A. (1989). *Structural Equations with Latent Variables*. Wiley, New York.

Boyd, B. (1990). 'Corporate linkages and organizational environment: A test of the resource dependence model', *Strategic Management Journal*, **11**, pp. 419–430.

Boyd, B. K. and W. O. Carroll (1993). 'Corporate governance and social performance'. Paper presented at the Strategic Management Society Annual International Conference, Chicago, IL.

Business Month (March 1990). 'A morning jolt for bored boards', pp. 80–81.

Business Roundtable (1978). *The Role and Composition of the Board of Directors of the Large Publicly Owned Corporation*. Business Roundtable, New York.

Business Week (July 3, 1989). 'A seat on the board is getting hotter', pp. 72–73.

Business Week (May 6, 1991). 'Directors' pay is becoming an issue, too', p. 94.

Carmines, E. G. and J. P. McIver (1981). 'Analyzing models with unobserved variables: Analysis of covariance structures'. In G. W. Bohrnstedt and E. F. Borgatta (eds), *Social Measurement: Current Issues*. Sage, Beverly Hills, CA, pp. 65–115.

Chaganti, R. and F. Damanpour (1991). 'Institutional ownership, capital structure, and firm performance', *Strategic Management Journal*, **12**, pp. 479–491.

Cicsel, D. and T. Carroll (1980). 'The determinants of executive salaries: An econometric survey', *Review of Economics and Statistics*, **62**, pp. 7–13.

Conference Board (1991a). *Top Executive Compensation*, 1991 edition. Conference Board, New York.

Conference Board (1991b). *Corporate Directors' Compensation*, 1991 edition. Conference Board, New York.

Coughlan, A. T. and R. M. Schmidt (1985). 'Executive compensation, managerial turnover, and firm performance', *Journal of Accounting and Economics*, **7**, pp. 43–66.

Deckop, J. R. (1988). 'Determinants of chief executive officer compensation', *Industrial and Labor Relations Review*, **41**, pp. 215–226.

Dess, G. G. and D. Beard (1984). 'Dimensions of organizational task environments', *Administrative Science Quarterly*, **29**, pp. 52–73.

Eisenhardt, K. M. (1988). 'Agency theory: An assessment and review', *Academy of Management Review*, **14**, pp. 57–74.

Fama, E. F. (1980). 'Agency problems and the theory of the firm', *Journal of Political Economy*, **88**, pp. 288–307.

Fama, E. F. and M. N. Jensen (1983). 'Separation of ownership and control', *Journal of Law and Economics*, **26**, pp. 301–325.

Finkelstein, S. and D. C. Hambrick (1989). 'Chief executive compensation: A study of the intersection of markets and political processes', *Strategic Management Journal*, **10**, pp. 121–134.

Fortune (April 1, 1985). 'Why chief executives' pay keeps rising', pp. 66–76.

Fortune (May 6, 1991). 'Do directors earn their keep?', pp. 78–80.

Hambrick, D. C. and S. Finkelstein (1987). 'Managerial discretion: A bridge between polar views of organizational outcomes', *Research in Organizational Behavior*, **9**, pp. 369–406.

Harrison, J. R., D. L. Torres and S. Kukalis (1988). 'The changing of the guard: Turnover and structural change in the top-management positions', *Administrative Science Quarterly*, **33**, pp. 211–232.

Hayduk, L. A. (1987). *Structural Equation Modeling with LISREL: Essentials and Advances*. Johns Hopkins University Press, Baltimore, MD.

Herting, J. R. (1985). 'Multiple indicator models using LISREL'. In H. M. Blalock, Jr. (ed.), *Causal Models in the Social Sciences*. Aldine, New York, pp. 263–319.

Hill, C. W. and P. Phan (1991). 'CEO tenure as a determinant of CEO pay', *Academy of Management Journal*, **34**, pp. 707–717.

Holderness, C. G. and D. P. Sheehan (1988). 'The role of majority shareholders in publicly held corporations', *Journal of Financial Economics*, **20**, pp. 317–346.

Ichan, C. (October 27, 1986). 'What ails corporate America—and what should be done?' *Business Week*, pp. 98–104.

James, L. R., S. A. Mulaik and J. M. Brett (1982). *Causal Analysis*. Sage, Beverly Hills, CA.

Jensen, M. C. and K. J. Murphy (1990). 'Performance

pay and top management incentives', *Journal of Political Economy*, **98**, pp. 225–264.

Joreskog, K. G. and D. Sorbom (1988). *LISREL VII: A Guide to the Program and Applications*. Scientific Software, Mooresville, IN.

Kerr, J. and R. A. Bettis (1987). 'Boards of directors, top management compensation, and shareholder returns', *Academy of Management Journal*, **30**, pp. 645–664.

Kimberly, J. R. and E. J. Zajac (1988). 'The dynamics of CEO/board relations'. In D. C. Hambrick (ed.), *The Executive Effect: Concepts and Methods for Studying Top Managers*. JAI Press, Greenwich, CT, pp. 179–204.

Kosnik, R. D. (1987). 'Greenmail: A study of board performance in corporate governance', *Administrative Science Quarterly*, **32**, pp. 163–185.

Kosnik, R. D. (1990). 'Effects of board demography and directors' incentives on corporate greenmail decisions', *Academy of Management Journal*, **33**, pp. 129–150.

Lambert, R. A., D. F. Larcker and K. Weigelt (1991). 'How sensitive is CEO compensation to organizational size?', *Strategic Management Journal*, **12**, pp. 395–402.

Lewellen, W. G. and B. Huntsman (1970). 'Managerial pay and corporate performance', *American Economic Review*, **60**, pp. 710–720.

Lorsch, J. W. (1989). *Pawns or Potentates: The Reality of America's Corporate Boards*. Harvard Business School Press, Boston, MA.

Mace, M. L. (1971). *Directors: Myth and Reality*. Harvard Business School Press, Boston, MA.

Mizruchi, M. S. (1983). 'Who controls whom? An examination of the relation between management and boards of directors in large corporations', *Academy of Management Review*, **8**, pp. 426–435.

Morck, R., A. Shleifer and R. W. Vishny (1989). 'Alternative mechanisms for corporate control', *American Economic Review*, **79**, pp. 842–852.

Murphy, K. (1985) 'Corporate performance and managerial remuneration', *Journal of Accounting and Economics*, **7**, pp. 11–42.

Murphy, K. (1986). 'Incentives, learning, and compensation: A theoretical and empirical investigation of managerial labor contracts', *Rand Journal of Economics*, **17**, pp. 59–76.

Patton, A. and J. C. Baker (1987). 'Why won't directors rock the boat?', *Harvard Business Review*, **65**(6), pp. 10–12, 16, 18.

Pearce, J. A. and S. A. Zahra (1991). 'The relative power of CEOs and boards of directors: Associations with corporate performance', *Strategic Management Journal*, **12**, pp. 135–153.

Rajagopalan, N. and J. E. Prescott (1990). 'Determinants of top management compensation: Explaining the impact of economic, behavioral, and strategic constructs and the moderating effects of industry', *Journal of Management*, **16**, pp. 515–538.

Saris, W. and H. Stronkhorst (1984). *Causal Modelling in Nonexperimental Research*. Sociometric Research Foundation, Amsterdam.

Schellenger, M. H., D. D. Wood and A. Tashakori (1989). 'Board of director composition, shareholder wealth, and dividend policy', *Journal of Management*, **15**, pp. 457–467.

The Wall Street Journal (March 20, 1991). 'More directors are recruited from outside', pp. B1, B3.

Shleifer, A. and R. W. Vishny (1986). 'Large shareholder and corporate control', *Journal of Political Economy*, **94**, pp. 461–488.

The Los Angeles Times (September 7, 1986). 'Bank America board: A study in inertia.' IV, pp. 4–5.

The Wall Street Journal (April 22, 1991). 'While outside directors' pay increases, independence from managers may fade', pp. B1, B2.

The Wall Street Journal (April 14, 1992a). 'Agencies probe executive pay at hospitals', pp. B1, B5.

The Wall Street Journal (February 14, 1992b). 'Shareholder groups cheer SEC's move on disclosure of executive compensation', p. B6.

The Wall Street Journal (October 12, 1992c). 'Managers' incomes aren't worlds apart', p. B1.

The Wall Street Journal (November 23, 1992d). 'Shield outside directors from inside seduction', p. A.14.

Tosi, H. L. and L. R. Gomez-Mejia (1989). 'The decoupling of CEO pay and performance: An agency theory perspective', *Administrative Science Quarterly*, **34**, pp. 169–189.

Walsh, J. P. and J. K. Seward (1990). 'On the efficiency of internal and external corporate control mechanisms', *Academy of Management Review*, **15**, pp. 421–458.

Weidenbaum, M. L. (1986). 'Updating the corporate board', *Journal of Business Strategy*, **7**, pp. 77–83.

Weisbach, M. S. (1988). 'Outside directors and CEO turnover', *Journal of Financial Economics*, **20**, pp. 431–460.

Zajac, E. J. (1990). 'CEO selection, succession, compensation and firm performance: A theoretical integration and empirical analysis', *Strategic Management Journal*, **11**, pp. 217–230.

Zald, M. N. (1969). 'The power and functions of boards of directors: A theoretical synthesis', *American Journal of Sociology*, **75**, pp. 97–111.

JOURNAL OF FINANCIAL AND QUANTITATIVE ANALYSIS VOL. 32, NO. 3, SEPTEMBER 1997

Reciprocally Interlocking Boards of Directors and Executive Compensation

Kevin F. Hallock*

Abstract

Is executive compensation influenced by the composition of the board of directors? About 8% of chief executive officers (CEOs) are reciprocally interlocked with another CEO—the current CEO of firm A serves as a director of firm B and the current CEO of firm B serves as a director of firm A. Roughly 20% of firms have at least one current or retired employee sitting on the board of another firm and vice versa. I investigate how these and other features of board composition affect CEO pay by using a sample of 9,804 director positions in America's largest companies. CEOs who lead interlocked firms earn significantly higher compensation. Also, interlocked CEOs tend to head larger firms. After controlling for firm and CEO characteristics, the pay gap is reduced dramatically. However, when firms that are interlocked due to documented business relationships are considered not interlocked, the measured return to interlock is as high as 17%. There also is evidence that the return to interlock was higher in the 1970s than in the early 1990s.

I. Introduction

Why are Chief Executive Officers (CEOs) of major American companies paid such large sums for their services? In the last decade, a literature has grown to offer competing explanations. Pay-for-productivity theories (Murphy (1985)) suggest that CEOs are extraordinarily productive and worth what they are paid. Tournament models (Lazear and Rosen (1981)) propose that each firm offers an optimal prize to the CEO and that lower level managerial workers strive for that prize. Neither of these theories directly considers the role of the board of directors—the body that formally sets executive salaries. In this paper, I propose a test for the explicit role of the boards of directors in determining CEO salaries. CEOs and

*Department of Economics and Institute of Labor & Industrial Relations, University of Illinois at Urbana-Champaign, 1206 South 6th Street, Champaign, IL 61820. I am grateful for comments from and/or discussions with Orley Ashenfelter, Sanjai Bhagat, William Bowen, David Card, Kenneth Chay, Wallace Hendricks, Dean Hyslop, Jonathan Karpoff (the editor), Alan Krueger, Owen Lamont, Richard Lester, Burton Malkiel, Randall Morck (the referee), Paul Oyer, Jin Heum Park, John Penrod, Jörn-Steffen Pischke, Richard Quandt, Anju Seth, Charles Thomas, and Ralph Walkling. Benjamin Gordon provided excellent research assistance. I also thank participants in seminars at the University of Arizona, the University of Chicago, Harvard University/MIT, the University of Illinois, the University of Michigan, Princeton University, the Federal Reserve Bank of Philadelphia, and the Princeton Association of New England. The Industrial Relations Section at Princeton University, the Jacob Javits Fellows Program, and the Princeton Association of New England provided generous financial support.

their subordinates often are directors of other boards, and CEOs often have much discretion in choosing new board members. If two CEOs, or their subordinates, serve on each other's boards (they are reciprocally interlocked), then these CEOs may have both the incentive and the opportunity to raise each other's pay.

I use data on the full names, occupations, and employers of nearly 10,000 directors from more than 700 of America's major corporations to construct two measures of interlock of the boards, CEOs, and directors. I then use CEO compensation data from 1992 and other CEO-specific and firm-specific data to study the effect of interlock on CEO pay.

I find that 20% of firms are any-employee interlocked, that is any current or retired employee (including the CEO) from firm A sits on firm B's board *and* any current or retired employee (including the CEO) from firm B sits on firm A's board. Eight percent of firms are current-CEO interlocked—the current CEO of firm A serves as a director of firm B and the current CEO of firm B serves as a director of firm A. Salaries of CEOs in interlocked firms are higher than in other firms. After controlling for firm and CEO characteristics, this pay gap is reduced dramatically. However, when firms that are interlocked due to documented business relationships are considered not interlocked, the measured return to interlock is as high as 17%. There also is evidence that the return to interlock was higher in the 1970s than in the early 1990s.

II. Summary Statistics and Estimation

The sample of firms is from the Forbes magazine 500s list, so called because it is a list of the 500 largest American companies in each of four different categories: sales, profits, assets, and market value. The combined sets in 1992 yield 773 companies.

A. Summary Statistics and Data

I collected data from 1992 on the board of directors from the individual annual reports and proxy reports of each of the firms in the sample. For each director, the data include seven variables: the name of the firm for which he serves as director, his first, middle, and last name, his occupation, his principal employer, and whether he is retired. The data cover 9,804 director seats held by 7,519 individuals. There are fewer individuals than seats since some directors serve on more than one board.

When there was missing information, I supplemented the data from annual reports and proxy statements with data from The Million Dollar Directory, Standard & Poor's Register of Corporations, Directors, and Executives, The Directory of Corporate Affiliations, Who's Who in Finance and Industry, the Lexis-Nexis System, and Laser Disclosure. It was vital to collect information on all firms since the exclusion of one firm, which might be interlocked with others, could incorrectly label the remaining firms as not interlocked.

The data on the 1992 CEO salaries and personal information were collected from Forbes magazine's Annual Survey of CEO Compensation from 1993. These data cover many of the largest corporations in the U.S. and include the CEO's age, years with the firm, and years as CEO. Included are bonuses and other compensation such as insurance policies, restricted shares that vested during the year, savings plan contributions, and club memberships. Forbes also reports stock gains, which are the value realized by the exercise of options. I primarily use three measures of compensation: salary plus bonus, salary plus bonus plus other compensation, and total compensation. Total compensation is the sum of salary, bonuses, other compensation, and exercised options. Because total compensation includes exercised options, it may not reflect current compensation as accurately as the other measures.[1]

Table 1 describes some of the characteristics of the boards of directors, the CEOs, and the firms. The sample size is 602 because data on compensation and other CEO and firm characteristics are not available for all of the original firms. The summary statistics are broken down into five groups: all firms, non-any-employee interlocked firms, any-employee interlocked firms, non-current-CEO interlocked firms, and current-CEO interlocked firms. The average number of directors per firm is 12.71. Forty-four percent of the directors are principally employed by one of the original firms in the sample.

Table 1 also includes other characteristics of the firm such as market value of equity from COMPUSTAT and annual stock return from CRSP. Interlocked and non-interlocked firms are statistically significantly different on a number of dimensions. CEOs from interlocked firms have higher pay, more directors on their boards, and longer tenure with their firms. Interlocked firms have market value of equity more than twice that of non-interlocked firms. However, the previous year's mean cumulative stock returns for interlocked and non-interlocked firms are not significantly different.

B. Estimation

Even though CEOs may not necessarily sit on each other's compensation committees, the potential for conflicts of interest is likely to be more severe for firms that are current-CEO interlocked rather than any-employee interlocked. This is because each CEO in the pair actually interacts with other board members at board meetings roughly once each month. A positive link between any-employee interlock and CEO pay is still plausible, however, for several reasons. The pay of non-CEO managers is linked to that of the CEO. They may also strive to become the CEO. Additionally, non-CEO-interlocked employees from two firms who sit on each other's board can report information to the CEOs about the board proceedings. By providing a conduit for information, non-CEO employees can convey information to the CEOs that allows them to manipulate the compensation process or modify their own behaviors to elicit higher pay. The fact that non-CEOs can provide information to the CEOs might also encourage other board members to support higher CEO pay.

Table 2 presents compensation regressions for the three different compensation variables, measured in natural logs: ln(salary + bonus), ln(salary + bonus +

[1]For approximately half of the firms, I also analyzed, but do not report in the tables, the value of stock options granted to the CEO using data from William Mercer Inc. I added this measure of pay to salary, bonus, and other. The returns to interlock reported in this paper are similar whether including or excluding these option grants.

TABLE 1

Summary Statistics

	(1)	(2)	(3)	(4)	(5)
	All	Non-Any-Employee Interlocked	Any-Employee Interlocked	Non-Current-CEO Interlocked	Current-CEO Interlocked
CEO's Age (years)	56.98 (0.27)	56.75[b] (0.32)	57.88[b] (0.43)	56.82[c] (0.29)	58.93[c] (0.71)
CEO's Firm Seniority (years)	23.72 (0.49)	22.62[b] (0.56)	28.02[b] (0.87)	23.27[c] (0.51)	29.31[c] (1.38)
CEO's Seniority as CEO (years)	8.52 (0.31)	8.87[b] (0.36)	7.17[b] (0.28)	8.35[d] (0.32)	10.60[d] (1.01)
CEO's Salary + Bonus ($millions)	1.10 (0.04)	1.05[b] (0.05)	1.27[b] (0.06)	1.07[c] (0.04)	1.42[c] (0.21)
CEO's Salary + Bonus + Other ($millions)	1.35 (0.05)	1.28[b] (0.06)	1.64[b] (0.08)	1.32[c] (0.05)	1.71[c] (0.13)
CEO's Total Compensation ($millions)	2.57 (0.23)	2.45 (0.23)	3.05 (0.63)	2.45 (0.21)	4.02 (1.47)
Market Value of Equity ($millions)	4843 (336)	3783[b] (324)	8973[b] (975)	4498[c] (340)	9121[c] (1466)
Stock Return[a] in Year $t-1$	0.48 (0.03)	0.49 (0.03)	0.44 (0.04)	0.48 (0.03)	0.51 (0.08)
Number of Directors on Board	12.71 (0.16)	12.32[b] (0.19)	14.24[b] (0.29)	12.55[c] (0.17)	14.73[c] (0.53)
Proportion of Directors Employed by One of Original Sample Firms	0.44 (0.01)	0.41[b] (0.01)	0.54[b] (0.01)	0.43[c] (0.01)	0.54[c] (0.08)
N	602	479	123	557	45

Summary statistics are presented for all, for non any-employee interlocked firms, any-employee interlocked firms, non current-CEO interlocked firms, and for current-CEO interlocked firms in the five columns, respectively. Two firms are any-employee interlocked if any current or retired employee (including CEOs) of firm A serves as a director of firm B and if any current or retired employee (including CEOs) of firm B serves as a director of firm A. Two firms are current-CEO interlocked if the current CEO of firm A serves as a director of firm B and vice versa. Data on CEO pay and characteristics are collected from Forbes, accounting data are from COMPUSTAT, and return data are from CRSP. Standard errors are in parentheses.

[a] Annual stock return computed from CRSP. Stock return data from 1991. All other data from 1992.

[b] Indicates that the mean value for this variable is statistically different for non-any-employee interlocked firms relative to any-employee interlocked firms at the 1% level of significance.

[c] Indicates that the mean value for this variable is statistically different for non-current-CEO interlocked firms relative to current-CEO interlocked firms at the 1% level of significance.

[d] Indicates that the mean value for this variable is statistically different for non-current-CEO interlocked firms relative to current-CEO interlocked firms at the 5% level of significance.

other compensation), and ln(total compensation). The table is arranged into two panels: Panel A shows the effects of any-employee interlock on CEO pay and Panel B shows current-CEO interlock. Without controlling for other firm and individual characteristics, the coefficients in Table 2, Panel A, row 1, columns 1 (0.291), 4 (0.357), and 7 (0.314), imply that compensation of CEOs in any-employee interlocked firms is estimated to be 34 to 43% higher than in other firms. These pay gaps are estimated using the standard conversion $e^{\beta}-1$, where the βs come from the coefficients on interlock from the regressions in Table 2. Using the same simple conversion, the regressions from columns 1, 4, and 7 of Table 2, Panel B imply that CEO compensation in current-CEO interlocked firms is estimated to be 46 to 52% higher than in other firms. All of these differences are statistically significant at the 1% level. There is a substantial difference in CEO pay for interlocked CEOs relative to non-interlocked CEOs, no matter how interlock or pay are measured.

Columns 2, 5, and 8 of Table 2, Panel A include as additional regressors the age of the CEO and its square, the CEO's seniority in the firm and its square, the

TABLE 2

Least Squares Regressions for Estimates of the Return to Interlock and Other Determinants of CEO Pay

	ln(salary + bonus)			ln(salary + bonus + other)			ln(total compensation)		
	(1)	(2)	(3)	(4)	(5)	(6)	(7)	(8)	(9)
Panel A. Focus on ANY-EMPLOYEE interlock. Two firms are any-employee interlocked if any current or retired employee of firm A serves as a director of firm B and vice versa. Interlock measures constructed by the author from various sources.									
ANY-EMPLOYEE Interlock	0.291***	0.092		0.357***	0.142**		0.314***	0.060	
	(4.716)	(1.583)		(5.289)	(2.204)		(3.323)	(0.665)	
ANY-EMPLOYEE Interlock (with any business relationships considered not interlocked)			0.116*			0.165**			0.045
			(1.805)			(2.309)			(0.448)
CEO's Age (years)		0.137***	0.137***		0.156***	0.156***		0.195***	0.196***
		(3.832)	(3.827)		(3.932)	(3.935)		(3.517)	(3.530)
$(\text{CEO's Age})^2/100$		−0.118***	−0.118***		−0.133***	−0.133***		−0.164***	−0.164***
		(3.695)	(3.684)		(3.752)	(3.747)		(3.292)	(3.302)
CEO's Firm Seniority (years)		−0.020**	−0.020**		−0.021**	−0.021**		−0.019	−0.019
		(2.507)	(2.536)		(2.360)	(2.387)		(1.526)	(1.518)
$(\text{CEO's Firm Seniority})^2/100$		0.032*	0.032*		0.032*	0.032*		0.021	0.021
		(1.830)	(1.842)		(1.653)	(1.664)		(0.804)	(0.801)
CEO's Seniority as CEO (years)		0.028***	0.029***		0.028***	0.029***		0.032***	0.032***
		(3.621)	(3.673)		(3.272)	(3.329)		(2.657)	(2.650)
$(\text{CEO's seniority as CEO})^2/100$		−0.042*	−0.043*		−0.040	−0.042		−0.030	−0.030
		(1.796)	(1.842)		(1.566)	(1.621)		(0.828)	(0.833)
ln(Market Value of Equity) in ln($millions)		0.232***	0.231***		0.250***	0.251***		0.332***	0.334***
		(10.470)	(10.499)		(10.225)	(10.290)		(9.682)	(9.788)
$(\text{Stock Return})_{(t-1)}$		0.030	0.028		0.017	0.014		0.180***	0.178***
		(0.754)	(0.703)		(0.401)	(0.328)		(2.934)	(2.913)
Number of Directors on Board		0.011*	0.012*		0.013*	0.013*		0.001	0.002
		(1.784)	(1.833)		(1.774)	(1.851)		(0.141)	(0.176)
20 Industry Indicators	no	yes	yes	no	yes	yes	no	yes	yes
Constant	13.646***	8.813***	8.190***	13.806***	7.584***	7.573***	14.105***	5.953***	5.912***
	(489.639)	(8.235)	(8.255)	(451.927)	(6.898)	(6.897)	(330.467)	(3.862)	(3.839)
R^2	0.034	0.306	0.307	0.043	0.299	0.300	0.016	0.275	0.274

(continued on next page)

TABLE 2 (continued)

Least Squares Regressions for Estimates of the Return to Interlock and Other Determinants of CEO Pay

	ln(salary + bonus)			ln(salary + bonus + other)			ln(total compensation)		
	(1)	(2)	(3)	(4)	(5)	(6)	(7)	(8)	(9)
Panel B. Focus on CURRENT-CEO interlock. Two firms are current-CEO interlocked if the current CEO of firm A serves as a director of firm B and vice versa.									
CURRENT-CEO Interlock	0.381***	0.068		0.377***	0.039		0.418***	0.004	
	(4.011)	(0.793)		(3.591)	(0.413)		(2.878)	(0.032)	
CURRENT-CEO Interlock (with any business relationships considered not interlocked)			0.158			0.130			−0.028
			(1.528)			(1.134)			(0.177)
CEO's Age (years)		0.139***	0.138***		0.160***	0.159***		0.197***	0.198***
		(3.895)	(3.867)		(4.034)	(4.006)		(3.557)	(3.564)
$(\text{CEO's Age})^2/100$		−0.120***	−0.119***		−0.137***	−0.136***		−0.165***	−0.166***
		(3.753)	(3.725)		(3.846)	(3.820)		(3.328)	(3.335)
CEO's Firm Seniority (years)		−0.019**	−0.020**		−0.020**	−0.020**		−0.018	−0.018
		(2.428)	(2.470)		(2.243)	(2.274)		(1.494)	(1.489)
$(\text{CEO's Firm Seniority})^2/100$		0.031*	0.031*		0.031	0.031		0.021	0.021
		(1.792)	(1.824)		(1.601)	(1.623)		(0.791)	(0.788)
CEO's Seniority as CEO (years)		0.027***	0.026***		0.027***	0.026***		0.032***	0.032***
		(3.410)	(3.367)		(3.064)	(0.009)		(2.599)	(2.626)
$(\text{CEO's Seniority as CEO})^2/100$		−0.039*	−0.039*		−0.038	−0.037		−0.029	−0.030
		(1.679)	(1.652)		(1.471)	(1.435)		(0.808)	(0.825)
ln(Market Value of Equity) in ln($millions)		0.238***	0.237***		0.262***	0.261***		0.338***	0.339***
		(10.927)	(11.018)		(10.880)	(10.941)		(10.031)	(10.150)
$(\text{Stock Return})_{(t-1)}$		0.029	0.027		0.015	0.014		0.178***	0.178***
		(0.723)	(0.681)		(0.336)	(0.310)		(2.911)	(2.913)
Number of Directors on Board		0.012*	0.011*		0.014*	0.013*		0.002	0.002
		(1.849)	(1.779)		(1.921)	(1.854)		(0.196)	(0.215)
20 Industry Indicators	no	yes	yes	no	yes	yes	no	yes	yes
Constant	13.676***	8.079***	8.122***	13.851***	7.366***	7.417***	14.138***	5.850***	5.829***
	(526.578)	(8.138)	(8.198)	(483.014)	(6.690)	(6.746)	(356.382)	(3.805)	(3.792)
R^2	0.025	0.303	0.305	0.019	0.293	0.295	0.012	0.274	0.274

The dependent variables are, respectively, ln(salary + bonus), ln(salary + bonus + other compensation), and ln(total compensation). Other compensation includes such items as insurance policies, restricted shares that vested during the year, savings plan contributions, and memberships to clubs. Total compensation = salary + bonus + other compensation plus exercised options. These salary data are from Forbes magazine and are for 1992.

***significant at 0.01, **significant at 0.05, and *significant at 0.10.

There are 602 observations. (*t*-statistics are in parentheses).

CEO's seniority as CEO and its square, ln(firm market value), the lagged annual stock market return, and the number of directors on the board. The regressions also include 20 industry indicator variables collected from Forbes, which are not reported in the table. Compensation increases at a declining rate with the CEO's age and seniority. The coefficient on lagged stock return is positive, but statistically significant only for the total compensation measure.[2]

The effect of market value of equity is highly statistically significant. The functional form for this variable in a compensation regression is important not only for its own sake, but also for the effect it has on the other covariates. For example, if I use the actual level (instead of the natural log) of the firm's market value as a control, the coefficient on any-employee interlock in Table 2, Panel A, column 2, row 1 is 0.179 with a t-statistic of 3.0 rather than 0.092 with a t-statistic of 1.58. As reported in Table 1, larger firms are more likely to interlock than smaller firms. Market value and interlock are so highly correlated that specifying market value as linear seriously affects the coefficient on interlock. The Appendix and Appendix Figure 1 describe in more detail why it is more appropriate to specify ln(market value of equity) than levels as a covariate. The ln(market value) specification is also consistent with the literature (see, for example, Murphy (1985)). Alternative ways to control for firm size, such as that described in the Appendix, yield estimates of the return to interlock almost identical to those reported in Table 2. The coefficient on the any-employee interlock variable falls to 0.092 (Table 2, Panel A, column 2) and becomes statistically insignificant at conventional levels when the control variables are included in the regression.

Column 5 of Table 2, Panel A repeats the analysis of column 2 while using ln(salary + bonus + other compensation) as the dependent variable. The results are similar to those presented in column 2, except that the return to any-employee interlock is higher (0.142) and significant at the 5% level. Since any-employee interlock produces a larger effect on this dependent variable, I investigated other compensation more closely. Ninety-three percent of the firms in the sample offer their CEOs at least some other compensation. Other compensation is, on average, 13.5% of salary plus bonus plus other. If I use the 93% of firms with non-zero other compensation and run a least squares regression of ln(other compensation) on the complete list of control variables from Table 2, the return to interlock is much higher than reported in the table. The coefficient on any-employee interlock implies a difference of 57.1% with a t-statistic of 3.0. The coefficient on current-CEO interlock implies a relatively smaller difference of 25.9%, however. If, instead, I use the entire set of data, including observations with zero other compensation, tobit specifications censoring either at 1 or at the minimum of other non-zero compensation yield even larger effects. Even though other compensation is a relatively small part of remuneration, interlocking has a significant effect on it. Because it is less tangible than salary, individual directors may be able to influence other compensation more easily than salary.

Column 8 of Table 2 uses ln(total compensation) as the dependent variable and includes the same set of control variables as reported in columns 2 and 5.

[2]Although there are some significant outliers in CEO pay, results are similar if I use median regressions (Koenker and Bassett (1978)) rather than OLS. The OLS estimates are reported in this paper.

The coefficient on the interlock variable is smaller than those reported in columns 2 and 5 and insignificant. I have reported the results for total compensation for completeness even though, as I mentioned earlier, this dependent variable includes the value of exercised options and not the value of options when granted. This variable potentially has a lot of noise associated with it as the exercise of options can be quite irregular over time.

Interlocks may simply reflect legitimate business relationships such as customer/supplier, banking, or other business relationships, and not the cronyism implied by Rees (1992). For each interlocked firm, I examined annual reports, proxy statements, 10Ks, and 10Qs to determine why these firms were interlocked with one another. For each firm, I searched by computer through the reports for the name of the firm to which it was interlocked. When I found the name of an interlocked firm, I made a determination as to why the interlocks took place. For example, firms can be interlocked because one firm supplies goods or services to the other or because they participate in a joint venture with one another. A number of firms seem to be interlocked because of documented business relationships. For example, 26% of any-employee interlocked firms and 36% of current-CEO interlocked firms had identifiable business relationships. Although a large fraction of interlocks remains unexplained by these relationships, it is plausible that cronyism is less of a problem in firms with such formal business arrangements.

In columns 3, 6, and 9 of Table 2, Panel A, those interlocked firms that have documented business relationships are redefined as not interlocked and the analysis of columns 2, 5, and 8 is repeated. For the first two measures of compensation, when controlling for firm and CEO characteristics, the point estimates for the return to interlock are higher when firms with business relationships are considered to be *not* interlocked (compare column 3 to column 2 and column 6 to column 5). Redefining interlock leaves only those firms with potentially the largest opportunity for agency problems.

Panel B of Table 2 repeats the analysis of Panel A but focuses on current-CEO interlocks. Without conditioning on other covariates, firms that are current-CEO interlocked pay their CEOs substantially higher pay. In columns 2, 5, and 8, when covariates are introduced, the point estimates on interlock fall and are insignificant. However, when interlocks that can be explained by business relationships are considered not interlocked, in columns 3, 6, and 9, the return to interlock rises substantially for the first two measures of pay. Given the earlier discussion of the differences in the two types of interlock, it is plausible to expect a higher return for current-CEO interlock relative to any-employee interlock. In fact, however, it is not higher. But when interlocks explained by business relationships are redefined as not interlocked, the current-CEO interlock coefficients are larger compared with the any-employee interlock coefficients than discussed earlier, at least for the first two measures of pay.

I have repeated the analyses reported earlier using compensation data for the years before and after the focus of this study, 1991 and 1993. Results using the compensation data from 1991 and 1993 are qualitatively similar to those reported above for 1992.

III. Return to Interlock over Time

To study the effects of interlock over time, I obtained a data set from Bearden and Mintz (1985) who studied the largest 252 firms in terms of sales in 1976. Their data are quite similar to mine in that they also study very large firms. I was able to construct any-employee interlock measures for 1976 using their data. The fraction of any-employee interlocked firms in the sample constructed from their data is 7.54%. Following their selection procedure and using my 1992 data yields an any-employee interlock fraction of 28.57%. Note that this is higher than the 20% reported earlier for the 1992 data—as the very largest firms are more likely to interlock. For the comparison described in this section, the sample construction of the data sets is identical, although the fraction interlocked in 1992 is much higher.

Table 3 presents a comparison of the returns to interlock in 1976 with those in 1992 and shows that the return to interlock is higher in 1976. Panel A of Table 3 presents results for the dependent variable ln(salary + bonus) and Panel B for ln(total compensation). The middle compensation category from Table 2, which includes other compensation, is not included in Table 3 since data on other compensation are not available for 1976. Column 1 presents regression results using the full sample from 1992 and column 2 presents results for the 1992 subsample, which only includes the largest 252 firms in terms of sales. There is not a significantly different return to interlock using the entire 1992 data set rather than the smaller subset of firms. Column 3 uses the same sample selection criteria as column 2 but uses data from 1976 instead of 1992. In column 3, the return to any-employee interlock is very high and statistically significant, 21.3 and 16.6%, respectively, for the dependent variables.

TABLE 3

Return to Any-Employee Interlock Using Data from Two Periods, 1992 and 1976

	(1) Full Sample 1992	(2) Largest Firms by Sales 1992	(3) Largest Firms by Sales 1976
Panel A. Dependent Variable: ln(salary + bonus)			
ANY-EMPLOYEE Interlock	0.092	0.115	0.213***
	(1.583)	(1.603)	(2.696)
$\bar{R}^2$	0.306	0.225	0.295
Panel B. Dependent Variable: ln(total compensation)			
ANY-EMPLOYEE Interlock	0.060	0.139	0.166**
	(0.665)	(1.240)	(1.983)
$\bar{R}^2$	0.275	0.210	0.340
N	602	213	232

The dependent variables in Panels A, and B, respectively, are ln(salary +bonus) and ln(total compensation). Total compensation = salary + bonus + other compensation (which includes such items as insurance policies, restricted shares that vested during the year, savings plan contributions, and memberships to clubs) + exercised options. The data in columns 1 and 2 are for 1992 and the data in column 3 are from 1976. The data used to construct the interlock variables used in column 3 are from Bearden and Mintz (1985). All specifications also control for 20 industry indicator variables, age of the CEO and its square, seniority of the CEO in the firm and its square, seniority of the CEO as CEO and its square, ln(firm value), and the number of directors on the board. The largest 252 firms in 1992 (column 2) and the largest 252 firms in 1976 (column 3) were used to construct the any-employee interlock variables. Sample sizes differ from 252 as not all other information is available for all firms.

***significant at 0.01, and **significant at 0.05. (*t*-statistics are in parentheses).

It is particularly interesting that the *return* to interlock is higher in 1976 than 1992, especially given that the *fraction* of interlocked firms is much higher in 1992 than in 1976. In light of a comment by Jensen and Murphy (1990) that "disclosure of top-management compensation can guard against 'looting' by management (in collusion with 'captive' boards of directors)," it is surprising that the true fraction interlocked is smaller in the later period since disclosure has become more common and SEC rules more strict. The data suggest that although firms are more likely to have interlocking relationships, these are not being translated into substantially higher pay for CEOs.

IV. Agency

To study whether the fraction of employees interlocked is larger than would be expected by chance, I ran simulations to examine what fraction of firms would be interlocked if directors were randomly assigned to board positions. We should not think a priori that this fraction is zero. To test whether the portion of firms that are any-employee interlocked is simply an artifact of random assignment, I simulated what the true fraction interlocked would be under a set of simple assumptions. First, I assumed that the directors who are currently in my sample are the entire population of potential directors. Second, I assumed that for each of 999 iterations of randomly assigning directors, each director had a probability of 1 of being reassigned a spot in the pool. Finally, I assumed that interlocks are allowed within an industry.[3] I effectively sorted each of the 9,804 director positions and randomly put directors back into positions. I did this 999 times and each time computed the fraction interlocked. Although each of the assumptions tends to overestimate the simulated fraction interlocked, actual board directors interlock much more often than would occur by random chance: the actual number interlocked is five times the simulated level.

There is some reason to believe that interlock is due to agency conflicts. First, simulation estimates suggest that interlocking happens far more often than can be explained by random chance. Second, although up to one-third of interlocks can be explained by business relationships, a large fraction of interlocking cannot be explained in this way. Finally, the return to interlock is higher when firms with documented business relationships are considered not interlocked. Taken together, these facts suggest that interlock could be due to agency problems.

V. Econometric Issues

A. Sample Selection

Because of the way I constructed the sample, some firms that may actually be interlocked may artificially look not interlocked. If directors tend to associate with directors of firms like their own in terms of firm value, then firms near the bottom of the sample may be interlocked with firms just below them (who are out of the sample). Also, firms high in value have fewer directors to choose from if

[3] According to the Clayton Act of 1914, employees of one firm cannot serve as directors of another firm in the same industry.

they want directors from like firms. To study this possibility, I split the sample in half in terms of the market value of equity of the firms. If the sample construction is a problem, then there should be a larger effect of interlock on CEO pay for firms with high equity value than for firms with low equity value.[4] Firms in the upper half of the value distribution are any-employee interlocked 33% of the time, and those in the lower half of the value distribution are any-employee interlocked only 8% of the time. However, selection is not systematically driving the results, since the coefficient on interlocked is higher and more significant in high value firms if the dependent variable is a function of salary plus bonus, but lower if the dependent variable is a function of either salary plus bonus plus other compensation or total compensation.

B. Unobserved Heterogeneity

The interpretation of the models in Tables 2 and 3 depends on the assumption that CEOs in companies with different levels of interlock are otherwise identical, conditional on the observed control variables. However, there is some reason to suspect this is not the case. Since there are large differences in the observable characteristics of CEOs of interlocked and non-interlocked firms, it is likely that there are additional explanations for CEO pay beyond those already stated, including interlock. If interlock is just a proxy for other, unobserved variables, then controlling for other variables as well may at least partially reduce the effect of interlock.

I have considered several possibilities for additional controls. One is the fraction of the board of directors that is principally employed by one of the firms in the sample. Forty-four percent of the directors are employed by one of the large firms. The coefficient on this variable in a compensation regression could have a few interpretations. First, it could be interpreted as a measure of cronyism. Second, it could be interpreted as a measure of firm quality. If a higher fraction of the board members from large firms implies a more prestigious firm, this could translate into higher CEO pay. Also, Morck, Schliefer, and Vishny (1989) have suggested that Tobin's Q may proxy for the ability of the managers. Additionally Abowd, Kramarz, and Margolis (1993) and Rosen (1982) have argued that firms with above average wages may have workers of above average ability, so I have controlled for a crude measure of the average firm wage by using the total labor and related expenses of the firm divided by the total employees (collected from COMPUSTAT). Finally, I controlled for the occupational distribution of the board members by including 12 indicator variables for board member occupations: CEO, chairman, president, vice-chairman, vice-president, professor, attorney, doctor, government official, consultant, businessman, and other. If boards organized in particular ways are more likely to be interlocked and more likely to have higher paid CEOs, then interlock could be a proxy for good management and not cronyism. Collectively controlling for these measures reduces the return to interlock slightly. Although the

[4] Another way to see if directors tend to come from similar firms in terms of firm market value of equity is to measure the correlation between firm value and average value of the firms that principally employ the directors. This is difficult, however, as many directors are employed by organizations outside of the sample of firms, such as universities and foundations.

data do not allow for more sophisticated tests for unobserved heterogeneity, these results using additional controls suggest that additional covariates might further reduce the measured return to interlock.

VI. Concluding Comments

Previous study of the compensation of CEOs has excluded detailed analysis of the group that actually sets CEO pay, the board of directors. This work uses data on the composition of the boards of directors of America's largest firms as well as information on CEO compensation and firm characteristics to test the hypothesis that CEOs who are reciprocally interlocked with other CEOs via their boards of directors can raise their wages above those of their counterparts who are not interlocked. There is a substantial amount of interlock. About 20% of firms are any-employee interlocked. Roughly 8% of firms are current-CEO interlocked. Interlocked CEOs earn, on average, significantly higher pay than non-interlocked CEOs. After controlling for firm and CEO characteristics, this pay gap is reduced dramatically. However, when firms that are interlocked due to documented business relationships are considered not interlocked, the measured return to interlock is as high as 17%. There is also evidence that the return to interlock was higher in the 1970s than in the early 1990s.

Appendix. Discussion of ln(Firm Market Value of Equity) Functional Form Assumption in the ln(Compensation) Regression

Table 1 demonstrates that interlocked firms are, on average, twice as large as non-interlocked firms. In the regressions of CEO pay on firm characteristics, the specification of functional form of the market value of the firm is crucial to the coefficient on interlock.

To test what specification for firm size was appropriate, I ran a series of regressions like the following,

$$\begin{aligned}\ln(\text{salary} + \text{bonus}) = {} & \alpha + \beta_1(\text{CEO's Age}) + \beta_2(\text{CEO's Age})^2 \\ & + \beta_3(\text{CEO's firm seniority}) + \beta_4(\text{CEO's firm seniority})^2 \\ & + \beta_5(\text{CEO's seniority as CEO}) + \beta_6(\text{CEO's seniority as CEO})^2 \\ & + \beta_7(\text{stock return})_{t-1} + \beta_8(\text{number of directors on board}) \\ & + \sum_{i=2}^{20} \text{Industry}_i \Gamma_i + \sum_{j=2}^{20} \left[(\text{value size group})_j\right] \theta_j + \epsilon.\end{aligned}$$

This regression is simply ln(salary + bonus) on many standard CEO and firm-level characteristics as well as 19 other variables that are indicators for firm market value of equity. Since there is a constant, one of the group of 20 is omitted from the regression. To construct these firm market value of equity size groups, I sorted the data by market value and assigned the smallest 5% to $(\text{value size group})_1$ and so on up to the largest 5% in $(\text{value size group})_{20}$. The coefficients of interest are the 19

$\widehat{\theta}_j$ coefficients. Appendix Figure 1 plots these 19 coefficients on the vertical axis and ln(average of each of the 19 firm value size groups) on the horizontal axis. The straight line in the figure suggests that a log-linear specification is appropriate—that is, the regressions should include ln(firm market value of equity) and not the level. The results of this analysis are robust to changes in the covariates and dependent variables in the equation above.

APPENDIX FIGURE 1

Coefficients on Value Indicator Variables

Points in the figure are the 19 $\widehat{\theta}_j$ estimates from the following regression:

$$\begin{aligned}\ln(\text{salary} + \text{bonus}) = {} & \alpha + \beta_1(\text{CEO's age}) + \beta_2(\text{CEO's age})^2 \\ & + \beta_3(\text{CEO's firm seniority}) + \beta_4(\text{CEO's firm seniority})^2 \\ & + \beta_5(\text{CEO's seniority as CEO}) + \beta_6(\text{CEO's seniority as CEO})^2 \\ & + \beta_7(\text{stock return})_{t-1} + \beta_8(\text{number of directors on board}) \\ & + \sum_{i=2}^{20} \text{Industry}_i \Gamma_i + \sum_{j=2}^{20} \left[(\text{value size group})_j\right] \theta_j + \epsilon.\end{aligned}$$

To construct the market value of equity size groups, I sorted the data by firm market value of equity and assigned the smallest 5% to (value size group)$_1$ and so on up to (value size group)$_{20}$. Since there is a constant, one of the group of 20 is omitted from the regression. The other variables are described in the text and other tables.

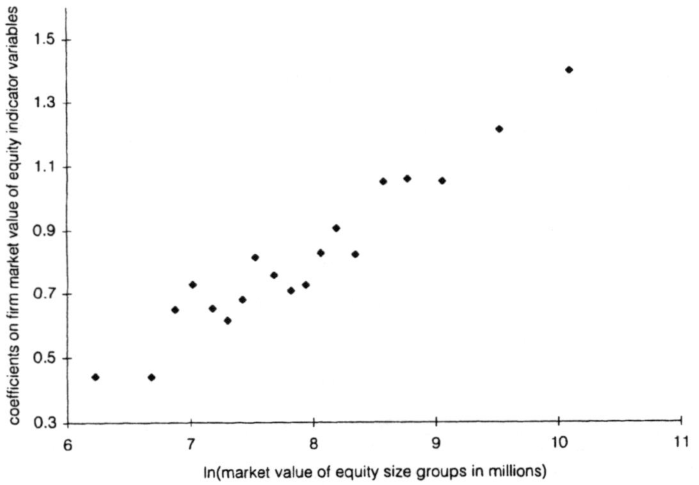

References

Abowd, J.; F. Kramarz; and D. Margolis. "High Wage Workers and High Wage Firms: Compensation Policies and Firm Performance in France." Mimeo, (March 1993).

Bearden, J., and B. Mintz. "Regionality and Integration in the American Interlock Network." In *Networks of Corporate Power,* F. N. Stockman, R. Ziegler, and J. Scott, eds. Cambridge, U.K.: Polity Press (1985), 234–249.

The Directory of Corporate Affiliations. National Register Publishing (1992).

Jensen, M. C., and K. J. Murphy. "Performance Pay and Top Management Incentives." *Journal of Political Economy,* 98 (No. 2, 1990), 225–264.

Koenker, R., and G. Bassett. "Regression Quantiles." *Econometrica,* 46 (No. 1, 1978), 33–50.

Lazear, E. P., and S. Rosen. "Rank-Order Tournaments as Optimum Labor Contracts." *Journal of Political Economy,* 89 (No. 5, 1981), 841–864.

Million Dollar Directory. Dunns Marketing Services (1992).

Morck, R.; A. Schliefer; and R. Vishny. 'Alternative Mechanisms for Corporate Control." *American Economic Review,* 79 (Sept. 1989), 842–852.

Murphy, K. J. "Corporate Performance and Managerial Remuneration: An Empirical Analysis." *Journal of Accounting and Economics,* 7 (1985), 11–42.

Rees, A. "The Tournament as a Model for Executive Compensation." *Journal of Post Keynesian Economics,* 14 (Summer 1992), 567–571.

Rosen, S. "Authority, Control, and the Distribution of Earnings." *Bell Journal of Economics,* 13 (Autumn 1982), 311–323

Standard and Poor's Register of Corporations, Directors, and Executives. McGraw Hill (1992).

Who's Who in Finance and Industry, 27th Edition. Marquis (1992).

[22]

Golden Parachutes: CEOs and the Exercise of Social Influence

James Wade
Charles A. O'Reilly, III
Ike Chandratat
University of California at Berkeley

Using an agency theory framework and data on 89 Fortune 500 firms, we assess whether the granting of golden parachutes to chief executive officers is the result of an economically rational process or determined by the social influence of the CEO. While increased takeover risk is associated with a higher incidence of GPs, as predicted by economic theory, CEOs who are able to appoint more outsiders to their board are also more likely to have GPs. These results suggest that both economic and social influence perspectives have merit and that the importance of each may depend on the ownership structure of the firm.•

Along with the recent trend in corporate mergers and takeovers have emerged new incentive packages for incumbent management teams as insurance against takeovers. Generally referred to as "golden parachutes" (or GPs), these are contracts between the executive and the employer that provide for additional compensation should a change in control or ownership occur (Krueger, 1985). The magnitude of these payouts can be significant. For instance, ten executives from Primerica recently received $98.2 million as a result of a takeover (Winkler, 1988). Estimates are that approximately 30 percent of the top 250 industrial companies have these, and the proportion is growing rapidly (Adair, 1987). But are golden parachutes a sound idea? Who actually benefits from them, the shareholders or top management? What rationale is used by the board of directors in the decision to grant GPs to management?

Thus far, these issues have generated far more controversy than research. The general argument in favor of GPs is one of aligning incentives between shareholders and management. The logic is that an entrenched management, faced with a takeover bid that may lead to job loss, is likely to resist the offer in order to protect management's jobs, even though such an offer might be in the shareholders' interest (e.g., Jensen and Ruback, 1983). Walkling and Long (1984), for instance, demonstrated empirically that the probability of management resisting a takeover bid is directly related to the takeover's effect on management's personal wealth. Some evidence is also available suggesting that the adoption of a golden parachute is associated with a positive security market reaction (Lambert and Larcker, 1985). From this perspective, GPs provide incentives to management to pay attention to the stockholders' interests and not to the top managers' potential job loss.

But is the decision by the board of directors to award GPs to management solely one dictated by economic rationality? Although the board has the legal right and formal power to hire, evaluate, reward, and fire the chief executive officer (CEO), it has been widely noted that the CEO can also influence the board through persuasion, the selective use of information, control over the agenda, and other tactics designed to influence its deliberations and decisions (e.g., Zald, 1969; Mace, 1971; Mizruchi, 1983; Patton and Baker, 1987). While not possessing formal power over the board, the CEO may be able to exert what social psychologists refer to as "social influence" (Cialdini, 1984), relying on norms of reciprocity,

0001-8392/90/3504-0587/$1.00.

•

The authors gratefully acknowledge the helpful criticisms and comments of Peter Cappelli, Glenn Carroll, Heather Haveman, David Levine, Brian Main, Trond Petersen, and the anonymous reviewers on an earlier version of this manuscript and the Institute of Industrial Relations and the Center for Research in Management for research support.

liking, and social consensus to shape the board's decision making. Consistent with this view, an argument sometimes made in the business press is that boards of directors often rubberstamp management's requests, including providing undeserved compensation such as GPs (e.g., Sherman, 1988). Several studies have suggested that actual relationships between boards and CEOs may be quite different than that assumed in conventional economic theory (e.g., Baker, Jensen, and Murphy, 1988). O'Reilly, Main, and Crysta (1988), for example, have shown that CEO compensation may be strongly affected by social comparison processes operating within the compensation committee. More recently, O'Reilly, Wade, and Chandratat (1990) have extended these findings to show that CEOs may be able to use social influence to affect their compensation. They show that, independent of economic determinants, a CEO's compensation is likely to be significantly higher if the CEO was appointed to the board of directors before the chairman of the compensation committee was appointed. This and other findings led O'Reilly, Wade, and Chandratat (1990) to conclude that compensation decisions by the board of directors may be affected through the exercise of social influence by the CEO over the board.

From an agency theory perspective (Gibbons and Murphy, 1988), there are two possible explanations for the existence of golden parachutes. On the one hand, GPs may act to align the interests of management and shareholders and thus be economically efficient. On the other hand, CEOs (agents) with a high degree of social influence may be able to circumvent the interests of shareholders (the principal) and opportunistically acquire GPs irrespective of the GP's economic value to the shareholders. The purpose of this study is to explore the relative associations of both economic and social influence variables with the incidence of golden parachutes.

Agency Theory and Golden Parachute Adoption

Takeover risk. The primary argument for granting golden parachutes is predicated on the notion that, under some circumstances, top executives may resist takeover attempts in order to protect their jobs, even though such attempts may be in the shareholders' interest. From an agency theory perspective (Eisenhardt, 1989; Tosi and Gomez-Mejia, 1989), managers can be conceived of as agents who are in control of the firm's assets and receive compensation for their performance. The board of directors acts as the principal on behalf of the stockholders and is charged with monitoring management to insure that it fulfills its fiduciary duties of maximizing shareholder wealth. Since a takeover may result in top management's loss of jobs while also providing substantial benefits to shareholders, an argument can be made that contingent compensation contracts, in the form of golden parachutes, can help align principal-agent interests in the event of a takeover (Jensen and Ruback, 1983; Lambert and Larcker, 1985; Singh and Harianto, 1989). Therefore, from this perspective, factors that make a takeover significantly more or less likely should be related to the incidence of golden parachutes. Previous research has provided empirical support for this claim (Cochran, Wood, and Jones, 1985; Singh and Harianto, 1989).

Social influence. In a recent paper, Jensen and Murphy (1987: 43) observed that "actual executive compensation contracts look very different from those predicted by economic theory. The failure of the theory to explain actual compensation arrangements suggests that the theory is wrong." The authors suggested that what is missing from the economic view is any consideration of the political processes that characterize the executive wage-setting process. O'Reilly, Main, and Crystal (1988: 272) provided some evidence in support of this more political view, demonstrating that CEO salaries are strongly related to the salaries of the outside directors who sit on the compensation committee of the board of directors. They raised the possibility that "CEOs can, under some circumstances, influence the decision making process of the board—either subtly through increased similarity, or more directly through social influence." O'Reilly, Wade, and Chandratat (1990) investigated directly the possibility of CEOs using social influence to enhance their compensation. They found that CEOs who were appointed to the board of directors before the chairman of the compensation committee was appointed and CEOs whose tenure relative to the tenure of members of the board is higher have significantly higher compensation. They argued that under these circumstances CEOs are able to select individuals for board membership who may be more similar to themselves and such directors will also be more likely to feel an obligation to the CEOs and, hence, be more willing to grant higher levels of compensation. These findings are consistent with a view suggesting that CEO compensation may reflect social influence processes as well as being determined by economic factors.

The proposition that CEO compensation is influenced by an executive's social influence can be readily accommodated within an agency theory framework. Tosi and Gomez-Mejia (1989: 171) noted that "because agents control organizational resources and are likely to know more about the tasks that they perform for the principal, an information asymmetry exists that could give an advantage to the agents." Social influence can be thought of as an organizational resource that can enable the agent (the CEO) to act opportunistically in his or her own interest at the expense of the principal (shareholders). Social influence might be one mechanism that renders shareholder monitoring devices, such as the board of directors, ineffective and allows influential CEOs to obtain GPs. Therefore, the primary purpose of this paper is to determine if GP adoption is an efficient incentive alignment device (e.g., predicted by takeover threat) or an example of opportunism by influential and powerful CEOs.

Determinants of Golden Parachutes

We have developed a series of hypotheses concerning the determinants of golden parachutes. The first three hypotheses reflect the economic rationale for the adoption of golden parachutes. Both a firm's size and its market value relative to book value are postulated to affect GPs through takeover risk. Consistent with principal-agent theory, owner control is expected to increase the ability of the principal to monitor the agent and decrease the likelihood of a GP. While the logic is not as clear, the effects of human capital variables and the role of a CEO's board tenure are also investigated, although no formal hypotheses are offered. Hypotheses 4 through 6 explore possible social influence determinants of GPs. After controlling for economic variables, the effects of a CEO's reputation, relative tenure on the board, and the appointment of outsiders after the CEO is on the board (controlling for board size) are investigated. These measures are derived from a consideration of how social influence could be used by the CEO to manage the board. Finally, hypothesis 7 draws on principal-agent theory to explore how social influence may be more likely to occur in management-controlled firms.

Firm size. Until quite recently, large firms were considered to be less likely to be takeover targets than small ones since their size made them more expensive to acquire. This cost made it less likely that other firms or individuals could amass the capital necessary to engage in a takeover contest. Further, size also increases the differentiation and structural complexity of firms (e.g., Meyer, 1972), thereby making it potentially more difficult for an acquirer to integrate the assets easily (Jemison and Sitkin, 1986; Jensen, 1988). Empirically, this position is supported by Palepu (1986), who found that after controlling for growth, increases in size (as measured by assets) decreased the probability that a firm would be taken over.

The economic argument suggests that since larger firms may be more difficult to acquire, their boards of directors should be less likely to offer GPs to management. In addition, because top managers in these firms may feel less threatened by the possibility of a takeover, they may also be less likely to request them. What little empirical evidence exists generally supports this relationship. Cochran, Wood, and Jones (1985) found a significant negative relationship between firm size, indexed by the rank of the firm in the Fortune 500 listing, and the incidence of golden parachutes. Knoeber (1986) also found that CEOs of firms with fewer assets are more likely to have GPs. However, previous studies have not examined size while controlling for industry effects. Using a set of firms across industries may confound size effects with industry, since some industries may have characteristically larger or smaller firms and, in some instances, be exposed to more systematic risk of takeover. This suggests the following hypothesis:

Hypothesis 1: CEOs of larger firms will, all other things being equal, be less likely to have golden parachutes than CEOs of smaller firms.

Owner control. From a principal-agent perspective, a large group of small shareholders (the principal) will have more difficulty in ensuring that the actions of management are in their interests than would a small group of large shareholders. In effect, the dispersed shareholders will have more difficulty in coordinating their efforts to exert control over management. Thus a CEO in this type of firm (management-controlled) may be freer to pursue his or her self-interests at the expense of shareholders. Tosi and Gomez-Mejia (1989), for instance, found that in management-controlled firms the board has less influence over the CEO than in owner-controlled firms. If golden parachutes are an agency cost associated with ineffective monitoring by shareholders, one might expect that GPs might be more common in management-controlled firms. Consistent with these arguments, both Singh and Harianto (1989) and Knoeber (1986) found that the greater the concentration of stock ownership, the less likely the incidence of a golden parachute.

In the relatively rare circumstance in which the CEO owns a substantial amount of the stock, the prediction would be the same. Because a takeover typically generates wealth for the acquired company's shareholders, a CEO in this position needs no insurance against job loss. In addition, since, in effect, the principal and the agent are the same in this situation, there is no need to align their interests. Thus, the following hypothesis is offered:

Hypothesis 2: CEOs in owner-controlled firms are less likely to have golden parachutes than are CEOs in management-controlled firms.

Market performance. Another variable that may increase the incidence of golden parachutes is market performance. When the value of the firm's assets is not adequately reflected in the stock price, there may be an opportunity for new owners to capitalize on the undervalued assets (e.g., Jensen, 1988). Cochran, Wood, and Jones (1985) have suggested that one measure (hereafter called EXCESS) that may reflect this is the difference between a firm's market value (defined as market value of common stock + book liabilities) and the book value of the firm's assets normalized by sales. The logic here is that a firm whose assets are undervalued by the market will have a low market value relative to its book value. Hence, the lower the value of EXCESS, the greater will be the risk of a takeover. Because an increased probability of a takeover will make job loss more salient to the CEO, we expect that the lower EXCESS is, the greater the incidence of golden parachutes. In fact, Cochran, Wood, and Jones (1985) found a strong negative association between EXCESS and the adoption of GPs. The above discussion leads to the following hypothesis:

Hypothesis 3: Ceteris paribus, the greater a firm's takeover susceptibility (the lower a firm's EXCESS value), the greater the likelihood is that the CEO will have a golden parachute.

CEO tenure on the board. From one perspective, the longer the CEO's tenure, the more likely it is that he or she will be able to influence the board and have greater social influence. Thus, the longer the board tenure, the greater the likelihood of a golden parachute. However, this argument is not completely straightforward. It could also be argued that while CEOs with short tenure may have little ability to influence the board, those with very long service may have such strong control over the board that a GP is not seen as necessary (e.g., Salancik and Pfeffer, 1980). In addition, very long-tenured CEOs may be at an age and level of personal wealth that insurance against job loss is seen as less important. This possibility is all the more likely, given that GPs are a relatively recent phenomenon and more likely to be relevant for CEOs appointed after 1980. This interpretation would suggest a curvilinear association between tenure and the incidence of GPs, with the linear term being positive and the squared term being negative.

In contrast, Gomez-Mejia, Tosi, and Hinkin (1987) found a negative relationship between tenure and several compensation measures. They speculated that it simply costs more to attract newer CEOs. It may also be that newer CEOs may bargain for GPs in order to reduce their employment risk. This interpretation, consistent with economic reasoning, would suggest a negative relationship between CEO board tenure and GP adoption. A priori, the general effects of tenure on the likelihood of a GP are not easily predicted. Because of this ambiguity, we make no specific predictions regarding board tenure but explore the issue empirically.

External reputation. Kreps and Wilson (1982) have shown that one's reputation may have powerful effects on the behavior of others. One possible indicator of this may be the number of other corporate boards of directors on which the CEO serves. A signal that the CEO is valued by relevant others may give the focal CEO leverage in bargaining with the board. As Cialdini (1984: 119) noted, "people are persuaded more by the actions of others than by any proof we can offer." If other corporations value the CEO's advice, then shouldn't the board of directors also value his or her service?

It should be noted, of course, that reputation can be deserved or not; that is, the number of other corporate boards that a CEO serves on could be a genuine indicator of quality. While one cannot clearly distinguish between reputation based on social consensus or reputation based on objective quality, it is likely that, over time, high-quality CEOs will tend to be associated with high-performing firms. Thus, if the effects of CEO reputation remain after controlling for firm performance, the reputational effect may be one of social consensus and support the case for social influence. This argument suggests the following hypothesis:

Hypothesis 4: Controlling for economic indicators of quality, the more corporate boards on which a CEO serves, the greater the likelihood of a golden parachute.

CEO's relative tenure. In principle, boards are expected to be independent evaluators of the CEO (e.g., Vance, 1983). In fact, board members are typically appointed with the approval of the CEO and, as Patton and Baker (1987: 10) noted, once appointed, "value each other's friendship and want to keep their seats." Given norms of reciprocity and the fact that the directors are most often themselves executives (Kesner, 1988), it may be that if the CEO's board tenure is long compared to the board, the board may feel less expert and more obligated and, hence, be more likely to grant a GP. Board members who have longer tenures than the CEO may feel less obligation to the CEO, be more experienced in governance matters, and be less likely to award GPs.

Although much has been written about the roles, functions, and responsibility of the board of directors (e.g., Mace, 1971; Vance, 1983), only O'Reilly, Wade, and Chandratat (1990) and Singh and Harianto (1989) have directly examined the relative tenures of the CEO and the board. O'Reilly, Wade, and Chandratat (1990) reported significant positive relationships between CEO relative tenure and CEO compensation. They interpreted this as evidence for possible social influence in determining CEO salary. Singh and Harianto (1989), using a slightly different formulation of CEO relative tenure, investigated the relationship between CEO tenure relative to the tenure of outside directors and found this to be a significant positive predictor of GP adoption. Thus, consistent with a social influence perspective, the following hypothesis is suggested:

Hypothesis 5: The higher the CEO's board tenure relative to the board's average tenure, the higher the likelihood that the CEO will have a GP.

Appointment of outside directors. The role of outside directors has long been seen as an important counterweight to management interests (e.g., Mizruchi, 1983). While inside directors are assumed to be responsive to the desires of the CEO, outside directors generally have been assumed to be more able to represent shareholders' interests impartially (e.g., Fama, 1980). Thus, previous studies have typically hypothesized that an increased number or percentage of outsiders would diminish the ability of management to exploit insider information (e.g., Kesner, Victor, and Lamont, 1986; Hermalin and Weisbach, 1987).

The two empirical studies that have examined the effect of the percentage of outsiders on the granting of GPs, however, have not supported this thinking. Quite the opposite effects were found. Cochran, Wood, and Jones (1985: 670) reported: "The principal and surprising result of this study was that firms with comparatively higher percentages of directors who are insiders are less likely to give management golden parachute contracts." Singh and Harianto (1989: 20) reached a similar conclusion: "Contrary to our hypothesis . . . firms that adopted golden parachutes had higher percentages of outside directors on their boards than firms that did not adopt golden parachutes." Although these findings are puzzling, it may be that the true variable of interest is not simply the percentage of outsiders on the board, but the percentage of the board that is composed of outsiders appointed *after* the CEO. If the CEO has been appointed to the board before an outsider, he or she will likely have had a hand in selecting the new director. Although outside board members are often nominated by a committee, the CEO almost invariably is consulted before candidates are put forward. Thus, the CEO is able to nominate and select board members who are sympathetic to his or her desires. In addition, as noted earlier, given norms of reciprocity, outside board members are likely to feel a sense of obligation and liking for the CEO who was responsible for their appointment (Regan, 1971; Cialdini, 1984). In addition, if the number of outsiders appointed after the CEO is on the board (controlling for board size) is an important determinant of GPs, this variable should have a stronger and more significant effect than would be obtained by simply using the percentage of outsiders. The above discussion suggests the following hypothesis:

Hypothesis 6: The greater the percentage of the board that is composed of outside directors appointed after the CEO, the greater the likelihood that the CEO will have a GP.

Owner control as a moderator. Throughout this study we investigate the effects of owner control by using a dummy variable in the multivariate analyses. However, this formulation assumes that the relationships in the models are the same across observations. Thus, the effect of the number of boards the CEO serves on is presumed to be the same for both owner-controlled and management-controlled firms (i.e., they should have the same coefficients). However, recent research by Tosi and Gomez-Mejia (1989) raises the possibility that this may not be the case. They found that the board exerted more influence over CEO pay in owner-controlled firms. In the case of GPs, for example, it could be that in owner-controlled firms the CEO would be unable to exercise influence over the board even if he or she were appointed before many of the outsiders. If this is the case, the relationships between GPs and the social influence variables should be weaker for owner-controlled firms than for management-controlled firms. The following hypothesis is suggested:

Hypothesis 7: The relationship between the incidence of GPs and social influence variables (such as the number of boards on which the CEO serves) should be stronger for management-controlled firms than for owner-controlled firms.

METHOD

Sample. A sample of 105 firms, representing nine industries, was drawn from *Business Week*'s (May 6, 1985) annual survey of executive compensation for the year 1984. Because of the nature of the survey, the firms in the sample are quite large, and the sample is thus not a random sample of firms. However, firms ranged widely in size from $320 million to $42 billion in assets. In addition, since corporations with more than $250 million in assets accounted for more than 50.8 percent of all corporate assets in 1972 (Aldrich, 1979), we feel that large firms are important to study in their own right.

Given the need to control for industry when examining determinants of golden parachutes, the nine industries selected from *Business Week*'s (May 6, 1985) sample were those with the largest number of firms per industry represented. Because of data problems, 16 firms were deleted from the sample. For instance, six firms were eliminated because no data were available for the tenure of board members. Six others were dropped because compensation data were not included on the proxy or the proxy itself was not available. Because of T. Boone Picken's emphasis on takeover activities rather than traditional business operations, his firm, Mesa Petroleum, was also eliminated from the sample. Two other firms were eliminated because they were subsidiaries (e.g., North American Philips).

Measures

A golden parachute was defined as any contractual agreement that will potentially provide the CEO with a payment contingent upon a change in control of the company (McMillan and Reisinger, 1983; Krueger, 1985). Sometimes this payment is awarded only if the CEO is fired following the change in control, but many times it is awarded even if the CEO does not leave or leaves voluntarily. The data on GPs were obtained from the 1984 proxy statement for each company. Firm size was measured using the log of sales in 1984. The logarithm of the size variable was used so that extreme values would not bias the results. Nine industry dummy variables were constructed as controls.

While the precise relationship between concentration of ownership and control is unknown, researchers have long argued that the fraction of ownership needed to exercise a substantial degree of influence is quite small. Since the 1960s, a cutoff of 5 percent stock ownership has been used to distinguish between owner- and management-controlled firms (Glassman and Rhoades, 1980; Gomez-Mejia, Tosi, and Hinkin, 1987). Therefore, a dummy variable was used for firms designated as owner-controlled if at least 5 percent of the stock was beneficially owned by an individual or organization. The measures and data on the board of directors, including the percentage of outside directors, the percentage of the board that was composed of outside directors appointed after the CEO, CEO board tenure and relative tenure, and the number of boards the CEO served on were obtained from 1984 proxies. Since the number of boards was meant to measure prestige, we only counted major boards, specifically those listed in Moody's industrial, finance, or transportation manuals. Not surprisingly, the number of board memberships that were excluded as a result of this selection rule was negligible—these CEOs almost exclusively served on the boards of major corporations. Directors were classified as outsiders if we judged that they would not have detailed knowledge and experience in the internal operations of the firm. Our general rule was that directors were classified as outsiders if they had never worked for the firm or one of its subsidiaries in a high-level executive position. CEO relative tenure was defined as the board tenure of the CEO divided by the average board tenure of the other directors.

EXCESS was computed for 1984 by taking the difference between a firm's total market value (market value of equity + book value of liabilities) and the book value of its assets and normalizing by sales. For purposes of comparison, we also computed each firm's market-to-book ratio (market value of equity/book value of equity), which is a more traditional measure of takeover risk. The logic underlying this measure is virtually identical to that of EXCESS. In general, the lower a firm's market-to-book ratio is, the greater the threat of a takeover, and, thus, we expect a greater incidence of GPs. These data were obtained from *Fortune*'s annual listing of the largest industrial corporations (April 29, 1985), *Moody's Industrial Manual* (1985), and from COMPUSTAT services.

RESULTS

Table 1 presents the correlation matrix as well as variable means and standard deviations. Most of the bivariate relationships are generally consistent with the multivariate results reported in Table 2 and will not be discussed here.

Table 2 presents tests of the hypotheses, using logit analysis. Logistic estimation was used in lieu of ordinary least squares (OLS) because OLS assumes a linear additive model, while it is more reasonable to assume that the true probability model is nonlinear (Hanushek and Jackson, 1977). Using OLS would thus introduce systematic errors in the model and could produce unrealistic predicted probabilities that are greater than one (Hanushek and Jackson, 1977; Pindyck and Rubinfeld, 1981). The coefficients in the logistic model represent the change in the log odds of the dependent variable that would result from a unit increase in the independent variables. The model can be represented as follows:

Table 1

Correlations among Variables

Variables	$\bar{X}$	S.D.	1	2	3	4	5	6	7	8
1. Golden parachutes	.371	.486								
2. Log sales	5.79	.936	−.326••							
3. Investor control dummy	.438	.499	−.068	−.368••						
4. EXCESS	.366	.475	−.19	−.251•	.126					
5. CEO board tenure	13.38	6.88	−.26••	−.042	.146	.037				
6. Number of corporate boards CEO serves on	1.88	1.35	.081	.196	−.095	−.153	.122			
7. CEO relative board tenure	1.59	.87	−.118	−.028	.132	−.007	.80••	.078		
8. Number of outsiders appointed to board after CEO	6.39	2.82	−.016	.082	.054	−.034	.495••	.199	.673••	
9. Board size	13.69	3.24	−.084	.329••	.009	.051	−.111	.036	.057	.441••

• $p < .05$; •• $p < .01$.

$$L = \log\left[\frac{p}{1-p}\right] = B_iX_i, \tag{1}$$

where L is called the log odds ratio, p is the probability of having a golden parachute, X_is are independent variables, and B_is are the estimated coefficients of the independent variables. The magnitude of the effects of the independent variables cannot be ascertained simply by comparing the values of their coefficients. Instead, the following formula can be used to find the change in probability of the dependent variable resulting from a change in the independent variable (Petersen, 1985):

$$P = \exp(L_1)/[1 + \exp(L_1)] - \exp(L_0)/[1 + \exp(L_0)], \tag{2}$$

where L_0 is the logit before the change in the independent variable, and L_1 is the logit after the change in the independent variable.

Model 1 tests the effects of the three primary economic variables: size, owner control, and takeover risk as indexed by the EXCESS ratio. As can be seen, the first three hypotheses, based on economic reasoning, were strongly confirmed in that size, owner control, and takeover susceptibility were all negatively related to the incidence of GPs. As mentioned earlier, we also computed each firm's market-to-book ratio. While this variable was negative and significant, EXCESS was of both greater magnitude and significance and appeared to be the better measure of takeover risk.

Model 2 investigated the effects of CEO tenure on the board and the number of outside boards on which the CEO serves, while continuing to control for firm size, owner control, and takeover susceptibility. The effect of CEO board tenure is negative and significant, suggesting that comparatively new CEOs are more likely to have a GP. This result is also consis-

Table 2

Logit Analysis of Six Models of Effects on Golden Parachutes*

Independent variables†	Model 1	2	3	4	5	6
1. Log Sales	−1.94***	−2.67***	−2.66***	−3.57***	−4.71***	−5.80**
	(.535)	(.692)	(.692)	(.934)	(1.82)	(2.89)
2. Investor-control dummy	−1.63*	−1.54**	−1.39*	−1.79**	–	–
	(.691)	(.767)	(.790)	(.863)		
3. EXCESS	−2.69***	−2.97***	−2.75***	−3.25***	−3.32	−5.59**
	(.975)	(1.11)	(1.11)	(1.15)	(2.78)	(2.81)
4. Board tenure of CEO		−.129***	−.247***	−.275***	−.620**	−.311*
		(.0492)	(.0963)	(.0941)	(.294)	(.177)
5. Number of corporate boards CEO serves on		.747***	.799***	.771**	1.68**	.675
		(.295)	(.307)	(.324)	(.847)	(.585)
6. CEO relative board tenure			1.06			
			(.668)			
7. Number of outsiders appointed after CEO				.453**	.934*	.529
				(.200)	(.507)	(.431)
8. Board size				.0420	.338	.124
				(.153)	(.368)	(.235)
Constant	12.23***	17.31***	16.97***	21.21***	22.13**	36.98**
	(3.48)	(4.57)	(4.52)	(5.44)	(9.88)	(18.74)
χ^2	30.71	43.77	46.54	51.85	43.08	27.24
N	89	89	89	89	50	39

* $p < .10$; ** $p < .05$; *** $p < .01$.
* Industry dummies included but coefficients not reported.
† Standard errors are in parentheses.

tent with economic reasoning. Although results are not presented here, to further explore the social influence approach, we added board tenure squared to see if tenure had a curvilinear effect and found that it did not.

Since GPs are a relatively recent innovation, CEOs who have been recently appointed to the board may use the bargaining leverage that they have upon their appointment to the board to procure a GP. This is also consistent with Gomez-Mejia, Tosi, and Hinkin (1987), who found a negative relationship between CEO tenure and several compensation measures.

Hypothesis 4 postulated that social influence might operate through the social reputation of the CEO. A CEO who serves on many corporate boards may be seen as more knowledgeable, competent, and valuable. Model 2 provides strong support for this in that the more corporate boards the CEO serves on, the higher the probability of a GP ($p < .05$).

While the results regarding the number of boards served on are consistent with a social influence interpretation, they are also consistent with a human capital argument (Hogan and McPheters, 1980). The number of boards may represent the true quality of the CEO; that is, a GP may be awarded based on merit rather than social influence. Although results are not reported in Table 3, several variants of model 2 were estimated after including additional human capital variables that can index CEO quality (e.g., company and job tenure, education, overall compensation, and other measures of firm performance). In all formulations, the number of boards served on by the CEO remained significant. Because these other controls for CEO quality are admittedly imperfect, the results are not definitive, but they do suggest that it may be social reputation rather than objective quality that is associated with the increased likelihood of a GP.

Model 3 investigated a more direct indicator of social influence, the CEO's board tenure relative to the average tenure of other board members. Although it is in the expected positive direction, this variable is not quite significant. However, it should be noted that since hypothesis 5 is directional, a one-tailed test is more appropriate than the two-tailed test reported. Using a one-tailed test, CEO relative tenure is marginally significant ($p < .10$). This finding suggests, consistent with Singh and Harianto (1989), that the higher a CEO's tenure relative to the board, the greater the probability that the CEO will have a GP. This finding is also consistent with a social influence perspective, in that CEOs who were able to have a hand in the appointment of members of the board are more likely to have a GP.

Model 4 dropped the relative tenure variable and added to the analysis the number of outsiders appointed after the CEO and the size of the board.[1] Thus, the coefficient on the number of outsiders appointed after the CEO effectively represents the percentage of the board that is composed of outsiders appointed after the CEO, given that the size of the board is held constant. As suggested by hypothesis 6, the larger this percentage, the greater the probability that the CEO will have a golden parachute ($p < .05$). Presumably, the more outsiders that a CEO has had a hand in appointing, the greater his or her influence over them with regard to perks such as GPs and compensation. This finding has no obvious economic rationale and is clearly and logically consistent with a social influence perspective.

Although these results are not presented here, several analyses were run using the percentage of outside directors rather than the percentage appointed after the CEO. While this variable was in the expected positive direction, it was not significant. Thus, as expected, it appears that the percentage of the board that are both outsiders and appointed after the CEO best captures the phenomenon of social influence

It was also expected that CEOs of firms performing below the industry average (as measured by 1984 return on equity) and whose compensation was above the industry median would be those most likely to exert social influence to obtain a GP, even though from an economic perspective these would be the least deserving. If a CEO is paid above average despite the fact that his or her firm is a poor performer, it is plausible that he or she might feel more susceptible to job loss in the event of a takeover, since the CEO's salary cannot be justified by the firm's performance. At the same time, a CEO who is able to maintain a high salary despite poor firm performance is likely to have a great deal of influence. Using a dummy variable to index this category, model 4 was reestimated. Results showed that CEOs whose firms performed above the industry median were significantly more likely to have a GP than CEOs whose firms were underperforming and whose salaries were below average. Of most interest was the finding that CEOs who were overpaid relative to the in-

1
Although results are not presented here, we also ran a model that included both CEO relative tenure and the number of outsiders appointed after the CEO. Since CEO relative tenure became insignificant, while the number of outsiders retained significance, CEO relative tenure was not included in succeeding models.

dustry and were underperforming were also more likely to have a GP. This suggests that both economic factors and social influence appear to be determinants of GPs.

Hypothesis 7 proposed that social influence effects would be more likely to operate in management-controlled than in owner-controlled firms. Models 5 and 6 investigated this possibility using two separate samples, one consisting of owner-controlled firms and the other of management-controlled firms. Model 4 was reestimated separately for owner- and management-controlled firms. The results, shown in models 5 and 6, are striking.[2] Model 5 investigated the effects for management-controlled firms. Both the number of boards that the CEO serves on and the number of outsiders appointed after the CEO increase in magnitude beyond the effects shown in model 4. For example, the coefficient for the number of boards on which the CEO serves increases from .771 to 1.68. In contrast, model 6 shows that both the percentage of outsiders appointed after the CEO and the number of boards that the CEO serves on have no significant effects for owner-controlled firms. In addition, the EXCESS variable, indexing takeover risk, is only significant for the owner-controlled firms, further indicating that economic determinants of GP adoption are more important in owner-controlled firms. Although a Chow test reveals that there is not a significant difference between the coefficients of the two groups, the separate analyses suggest that the social influence variables are stronger predictors of GP adoption for the management-controlled group.

These results also cast some doubt on the explanation that the number of boards served on is simply an objective measure of quality. We can see no reason why a "valuable" CEO should be rewarded less in an owner-controlled firm. A likely explanation is that the number of boards on which the CEO serves is a good index of the CEO's reputation and influence, which he or she can more easily exploit in management-controlled firms. These findings, while not definitive, are consistent with those of Tosi and Gomez-Mejia (1989), who suggested that CEOs in owner-controlled firms may be monitored more effectively by their boards and thus be less able to gain and exercise social influence. In this sense, social influence processes may be thought of as agency costs; that is, CEOs are able to take advantage of ineffective monitoring in management-controlled firms for their own benefit. Agency theory predicts that there will be a divergence of interests between managers and owners. Owners are most interested in profits, while managers are most interested in their pay and security. Not surprisingly, with regard to the security offered by a GP, it appears that managers in management-controlled firms are better able to pursue their own interests.

Magnitude of Effects

The preceding analyses have addressed the significance and directionality of both takeover risk and social influence variables. However, in order to assess fully the merits of social influence effects, the relative strength of these need to be investigated. In order to examine the relative magnitudes of takeover risk, social influence, and control variables, several comparisons were made. Table 3 presents the changes in the

2 We were unable to obtain estimates for one industry dummy in the management-controlled group and two industry dummies in the owner-controlled group because the dependent variable was exactly identified. To check the robustness of the results, we reran the analyses without industry dummies and the results did not change.

Table 3

Analyses of the Strength of Economic and Social Influence Variables (Evaluated at the Mean of the Dependent Variable y = .37)

Independent variables	Changes in independent variables	% Change in the probability of granting a golden parachute
1. Owner control	Change from management- to owner-controlled	−28.1
2. EXCESS	Increase of 1 S.D.	−25.9
3. Log sales	25% Increase in sales	−17.6
4. Board tenure of CEO	Increase of 5 years in CEO board tenure	−24.1
5. Number of boards CEO serves on	Increase of 1 board served	18.9
6. Number of outsiders appointed after CEO	Increase of 2 outsiders	22.2

probabilities of the incidence of a GP resulting from a change in the independent variable. These changes were evaluated at the mean of the dependent variable and were computed using the formula specified earlier (Petersen, 1985). The coefficients used to estimate the changes in probabilities were those from model 4. Petersen (1985) presented a more detailed description of this technique.

As Table 3 shows, the impacts of the control variables, CEO board tenure, and owner control were substantial. A CEO whose firm changed from management- to owner-controlled decreased his or her chances of receiving a GP from the sample mean of 37 percent to 9 percent, or a net decrease of 28 percent. Similarly, an increase of five years in the board tenure of the CEO will lower the probability of a GP by 24 percent. The impact of size on GP adoption was assessed by examining the effect of a 25-percent increase in sales. This change lowered the probability of a golden parachute by about 18 percent.

Increases of the social influence variables and EXCESS were chosen so that the change in probabilities would be less than one standard deviation and thus well within the range of the sample. As Table 3 shows, an increase of two outsiders appointed after the CEO or an increase of one board served on by the CEO increases the probability of a GP by 22 and 19 percent, respectively. These are comparable in size to a one-standard-deviation change in EXCESS, which reduces the probability of a GP by about 26 percent. As a whole, these results suggest that the effects of social influence are substantial and of the same general magnitude as those reflecting takeover threat.

DISCUSSION

Is a golden parachute simply an incentive alignment device, as economic theory suggests, or is it an example of the board of directors failing to represent adequately the shareholders' interests by allowing the agent (the CEO) to behave opportunistically? Overall, the results of this study suggest that the truth lies somewhere in between. Evidence was found consistent with economic arguments regarding takeover risk. Larger firms were shown to have a lower likelihood of the CEO having a GP. Although this finding is not the result of a direct test, it is consistent with the notion that larger firms are less likely to become takeover targets; hence, there is less need to use GPs to align shareholder and management interests (Jensen and Ruback, 1983). Also consistent with an economic rationale for GPs, there was strong evidence of a negative association between GPs and takeover risk as indexed by EXCESS. Although not the result of a formally tested hypothesis, the finding that newer CEOs are more likely to have a GP is consistent with economic logic and runs counter to the social influence argument that suggests a positive association between tenure and the CEO's ability to influence the board.

The results in Table 2 also provide some evidence consistent with the argument that the social influence of the CEO over the board of directors may be associated with the incidence of GPs. Of course, this evidence is inferential, in that the social influence variables are structural measures (e.g., the number of outsiders appointed to the board after the CEO) and not direct assessments of process. In this regard, the social psychology of influence was used as a basis for the construction of the measures. The results are consistent with this underlying theory and research (Cialdini, 1984), but no measures of actual process were taken. Consistent with predictions derived from the theory, we find that CEOs who serve on many outside boards, and therefore are likely to have a better social reputation and be more familiar with GPs, are more likely to have a golden parachute. These effects remain even after controlling for human capital variables. Similarly, CEOs with a higher tenure relative to the board are more likely to receive a GP (one-tailed test, $p < .10$). From a social influence perspective, CEOs with a higher relative tenure are more likely to have appointed other board members who may then feel a reciprocal obligation. This supposition is strengthened by our finding that the percentage of the board that is composed of outsiders appointed after the CEO is even more important than relative tenure. These results suggest that it is more important that a CEO simply be appointed before outside board members than it is for him or her to be appointed a long time before members of the board. Presumably, this enables the CEO to influence the selection process. This finding is not surprising, given Pfeffer's (1972: 220) assertion that "in most cases board members are handpicked by management. In many practical respects, then, management is, therefore, in control of the board."

Support for both the economic and social influence perspectives is evident in the results showing that the social influence variables are only significant for management-controlled firms. Consistent with Tosi and Gomez-Mejia (1989), our findings indicate that CEOs may be better monitored by the board in owner-controlled firms and be less able to gain and use social influence for their own purposes. Thus, the effects of social influence seem to be an agency cost produced by ineffective monitoring systems.

While generally consistent with the opportunism suggested by principal-agent theory (Gibbons and Murphy, 1988), the results suggest a more subtle and dynamic process than simply withholding information. If the agent (the CEO) is able to exercise influence to select representatives of the principal (members of the board), the agent may be able to frame subsequent decisions in such a way that the principals are likely to "see" the problem in a manner favorable to the agent. As March (1984) has noted, judging a CEO's performance is an ambiguous task. If the CEO can exert influence over those who judge his or her performance, these evaluators may be predisposed to agree with the agent. F. Ross Johnson, former CEO of RJR-Nabisco, is quoted as saying, "one of the most important jobs a CEO has is the care and feeding of his directors" (Burroughs and Helyar, 1990: 26).

These findings have potentially important ramifications for corporate governance. As Fama (1980: 294) has noted, the board's "most important role is to scrutinize the highest decision makers in the firm." If, intentionally or unintentionally, the board is unable to fulfill this mission impartially, the shareholders' interests may not be well represented. Unfortunately, the evidence here suggests that outside directors may actually be more responsive to management's interests than those of the shareholders. The extent to which CEOs may be influencing or co-opting the so-called impartial outsider directors strikes at the heart of the role of the board and may even undermine the ability of the board to design incentive-aligning compensation contracts (Jensen and Murphy, 1987). It may be that to ensure that the shareholders' interests are fully represented, more careful consideration needs to be given to limiting the CEO's ability to influence the board, perhaps by restructuring the roles of the board to eliminate the CEO's role as a board member entirely.

REFERENCES

Adair, Donald R.
1987 "Golden parachutes can be more than an executive's bailout." Bottomline, March: 39–43.

Aldrich, Howard E.
1979 Organizations and Environments. Englewood Cliffs, NJ: Prentice-Hall.

Baker, George, Michael C. Jensen, and Kevin C. Murphy
1988 "Compensation and incentives: Practice vs. theory." Journal of Finance, 43: 593–616.

Burroughs, Bryan, and John Helyar
1990 Barbarians at the Gate: The Fate of RJR-Nabisco. New York: Harper and Row.

Cialdini, Robert B.
1984 Influence: The New Psychology of Modern Persuasion. New York: Quill Press.

Cochran, Philip L., Robert A. Wood, and Thomas B. Jones
1985 "The composition of boards of directors and the incidence of golden parachutes." Academy of Management Journal, 23: 664–671.

Eisenhardt, Kathleen
1989 "Agency theory: An assessment and review." Academy of Management Review, 14: 57–74.

Fama, Eugene F.
1980 "Agency problems and the theory of the firm." Journal of Political Economy, 88: 288–307.

Gibbons, Robert, and Kevin J. Murphy
1988 "Agency theory and the determinants of executive compensation." Working Paper, Simon School of Business, University of Rochester.

Glassman, Cynthia A., and Stephen A. Rhoades
1980 "Owner vs. manager control effects on bank performance." Review of Economics and Statistics, 27: 263–270.

Gomez-Mejia, Luis, Henry Tosi, and Timothy Hinkin
1987 "Managerial control, performance, and executive compensation." Academy of Management Journal, 30: 51–70.

Hanushek, Eric A., and John E. Jackson
1977 Statistical Methods for Social Scientists. Orlando, FL: Academic Press.

Hermalin, Benjamin E., and Michael S. Weisbach
1987 "The effect of board composition on corporate performance." Working Paper, Simon School of Business, University of Rochester.

Hogan, Timothy D., and Lee R. McPheters
1980 "Executive compensation: Performance versus personal characteristics." Southern Economic Journal, 46: 1060–1068.

Jemison, David B., and Sim B. Sitkin
1986 "Corporate acquisitions: A process perspective." Academy of Management Review, 1[illegible]: 145–163.

Jensen, Michael C.
1988 "Takeovers: Their causes and consequences." Journal of Economic Perspectives, 2: 21–48.

Golden Parachutes

Jensen, Michael C., and Kevin J. Murphy
1987 "Are executives' compensation contracts structured properly?" Working Paper, 86-14 (June), Managerial Economics Research Center, University of Rochester.

Jensen, Michael C., and Richard Ruback
1983 "The market for corporate control: The scientific evidence." Journal of Financial Economics, 11: 5–50.

Kesner, Idalene F.
1988 "Directors' characteristics and committee membership: An investigation of type, occupation, tenure, and gender." Academy of Management Journal, 31: 66–84.

Kesner, Idalene F., Bart Victor, and Bruce T. Lamont
1986 "Board composition and the commission of illegal acts: An investigation of Fortune 500 companies." Academy of Management Journal, 29: 789–799.

Knoeber, Charles R.
1986 "Golden parachutes, shark repellants, and hostile tender offers." American Economic Review, 76: 155–167.

Kreps, David M., and Robert Wilson
1982 "Reputation and imperfect information." Journal of Economic Theory, 27: 253–279.

Krueger, Herbert W.
1985 "Opportunities and pitfalls in designing executive compensation: The effects of the golden parachute tax penalties." Taxes, 63: 846–861.

Lambert, Richard A., and David F. Larcker
1985 "Golden parachutes, executive decision making, and shareholder wealth." Journal of Accounting and Economics, 5: 3–30.

Mace, Myles L.
1971 Directors: Myth and Reality. Boston: Division of Research, Graduate School of Business, Harvard University.

March, James G.
1984 "Notes on ambiguity and executive compensation." Scandinavian Journal of Management Studies, August: 53–64.

McMillan, John D., and Gregory S. Reisinger
1983 "Takeover protection for executives: The golden parachute." Compensation Review, First quarter: 34–43.

Meyer, Marshall W.
1972 "Size and structure of organizations: A causal analysis." American Sociological Review, 37: 434–441.

Mizruchi, Mark S.
1983 "Who controls whom? An examination of the relation between management and boards of directors in large corporations." Academy of Management Review, 8: 426–435.

O'Reilly, Charles A., Brian Main, and Graef Crystal
1988 "CEO compensation as tournament and social comparison: A tale of two theories." Administrative Science Quarterly, 33: 257–274.

O'Reilly, Charles A., James B. Wade, and Ike Chandratat
1990 "The CEO, the board of directors, and executive compensation: Who manages whom?" Working Paper, School of Business, University of California, Berkeley.

Palepu, Krishna G.
1986 "Predicting takeover targets: A methodological and empirical analysis." Journal of Accounting and Economics, 8: 3–35.

Patton, Arch, and John C. Baker
1987 "Why don't directors rock the boat?" Harvard Business Review, 65 (Nov.–Dec.): 10–18.

Petersen, Trond
1985 "A comment on presenting results from logit and probit models." American Sociological Review, 50: 130–131.

Pfeffer, Jeffrey
1972 "Size and composition of corporate boards of directors." Administrative Science Quarterly, 17: 218–228.

Pindyck, Robert S., and Daniel L. Rubinfeld
1981 Econometric Models and Economic Forecasts, 2d ed. New York: McGraw-Hill.

Regan, D. T.
1971 "Effects of favor and liking on compliance." Journal of Experimental Social Psychology, 7: 627–639.

Salancik, Gerald R., and Jeffrey Pfeffer
1980 "The effects of ownership and performance on executive tenure in U.S. corporations." Administrative Science Quarterly, 30: 46–60.

Sherman, Stratford P.
1988 "Pushing corporate boards to be better." Fortune, 118 (July 18): 58–67.

Singh, Habir, and Farid Harianto
1989 "Management board relationships, takeover risk, and the adoption of golden parachutes." Academy of Management Journal, 32: 7–24.

Tosi, Henry L., and Luis Gomez-Mejia
1989 "The decoupling of CEO pay and performance: An agency theory perspective." Administrative Science Quarterly, 34: 169–189.

Vance, Stanley C.
1983 Corporate Leadership: Boards, Directors, and Strategy. New York: McGraw-Hill.

Walkling, Ralph A., and Michael S. Long
1984 "Agency theory, managerial welfare, and takeover bid resistance." Rand Journal of Economics, 15: 54–68.

Winkler, Matthew
1988 "Ten Primerica Executives' parachutes gilded in $98.2 million severance pact." Wall Street Journal, November 29: 23.

Zald, Mayer N.
1969 "The power and functions of boards of directors: A theoretical synthesis." American Journal of Sociology, 75: 97–111.

Journal of Management Studies 39:2 March 2002
0022-2380

PAY COMPARABILITY ACROSS AND WITHIN UK BOARDS: AN EMPIRICAL ANALYSIS OF THE CASH PAY AWARDS TO CEOs AND OTHER BOARD MEMBERS*

MAHMOUD EZZAMEL

Cardiff University

ROBERT WATSON

University of Glasgow

ABSTRACT

Drawing on the literature on social comparison and equity theories, this paper analyses the determinants of, and the relationships between, the cash pay awards of CEOs and other board members for a sample of large UK companies over the period 1992–95. Our results suggest that external labour market and internal (i.e., within board) pay comparisons are important in explaining both CEO and other directors' pay awards. In the case of CEOs, however, there is evidence of an asymmetric adjustment to prior period pay anomalies, whereby the pay of the relatively underpaid executives displays significantly greater sensitivity to external market comparison pay levels. This asymmetric adjustment process results in a 'bidding-up' of average CEO pay relative to other board members over the four year period investigated.

INTRODUCTION

This paper examines the influence of external labour market and internal (i.e., within the board) pay comparisons upon the cash pay awards of the CEO and other board members for a sample of large UK, public-listed, companies covering the four year period from 1992 to 1995. An analysis of the relationship between executive cash pay awards and firm performance is also undertaken, even though our primary focus is not the incentive alignment issues that motivate agency theory models and their predictions of a significantly positive empirical relationship between executive pay and firm performance metrics (see Ross, 1973). Rather, given an external labour market that reflects executive risk-aversion, the optimal employment contract can be expected to include a significant fixed salary component that is wholly independent of any firm performance related metric.

Address for reprints: Mahmoud Ezzamel, Cardiff Business School, Cardiff University, Cardiff CF10 3EU, Wales, UK (ezzamel@cf.ac.uk).

In such a context, there will be an agency cost trade-off between insuring executives against poor outcomes (i.e., a fixed salary which represents the insurance element of the compensation contract) and incentive alignment concerns (see Garen, 1994; Haubrich, 1994). Moreover, there may be various other institutional and internal and external labour market constraints upon how far executive pay can be made contingent upon firm performance. For example, as Jensen and Murphy (1990) have argued, there may be non-trivial private and public political costs associated with the disclosure and wide dissemination of executive pay details. They also suggested that the low empirical sensitivity of executive pay to firm performance found by many studies, including their own, may be due to the potentially high political costs that arise whenever an unusually high cash bonus or share option arrangement is disclosed. Even so, if significant private and political costs are important considerations with regard to performance-related pay, they can also be expected to have an impact upon the level and/or changes in executives' risk-free pay. The details relating to executives' fixed salaries are widely reported and, being already expressed in cash terms, relatively easy for others to value and compare across different firms and individuals.

This trade-off between incentive alignment concerns and the need to provide some acceptable level of risk-free pay to executives provides the main motivation for investigating the influence of external (market) and internal-to-the-board pay comparisons on the cash pay awards to both CEOs and the other board members. Specifically, in this paper we empirically examine:

(1) Whether the cash pay awards for CEOs and other directors are both determined with reference to external pay norms.
(2) The extent to which asymmetric adjustment (i.e. 'bidding-up') of underpaid directors cash awards exists and whether it is more apparent in the case of CEOs compared to the other board members.
(3) Whether a significant element of within-board comparability is maintained in determining the cash awards of CEOs and other board members.
(4) The extent to which the 'bidding-up' of CEO cash pay is most apparent in firms where other board members are well paid compared to external norms.

Of these possibilities, only the influence of external market comparisons for CEO cash compensation has been examined before (Ezzamel and Watson, 1998). In contrast to the overwhelming emphasis by previous researchers upon agency theory, we draw upon relevant literature from equity/fairness theory dealing with issues of distributive justice (Adams, 1963; Bazerman and Neale, 1992; Deutsch, 1975, 1984; Kahneman et al., 1986, 1987) and social comparison theory in which executives' expectations for pay are anchored (Festinger, 1957; Goodman, 1974; O'Reilley et al., 1988). We argue that this management-based literature yields powerful and valuable insights in explaining within and across board pay comparability.

The remainder of the paper is organized as follows. The next section reviews the literature on executive pay and the influence of external and internal pay comparisons and develops our research hypotheses. This is followed by a description of our modelling approach to test the hypotheses, the sample, data and variables used in the empirical analysis. The main empirical results are then presented, followed by a concluding section which summarizes the main issues raised by the paper, their implications for corporate governance, and some future research possibilities.

LITERATURE REVIEW AND RESEARCH HYPOTHESES

Previous Research

The agency theory model that provides the theoretical foundation for much of the research into executive pay appears to focus exclusively on incentive alignment issues. Basically, it is assumed that, in order to motivate executives to supply sufficient effort in pursuing activities that increase shareholder value, the optimal employment contract will render executive remuneration *partly contingent* upon a performance measure related to shareholder value creation, such as profitability or share prices. Note, however, that agency theory does not deny that other factors may be important determinants of executive pay. Fama (1980), for example, has argued that in an efficiently functioning executive labour market, compensation levels cannot deviate significantly from what is deemed appropriate by the market, otherwise under-paid executives are likely to be bid away by competitor firms prepared to pay the market rate. The influence of external and internal peer group comparisons is therefore implicitly acknowledged and, as we argue below, such comparisons are likely to be particularly strong in determining the minimum level of risk-free pay necessary in order for the firm to attract and retain executives of the requisite quality (Smith and Szymanski, 1995). Hence, because incentive alignment has normally been the central concern of researchers, agency models simply consign the factors that account for the non-contingent (fixed salary) element of pay under the title 'insurance' or, more generally, the 'participation constraint'.

When the agency problem is, however, set within a more descriptively realistic institutional framework, characterized by information asymmetries and costly and incomplete contracting (see Hart, 1995) the role of incentive alignment via performance related pay becomes problematic due to the difficulties in measuring individual inputs, particularly within a team-based working environment. When coupled with significant levels of executive risk aversion (Garen, 1994; Haubrich, 1994), and non-trivial private and political contracting costs (Jensen and Murphy, 1990) the scope for making executive pay contingent upon firm performance is further limited. In such a context, factors other than incentive alignment, such as corporate governance, maintaining executive pay comparability, team cohesion, matching alternative employment opportunities and signalling to outside stakeholders that the firm has high quality management in post, are likely to be important considerations in the pay setting process.

The extensive empirical research on executive cash pay has typically found a positive, though usually statistically weak, relationship between executive cash pay and firm performance.[1] Barkema and Gomez-Mejia (1998, p. 143) have concluded that 'adding more empirical studies on the statistical relationship between executive pay and firm performance to the vast literature that already exists on this issue leads researchers into a blind alley'. These authors have also suggested that future research should focus on 'other criteria, such as the market, peer compensation and behaviour, and how the definition, measurement, and relative importance of these criteria depend on a firm's governance structure and on contingencies such as its strategy and R&D level, market growth, industry concentration and regulation, and national culture'.

There is already some research which suggests that other variables, such as firm size and peer group comparisons, are frequently important in determining pay and that different institutional settings and organizational contexts have an influence on how these variables are likely to be incorporated into pay awards. For example, most empirical studies have reported a highly significant positive relationship between firm size and the level of executive pay. Large firms pay larger salaries and typically the elasticity of pay with respect to firm size measures such as sales is in the region of 0.30, i.e., executive pay rises by 30 per cent for every doubling of sales revenue. In a labour market which, though competitive, is characterized by costly and incomplete contracting, firm size is an easily observable proxy for several supply and demand relevant factors, such as relative workloads, responsibilities, managerial quality and ability to pay. As information on such factors is particularly difficult and costly for an outsider to acquire, the analyses of outside professional pay consultants typically brought in to advise compensation committees largely consists of the production of comparison levels of pay across firms in different size bands (Baker et al., 1988). Apparently objective external market pay comparisons based on firm size are particularly favoured by remuneration (compensation) committees precisely because they have to legitimize to shareholders and other outside stakeholders both their own and the other board members' pay awards. Moreover, since the compensation committee members, the CEO and other executives on the board are all members of the same management team that is legally and jointly responsible for the strategic direction and governance of the firm, the use of external benchmarks to determine executive pay helps avoid any highly contentious judgements on the 'quality' and skills of individual executives that might undermine team cohesion and purpose.

In practice then, compensation committees have to strike a balance between providing financial incentives to executives to improve firm performance whilst avoiding a binding 'participation constraint', that is, ensuring that executives remain loyal to the firm by offering a level of pay comparable to the perceived external labour market alternatives.

The desire to maintain a good working relationship with the CEO and avoid adverse signals to outsiders by appearing to pay below the market rate, provides a strong motive for remuneration committees to award remuneration packages that are *at least* comparable to external alternatives. Several writers (Wade et al., 1990; Zajac and Westphal, 1995) have also questioned the independence of non-executive directors because of their close social ties with executive directors (or what Westphal and Zajac (1997) call 'generalized norms of reciprocity' among CEOs), and the tendency of compensation committees to award large pay rises unrelated to company performance. Studies by Main (1991), Main and Johnston (1993), O'Reilly et al. (1988) and Belliveau et al. (1996), for example, indicate the presence of 'strong social influence considerations' that affect the pay awards granted by compensation committees, suggesting that the compensations received by non-executive directors in their own companies largely condition what is deemed to be a 'reasonable' pay award when serving on the compensation committees of other companies. Furthermore, as O'Reilly et al. (1988, p. 258) have stated: 'since the CEO exerts considerable informal influence in selecting new members of the board, it may be also that the selection process itself can raise CEO compensation if new members are selected whose compensation exceeds that of the focal CEO'.

These empirical findings are not necessarily evidence of a lack of independence since they appear to be equally consistent with theories which suggest that 'social comparison processes' of this nature are both ubiquitous and inescapable. Festinger (1957) has argued that social actors routinely rely upon a whole range of social comparisons to secure equity in their expected rewards. According to Festinger, individuals have a need to evaluate their abilities and, in the absence of objective, non-social means, this need is fulfilled by choosing for comparison other individuals who are perceived to have similar abilities. These comparisons help in reassuring an individual of the adequacy of his performance which leads to greater satisfaction (Festinger, 1957, pp. 135–6). Individuals are also assumed to have a need to evaluate their opinions and abilities by comparing themselves with others that are perceived to have attitudes or abilities similar to themselves (Goodman, 1974). Indeed, O'Reilly et al. (1988, p. 262) have indicated that 'when making comparisons, individuals are likely to select as comparisons others who are seen as slightly better or more expert'.[2] Non-executive directors selected to serve on compensation committees are likely to be chosen because of their similarity to those involved in the selection process. Similarity between executives and non-executives in terms of earnings levels ensures that, in order to minimize cognitive dissonance, compensation committee members will tend to anchor their judgements regarding what the appropriate level of earnings for senior executives should be on the basis of their own earnings (Tversky and Kahneman, 1974).

Evidence from the UK that remuneration committees make pay awards to their CEOs that reduce external market pay anomalies is provided by Ezzamel and Watson (1998). They reported that the process by which CEO pay was kept in line with external market comparisons was not neutral, but rather, the adjustment process was particularly evident in relation to apparently underpaid (relative to the external comparison) executives. This asymmetric pay adjustment process produced a significant 'bidding up' in the average level of CEO pay over the period they examined. As indicated above, interpreting this as clear evidence of a lack of board independence is highly contentious. Given that in the UK information on executive pay levels is now widely reported, the potential costs in terms of lowered executive motivation and the loss of external credibility that may result from appearing to pay below the going rate can be expected to impart an upward bias to CEO pay awards. Hence, this bidding-up of CEO pay may simply reflect the external signalling and figurehead concerns discussed earlier.

One of the limitations of previous literature is its predominant focus on the remuneration of the CEO or the highest paid director to the exclusion of other board members. Although some researchers included other board members in their analyses (Main et al., 1996; Murphy, 1985; O'Reilly et al., 1988; Smith and Szymanski, 1995; Westphal and Zajac, 1997), none of them: (1) incorporated external benchmarks (with the exception of Smith and Szymanski (1995), who used a rather crude sector-average benchmark); and (2) considered within-board comparability relative to CEO pay. This may be because the CEO is widely recognized as 'the main strategist of the firm' and hence the CEO compensation package 'may have a direct bearing on business decisions affecting the future of the entire organization' (Gomez-Mejia, 1994, p. 162). While not wishing to deny the crucial importance of the CEO, the importance of other board members needs to be recognized. The board of directors is the locus of ratifying and monitoring crucial strategic decisions, and of hiring, rewarding, and firing top managers (Fama and Jensen, 1983, p. 311).

In both the USA and the UK, the legal situation is that all directors are equally responsible to the company; the directors' power is 'conferred upon the directors collectively as a board' (Gower, 1992, p. 160). As Main et al. (1996, p. 1634) have noted: 'The posts of chairman or chief executive officer describe administrative specialisms, but the authority for final decisions rests with the board.' As discussed earlier, social comparisons with similar directors in similar companies (e.g. O'Reilley et al., 1988) will inevitably create pressure on remuneration committees to be relatively generous in redressing any pay anomaly in order to avoid any possibility that executive talent may be bid away by competitors prepared to match the market pay rate.

It is interesting to interpret some of the results of previous research in the context of our broader interest in board remuneration. For example, under tournament theory, the larger the number of senior executives the greater is the expected pay differences between CEO and average senior executives; however, O'Reilly et al. (1988) uncovered a negative association between these two variables. They also reported a significantly positive relationship between CEO pay and pay for members of the compensation committee. Similarly, if signalling and figurehead motivations provide the explanation for the asymmetric adjustments observed by Ezzamel and Watson (1998), there would be less reason to expect that the pay of the other board members will also exhibit a similar bidding up pattern. Ezzamel and Watson did not, however, examine whether the pay of the other board members was also influenced by external market comparisons.

An, as yet, unexplored empirical corollary of recognizing that common (market wide), peer group and internal (to-the-firm) comparability concerns may influence pay awards is that this should produce a positive contemporaneous relationship between the CEO's pay award and the average pay awards to the other board members. It is important to investigate the extent to which common, within-board pay adjustments to external market pay rates can explain a significant element of CEO pay awards. Researchers have been concerned with the magnitude and perception of fairness in rewarding senior executives (Gomez-Mejia, 1994). Research on the multiplier effect on the compensation structure of different managerial levels has suggested that higher pay at the top is associated with higher pay at lower levels (Mahoney, 1979). This pattern has its roots in equity and fairness theories as means of distributive justice and mechanisms for regulating social exchange relationships between members of an organization.

According to equity theory (Adams, 1963), an individual gives something (input) in return for something (outcome). If input is not recognized as relevant or 'appropriately' valued by the other party in the exchange, then inequity is perceived to occur. In exchange relationships a reference is used in evaluating equity, and while this reference is typically assumed to be someone of a similar standing, individuals can also compare the outcomes they receive against individuals in higher or lower levels. Hence, equity has both lateral and vertical dimensions. In the context of this paper, a member of the board of directors, e.g. production director, could compare his/her compensation against another member perceived to be of a similar standing, e.g. finance director. Moreover, while not expecting parity, the same director is also likely to compare *changes* in his/her compensation over time with the *changes* in the compensation of the CEO. Inequity would be perceived to occur if the compensation of the director is less than that of the direct comparator (a director of similar standing), and if the *pattern*, but not necessarily the magnitude, of change in his/her compensation is disadvantageous compared to that of the CEO. Thus, if the CEO is offered an increase in his/her compensation, the other director would also expect an increase, even though possibly of a lower magnitude, otherwise inequity occurs. This concession to the CEO to obtain a higher level of remuneration and possibly higher percentage increases over time is a reflection of the widely held view that 'CEOs are seen as the ultimate power brokers not only internally, as managerialism predicts, but also in collusion with board members and CEOs of other firms' (Gomez-Mejia, 1994, p. 180). This argument is also consistent with the hierarchical pecking order, or the social stratification norms argument (Mahoney, 1979; Simon, 1957) and figurehead theory (Steers and Ungson, 1987).

Subsequent writers developed and expanded Adams' work on equity by exploring the concept of fairness and equality (Deutsch, 1975, 1984; Kahneman et al., 1986, 1987; Bazerman and Neale, 1992). Fairness (or unfairness) is not an objective state since it depends on personal perceptions. As Kahneman et al. (1987) have demonstrated, perceptions of fairness often dominate economic considerations. Fairness could be taken to mean equal allocation of resources, or allocation in proportion to individual contributions (which is particularly relevant in the case of incentive and merit-based compensation schemes), or allocation on the basis of need (Bazerman and Neale, 1992). Kahneman et al. (1986, 1987) have shown that judgements of fairness can be susceptible to the effects of framing: their results revealed that a pay cut of a given percentage was considered unfair, whereas a nominal gain that was below inflation by the same percentage (i.e. the direct pay cut and the real terms loss were equivalent in terms of their wealth effects) was more acceptable to their subjects. It seems that organizations develop rules of fairness (e.g. that pay should go up, not down) and pay awards are expected to follow these rules, otherwise unfairness will be perceived to occur. Moreover, in situations where it is difficult for pay to go up for everyone, the importance of equality could become paramount as it would be best if 'things are equally bad for everybody' (Bazerman and Neale, 1992, p. 120). In all pay negotiations, the outcome of other parties is a key reference point for evaluating one's own outcome (Kahneman et al., 1986). In team situations (such as corporate executives) group behavioural norms will be important in framing expectations, pay relativities and notions of fairness and equity between team members. While remuneration committees may wish to award the CEO with a high percentage pay increase to reflect his greater strategic importance and visibility to outsiders, such awards could create friction and resentment within the senior management team if the award is seen to violate existing within-board pay comparability. Hence, it is likely that remuneration committees will award similar (across-the-board) percentage pay rises to all board members and that any additional percentage pay rises received by the CEO will be closely related to external changes in the pay levels of the CEO's external benchmark.

Research Hypotheses

The literature reviewed above suggests that in setting cash pay for board members, members of the compensation committee can be expected to base their views on what constitutes a 'reasonable' level of pay on three factors. First, their own experiences, either as serving executives or as non-executives elsewhere; second, the analyses provided by external pay consultants concerning similar executives in comparator firms and/or those which provide better-than-average pay levels; and third, the level of pay of organizational peers, that is, other senior executives and board members within the same firm. The above discussion gives rise to the following hypothesis:

> *Hypothesis 1*: Both the CEO's and the other board members' pay awards will be partly explained by an adjustment process which keeps their pay in line with appropriate external market pay levels and, therefore, prior period pay anomalies will be significantly related to subsequent period pay awards.

The case made above for emphasizing the importance of examining the remuneration of board members is still consistent with the literature positing a crucially significant role for the CEO. Generally speaking, the remuneration committee will be motivated to move quickly to bid up the pay of underpaid executives (the CEO and others) than to adjust the pay of those overpaid, since feelings of unfairness will be much greater in the first case. As indicated earlier, the CEO is typically the main strategist and the one who ultimately drives the most important corporate decisions. Figurehead, signalling, and tournament theories (Gomez-Mejia, 1994) will all support a more careful (and generous) treatment when deciding the pay of CEOs compared to the other board members. Turnover of successful CEOs is something that most firms wish to avoid because of the loss of major executive talent and because CEO succession can cause turbulent and, at times, difficult to predict changes with wide implications for other senior executives and the firm. Hence, while firms would in general be motivated to offer competitive remuneration to the other board members, their concern to retain the CEO would be even greater. This gives rise to the following hypothesis:

> *Hypothesis 2*: Asymmetric adjustments to reduce underpayment anomalies, i.e. 'bidding up', will be most apparent in the case of CEO pay changes than in the case of the pay changes of the other board members.

An important implication that emerges from the literature on social comparisons, is that within board comparisons in individuals' pay will also be easy to make. Team cohesion and equity concerns are therefore likely to be important considerations when setting both CEO and other board members' pay. Moreover, since remuneration committee members bring their own experiences and perceptions into the board room, the extent to which they are themselves influenced by how under- or over-paid they are relative to their implied external benchmark may be an important factor in explaining CEO pay awards. For example, if the CEO is underpaid relative to his/her externally derived benchmark, the adjustment factor by which the CEO's pay is subsequently brought into line with comparable cases can be expected to be higher if the other board members are generously paid relative to comparison levels than if they were underpaid. Similarly, if the other board members are themselves relatively underpaid, it might be expected that remuneration committees would make CEO pay awards that are less generous relative to market rates than otherwise. In short, it is to be expected that any 'bidding-up' behaviour in respect of CEO pay, of the type investigated by Ezzamel and Watson (1998), will be more apparent in the case of relatively well-paid boards than in the case of boards in which the other board members appear to be underpaid relative to the market. The above discussion gives rise to the following two hypotheses:

> *Hypothesis 3*: Remuneration committees will give similar percentage pay awards to all their board members, but changes in CEO pay will be closely related to the change in the comparison level of pay rather than the actual change of pay of the other board members.

> *Hypothesis 4*: Asymmetric adjustments to prior period pay anomalies that result in the 'bidding-up' of CEO pay will be most apparent in the case of firms in which the other board members are themselves relatively generously paid with respect to the external comparison level of pay.

Hypotheses 1 and 2 focus on the external comparison, i.e. the between-board, aspects of directors' pay awards. The basic issue addressed by Hypothesis 1 is to explore whether there is any evidence to suggest that in determining the pay awards for CEOs and other directors, remuneration committees take account of external and easily observable pay norms. The Ezzamel and Watson (1998) study tested Hypothesis 1 in respect of CEOs and it also established that CEO pay awards exhibited a significant element of 'bidding-up', which is of obvious relevance to Hypothesis 2. No study has to date undertaken a similar analysis in respect of the other board members' pay. Hypothesis 2 examines the precise nature of the mechanism by which both CEO and other board members' pay is kept in line with the external comparison pay measure. The theoretical literature and empirical findings to date suggest that remuneration committees can be expected to be relatively more responsive in respect of apparent underpayments than overpayments, particularly in regard to CEO pay.

Hypotheses 3 and 4 examine the nature of the contemporaneous relationship between CEO and other board members' pay, i.e., the within-board pay comparisons. Hypothesis 3 examines whether remuneration committees attempt to maintain an element of within-board comparability by awarding both the CEO and the other board members similar (rather than the same) percentage pay rises. It suggests that the CEO can be expected to receive a percentage change in pay that is most closely related to changes in the external comparison level of pay experienced by the other board members. In our analysis we distinguish between and evaluate the relative explanatory power of Hypothesis 3 and the simple 'across-the-board' common percentage pay change explanation. Hypothesis 3 implies that CEO pay changes will be positively related, not merely to the actual percentage change in the pay of the other board members, but also to the other board members' prior period pay anomaly and that empirically the estimated coefficients on these two variables will be of roughly the same magnitude and sign.

Hypothesis 4 focuses on the relationship between CEO pay changes and the extent to which the other board members appear to be under or overpaid relative to their peers in other firms. It tests whether the other directors' pay anomaly has a positive influence on the degree to which remuneration committees are willing to award generous pay rises to underpaid CEOs relative to their external comparison pay level. In cases where the other board members are relatively well-paid, it is to be expected that the remuneration committee will tend to bid-up CEO pay by awarding a proportionately high pay adjustment to an underpaid CEO whilst making a proportionately lower adjustment in the pay levels of overpaid CEOs. Similarly, in cases where the other board members are relatively less well paid than their peers in other firms, it is to be expected that the remuneration committee will be less willing to significantly adjust the pay levels of underpaid CEOs to bring them into line with the external market comparison level. Given a high enough concern for enhancing the degree of within-board comparability (equity), it is possible that in such cases the remuneration committee will take action to significantly reduce the pay of overpaid CEOs.

RESEARCH METHOD

Modelling Changes in CEO's and Other Board Members' Pay

In this section we explain how the typical agency theory model used in the literature will be augmented so as to allow us to empirically test each of the across and within board hypotheses introduced in the previous section. We retain the agency theory assumption that the 'optimal' pay scheme will consist of both insurance (fixed salary) and incentive (performance-related) components and that in order to retain the services of the executive, the minimum guaranteed salary offered must be at least as much as comparable executives in comparable firms earn (the participation constraint). At time t−1 the remuneration committee decides on the level of pay for its CEO and the other board members (including themselves) for the coming period to time t. The actual level of pay determined at t−1 and paid throughout the period to time t, W_t, will be reported in the financial statements at time t. As noted earlier, firm size is an easily observed measure which is empirically strongly positively related to pay levels. This is because it proxies for a number of supply and demand relevant factors and is therefore a major determinant of the participation constraint. Many empirical studies have produced a pay function (W^*_t) that isolates the participation constraint from the incentive alignment component of the contract by assuming a firm-size and firm-performance relationship to pay of the following form:

$$(W^*_t) = a\text{Sales}^b_{t-1}P^c_{t-1} \quad (1)$$

where:

a	= a constant representing the demand-relevant human characteristics of the executive concerned
Sales	= the firm size measure that proxies for the supply relevant job and firm characteristics
P	= the firm performance measure
b and c	= parameters that determine the sensitivity of pay to differences in, respectively, firm size and performance.

The first term on the right-hand-side of (1) above ($a\text{Sales}^b_{t-1}$) can be interpreted as capturing the factors that determine the participation constraint, whilst the second term (P^c_{t-1}) captures the incentive alignment component, the usual focus of agency theory models.

By rewriting (1) in log-form and recognising that at time t the actual market pay level could differ from the pay level decided at the start of the period and so $W_t = W^*_t + u_t$, we get the estimating equation that the majority of empirical executive pay-level studies have adopted:

$$\ln(W_t) = \ln(a) + b\ln(Sales_{t-1}) + c\ln(P_{t-1}) + \ln(u_t). \quad (2)$$

As noted earlier, pay-level models of this nature generally find a highly significant positive coefficient of around 0.30 on the firm size variable though, due to the multiplicity of absolute and relative, firm performance measures tested and the greater cross-sectional heterogeneity in the use of performance-related pay systems, there is less consistent empirical support in respect of the incentive alignment hypothesis. A major difficulty associated with cross-sectional estimates of the above types of pay-level model is that it is unable to control for any unobservable firm-specific characteristics, such as differences in risk, management quality, etc. Consequently, many researchers have chosen to focus on the dynamics of the pay setting process and have estimated the first difference version of (2):

$$\ln(W_{t+1}) - \ln(W_t) = \beta_0 + \beta_1 \ln\Delta Sales_t + \beta_2 \ln\Delta P_t + u_{t+1}. \quad (3)$$

Thus, the log change in reported pay between time t and t+1 is simply a function of common, across-sample, average change in pay (the constant), the change in firm size (Sales) and the firm performance measure (P). An advantage of this model is that the omitted variables problem associated with the pay level models, if they arise from unobservable firm-level fixed effects such as differences in firm and individual characteristics, drop out of the equation and can, therefore, be ignored. However, empirical testing of models along the lines of (3) above do not take into account the element of the change in pay that represents the remuneration committee's attempt to keep pay aligned with external market pay rates. The empirical implication arising from such pay-alignment behaviour is that the prior year's deviation from market comparison pay levels (i.e., u_t in equation (2)) can be expected to have a significant effect upon subsequent (t+1) changes in pay. To see why, assume that at time t, the remuneration committee believes that the (as yet unobservable) comparison pay level for the coming period will be related to the observed level today as follows:

$$W_{t+1} = (1+\alpha)W^*_t \quad (4)$$

If the remuneration committee attempts to keep pay aligned with the new market rate for the period t to t+1, then empirically (omitting the log notation and other terms in the equation for convenience) the actual change in pay will be

$$W_{t+1} - W_t = W^*_t(1+\alpha) - (W^*_t + u_t) + u_{t+1} \quad (5a)$$

$$W_{t+1} - W_t = \alpha W^*_t - \delta u_t + u_{t+1} \quad (5b)$$

The estimated coefficient (δ) on the prior year's pay anomaly (u_t) will be negative and equal to −1 if there is full adjustment to the pay anomaly. Also, the anticipated change in the market pay level between time t and t+1 (αW^*_t) will be reflected in the constant term. Ezzamel and Watson (1998) tested several formulations of the above model for changes in UK CEO pay. They investigated the claims that CEO pay was being 'bid up' by remuneration committees by testing for differences in the pay anomaly δ between under and overpaid executives, hypothesizing that underpaid executives would experience a more significant adjustment to the market rate than overpaid executives. We follow Ezzamel and Watson (1998) in estimating the model:

$$\ln W_{it+1} - \ln W_{it} = \Sigma \ln(\alpha W^*_t) + \beta \ln(\text{RETURNS}_{it}) + \beta \Delta \ln(\text{SALES}_{it}) + \delta_u(\ln W_{it} - \ln W^*_{it}) + \delta_o(\ln W_{it} - \ln W^*_{it}) + u_{it} + 1 \quad (6)$$

where:

$\ln W_{it+1} - \ln W_{it}$	= the reported log change in executive i's pay between time t and t+1
$\Sigma \ln(\alpha W^*_t)$	= the constant term and year dummy variables
$\delta_o(\ln W_{it} - \ln W^*_{it})$	= the adjustment process for the 'overpaid' executives, i.e., all i's where $(\ln W_{it} - \ln W^*_{it}) > 0$, and 0 otherwise
$\delta_u(\ln W_{it} - \ln W^*_{it})$	= the adjustment process for the 'underpaid' executives, i.e., all i's where $(\ln W_{it} - \ln W^*_{it}) < 0$, and 0 otherwise
Returns_{it}	= the sector-relative total (dividend and capital gain) return to shareholders of firm i in time t
$\ln\Delta(\text{Sales}_{it})$	= log change in company i's sales revenue in time t.

Empirical support for the 'bidding-up' hypothesis would imply that: $\delta_u < 0$ and $\delta_o > \delta_u$. Our proxies for the comparison level of pay used to estimate the executive pay anomaly variables are likely to be noisy because compensation committees may only adjust executive pay in response to relatively large deviations (positive or negative) from the implied market rate of pay. However, we also evaluate non-linear specifications of equation (6), but we report only the specification in which the deviations from the implied external market comparison rates of pay $(\ln W_{it} - \ln W^*_{it})$, are squared.[3] Hypotheses 1 and 2 are evaluated for both the CEO's and other board members' pay changes by estimating equation (6), using both linear and squared versions of the pay adjustment variables.

Ezzamel and Watson (1998) assumed that the remuneration committee adjusts the CEO's pay in line with changes in comparison (market) pay levels. What, according to Hypothesis 3, seems more likely is that the remuneration committee will also attempt to maintain an element of comparability with the pay awards of other board members. Basically, in order to maintain top-team cohesion and avoid offending existing equity and fairness notions within the board of directors, changes in CEO pay will also be partly explained in terms of the pay awards received by the other board members. The average actual change in pay of the other board members will be $(W_{(OB)t+1} - W_{(OB)t})$ and this will consist of the same two elements as for CEOs: one related to the anticipated general change in the market level of pay, $\alpha W^*_{(OB)t}$, and the other associated with the firm-specific adjustment to the prior period pay anomaly, $u_{(OB)t}$, i.e.,

$$W_{(OB)t+1} - W_{(OB)t} = \alpha W^*_{(OB)t} - u_{(OB)t} \quad (7)$$

The CEO's change in pay is not expected to be related to the prior period pay anomaly adjustment associated with the other directors ($-u_{(OB)t}$). This element of the other board members' pay change is independent of anticipated changes in the external market rate, and it is in this respect that Hypothesis 3 does not simply imply that remuneration committees use the actual change in the other board members' pay as the within-board comparability criterion. Under Hypothesis 3, the remuneration committee is expected to only adjust the CEO's pay in line with the anticipated general change in board members' pay ($\alpha W^*_{(OB)t}$). Note that $\alpha W^*_{(OB)t}$ differs from the actual change in the other board members' pay by ($-u_{(OB)t}$) and hence:

$$\alpha W^*_{(OB)t} = (W_{(OB)t+1} - W_{(OB)t}) + u_{(OB)t} \quad (8)$$

To empirically test Hypothesis 3, both terms on the right-hand-side of equation (8), the actual change in the other board members' pay ($W_{(OB)t+1} - W_{(OB)t}$) and their prior period pay anomaly estimate ($u_{(OB)t}$), are included in an augmented version of equation (6). Empirical support for Hypothesis 3 requires that both of these variables have positive coefficients that are statistically identical in magnitude. The change in the other board members' pay relative to the prior period's estimated market level of pay ($W_{(OB)t+1} - W^*_{(OB)t}$) is an alternative definition of both sides of equation (8) i.e.,

$$(W_{(OB)t+1} - W^*_{(OB)t}) = \alpha W^*_{(OB)t} = (W_{(OB)t+1} - W_{(OB)t}) + u_{(OB)t} \quad (9)$$

Hypothesis 3 implies that the left-hand side of equation (9) may be inserted into the CEO pay change equation in place of both the actual change in other board members' pay and their prior period pay anomalies. Hypothesis 4 assumes that relatively well paid boards will be more generous in respect of CEO pay, particularly in relation to underpaid CEOs relative to their peers in similar sized firms. To test Hypothesis 4, a dummy variable is created, which has a value of one if the other board members were overpaid in the previous period and zero otherwise. This is then multiplied by the CEO's prior period under and overpayment anomaly variables. This results in the creation of two new interaction terms whose estimated coefficients represent the differential impact that relatively overpaid boards have upon the responsiveness of CEO pay to prior period pay anomalies. Empirical results consistent with Hypothesis 4 would require that the coefficient on the underpaid CEO interaction term is significantly less than zero and that of the overpaid CEO interaction term greater than zero. The use of the interaction terms does not, however, allow the slope coefficients on the other variables in the model to vary across the two groups of firms (i.e., those with overpaid and those with underpaid boards). To overcome this limitation we partition the sample on the same basis (i.e., in terms of under and overpaid other board members) and separately re-estimate the models (without the interaction terms included in the estimation equation).

The Sample

Our sample was drawn from all the listed companies in the Times 1000, which is a ranking by turnover of the 1000 largest UK companies. We excluded financial

Table I. Descriptive statistics

Variable	*Year*	*N*	*Mean*	*Standard deviation*
CEO cash compensation (salary + bonus) (£'000)	1992	196	242.0	174.1
	1993	195	300.7	220.0
	1994	188	362.4	273.2
	1995	178	387.6	278.0
Average cash compensation of the other board members (£'000)	1992	194	117.0	85.3
	1993	195	124.4	86.6
	1994	182	138.9	123.5
	1995	178	138.6	88.2
Total sales (£m)	1992	191	1827	7888
	1993	192	1423	4091
	1994	187	1555	4480
	1995	189	1556	4395
Ind relative profit/equity	1992	195	5.7%	86.7
	1993	195	2.8	103.1
	1994	196	−2.1	35.5
	1995	193	5.2	79.4
Ind relative market return	1992	187	−5.9	37.1
	1993	187	−2.5	52.3
	1994	182	4.0	35.5
	1995	182	1.1	30.4
Percentage of non-executives	1992	185	39.2	14.3
	1993	188	40.7	14.0
	1994	196	41.6	13.8
	1995	182	43.3	13.3

companies and companies with year ends other than December–January, which produced 223 companies.[4] This number was reduced to 199 due to some companies not having a full UK listing (primarily the subsidiaries of non-UK companies) and others losing their separate listing through mergers and takeovers since the publication of the Times 1000. Because of the presence of lagged performance variables in the equations, three years accounting data was required to estimate each one period cash compensation change model. As we wished to estimate as many pay change relationships as possible, the number of companies for which we were able to obtain full data varies by year (see table I).[5] In estimating the empirical models of the relationship between cash compensation changes, payment anomalies and firm performance, we used sector relative measures of firm performance by deducting the sector average (for all Times 1000 firms) shareholder returns from the actual shareholder returns of each company in each time period.

As table I shows, both CEO and other board members experienced increases in their average pay over the period 1992 to 1995. Two points are worth noting, however. First, the average total cash compensation per other board member as a percentage of the total cash compensation of the CEO declined sharply over the four year period from 48.3 to 35.8 per cent. Second, the average annual increase in cash compensation for the CEOs was 17.3 per cent compared to only 5.9 per cent for the other board members (indeed, in 1995, CEOs' cash compensation compared to 1994 increased by 7 per cent, whereas the other board members experienced on average a decline of 0.02 per cent). The Cadbury report recommended that companies have a minimum of three non-executive directors; this appears to have had a positive effect upon the percentage of non-executive directors, which shows a consistent, though fairly small, year-on-year increase.

Variables and Estimation

Our dependent variables are the cash payments (salary plus bonuses) to the highest paid executive, and the average amount of cash payments to the other (remaining) board members. Clearly, cash compensation is only part of the total pay received by executives as it does not include long-term incentive plans (in particular stock options), nor other benefits/perquisites. It could be argued that stock options contain an element of comparison with what other firms offer, and hence the 'bidding-up' process on which we focus here could be capable of being empirically tested for this element. However, in theory and for the period we study, long-term incentive plans, such as stock options, are aimed at aligning managerial incentives with shareholders' interests during the period between issue and exercise. Hence, current period option awards are likely to be noisy indicators of performance-related pay and more likely to depend upon factors such as how many unexercised options the executive holds (and/or has exercised recently), whether there are other ways of aligning incentives (e.g. internal or external governance mechanisms), etc. Moreover, as Gomez-Mejia (1994, pp. 167–8) has noted, attempts to specify the timing of generating income from such plans is fraught with serious measurement and information problems.[6] In addition, in the UK during the period covered by this study, the ability of compensation committee members to evaluate and compare executive share option awards external to their own firm will be extremely difficult, due to the lack of adequate statutory reporting requirements concerning the disclosure of the details of executive share option awards.

Our estimate of the comparison level of pay is the predicted pay level in time t derived from empirically estimating an OLS regression of the pay variables of executives' current cash compensation level using the t–1 firm size (log of sales), and in the case of the other board members' pay level model, the proportion of non-executives on the board (excluding the CEO in the denominator), as explanatory variables. Hence, the estimated pay anomaly experienced by each CEO and the other board members in time t ($\ln W_{it} - \ln W^*_{it}$), is simply the residual from these annually estimated models. The pooled versions of these two models, which include three dummy variables in addition to the constant to represent the differential intercepts for each annual cross section, are presented in the Appendix.[7]

Table II. Full information for all variables sample (N = 675)

	$\ln\Delta(\text{sales}_t)$	Relative market return$_t$	CEO pay anomaly $(\ln W_{it} - \ln W^*_{it})$	Other directors' pay anomaly $(\ln W_{it} - \ln W^*_{it})$	CEO $\ln\Delta pay_{it+1}$
Relative market return$_t$	0.01				
CEO pay anomaly $(\ln W_{it} - \ln W^*_{it})$	0.17***	−0.04			
Other directors' pay anomaly $(\ln W_{it} - \ln W^*_{it})$	0.14***	−0.05	0.43***		
CEO $\ln\Delta pay_{it+1}$	0.01	0.14	−0.30***	0.02	
Other directors' $\ln\Delta pay_{it+1}$	−0.00	0.02	0.04	−0.42***	0.02

Variable definitions

$\ln\Delta pay_{t+1} = \ln(W_{t+1}) - \ln(W_t)$ where pay_t and pay_{t-1} are the actual cash compensation payments (salary plus bonuses) to the CEOs and other board members (other directors) reported at times t and t−1 respectively.

$\ln\Delta sales_t = \ln(sales_t) - \ln(sales_{t-1})$

Relative return$_t$ = $\{\ln(\text{share price}_t + \text{dividend}_t) - \ln(\text{share price}_{t-1})\}$ − sector return in time t.

CEO pay anomaly $(\ln(W_t) - \ln(W^*_t))$ = actual pay in time t − market comparison pay at time t.

Other directors' pay anomalies = $(\ln(W_t) - \ln(W^*_t))$ = actual pay in time t − market comparison pay at time t.

What is particularly striking about these estimates is that the firm-size slope coefficients are almost identical in magnitude and statistical significance levels for both the CEOs and the other directors.

Table II presents a correlation matrix of the univariate linear relationships between the variables used in the empirical analyses. As can be seen from the table, there is a highly significant positive relationship of 0.43 between the two pay anomaly variables relating to the CEOs and the other board members. Hence, there appears to be some within-board common characteristics with respect to the externally derived pay anomalies, i.e., relatively well-paid (poorly-paid) CEOs are associated with relatively well-paid (poorly-paid) other board members. But note that no statistically significant relationship exists between the actual subsequent changes in the pay of CEOs and other board members. In both cases, however, there is a significant negative relationship between payment anomalies and subsequent pay changes, which is consistent with Hypothesis 1. The correlation between pay anomalies and subsequent pay changes is stronger for the other board members than for CEOs. However, this only measures the simple linear relationship between these two variables and Hypothesis 2 suggests that a non-linear asymmetric adjustment to pay anomalies will exist in relation to CEO pay anomalies.

RESULTS

Table III presents the empirical estimates of the model described by equation (6) which is used to test Hypotheses 1 and 2. As a benchmark to indicate the difference that our pay anomaly variables make upon the ability to explain changes in CEO and other board members' pay, we have estimated an initial pay change

Table III. Changes in CEO and other directors' remuneration (dependent variable = lnΔ(salary + bonus) (1992–95))

Variable	Other directors' remuneration			CEO remuneration		
	Model 1	Model 2	Model 3	Model 1	Model 2	Model 3
Constant	0.067***	0.087***	0.065***	0.062***	0.057**	0.051**
	(2.75)	(2.94)	(2.74)	(3.03)	(2.01)	(2.27)
$\ln\Delta sales_t$	−0.002	0.057	0.060	0.016	0.080**	0.101**
	(0.07)	(1.31)	(1.08)	(0.70)	(2.28)	(2.15)
Relative return$_t$	0.012	−0.013	−0.012	0.069**	0.059**	0.065**
	(0.36)	(0.42)	(0.37)	(2.02)	(2.07)	(2.10)
Underpaid$_t$		−0.248***			−0.257***	
		(3.72)			(2.41)	
Overpaid$_t$		−0.455***			−0.262***	
		(4.65)			(3.59)	
Underpaid$_t^2$			−0.411***			−0.438***
			(4.85)			(3.09)
Overpaid$_t^2$			−0.340***			−0.286***
			(8.05)			(4.07)
Year dummies	Yes	Yes	Yes	Yes	Yes	Yes
Adjusted R^2	0.7	18.9	19.6	3.3%	13.1	15.4
Equation F-ratio	1.9*	23.8***	24.9***	5.7***	15.8***	19.0***
F-ratio for new variables		66.3***	81.2***		39.5***	50.2***
N =	686	686	686	693	693	693

White (1980) heteroskedasticity-consistent t-statistics in parenthesis

Significance levels: * ≤ 0.10; ** ≤ 0.05; *** ≤ 0.01

Variable definitions

$\ln\Delta sales_t = \ln(sales_t) - \ln(sales_{t-1})$

Relative return$_t$ = ln(share price$_t$ + dividend) − ln(share price$_{t-1}$)

Underpaid$_t$ = $(\ln(W_t) - \ln(W^*_t))$ if $(\ln(W_t) - \ln(W^*_t)) < 0$ and 0 otherwise

Overpaid$_t$ = $(\ln(W_t) - \ln(W^*_t))$ if $(\ln(W_t) - \ln(W^*_t)) > 0$ and 0 otherwise

Underpaid$_t^2$ = underpaid$_t$ × underpaid$_t$ x − 1 (to retain negative sign)

Overpaid$_t^2$ = overpaid$_t$ × overpaid$_t$

model, Model 1, which does not include any of our measures of pay anomalies. The two versions of Model 1, based upon CEO and the other board members' data, are replications of the traditional agency models that focus solely on the pay and firm-performance link.

As can be seen from table III, neither version of Model 1 is able to explain a substantial proportion of the cross-sectional variance in the changes in board members' pay. Only the constant term is statistically significant in the other directors model, and in the CEO model, relative shareholder returns are significantly positively related to changes in CEO pay. Model 2 is Model 1 with the additional prior period pay anomaly variables included. The inclusion of these variables results in a large and highly significant increase in the explanatory power of the estimates. Moreover, for both versions of Model 2, the estimated coefficients are statistically highly significant and negative as anticipated by Hypothesis 1; hence, prior period pay anomalies have a significant impact upon subsequent pay awards to both the CEOs and the other board members. Model 3 replaces the pay anomaly variables with the original pay anomaly variables squared. The squared pay anomaly estimates lead to a further increase in the explanatory power of the models, though only in the case of the CEO model is the increase in explanatory power statistically significant at the 1 per cent confidence level. These results confirm the findings of Model 2 and, therefore, give further support to Hypothesis 1.

Model 3 estimates indicate that the (absolute size of the) coefficient on the underpayment variable is greater in magnitude than the coefficient on the overpayment variable, which is consistent with 'bidding-up' behaviour according to which the response to underpayment anomalies is greater than the response to overpayment anomalies. However, only in the case of the CEOs is the difference in the absolute size of the coefficients of statistical significance at the 5 per cent confidence level. These results give some support for Hypothesis 2 which assumes that any bidding-up behaviour will be most apparent in the case of CEOs.

Table IV presents the results relating to the relationship between CEO pay changes and the relative pay of the other board members; Panel A shows the full sample estimates while Panel B shows the separate estimates for the under and overpaid other board member sub-samples. Model 3 in Panel A is taken from table II and is our benchmark for evaluating the incremental explanatory power associated with the within-board pay comparisons assumed by Hypotheses 3 and 4. Models 4 and 5 examine the empirical plausibility of Hypothesis 3. As explained earlier, and shown by equation (9), for Hypothesis 3 to hold the difference between the two estimates should be minor, since the aggregate of the two new variables included in Model 4 is statistically equivalent to the one new variable included in Model 5, i.e. $(W_{(OB)t+1} - W^*_{(OB)t})$, the change in the other board members pay to t+1 relative to the estimated external comparison pay level at time t. Both of the estimated coefficients on the new variables included in Model 4 are positive, statistically significant at 1% confidence levels and, on the basis of a Wald test, the difference in the sizes of the two coefficients is not significant at conventional levels of confidence. This provides empirical support for Hypothesis 3 which assumes that remuneration committees adjust CEO pay in line with anticipated changes in the market rates for the other board members and not simply by awarding a uniform percentage pay change 'across-the-board'. This is supported by the estimates of Model 5 which includes only the $(W_{(OB)t+1} - W^*_{(OB)t})$ variable. The explanatory power of the model is essentially identical to that of Model 4 and as hypothesized, the size of the estimated coefficient on the new variable is statistically indistinguishable from the coefficients on the two variables included in Model 4.

Model 6 is Model 5 after the addition of two interaction terms to distinguish the differential slope coefficients relating to the CEO's pay anomaly variables for those cases where the other board members are paid more than the comparison level of pay. This model is designed to test Hypothesis 4 which assumes that in instances where the other board members are overpaid relative to their peers, there will be a greater element of bidding-up in respect of the CEO's pay. Support for Hypothesis 4 requires a significantly negative coefficient on the underpayment interaction term and/or a significantly positive coefficient on the overpayment interaction term. Note that the coefficients on the original under and overpayment (squared) terms represent the responsiveness of CEO pay to payment anomalies associated with boards that are relatively underpaid *vis-à-vis* their external bench-

Table IV. Changes in CEO remuneration and the relationship to other directors' remuneration (dependent variable = lnΔ(salary + bonus) (1992–95))

Panel A: All observations

Variable	*Model 3*	*Model 4*	*Model 5*	*Model 6*
Constant	0.051**	0.049***	0.046**	0.060***
	(2.27)	(2.25)	(2.13)	(2.86)
$\ln\Delta sales_t$	0.101**	0.080**	0.083**	0.053*
	(2.15)	(2.03)	(2.09)	(1.75)
Relative $return_t$	0.065**	0.078***	0.076***	0.073***
	(2.10)	(2.63)	(2.57)	(2.46)
$Underpaid_t^2$	−0.488***	−0.538***	−0.534***	−0.180
	(3.09)	(3.79)	(3.73)	(1.09)
$Overpaid_t^2$	−0.286***	−0.352***	−0.344***	−0.449***
	(4.07)	(5.08)	(4.97)	(7.45)
Year dummies	Yes	Yes	Yes	Yes
Other directors' pay anomaly ($\ln W_{it} - \ln W^*_{it}$)		0.169***		
		(4.42)		
Other directors' change in pay ($\ln W_{it+1} - \ln W_{it}$)		0.117***		
		(2.53)		
Other directors' change in pay relative to $\ln W^*_{it}$ i.e. ($\ln W_{it+1} - \ln W^*_{it}$)			0.147***	0.093***
			(4.13)	(2.45)
$Underpaid_t^2$ *overpaid other directors' dummy				−0.657***
				(3.50)
$Overpaid_t^2$ *overpaid other directors' dummy				0.157
				(1.49)
Adjusted R^2	15.4	18.4	18.2	21.3
Equation F-ratio	19.0***	18.1***	20.1***	19.5***
F-ratio for new variables	50.2***	12.8***	17.0***	66.3***
N =	693	686	686	686

Panel B: Model 5 partitioned by other directors' pay anomaly

Variable	*Model 5* *Overpaid boards*	*Model 5* *Underpaid boards*
	($\ln W_{it} - \ln W^*_{it}$) > 0	($\ln W_{it} - \ln W^*_{it}$) < 0
Constant	0.043	0.080***
	(1.16)	(3.44)
$\ln\Delta sales_t$	0.035	0.052
	(1.06)	(1.04)
Relative $return_t$	0.047	0.099***
	(0.99)	(2.73)
$Underpaid_t^2$	−0.877***	−0.136
	(9.25)	(0.70)
$Overpaid_t^2$	−0.264***	−0.491***
	(3.03)	(8.07)
Year dummies	Yes	Yes
Other directors' change in pay relative to $\ln W^*_{it}$ i.e. ($\ln W_{it+1} - \ln W^*_{it}$)	0.087*	0.117**
	(1.71)	(1.94)
Adjusted R^2	27.8	13.2
Equation F-ratio	15.7***	8.2***
N =	338	348

White (1980) heteroskedasticity-consistent t-statistics in parenthesis

Significance levels: * ≤ 0.10; ** ≤ 0.05; *** ≤ 0.01.

Variable definitions

$\ln\Delta sales_t = \ln(sales_t) - \ln(sales_{t-1})$

Relative $return_t = \ln(\text{share price}_t + dividend_t) - \ln(\text{share price}_{t-1})$

$Underpaid_t = (\ln(W_t) - \ln(W^*_t))$ if $(\ln(W_t) - \ln(W^*_t)) < 0$ and 0 otherwise

$Overpaid_t = (\ln(W_t) - \ln(W^*_t))$ if $(\ln(W_t) - \ln(W^*_t)) > 0$ and 0 otherwise

$Underpaid_t^2 = underpaid_t \times underpaid_t \times -1$ (to retain negative sign)

$Overpaid_t^2 = overpaid_t \times overpaid_t$

mark level of pay. As can be seen from the table, underpaid CEOs with boards that are themselves underpaid do not appear to receive a subsequent pay award, which removes this pay anomaly. Indeed, only the overpayment coefficient is statistically significant, and its absolute magnitude is statistically larger than the size of the coefficient on the underpayment term, which implies that these CEOs appear to experience a significant 'bidding-down' of their pay relative to the external benchmark. The estimated coefficient on the underpayment interaction term is, however, significantly negative, which implies that the responsiveness of CEO pay to prior period underpayment anomalies when the other members of the board are relatively well paid is 0.837 (i.e., 0.180 + 0.657). The coefficient is positive, but not statistically significant for the overpayment interaction term, implying that relatively well-paid CEOs with relatively well-paid boards experience a smaller negative increment in their pay to time t+1. In addition, the explanatory power of the model *vis-à-vis* Model 5 has increased significantly, which implies that the inclusion of the two interaction terms improves the efficiency of the model; this is consistent with Hypothesis 4.

In Panel B of table IV, Model 5 has been separately estimated for the two sub-samples, i.e., firms with relatively under and overpaid boards. The estimates included here are less restrictive than the estimates shown as Model 6 in Panel A since the coefficients on all the variables were allowed to vary across the two sub-samples. These estimates show the differences in the slope coefficients relating to the CEOs' payment anomalies. The results show that CEOs with relatively overpaid boards experience a significant element of bidding-up in their pay which is related to their prior period payment anomalies whilst CEOs with relatively underpaid boards experience a significant element of 'bidding down' since the negative coefficient on the overpayment variable is significantly larger in absolute magnitude than the coefficient on the underpayment variable. Whilst none of the other coefficients in the models differ significantly between the two sub-samples, it appears that CEOs with relatively underpaid boards have their pay more closely linked to changes in shareholder value than do CEOs with relatively well-paid boards. Empirically, however, this greater sensitivity to firm performance does not explain the depressive effect associated with the failure to reduce CEOs' external pay anomalies since they received on average an annual 12.2 per cent rise in their pay versus an average annual pay rise of 13.8 per cent for CEOs with relatively well-paid boards.

DISCUSSION AND CONCLUSIONS

This paper has investigated the issues and empirical evidence relating to the determinants of executive cash pay in large publicly listed UK companies. The focus has been on how various pay comparisons influence executive pay awards rather than on the incentive alignment issues that have motivated most of the previous (agency theory derived) attempts to empirically model executive pay. The paper has shown, however, that it is possible to incorporate pay comparability concerns into the agency theory framework without violating any of its assumptions, simply by investigating the implications of the insurance or participation constraint element of the optimal employment contract. The empirical estimating model was then augmented so as to include external market (across-board) pay comparison variables and internal (within-board) pay comparability measures which enabled the empirical testing of the four main hypotheses detailed in the text concerning the influence of pay comparability upon pay awards.

The first hypothesis was concerned with establishing the extent to which remuneration committees appeared to be making pay awards to both the CEO and the other board members that attempted to reduce any pay anomalies relative to what other similar-sized firms were paying the members of their board of directors, to explain the changes in cash compensation to CEOs and the other board members. Minimizing such deviations from the 'going rate' was thought likely to be an important consideration if the firm was to avoid motivational, retention and recruitment problems and compromised external credibility. Since the non-executives serving on the compensation committees are usually senior executives elsewhere, comparisons with their own pay levels are probably inevitable. When coupled with the advice of external pay consultants, it is likely that external pay comparisons will have an important impact upon compensation committee decisions on executive pay.

Our results suggest that the external labour market comparisons are important in explaining the cash pay awards to CEOs and also the other board members. In the case of the CEOs, however, there is clear evidence of an asymmetric adjustment to prior period pay anomalies which results in a 'bidding up' of CEO cash pay relative to other board members, which is consistent with our second hypothesis. Furthermore, we found evidence in support of our third and fourth hypotheses relating to the within-board pay comparability concerns. The estimated coefficient on the prior period pay anomaly variable for the other board members and that on their current period percentage cash pay award were both significantly positively related to the CEO's current period award. This we interpret as evidence consistent with Hypothesis 3, namely, that remuneration committees are concerned to maintain a significant element of within-board pay comparability. Finally, Hypothesis 4, which suggested that CEO pay was most likely to be 'bid-up' when the other board members were themselves generously paid relative to the external market benchmark pay level, was also supported by the empirical results. These results suggest that members of remuneration committees in the UK tend to determine CEO pay awards on the basis of: (1) their own pay levels; (2) the percentage change (typically increase) in their own pay awards; and (3) an element which attempts to maintain parity with comparable CEOs in other firms. This latter element is more significant in the case of 'underpaid' executives. As with many previous studies, relatively little of the CEO's change in pay is related to relative shareholder returns or sales growth, though it is interesting to note that with the introduction of the pay comparability variables, the statistical significance of returns and sales growth increases markedly. This suggests that some of the negative results of previous studies regarding the empirical pay–performance link, may be due to the omission of the pay comparability variables.

It is worth stressing that these results are consistent with the literature on equity theory on the one hand, and hierarchical pecking order/social stratification norms, and social comparison/figurehead theory on the other hand. First, equity theory (Adams, 1963) is underpinned by the notion of perceived fairness by the individual. For the CEO, equity/fairness implies outcomes consistent with the CEO's input (which is difficult to observe objectively) and pay parity with comparable CEOs in similar firms (which is relatively easier to establish). For the other board members equity entails, again, matching inputs with outcomes, but more visibly lateral (across-board) and vertical (within-board) fairness. Lateral fairness implies pay parity with other firm directors and outside directors of a similar standing (Festinger, 1957; O'Reilley et al., 1988). Vertical fairness for the other board members implies similar (rather than identical) changes in pay awards over time to those offered to the CEO. Thus, for any given year, if the remuneration committee awards an increase to the CEO, inequity will be perceived to occur if the other board members are not awarded an increase.

The increase in remuneration offered to the other board members, however, need not be identical to that received by the CEO for equity to occur. This is because a variety of theories accord the CEO special significance compared to the other board members. Thus, social norm theory (Mahoney, 1979; Simon, 1957) advances the argument that rewards to organizational members should reflect social stratification norms by appropriately differentiating rank through pay; this clearly involves both differences in pay magnitude and level of pay increases over time. Hierarchical rank is assumed to reflect the relative importance of the occupant of the rank to the organization. The CEO is typically viewed as the chief strategist and the key executive whose decisions and performance have the greatest impact on the entire organization (Gomez-Mejia, 1994). The CEO is also widely viewed, both internally and externally, as the ultimate power broker (Muckley, 1984). Moreover, figurehead theory (Steers and Ungson, 1987) emphasizes the symbolic importance of the CEO and the need to reflect this in the form of higher rewards; again this entails greater magnitude of reward and possibly higher percentage increase in pay over time compared to the other board members.

Our results therefore have some clear implications in regard to helping align public expectations regarding the typically multidimensional considerations and complex trade-offs that constitute the executive pay-setting process, and why in practice it is unlikely that incentive alignment issues will (or should) ever have much of an influence upon executive cash pay awards. First, remuneration committees appear to act as if it is important that equity is maintained within the board of directors, while simultaneously recognizing the external labour market alternatives for the strategic and leadership qualities of the firm's most senior executives, in particular the CEO. Clearly, if a significant degree of inequity is perceived, this is likely to breed dissatisfaction, tensions within the team, internal conflicts, and ultimately lead to the resignation of executives with the greatest job mobility (Adams, 1963) which is likely to be detrimental to the firm. Second, equity is a multidimensional concept. When one is comparing one's own compensation against those of similar attributes or equal standing in similar sized firms, equity means compensation parity as proposed by the market for managerial labour argument (Fama, 1980) and social comparison theory (Festinger, 1957; O'Reilley et al., 1988; Steers and Ungson, 1987). If firms wish to minimize the chances of their most talented executives being bid away by other competitors, their remuneration has to be kept in line with the 'going' market rate which we here denote lateral equity. This argument applies not only to the CEO but also to all board members. Another dimension of equity discussed in this paper is vertical equity; here vertical differences in the magnitude of the compensations and the percentage increases (or decreases) over time are acknowledged to reflect hierarchical, symbolic, and political differences between executives, so that strict parity in both these dimensions of compensation are not expected. However, high levels of inequity or unfairness are likely to be experienced if some executives (e.g. the CEO) are offered pay rises when the other board members are offered no or comparatively low pay rises. So, remuneration committees have to carefully balance these two dimensions of equity (lateral and vertical) in a manner that rewards the unique attributes of CEOs while ensuring that the other board members are appropriately remunerated.

One of the limitations of this study is that we have not been able to conduct separate analyses for salaries and bonuses for the whole period because of data unavailability. Although the limited analysis we have been able to conduct on these two variables separately strongly supports the findings for the salary plus bonus analysis, it would be desirable to test this further using separate data for salaries and bonuses over a longer time span. Another limitation is that we only focused on cash pay to the exclusion of stock options and other fringe benefits. We have suggested that for the period of our study UK data is highly noisy; however an extension of our analysis to incorporate non-cash elements of the remuneration package is likely to shed further interesting insights upon compensation comparability across and within boards of directors.

NOTES

*We are grateful to the Institute of Chartered Accountants in England and Wales (ICAEW) who provided the funding for this study, and the two anonymous reviewers. This paper was presented at the Conference of Business, Honolulu, June 2001.

[1] Given the high dependence of option value upon share price changes, when the pay variable includes changes in the value of executive share option holdings, the estimated pay–performance relationship is considerably strengthened (Main et al., 1996; Murphy, 1985).

[2] Equity, efficiency wage, signalling and figurehead theories, each in their different ways also suggest an upward bias in executive pay comparisons because payments in excess of the 'going rate' can be expected to minimize internal motivational and retention problems whilst enhancing the firm's external credibility (see Gomez-Mejia (1994) for a review).

[3] As squaring the underpaid CEO's and other board members' pay anomalies removes their negative signs, we multiply these by −1 to maintain consistency with the linear specifications.

[4] The restriction of our sample to firms with turn-of-the-year financial year ends ensured that the t−1 financial data of these firms was in the public realm when the compensation committees considered the time t awards. Our sample contains a slightly (but statistically insignificant) higher proportion of construction firms and stores than for the Times 1000 list. Using the SIC 2-digit definition, the sample covers seven sectors which accounted for over 70 per cent of all non-financial firms in the Times 1000.

[5] The data sources used to construct our dataset, included the published annual accounts, the Stock Exchange Year Book, The Hambro Corporate Register, Directors Guides and Datastream.

[6] Similar informational problems have also proved to be a major inhibition to research into many of the other non-cash benefits/perquisites received by executives.

[7] The precise specification of the pay level model used for estimating $\ln W^*_{it}$, along with the results of the estimated parameters using the pooled dataset can be obtained from the authors.

APPENDIX: CEO AND OTHER DIRECTORS REMUNERATION LEVEL MODELS FOR ESTIMATING PAY ANOMALIES

$$\text{Dependent variable} = \ln(\text{salary} + \text{bonus})_t \quad \text{where } t = 1991 - 94$$

Variable	*CEO pay*	*Other directors' pay*
Constant	1.638***	1.340***
	(9.89)	(8.06)
$\ln(\text{sales})_{t-1}$	0.283***	0.276***
	(21.97)	(21.60)
Proportion of non-executives$_{t-1}$		−0.737***
		(8.10)
Year dummies	Yes	Yes
Increasing over time?	Yes	Yes
Adjusted R^2	47.9%	48.5%
Equation F-ratio	165.5***	133.9***
N =	717	708

Individual year versions of the above pooled data models, i.e., using data for an individual year and excluding the year dummy variables, were used to produce the estimates of the market-based pay anomalies for both CEOs and other directors, i.e., $\ln(W_t) - \ln(W^*_t)$.

REFERENCES

ADAMS, J. S. (1963). 'Towards an understanding of inequity'. *Journal of Abnormal and Social Psychology*, **67**, 422–36.

ANDERSEN, C. A. and ANTHONY, R. N. (1981). *The New Corporate Directors: Insights for Board Members of Executives*. New York: Wiley.

BAKER, G. P., JENSEN, M. C. and MURPHY, K. J. (1988). 'Compensation and incentives: practice vs. theory'. *Journal of Finance*, **43**, 593–616.

BARKEMA, H. G. and GOMEZ-MEJIA, K. R. (1998). 'Managerial compensation and firm performance: a general research framework'. *Academy of Management Journal*, **41**, 2, April, 135–45.

BAZERMAN, M. H. and NEALE, M. A. (1992). *Negotiating Rationally*. New York: The Free Press.

BELLIVEAU, M. A., O'REILLY, C. A. and WADE, J. B. (1996). 'Social capital at the top: effects of social similarity and status on CEO compensation'. *Academy of Management Journal*, **39**, 6, 1568–93.

CADBURY COMMITTEE (1992). *Committee on the Financial Aspects of Corporate Governance*. Draft Report, May, Final Report, December.

CONYON, M. and LEECH, D. (1994). 'Top pay, company performance and corporate governance'. *Oxford Bulletin of Economics and Statistics*, **56**, 229–47.

CONYON, M., GREGG, P. and MACHIN, S. (1995). 'Taking care of business: executive compensation in the United Kingdom'. *The Economic Journal*, **105**, 704–14.

Cosh, A. and Hughes, A. (1995). 'Executive Remuneration, Executive Dismissal and Institutional Shareholdings'. University of Cambridge, Working Paper No. 19.

Deutsch, M. (1975). 'Equity, equality, and need: what determines which value will be used as the basis of distributive justice'. *Journal of Social Issues*, **31**, 137–49.

Deutsch, M. (1984). *Distributive Justice.* New Haven: Yale University Press.

Ezzamel, M. and Watson, R. (1997a). 'Wearing two hats: the conflicting management and control roles of non-executive directors'. In Keasey, K., Thompson, S. and Wright, M. (Eds), *Corporate Governance, Economic and Financial Issues.* Oxford: Oxford University Press, 54–79.

Ezzamel, M. and Watson, R. (1997b). 'Executive remuneration and corporate performance'. In Keasey, K. and Wright, M. (Eds), *Corporate Governance: Responsibilities, Risks and Remuneration.* New York: Wiley, 61–92.

Ezzamel, M. and Watson, R. (1998). 'Market comparison earnings and the bidding-up of executive cash compensation: evidence from the United Kingdom'. *Academy of Management Journal*, **41**, 2, 221–31.

Fama, E. G. (1980). 'Agency problems and the theory of the firm'. *Journal of Political Economy*, **88**, 280–307.

Fama, E. F. and Jensen, M. C. (1983). 'Separation of ownership and control'. *Journal of Law and Economics*, **26**, 301–26.

Festinger, L. (1957). 'A theory of social comparison processes'. *Human Relations*, **7**, 117–40.

Garen, J. E. (1994). 'Executive compensation and principal-agent theory'. *Journal of Political Economy*, **102**, 1175–99.

Gomez-Mejia, L. R. (1994). 'Executive compensation: a reassessment and a future research agenda'. *Research in Personnel and Human Resources Management*, **12**, 161–222.

Gomez-Mejia, L., Tosi, H. and Hinkin, T. (1987). 'Managerial control, performance, and executive compensation'. *Academy of Management Journal*, **30**, 51–70.

Goodman, P. S. (1974). 'An examination of referents used in the evaluation of pay'. *Organizational Behavior and Human Performance*, **12**, 170–95.

Gower, L. C. B. (1992). *Principles of Modern Company Law.* London: Sweet and Maxwell.

Gregg, P., Machin, S. and Szymanski, S. (1993a). 'The disappearing relationship between directors pay and corporate performance'. *British Journal of Industrial Relations*, **31**, 1–9.

Hart, O. (1995). 'Corporate governance: some theory and implications'. *Economic Journal*, **105**, May, 678–89.

Haubrich, J. G. (1994). 'Risk aversion, performance pay and the principal-agent problem'. *Journal of Political Economy*, **102**, 258–76.

Incomes Data Services (IDS) (1993). *Setting Pay at the Top.* IDS.

Institute of Directors (1995). *The Remuneration of Directors: A Framework for Remuneration Committees.* London.

Jensen, M. C. and Murphy, K. J (1990). 'Performance pay and top management incentives'. *Journal of Political Economy*, **98**, 225–64.

Kahneman, D., Knetsch, J. L. and Thaler, R. (1986). 'Fairness and the assumptions of economics'. *Journal of Business*, **56**, 285–300.

Kahneman, D., Knetsch, J. L. and Thaler, R. (1987). 'Fairness as a constraint on profit seeking: entitlements in the market'. *American Economic Review*, **76**, 728–41.

Kesner, I. F. (1988). 'Directors' characteristics and committee membership: an investigation of type, occupation, tenure and gender'. *Academy of Management Journal*, **31**, 66–84.

Mahoney, T. A. (1979). 'Organizational hierarchy and position worth'. *Academy of Management Journal*, **22**, 726–37.

Main, B. G. M. (1991). 'Top executive pay and performance'. *Managerial and Decision Economics*, **12**, 219–29.

Main, B. G. M. and Johnston, J. (1993). 'Remuneration committees and corporate governance'. *Accounting and Business Research*, **23**, 351–62.

MAIN, B. G. M., BRUCE, A. and BUCK, T. (1996). 'Total board remuneration and company performance'. *The Economic Journal*, **106**, November, 1627–44.

MUCKLEY, J. E. (1984). 'From the board room'. *Harvard Business Review*, **63**, 2, 46–64.

MURPHY, K. J. (1985). 'Corporate performance and managerial remuneration: an empirical analysis'. *Journal of Accounting and Economics*, **7**, 11–42.

MURPHY, K. J. (1997). 'Executive compensation and the modern industrial revolution'. *International Journal of Industrial Organization*, **15**, 417–25.

O'REILLEY, C., MAIN, B. and CRYSTAL, G. (1988). 'CEO salaries as tournaments and social comparisons: a tale of two theories'. *Administrative Science Quarterly*, **33**, 257–74.

ROSS, S. A. (1973). 'The economic theory of agency: the principal's problem'. *American Economic Review*, **63**, 134–9.

SIMON, H. A. (1957). 'The compensation of executives'. *Sociometry*, **20**, March, 52–6.

SMITH, R. and SZYMANSKI, S. (1995). 'Executive pay and performance: the empirical importance of the participation constraint'. *International Journal of the Economics of Business*, **2**, 485–95.

STEERS, R. and UNGSON, G. R. (1987). 'Strategic issues in executive compensation decisions'. In Balkin, D. B. and Gomez-Mejia, L. R. (Eds), *New Perspectives on Compensation*. Englewood Cliffs, NJ: Prentice-Hall, 315–27.

TATTON, A. (1992). 'Top people's pay is called to account'. *Independent on Sunday*, 20 September, 21.

TVERSKY, A. and KAHNEMAN, D. (1974). 'Judgement and uncertainty: heuristics and biases'. *Science*, **185**, 1124–31.

WADE, J. B., O'REILLY, C. A. and CHANDRATAT, I. (1990). 'Global parachutes: CEOs and the exercise of social influence'. *Administrative Science Quarterly*, **35**, 587–603.

WESTPHAL, J. D. and ZAJAC, E. J. (1997). 'Defections from the inner-circle: social exchange, reciprocity, and the diffusion of board independence in U.S. corporations'. *Administrative Science Quarterly*, **42**, 161–83.

ZAJAC, E. J. and WESTPHAL, D. J. (1995). 'Accounting for the explanation of CEO compensation: substance and symbolism'. *Administrative Science Quarterly*, **40**, 283–308.

Name Index